Encyclopedia Of
TREKKIE MEMORABILIA
Identification and Value Guide

by

Sally Gibson-Downs / Christine Gentry

Cover Photo - Courtesy Six Flags Movieland Wax Museum

DEDICATION

For our husbands, Doug and Milo, who paid the phone bills and for our children, Alesha Heather, Courtney Lynn and Jack Aaron who left our typewriters alone.

BOOKS AMERICANA INC

ISBN 0-89689-066-X

TABLE OF CONTENTS

ACKNOWLEDGEMENTS

Thanks to the following companies, retailers and private collectors who supplied information or photographed materials:

David Bostwick
Bradley Time, Division of Elgin Industries
Ertl Company
General Mills Inc.
John F. Green
Robert Jaiven
K-Tel International, Inc.
June Stoops
Uncle Hugo's Science Fiction Bookstore
Robert Wilson

Special thanks to individuals and groups who supplied photographs:

Ruth Berman
Loch David Crane
Douglas Downs
Ernst Limited Editions
Hollywood Wax Museum
Cynthia Levine
Kathi and Rick Mingo
Rocketships and Accessories
Running Press
David Thompson

INTRODUCTION

This handbook has been designed for practical use by collectors who have either been in the Star Trek hobbyist field for twenty years or who have just decided to begin collecting Trek memorabilia. This handbook is also the product of two decades of collecting and enjoying Star Trek collectibles by the authors in an ever-expanding marketplace.

No two Star Trek collections are alike, either in material content or in the overall value of the merchandise that constitutes them. Star Trek collections are as individual and unique as the infinite variety of collectors that create them. Therefore it is crucial that you know your own collection and establish some kind of organization to your purchasing endeavors.

This handbook is designed to help you, as a seasoned veteran or as a novice, understand, acquire and organize your collection. The authors have also designed this handbook to be as concise as possible so that memorabilia can be identified accurately and evaluated with a fair market value.

How To Use This Book

THIS IS A HANDBOOK. It is a functional log for maintaining a Star Trek collection.

USE this book before you go out in the marketplace to shop for wares. It is an information guide for the available types of Star Trek merchandise that exist. It will aid you in determining what particular kinds of collectibles you are most interested in acquiring.

USE this book to determine the nature of the collectibles you find available. It will be an invaluable reference in deciding the originality of certain merchandise; paring out the reprints and re-issues from first productions and helping you as a collector to authenticate the manufacturer/publisher for unboxed or unrecognizable wares.

USE the price listings as a tool in making your purchases. The relative price ranges will tell you what observed prices are generally in line from available sources in different locations across the country. The addition of original issue prices is unique and imperative for making comparisons between quickly escalating Star Trek memorabilia and items which tend to accrue value more slowly. Certain categories of collectible types do increase in value quicker than others as well.

USE this handbook when you shop. You can't remember all of the important details and there's no need for you to have to try! Carry this book with you as a workbook to jot down notes, prices, purchases, etc. Don't keep it home on the bookshelf. It's not designed to function that way.

USE this book as a permanent log for cataloging your own collection. The blank lines in this test are for you to fill out as more and more items in your individual collection are added. Record everything. Your Star Trek collection is unique.

CHAPTER 1

What's It All About?

Anyone who enjoys Star Trek in any of its various entertainment formats is considered a fan. They may or may not collect Star Trek memorabilia as well. Star Trek fans come in all shapes, colors, ages and dispositions. This is partially the reason for the success of the television series. The show, its concepts and moral philosophies, appeals to people of all walks of life.

What exactly is it about Star Trek that attracts more people year after year? That is a question that even the show's creator Gene Roddenberry has been asked countless number of times. The answer must be the result of several considerations.

First, we should look at Star Trek as it relates to the science fiction media itself. Isaac Asimov, Professor of Biochemistry and world renowned science fiction author, has described science fiction as being speculative fiction which takes place in a surreal background. That is to say that if the appropriate changes were made in our levels of science and technology today, the events, lifestyles and mechanizations represented in science fiction could conceivably exist. Therefore, the prospect that 200 years from now a spaceship like the Enterprise could exist is scientifically sound. This same ship could also have a crew of 400 people whose mission was to traverse the universe seeking out new contacts with extraterrestrials.

In fact, making Star Trek a scientifically sound series was a major concern of the show's writers. The entire series, episode by episode, was a logical projection of current scientific knowledge. It is quite conceivable that the Apollos, Geminis and space shuttles of our century could eventually evolve into a space vehicle of the size and scope of the U.S.S. Enterprise.

To its credit, Star Trek was, and still is, the only television science fiction show in history that engaged the advice of the National Aeronautics and Space Administration when preparing scripts. Their job was to eyeball scripts and weed out false or erroneous imaginings untrue to scientific theory.

The functional realism of the Enterprise is the result of more than five months of planning and the legacy of more than 200 design drawings accomplished with the assistance of the Jet Propulsion Laboratory of the RAND Corporation. Their intensive, creative research and development lead to a very convincing reality projected from scientific fact.

Everything aboard the mythical Enterprise was designed to be technically accurate. The matter/antimatter engines were based on accepted theory so that the ship's warp factors 1-8 are made up of a geometric progression of light velocities. Warp 1 is the speed of light or 186,000 miles per second. Warp 2 is 8 times the speed of light. Warp 4 is 64 times the speed of light and so on.

The ship's phasers, hand phasers and phaser pistols are only speculative refinements of today's lasers. The deflector beams are refined super-radar which sweep far into space before the Enterprise to deflect asteroids or space debris. We see that tricoders are the epitomy of miniature solid-state electronics and that the transporter which "beams" crewmembers everywhere is a gadget that converts matter to energy, sends it to a fixed point and re-converts it into its original shape and texture.

It's no wonder that Star Trek appeals to the mature viewing audience. A large proportion of Trek viewers of the 1960's were space technicians, scientists, college professors and higher-education students.

Star Trek is also a magnet for viewers because of the show's willingness to express thoughts on controversial problems. Constantly at odds with television censors of the 60's, Star Trek writers still managed to establish or present various points of view on a wide range of subjects from politics to ecology.

Star Trek wasn't only a thought provoking show but a positive one as well. Fans were shown that all the mysteries of the universe hadn't been discovered, that challenges still remained to be met and conquered. The characters of the show were heroes to admire and to emulate. Star Trek appeared on television at a time when most other T.V. leads were anti-heroes. For the first time, educated people could watch a series that both stirred their imaginations and that said meaningful things.

No other segment of science fiction fandom can claim to have saved the object of their love from a cancellation demise either. Star Trek fans did so in 1967 merely by the number of letters they wrote to NBC President Julian Goodman. On the average, Star Trek admirers sent 6,000 letters a week praising the show's qualities. However, when Star Trek was threatened with a premature burial after only one season on the air with favorable ratings, letters of protect escalated to a total of almost 115,000 individually written complaints.

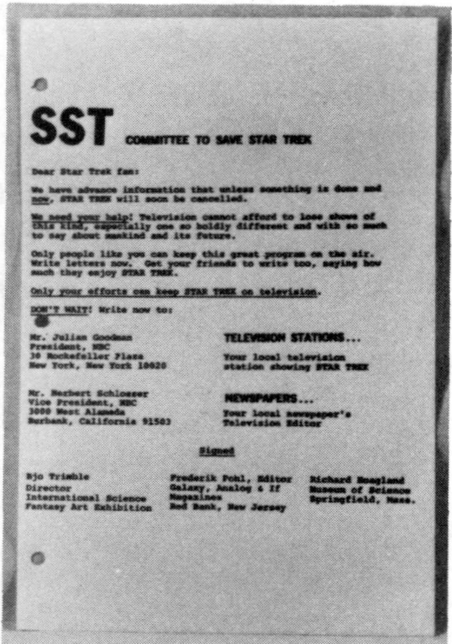

SST COMMITTEE TO SAVE STAR TREK

Dear Star Trek fan:

We have advance information that unless something is done and now, STAR TREK will soon be cancelled.

We need your help! Television cannot afford to lose shows of this kind, especially one so boldly different and with so much to say about mankind and its future.

Only people like you can keep this great program on the air. Write letters now. Get your friends to write too, saying how much they enjoy STAR TREK.

Only your efforts can keep STAR TREK on television.

DON'T WAIT! Write now to:

Mr. Julian Goodman
President, NBC
30 Rockefeller Plaza
New York, New York 10020

TELEVISION STATIONS...
Your local television station showing STAR TREK

Mr. Herbert Schlosser
Vice President, NBC
3000 West Alameda
Burbank, California 91503

NEWSPAPERS...
Your local newspaper's Television Editor

Signed

Bjo Trimble
Director
International Science Fantasy Art Exhibition

Frederik Pohl, Editor
Galaxy, Analog & If Magazines
Red Bank, New Jersey

Richard Hoagland
Museum of Science
Springfield, Mass.

The original **Save Star Trek** letter, 1967.

Students of Cal Tech marched on NBC in Burbank to present a petition of objection. Berkley students demonstrated at NBC's San Francisco outlet while MIT students converged on Rockefeller Center to register their feelings. Canadians, too, responded angrily to the threat of a cancellation of their number one ranked television show in the land. Throughout the North American continent, thousands of Star Trek followers watched the show and came to its rescue when they were needed the most.

Star Trek Genealogy

Throughout the past two decades, there have been several terms in circulation which denoted that a person was a Star Trek fan or collector. Star Trek fans come in many varieties and the differences between one type and another have evolved in relation to their particular date of origin and purpose.

Star Trekkers – Throughout their public exposure during the years 1966-1969, this was the name given to the first devotees of Star Trek and its fundamental teachings. The term was straight-forward and identified about 20 million Star Trek viewers.

Trekkies – This term appeared in 1971 in several professional publications. Almost overnight this tabloid label emcompassed the majority of Star Trek fandom as one united group. The word was derived from the name "groupie" as a few teen magazines had occasionally referred to Trek fans as Star Trek groupies. Trekkie can also trace its origins directly to the greatly successful Star Trek Con of 1972. The title appeared simultaneously via convention coverage in *T.V. Guide.* A Trekkie was a fan who haunted Star Trek conventions throughout the country.

Trekker – It is generally acknowledged that Trekkers are the workers and doers of Star Trek fandom. They organize, promote and supervise Trek conventions and clubs. They also feed information and literature to a hungry fandom with private and commercially produced Star Trek related materials. Trekkers may also be fans that have remained loyal to the show since its beginnings in 1966.

Trekkist – This is a rarer term which applies to a person who may follow the syndicated Star Trek episodes on occassion or attend a few conventions but who is not actively involved in collecting memorabilia or in a fan movement.

Trekster – This term has been created from the Star Trek phenomenon as it has occured through promotion of Trek on the Big Screen. A Trekster is an 80's fan who enjoys Star Trek the most on the theater marquee and who returns to see the same movie over and over again.

Types of Collectors

Just as there are different types of Star Trek enthusiasts, there are different types of memorabilia collectors who have also helped to make Star Trek the most popular television program in science fiction history. What variety of collectibles a fan will gather depends, of course, on his or her predispositions, number of years involved in the Star Trek movement and on personal finances. Over the years, a definite categorical hierarchy has developed in Star Trek fandom which determines what individuals prefer to build upon in their personal collections.

1. Character Collectors – This is the most common type of Star Trek memorabilia fan. Since the appearance of the first episode, fans have leaned towards enjoying one or two characters from the series, or its real-life actors and actresses. Star Trek polls have long since indicated that the most favorite characters of the show are Captain Kirk and First Officer Spock. Many Star Trek collections feature the Star Trek character of their owner's preference. Memorabilia featuring only one or two of the show's heros may set the entire theme for a collector's enjoyment and pursuant behavior. A character collector seeks only items that sport the likeness of his favorite actor. This is the only impetus for an initial outlay of cash for any Star Trek item.
2. Serial Collectors – A serial collector builds his Star Trek collection with items that represent moments from his favorite episodes. These collectors view the Trek universe as being built upon a foundation of indispensible parts that highlight the whole. Serial collectors can produce a wealth of detailed trivia about specific television episodes. They are most likely to collect photographic stills and clips, scripts, outlines and storyboards. The marketing of new episode videos is a dream come true to this group of collectors as well.
3. Media Collectors – These collectors are people who tend to acquire merchandise manufactured in the same way or by a similar process. Generally speaking, Star Trek collectibles fall into a distinct production taxonomy. Divisions in the commercial fabrication of memorabilia include the print media, photographic media, audio-visual media, recreational media, household wares and apparel. A media collector, for instance, may collect only Star Trek books, magazines, comics, scripts, sheet music, stationary, diplomas, certificates and any other item which is in print form. Another might collect photographs, slides, clips, posters and postcards.
4. Technology Collectors – This is a very recent and growing population of Star Trek merchandise collectors. Because Star Trek features such an array of accurate scientific information within its storylines, many fans are becoming quite intrigued with the sophisticated graphics and lofted renderings of the functional aspects of the Trek universe. Since the passing of the 70's, detailed reference manuals have appeared flashing to-scale alien anatomies, astrological maps and blueprints for medical equipment, weapons and ships. Until 1980, few collectors bothered with blue-print materials. Technological collectors are also interested in acquiring realistic, functional and non-functional hand props. Usually these are professional quality plastiformed weapons, communicators and tricorders.
5. Gaming Collectors – Gaming collectors come in two varieties. They are separated subtly not only by their area of interest but by their dates of origin. The first group is comprised of computer buffs who began incorporating Star Trek themes into their nearest computer systems during the 1960's. A myriad of Star Trek software programs have grown and diversified since then. Now computer gamers have no problem adjourning to their bedroom personal computer and playing rousing, multi-round battles between the legendary Enterprise and Klingon warships. The manufacturing heyday for Star Trek of the 1980's has brought a new breed of gaming collector. These are sophisticated battle gamers or role-playing enthusiasts. A role player is usually a teenager who is a second generation Star Trek fan weaned on the show as it has appeared on the syndicated airings of the series during the 1970's. Gaming collectors are intellectual activists. They, like their computer buff predecessors, prefer the visual imagery of commanding their own Constellation Class starships through space. The memorabilia of the board gamer will mostly be an extensive array of battle damage charts, characterization booklets, construction manuals and die-cast metal microships.

Very early fanzines relay the quick popularity of Star Trek.

6. Fanzine Collectors – On the average, fanzine collectors purchase little else but fanzines. Fanzine collections are one of the most expensive to maintain because of the initial price of each individual book. Fanzine collectors are also the least likely to sell their merchandize later on, although there is a quaint fan custom of passing them from hand to hand to be read by other enthusiasts.

Buyer Personalities

Many people consider Star Trek collectors to be fanatics. They seem to show no limit to what they will do to collect that one last item they've been looking for. They are persistant and scrutinizing. They attend conventions wearing outrageous outfits or T-shirts of their favorite Star Trek character years after the show is defunct. Who are these people?

Star Trek fans may be many things, but the majority are intelligent, well-educated, interested in current realms of scientific inquiry and prolific in hopes for the future. Are these qualities fanatical? If anything unflattering could be said about the average Star Trek collector, it might be that he or she bought his collectibles illadvisedly, failing to purchase merchandise selectively or by making unshrewd appraisals as to a collectible's condition and relative value.

There are basically two legions of Star Trek memorabilia buyers. Consumers may be either Focus buyers or Spontaneous buyers. A brief list of the differences between the two follows.

	Focus Buyer	**Spontaneous Buyer**
Type of merchandise bought	Specialized & the most desired	Any kind
Where shopped for	With previously established dealers	Anywhere
Why purchased	Fills a collectible niche (want-list buying)	Appeals to at the moment
Knowledge of subject and worth to a novice	Limited to collection type but a specialist in certain merchandising categories	A wide horizon of collecting information but of a more generalized nature

No matter how a Star Trek collector gathers his memorabilia, he should be cautious, patient and discriminating. Arbitrary buying on a helter-skelter spree is self defeating in the long run. The quality and condition of your collection will be as sporatic as your whims. You will inevitably be swindled at some point into paying too much for inferior items, or continually wishing later that you had waited before buying them.

Half the fun of building any Star Trek collection should stem from the searching of collectibles to comprise it. It is only sensible that a Trek investor use common sense when laying money on the table for merchandise. When buying any Star Trek material consider the five iron-clad rules below.

1. **Old is not necessarily good.**
It is true that many older Star Trek items have much higher prices today then when they were originally issued. Still the age of a collectible must take second place to both its condition and rarity. Some newer items (Goldkey Comic volumes No. 1 - 4 and the 1980, 12 inch Mego *Star Trek The Motion Picture* dolls) command high prices because warehouse fires destroyed the majority of those intended for shipment to retailers.
2. **Popularity creates demand.**
The more popular an article is today, the more in demand it is likely to be tomorrow. Books and magazines are particularly popular with Star Trek collectors. In the last 7 years, written materials concerning Star Trek have escalated at a phenomenal rate.
3. **Look before you leap.**
Price ranges for any Star Trek collectible are subject to the price tag parameters imposed upon it by the person desiring to sell it. On commercially produced items such as posters, records, videos and new book or magazine releases, a collector is not liable to find large price disparities from retailer to retailer. Vintage books, magazines, trading cards, show props, toys, dolls, glassware and non mass-produced memorabilia will vary considerably from dealer to dealer.

4. **Geography is money.**
There are wide differences in the sale price of many Star Trek items from two geographically independent locales. This is a persistant problem encountered in the Trek collectible marketplace. Star Trek items from the east coast are substantially higher than those in the midwest. Also, items considered scarce in one part of the country may carry a higher price when located even if they are still available in profusion directly off the store shelf somewhere else. Try to pick up as many complimentary catalogs from around the country as possible and compare them.
5. **Cost is everything.**
Every Star Trek collector must establish for himself a personal, financial limit. Such a consideration will systematically eliminate overspending when collectible prices appear to be above one's means, expectations or monetary boundaries. Setting "financial curbstones" for oneself is not only being budget-wise but discriminating.

Early publicity coverage in a local newspaper supplement, Aug. 1967.

Retail store displays call attention to Star Trek items.

CHAPTER 2

Your Star Trek Collection

A novice or veteran Star Trek collector has a variety of sources from which to purchase his merchandise. The first question asked will be, how do I do this? Usually the search for Star Trek collectibles is a step-by-step adventure. A collector starts looking for merchandise on his home stomping ground and eventually is lead farther afield. Finding sources from which to buy memorabilia takes patience, legwork and a level head. Finding that rare, one-of-a-kind item at a good price can involve many dead ends and true investigative research.

Retail Stores – Check with local toy stores, book stores and hobby stores. These outlets provide access to memorabilia which has attained the greatest distribution and promotion.

Hardware Stores and Drug Stores – More aged Star Trek items appear in small, privately owned retail outlets not associated with larger corporate chains. In these sequestered hideaways, Star Trek merchandise may languish for years.

Holiday Specials – Sometimes vintage Trek memorabilia surfaces near holidays. During Christmas months, many stores clean out their stockrooms and unload everything for possible sale. This is especially true of children's toys. During Halloween, it is still possible for 1975 Star Trek T.V. costumes to make their battered way onto toystore bargain racks.

Merchant Specials – It is possible to try and order specific Star Trek items through dealers in the area. Most retailers are helpful in providing suggestions as to the location of other distributors for material which they don't stock. Possibly the dealer can order the collectible direct for you.

Conventions – Thousands of Star Trek collectors have discovered the appeal of these events as a haven for memorabilia collecting. No greater variety and quantity of Trek wares can be found assembled under one roof than those souvenirs residing at convention dealer's tables. Fans no longer have to migrate en masse in order to attend a convention. Virtually any collector has access to some type of science fiction con. They are usually as close as the nearest well populated city. Be sure to compare prices. There is a wide diversity of Star Trek wares and prices. Be acquainted with the price ranges for the items you want before you get caught up in the spontaneity of a mass buying frenzy.

Auctions – Mail-in auctions represent one of the newest methods available for chasing down Star Trek wares. The procedure is a simple one. Generally, collectors must request a bid sheet which lists all of the items for sale (known as "on the block"). This list provides very basic information such as a collectible's manufacturer/publisher, date of origin and the minimum dollar bid acceptable. A collector's bid for purchase and a SASE are considered providing they are received before a posted closing date. After round one, those items which have attracted multiple bids may be entered into a final bidding round into which anyone may once again participate. Winners are notified of their success by mail and must forward payment in full along with the proper return postage for the memorabilia purchased. Auctions are often sponsored by fan clubs and Star Trek organizations.

Fan Clubs – Another choice for locating hard-to-find merchandise is through contact with one of many Star Trek leagues or clubs. There is a fan club, authorized or unauthorized, for each major Star Trek actor and actress. Most clubs publish monthly or quarterly newsletters which feature new Trek collectible releases, penpal lists, advertisements and fan swaps.

Direct Order – A collector can write directly to the manufacturer of a product for retail information and acquisition. If he knows who the manufacturer or publisher is, he can find an address or phone number for them, provided they are still in operation, as well. Most public libraries carry guides to U.S. manufacturers and corporations in their reference sections. Enclose a SASE with your query and allow up to 4 weeks for a response. Many times letters must be re-routed to other parts of the country to specific merchandising offices or publishing warehouses.

Mail-Order – Without a doubt, the Star Trek collector of today will come into contact with mail-order houses who specialize in or stock Trek merchandise. Some mail-order houses are better than others. To locate the good ones a collector can consult fan networks. Sending for catalogs from around the country is a good way to feel out price ranges on an item you're interested in. When interested in purchasing old memorabilia, it is prudent to request information about the overall condition of the collectible if it is not indicated in the catalog provided. Make your decision to buy the best you can under the circumstances. Beware of mail-order houses who do not provide this information. Reputable houses will provide condition information along with their price lists or offer to send polaroids of expensive Star Trek collectibles for a small fee (about $1.00 a copy).

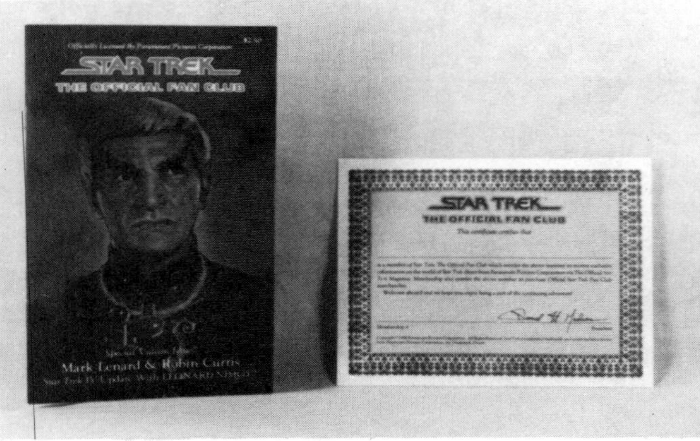

Fan clubs are a good source for obtaining memorabilia.

Mail order ads like this often appear in science fiction magazines.

Star Trek packaging is as collectible as the item it contains.

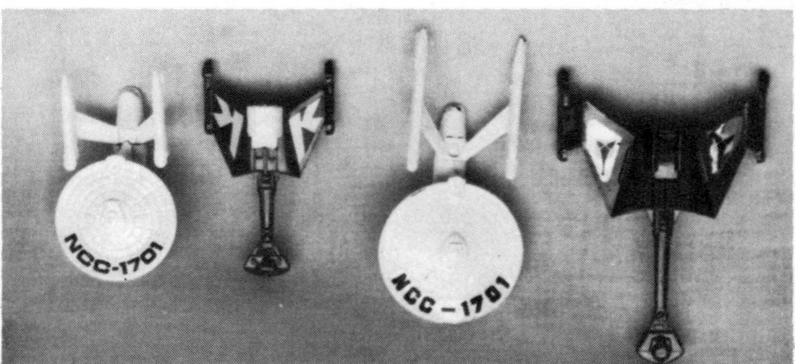

Comparison between Corgi & Dinky die-cast ships. As packaged memorabilia, their value would be more.

Selling Collectibles

A Collector must utilize the same sources in selling his memorabilia as he used acquiring it. However, this time around you'll be sitting on the other side of the dealing table. If a collector finds himself in this position, he should note the following retail pitfalls and avoid them.

Don't see dollar signs.

Usually the first mistake a novice collector makes when deciding to sell his collection or a portion of it, is to pick up a price guide, read the high end of the possible value scale for their memorabilia and see dollar signs flash before their eyes. If you try this maneuver, you're likely to find yourself saddled with virtually unmovable collectibles. It might cost you to keep providing free merchandise lists, postage stamps or advertisements.

It's all used merchandise.

No matter how excellent its condition (which it usually is not), secondhand merchandise is still considered to be used. That automatically drops the value of an item. It is rare to find collections where memorabilia hasn't been tampered with in some way (items have been removed from their blister packs, cartons, cellophane wraps, etc.) that alters its original mint, off-the-production line condition. This status of perfection is extremely important to keep in mind when collecting Star Trek memorabilia. To be worth its ultimate value, a collectible must, in essence, be perfect, unmarked, unblemished, virtually untouched and sealed in its original packaging if it was issued in such a manner.

Don't try to improve on a good thing.

In the collectible field, an item is always worth more if it comes in its original packaging materials, no matter what the condition of that commercial enclosure itself. Items removed from boxes or protective wraps are being altered, even if the intent is to store them more conveniently or in what is possibly a better container. The more a Star Trek collectible deviates from its issue appearance, the less its value and this fact should be chorused by its asking price.

Differentiate between the saleable and the unsaleable.

Know the difference between cannibalized items and items which still retain a collectibility status. No one wants your junk. Anything painted, glued, broken or in any other way tampered with is difficult to sell. Often plastic model kits, juvenile hobby and craft sets and activity games suffer irrevocable damage and wear. Collectors can't increase the value of their model kits by customizing them. Out of the box and assembled they become only ornaments. Display items are novelties of minimum worth unless they are professional quality, prop-style models which originally sell for high prices. Buy two items if necessary. One to remain untouched as an investment, the other to be used.

Services cost.

Anytime a collector tries to sell his Star Trek memorabilia through a representative, he must expect to pay in some manner for those services. Entire collections can be sold in bulk to local science fiction/nostalgia retailers or exhibited in their stores for possible piece-meal sales. Be forewarned that dealer purchases of entire collections often yields a seller only 30-50% of their **total estimated value.** Likewise, commission rates (monies paid to a storekeeper for handling and displaying your items on the premises) run around 10-20% for each item sold. In some cases collectors who have no idea how much their collection is worth can have it priced by knowledgeable dealers who will charge an assessment fee. Usually this fee will run a collector up to 20% of the final estimated value of the entire collection.

CHAPTER 3

Storing Your Collectibles

The only way to keep your collectibles in as good a condition as possible is to store them properly. The shortage of the average Star Trek collectible's numbers in good, saleable condition is usually the result of neglect for the proper storage practices.

Some basic rules for storing any piece of Star Trek memorabilia include:

1. Sealing out oxygen. Wrap or enclose unsealed items in polyester film bags of various sizes. These can be purchased at most comic stores and include Mylar, Melinex, Mylite or Scotchpar archival-quality bags. Avoid the easy temptation of just any plastic bag. The polyvinyl chlorides (PVC's) found in ordinary plastic bags can be detrimental to paper collectibles. Other memorabilia such as gum cards, business cards, photo cards, I.D. cards, badges, etc. may be stored in plastic-pouched vinyl sheets designed for baseball cards.
2. Store larger collectibles in metal containers or acid-free buffered cardboard boxes. Be careful about laying memorabilia directly on wooden surfaces such as shelves or in drawers. Acid hydrolysis could damage perishable paper products. If employed, wooden surfaces should be pre-sealed with a polyurethane coating.
3. Sealing out ultraviolet light. Professional display cases are often manufactured with plexiglass for this purpose. Expose collectible reading material to incandescent light only.
4. Keeping the collection cool and dry. It only stands to reason that excessive heat or dampness will damage certain memorabilia collectibles. Don't store anything in either the attic or the cellar without first considering these environmental factors.
5. Trying to avoid excessive handling. Any exposure to man-handling increases the likelihood of the destruction of valuable items. Aside from the actual physical damage inflicted, chemical blemishes from contact with human skin is usually unavoidable. Make sure the potential enjoyment outweighs the potential risks.

Storing Specific Items

Usually the collector's dilemma of how to store an item easily and efficiently has already been solved for him by the production of commercial enclosures on sale at nearby retail stores. Many collectibles, however, are prone to their own unusual storing problems. These will be focused upon here, along with their appropriate solutions. The most perishable Star Trek collectibles are those made from paper products.

Books – Books are extremely sensitive to damage from a variety of sources. A relative humidity of over 70% will promote the growth of damaging molds and a relative humidity of less than 40% will cause book pages to dry out and yellow. The perfect temperature for storage is 68°F or less with a humidity of 50%. Excessive temperatures, moisture, sunlight and excesses of artificial light will also damage Star Trek books. Collectors should keep them in plastic book sleeves made of stable chemicals such as Dupont's Mylar brand. Plastic seals which aren't chemically inert will react with book materials and disfigure them. Books with dark colors (black, purple) and metallic blends are very prone to destruction if not properly preserved.

Comics – Comic books are an excellent example of the many horrors inherent to other perishable Star Trek items. They are printed on newsprint paper. Their primary physical content of 80% of ground wood and 20% unbleached fiber predisposes them to ready deterioration when exposed to certain chemical and biological agents. The acid generated in common corrugated boxes can lead to hydrolysis of cellulose out of the comic. This results in embrittled paper. Oxidative attack on the same comic from exposure to air can cause both discoloration and an increase in the acidic quality of the newspaper stock itself. Humid conditions work to erode the comic's paper quality in general, plus serve as the breeding grounds for destructive types of fungi. In regions where the RH (relative humidity) regularly exceeds 65%, biological attack on Star Trek comics can become a serious problem. These collectibles should be maintained in standard Mylar comic bags and stored upright in specifically constructed comic boxes sold by comic dealers.

Magazines – Star Trek magazines are best maintained intact in Mylar magazine bags sold at most comic stores. To prevent an ever-growing attack of slippery-coated periodicals, it is convenient to store them in magazine boxes similar to those manufactured for comic books. It is also possible to remove the magazine pages you want from a periodical and slip them into plastic protector sheets sold at most drug stores. Since the sheets contain holes for clip binders, regular school notebooks or double-sized binders can be employed to store those pages in succession. The result is a handy reference book for pinpointing specific articles. Keep in mind that such separated pages will not bring top value when sold because they have been sliced from a once intact magazine. Magazines which have a good history of continually escalating prices and which feature full color fronts of Star Trek topics should be spared slicing. Prozine periodicals should not be cut up at all.

Posters – Posters should not be maintained in their original mailing tubes for any duration of time. The cardboard interiors aren't waxed or laminated to protect against the destruction of poster papers by the inherent acid content of tube fibers. If posters aren't to be displayed they should be uncurled and placed in 8 Mil Vinyl poster sleeves with specially designed cardboard backings. Such sleeves (usually sold in sewn together groups of six) may be bought with either horizontal or vertical openings. The clear front vinyl side allows for viewing. The backside is black and laminated. Combination, six capacity poster protectors for insert sheets and half sheets run about $95. A less expensive option for storing posters in quantity are 2 Mil poster bags with acid free cardboard backings to keep them stiff. Twenty-five half sheet bags will cost about $27. Twenty-five one-sheets with accompanying backings will run about $42. Never tape or tack posters to walls. Such abuse will mutilate and discolor potentially valuable collectibles. Collectors may have Star Trek posters professionally mounted onto ¼ inch foam backings for hanging on walls or displayed beneath glass. Please note that this method has inherent drawbacks. If improperly mounted, bulges and creases may occur and this type of mounting doesn't allow posters to shrink or expand well under temperature fluctuations. Also, a bonding glue is present to attach the foam to the poster. This is not easily removed later on. The best way to display posters on walls is to have them professionally framed as museum quality pieces. They are unmounted, allowing for thermal conditions and sealed behind glass. To prevent exposure to damaging ultraviolet light which causes fading, some poster collectors use plexiglass on frame fronts to protect their poster sheet collectibles.

Trading Cards – Trading cards should be stored to prevent against damage from ultraviolet light, high humidity and excessive handling. Plastic sheets made of .066 gauge vinyl are readily available to the collector. Many sleeve sizes are sold at retailer's shops dealing with standard baseball card collectibles. Special "D" ring binders can also be obtained for storing sheets in 50 page capacities per album.

Records – Star Trek records deserve proper protection. All 33⅓ LPs and 45 RPM singles should be stored upright in solid record stands to prevent warping. Don't stack records on their sides. Older albums especially need extra protection from deterioration by mildew, destructive insects and aging ills such as brittleness. High density, anti-static inner sleeves made for slipping over records inside album jackets are an inexpensive maintenance technique worth using. These plastic sleeves protect records from scratches, dust and moisture. Album jackets are also prone to destruction because of their paper components. For about $2, collectors can purchase ten vinyl album cover protectors.

Toys and Dolls – Collectors will rarely want to display all of their Star Trek toys, action figures, dolls, model kits or art kits. Usually smaller collectibles are sealed with blister packages, window box cartons or some sort of cellophane wrap, and exhibit some type of paper constructed support backing. Such cardboard backings are prone to wear and deterioration. Small collectibles can be placed into Mylar protectors used for comics or magazines. Even album jacket covers will do. If items are to be deep stored for a long time, they can be wrapped in disposable diapers and sealed in bulk within acid free cardboard boxes. Larger toys made of wood, rubber or metal are subject to damage from moisture if not properly sealed in chemically stable plastic sheets and tissue. Avoid undue shocks or pressure on sealed cartons. Also be aware of potential problems with insect pests and mice which will eat glued surfaces on collectibles or gnaw through boxes.

Buttons – The component metal for logo and photo buttons is steel of varying degrees of texture and rust-proofing. A button composed of bright, shiny silver is made from raw, untreated steel and is highly vulnerable to corrosion. High humidity environments or exposure to water will discolor button backings and clips. They should be kept in water resistant plastic sleeves (possibly trading card protectors) or individual zip-lock jewelry bags. Anodized buttons, those with steel reverses subjected to electrolyte action which coats them with a thin protective or decorative film, are more resistant to discoloration but deserve adequate care. Backings of anodized buttons are usually dull silver, gray, green and brown.

Jewelry – Star Trek jewelry may be an expensive investment. Silver and brass pieces can tarnish quickly. Gold, silver, nickel and brass filled collectibles can be chipped accidentally and expose baser metal cores to corrosion. To prevent the unwanted oxidation of metal surfaces, collectors should seal jewelry pieces in individual Mylar packets and box them to prevent exposure to excessive light. Don't let jewelry pieces rub against each other or they will scratch one another.

Clothes –Several factors effect the relative condition of Star Trek uniforms, costumes and other types of wearing apparel. Cloth fibers are extremely sensitive to discoloration and damage by sunlight. Other detrimental conditions include molds, insects, air pollutions, dust and relative humidity. Don't hang clothes on hangers for extended periods of time. This exposes them to insects such as moths, roaches and silverfish. It is best to box up clothes collectibles. Stuff them with wrapping tissue to prevent flattening and then wrap them in pieces of white sheet or white towels. To wash lightly soiled clothes, use mild soap and distilled water. Very collectible, prop quality pieces should be dry cleaned only.

Odds and Ends – Actually, every Star Trek collectible that you own should be enclosed in protective Mylar bags, plastic sheets, acid-free boxes or vinyl sleeves of some sort. Using the basics, there is a way to protect every piece of memorabilia owned. Use your imagination. Cut standard protectors down to useable size when needed. Remember, all paper goods need artificial protection.

Insuring Your Collection

If you are like most Star Trek fans, you probably keep your Star Trek collectibles in your home. Not only is this an inexpensive manner in which to store your bulging collection, it is also advantageous for insuring your memorabilia against such disasters as flood, fire, etc.

Under the terms and policies of most types of homeowners insurance policies, private collections are covered along with all other personal possessions such as furniture, appliances, clothing, etc. that comprise insurable properties. However, just as it is wise to photograph and inventory the everyday items in your house that may be damaged by unforseen events, it is prudent that you inventory your Star Trek collection as well.

The best way to do this is by keeping a running log of the type of item, the date of purchase and its relative retail value and condition. Conscientious collectors may desire to take individual photos of their memorabilia for safe keeping, but group shots are perfectly acceptable for insurance purposes. Such a collectible's log is also an invaluable reminder about what items you have and don't have in your collection when you have your doubts.

CHAPTER 4
Alphabetical Listings

Artwork and Cels

Art and illustrations have always been an important part of Star Trek fandom. The list of early amateur artists who extended their talents into the Star Trek universe is now filled with the names of individuals who are recognizable for their professional contributions to Star Trek merchandise or to science fiction genres as a whole. Such notables are Alicia Austin (stationary designs), George Barr (the original *Star Trek Concordance*), Mattewillis Beard (award-winning Trek poster design), Phil Foglio, Joan Winston and Allan Asherman (writer).

Artists may render their works in pastels, acrylics, oils, charcoal or pen and ink. Since black and white artwork reproduces the clearest through offset printing, pen and ink or charcoal drawings are the preferred artistic medium for amateur press releases.

The individual style of an artist also determines where the finished product will be used. Portrait artists generally work from still-life promotional or publicity photographs to produce detailed character studies or group portfolios. An excellent example of this technique carried to commercial level is the artwork of Susie Morton as it has now appeared on Ernst Limited Edition collector plates, mugs and steins.

Besides artwork that comes to Star Trek fans through amateur presses, other artwork comes to the public market through convention viewings. Reprinted lithos, scratchboards and photographic prints are clearly designated by convention Art Directors for sale or auction. Collectors can also find artwork relegated to dealer's tables. Signed, special edition "complete story sets" consisting of 10-15 individual reprints can be acquired for about $10-20.

Original oil canvases can command impressive price tags of $300 or more. One exquisite canvas executed by Barbara Fister-Litz holds the Star Trek fan art auction record price of $750. The very high value assigned to this piece resulted in part from the fact that the artist had produced the cover art for professional magazines.

Star Trek fans should take note that in 1991 the Smithsonian Institution is planning to have a 25th Anniversary display featuring Star Trek props and paraphernalia. There will also be a series of Robert McCall paintings featuring Star Trek themes.

- **Aliens of Star Trek**
Gary Hawfitch, c. 1975. Black and white, nine drawings of Star Trek aliens, plus one drawing of a Klingon Battle Cruiser, profiles in ink media. This is set II of Hawfitch's series.

	Issue	Current	Cost/Date
Klingon Battle Cruiser, 9" x12"	—	$2-4	______
Salt Monster, "The Man Trap", 8½"x11"	—	2-4	______
Alien "The Empath", 8½"x11"	—	2-4	______
T'Pring, 8½"x11"	—	2-4	______
Amanda and Sarek, 8½"x11"	—	2-4	______
Talosian, 8½"x11"	—	2-4	______
Gorn, 8½"x11"	—	2-4	______
Andorian Ambassador Shras, 8½"x11"	—	2-4	______
Female Romulan Commander "The Enterprise Incident", 8½"x11"	—	2-4	______
Klingon Kor, 8½"x11"	—	2-4	______
Complete set of 10	6.50	15-35	______

Animated Series Artwork

- **Cels-Original Handpainted**
Filmation Studios, 1977. Paintings on transparent celluloid made from drawings, cels overlayed on colorful background and mounted in mat folder, come bearing studio seal and/or limited edition issue numbers, 14"x18".

	Issue	Current	Cost/Date
ST 00 **Title Scene** from Star Trek animated series, small Enterprise with show title.			
Limited Edition, sealed/numbered	20	20-30	______
ST 1A **The Crew of the Enterprise.** Spock with camera and 6 crewmembers.			
Limited Edition, sealed/numbered	20	20-30	______
Studio Seal only	15	15-20	______
ST 4 The Enterprise escapes from a fiery exploding planet			
Limited Edition, sealed/numbered	20	20-30	______
Studio Seal only	15	15-20	______
ST 5 **Yesteryear,** Spock pointing finger at winged Aurelian, Aleek-Om. Limited Edition, sealed/numbered	20	20-30	______
Studio Seal only	15	15-20	______
ST 6 **More Tribbles, More Troubles,** bridge scene with tribbles.			
Limited Edition, sealed/ numbered	20	20-30	______
Studio Seal only	15	15-20	______
ST 8 The Enterprise encounters a Klingon ship, green planet in background. Limited Edition, sealed/numbered	20	20-30	______
ST 9 **The Ambergris Element** - Sursnake, Red serpent creature and green aliens called Aquans. Limited Edition, sealed/numbered	20	20-30	______
Studio Seal only	15	15-20	______

ARTWORK

	Issue	Current	Cost/Date
ST 11 **Jihad - Composite of Aliens** Crewmembers with one female crewmember. Limited Edition, sealed/numbered	20	20-30	_____
Studio Seal only	15	15-20	_____
ST 12 **Spock, the Boy Atop L'Chaya,** young Spock on back of his pet Sehlat facing Vulcan mountain cat, Yesteryear. Limited Edition, sealed/numbered	20	20-30	_____
Studio Seal only	15	15-20	_____
ST 14 **The Time Trap,** Enterprise in ship graveyard. Limited Edition, sealed/numbered	20	20-30	_____
Studio Seal only	15	15-20	_____
ST 15 **The Enterprise and Aqua Shuttle** The shuttle as it leaves hangar bay. Limited Edition, sealed/numbered	20	20-30	_____
Studio Seal only	15	15-20	_____
ST 16 **Beyond the Farthest Star,** Enterprise entrapped by a giant pod-like ship. Limited Edition, sealed/numbered	20	20-30	_____
Studio Seal only	15	15-20	_____
ST 20 **Kukulan and the Enterprise,** Enterprise and Aztec serpent-ship. Limited Edition, sealed/numbered	20	20-30	_____
Studio Seal only	15	15-20	_____
ST 22 **Time Warp** (Classic), blue, red and yellow Enterprise going through a black hole time warp. Limited Edition, sealed/numbered	20	20-30	_____
Studio Seal only	15	15-20	_____
ST 23 **About to Battle a Klingon,** Enterprise in deep dive on left, Klingon ship on right under green planet. Limited Edition, sealed/numbered	20	20-30	_____
Studio Seal only	15	15-20	_____
ST 24 **Star Trek,** Enterprise before red planet. Limited Edition, sealed/numbered	20	20-30	_____
Studio Seal only	15	15-20	_____
ST 25 **The CounterClock Incident**, Enterprise from rear approaching alien ship and purple planet. Limited Edition, sealed/numbered	20	20-30	_____
Studio Seal only	15	15-20	_____

• **Cels**

Lincoln Enterprises. Cartoon reproductions on clear acetate film, copies of original drawings by the studio animators, unmounted:

	Issue	Current	Cost/Date
Crew Figures, 1983. Ten standing portraits: Kirk, Spock, McCoy, Scotty, Uhura, Sulu, Chapel, Lt. M'Hress, Lt. Arex and the Enterprise, set of 4"x8"	4	6-9	_____
Enterprise, 1979. Overlay of the t.v. starship designed so you can mount it over the constellations or planets of your choice, 10"x14"	2.50	4-6	_____

• **Drawings.** Filmation Studios, 1974. The original drawings from which the t.v. animated cels were painted. Sizes vary.

	Issue	Current	Cost/Date
Kirk with phaser			_____
Kirk head profile			_____
Kirk pushing a rock			_____
Kirk holding communicator			_____
Kirk - close up			_____
Kirk falling			_____
Kirk with arms folded			_____
Kirk with eyes closed			_____
Kirk (old)			_____
Spock kneeling			_____
Spock lying down (old)			_____
Spock, waist-shot			_____
Spock leaning			_____
Spock holding phaser			_____
Spock painting			_____
Spock - rear view			_____
Spock, Markel and Randi			_____
Kirk helping Spock stand up			_____
Uhura - waist shot			_____
Kirk and Spock			_____
Harry Mudd			_____
Chapel carrying tricorder			_____
Chapel profile			_____
Chapel, waist shot			_____
Male and Female Ursinoids			_____
Two Rock Creatures fighting			_____
Three-eyes Rock Creature			
Sold individually	—	5-8	_____

• Prints

	Issue	Current	Cost/Date
Enterprise Art Print. Star Trek The Official Fan Club, 1986 Twentieth Anniversary, limited edition print, full color rendition of the Enterprise over planetscape by Gerard W. Roundtree, 3,500 signed & numbered, 11"x17"	15	15-16	_____
Enterprise Computer Print-Out. Lincoln Enterprises, 1979. Five-color printout of the t.v. starship in starboard profile. Intricately detailed dot matrix reproduction in a mural size, 12"x38"	4	4-7	_____
Enterprise Evolution Packet. Lincoln Enterprises, 1983. Full color art rendering of ship designs bearing the name of "Enterprise" from Star Trek archives, 12 drawings, 11"x17", P2192, set of 12	4.95	5-7	_____

ARTWORK

Seven Star Portfolio. Kelly & Feas, 1976. Seven specially commissioned paintings in full color rendered by the ST artist Kelly Freas. 12½"x19" color prints on heavy textured white paper. Original paintings were on tour with Strekcons during 1976-1977. [1]

Set includes:
S-1 Kirk against star map
S-2 Spock in environsuit at transporter controls
S-3 Scotty, in kilt wearing a moustache
S-4 McCoy, smiling
S-5 Sulu, without shirt with fencing foil
S-6 Uhura, sitting at Communications
S-7 Chekov, against starfield

	Issue	Current	Cost/Date
Individual print, unsigned	1.50	3-5	______
Individual print, signed by Freas	3.00	5-7	______
Set of 7 prints, unsigned	9.95	10-15	______
Set of 7 prints, signed	19.95	25-30	______

Seven star portfolio, 1976.

Star Trek Crew - Future Fantasy. Cousins Publishing, 1977. Full color, drawing by Ken Barr on 8-point coated board, wispy-style montage of Kirk in forefront holding phaser and communicator with Spock, McCoy, Sulu, Uhura and Scotty behind, Enterprise above firing phasers, planetscape below, mailed flat. [2]

	Issue	Current	Cost/Date
11"x14" artboard	1.50	6-12	______

Star Trek Color Portraits. Lincoln Enterprises, 1970. Color drawings by Probert, reproductions of oil paintings, includes Kirk, Spock, McCoy, Uhura, Chekov and Chapel, 8½"x11", thin glossy paper.

	Issue	Current	Cost/Date
No. 2141, Set of 8 portraits	3.50	5-7	______
No. 2200, 1983 Set of 9 portraits plus a special print of the Enterprise	3.95	4-6	______

An ad for Filmation Studio - Cels, 1977

Stars of Star Trek. Gary Hawfitch, c. 1974. Black and white, nine portrait studies of the Star Trek characters plus one drawing of the Enterprise, profiles in ink media. This is set I of Hawfitch's series.

	Issue	Current	Cost/Date
Enterprise firing twin phasers, reads "The Stars of Star Trek, 9"x12"	—	2-3	______
Captain Kirk, 8½"x11"	—	2-3	______
Mr. Spock, 8½"x11"	—	2-3	______
Dr. McCoy, 8½"x11"	—	2-3	______
Scotty, 8½"x11"	—	2-3	______
Sulu, 8½"x11"	—	2-3	______
Uhura, 8½"x11"	—	2-3	______
Chekov, 8½"x11"	—	2-3	______
Nurse Chapel, 8½"x11"	—	2-3	______
Yeoman Rand, 8½"x11"	—	2-3	______

Star Trek Folio. Lincoln Enterprises, 1983. Eleven color portraits of Star Trek characters by Doug Little. Features STTMP stars Nimoy, D. Kelley, James Doohan, G. Takei, Nichelle Nichols, Majel Barrett Roddenberry, Mark Lenard (as a Klingon), Persis Kimbatta and Steve Collins; plus STWOK Kirstie Alley, 11"x14".

	Issue	Current	Cost/Date
P 2140 Set of 11	9.95	10-12	______

[1] Kelly Freas' portfolio of artwork was reprinted in book format as a special amateur press release in 1976, entitled *Officers of the Bridge.*

[2] This drawing also appeared as a 20"x28" poster.

Color portrait by Probert, 1970.

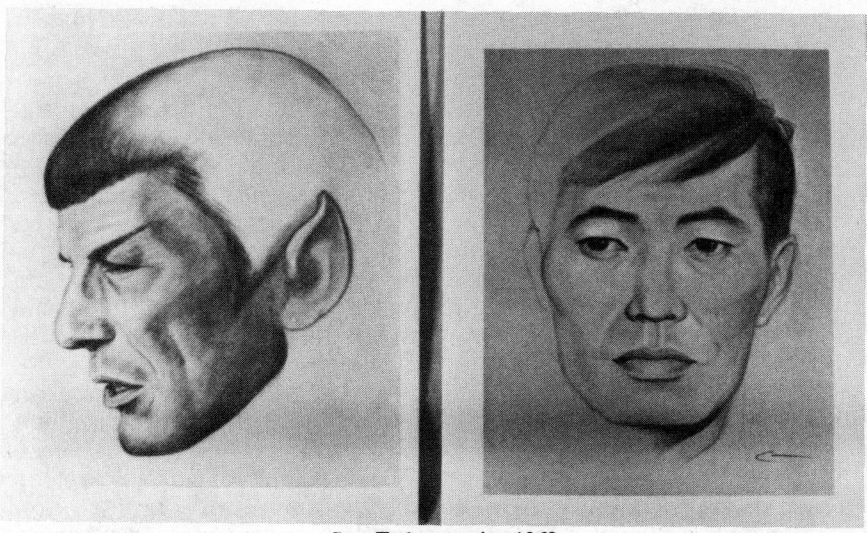

Star Trek portraits, 1968

	Issue	Current	Cost/Date
Star Trek Portraits. Star Trek Enterprises, 1968. Art folio by Criss. Nine 8½"x11" reproductions from charcoal portraits, includes the Spock portrait which appeared in *Sixteen Magazine* in 1967. Facial poses of Kirk, McCoy, Scotty, Uhura, Sulu, Chekov, Nurse Chapel and Gene Roddenberry also. Ready to frame on medium gauge white paper.			
Complete portfolio	2	12-16	_____
Star Trek Ships. M-5 Productions, 1974. Collection of glossy prints from original art drawings and photo overlays. Set contains 30 individual prints in art or photo styles, sold separately. Renderings of the U.S.S. Enterprise, the Klingon Battle Cruiser and the Romulan Bird of Prey as seen from different perspectives. Works are untitled and come available in three sizes:			
3½"x5" format.................	1.00	1-3	_____
5"x7" format....................	3.00	3-4	_____
8"x10" format..................	5.00	6-8	_____
Star Trek Spaceship Folder Lincoln Enterprises, 1980. Full color artwork prints of the six spaceships used in Star Trek. Includes the Federation Grain Cargo Ship, Klingon Battle Cruiser "Devisor," Romulan Raider (Bird of Prey), Beyond the Farthest Star, Galileo Shuttlecraft and the U.S.S. Enterprise, 12" x 12"			
P2190 Folder of 6	3.50	4-6	_____

	Issue	Current	Cost/Date
Star Trek Universe. Rivoche, Destination Enterprises, 1976. Special art portfolio featuring nine black and white prints in 11"x14" format. Art inset measures 9"x12" with a 2" white frame border. Studies are detailed technical drawings of vessels and planetscapes, plus portraits. Titles appear along the bottom, printed in Canada. Packaged in a clasp envelope with a portion of the Nova Rescue illustrated. "Aftermath," Downed Klingon Battle Cruiser on an alien moonscape			
Sold as a set of nine prints......	5	15-20	_____
• **Storyboards.** Lincoln Enterprises, 1980. Xeroxed copies of the pen and ink storyboards which trace the action sequences of each individual Star Trek cartoon. One booklet for each animated episode nine panels per sheet, or approx. 300-400 illustrations per book. Yellow construction paper covers have no ornamentation other than a stenciled "Star Trek" imprint. Invidividual Storyboards ordered by the 22 episode titles, each	4.50	5-7	_____

BLUEPRINTS

Star Trek blueprints represent fandom's fascination with the physical military and engineering paraphernalia of Starfleet and all of its associated weapons, field equipment or assorted alien craft. This technical application of the Trek universe has been propogated by professional and semi-professional artists since the early 1980's.

The first conception of Star Trek as a schematic medium appeared through the mail order lists of Star Trek Enterprises in 1968 when Matt Jeffries (Art Director for T.V. Trek) penned six 8½" x 11" blueprint sheets for sale in the catalog. The sheets contained very simple designs for the Enterprise and the Galileo shuttlecraft, focusing only on their weaponry, structural dimensions and multi-angle perspectives or comparisons. These sheets were the first of their type ever.

In 1974 Franz Joseph began work on both the *Star Trek Blueprints* and the *Star Trek Star Fleet Technical Manual* as a direct result to produce more accurate drawings than those available by Matt Jeffries. All of Jeffries blueprints are considered, despite their historical significance, to be inaccurate and out-of-scale.

Originally conceived as only a hardback technical manual, Franz Joseph decided to produce independent blueprint sheets of the U.S.S. Enterprise for the benefit of enthusiastic friends and convention goers.

The only other professionally produced publication to appear in blueprint form on bookstore racks are the *Official Blueprints Star Trek The Motion Picture* drawn by David Kimble. Simon & Schuster released this set of 14 sheets in a plastic vinyl case with a snap enclosure similar to that released by Ballantine in 1975.

Generally, blueprints come in paper pockets of various sizes according to their interior sheet content. Storing can be a problem to prevent bending and tearing. It is best to store blueprints upright in acid-free environments or to enclose them in Mylar protector bags.

More recently, there has been a trend by amateur presses to follow Franz Joseph's lead and incorporate multi-faceted blueprints into softbound volumes for convenient handling. For modeling or prop building purposes, to-scale blueprint sheets are preferable.

	Issue	Current	Cost/Date
Animated Freighter Blueprint Set. Geoffrey Mandel. 12 sheets	5	6-8	_____
Assorted Ship Profiles (Great Ships). Allen Everhart, Starcraft Productions. Exterior views of 4 famous spacecraft includes U.S.S. Enterprise, Valley Forge (Silent Running), Battlestar (Battlestar Galactica) and Orion Shuttle (2001), sheets 8½"x22", set of four	5.95	6-8	_____
Avenger Class Heavy Frigate. David John Neilson, Starfleet Printing Office. Interior and exterior, Killer Bee Assault Pod, 6 sheets, 14"x20"	7.95	8-10	_____
Blueprinting the Science Fiction Universes New Media Publishing. A collection of SF designs by Shane Johnson representing the blueprints from ships, weapons and equipment of Star Trek, Star Wars, Battlestar Galactica and other future worlds, available in four individual golden art folios.			
Gold Folio Volume I	12	12-15	_____
Gold Folio Volume II	12	12-15	_____
Gold Folio Volume III	12	12-15	_____
Gold Folio Volume IV	12	12-15	_____

	Issue	Current	Cost/Date
Communicator Blueprints (Star Fleet) Nova Productions, 1986. Eight views of the workings of one of Star Trek's most critical pieces of equipment	3	3-5	_____
Dreadnaught Comparison Chart Todd Guenther, Starstation Aurora Two configurations, giant 1 sheet, 24"x34"	3	4-6	_____
Durance Class Cargo/Tug Starstation Aurora. External and cut-away views of ship, 5 sheets, 8"x 17"	4	5-7	_____
DY 500 Series Comparison Chart Michael Morrissette, Starstation Aurora. Blueprints of Botany Bay Sleeper Ship ("Space Seed"), 1 sheet	3.95	4-6	_____
Federation Size Comparison Chart Todd Guenther, Starstation Aurora Chart I Exteriors of cruisers, heavy cruisers, tugs, freighters and scouts of the Federation, twelve different ships, two sheets, 20"x28"	5	6-8	_____

BLUEPRINTS

	Issue	Current	Cost/Date
Chart II Supplement featuring the Enterprise, Belknap, Avenger, Knox, Federation, Ascension and K'teremny Class vessels, one sheet 21"x26"...	6	7-9	______
Flagstaff Series Drone Spy Reconnaissance Ship March E. Shammai Blueprints of sensor-carrying drone used to explore dangerous phenomenon by the Federation, 4 sheets........................	4.95	5-7	______
Glenn Class, Eberhardt Design, 1985 Four sheets in set, views with stats and the details..................	5.95	6-8	______
Gorn Defense Battlecruiser Allen C. Peed III, Stardraft Productions. Exteriors of previously unknown ships, 2 sheets, 8½"x14".	3.50	4-6	______
Hornet Class Starship, 1985 Full exterior and interior views of this new SFC vessel. Package contains seven large sheets plus supplements.....................	10.95	12-14	______
J-Class, Eberhardt Design, 1985 Top, bottom, side, front and cutaway profiles for this ship.........	6.95	7-9	______
K-7 Space Station, Geoffrey Mandel Exterior only, four sheets, 15½"x22½"...................	3	4-6	______
Revised, 1986. Extended plans for this Class K Rest and Recreation Facility design. Six 17"x22" sheets featuring exterior as well as interior layout plans...................	5.95	6-8	______
Kantanga Class Klingon Vessel Stardraft Productions. Exterior profiles only........................	6	6-8	______
Giant Blueprint Set. The D-7/5 Star Vessel from STTMP in large detail, 24"x60" format.................	6	7-9	______
Klingon Battlecruiser Michael McMaster Galactic Designs and Productions Exterior and interior of ship, 8 sheets, 13½"x29". Envelope is white with blue lettering and diagram, 10"x15"......................	7.95	8-10	______

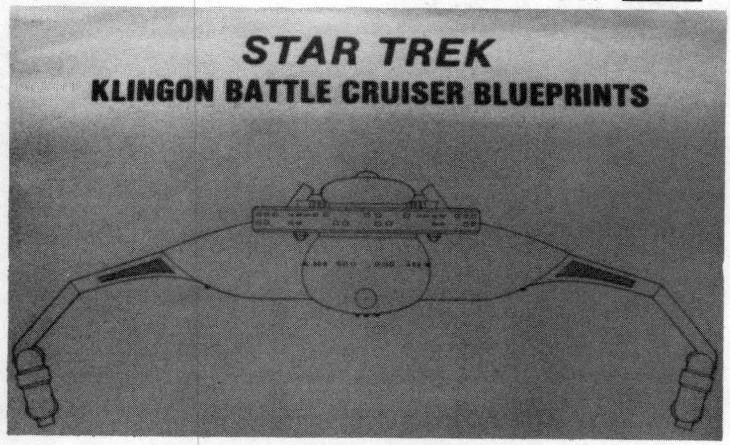

Klingon Battle Cruiser by Michael McMaster.

	Issue	Current	Cost/Date
• **Klingon Bird of Prey Scout Vessel** Kruge's battlecruiser from ST III. Outboard profile, outboard top and bottom plan, outboard bow and stern, plus inboard deck plans – elevations 1-10, eight sheets, 12"x28".......................	6.95	7-9	______
Klingon-Romulan hybrid design scout ship as seen in ST III, exterior and interior layouts, plus cloaking device technology, six sheets, 18"x24"......................	10.95	12-14	______
Klingon Destroyer K'T'Orr Full specifications, plus interior and exterior details, nine sheets, 11"x16"	8.95	9-10	______
Kobayashi Maru Neutronic Fuel Carrier Roger Sorenson, Starfleet Printing Office Five sheets detailing this "unseen" ship from ST II. Exteriors only, cross sections and specs, four sheets, 14"x17"......................	4.95	5-7	______
Major Deep Space Craft Size Comparison Chart Michael McMaster, Galactic Designs and Productions Exteriors of U.S.S. Enterprise, Romulan, Klingon D-7 and Tholian ships, 1 sheet, 24"x36"...........	3	4-5	______
Regula 1 Space Laboratory Full interior layout designs plus exploded views, outboard and cutaway views included, 5 sheets, 9"x16"...	8.95	9-12	______
Romulan Bird of Prey Cruiser Michael McMaster, Galactic Designs and Productions Interior and exterior designs plus plasma weapon, 5 sheets, 18"x24"..	6	6-8	______

Enterprise Blueprints

BLUEPRINTS

	Issue	Current	Cost/Date
Selayna Class Starship Corellian Freighter S. Johnson and D. Holt 4 sheets	4.95	5-7	______
Sherman Class Cargo Drones Todd Guenther, Starstation Aurora Interior and exterior of ship from Star Trek animated series, 10 sheets, 8½"x17"	5.95	6-8	______
Shuttlecraft Galileo-7 Allen Everhart, Starcraft Productions Designs for the Enterprise shuttle, 2 sheets, 18"x24"	3	4-6	______
Starship Fleet Blueprings Allen H. Fishbeck, Fishbeck Designs 12 sheets	7	7-9	______
S.S. Valenda Class (Giant Cargo Spaceship) Northstar Corp, 1980 Non-homebased spacecraft based on Federation designs which doesn't carry a planetary designation letter. Twelve large pages, 14"x22" in carrying envelope	6.95	7-9	______
• **Star Trek Blueprints** Franz Joseph, Franz Joseph Designs Blueprint sheet package produced for ltd. distribution and never mass marketed. Sheets are rolled copies detailing every facet of the t.v. Starship Enterprise		60-100	______
Franz Joseph Ballantine Books, 1975 Original mass-produced package of the starship Enterprise from the t.v. series. Every foot of the ship, to scale: bridge, sickbay, crew's quarters, shuttlecraft bay, photon torpedo banks, science labs, etc. Twelve sheets, 9"x30", folded in brown vinyl/plastic pocket with snap closure.[1]	5	25-40	______
Star Trek The Motion Picture – Official Blueprints David Kimble, Wallably Books, 1979 Assorted ship profiles from STTMP, includes new Klingon ship, Vulcan Shuttle, new version Enterprise, Work Bee and more. Packaged in vinyl and plastic pocket with snap closure. Blue cardstock insert, 14 sheets, 13⅓"x19"	6.95	15-20	______

Star Trek The Motion Picture Blueprints, 1979.

	Issue	Current	Cost/Date
Star Trek III The Search For Spock, Advance Prints Starstation Aurora Preview designs for the spacecraft to appear in the third movie, one sheet, 24"x36"	5	6-7	______
U.S.S. Almeida Heavy Cruiser Freighter Michael Morrissette, Starstation Aurora Five sheets, 18"x22"			______
U.S.S. Aurora Class Space Cruiser Todd Guenther, Starstation Aurora Cruiser which travels between the Sol and Eridani star systems from Star Trek t.v. series, 2 sheets, 16"x22"	4.95	5-7	______
U.S.S. Caracal Class Command Cruiser Todd Guenther, Starstation Aurora Designs for ship which preceeds the Reliant in construction, 12 sheets, 8½"x28"	7.50	8-12	______
U.S.S. Decateur Prototype Cruiser Todd Guenther, Starstation Aurora Printed on heavy gold paper, 1 sheet, 23"x29"	3.95	4-6	______
U.S.S. Destroyat Class Heavy Cruiser Todd Guenther, Starstation Aurora General plans, 6 sheets, 10½"x28".	7	7-9	______
• **U.S.S. Enterprise Bridge Blueprints** Michael McMaster, Galactic Designs and Productions The starship, all bridge stations, switches and functions, ten sheets, 17"x22", three renditions:			
First Edition – blue vertical design cover, t.v. Enterprise	5.95	6-8	______
Second Edition – "Revised", black horizontal cover, STTMP ship	6.95	7-9	______

1. **This packet was the first mass-produced commercial printing of Star Trek blueprints. Franz Joseph, a Technical Artist at General Dynamics, Convair Division began work on these prints in 1973, the same time he initiated the** *Star Fleet Technical Manual* project. Within 6 months after hitting the newsstands, this blueprint package went through 3 consecutive printings: 50,000; 100,000 and 60,000 copies were produced and sold.

Second Edition Bridge Blueprints.

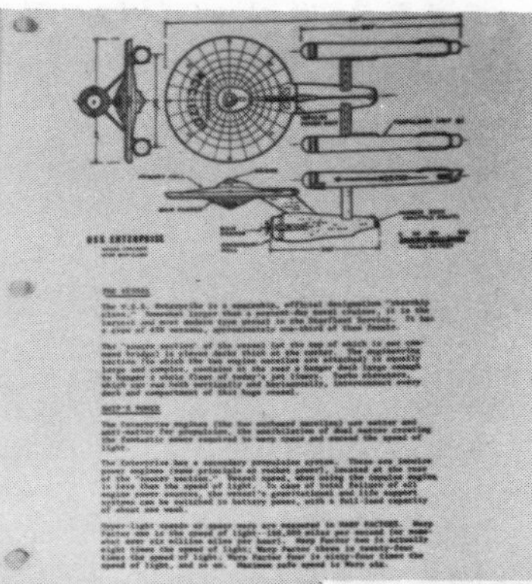

Original Matt Jeffries Plans, 1968.

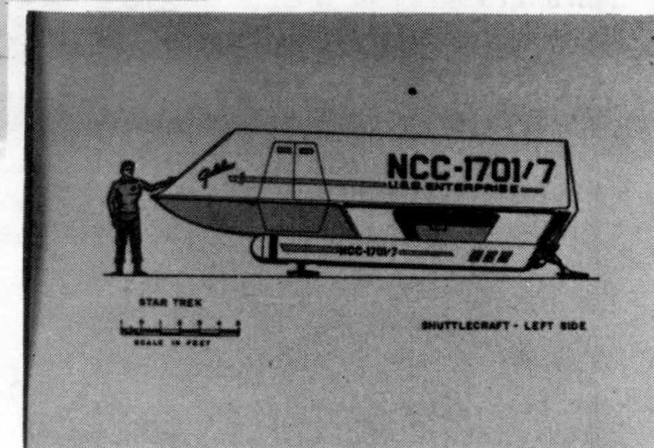

Enterprise Blueprints	**Issue**	**Current Cost/Date**	
Pan Galactic Press, 1974 Franz Joseph's release of these famous blueprints, exterior and interior profiles, 12 sheets, 9"x29", folded and packaged in white envelope packet [2]	7.95	10-12	______
Enterprise Giant Blueprints Two sheets, large 24"x60" format:			
T.V. starship	6.95	7-9	______
STTMP starship	6.95	7-9	______
Enterprise-Construction Profiles			
New Eye, distrib., 1985 Four sheets detailing the starship as it was constructed, 17"x22"	6.95	7-9	______
Enterprise-Type Profiles			
New Eye, distrib. Compares the two Enterprise models as seen in the television series and the pilot film:			
Type I (from the pilot film "The Cage")	6.95	7-9	______
Type II (seen in the aired series)	6.95	7-9	______

Enterprise and Shuttlecraft Galileo Set
Star Trek Enterprises, 1968
Official plans from the drawing board of Matt Jeffries, Art Director for Star Trek t.v. series, Set of 6 pen and ink drawings of deck plans on white bond paper, 8½"x11". Details focus only on weaponry, structural dimensions and multi-angle perspectives. Very simple blueprints, but the first of a whole range of prints devoted to Star Trek's spacecraft:

	Issue	**Current Cost/Date**	
1. Starship Enterprise, size comparison to CVA-65 Enterprise Aircraft carrier 2. U.S.S. Enterprise (top, front and side schematics) 3. Galileo 1707'7 Shuttlecraft, exterior and interior seating plans, 2 sheets 4. Hangar Deck, bay and aft sections, 2 sheets			
Sold as a set [3]	.50	4-6	______
U.S.S. Excelsior			
Jason Genser, Starstation Aurora Official S.F.C. Datapack designs of the Ingram Class starship. Eight sheets in a special collector's edition, plastic wrap packaged set	9.95	10-12	______

U.S.S. Excelsior Blueprints, 1986.

2. This amateur press release of Franz Joseph's Enterprise blueprints occurred before the commercial 1975 printing by Ballantine books.
3. With this entry, Star Trek Enterprises began the very prolific age of Star Trek starships in blueprint format. These six pen and ink illustrations appeared in the Roddenberry/Whitfield paperback book *The Making of Star Trek* published by Ballantine in September 1968.

BLUEPRINTS

	Issue	Current Cost/Date	
U.S.S. Federation Class Dreadnaught Allen C. Peed III, Starcraft Productions Designs for largest starfleet starship, 10 sheets, 9"x27" in carrying envelope. Includes inboard deck plans, sickbay, engineering, hangar decks, deflector shields, cloaking device room, etc.	9.95	10-12	_____
U.S.S. Independence Class Freighter Geoffrey Mandel, Interstellar Associations Interior and exterior plans, 11 sheets, 8½"x14". Envelope is white with blue lettering, folded 10"x15".	4	5-8	_____
U.S.S. Menahga Class Battlecruiser Michael Morrissette, Starstation Aurora 1 sheet, 24"x36"	3.50	4-6	_____
U.S.S. Reliant Starstation Aurora Interior and exterior of this Avenger Class starship, ten sheets, 16"x28", vinyl and plastic pouch with snap closure	9.95	10-12	_____
Development Chart, 1986 The evolution of this ship, includes Coventry, Destroyat, Surya and Ptolemy Class vessels and history, 24"x36"	3	3-5	_____
U.S.S. Renner Class Escort Destroyer New Eye, distrib., 1986 Four sheets, 11"x17"	4.95	5-7	_____
U.S.S. Saladin Class Destroyer Scout Allen Everhart, Starcraft Productions Exterior and interior blueprints, 9 sheets	7.95	8-9	_____

	Issue	Current Cost/Date	
U.S.S. Valenda Class Star Freighter Allen C. Peed III, Starcraft Productions New ship, 12 sheets	9.95	10-12	_____
• **Weapons and Field Equipment Prints** Individual packaged sets containing five sheets each, paper envelopes are white with blue lettering, folded prints are 9½"x12", covers entire S.F. media range:			
Number 1 - Details on phasers, communicators, Jupiter II laster pistol, Sandman gun, light sabres and phaser rifles. Assorted other weaponry	7.95	8-10	_____
Number 2 - Star Trek phasers III and IV, Jupiter II laser rifle, Colonial blaster, Sandman follower types I & II, Alpha Stungun	7.95	8-10	_____
Number 3 - More assorted S.F. weapons and field equipment blueprints	7.95	8-10	_____

CLOTHES AND ACCESSORIES

Few Star Trek collectors engage actively in the purchasing of Trek apparel and clothing accessories unless they intend to use an item for daily wear. Since most clothing merchandise designed for adults is a moderately high financial investment, fans are less likely to buy something which they can't expect to be able to don and enjoy. This is especially true of high-quality Star Trek promotional jackets, uniforms and caps.

Some of the most interesting apparel collectibles are those vintage items produced for children during the 60's. Kids' pajamas, underwear and socks are definitely rare memorabilia. Like children's toys, clothes for children seldom survived the ravages induced upon them by everyday use. Few apparel collectibles of this type exist in their original packaging sealed and untouched.

Probably the most popular general clothing item which Star Trek fans tend ot buy is the T-shirt. There is no limit to the diversity of commercial or fan-generated T-shirts available on the market today.

In retrospect, T-shirts which serve as pre-promotion displays for upcoming motion pictures such as "Waiting For Star Trek III", are unusual memorabilia which tend to disappear quickly. Vintage *Star Trek The Motion Picture* T-shirts bearing photo transfers are also good collectibles. Convention T-shirts of the early 70's can be irreplaceable collector's items as well. Fan artists also use the T-shirt surface as a medium for fine silkscreen designs or airbrush renderings. Some of these, although expensive, can be one-of-a-kind investments.

UNIFORMS AND COSTUMES

Excluding special offers for customized jackets and shirts which accompanied the purchase of certain children's toys of the 1970's, marketing Star Trek uniforms has traditionally been the merchandising vehicle of amateur fans. Costumes celebrating the tunics worn by Captain Kirk and Mr. Spock as well as the Yeoman's uniform have become an integral part of Star Trek fandom.

From 1973 to 1977, a New York based costume outlet known as Enterprise Outfitters began its business by providing custom, mail-order shirts and tunics from Star Trek. The operation eventually expanded to display its wares on the racks of a Chicago novelty store. A similar venture evolved with Starfleet Fabrications. In addition to providing completed Star Trek uniforms, this fan endeavor also marketed a variety of home-grown sewing patterns which could be "authenticated" by purchasing the proper insignia patches being sold by Star Trek Enterprises.

A more recent market has developed from professional manufacturers centering around adult Star Trek partywear. Headmasks constructed of latex and other synthetic fibers have been produced which model alien characters from *Star Trek The Motion Picture.* Besides the ageless quantities of molded latex Vulcan ears fans have enjoyed for years, complete head masks of Klingon or Vulcan Master personas also hit the market.

Perhaps the most collectible partywear item for memorabilia fans is the Halloween costume sets designed for children. In the mid 1970's, following the appearance of the Star Trek animated series, Trek characters were marketed as "Super Hero," "Science Fiction Hero" or "Star Trek Star" fashionables during October Trick or Treat blitzes.

Collectors in pursuit of Star Trek children's costumes of this caliber should be aware of the very subtle costume changes that went towards producing "new line" outfits. Annual alterations can be as inconsequential as the hemming of a pants leg or the addition/deletion of a sleeve.

Color costume logos may also be relocated. In the case of the Ilia costume from *Star Trek The Motion Picture,* the decal character disappears one year only to reappear on the following. Generally, the face masks accompanying a costume will remain unchanged for years. However, identical face molds did on occasion receive heavier doses of makeup or show deeper facial etchings and slightly different hair shadings.

Packaging is the most crucial element in the marketing of Halloween costumes. It is also important to collectors. Usually the mask is partially visible through a tightly shrink wrapped window box. Box features changed quite regularly even if the interior costume didn't.

Ad for two hats produced by The Thinking Cap Company, 1982.

Jacket and T-shirt ad released with promotion associated with STTMP.

CLOTHING

STTMP T-shirt. Photo style transfer, 1979.

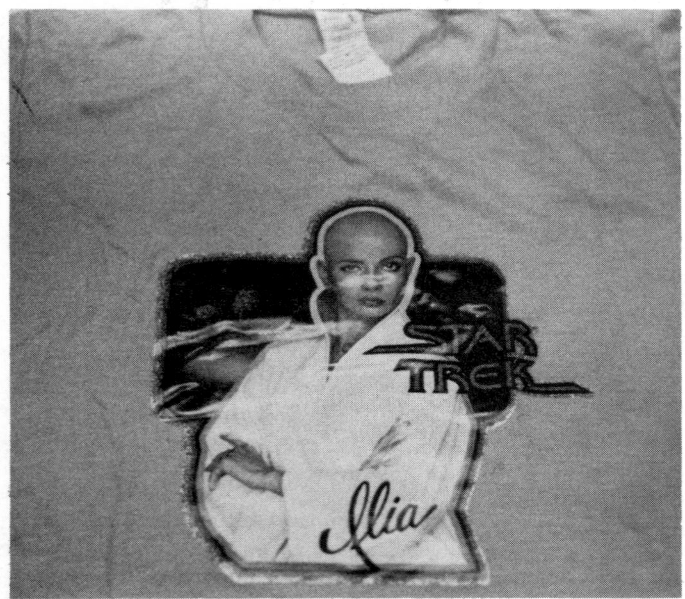

STTMP T-shirt featuring Ilia.

T.V. Enterprise T-shirt, circa 1976.

Kirk Costume, STWOK, 1979.

Spock Super Hero Costume, Ben Cooper, 1973.

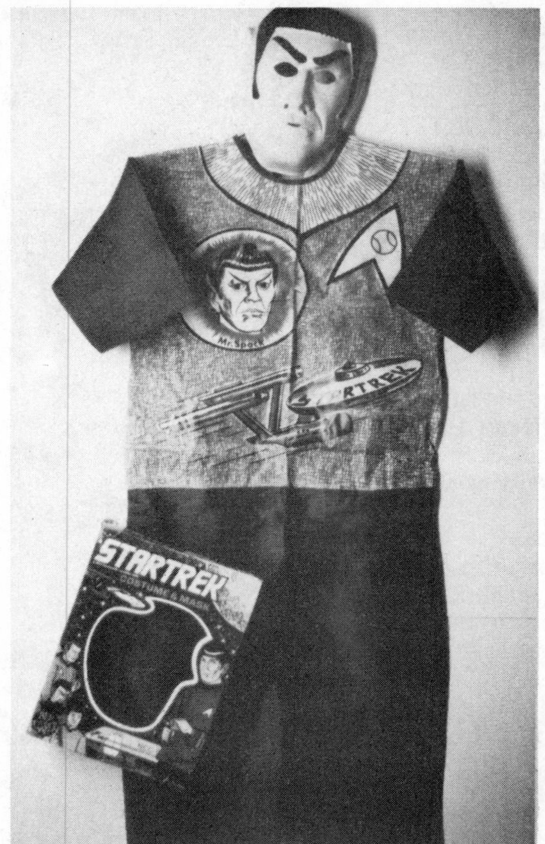

Spock Costume, 1975. Very similar to #293 but lacks plastic cuffs.

Spock costume #293. Notice no sleeves, 1975.

Spock face mask for adults, Ben Cooper, 1976.

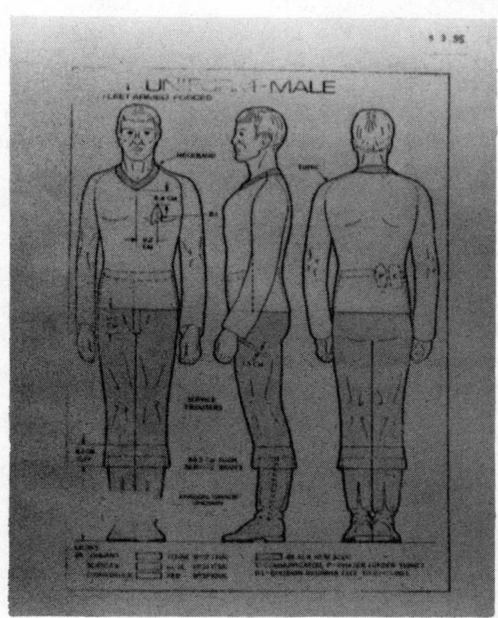

Pattern for Star Trek uniforms - men.

Vulcan ears by Franco, 1975 and by unknown manufacturer, 1980.

CLOTHING AND ACCESSORIES

BELT POUCHES

	Issue	Current	Cost/Date
•Belt Pouches. T-K Graphics Various shades of tan and brown, polyester-lined and hand sewn, water resistant, assorted textures with metal snap closures. Designs are silk-screened on the front, 6"x9" sizes:			
Imperial Klingon Fleet. Design shows Klingon Cruiser	4.50	4-6	_____
Star Fleet Academy. Design shows Janus Head Emblem	4.50	4-6	_____
Star Fleet Command Intelligence Division Assorted textures	4.50	4-6	_____
Star Fleet HQ Tactical Operations Center Design shows UFP Pennant	4.50	4-6	_____
UFP Diplomatic Service Design shows Janus Head Emblem	4.50	4-6	_____
U.S.S. Enterprise Design shows schematic of the starship Enterprise	4.50	4-6	_____
U.S.S. Enterprise/NCC 1701 Assorted textures	4.50	4-6	_____

BILLFOLDS

	Issue	Current	Cost/Date
• **Enterprise Billfold.** Larimi, 1977 Zippered wallet for children. Available in black or brown vinyl with circle decal feturing the t.v. Enterprise engaged in a torpedo battle with a Romulan Bird of Prey vessel	2	3-6	_____
"Star Trek The Motion Picture" Billfold. Larami, 1979 Vinyl, child's wallet with the STTMP letter logo. Blister packed on cardstock which features photo scenes from the movie	2	3-5	_____

OUTERWEAR

	Issue	Current	Cost/Date
• **"Beam Me Up, Scotty" Interstallar Propellar Cap** Fantastic Films Magazine, 1983 Beanie style cap with rectangular patch and lettering. Multicolored, includes a plastic spaceship with a propeller on top, adjustable band, sizes SML	10	12-15	_____
• **"Enterprise, U.S.S." /Insignia Patch Cap** The Thinking Cap Co., 1982 100% cotton sports cap in red, white background embroidered patch features golden encircled insignia design from the movies	8.95	9-12	_____
• **"Enterprise, U.S.S. /Star Trek" Stocking Cap** Acrylic yarn hat with ribbed headband and fluffy pom-pom on top. Oval patch has imprinted starboard profile t.v. starship between embroidered lettering. Assorted color combination	3	7-10	_____
• **"Enterprise, U.S.S." Design Jacket** Hollywood On Location, 1985 Satin-finish jacket in black with red trim. Embroidered in white lettering above the left pocket and features a silk screen design starship across the back. Jacket	65	65-75	_____
Jacket personalized with your own name	73	75-80	_____
• **"Enterprise, U.S.S." Letter Jacket** Lincoln Enterprises, 1984 Blue satin-finish crew jacket with navy and gold striped banding for fold-down collar, cuffs and waistband. Navy colored snap closures. Lettering in white. SMLXL	45	50-60	_____
• **"Star Trek The Motion Picture" Letter Windbreaker**[1] D.D. Bean & Sons, Inc., 1980 Also called the "Standard Duty Jacket". Lightweight polyurethane windbreaker with nylon piping and no lining. Front has movie style encircled Command Insignia in red. Silver cloth. Child SML; Women SML; Men SMLXL	40	45-50	_____
• **"Star Trek The Motion Picture" L.E.D. Design Jacket** D.D. Bean & Sons, Inc., 1980 Also called the "Deluxe Duty Jacket" Outer shell of metallic, silver-fleck polyurethane with 100% nylon, silver lining. "Neru-style" collar, U.F.P. emblem patch on breast, right sleeve embroidered with gold, white and black rank braid. Back has printed official Movie Letter Logo and outline of Enterprise in front-portside profile. Seven ruby L.E.D. lights illuminate dome, saucer, torpedo bay and nacelles. Padded shoulders, elastic waist and sleeves. Black nylon accent piping. Operates by battery pack. Child SML; Women SML; Men SMLXL	95	120-150	_____
• **"Star Trek The Wrath of Kahn" Design Cap** Sports cap in assorted colors, featuring a blue-background patch and "starburst" design logo from the second movie, 1982	3.95	6-9	_____

1. This windbreaker was used as a special offer from D.D. Bean as advertised in bookcovers of Star Trek The Motion Picture matchbooks given away as theater promotions.

CLOTHING AND ACCESSORIES

Item	Issue	Current	Cost/Date
• **"Star Trek III: The Search For Spock" Official Commemorative Patch Cap** Lincoln Enterprises, 1984 Sports cap in black with official embroidered commemorative patch for the third movie (Enterprise and planet Genesis). The cap's bill has military "scrambled eggs" laurels in gold. (Cap goes with Lincoln's STSFS windbreaker listed below)...	9.95	10-12	_____
• **"Star Trek III: The Search For Spock" Official Commemorative Patch Jacket** Lincoln Enterprises, 1984 White satin-finsih crew jacket. Black banding for stand-up collar, black cuffs and waistband, black piping on raglan sleeves. Snap closures are black. Breast patch is official Enterprise/Genesis planet commemorative sewn on left. SMLXL............	45	50-70	_____
• **"Star Trek III: The Search For Spock" Official Commemorative Patch Windbreaker** Lincoln Enterprises, 1984 Black nylon windbreaker with 3/4 length sleeves, White trim and zipper, white flashing on stand-up collar. Left chest has official Enterprise/Genesis planet patch. (Matches the above Commemorative Cap). SMLXL.......................	25	30-35	_____
• **"Star Trek IV: The Voyage Home" Letter Jacket** Star Trek Official Fan Club, 1987 Silver satin-finish jacket with kasha lining, water repellent shell, washable. Black and white piping trim. Has 2-color Official Movie Letter Logo, plus lettering "Star Date 1986. How on Earth ..." SMLXL......................	45	45-50	_____
• **"Star Trek IV: The Voyage Home" Letter Cap** Star Trek Official Fan Club, 1987 Corduroy sports cap, embroidered in red with full movie Letter Logo, one size..........................	14	14-16	_____
• **"Star Trek IV: The Voyage Home" Deluxe Design Jacket** Paramount Pictures, 1987 White satin-finish jacket with blue and aqua piping, white quilted lining, blue ribbed collar and cuffs, zipper packet on lower left sleeve, snap closures, TVH Letter Logo over left breast, full width back embroidered scene of Enterprise and San Francisco Bay with Letter Logo. SMLXL......................	90	90-95	_____
• **"United Federation of Planets/Starfleet Headquarters" Patch Cap** The Thinking Cap Co., 1982 Blue and white galaxy emblem with golden laurels on patch, cap's bill has twin gold laurels, 100% cotton hat in navy, white or red..........	5.95	6-8	_____
• **United Federation of Planets Patch Windbreaker** [2] Great Lakes Sportswear, 1974 Light weight windbreaker with embroidered U.F.P. patch. Silver jacket, SMLXL.................	7.95	14-20	_____
• **Vulcan Ear Hat** A & D Company Navy blue flannel-material sports cap with two flesh-tone pointed ears sprouting through the top.........	5.95	6-8	_____

SHIRTS

Item	Issue	Current	Cost/Date
• **"Beam Me Up, Scotty. There's No Intelligent Life Down Here" Letter Shirt #11051** Mellow Mail Disturb., 1986 Navy shirt in 50/50 cotton, polyester with white lettering, SMLXL......................	9.95	10-12	_____
• **"Beam Me Up Scotty. There's No Intelligent Life Down Here!" Design Shirt** Intergalactic, distrib., 1985 Crew neck, short sleeves with ribbing. 50/50 cotton. Design shows cartoon droid punching into a computer terminal, color silk screen on grey shirt. SMLXL..............	9.95	10-12	_____
• **"Beam Me Up Scotty. There's No Intelligent Life On This Planet." Design Shirt** Fantasy Trader T-Shirts Powder blue decal of t.v. Enterprise over planet, wide-neck style shirt in assorted colors.................	7.95	8-10	_____
• **"Beam Me Up, Scotty. This Planet Sucks" Shirt** Letter, Mellow Mail, 1986 #10365 Black 50% shirt with white letters, SMLXL	9.95	10-12	_____
Design, Fantasy Traders T-Shirts Silver decal of t.v. Enterprise over planet on black shirt, crew neck; or assorted other colors available.....	7.95	8-10	_____

2. This windbreaker was used as a special offer inside boxes of plastic model kits sold by AMT Corporation from 1974 to 1976.

SHIRTS

	Issue	Current	Cost/Date
• **Enterprise Bridge/Blish Design Tank Top** [3]			
Lincoln Enterprises, 1980			
Features full color repro of NBC's one and only official Star Trek poster – Spock, Kirk and Enterprise over planet. Tank top in yellow, blue or orange with black trim. Silkscreen design on 100% cotton.			
SML	6.95	8-10	_____
• **Klingon Empire Design Shirts**			
Star Base Central, distrib. 1986			
Two styles:			
I - Klingon script (hieroglyphics) with Klingon Empire insignia design			
II - Same as above with additional lettering, "Klingons Don't Take Prisoners" in 1-inch letters, front or back.			
1. Tapered crew-neck, 50%, red print on white. Style I	12.95	12-13	_____
Style II	13.95	13-14	_____
2. Sand color shirt, 100% burnt orange printing. Style I	13.50	13-14	_____
Style II	14.95	14-15	_____
3. Sweat shirt in white with dark red design, 50%, raglan sleeves, opt. hood. Style I	15.95	15-16	_____
Style II	16.95	16-17	_____
4. Sand colored sweat shirt, burnt orange design, optional hood. Style I	17.95	17-18	_____
Style II	18.95	18-19	_____
• **"Property Of Star Fleet Command - U.S.S. Enterprise Rec Room" Letter Shirt**			
Space Station Studios, 1987			
Gym-style work-out T-shirt for the athletically minded crewmembers,			
SMLXL	6.95	7-8	_____
• **"Property of William Shatner Fan Club" Letter Shirt**			
William Shatner Fan Club, 1983			
Lettering on choice of four color shirts, white, navy, maroon or light blue. Two styles, SML:			
Polo Shirt	19.95	20-22	_____
Sweatshirt	19.95	20-22	_____
• **"Riverside, Iowa" Birthplace Letter Shirts** [4]			
Riverside Area Community Club, 1986			
Black letters with multi-color designs on solid color shirts: yellow, red, gray, blue, black or pink, two styles:			
Style I - "Where the TREK begins"			
Style II- "Future Birthplace of Captain Kirk" Child sizes 2-16	8	8-10	_____
Adult SMLXL	12	12-14	_____
• **"Starfleet Academy Training Command" Design Shirts**			
Star Base Central, distrib., 1986			
Lettering below an encircled command star design, SMLXL			
1. White 50%, navy trim and design	12.95	12-13	_____
2. Blue, high crew-neck, 100%, with white design	13.50	13-14	_____
3. White sweatshirt, navy blue design (optional hood for $2.00)	15.95	16-17	_____
4. Royal blue sweat shirt, white design (optional hood for $2.00)	15.95	16-17	_____
• **"Starship Security" Design Shirt**			
Intergalactic, distrib., 1985			
Crew neck with shirt sleeves and ribbing, 50% white shirt, silk screen lettering in red around a target-bullseye, SMLXL	6.95	7-8	_____
• **"Star Trek"/Enterprise Design Shirt**			
April Publications, 1984			
50% cotton blend, machine washable shirt. Litho design shows lettering above photo of t.v. Enterprise, has sparkling silver glitter on midnight black shirt, SMLXL	7	9-12	_____
• **"Star Trek Lives!" / Enterprise Design Shirt** [5]			
Albert Schuster, distrib. 1972			
The 1972 New York Star Trek Con Commemorative T-Shirt. Lettering in bright orange block letters inside solid black block frame. Black outline of t.v. Enterprise underneath in starboard profile, white shirt.			
Childs sizes 6-16	3	5-8	_____
Adult SMLXL	3	5-10	_____
• **Star Trek Lives T-Shirt**			
Furry, 1976			
White cotton T-shirt with silk screen designs, blue t.v. Enterprise in starfield, reads "Star Trek Lives" underneath, sizes SML	8	8-12	_____
Lincoln Enterprises, 1980			
100% cotton, crew neck shirt showing movie version starship, two colors: White shirt, Childs 10, 14, 18	3.95	4-6	_____
Adult SML	5.95	6-8	_____
Sky blue shirt, SMLXL	6.95	7-9	_____
• **"Star Trek 20 Years 1966-1986" Design Shirt**			
Star Trek The Official Fan Club, 1986			
Official circular design logo with "20" number in center, blue and gold on 50% shirt, either white or gray, SMLXL	9	9-10	_____
Paramount Label, 1986			
Same official design in pink and black, white shirt, SMLXL	10	10-11	_____

3. This NBC promotional artwork appeared in poster form (also distributed through Lincoln Enterprises, see Poster listings) and was used as the cover art for Bantam's *Star Trek I,* the first in the James Blish episode novelizations.
4. The Riverside Area Community Club proclaimed itself the town of origin for James T. Kirk. Captain Kirk's birthplace was quoted as being "a small town in the state of Iowa" in the book *The Making of Star Trek* written by Rodenberry and Whitfield and published in 1968 by Ballantine..
5. This T-shirt was sold as a promotion for the 1972 NYC Star Trek Convention, the first exclusively Trek convention sponsored by its fans. It's the first fan promo shirt of its kind.

SHIRTS

	Issue	Current	Cost/Date
• **"Star Trek 20 Years 1966-1986" Insignia Design Shirt** Star Trek Official Fan Club, 1986 Design of the anniversary color insignia logo on white 50% cotton blend, SMLXL	12	12-14	______
• **Star Trek The Motion Picture T-Shirts** Kmart, 1979 Kids T-shirts, 50% dacron polyester & 50% cotton, blue with photo transfers, sizes 2-4, 6-8, 10-12, 14-16			
Kirk & Spock, front profiles with Enterprise in background	3.59	5-15	______
Ilia, front profile, cut-out photo with silver and orange glitter border	3.59	5-15	______
• **"Star Trek" The Motion Picture Design Shirt** Star Base Central, distrib. 1980 Exclusive design with silk screen white on black square: photostyle Enterprise and busts of Kirk and Spock below, lettering in lower left corner, SMLXL	7.95	12-14	______
• **Star Trek The Motion Picture" L.E.D. Design Shirt** D.D. Bean & Sons, 1980 100% cotton pull-over with crew neck. Front has large square design print of full-front movie Enterprise over red starburst and official movie Letter Logo. Four ruby L.E.D. lights flash over the saucer's width. Battery operated. Child SML; Women SML, Men SMLXL	35	45-50	______
• **Star Trek The Wrath of Kahn/"He Lives" Design Shirt** Kirk Enterprises, 1982 Silkscreened navy outline of the Vulcan salute with border and lettering. White shirt has navy blue collar and sleeve ribbing	8.50	10-12	______
• **Star Trek The Wrath of Kahn/ "He Will Never Die!" Design Shirt** Birnbaum Productions, 1982 Also known as the "ST:WOK Memorial Shirt". Black transfer shows head portrait of Spock on light blue, 100% cotton, black letters	9.95	10-12	______

	Issue	Current	Cost/Date
• **"Star Trek III, Coming in 1984, The Adventure Continues"** Letter Shirt, Fantasy Trader T-shirts Black with white lettering, or in assorted other colors	9.95	12-14	______
Design Shirt, Star Realm, distrib. Black crew neck shirt with full front decal - white nova with yellow, red and white rays and white front view Enterprise. Lettering in 3 segments around illo, white block style, SML	10.95	15-17	______
• **"Star Trek III, Return to Genesis" Letter Shirt** Star Realm, distrib., 1984 Short sleeve, crew neck in medium blue with two rows of white block letters, SML	8.95	9-12	______
• **"Star Trek III, The Search For Spock" Design Shirt** Star Realm, distrib., 1984 Black crew neck with full front decal. Has official STSFS letter logo with Enterprise. Logo in white over solid red, black and yellow Genesis planet and bust of Spock executed in black, flesh, red, white and yellow, SML	12.95	15-20	______
• **"Star Trek IV - The Voyage Home" Letter Shirt** Star Trek Official Fan Club, 1987 Full official movie Letter Logo on aqua blue shirt, SMLXL	9	9-10	______
• **Star Trek IV - "The Voyage Home" /Klingon Vessel Design Shirt** 1986 Decal, green Klingon vessel over yellow planet, with lettering, SMLXL	10	10-12	______
• **Star Trek IV - "The Voyage Home/ Christmas 1986" Design Shirt** 1986 Blue cotton shirt with blue and white letters, plus Paramount Seal, SMLXL	10	10-11	______
• **Star Trek IV - "The Voyage Home /20th Anniversary Celebration Design Shirt** 1986 Black cotton shirt with white lettering and white decal Enterprise, SMLXL	10	10-11	______

UNDERWEAR AND PAJAMAS

Issue | Current | Cost/Date

• "Trekkers Do It Under The Stars" Letter Shirt
William Shatner Fan Club, 1983
Lettering on choice of three shirt styles and in four colors, SML

	Issue	Current	Cost/Date
T-Shirts (white, navy, maroon, lt. blue)	10.95	11-13	______
Sweatshirt (white, navy, maroon, lt. blue)	19.95	20-22	______
Polo Shirt (white, navy, maroon, gray)	19.95	20-22	______

• "United Federation of Planets-UFP" Design Shirts
Intergalactic, distrib., 1985

	Issue	Current	Cost/Date
Long-sleeve shirt, galazy and laurels emblem in silver and blue on black jersey, writing appears in silver down the inside of the sleeve, SML	15	15-18	______
Short-sleeve shirt with neck and sleeve ribbing, emblem in:			
Black on assorted colors	5.95	7-9	______
Silver on black shirt only	5.95	7-10	______
Star Base Central, distrib. 1986			
Navy trim and design on white, 50%	12.95	12-13	______
Blue, high crew, white design, 100%	13.50	13-14	______
Sweatshirt, navy with white design	15.95	16-17	______
Sweatshirt, white with royal blue design	15.95	16-17	______

• "William Shatner" Signature Sweatsuit
William Shatner Fan Club, 1983

	Issue	Current	Cost/Date
Shatner's personal autograph on choice of two colors, two-piece outfit with top and warm-up pants, SML white or navy	37.50	40-42	______

UNDERWEAR AND PAJAMAS

• Pajamas - Star Trek The Motion Picture
Pajama Corp., 1980
100% polyester knit two-piece pajamas for children. Tops are white with light blue short sleeves; pants are light blue. Two Star Trek transfer tops available, sizes 4-14 (up to a weight of 100 lbs.)

	Issue	Current	Cost/Date
Enterprise Transfer - oblong rectangle with yellow border and front-view STTMP Enterprise over star-burst in red, "Star Trek" lettering above	8.95	15-17	______
Mr. Spock - oval, borderless transfer with color head photo of Spock at bridge station, "Star Trek" lettering below	8.95	15-17	______

• Socks, 1976
White cotton crew socks with white ribbing. Iron-on appliques show standing figures from t.v. series on the transporter pad wearing holstered phaser; block lettering above reads "Star Trek" with name caption at figure's feet. Hanger manufacturer is Batts Co., Inc.:

	Issue	Current	Cost/Date
"Captain Kirk"	—	7-9	______
"Mr. Spock"	—	7-9	______

Charleston Hosiery, Inc., 1979
White polyester and cotton crew socks with multi-colored ribbing and iron-on transfer photos of the movie cast:

	Issue	Current	Cost/Date
Kirk	—	5-7	______
Spock	—	5-7	______
Ilia	—	5-7	______
Decker	—	5-7	______
Kirk and Spock	—	5-7	______

• Underwear
Nazareth Mills, 1979

	Issue	Current	Cost/Date
"Star Trek The Motion Picture Fundy-Undies" Boys T-shirt and briefs packaged underwear set. Plastic wrapped with photo insert of Kirk and Spock busts with Enterprise over a cartoon illo of a boy reclining in the clothing. Usual hosiery style wrapping, sizes SML	4	7-10	______

UNIFORMS AND COSTUMES

• "Ilia - Star Trek The Motion Picture"
#2490-E151
Collegeville Flag Mfg., 1980

	Issue	Current	Cost/Date
Children's Halloween party costume with yellow, shirt-style dress, sleeveless, cloth front ornamentation in pink, brown and black. Shield cartoons standing Ilia, encircled insignia and her name beneath the "STTMP" letter logo. Mask is pinkish, bald, full-lipped with black eyeliner and gray eye shadow. 10"x12" boxed, window-cut with "Rainbow" design movie poster on lid	4.49	5-10	______

• Kirk Costumes
Collegeville Flag Mfg.
Line of children's Halloween and party costumes with one-piece fabric tie-on suits and plastic face masks with elastic bands, a variety of packages:

UNIFORMS AND COSTUMES

	Issue	Current	Cost/Date
1980 **"Kirk - Star Trek The Motion Picture"** #2491-E148. Long silver pants, shirt sleeves. Ornamentation in neon-glo pink and green, plus silver, black and yellow. Shield photos Kirk seated with Spock and Ilia standing. encircled insignia, front view Enterprise and solar flare. Letters STTMP logo. Mask is pink complected, without facial etching, auburn hair with black highlights. 10"x12" boxed, window-cut, features the "rainbow" promo poster.	4.49	5-8	_____
1982 - **"Kirk - Star Trek The Wrath of Kahn"** #2476-9576. Long silver pants, sleeveless shirt. Ornamentation colors the same as above #2491. Shield differs in that Ilia is removed and there is a rear-view Enterprise. Mask 10"x12" window cut box	4.49	5-8	_____
1984 - **"Kirk - Star Trek"** #2476-9776 Long silver pants, shirt sleeves. Ornamentation returns to the shield of #2491. Only difference is the deletion of the "STTMP" logo lettering. Includes Ilia. Mask shows fuller hairstyling with blue highlights. Flresh complected with some etching in darker pink. 10"x12" boxed, window-cut	4.99	5-7	_____

• Klingon Costumes

	Issue	Current	Cost/Date
1980 **"Klingon - Star Trek The Motion Picture"** #2489-E150 Collegeville Flag. Mfg. Long-legged pants, shirt sleeves. Ornamentation in neon-glo pink and yellow with green, silver and black. Shield cartoons detailed movie race Klingon equipped with holstered disrupter. Pants are olive green in pseudo-suede. Mask is pink, gray, black, blue with yellow skull ridge and orange facial highlights. Bearded. 10"x12" boxed, window-cut with "rainbow" promo poster	4.49	8-10	_____
"Klingon Head Mask" - Star Trek The Motion Picture Don Post Studios Warrior from the first movie, latex slip-over head mask with prominent skull ridges, bone studded scalp and coarse, black yak hair	51.95	45-65	_____

• Spock Costumes

	Issue	Current	Cost/Date
1973 **"Spock - Star Trek, Super Hero Costume"** #254 Ben Cooper, Inc. Knee-length black pants, shirt sleeves. Ornamentation is blue, silver, yellow and black. Shield cartoons stylized standing Spock with communicator, sketchy outline of Enterprise, a lunarscape and an inaccurate t.v. version of insignia. Mask is pink with blue highlighted hair, full pink lips, heavy shadow and long, exaggerated pointed ears. 10"x12" window-cut box front has a lightning bolt. Side panels cartoon a big-eared Spock, Batman, Planet of the Apes star and Superman in flight	3.98	10-15	_____
1975 **"Spock-Star Trek Costume"** #246 Ben Cooper, Inc. Long black pants, shirt sleeves. Ornamentation is identical to #293 above, same shield and mask. Pants are without cuffs. 10"x12" window-cut box front cartoons portraits of Kirk, Klingon, McCoy, 3/4 figure Spock with phaser and Enterprise oribiting the moon. Side panel has bust of Spock and Enterprise	3.98	10-12	_____
"Spock-Star Trek, Science Fiction Costume" #293 Ben Cooper, Inc. Long black pants with heavy vinyl cuffs which simulate boots, sleeveless. Ornamentation is blue, yellow, red and black. Shield cartoons Spock's head, inaccurate t.v. version insignia and Enterprise, with "Star Trek" lettering across the saucer. Mask is pink, black red-highlighted hair, long ears and heavy eye shadow. 10"x12" window-cut box is blue with cartoon giant insect, astronauts with an American flag on the moon, and an orbital satellite	3.98	8-10	_____
1976 **"Spock Face Mask, Super Hero"** Ben Cooper, Inc. Adult size plastic face mask with elastic string. Pink complected face and lips, long ears and solid black hair and eye liner	.79	2-4	_____

UNIFORMS AND COSTUMES

	Issue	Current	Cost/Date
1980 **"Spock-Star Trek The Motion Picture Costume"** #2488-E149 - Collegeville Flag Mfg. Long silver pants, shirt sleeves. Ornamentation and shield are the same as Captain Kirk STTMP #2491. Mask is dark pink with heavy etching, black blue-highlighted hair, small/short ears, 10"x12" window-cut box with "rainbow"	4.49	5-8	_____
1980 **"Spock Head Mask - Star Trek The Motion Picture"** Don Post Studios Latex mask to slip over head, the legendary Mr. Spock with synthetic eyebrows and simulated hair	51.95	45-70	_____
1983 **"Spock - Star Trek The Wrath of Kahn Costume"** #2488-9588 Collegeville Flag Mfg. Long silver pants, sleeveless. Ornamentation and shield identical to Captain Kirk STWOK #2476. Mask is the same as Spock STTMP #2488, but with all of the facial etching removed. 10"x12" window-cut box	4.39	5-9	_____
1984 **"Spock - Star Trek Costume"** #2488-9788 Collegeville Flag Mfg. Long silver pants, shirt sleeves. Ornamentation and shield identical to Captain Kirk #2476-9776. Mask is flesh complected, black blue highlighted hair, sky blue heavy eye shadow and some pink etching. 10"x12" window-cut box	4.99	5-8	_____
• **"Star Trek Mask"** #2800· Lincoln Enterprises, 1984 One of a series of 24 original felt, fabric, embroidery thread and paint face masks designed by Maureen Culligan and distributed by Lincoln. Only one is "authentic" Trek creation: a red and purple starburst-style mask	19.95	19-20	_____

• **Uniforms**

One-time distributors of custom-order outfits:

	Issue	Current	Cost/Date
1973-1977 **Enterprise Outfitters,** NYC Fan Issue, custom made regulation tunics and shirts from the t.v. series. Velour fabrics with gold braids and insignias. Sized to order, for men, women and children	5.50	15-25	_____
1976 **Star Fleet Fabrications,** MA Uniforms and accompanying accessories for a complete Trekker wardrobe. By order, fan issue, uniforms, phasers, communicators, tricorders, misc.	—	15-25	_____

• **Uniform Patterns**

Lincoln Enterprises
Authentic patterns of the uniforms as created by William Ware Theiss (t.v. series) and for the movies, braids and rank insignia optional and extra:

	Issue	Current	Cost/Date
1976 **Series Costumes**			
#1006A Men's Uniform Shirt (SML)	1.50	3-5	_____
#1006B Women's Uniform (Sizes 8-18)	3	4-8	_____
#1006C Command Insignia, plus one yard of gold sleeve braiding	1.50	3-5	_____
#1006E Engineering Insignia, plus braiding	1.50	3-5	_____
1984 **Motion Picture Uniforms** the new uniforms worn in the movies:			
#0800 Men's Jacket (SML in one)	6.95	7-9	_____
#0801 Women's Jacket (All sizes in one)	6.95	7-9	_____
#0802 Trousers (Men's and Women's)	4.95	5-7	_____
#0803 Undershirt (Women's with darts)	3.95	4-5	_____
#0804 Recreation Jumpsuit (All sizes)	6.95	7-9	_____

• **Vulcan Ears**

	Issue	Current	Cost/Date
1975 **"Vulcan Ears"** #3295 Franco Fleshtone, pointed ears molded in latex. Bagged with orange cardstock header showing Ling illustration of Spock, a shuttlecraft and planet. Ears measure 2¼"x4¼"	2	3-5	_____
1980 **"Vulcan Ears"** Fleshtone latex molds. Bagged with white header showing a Vulcan Master over an alien planetscape. Ears measure 2½"x4¼"	2	2-4	_____
1982 **"Vulcan Ears"** - Star Trek Wrath of Kahn Don Post Studios Molded latex ears. Packaged under plastic form on cardstock that photos scenes from the bridge crew of Star Trek the Wrath of Kahn movie	7	9-12	_____
• **Vulcan Master Head Mask - Star Trek Motion Picture** Don Post Studios, 1980 Latex slip-over head mask, bald-headed male Vulcan Priest as seen in first movie	36.95	40-60	_____

FILM AND PHOTOGRAPHY

The photographic media comprises a very large collectible sector of Star Trek merchandise. Film and photographic memorabilia had their beginnings with fan issue photo reprints offered by individuals and Star Trek fan clubs. Since that time, many professional photographic houses have become involved in marketing Star Trek photos and prints. At the moment there are literally thousands of individual photographs from Trek in circulation. Their quality and content can range dramatically as both amateur and commercial products.

Collectors of vintage film and photographic memorabilia associated with Star Trek will come across six basic types of collectible categories.

Film Clip Frames – These individually cut frames from actual Star Trek T.V. episode out-takes were first marketed by *Star Trek Enterprises* in mid 1968. They were originally 35mm. With the release of *Star Trek The Motion Picture* in 1979, movie clip frames appear as 70mm size.

Photo Glossies – Star Trek episode glossies have been reprinted from T.V. frame clips and pre-mounted slides and are commonly referred to as 5"x7"s or 8"x10"s. They can be either color or black and white reprints taken from actual film footage. Usually they are action scenes or character profiles.

Photo Sheets - Photo sheets are photo lithographs which are reproduced on slick bond or glossy periodical paper. Langley Associates produced an extensive line of top quality, full color photo sheets throughout the 1970's. The sheets featured scenes, characters and planetscapes produced from T.V. film footage.

Starlog Magazine ad, 1978.

Photo Stills - A relatively new format since the mid 1970's, photo stills are full color photographic reproductions which depict action scenes or character profiles from Star Trek and which are printed on paper bonds with a flat finish. Photo stills are also issued as prescribed sets and lack identifying legends on their backside. They have appeared as wallet photos (2½"x4½"), photo cards (4"x5") and photo montages (8½"x11").

Reels - These are 8 mm film versions which must be viewed with a projector and screen. Star Trek reels are expensive but represent archival quality collectibles that are immeasurably superior to commercial videos as far as durability and quality of photographic clarity after successive showings.

Slides - Slides may be reproduced from frame clips or from existing photo glossies. Individual transparencies are mounted on 2"x2" cardstock holders for viewing in a slide projector. Thousands of Star Trek slides exist, but those produced by Langley Associates in 1976 are notable photographic memorabilia.

Close up of Episode Card C-3.

A sampling of wallet photos, Lincoln Enterprises.

Viewers

Film viewers are excellent collectibles as are viewing reels designed for use with specific viewer mechanisms. Generally speaking, celluloid strips and/or photo panels found in Star Trek viewing devices were designed for children's merchandising.

Videos and Video Discs

The affordable availability of video in its various formats has been a commercial boon to Star Trek. There is no dispute that the coming of the video age has opened unlimited potential, creative and financial, for the merchandising of Star Trek.

The typical Star Trek fan and collector will probably already have had some experience with the increasingly popular world of video viewing and taping in the home environment. Essentially, video taping the syndicated Star Trek episodes from T.V. has replaced the reel-to-reel and audio cassette taping craze of the 1960's.

Star Trek videos first appeared in video stores in 1979 with Paramount promotion associated with *Star Trek The Motion Picture.* Every succeeding movie video release since then has been immensely successful with video fans who continue to purchase home videos for their own personal video libraries.

In early 1985, Paramount began releasing the original, uncut episodes from the T.V. series. The groupings are being released in lots of ten meant to coincide with the original airdates occurring during the 60's. Collectors will note, however, that numerical gaps do exist in the packaging sequences currently being issued on the slipcover boxes.

There is no comparison with the packaging between that of video tapes and that of video discs such as those released by RCA. These CED discs come in colorful, profusely illustrated photo collage covers, approximately 12 inches wide.

Collectors should also be appraised of the fact that video discs are a dying commodity. Only two American companies ever produced CED format discs. Both RCA and CBS have decided to drop the production of video discs in the future. The result could be to make video discs good collectibles even if you have the potential to view them or not. They will probably never be produced again.

Advance display card for video classics.

Star Trek Viewmaster Disc Packet & Booklet, 1968.

Enemy Within video with photo from *What Are Little Girls Made Of?*

Second issue video cover with corrected photo front.

Star Trek The Motion Picture, Video, 1979.

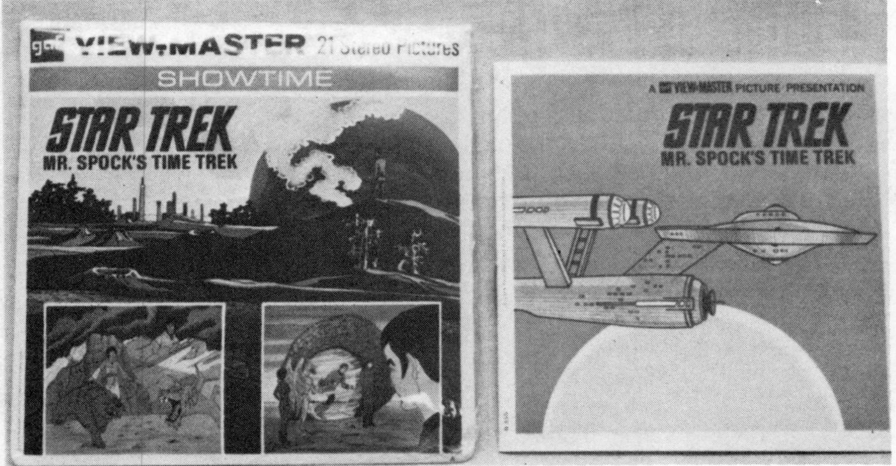

Mr. Spock's Time Trek, GAF, 1974.

STTMP doubleview, GAF, 1981.

STTMP Viewmaster Disc, 1979.

Laramie Space Viewer, 1979.

Star Trek *Wrath of Kahn* Viewmaster Disc, 1982.

FILMS AND PHOTOGRAPHY

(Clips, Reels, Slides, Stills, Videos, Viewers)

Clips	**Issue**	**Current**	**Cost/Date**
• **Star Trek Clip Frames** Star Trek/Lincoln Enterprises 1968-1980. Individual frames from the actual 35mm film, first print "daily" originals. Each set contains 8 different shots. Can be mounted in half-frame slide mount holders. Priced per set of 8 clips:			
#1301 Capt. Kirk.	1	2-3	______
#1302 Mr. Spock.	1	2-3	______
#1303 Dr. McCoy.	1	2-3	______
#1304 Lt. Crd. Scott.	1	2-3	______

SLIDES

	Issue	Current	Cost/Date
#1305 Lt. Uhura	1	2-3	______
#1306 Lt. Sulu	1	2-3	______
#1307 Ens. Chekov	1	2-3	______
#1308 Nurse Chapel	1	2-3	______
#1311 Interior of the Enterprise, equipment and gadgetry	1	2-3	______
#1312 Action Scenes	1	2-3	______
#1313 Planet Interiors	1	2-3	______
#1314 Planet Exteriors	1	2-3	______
#1315 Monsters and Alien Beings	1	2-3	______
#1316 Wardrobe, Makeup, Hairstyling (*)	2	2-3	______
#1317 Grab Bag (*)	2	2-3	______
#1318 Single frame U.S.S. Enterprise (*)	2	2-3	______
#1319 Single frame of another spaceship (*)	2	2-3	______

- **Star Trek The Motion Picture Film Clip Frames**
  Lincoln Enterprises, 1980
  70mm film clips in assorted packs which represent the scope of the movie. Each set contains 20-25 individual frames. 8 different sets available. #1320 through #1327, priced per set — Issue 5, Current 5-6 ______

- **Star Trek The Wrath of Kahn Film Clip Frames**
  Lincoln Enterprises
  70mm film clips in assorted packs which represent the scope of the movie. Each set contains 20-25 individual frames. 4 different sets available. #1330 through #1333, priced per set — Issue 5, Current 5-7 ______

- **Star Trek The Search For Spock Film Clip Frames**
  Lincoln Enterpriese, 1984
  Anamorphic frames from the outtakes of the movie. 70mm makes the shots taller and thinner than 35mm frames. Sets contain 20-25 individual clips which represent the scope of the movie. 4 different sets available, #1334 through #1337, priced per set — Issue 5, Current 5-7 ______

Reels

- **Star Trek Bloopers**
  Reel Images, 1986
  Blooper series out-takes, one reel each, sound and color:

	Issue	Current	Cost/Date
Bloopers #1 - Super 8 Sound, 10 min	34.98	35-38	______
Bloopers #2 - Super 8 Sound, 7 min	32.98	33-35	______
Bloopers #2 - 16mm Sound, 7 min.	79.98	80-85	______

(*denotes new sets offered in 1980)

- **Star Trek Episodes**
  Reel Images, 1978
  Original t.v. films in Super 8 mm sound and color three reels per show with 18 minutes on each reel, 54 minute episodes, distributed by Select Film Library:

	Issue	Current	Cost/Date
"City on the Edge of Forever"	160	150-175	______
"Squire of Gothos"	160	150-175	______
"The Trouble With Tribbles"	160	150-175	______
"Miri"	160	150-175	______
"Space Seed"	160	150-175	______
"Shore Leave"	160	150-175	______
"Man Trap"	160	150-175	______
"The Menagerie, Part I"	160	150-175	______
"The Menagerie, Part II"	160	150-175	______

- **Star Trek The Motion Picture - Preview**
  Paramount Pictures, 1980
  Library preview edition for the first movie, one reel Super 8mm sound and color, featuring edited preview of the feature length film, distributed by Marketing Film International, 18 minutes — Issue —, Current 50-60 ______

Slides

- **Star Trek Episode Slides**
  Langley & Associates, 1976
  Full-frame 35mm slides, mounted in plastic, scenes cut from the films and include character and action shots from Space, Shipboard Scenes, Planetscapes, Viewscreen Displays, Aliens, Gadgetry and Close-ups of the stars and guest stars from Trek:

	Issue	Current	Cost/Date
#501 Space, the moonsize flagship owned by Balok (CMn)	.15	.50-1	______
#502 Viewscreen, bridge imaging the spectral U.S.S. Defiant (TW)	.15	.50-1	______
#503 Space, half-shot of the Enterprise with the shimmering hulk of the Defiant in the background (TW). Also Langley Photo #ST-126	.15	.50-1	______
#504 Aliens, the Amoeba life form (IS)	.15	.50-1	______
#505 Shipboard, Spock and McCoy standing before overhead image of Professor John Gill (PF)	.15	.50-1	______
#506 Close-up, Spock, sitting before laboratory console	.15	.50-1	______
#507 Planet Ekos, McCoy and Kirk as Nazis (PF)	.15	.50-1	______
#508 Close-up, Kirk wearing environsuit after beaming back from the Defiant (TW)	.15	.50-1	______
#509 Shipboard - Romulan, female Commander embraces Spock as he dematerializes from her ship (EI)	.15	.50-1	______

SLIDES

	Issue	Current	Cost/Date
#510 Close-up Kirk wearing alternate universe tunic (MM)	.15	.50-1	_____
#511 Planet 892-IV, Capt. R. M. Merik/Merikus and Kirk, seated	.15	.50-1	_____
#512 Planet 892-IV, McCoy in slave apparel, seated (BC)	.15	.50-1	_____
#513 Aliens, shimmering coaliting of entities in space (LZ)	.15	.50-1	_____
#514 Shipboard, the Klingons Kang and Mara plot a takeover from Engineering (Dv)	.15	.50-1	_____
#515 Close-up, Kirk and McCoy	.15	.50-1	_____
#516 Planet Elba II, Kirk and former starship Captain Garth (WGD)	.15	.50-1	_____
#517 Space, the Enterprise ensnared and the Tholian scoutship as it completes its energy field (TW)	.15	.50-1	_____
#518 Shipboard, bridge, Spock, Kirk and McCoy engage a conversation	.15	.50-1	_____
#519 Shipboard, decompression chamber, Lt. Mira Romaine as the alien entities flee (LZ)	.15	.50-1	_____
#520 Aliens, close-up of Sarek of Vulcan among other ambassadors and dignataries (JB)	.15	.50-1	_____
#521 Planet Organia, Klingon Capt. Kor, his military aide and Kirk (EM)	.15	.50-1	_____
#522 Aliens, close-up of Vina as the green-skinned Orion Slave girl (Me)	.15	.50-1	_____
#523 Planet Beta III, Kirk's landing party is betrayed by the natives Reger and Tamar to Landru's disciples (RA)	.15	.50-1	_____
#524 Shipboard, Nomad tours the Enterprise (Cg)	.15	.50-1	_____
#525 Shipboard, Spock, McCoy and Kirk confer in the sickbay	.15	.50-1	_____
#526 Aliens, the Romulan Commander aids his dying Centurian friend (BT)	.15	.50-1	_____
#527 Planet Capella IV, the Enterprise party confronts Maab and his Klingon ally Kras inside the council tent (FC)	.15	.50-1	_____
#528 Planet Riegel IV, moonrise over the gothic fortress, Capt. Pike and Vina (Me). Also Langley Poster #P1013	.15	.50-1	_____
#529 Space, a Klingon Cruiser, front view	.15	.50-1	_____
#530 Aliens, close-up of a Mugato from the planet Neural, an albina one-horned ape (PLW)	.15	.50-1	_____
#531 Viewscreen, bridge, imaging Deela and Rael with five other survivors of Scalos (WE)	.15	.50-1	_____
#532 Shipboard - Romulan, the female Commander and Spock, reclining (EI)	.15	.50-1	_____
#533 Shipboard - Romulan, security guards detain Kirk (EI)	.15	.50-1	_____

	Issue	Current	Cost/Date
#534 Shipboard, Kirk and Klingon Capt. Kang face-off, close-up (Dv)	.15	.50-1	_____
#535 Shipboard, bridge, Kirk, Uhura and Chekov seated at their stations	.15	.50-1	_____
#536 Shipboard, Spock amidst the many alien dignitaries in conference room	.15	.50-1	_____
#537 Close-up, Spock, in full dress uniform	.15	.50-1	_____
#538 Planet Omicron Ceti III, Leila Kalomi and Spock recline to watch the clouds (TSP)	.15	.50-1	_____
#539 Close-up, alternate universe bearded Spock (MM)	.15	.50-1	_____
#540 Viewscreen, bridge, a shot over the Helmsman's shoulder to see Space Station K-7 (TT)	.15	.50-1	_____
#541 Planet Rigel IV, the attacking barbarian warrior strikes	.15	.50-1	_____
#542 Shipboard - Romulan, Kirk in Romulan disguise beams out with their cloaking device (EI)	.15	.50-1	_____
#543 Space, Enterprise under seige by three Klingon class Romulan ships (EI). Also Langley Photo # ST-134	.15	.50-1	_____
#544 Shipboard, sickbay, Kirk confronts the two Cherons, Bele and Lokai (LB)	.15	.50-1	_____
#545 Aliens, close-up of the androids Ruk and Andrea (LG)	.15	.50-1	_____
#546 Planet Janus VI, cavern mines, Kirk with Spock as he mind-melds with the horta (DD)	.15	.50-1	_____
#547 Shipboard, Kirk questions two Andorian Ambassadors Thelev and Shras (JB)	.15	.50-1	_____
#548 Planet Beta III, Kirk and Spock in native business suits survey the damage to the Landru computer complex	.15	.50-1	_____
#549 Shipboard - Romulan, close-up of the female Commander reclining in her chair (EI)	.15	.50-1	_____
#550 Planet Capella IV, the High Teer Akaar and his wife Eleen (FC)	.15	.50-1	_____
#551 Shipboard, hangar bay, shuttle docking	.15	.50-1	_____
#552 Space, planetsize weapon devours Capt. Mathew Decker's shuttlecraft (DMa)	.15	.50-1	_____
#553 Aliens, close-up of the Andorian Ambassador Thelev, really an Orion spy with a broken antenna (JB)	.15	.50-1	_____
#554 Space, shuttlecraft in flight into bay	.15	.50-1	_____
#555 Space, lateral view of the Enterprise	.15	.50-1	_____
#556 Planet Pyris VII, dungeons, Kirk, Spock and a skeleton in chains (Cp)	.15	.50-1	_____

SLIDES

	Issue	Current	Cost/Date
#557 Shipboard, corridor, Kirk draws his sword as the Klingons watch, against the energy being invading the ship (Dv)	.15	.50-1	
#558 Close-up, Capt. Pike, young and well (Me)	.15	.50-1	
#559 Space Station K-7, Kirk catches tribbles as they plummet from the grain hatch (TT)	.15	.50-1	
#560 Space Station K-7, classic shot of Kirk chest deep in gorged tribbles (TT). Also Langley Photo #ST-132.	.15	.50-1	
#561 Shipboard, sickbay, Chapel, McCoy and Spock watch as Nomad repairs the biological unit known as Scotty (Cg)	.15	.50-1	
#562 Aliens, the reptilian Gorn Captain (Ar)	.15	.50-1	
#563 Planet Sigma Dricomas VII, McCoy works to replace Spock's brain as Kirk and Scotty offer support	.15	.50-1	
#564 Planet Sigma Iotia II, game room, Kirk, Spock and McCoy are introduced to Bela Oxmyx (PA)	.15	.50-1	
#565 Planet Gamma Trianguli VI, native supplicants entreat Vael with food (Ap)	.15	.50-1	
#566 Shipboard, bridge, Spock at the con, McCoy, Uhura and Sulu	.15	.50-1	
#567 Space, the shuttlecraft in flight	.15	.50-1	
#568 Space, Enterprise entrapped by Apollo's energy "hand" (WM)	.15	.50-1	
#569 Viewscreen, bridge, front view of a Tholian scout ship	.15	.50-1	
#570 Planetside, front view of the Guardian of Forever (CEF)	.15	.50-1	
#571 Space, long shot of the weapon (DMa)	.15	.50-1	
#572 Space, front view of the weapon's maw (DMa)	.15	.50-1	
#573 Viewscreen, transporter room, the U.S.S. Constellation ramming down the throat of the Doomsday Machine (DMa)	.15	.50-1	
#574 Space, Enterprise in standard orbit over dark blue planet	.15	.50-1	
#575 Space, lateral view of the U.S.S. Defiant (TW)	.15	.50-1	
#576 Shipboard, sickbay, a prone Kahn secures McCoy by the throat	.15	.50-1	
#577 Shipboard, Engineering, Scotty and four crewmen face off Nomad (Cg)	.15	.50-1	
#578 Planet Sigma Iotia II, Spock in gangster garb holds machine gun on Bela Oxmyx (PA)	.15	.50-1	
#579 Shipboard, outside shuttlecraft bay, Ambassador Sarek and Amanda come aboard (JB)	.15	.50-1	
#580 Planetside, 'Gem' from Gamma Vertas IV, listens to Kirk, Spock and McCoy (Em)	.15	.50-1	
#581 Planet Ardana, City of Stratos, the rebel Vanna is "questioned" by the High Advisor Plasus (Cms)	.15	.50-1	
#582 Planetside, episode finale, seven members of the landing party beam off planet where "All is as it was"	.15	.50-1	
#583 Aliens, close-up of the Telarite Ambassador Gav (JB)	.15	.50-1	
#584 Aliens, close-up of the Andorian Ambassador Thelev (JB)	.15	.50-1	
#585 Close-up, Spock's betrothed, T'Pring (AT)	.15	.50-1	
#586 Planet Elba II, 'Lord' Garth reviews his motley subjects in the asylum (WGD)	.15	.50-1	
#587 Aliens, the lion-like figure of a Melkotian (SGn)	.15	.50-1	
#588 Close-up, Marta resting her head against 'Lord' Garth's shoulder (WGD)	.15	.50-1	
#589 Aliens, the 'salt-vampire' of planet M-113 as it dies aboard the Enterprise (MT)	.15	.50-1	
#590 Space, rear view Enterprise as it penetrates the galactic barrier (WNM) Also available as Langley Photo #ST-117	.15	.50-1	
#591 Planet Elba II, Kirk confronts Garth and Marta (WGD)	.15	.50-1	
#592 Space, U.S.S. Constellation ramming down the throat of the Doomsday Machine (DMa). Also Langley Slide #573 - only viewscreen shot	.15	.50-1	
#593 Space, unusual overhead half-shot of the Enterprise, panned down the right nacelle	.15	.50-1	
#594 Space, unusual overhead shot of the Enterprise, panned directly at the front of the saucer	.15	.50-1	
#595 Space, rear view Enterprise as it faces the asteroid endangering Miramanee's tribe (PS)	.15	.50-1	
#596 Space, the derelict Romulan Bird of Prey following battle (BT)	.15	.50-1	
#597 Planetside, 'Gem' empathically heals an unconscious McCoy (Em)	.15	.50-1	
#598 Space, close-up of the Enterprise dwarfed by Balok's moonsize flagship (CMn)	.15	.50-1	
#599 Space, the Romulan Bird of Prey making its attack run (BT)	.15	.50-1	
#600 Space, Enterprise firing twin phasers. Also Langley Photo # ST-102 and Poster #PL1008	.15	.50-1	
#601 Space Station K-7, a horrified Mr. Lurry and Nilz Barris watch with Spock as Kirk is buried in tribbles (TT)	.15	.50-1	
#602 Planet Talos IV, the laser cannon blasting the door to the Keeper's retreat (Me)	.15	.50-1	

SLIDES

	Issue	Current	Cost/Date
#603 Planetside, Kirk staying his hand to kill the Gorn enemy (Ar)	.15	.50-1	______
#604 Planetscape, remote lithium cracking station (WNM). Also Langley Photo #ST-101	.15	.50-1	______
#605 Close-up, Vina as the green-skinned Orion Slave girl (Me)	.15	.50-1	______
#606 Space, lateral view of the Enterprise with Kahn's sleeper ship (S.S. Botony Bay) in tow (SS)	.15	.50-1	______
#607 A Planet in Quadrant 904, Kirk draws his breech-loader to persuade Trelane (SG)	.15	.50-1	______
#608 Aliens, close-up of the wounded mother horta (DD)	.15	.50-1	______
#609 Planet Gamma Canaris N, the missing inventor Zephram Cochrane welcomes the party of the Galileo '7 (Mt)	.15	.50-1	______
#610 Planet Sarpeidon, its arctic past, a tender embrace between reclining Spock and Zarabeth	.15	.50-1	______
#611 Shipboard, Commodore Jose Mendez leads the court-martial proceedings against Spock (Me)	.15	.50-1	______
#612 Space, front view of Tholian scout ship (TW)	.15	.50-1	______
#613 Aliens, 'The Companion' of Gamma Canaris N (Mt)	.15	.50-1	______
#614 Planet Beta XII-A, Klingon Capt. Kang and his war party beam down to intercept Kirk (Dv)	.15	.50-1	______
#615 Planet Gamma Trianguli VI, computer-god Vaal under twin phaser fire from the Enterprise (Ap)	.15	.50-1	______
#616 Space, front view of the maw of the Doomsday Machine (DMa). Similar to Slide #572, but closer	.15	.50-1	______
#617 Shipboard, Spock's Quarters, Spock with Vulcan harp (WEd)	.15	.50-1	______
#618 Planet Gamma Canaris N, 'The Companion' enfolding Cochrane (Mt)	.15	.50-1	______
#619 Shipboard, Spock at the con with full helm view of a Tholian scout ship on screen	.15	.50-1	______
#620 Planet M-113, Kirk and Spock aide the stricken Dr. Robert Crater (MT)	.15	.50-1	______
#621 Planetscape, city metropolis	.15	.50-1	______
#622 Space, Enterprise firing bridge phasers	.15	.50-1	______
#623 Space, the spectral U.S.S. Defiant (TW)	.15	.50-1	______
#624 Space, four Tholian scout ships align to weave their energy web (TW)	.15	.50-1	______
#625 Close-up, Uhara wearing an audio transceiver, at the communications station	.15	.50-1	______
#626 Shipboard, alternate universe sickbay, Scotty, McCoy and Kirk parlay (MM)	.15	.50-1	______
#627 Planet Earth, circa 1930, Kirk and Spock explain to an impatient policeman how they came about an armful of clothes (CEF)	.15	.50-1	______
#628 Close-up, radiation deformed Pike (Me)	.15	.50-1	______
#629 Planet Elba II, Marta struggles outside in the lethal atmosphere (WGD)	.15	.50-1	______
#630 Planet Gamma II, subterranean vault, Kirk in harness wagers quatloos with the three brain-like Providers (GT)	.15	.50-1	______
#631 Shipboard, transporter room, Spock and Crewman Joe Tormolen in orange radiation suits ready to beam down (NT)	.15	.50-1	______
#632 Planet Psi 2000, Spock and Crewman Tormolen explore the frozen remains of the research station (NT)	.15	.50-1	______
#633 Shipboard, Kirk in full dress uniform conversing with Uhura via tabletop viewer	.15	.50-1	______
#634 Shipboard, alternate universe, Kirk, bearded Spock and the helm crew on bridge (MM)	.15	.50-1	______
#635 Shipboard, alternate universe corridor, Spock walks with Kirk as their security details follow (MM)	.15	.50-1	______
#636 Space "Star Trek" title clip, Enterprise orbiting planet. Similar to Langley Photo #ST-121	.15	.50-1	______
#637 Shipboard, alternate universe helm, Sulu speaking into communicator. Dagger-thru-Earth emblem is on turbo doors (MM)	.15	.50-1	______
#638 Viewscreen, bridge, Romulan Bird of Prey on its attack run, head on (BT)	.15	.50-1	______
#639 Close-up, mutants Gary Mitchell and Dr. Elizabeth Dehner observe themselves in the mirror (WNM)	.15	.50-1	______
#640 Close-up, group shot, Dr. Elizabeth Dehner, Scotty, Dr. Mark Piper and Sulu (WNM)	.15	.50-1	______
#641 Planet Vulcan, ceremonial arena, Spock with hands in pyramid, deep in Plak-tow, T'Pau, Bell-bearer and Kirk (AT)	.15	.50-1	______
#642 Close-up, Spock engaging Kirk in hand-to-hand combat with lirpas (AT)	.15	.50-1	______
#643 Planet Vulcan, arena, Spock holding the ahnwoon around Kirk's limp neck (AT)	.15	.50-1	______
#644 Close-up, Christine Chapel and Spock as they are manipulated in a love scene (PSt)	.15	.50-1	______
#645 Planet Earth, circa 1930, Spock and Kirk in period attire work in the basement of the 21st Street Mission (CEF)	.15	.50-1	______

SLIDES

	Issue	Current	Cost/Date
#646 Planet Argelius Two, Kirk and McCoy, the Prefect, Mr. Hengist, Morla and Kara's father (WF)	.15	.50-1	_____
#647 Planetside, the Vian captors Lal and Thann administer to 'Gem' after freezing Kirk, Spock and McCoy in a force field (Em)	.15	.50-1	_____
#648 Close-up, Uhura wearing formal gown (PSt)	.15	.50-1	_____
#649 Aliens, the tiny vegetable-like creatures known as 'Sylvia' and 'Korob' as they disintegrate (Cp)	.15	.50-1	_____
#650 Shipboard, transporter room, Kirk wearing environsuit, standing on pad (TW)	.15	.50-1	_____
#651 Aliens, the light entity invader (Dv)	.15	.50-1	_____
#652 Planet Earth, circa 1930, the 21st Street Mission as Edith Keeler pours coffee (CEF)	.15	.50-1	_____
#653 Planet Ardana, City of Stratos, Kirk thwarts the rebel Vanna's attempt on his life (Cms)	.15	.50-1	_____
#654 Shipboard, briefing room, Commodore Jose Mendez, Spock and Kirk watch scenes of the Orion escapade involving Pike on screen (Me)	.15	.50-1	_____
#655 Planet Orion, the romanesque tabloid of festivities to induce Pike, including the green-skinned slave girl, Vina (Me)	.15	.50-1	_____
#656 Planet Omicron Ceti III, Leila Kalomi and Spock tour the fields (TSP)	.15	.50-1	_____
#658 Planet Mudd, Harcourt Fenton enjoys the lecture by Stella #1 (IM)	.15	.50-1	_____
#659 Planet Ardana, skyline showing the floating City of Stratos (Cms)	.15	.50-1	_____
#660 Planet Ardana, City of Stratos, Droxine and her father, Plasus, converse (Cms)	.15	.50-1	_____
#661 Planet Janus VI, mother horta blazes a tunnel to her eggs (DD)	.15	.50-1	_____
#662 Planet Janus VI, in the Vault of Tomorrow, Kirk cradles an egg (DD)	.15	.50-1	_____
#663 Planetside, the Tribal Chief and his daughter, Miramanee, instruct a newly arrived and disoriented Kurok (PS)	.15	.50-1	_____
#664 Planetside, Indian attired 'Kurok' mourns over the prone body of his wife Miramanee (PS)	.15	.50-1	_____
#665 Planetside, Mistress Kara employs the Controller's teaching helmet (SB)	.15	.50-1	_____
#666 Shipboard, Yeoman Janice Rand's Quarters, mirror-image Kirk touts his Saurian Brandy bottle before an astounded Janice (EW)	.15	.50-1	_____
#667 Planet Deneva, Kirk, Spock and two crew members search buildings for the killer protoplasts (OA)	.15	.50-1	_____
#668 Space, ship's phaser on target re-directs the errant asteroid imperiling Miramanee's civilization (PS)	.15	.50-1	_____
#669 Viewscreen, bridge, the starships Excaliber, Hood and Potemkin readied for war games (UC)	.15	.50-1	_____
#670 Space, shuttlecraft	.15	.50-1	_____
#671 Planet Gamma Trianguli VI, landing party at ease, Spock, Kirk, McCoy, Lt. Martha Landon and Chekov (Ap)	.15	.50-1	_____
#672 Shipboard, bridge, Uhura and Capt./Pilot John Christopher fingering his ear at the precise moment he discovers Spock (TY)	.15	.50-1	_____
#673 Space, Enterprise in orbit over blue, Class M planet	.15	.50-1	_____
#674 Planet Talos IV, the original landing party including Capt. Pike and Spock (Me)	.15	.50-1	_____
#675 Shipboard, transporter room, the above Talos IV party beaming down (Me)	.15	.50-1	_____
#676 Close-up, Vina as a blonde, role-playing Pike's hometown girl (Me)	.15	.50-1	_____
#677 Planetside, Kirk, Spock and landing party watch the 'Guardian's' relay of Earth history to find McCoy's exact point of entry (CEF)	.15	.50-1	_____
#678 Space, the Doomsday Machine as it implodes into the void (DMa)	.15	.50-1	_____
#679 Planet talos IV, caged Number One, Pike, Yeoman J.M. Colt and Vina speak to one of the Keepers (Me)	.15	.50-1	_____
#680 Shipboard, bridge, six crew team in conversation at the helm, including Number One (Me)	.15	.50-1	_____
#681 Aliens, the Organians Ayelborne and Trefayne after they have transformed into their pure energy forms (EM)	.15	.50-1	_____
#682 Viewscreen, bridge, the image of Apollo's giant head (WM)	.15	.50-1	_____
#683 Planet Triskelion, the arena, Galt the Master Thrall, Kloog, Lars the Drill Thrall and Uhura in harness (GT)	.15	.50-1	_____
#684 Shipboard, bridge, Uhura attempts to explain her singing to Nomad (Cg)	.15	.50-1	_____
#685 Aliens, the Tholian Commander Loskene delivering a warning from space (TW)	.15	.50-1	_____
#686 Planet M-113, Kirk and McCoy conduct routine examination of archeologist Dr. Robert Crater (MT)	.15	.50-1	_____

SLIDES

	Issue	Current	Cost/Date
#687 Planetside, McCoy, Dr. Anne Muhall, Kirk and Spock investigate a 2-million year old life vault (RT)	.15	.50-1	
#688 A Planet in Quadrant 904, McCoy, Uhura and Yeoman Teresa Ross at Trelane's estate (SG)	.15	.50-1	
#689 Aliens, the mock-up manikin used by Balok to disuade visitors (CMn)	.15	.50-1	
#690 Aliens, the boyish but ancient figure of a Metron (Ar)	.15	.50-1	
#691 Planetside, remote lithium cracking station, mutants Gary Mitchell and Elizabeth Dehner create their world (WNM)	.15	.50-1	
#692 Shipboard, alternate universe bridge, Sulu accousts Uhura at her station (MM)	.15	.50-1	
#693 Gadgetry, the Pyris VII tablesetting, Enterprise in lucite, phaser pistol, communicator and a spoon	.15	.50-1	
#694 Planetscape, Eminiar VII, the city as the landing party and reception party meet (TA)	.15	.50-1	
#695 Planet Pyris VII, castle, Korob, Kirk and Spock (Cp)	.15	.50-1	
#696 Planet Ardana, City of Stratos, Droxine and Spock converse (Cms)	.15	.50-1	
#697 Amusement Planet, Sulu examines the White Knight dummy after it loses in a joust (SL)	.15	.50-1	
#698 Shipboard, transporter room, Uhura, Kirk, McCoy and Scotty as they beam into the alternate universe ship (MM)	.15	.50-1	
#699 Shipboard, sickbay, altered-state Gary Mitchell scans the video tape library store (WNM)	.15	.50-1	
#700 Planet Janus VI, mining HQ, Chief Engineer Vanderberg and Scotty discuss the damaged generator (DD)	.15	.50-1	
#701 Shipboard - Romulan, aboard the flagship Spock and the female Commander court (EI)	.15	.50-1	
#702 Viewscreen, bridge, the space marker buoy for Melkotian Space (SGn)	.15	.50-1	
#703 Close-up, Miramanee (PS)	.15	.50-1	
#704 Planet Platonius, Alexander, Spock, Kirk and McCoy are detained (PSt)	.15	.50-1	
#705 Planet Platonius, Kirk persuades Alexander not to harm himself (PSt)	.15	.50-1	
#706 Planet 892-IV, Roman palace interior, Spock in slave's tunic, seated (BC)	.15	.50-1	
#707 Planet Ekos, underground HQ, Spock and Kirk in Nazi uniforms are tested at gunpoint by Darus (PF)	.15	.50-1	
#708 Planet 892-IV, Roman palace interior, Claudius Marcus toasts Kirk (wearing slave's tunic) (BC)	.15	.50-1	
#709 Shipboard, ship's theatre, Kirk wrestles the phaser away from the crazed actress Lenore Karidian (CK)	.15	.50-1	
#710 Viewscreen, bridge as it images Surok of Vulvan; Sulu at the helm (SC)	.15	.50-1	
#711 Close-up inside wigwam, Kurok comforts a frightened Miramanee (PS)	.15	.50-1	
#712 Planetside, exterior of the obelisk, Kirk recreates signal to enter by using communicator; Spock (PS)	.15	.50-1	
#713 Planet Ikos, Gestapo HQ, McCoy, Kirk, Darus and Spock as they try to revive the drugged John Gill (PF)	.15	.50-1	
#714 Planet Exo III, the caverns, view of the android duplicator and the humaniform destined to become Kirk (LG)	.15	.50-1	
#715 Planet Elba II, two asylum inmates enjoy Marta's dancing (WGD)	.15	.50-1	
#716 Close-up, Harry Mudd and Uhura (IM)	.15	.50-1	
#717 Planet Memory Alpha archives, Spock, Scotty, Lt. Mira Romaine, McCoy and Kirk discover the aftermath of the alien 'storm'	.15	.50-1	
#718 Planet Ekos, detention cell, Spock uses a light fixture to create a primitive kind of laser beam (PF)	.15	.50-1	
#719 A Planet in Quadrant 904, the landing party and the Squire square-off in the music room (SG)	.15	.50-1	
#720 Planet Sarpeidon, its arctic past, Spock tending to the stricken McCoy discovers their host's identity - Zarabeth (AY)	.15	.50-1	
#721 Planet Ekos, Gestapo HQ, group close-up of Kirk, Spock and McCoy in Nazi dress (PF)	.15	.50-1	
#722 Space, Enterprise rear angle shot, panning the saucer, completed Tholian field in the background (TW)	.15	.50-1	
#723 Shipboard, ship's theatre, Lenord Karidian delivers a soliloquy alone on stage (CK)	.15	.50-1	
#724 Planet near Pollux IV, exterior of the ruined temple as Apollo beseeches his long lost comrades (WM)	.15	.50-1	
#725 Planet Triskelion, in the Thrall arena, Kirk and Uhura conclude their stay; Kloog, Galt, Shahna and Tamoon (GT)	.15	.50-1	
#726 Planet Pyris VII, throneroom, Korob is seated as the landing party meets him (Cp)	.15	.50-1	

SLIDES

	Issue	Current	Cost/Date
#727 Planet Gamma Triangulu VI, Akuta, Makora and his girlfriend wrap up business with Kirk and Spock	.15	.50-1	______
#728 Shipboard, bridge, Kirk, Lee Kelso and a tech team effect repairs at the helm (WNM)	.15	.50-1	______
#729 Shipboard, bridge, full crew as they face the galactic barrier, Yeoman Smith, Gary Mitchell, Kirk, Elizabeth Dehner, Scotty, Dr. Mark Piper, Sulu and Lee Kelso	.15	.50-1	______
#730 Planet Sigma Draconus VII, subterranean abode, Luma holds Scotty and Kirk at phaser point (SB)	.15	.50-1	______
#731 Close-up, Flint's robot unit, M4, in mid-air flight (RM)	.15	.50-1	______
#732 Shipboard, bridge, Kirk and Spock with the Dohlman Elaan at the turbo (ET)	.15	.50-1	______
#733 Planet Sigma Draconus VII Spock's body walks by means of a robot control device (SB)	.15	.50-1	______
#734 Gadgetry, close-up, the bridge science station console	.15	.50-1	______
#735 Gadgetry, close-up, the transporter unit console	.15	.50-1	______
#736 Close-up, portrait of Mudd's three women; Eve McHuron, Ruth Bonadventure and Magda Kovas (MW)	.15	.50-1	______
#737 Planet Yonada, the temple, Kirk and Spock are zapped as they transgress the 'book' and altar (FW)	.15	.50-1	______
#738 Planet in Melkotian Space, corral scene, Spock, McCoy, Kirk and Scotty discuss the approaching possee (SGn)	.15	.50-1	______
#739 Planet Gideon, the mock-up bridge, Kirk questions the native girl Odona (MG)	.15	.50-1	______
#740 Ghost planet, the computer generated halograph of Losira (TWS)	.15	.50-1	______
#741 Aliens, close-up of Bele and Lokai from the planet Cheron (LB)	.15	.50-1	______
#742 Close-up, Flint and his lovely 'ward' Reena Kapec, from Holberg 917-G (RM)	.15	.50-1	______
#743 Close-up, Miranda Jones (TB)	.15	.50-1	______
#744 Close-up, Kirk in dress uniform proposes a toast	.15	.50-1	______
#745 Planet Ardana, City of Stratos, Spock converses with Droxine (Cms)	.15	.50-1	______
#746 Planet Ardana, City of Stratos, Droxine standing alone (Cms)	.15	.50-1	______
#747 Close-up, alternate universe Lt. Marlena Moreau (MM)	.15	.50-1	______
#748 Planet Gamma Canaris N Cochrane's home, as the shuttlecraft party arrives (Mt)	.15	.50-1	______
#749 Aliens, Mudd's androids, two of the Alices and Norman (IM)	.15	.50-1	______
#750 Planet Mudd, McCoy and Spock standing in between two Alices (IM)	.15	.50-1	______
#751 Shipboard, sickbay, Spock doubles over in pain as Gary Mitchell exerts his new-found powers (WNM)	.15	.50-1	______
#752 Shipboard, transporter room, Gary Seven materializing, sitting down (AE)	.15	.50-1	______
#753 Gadgetry, the atavacron device on the planet Sarpeidon (AY)	.15	.50-1	______
#754 Planet Earth, circa the 1960's Seven's office, Kirk and Spock in 20th century business suits (AE)	.15	.50-1	______
#755 Shipboard, the Jeffrey's tube, Scotty works to stabilize polarity flux	.15	.50-1	______
#756 Planetside, The Kelvan named Kelinda as she approaches Lt. Shea and Yeoman Leslie Thompson (AON)	.15	.50-1	______
#757 Planet Sigma Iotia II, window pan, Bela Oxmyx, Kirk, JoJo Krako, Spock and McCoy visible through the window panes (PA)	.15	.50-1	______
#758 Shipboard, bridge, the Scalosian Deela as she easily sidesteps Kirk's sluggish phaser stun ray (WE)	.15	.50-1	______
#759 Planet Capella IV, the Klingon Kras with Maab and two of his guardsmen (FC)	.15	.50-1	______
#760 Aliens, close-up of Balok (CMn)	.15	.50-1	______
#761 Planet Omicron Ceti III, spore-afflicted Spock hangs from a tree; close-up of the smile on his face (TSP)	.15	.50-1	______
#762 Close-up, Spock in mind-meld with the mother horta (DD)	.15	.50-1	______
#763 Planet Organia, the Council of Elders; Ayelborne, Trefayne and Claymare (EM)	.15	.50-1	______
#764 Planet Talos IV, Pike's dreamscape of a picnic back on Earth with Vina and his horse (Me)	.15	.50-1	______
#765 Planet Talos IV, one of the Keepers as it transforms into a beast in order to scare off Pike (Me)	.15	.50-1	______
#766 Aliens, group of four Talosians (Me)	.15	.50-1	______
#767 Shipboard, alternate universe transporter room, bearded Spock holds Kirk at phaser point (MM)	.15	.50-1	______
#768 Shipboard, alternate universe bridge, bearded Spock and Kirk (MM)	.15	.50-1	______
#769 Close-up, the Vulcan T'Pau seated with her staff (AT)	.15	.50-1	______
#770 Close-up, the Vulcans Stonn and T'Pring (AT)	.15	.50-1	______
#771 Planet Vulcan, arena, Spock and T'Pring as she invokes Kal-i-fee (AT)	.15	.50-1	______

SLIDES

	Issue	Current	Cost/Date
#772 Shipboard, Uhura's Quarters Kirk, the Elasian guardsman Kryton and the Troyan Ambassador Petri (ET)	.15	.50-1	______
#773 Shipboard, bridge, Kirk and Elaan (ET)	.15	.50-1	______
#774 Planet Elba II, Governor Donald Cory, Kirk and Spock converse (WGD)	.15	.50-1	______
#775 Close-up, two Elba II asylum inmates; a Telarite and an Andorian armed with phasers (WGD)	.15	.50-1	______
#776 Close-up, Akuta, the 'Eyes and ears of Vaal' (Ap)	.15	.50-1	______
#777 Planet Gamma Trianguli VI, Security Guard Kaplna is vaporized by a lightning bolt from Vaal (Ap)	.15	.50-1	______
#778 Planet Gamma Canaris N, outside Cochrane's home McCoy Spock and Kirk advance on the 'Companion' with a universal translator (Mt)	.15	.50-1	______
#779 Space, very unusual shot panned between the Enterprise pylons to the scarred hulk of the U.S.S. Constellation (DMa)	.15	.50-1	______
#780 Planet Excalbia, the enemy camp; Colonel Green, the Klingon Kahless, Zora and Genghis Kahn (SC)	.15	.50-1	______
#781 Aliens, Yarken, the master of ceremonies and molten rock creature from the planet Excalbia (SC)	.15	.50-1	______
#782 Shipboard, Nomad with a seated Spock and standing Kirk (Cg)	.15	.50-1	______
#783 Close-up, Dr. Severin, cult leader (WTE)	.15	.50-1	______
#784 A Planet near Pollux IV, Lt. Carolyn Palamas and Apollo in the gardens (WM)	.15	.50-1	______
785 Close-up, the new Ensign Pavel Chekov (WM)	.15	.50-1	______
786 A Planet near Pollux IV, Lt. Carolyn Palamas standing in gown in the statuary garden (WM)	.15	.50-1	______
787 Close-up, Harcourt Fenton Mudd (MW)	.15	.50-1	______
788 Shipboard, transporter room, three lovely ladies at beam-up; Eve, Ruth and Magda (MW)	.15	.50-1	______
789 Close-up, Spock, wearing the stage costume and laurel wreath chosen by the Platonians (PSt)	.15	.50-1	______
790 Close-up, Spock with Vulcan harp, Uhura (CX)	.15	.50-1	______
791 Shipboard, bridge, Spock at the science station	.15	.50-1	______
792 Close-up, Captain James T. Kirk	.15	.50-1	______
793 Shipboard, transporter room, Scotty and a crewman manning the controls	.15	.50-1	______
794 Close-up, Yeoman Janice Rand in the ship's botanical lab (CX)	.15	.50-1	______

Stills

	Issue	Current	Cost/Date
• **Spock Photo Card** [1] Trend Communications, 1973 B/w, features Spock bust as drawn by Virgin Finlay, 4"x5"	1	3-5	______
• **Starlog Magazine - 15 Card Set,** 1978 Full color cardstock cards featuring photo inserts of some of the most popular Trek episodes, each card contains one large photo on left with three small vertical photos on right, 8½"x11" format:			
#C-1 "City on the Edge of Forever"			______
#C-2 "The Tholian Web"			______
#C-3 "Amok Time"			______
#C-4 "The Trouble With Tribbles"			______
#C-5 "The Paradise Syndrome"			______
#C-6 "Patterns of Force"			______
#C-7 "What Are Little Girls Made Of?"			______
#C-8 "The Doomsday Machine"			______
#C-9 "Journel to Babel"			______
#C-10 "The Menagerie"			______
#C-11 "Where No Man Has Gone Before"			______
#C-12 "All Our Yesterdays"			______
#C-13 "Mirror, Mirror"			______
#C-14 Special Enterprise Card			______
#C-15 Special Bloopers Card			______
Individual cards	1	2-3	______
Complete set of 15 cards	9.95	10-30	______
• **Starpost - 12 Card Set** Twelve full-color cards featuring characters and planetscapes from the series, 4"x5" format:			
Bridge View Screen			______
Cityscape Eminiar VII (TA)			______
Enterprise			______
Guardian of Forever (CEF)			______
Janus VI Mining Complex (DD)			______
Kirk			______
Lithium Cracking Station, Delta Vega (WNM)			______
McCoy			______
Rigel Fortress (Me)			______
Spock			______
Starbase Eleven (CM)			______
Telarite (JB)			______
Individual cards	.39	.50-1	______
Complete set of 12 cards	4.50	6-12	______

1. This photo card features the artwork bust of Spock that appeared as a promotional candy wrapper on the sucker distributed by *Monster Times Magazine.*

STILLS

Star Trek Photo Sheets

• Photo Sheets

Langley and Associates, 1976 editions. 42 action photos in full color lithos on thin paper stock, ships and scenes from the t.v. series. 8"x10":

	Issue	Current	Cost/Date
ST101 Exterior planetscape of the lithium cracking station (WNM)	.50	1-2	______
ST102 Enterprise firing twin phaser banks. Also available in Langley Poster #P10008	.50	1-2	______
ST103 Enterprise in standard orbit (clockwise) over magenta planet and moon	.50	1-2	______
ST104 Spock in full dress uniform, close-up at bridge station	.50	1-2	______
ST105 Uhura, close-up, at bridge communications station	.50	1-2	______
ST106 Spock, in mid-sentence, bridge	.50	1-2	______
ST107 Kirk, facial close-up	.50	1-2	______
ST108 Enterprise, starboard profile	.50	1-2	______
ST109 Romulan Warclass with clear Bird-of-Prey design	.50	1-2	______
ST110 Chekov, sideview, seated at Science Station	.50	1-2	______
ST111 Pyros VII landing party at beamdown; Scotty, Spock, Kirk, McCoy, Sulu (Cp)	.50	1-2	______
ST112 Enterprise, frontal view in standard orbit (clockwise) over black and green planet	.50	1-2	______
ST113 Klingon Battle Cruiser, front view	.50	1-2	______
ST114 Kirk and Spock planetside, viewed through the Guardian of Forever portal (CEF)	.50	1-2	______
ST115 Spock, phaser dawn, Engineering	.50	1-2	______
ST116 Gamma Trianguli VI materialization of party; McCoy, Chekov, Kirk, Yeoman Martha Landon and Marpoi (TA)	.50	1-2	______
ST117 Enterprise, rear view as it enters galactic barrier (WNM)	.50	1-2	______
ST118 Kirk, with communicator, interior of Sylvia and Karob's castle (Cp)	.50	1-2	______
ST119 Scotty, close-up, in full dress kilt	.50	1-2	______
ST120 Mirror-Spock, close-up of bearded First Officer (MM)	.50	1-2	______
ST121 "Star Trek" title credit with Enterprise over planet	.50	1-2	______
ST122 Kirk, close-up, contemplative pose over the bridge	.50	1-2	______
ST123 Sulu, close-up, seated at the helm	.50	1-2	______
ST124 Kirk, close-up, dress uniform, in conference room	.50	1-2	______
ST125 Enterprise, front view, as Tholian Scout completes its energy field (TW)	.50	1-2	______
ST126 Enterprise, half-shot, before shimmering hulk of the U.S.S. Defiant (TW)	.50	1-2	______
ST127 Bridge crew, full complement around seated Kirk; Scotty, Chekov, Chapel, McCoy, Uhura and Sulu. Also available as Langley poster # P1016	.50	1-2	______
ST128 McCoy, close-up, in corridor	.50	1-2	______
ST129 Conference Room formal hearing; Scotty, Spock, Kirk and McCoy (SS)	.50	1-2	______
ST130 Spock giving Vulcan hand salute on planet Vulcan (AT)	.50	1-2	______
ST131 Kirk, close-up, before bridge viewscreen	.50	1-2	______
ST132 Kirk, chest-deep in tribbles on deep space station K-7 (TWT)	.50	1-2	______
ST133 Shuttlecraft Galileo '7, deep space	.50	1-2	______
ST134 Enterprise surrounded by three Klingon class Romulan ships (EI)	.50	1-2	______
ST135 Klingon Captain Kor, close-up (EM)	.50	1-2	______
ST136 Spock, profile, seated at station	.50	1-2	______
ST137 Enterprise, rear-view, as dwarfed by the amoeba entity (IS)	.50	1-2	______
ST138 Mirror-Spock, bearded Vulcan seated in his quarters (MM)	.50	1-2	______
ST139 Partial bridge crew, with Spock at the con; Uhuru, Sulu and McCoy	.50	1-2	______
ST140 Enterprise, in orbit (counter-clockwise) over blue planet	.50	1-2	______
ST141 Kirk, close-up, concerned expression	.50	1-2	______
ST142 Spock, close-up, horizontal pose of the spore-afflicted Vulcan smiling as he hangs from a tree (TSP)	.50	1-2	______

Star Trek T.V. and Motion Picture Still Sets

• Lincoln Enterprises

Wallet photos on thin stock featuring color scenes and action in assorted packaged sets:

Packets containing 2½"x3½" format photos:

	Issue	Current	Cost/Date
2151, Set No. 1	.50	1-2	______
2152, Set No. 2	1.50	2-3	______
2153, Set No. 3	1.50	2-3	______

1983 - 15 Color Photo sets in 2"x3" format:

	Issue	Current	Cost/Date
2110 STWOK cards	1.95	2-3	______
2111 STWOK cards	1.95	2-3	______
2112 STWOK cards	1.95	2-3	______
2113 STWOK cards	1.95	2-3	______
2114 Kirk (assorted)	1.95	2-3	______
2115 Spock (assorted)	1.95	2-3	______
2116 STTMP Cast and Various groups	1.95	2-3	______
2117 STTMP scenes	1.95	2-3	______

VIDEOS

	Issue	Current	Cost/Date
2118 STTMP action scenes	1.95	2-3	
2119 Make-up and aliens (assorted)	1.95	2-3	
2120 Costumes (assorted)	1.95	2-3	
2121 Costumes (assorted)	1.95	2-3	
2122 T.V. series (assorted)	1.95	2-3	
2123 T.V. series (assorted)	1.95	2-3	
2124 T.V. series (assorted)	1.95	2-3	
2125 STSFS (assorted)	1.95	2-3	
2126 STSFS (assorted)	1.95	2-3	
2127 STSFS (assorted)	1.95	2-3	
2128 STSFS (assorted)	1.95	2-3	

• **Star Trek Weapons and Gadgetry Folio**
Lincoln Enterprises, 1984
Color card package of 12 shots of the various weapons and equipment from the Star Trek universe, replica reproductions:

	Issue	Current	Cost/Date
Individual cards	.50	1-2	
Complete Set of 12 cards, No. 2142	3.95	5-7	

Video Cassettes

• **Best of John Belushi**
Warner Home Video, 1985
Collection of 16 skits as originally aired on *Saturday Night - Live!* during the 1975-79 seasons. Includes the classic Star Trek cancellation skit entitled "The Last Voyage of the Starship Enterprise," 60 min.

	Issue	Current	Cost/Date
VHS 34078	24.98	25-26	
Beta 34079	24.98	25-26	

• **Blooper Reels**
Assorted Distributors, 1985
All three blooper reels from the series on one cassette, color, 20 min.

	Issue	Current	Cost/Date
VHS	29.95	30-32	
Beta	29.95	30-32	

• **Star Trek Dream**
Star Base Central Dist., 1985
Made from the 1975 t.v. special of the same title, in depth analysis of Star Trek phenomenon, interviews with Gene Roddenberry, William Shatner and Leonard Nimoy, 60 min.

	Issue	Current	Cost/Date
VHS	39.95	40-42	
Beta	39.95	40-42	

• **Star Trek Origial Television Series Videos**
Paramount Home Video, 1985
Successive cassettes of all 79 t.v. episodes are being released in uncut format and in groups of ten. Group releases supposedly coincide with the original sequence of episode air dates. However, box numbers don't follow a sequential numbering system and gaps exist, all tapes are 51 min.

	Issue	Current	Cost/Date
All tapes (unless noted)	14.95	15-16	

•**Set 1**

	Issue	Current	Cost/Date
2 - "Where No Man Has Gone"			
VHS 60040-02			
Beta 60040-02			
3 - "The Corbomite Maneuver"			
VHS 60040-03			
Beta 60040-03			
4 - "Mudd's Women"			
VHS 60040-04			
Beta 60040-04			
5 - "The Enemy Within"			
VHS 60040-05			
Beta 60040-05[1]			
6 - "The Man Trap"			
VHS 60040-06			
Beta 60040-06			
7 - "The Naked Time"			
VHS 60040-07			
Beta 60040-07			
8 - "Charlie X"			
VHS 60040-08			
Beta 60040-08			
10 - "What Are Little Girls Made Of?"			
VHS 60040-10			
Beta 60040-10			
11 - "Dagger of the Mind"			
VHS 60040-11			
Beta 60040-11			
12 - "Miri"			
VHS 60040-12			
Beta 60040-12			

• **Set 2**

	Issue	Current	Cost/Date
9 - "Balance of Terror"			
VHS 60040-09			
Beta 60040-09			
13 - "The Conscience of the King"			
VHS 60040-13			
Beta 60040-13			
14 - "The Galileo 7"			
VHS 60040-14			
Beta 60040-14			
15 - "Court Martial"			
VHS 60040-14			
Beta 60040-14			
16 - "The Menagerie" Special double episode cassette, contains Part I & Part II			
VHS 60040-16	29.95	30-32	
Beta 60040-16	29.95	30-32	
17 - "Shore Leave"			
VHS 60040-17			
Beta 60040-17			
18 - "The Squire of Gothos"			
VHS 60040-18			
Beta 60040-18			

1. First productions of this video displayed a cover photo of a scene from "What Are Little Girls Made Of?" This error has just recently been corrected to show an appropriate still from "The Enemy Within."

VIDEOS

	Issue	Current	Cost/Date
19 - "Arena"			
VHS 60040-19			______
Beta 60040-19			______
21 - "Tomorrow is Yesterday"			
VHS 60040-21			______
Beta 60040-21			______
22 - "Return of the Archons"			
VHS 60040-22			______
Beta 60040-22			______

• Set 3

	Issue	Current	Cost/Date
#20 "The Alternative Factor"			
VHS 60040-20			______
Beta 60040-20			______
23 - "The Alternative Factor"			
VHS 60040-23			______
Beta 60040-23			______
24 - "Space Seed"			
VHS 60040-24			______
Beta 60040-24			______
25 - "This Side of Paradise"			
VHS 60040-25			______
Beta 60040-25			______
26 - "The Devis in the Dark"			
VHS 60040-26			______
Beta 60040-26			______
27 - "Errand of Mercy"			
VHS 60040-27			______
Beta 60040-27			______
28 - "The City On The Edge"			
VHS 60040-28			______
Beta 60040-28 [2]			______
29 - "Operation - Annihilate!"			
VHS 60040-29			______
Beta 60040-29			______
33 - "Who Mourns for Adonais?"			
VHS 60040-33			______
Beta 60040-33			______
34 - "Amok Time"			
VHS 60040-34			______
Beta 60040-34			______

• Set 4

	Issue	Current	Cost/Date
30 - "Catspaw"			
VHS 60040-30			______
Beta 60040-30			______
31 - "Metamorphosis"			
VHS 60040-31			______
Beta 60040-31			______
32 - "Friday's Child"			
VHS 60040-32			______
Beta 60040-32			______
35 - "The Doomsday Machine"			
VHS 60040-35			______
Beta 60040-35			______
37 - "The Changeling"			
VHS 60040-37			______
Beta 60040-37			______
38 - "The Apple"			
VHS 60040-38			______
Beta 60040-38			______
39 - "Mirror, Mirror"			
VHS 60040-39			______
Beta 60040-39			______
40 - "The Deadly Years"			
VHS 60040-40			______
Beta 60040-40			______
41 - "I, Mudd"			
VHS 60040-41			______
Beta 60040-41			______
44 - "Journey to Babel"			
VHS 60040-44			______
Beta 60040-44			______

• Set 5

	Issue	Current	Cost/Date
1 - "The Cage"			
Special Star Trek episode never aired, features Captain Pike, 73 min.			
VHS 60040-01	29.95	30-32	______
Beta 60040-01	29.95	30-32	______
36 - "Wolf in the Fold"			
VHS 60040-36			______
Beta 60040-36			______
42 - "The Trouble With Tribbles"			
VHS 60040-42			______
Beta 60040-42			______
43 - "Bread and Circuses"			
VHS 60040-43			______
Beta 60040-43			______
45 - "Private Little War"			
VHS 60040-45			______
Beta 60040-44			______
46 - "Gamesters of Triskelion"			
VHS 60040-46			______
Beta 60040-46			______
47 - "Obsession"			
VHS 60040-47			______
Beta 60040-47			______
48 - "Immunity Syndrome"			
VHS 60040-48			______
Beta 60040-48			______
49 - "Piece of the Action"			
VHS 60040-49			______
Beta 60040-49			______
50 - "By Any Other Name"			
VHS 60040-50			______
Beta 60040-50			______
51 - "Return To Tomorrow"			
VHS 60040-51			______
Beta 60040-51			______
52 - "Patterns of Force"			
VHS 60040-52			______
Beta 60040-52			______
53 - "The Ultimate Computer"			
VHS 60040-53			______
Beta 60040-53			______
54 - "The Omega Glory"			
VHS 60040-54			______
Beta 60040-54			______
55 - "Assignment: Earth"			
VHS 60040-55			______
Beta 60040-55			______

2. This slightly abridged video carries a special notation on the cover which advises collectors that it contains music changes not produced when the episode was aired on T.V.

VIDEOS

	Issue	Current	Cost/Date
56 - "Spectre of the Gun"			
VHS 60040-56			______
Beta 60040-56			______
58 - "The Paradise Syndrome"			
VHS 60040-58			______
Beta 60040-58			______
59 - "The Enterprise Incident"			
VHS 60040-59			______
Beta 60040-59			______
60 - "And The Children Shall Lead"			
VHS 60040-60			______
Beta 60040-60			______
61 - "Spock's Brain"			
VHS 60040-61			______
Beta 60040-61			______
62 - "Is There In Truth No Beauty"			
VHS 60040-62			______
Beta 60040-62			______

• **Star Trek The Motion Picture**
Paramount Home Video, 1979
Original, shorter version as viewed at movie theaters, 132 min.[3]

	Issue	Current	Cost/Date
VHS	39.95	40-41	______
Beta	39.95	40-41	______

• **Star Trek The Motion Picture Special Longer Version**
Paramount Home Video
Stereo & Dolby Sound, includes 12 minutes of new footage, 143 min.
Original "rainbow promo" on front, 1984

	Issue	Current	Cost/Date
VHS 8858A	24.95	25-26	______
Beta 8858A	24.95	25-26	______

Special Collector's Series, Paramount 75th Anniversary Edition, black & gold box, 1986

	Issue	Current	Cost/Date
VHS 8858	19.95	20-21	______
Beta 8858	19.95	20-21	______

• **Star Trek III, The Search For Spock**
Paramount Home Video
Hi-Fil quality movie-length video, 105 min.,
Movie promo cover, 1984

	Issue	Current	Cost/Date
VHS 1621	29.95	30-31	______
Beta 1624[4]	29.29	30-31	______

Special Collector's Series, Paramount 75th Anniversry Edition, black & gold box, 1986

	Issue	Current	Cost/Date
VHS 1621	19.95	20-21	______
Beta 1621	19.95	20-21	______

• **Star Trek: The Superfans, The Superstars**
1977,
Video of T.V. special with the same title, Hosted by Bob Williams, a look at Trek fans and stars, 60 min.

	Issue	Current	Cost/Date
VHS	39.95	40-41	______
Beta	39.95	40-41	______

• **Star Trek T.V. Classic: Space Seed**
The episode that insired *Star Trek The Wrath of Kahn,* plus the bonus trailer for ST II, slipcover box is silver with action scene of Kirk & Kahn from the episode, Gateway Video Distributors,

	Issue	Current	Cost/Date
VHS	39.95	40-41	______

• **Star Trek T.V. Episodes**
Paramount Home Video, 1982
Selected episodes from the series, two shows per cassette, 100 minutes each,

	Issue	Current	Cost/Date
Volume 1 - "The Menagerie"			
Parts I & II, VHS V0389	49.49	50-56	______
Beta B0389	49.95	50-56	______
Volume II - "Balance of Terror" & "The City on the Edge of Forever"			
VHS V0391	49.95	50-56	______
Beta B0391	49.95	50-56	______
Volume 3 - "Amok Time" & "Journey To Babel",			
VHS V0393	49.95	50-56	______
Beta B0393	49.95	50-56	______
Volume 4 - "Mirror, Mirror" & "The Tholian Web",			
VHS V0395	49.95	50-56	______
Beta B0395	49.95	50-56	______
Volume 5 - "The Trouble With Tribbles" & "Let That Be Your Last Battlefield"			
VHS V0397	49.95	50-56	______
Beta B0397	49.95	50-56	______

• **Star Trek II, The Wrath of Kahn**
Paramount Home Video, 1982
Recorded on Scotch tape with stereo & Dolby Sound, slipcase with "starburst" movie logo, four photo collage on rear, 113 min.[5]

	Issue	Current	Cost/Date
VHS 1180	24.95	25-26	______
Beta 1180	24.95	25-26	______

• **Vincent**
Leonard Nimoy as Vincent Van Gogh, one-man visual show,

	Issue	Current	Cost/Date
VHS	29.95	30-31	______
Beta	29.95	30-31	______

3. Both *Star Trek The Motion Picture* videos and *Star Trek II, The Wrath of Kahn* videos were originally issued at $39.95. Because of excellent sales, Paramount slashed video prices down to $29.95 in the summer of 1983 and then down to $24.95 for Christmas 1984.

4. *Star Trek III* was ranked as number 2 in overall video sales for 1985 after sales of 425,000 copies and a total revenue of nearly 13 million dollars.

5. By November 1982, *Star Trek II* videos had broken all video sales records to date in comparative categories. At that time, 1,000 videos per day were selling in video stores throughout the country. One hundred and ten thousand videos sold with the $39.95 price tag.

VIDEOS

Video Discs (Laser & CED)

	Issue	Current	Cost/Date
• **Star Trek The Motion Picture,** 1979 Selectra Vision, double disc package, side one: 1 hr., 34 min., side two: 38 min., slipcover case,			
Laser disc	39.95	35-40	______
CED 00636 (RCA)	34.98	30-35	______
• **Star Trek II, The Search For Spock,** 1984 Motion picture disc, 105 in.,			
Laser disc	29.95	25-30	______
CED (RCA)	29.95	25-30	______
• **Star Trek T.V. Episodes,** RCA Set of four special CED pressings containing two episodes per disc, 100 min. each,			
Volume I - "The Menagerie", Parts I & II	19.95	15-20	______
Volume II - "The City On The Edge of Forever" & "Let That Be Your Last Battlefield"	19.98	15-20	______
Volume III - "The Trouble With Tribbles" & "The Tholian Web"	19.98	15-20	______
Volume IV - "Mirror, Mirror" & "The Tholian Web"	19.98	15-20	______
• **Star Trek T.V. Episodes** (expanded set), RCA Star Trek T.V. disc library containing 6 volumes of double-episode discs, Selectra Vision 12-inch videos in colorful boxed slipcover cases, each with photo collages from the appropriate episodes, 100 min. each,			
Volume I - "The Menagerie", Parts I & II, CED 00631	19.98	15-20	______
Volume 2 - "The City On The Edge of Forever" & "Let That Be Your Last Battlefield" CED 00632	19.98	15-20	______
Volume 3 - "The Trouble With Tribbles" & "The Tholian Web" CED 00664	19.98	15-20	______
Volume 4 - "Space Seed" & "The Changeling" CED 03602	19.98	15-20	______
Volume 5 - "Balance of Terror" & "Mirror, Mirror" CED 00672	19.98	15-20	______
Volume 6 - "Amok Time" & "Journey To Babel" CED 03609	19.98	15-20	______
Star Trek T.V. Series Pioneer Video Corp., 1982 Set of five 12 inch video discs featuring two Trek episodes per disc, 100 min. each,			
1 - "Balance of Terror" & "Conscience of the King", Laser	29.95	25-30	______
2 - "Galileo Seven" & "Shore Leave" Laser	29.95	25-30	______
3 - "Arena" & "The Squire of Gothos" Laser	29.95	25-30	______
4 - "Court Martial" & "Tomorrow is Yesterday" Laser	29.95	25-30	______
5 - "Return of the Archons" &"Space Seed" Laser	29.95	25-30	______
• **Star Trek II, The Wrath of Kahn,** RCA, 1982 Selectra Vision, photo style slipcover case,			
CED 13605	19.98	15-20	______
• **Star Trek II, The Wrath of Kahn** Pioneer Video Corpo, 1982 Stereo Laser video disc, 12 inch diameter with slipcover case featuring 14 photo collage from the movie promo poster, rear cover with 6 action scenes and credits, 113 min.,			
Laser	29.95	25-30	______
• **Vincent** Laser video disc with Leonard Nimoy playing Vincent Van Gough,			
Laser	49.95	50-50	______

Viewers

	Issue	Current	Cost/Date
• **Star Trek Keychain Viewer** Lincoln Enterprises, 1974 1"x2½" pyramidal viewers with single frame clip from the series:			
1901 Kirk	1.00	1-3	______
1902 Spock	1.00	1-3	______
1903 McCoy	1.00	1-3	______
1904 Scotty	1.00	1-3	______
1905 Uhura	1.00	1-3	______
1906 Sulu	1.00	1-3	______
1907 Chekov	1.00	1-3	______
1908 Nurse Chapel	1.00	1-3	______
1909 Other Stars	1.00	1-3	______
1910 Space Ships	1.00	1-3	______
1911 Interior Enterprise and Gadgetry	1.00	1-3	______
1912 Action Scenes	1.00	1-3	______
1913 Interior/Exterior Sets	1.00	1-3	______
1914 Monsters/Aliens	1.00	1-3	______
1915 Phasers	1.00	1-3	______
1916 Communicators	1.00	1-3	______
• **Star Trek Movie Viewer - 8 mm - 225** Chemtoy Corporation, 1969 Red and black plastic monocular viewer with hand advance knob for viewing film strip, two boxed adventure strips included, blister packed 7"x9" cardstock that photos bridge scene of Kirk, McCoy, Spock and Uhura	.79	5-8	______
• **Star Trek Pocket Flix** 6571-4 Ideal, 1978 Hand-held viewer featuring "By Any Other Name" episode in unremoveable cartridge with crank advance, red plastic casing, approx. 7" long, in blister pack	2.98	15-25	______

VIEWERS

	Issue	Current	Cost/Date
• **Star Trek View Masters,** GAF **"The Omega Glory",** B499, 1968 episode in 21 scenes on three, 3-D discs, includes 16 page two-tone illustrated booklet, 4½" square paper pocket photos Exeter and Enterprise starships	1.25	8-12	_____
• **"Mr. Spock's Time Trek",** B555, 1974 21 view master scenes on three 3-D discs from the animated episode, includes 16 page two-tone illustrated booklet, 4½" square paper pocket illos three separate cels from the cartoon series	1.50	8-10	_____
• **"Mr. Spock's Time Trek"** ABV555, 1974. Talking viewmaster kit with 3 reels and scenes from this animated episode, box cover illos young Spock and the Guardian of Forever device	3.15	10-15	_____
• **Star Trek The Motion Picture - Automatic Double-Vue** GAF, 1981 The movie in two separate movie films permanently encased inside self-winding plastic cartridge - 2½"x5", requires the special Automati Double-Vuew viewer. Two advanture sequels titled "Galactic Adventure" and "Action in Space", cardboard mount on 6¼"x9" with official movie letter logo	3.99	10-15	_____
• **Star Trek The Motion Picture Space Viewer** 8053-1 Larami Corp., 1979 Red plastic body 3"x3" with gray bubble screen, gray knobs on right roll photo film sequences, one roll insert with two boxed rolls includes 6"x9" cardstock blister pack with alien stills on lower horizontal borders	2	7-10	_____
• **Star Trek The Motion Picture View Masters,** GAF, 1979 **Viewmaster** K57 21 scenes on three 3-D discs, includes a 16 page two-tone illustrated booklet, 4½" square paper pocket has art style yellow grid on black with the STTMP movie letter logo in white inside orange oval	2	5-10	_____
• **Viewmaster Kit** Packaged set containing one viewmaster viewer and 3 disc reels for STTMP, bonus pair of 3-D poster glasses included, enclosed inside a circular tub with purple lid	3.95	25-30	_____

	Issue	Current	Cost/Date
• **Star Trek II The Wrath of Kahn View Master** M38 View Master International Group, 1982. ST II in 21 scenes on three 3-D film discs. Story outline is written on the package back, no booklet included, 4½" x 8½" cardboard mount with "Starburst" movie logo and movie Enterprise	2.50	5-7	_____

GAMES

Board Games and Puzzles

The popularity of T.V. Trek made it a perfect action/adventure theme for incorporation into the children's market via board games, card games and jigsaw puzzles.

In 1966 Ideal Toy Corporation produced the first Star Trek game. Despite relatively poor sales, Star Trek would again be manufactured as a board game eight years later by Hasbro and again in 1979 by Milton Bradley. Just recently, the usual Trek board gaming format has undergone a metamorphosis to become a trivia game designed for more sophisticated fans.

The greatest flurry of Star Trek gaming paraphenalia has circulated around the release of both Star Trek the animated series and *Star Trek The Motion Picture.* Originally, all of these items made interesting and inexpensive collectible investments. Today they are hard to find in complete and unaltered condition. Since 1982 only two new memorabilia items have appeared on the market at all, the **Star Trek Trivia Game** (1985) and the **U.S.S. Enterprise** jigsaw puzzle by David Kimble (1986).

Gaming Programs

The growth of Star Trek themes for use bv adult fans in a gaming medium has been extensive during the 1980's. Gaming programs through computer software and video display have lifted Star Trek board games into a new, three-dimensional realm for advanced Trekker tastes. Video arcades, home video games and a variety of computer programs exist to test and tantalize individual gaming skills.

Arcade Games

Sega Enterprises was the first to produce a 3-D video simulation game in 1983. It appeared as either an upright, free-standing model or as a plexiglass command chair simulator. Tomorrow's video arcade games are expected to be functionally "sen-surround" with images so precise that Star Trek fans actually feel themselves sitting in the Captain's chair. Wraparound environments such as the one by Sega are unique annd experimental prototypes.

At a recent arcade display at the Simulation Tournament Center in San Diego, California, certain consoles were equipped with an advanced video game based upon **Star Trek The Motion Picture.** Video users sat in a replica of the Captain's chair wearing special earphones and watching three synchronized monitor screens which ran actual footage from the movie. Armed with joysticks and fire controls, adventurous video players squared off with Klingons for the rental fee of $10 per hour.

Computer Software

Long before companies began producing Star Trek in packaged home computer programs, fandom had discovered the novelty of using Trek war game scenarios. The earliest computer games were text-based. They didn't require a graphics card or a monitor in order to be played but consisted mainly of typed chain-order commands which the computer program responded to via a printed page or a text of consecutive actions and responses. Games were scored by printed documentation and players could review their strategies by studying the printed replies.

There are two basic types of computer software programs.

Commercial discs - These appear as pre-programmed diskettes which are expensively packaged and marketed. Elaborate programs may contain detailed instruction and scenario packets including graphs, artwork, mission briefings from Star Fleet, crew biographies, ship's systems descriptions and universe summaries. The **Kobayashi Alternative** packaged inside a hard-cover binding is an excellent sample.

Public domain software - Public domain Star Trek games consist of computer user manuals, magazines and discs for every type of home computer system. Such games may be acquired either as published step-by-step instructions for programming your own disc or as a pre-programmed disc containing assorted levels of documentation that explains the game and its objectives. An extensive library listing of public domain software designed for IBM and IBM compatibles is available from PG-SIG (the PC Software Interest Group) located in California. They supply an impressive directory of Star Trek software in addition to user support.

Well known computer systems which offer some sort of Star Trek game programming instructions include Arpannet, Micronet and The Source, along with Apple, Commodore, TRS-80, Texas Instruments and IBM.

Star Trek as a software theme has been used as a marketing strategy for selling computer systems as well. In 1982 William Shatner helped to promote a full line of Commodore business computers, including the VIC-20 personal computer, the CBM 8000 business computers and Super PET 9000 series. Shatner appeared in advertising seen in print, on radio and television. This was the largest advertising campaign in the history of Commodore Business Machine.

Star Trek's futuristic hardware has also shown up in the promotion programs of companies that manufacture CAD (Computer Aided Design) systems. Texas instruments used the schematics of the Enterprise to advertise the drafting capabilities of their new PC-CAD software targeted at home designers and architects. A Klingon Battle Cruiser reproduction was used to market a CAD drafting system used in the design and manufacturing of printed circuit boards as well.

Role Playing and Space Gaming

There are current four commercial gaming formats available to Star Trek fans. Lou Zocchi's **Star Fleet Battle Manual Game** traces its beginning to a non-board fanzine adventure book published in 1971 and titled **Battle Manual (for Alien Space).** In 1977 the newly renamed, boxed edition was released by Game Science Corp. It converted the earlier format game to board gaming with counters, playing pieces, miniature starships and mapsheets. Since the combination of Zocchi's two games, a rules supplement was added in 1979 to consolidate and broaden the scope of this universe.

In 1980, through the help of Lou Zocchi and Franz Joseph (designer of the **Star Trek Technical Manual** and blueprints), Steve Cole of Task Force Games produced its set called **Star Fleet Battles Game.** A distinct format with a confusingly similar title. This game is presently a widely played format for Star Trek that keeps the tactical/battle strategy approach of more traditional war-gaming. The Task Force line of 2200 Miniature Starships provides an elaborate array of metal and plastic replica ships, from tiny space buoys to giant Dreadnoughts. These ships are produced regularly to coincide with the company's updated rulesbooks and adventures.

Role-playing for Star Trek began in 1983 with the extensive Fasa Corp. line of gaming sets, modules and sourcebooks. Diverging away from the battle-forces play strategy, role-playing adventures involve resolving issues that don't necessarily require the use of military force. Fasa's own expansive line of character figurines as well as metal ships and booklet guides has sold over a million copies to date. This very prolific company packages its merchandise with attractive cover art by such artists as O'Connell and Martin, and is now re-releasing earlier editions with the artwork of Dietrick. Modules are continuously being updated to keep abreast of universe changes brought about by the Star Trek motion pictures.

The newest producer of space games is West End Games with its Star Trek Adventure Game series. Three sets have been released with storylines paralleling plots established on the t.v. and movie adventures. West End's independent and fully contained game packages are aimed at beginning gamers who wish to step into the universe of Star Trek gaming possibilities.

A distinction may be made between the collectors and the gamers in the particular field of role playing sets and accessories. While participating gamemasters will attach higher value to newly released updates, sourcebooks and scenarios from the standpoint of further enhancements to the intrigue of the game; collectors should be more attuned to the vintage, often very different packaging methods and contents of the earlier produced games as representing "original" game plots and formatting.

For those fans who don't have the time or patience to become involved with the intracacies of interactive group play, Entertainment Concepts launched the alternative Star Trek Correspondence Game in 1983. This approach represents a novel play-by-mail system of role playing via computer tracked situations, responses and outcomes.

• Board Game Sets

	Issue	Current	Cost/Date
Action and Adventure in Outer Space - Star Trek Game #2678-3, Hasbro, 1974 Children's fold-out board game with four playing pieces, pair of dice, 2 spinners and a peg-hole board. Animation-style box cover.........	5	12-18	_____
Star Trek Game #2293-9 Ideal Toy Corp., 1966 Board game for 2 to 4 players. Object is to race in space from Earth to designated planet and back, keeping your fuel ships within reach. 19" square board shows Earth cartwheeled by six alien planets. Includes one 6-sided die, 4 tokens, 4 cardboard mission cards, 36 fuel packs and color fuel discs. Boxed, 10¼"x19¼", cover artwork of t.v. Spock, Kirk and Uhura with bridge viewscreen action................	2.50	20-35	_____

Star Trek Trivia Game, 1985.

	Issue	Current	Cost/Date
Star Trek Trivia Game #4161 Golden Trivia Game, Star Trek Edition Western Publishing Co., Inc., 1985 Card and board tray set for 2 or more players. Quiz categories are: Aliens, Trek Trivia, Science Fiction, Alien Worlds, Quotes and The Ship's Crew. Includes 216 printed cards (1,296 questions), 1 die, 4-point value cards and instructions. Tray is plastic., Boxed 12½" x 12" with photo cover of t.v. Enterprise..	11	12-15	_____
Star Trek The Motion Picture Game #4913 Milton Bradley, 1979 Board game for 2 to 4 players. Object is to travel the galaxy seeking out alien phenomenon, complete 3 missions and return home. 26½" x 27" game board features six individual triangular Space Sector punch-ons. Central panorama is the Enterprise in pursuit of Klingon Cruisers. Includes two 6-sided dice, 4 miniature plastic starship pawns, 24 mission cards, 32 star cards, 6 clips and 60 control markers. Boxed 14" x 19", cover artwork Kirk, Spock, Uhura, McCoy, Scotty, Ilia and Enterprise..................	9	10-12	_____

• Cards

Playing card decks

	Issue	Current	Cost/Date
Enterprise Deck, Aviva, 1979 STTMP vintage starship appears on the card-backs, plastic coated cards.	4		_____
Fizzin Deck, Zolke and Davis, 1976 Card deck and playing rules for the card game "Fizzbin" as introduced by Kirk in the t.v. episode "A Piece of the Action". Photo cardbacks show a collage of four scenes from the show.....................	6		_____
Star Trek Wrath of Kahn Official Playing Cards Movie Players, Ltd, 1982 Complete deck featuring 52 different photo portraits and action scenes from the second move.			
1st edition - title reads above......	2.50	4-7	_____
2nd edition - adds Roman Numeral II to movie title................	3	3-5	_____

Star Trek Wrath of Kahn playing cards, 1982.

- **Colorforms – Star Trek Adventure Set,** Colorforms, 1975

	Issue	Current	Cost/Date
Sticker board showing cartoon transporter chamber, bridge stations and captain's chair. Red, blue, white and yellow colorform parts recreate action scenes of crew and aliens. Boxed, cover illos artwork Enterprise, Spock, Kirk and McCoy.....	3.50	10-15	_____

- **Color 'n Recolor Game Cloth – Star Trek**

	Issue	Current	Cost/Date
Avalon, 1979 STTMP vintage washable plastic game cloth, measures 36"x40" and includes eight coloring crayons, and wipe-off sponge.................	4	8-15	_____

- **Pinball - Lap board**

Azrak-Hamway International (AHI), 1976
Traditional clear plastic pinball lap tray with internal targets and metal balls with shooter. Base board features the Gold Key "Star Trek" comic letter logo with choice of characters:

	Issue	Current	Cost/Date
Captain Kirk	3	6-8	_____
Mr. Spock	3	6-8	_____

- **Puzzles**

Assorted photo and cartoon image puzzles with interlocking pieces.

Battle on the planet Klingon.

"Attempted Hijacking" H.G. Toys, 1974.

Captain Kirk & Officers beaming down.

	Issue	Current	Cost/Date
Aviva Enterprises, 1979 551-piece jigsaw puzzles featuring Star Trek The Motion Picture themes, 18"x24", boxed.			
"Enterprise"	4	6-10	_____
"Mr. Spock"	4	6-10	_____
H.G. Toys, 1974 Jigsaw puzzles with scenes from the Star Trek Animated Cartoon series. Packaged in two finished puzzles sizes and numbers of pieces, all are boxed:			
"Attempted Hijacking of the U.S.S. Enterprise and Its Officers" #496-02 Bridge scene, 14"x18", 150 pieces . .	2	7-10	_____
"Battle on the Planet Klingon" #495-02 Kirk, Spock and crewman firing phasers, 10" x 14", 150 pieces	1.50	7-10	_____

PUZZLES

Battle on the planet Romulan.

	Issue	Current	Cost/Date
H.G. Toys			
"Battle on the Planet Romulan" #495-03. Crewmembers under attack by dragon-like monster, 10" x 14", 150 pieces	1.50	7-10	______
"Captain Kirk and Officers Beaming Down" #495-01 Kirk, Spock and crewman in transporter, 10"x14", 150 pieces	1.50	7-10	______
"Force Field Capture" #495-05 Drawing of Kirk, Spock and hooded figure, 10" x 14", 150 pieces	1.50	7-10	______
"Starship U.S.S. Enterprise and Its Officers" #496-01. Busts of Kirk, Spock, McCoy and Sulu in corners with Enterprise orbiting planet, 14"x18", 300 pieces	2	8-12	______

Starship U.S.S. Enterprise and its officers.

Merigold Press, Frame-Tray Series 4599, 1979. Easy, 12-piece children's puzzles in cardboard frame trays. Have color cartoon series derived from the t.v. series, 8¼"x11" trays, cellophane wrapped. Untitled.

Two frame trays by Merrigold Press, 1979.

	Issue	Current	Cost/Date
Beam Down. Spock, Kirk and female crewmember on pads with Scott at the transporter controls	1	2-4	______
Enterprise Bridge Spock at the Con on top, bottom shows close-up of Kirk and Spock	1	2-4	______
Kirk The Captain in an environsuit outside the starship	1	2-4	______
Outer Space Montage Enterprise, Kirk, Spock and several planets in fanciful collage	1	2-4	______

Note artwork cover for "Forcefield Capture."

Milton Bradley, Series 4993, 1979 250-piece puzzles featuring photos from STTMP film, 13⅞"x19⅞" box with photo lid showing the puzzle:

	Issue	Current	Cost/Date
"Enterprise" Photo of the revised motion picture starship	2.50	5-10	______
"Faces of the Future" Movie action portrait photo	2.50	5-10	______

PUZZLES

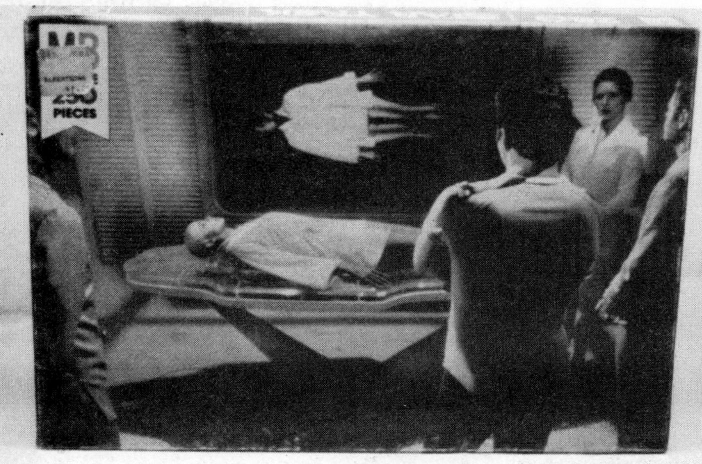

"Sick Bay" puzzle, Milton Bradley, 1979.

	Issue	Current	Cost/Date
Milton Bradley **"Sick Bay"** Ilia in sickbay with a concerned crew looking on	2.50	5-10	_____
Mind's Eye Press, 1986 **"U.S.S. Enterprise NCC-1701-A"** Photo puzzle of David Kimble's famous cut-away poster detailing compartments of the movie version Enterprise. The original poster is revamped to indicate the newly re-built Enterprise II that appeared at the end of Star Trek The Voyage Home, 18"x24", 551 pieces, photo box. 1	15	15-17	_____
Starlog Magazine Custom Jigsaw Puzzles Starlog Magazine, 1979 Personalized photo puzzle reproductions made from your own photographs, negatives or slides. Advertised with Star Trek repros, 8"x10" size, 110 interlocking pieces:			
Made from print or photo	3.50	5-10	_____
Made from negative or slide 2	7.50	5-10	_____
• **Target Game - Photon Balls** Lincoln Enterprises, 1973 Hanging target piece with Star Trek figures and 3 velcro-covered balls	4	5-7	_____

1. This puzzle made available as a special order direct from the manufacturer. Not sold originally through retail.
2. Custom puzzles would vary by content which would dictate the price range that resulted. Prices here reflect the average prices for similarly formated puzzles. This offer was a special order coupon through Starlog Magazine.

GAMING PROGRAMS

(For Arcades, Computers and Videos)

	Issue	Current	Cost/Date
ENTREP — Starship Enterprise on Printer Disk No. 44, Games #6, PC-SIG, 1985 Diskette with 20 Basic games, including a printer program for creating the starship and STAR-TREK, and adventure game in 45K version	6	6-8	_____
MEGATREK, Disk No. 299, Mixture. PC-SIG, 1985 Diskette with 22 simple utilities and assembler programs, includes MEGATREK game and NUTREK, a screen oriented program	6	6-8	_____
NEWTREK. Another Version of STARTREK Disk Bo. 24, Games #3, PC-SIG, 1985 Disk with 9 Basic games including Tic-Tac-Toe, pseudo PACMAN, moon survival and a Trek adventure	6	6-8	_____
PHASER, Disk No. 53, Sounds PC-SIG, 1985 Disk featuring 16 sound effects programs, two of which are phasers	6	6-8	_____
SPACWR/"Space War" Digital Equipment Corp., 1973 Paperback manual entitled *101 Basic Computer Games by David H. Ahl. Complete instructions for Basic-Plus. SPACWR program was the first version of the "Super Star Trek" game in Basic*	6	6-8	_____
"Star Trek" Winthrop Publishers, 1979 Paperback manual *Computer Games for Business, Schools and Homes* by J. Victor Nahigian and William S. Hodges. Instructions for Basic games. "Star Trek" game p. 123-127 involves battle sequence with Klingons, warp drive, phasers and diminishing life support. #0-87626-166-7	8	8-10	_____
Star Trek Electronic Pinball Arcade Machine Bally Manufacturers, 1979 Full-size table stand pinball game, featuring balls and shooter, flags, buzzers and bells and flashing electronic scoreboard with a lighted cartoon rendition of the main STTMP characters in their new regulation uniforms. Players fee: 1 Quarter per game		(Lease option)	

GAMING PROGRAMS

	Issue	Current Cost/Date	
Star Trek Evolution, Share Date, Inc., 1986 Disk for the Commodore 64 and 128 home computers. No manual required. Klingons attack a Federation home base and must be eliminated before they overrun the known universe. Three levels of play: Beginner's ST, ST Junior and ST Senior. Plastic pocket package............	6.50	7-8	_____

Star Trek: The Kobayashi Alternative, Micromosaics Products, Inc., Simon & Schuster Software.
Packaged disk detailing routine mission in the Trianguli sector when Lt. Sulu's ship vanishes. Enterprise must find him and neutralize the "Menace." Bookcover case is 32-page spiral bound hardcover with drawings, mission briefings, bios, ship stations. Three types:

	Issue	Current Cost/Date	
IBM PC, PC/XT, PC AT and PC Jr. #0-671-55771-8	39.95	35-40	_____
Apple II+, IIe and IIc, #0-671-557770-X	39.95	35-40	_____
Commodore Computers #0-671-557772-6	39.95	35-40	_____

Star Trek: The Promethean Prophecy
Simon & Schuster Software, 1987
Packaged story and disk detailing the Enterprise badly damaged and Kirk as he unravels the enigmatic Promethean culture to save the crew. One of the "lost adventures of the Starship Enterprise". Hardcover bookcover.

	Issue	Current Cost/Date	
IBM PC, PC/XT, PC AT and PC Jr. plus certain compatibles #0-13-842782-8	39.95	35-40	_____
Apple II+, IIe and IIc #0-13-842766-6	39.95	35-40	_____
Commodore 64 or 128 #0-13-842774-7	32.95	28-34	_____

	Issue	Current Cost/Date	
Star Trek Phaser Strike #4973 Milton Bradley, 1979 Interchangeable cartridge for the Mircrovision game. You battle attacking Klingon Warships. Graphics are cube shaped ships of varying sizes and speeds adjustable firing location and speed controls. Ending score appears on screen. Includes an instruction booklet. Ages 8 to Adult. Boxed 4"x9" with STTMP "Star Trek" letter logo in white on black, magenta and yellow cardstock box..	19	15-20	_____

Star Trek Strategic Operations Simulator
Sega Enterprises, 1983
Official arcade version video game cartridge for home computers and video consoles, one-player or two-player strategy, 3-way viewing screen, functions include thrust, warp drive, photo torpedos, phaser banks and energy fields with exclusive combat control overlay, joystick control or keyboard control, box cartoons the movie Klingons at the helm siting in on the starship Enterprise

	Issue	Current Cost/Date	
Atari 2600	29.99	25-35	_____
Atari 5200	29.99	25-35	_____
Coleco Gemini	29.99	25-35	_____
Coleco Vision Expansion Module	29.99	25-35	_____
Commodore 64 or Vic-20	29.99	25-35	_____
Sears Tele-Games	29.99	25-35	_____
400/800/1200 XL	29.99	25-35	_____

The TI Professional Computer takes CAD where no PC CAD has gone before.

Magazine ad for T.I. PC-CAD Computers. Note Enterprise Models.

Star Trek evolution disk, Share Data, Inc., 1986.

Simon & Shuster Software by Micromosaics Prod. Inc., 1985.

STTMP Video Game.

Star Trek Strategic Operations Video Arcade Game, 1983.

Issue | Current | Cost/Date

Star Trek Strategic Operations Simulator Video Arcade Game, Sega Arcade Rentals, 1983
Complete set-up, action packed video arcade game with joystick and push button command options:
1. Defend Starbase from Klingons
2. Dock Enterprise with Starbase to replenish supplies or effect repairs
3. Utilize Captain's controls to:
   Fire phasers
   Trust power
   Fire photon torpedos
   Warp drive out
"You are the Captain!"
Two Models:
Upright - standard standing arcade with screen on top of floor base control . . . .
Chair-molded plexiglass and plastic seat with front viewscreen visuals
Players Fee for both: 50¢ per game — (Lease option)

STARTREK, Disk No. 178, Miscellaneous Games PC-SIG, 1985
Disk with 7 Basic games including color chess, space travel and super color version of Trek . . . . — 6 — 6-8 — _____

STARTREK, Another Game, Disk No. 71, Games #9 PC- SIG, 1985
Disk with 8 Basic programs including memory game, speller and a Trek adventure . . . . — 6 — 6-8 — _____

Issue | Current | Cost/Date

STARTREK, The Game of, Disk No. 2, Spoolers PC-SIG, 1985
Basic program disk with mostly printer, file and graphics utilities, simple Trek game . . . . — 6 — 6-8 — _____

STARTREK, Questions, Disk No. 329 PC-SIG, 1985
Miscellaneous questions to play Star Trek trivia game. . . . . — 6 — 6-8 — _____

STARTREK, Starship Enterprise, Disk No. 13, PC-SIG, 1985
Disk with 3 Basic programs. Trek action game is to rid the galaxy of the Klingon menace by destroying their invasion force. You have 40 solar years to comlete mission. Includes instruction screen and sound effects for space war. . . . . — 6 — 6-8 — _____

STARTREK 2, Disk No. 17, Games #2 PC-SIG, 1985
10 Basic games on disk including a Trek adventure with overlay module. . . . . — 6 — 6-8 — _____

Star Trek The Motion Picture #HS-4110
Vectrex Arcade System Cartridge, General Consumer Electronics, 1982
Designed for 1-2 player game, features black hole, enemy Klingon mothership, enemy Romulans and Federation refueling space station, abilities for laser weapons and shields, includes 7"x8½" plastic screen overlay, boxed.
Cartridge and screen overlay . . . . . . — 29 — 30-35 — _____
Screen overlay #HO-4110 . . . . — 2 — 2-4 — _____

"Super Star Trek"
Workman Publishing Co., 1978
Tradepaper sequel to *101 Computer Games,* editor David H. Ahl. Titled *Basic Computer Games - Microcomputer Editon.* Super Star Trek game instructions for programming p. 157-163 for Microsoft 8K Basic Version 3.0 or higher. (This Trek program also appeared in *Creative Computing Magazine.*)
#0-89480-052-3 . . . . — 7.95 — 8-10 — _____

SUPERTREK, Disk No. 457 PC-SIG, 1985
Disk with full sound effects game plus vocal module that gives voice instructions from Spock, Sulu, etc. Disk plays the Star Trek theme song and provides phaser, photon effects, Klingon territory alarm siren, too. . — 6 — 6-8 — _____

GAMING PROGRAMS

	Issue	Current	Cost/Date
SUPERTREK, Another Version for Trekkies, Disk No. 16, Games PC-SIG, 1985 Disk with 6 Basic games including chess, craps, communications and undated version of the Trek game on Disk No. 13	6	6-8	_____
"TI-Trek", Texas Instruments, 1980 Commercial software package designed for the Texas Instruments 99/4A computer. Game of skill that uses the speech capabilities of the TI-99 console. You are responsible for the safety of a galaxy and have the ability to fire phasers, torpedos to destroy the enemy. A warp control is provided. Package comes as a module hook-up and plugs into the gaming console. #PHD 5002	15	16-20	_____
"3-D Star Trek", Norton Software, 1985 Program designed for the TI-99/4A computer. Here is an undated version of the classic space war game that uses TI graphics to add a new twist to the Trek adventure. Two formats:			
#10975 Cassette format for TI Basic/Ext. Basic Version	9.95	8-12	_____
#14994 Disk format for TI Extended Basic requires memory expansion	9.95	8-12	_____
"Trek" Softsync, Brady Communications Co. Book collection of short programs in Basic by John W. Stephenson entitled *Brain Games for Kids and Adults Using the Commodore 64.* "Trek" is a geometry game where goal is to coordinate your starship back home, p. 132-137. #0-89303-349-9, tradepaper	9	10-12	_____
TREK, Yet Another Star Trek Game, Disk No. 27 PC-SIG, 1985 Disk with 4 Basic games including Trek game that uses a color graphics monitor. Also has 4 utility programs and 3 printer spoolers.	6	6-8	_____
TREKRUN, Disk No. 197, Utilities #13, PC-SIG, 1985 Exclusive Trek games that work on color graphics or mono screen. Includes complicated games MS-TREK and Galaxy Trek using official SEC advice and command codes	6	6-8	_____

ROLE PLAYING GAMES AND ACCESSORIES

	Issue	Current	Cost/Date
• **Adventure Gaming in The Final Frontier** Heritage, 1980 Gaming booklet designed for use with this Company's metal miniature figures	5.95	8-12	_____
25mm Figures (1980) Unpainted, lead alloy castings designed for field play:			
1604 Captain Kirk, Yeoman, Scotty, Sulu	2.95	4-6	_____
1605 Mr. Spock, McCoy, Uhura, nameplate	2.95	4-6	_____
1612 6 Federation Crewmembers	2.95	4-6	_____
1613 6 Romulan Crewmembers	2.95	4-6	_____
1614 6 Klingon Crewmembers	2.95	4-6	_____
1615 6 Gorn Soldiers	2.95	4-6	_____
1618 4 Phylosians	2.95	4-6	_____
1619 6 Andorians	2.95	4-6	_____
1620 4 Skor	2.95	4-6	_____
1621 6 Talosians	2.95	4-6	_____
1622 4 Kzin	2.95	4-6	_____
1628 6 Tellerites	2.95	4-6	_____
1630 6 Federation Special Forces	2.95	4-6	_____
1632 6 Romulan Assault Units	2.95	4-6	_____
75mm Figures (1980) Unpainted, lead alloy castings			
1600 Captain Kirk	10.95	15-20	_____
1601 Mr. Spock	10.95	15-20	_____
• **Battle Manual,** Lou Zocchi, 1971 The original Zocchi game format in fanzine design. Technical strategies and Fleet tactics for space wargaming, complete playing set for 1 or more players. This book later became Alien Space Battle Manual (see below)	3	20-25	_____
• **Battle Manual, Alien Space,** Lou Zocchi, 1972 Non-board, paper game with rules for conducting ship to ship combat for Trek. Originally formated as a fan manual. Later re-formated for board use with figures and sold as a companion guide for the Star Fleet Battle Manual Game	3	8-10	_____
25mm Figures, Wee Warriors, 1979 To-scale (1/72 and 1/76) standard gaming figures sold in set through Anshell Miniatures. Six figures per set:			
WEST-LP Landing Part Set (Federation and one Vulcan. One may be painted as either Federation crew of Klingon	2.50	6-10	_____
WEST-AL Alien Set (Gorn, Romulan male, Andorian)	2.50	6-10	_____

ROLE PLAYING GAMES

Starships 1/4800 Scale. Attack Wargaming Association, 1979
Metal die-cast miniatures used with plastic stands. Sold individually through Anshell Miniatures. (Could also be used with companion game Star Fleet Battle Manual Game).

	Issue	Current	Cost/Date
WA-2 Federation Recharge Cruiser	2.25	4-6	_____
WA-10 Klingon Battle Cruiser	2.25	4-6	_____
WA-23 Tholian Scouts (4)	1	3-4	_____
WA-30 E'ckor Battleship	2.50	4-6	_____
WA-41 Gorn Marauder	4	5-7	_____
WA-53 Romulan Bird of Prey	2.25	5-7	_____
WA-62 Zellthon Heavy Cruiser	3	4-6	_____

• **Embattled Trek Game,** Anshell Miniatures
Role playing game for make-your-own hexboard. Requires one 6-sided die, one 12-sided die and two 20-sided dice. Rules and description of play. Uses metal microships. . . . . 4 10-12 _____

Ptolemy Class Transport Tug, 3/3788 scale, 1979.

Starships 1/4800 Scale, Valiant, 1979
Metal die cast miniatures, sold individually through Anshell Miniatures.

	Issue	Current	Cost/Date
VTSD-1 Intruder Scout (9)	3.50	4-6	_____
-2 Vigilante Interceptor (6)	3.50	4-6	_____
-3 Phantom Assault Ship (4)	3.50	4-6	_____
-4 Alien Banshee Scout (6)	3.50	4-6	_____
-5 Alien Vampire Interceptor (4)	3.50	4-6	_____
-6 Draco Class Destroyer (2)	3.50	4-6	_____
-7 Aries Class Escort Cruiser	3.50	4-6	_____
-8 Persus Class Cruiser	3.50	4-6	_____
-9 Orion Class Heavy Destroyer	3.50	4-6	_____
-10 Alien Sadr Destroyer (2)	3.50	4-6	_____
-11 Alien Sadr Destroyer (2 add'l)	3.50	4-6	_____
-12 Alien Mirazh Battle Cruiser	3.50	4-6	_____
-13 Alien Merak Heavy Battle Cruiser	3.50	4-6	_____
-14 Small stands (9) for 1-7, 10, 11	3.50	4-6	_____
-15 Large stands (6) for 8, 9, 12, 13	3.50	4-6	_____

• **Federation and Empire Game 5006**
Task Force Games, 1986
Self-contained space gaming set designed by Stephen Cole to be independent or used as a companion game set for Task Force Games

• **Star Fleet Battles Game** series. The results have been structured to give the same range of options to improve interchangeability. Boxed strategic battle game designed for fast-action movement combat systems. Includes:
Commander's Rulebook, Maps - 2, 864 playing pieces, reference cards and 8 charts.
For 2 to 8 players, duration several hours playing time a week. Box cover shows artwork Human and t.v. race Klingon profiles over space battle scene. . . . . 39.95 40-42 _____

Additional Pieces

	Issue	Current	Cost/Date
Rulebook 5006.1	6	6-7	_____
Map A 5006.2	5	5-6	_____
Map B 5006.3	5	5-6	_____
Counter Sheets 1, 3, 5, 7, 5006.4	14	14-15	_____
Counter Sheets 1-8 5006.5	28	28-29	_____
Counter 9 & 10 5006.6	4	4-5	_____
Set of 8 Charts 5006.7	8	8-9	_____

• **Star Fleet Battle Manual Game**
Game Science Corp.
Board game editions by designer Lou Zocchi.

10305 First Editions, 1977 [1]
Boxed set, includes counters, map-sheet, pieces. Requires special 20-sided die. Also contains formula for converting the companion Alien Space Battle Manual game into a board game scenario. . . . . 10 12-16 _____

10306 New Improved and Expanded Game, (5th Printing), 1979
Updated edition, 8½"x11" booklet containing rules for repair, economics, diplomacy, campaigns and production of ships. . . . . 7 9-12 _____

10307-D Deluxe Game Edition, 1979
Includes all of the above items in a special boxed set that supplies the required die and all the 1/3788 scale fleet of ships. . . . . 25 25-30 _____

Starships 1/3788 Scale (1979)
Scale plastic or metal ships that include stands. Packaged in plastic pouch stapled to 5½"x5½" schematic cardboard stock.

	Issue	Current	Cost/Date
GS-1 Federation Scout (plastic)	2	3-5	_____
-2 Federation Destroyer (plastic)	2	3-5	_____
-3 Federation Heavy Cruiser (plastic)	2	3-5	_____
(clear plastic)	2.25	3-5	_____

1. The game was the Winner of the 1981 England Games Day Award.

ROLE PLAYING GAMES

	Issue	Current	Cost/Date
(Glow in the dark, blue or green).	2.50	3-5	______
-4 Federation Dreadnought (plastic)	2	3-5	______
(clear plastic).	2.25	3-5	______
(Glow in the dark, blue or green).	2.50	3-5	______
-5 Ptolemy Class Transport Tug (plastic).	3	4-6	______
-6 Romulan Warship /Tholien Vessel (metal)	2	5-7	______
-7 Klingon Cruiser (metal)	2.50	4-6	______
Accessories (1980)			
Plastic Ship Stands for metal or plastic ships, each	.25	.50-1	______
Polydice Six color: red, yellow, orange, green, blue or white. Inked or uninked with numbers.			
Tholian dice, 4-sided, inked in black	1	1	______
uninked	.75	1	______
Romulan dice, 8-sided, inked	1	1	______
uninked	.75	1	______
Klingon dice, 12-sided, inked	1	1	______
uninked	.75	1	______
Vulcan dice, 20-sided, black or green/inked	1.25	1	______
red, uninked	.75	1	______
Regular 6-sided dice, inked	.15	.50	______

- **Star Fleet Battles Game,** Task Force Games
Basic sets, rule and supplemental adventures for war-gaming in the Star Trek universe.[2]

Basic Game Sets

	Issue	Current	Cost/Date
Star Fleet Battles Volume I 5001 (1980) Complete starter set for seven fleets, outposts, stations, starbases, asteroids, planets and monsters: Commander's Rulebook, Vol. I - 108 pages Ship System Chart and Display Book - 32 p. 216 die-cut counters, field map and dice Boxed, art cover shows t.v. Enterprise rear-view emitting phaser fire.	17.95	20-22	______
Commander's Rulebook (1983) Looseleaf, blue binder. Alpha-numeric system, index and rules from the original boxed set, update, 8½"x11"	9.95	12-14	______
Commander's Rulebook - New and Revised 3002 (1983) White cover, spiral bound additions and updates, 8½" x 11"	9.98	10-12	______
Expansion Set No. 1 1015 (1983) Plastic pocket kit, introduces new alien weapons, dog fighting drones, type "F" plasma torpedoes, 30 ships, 8 scenerios, 54 pieces, 5 SSD's.	6.95	7-9	______
Expansion Set No. 2, 1022 (1983) Plastic pocket kit, introduces Lyrans (Klingon allies) and Pseudo-fighters, 32 ships, weapons, Dreadnoughts and Fed. Carriers, Tomcats, 8 scenerios, 108 pieces, 4 SSD's.	6.95	7-9	______
Expansion Set No. 3 1025 (1983) Plastic pocket kit, introduces Wyn Star Cluster aliens, Light Cruiser classes, 86 new ships, mine warfare rules, 8 scenerios, 5 SSD's, 108 pieces	6.95	7-9	______
Rules Update No. 1, 3015 (1985) Updated pages for Star Fleet Battles Vol. I Revision 0 and Supplement #1 Revision 0. Pages reformatted and include errata data, 8½"x11" booklet sheets.[3]	5.95	6-8	______
Volume I - Additonal Pieces			
Counter Sheet No. 1 5001.5	2	2-3	______
Counter Sheet No. 2 5001.6	2	2-3	______
Energy Allocation Forms 5001.7 . .	.50	1-2	______
SSD Booklet 5001.8	5	5-7	______
Star Fleet Battles Volume II #5008 (1984 Revised to include Expansion Sets 1-3. Introduces the Hydrans, Andromedans, Lyrans, and Wyns. Includes as well: **Commander's Rulebook Vol. II** - 96 pages; SSD Book let - 32 pages; three solitaire scenerios; 150 new ships and weapons, six campaign games, 21 other adventures, 324 die-cut playing pieces; Boxed, cover t.v. Enterprise in pursuit of t.v. Klingon Battle Cruiser	19.95	20-22	______
Commander's Rulebook Vol. II #3011 (1984) Softbound, yellow booklet which is sold for additional players and updates and replaces Expansion Sets 1-3. 8½"x11" sheets have punched 3-ring binder holes, 96 pages.	9.95	12-14	______
Supplement #1 - Fighters and Shuttles #3003 (1984) Pocket folio kit including designs and rules for fighter action: fighter carriers, dog-fighting rules, direct fire drones, plus five scenerios, 216 pieces, 12 new SSD's, 20 pages.	6.95	8-9	______
Supplement # 2 X-Ships #3013 (1984) Pocket folio kit including how to control the powerful X-ships, the newest technological wonders to date; 108 pieces, 32 new SSD's, scenerios, 24 pages.	6.95	8-10	______

2. Task Force issues product ID #'s sequentially as games are produced (1015, 1016 . . .) so the number codes do not indicate the type or subset of the piece being released. Listings here are ordered alphabetically and according to the name of the Basic Game Set to which items belong, in cases where non-interchangeable supplements appeared.
3. Errata updates also appear in Task Force's press publication entitled *Nexus - The Gaming Connection* (See Amateur Press listings).

ROLE PLAYING GAMES

	Issue	Current Cost/Date	
Supplement 3 - Fast Patrol Ships #3019 (1986) Larger format kit for fast patrol ship technology; type PF Leaders and Interceptors, SSD's to create a flotilla, 8 new scenerios, special PF Campaign, 32 pages, playing aids.	9.95	9-10	______
Volume II - Additional Pieces			
Commander Rulebook and Charts 5008.1	10	10-12	______
SSD Booklet 5008.2	5	5-7	______
Counter Sheet #1 5008.3	2	2-3	______
Counter Sheet #2 5008.4	2	2-3	______
Counter Sheet #3 5008.5	2	2-3	______
Supplement #1, Counter Sheet #1 3003.2	2	2-3	______
Counter Sheet #2 3003.3	2	2-3	______
Supplement #2, Rulebook 3013.1	4	4-6	______
Counter Sheet 3013.2	2	2-3	______
SSD Booklet 3013.3	5	5-7	______
Supplement #3, Rulebook 3019.1	3	3-4	______
SSD Booklet 3019.2	5	5-7	______
Counter Sheet #1 3019.3	2	2-3	______
Counter Sheet #2 3019.4	2	2-3	______

Star Fleet Battles Volume III #5009 (1985)
Set that allows you to command the decisive battles; introduces the ISC (INterstellar Concordium) race that conquers the galaxy after the First General War, plus an Andromedan invasion, includes:

Commander's Rulebook, Vol. III - 80 pages; Commander's SSD Book - 48 pages; Updated anexes and charts; 216 die-cut pieces, 12 scenerios. Introduces new ships – ISC Star Cruiser, Lyran Prairie Cat Survey Cruiser and Tholian Dreadnought. Boxed, cover art shows t.v. Enterprise suffering a saucer hit	19.95	20-22	______
Volume III - Additional Pieces			
Commander's Rulebook 5009.1	11	12-14	______
SSD Booklet 5009.2	6	6-8	______
Counter Sheet #1 5009.3	2	2-3	______
Counter Sheet #2 5009.4	2	2-3	______

Introduction to Star Fleet Battles #3000 (1987)

Economical, easy format intro set for this gaming universe. Provides step-by-step instructions for play, solitaire and battle game included: Easy Rulebook - 8½" x 11" format; 54 die-cut pieces, map, playing time 1 hour. Cellophane wrapped, cover art t.v. Klingon Cruiser taking phaser fire from Enterprise in pursuit, over planet	5.95	6-7	______
Intro Game - Additional Pieces			
Introduction Book 3000.1	11	11-12	______
Intro. Counter Sheet 3000.2	1	1-2	______

STAR FLEET BATTLES - General Supplements / Companion Games

Supplement for Star Fleet Battles Game, #3001, 1983.

	Issue	Current Cost/Date	
Battle Damage: Code Red #3001 (1983) Playing aid to resolve the problem of battle damage during play, 64 card deck, 18 critical hits and damage allocations chart, 8½"x11" booklet	4.95	6-9	______

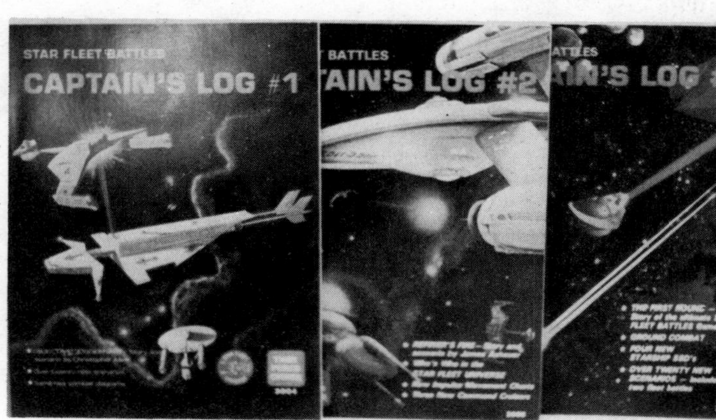

Captain's Log Series, 1983, 1984 & 1984.

Captain's Log Series
Package gaming scenerios with diagrams and charts for resolving problems, 8½"x11" books

Log No. 1 #3004 (1983) Adventure "Juggernaut" multi-player scenerio, plus 20 other games and diagrams to resolve combat in a single hex.	5.95	6-8	______

ROLE PLAYING GAMES

	Issue	Current	Cost/Date
Log No. 2 #3008 (1984) Adventure "Refiner's Fire" by James Ashauer, 3 new SSD's, 23 scenerios, "Breakthrough" campaign game, movement charts for 24, 16 and 8 impulses.	5.96	6-8	_____
Log No. 3 #3010 (1984) Story of "The First Round" an intergalactic tournament, 26 scenerios, rules for ground combat.	5.95	6-8	_____
Log No. 4 #3012 (1987) Story "Where Wisdom Fails", plus scenerio of contact with a new breed of Hydran, games and a consolidated addenda	5.95	6-7	_____

Commander's SSD Books (1983-1985)
Racing ship scenerios, 48 SSD's per book; easy play format, one-sheet chart for moving, firing and scoring, includes counters, 8½"x11" booklets.

	Issue	Current	Cost/Date
Book No. 1 #3005 Federation, Andromedans, Orions, Kzintis	4.95	5-7	_____
Book No. 2 #3006 Klingon, Lyran, Hydran, Wyn	4.95	5-7	_____
Book No. 3 #3007 Romulan, Tholian and Gorn	4.95	5-7	_____
Book No. 4 #3009 Tugs, starbases, battle stations and freighters	4.95	5-7	_____
Book No. 5#3016 Separate booms, light command cruisers, Q-ships and monitors	4.95	5-7	_____
Book No. 6#3018 Survey Cruisers, Police Ships, Space Patrolships and light tugs	4.95	5-7	_____
Book No. 7 #3020 More ships for Tholian, Gorns, Federation, Kzintis and Hydrans	4.95	5-6	_____
Book No. 8 #3021 Additional ships for Klingons, Lyrans, Orions and Romulans	4.95	5-6	_____
Book No. 9 #3022 26 new ships for Andromedans, Lyrans, Wyns and Hydrans	4.95	5-6	_____

	Issue	Current	Cost/Date
Reinforcements #3014 (1984) New playing pieces, including defense satellites, cloak markers, drones, shuttlecraft and planet cutouts	6.95	7-9	_____
Starships – Starline 2200 Rules Book (1983) Complimentary booklet explaining how to incorporate the Starline miniatures into the gaming set. Send SASE.	—	1-2	_____

Starline 2200 Series, Federation Dreadnought #10507, 1982.

Starships – Starline 2200 (1/3788 Scale) (1982)
Plastic replicas based on original designs from Franz Joseph's Star Fleet Technical Manual. Sold individually in foam-back blister packs, includes clear plastic stand.

	Issue	Current	Cost/Date
10504 Enterprise Cruiser: plain (P); Cloaking device (C), Blue-glo (B) or Green-glo (G) colors	2	3-5	_____
10505 Federation Destroyer (P,C,B,G)	2	3-5	_____
10506 Federation Scout (P,C,B,G)	2	3-5	_____
10507 Federation Dreadnought (P,C,B,G)	3	3-5	_____
10508 Ptolemy Class Transport Tug (P,C,B.G)	3.50	4-6	_____

Starships – Starline 2200 (1/3900 Scale)
Die-cast metal miniatures. Free conversion rules available. Packaged in foam-backed blister pack with clear stands (1982).

	Issue	Current	Cost/Date
7010 Federation Dreadnought	3.95	4-6	_____
7011 Federation Heavy Cruiser	3.95	4-6	_____
7012 Federation Light Cruiser	3.95	4-6	_____
7013 Federation Light Cruiser (2nd - 1985)	3.95	4-6	_____
7014 Federation Destroyer	3.95	4-6	_____
7015 Federation Scout	3.95	4-6	_____
7016 Federation Tug	3.95	4-6	_____
7017 Federation Frigate (two)	4.95	5-7	_____
7020 Federation Carrier	5.50	6-8	_____
7025 Federation Starbase	7.95	8-10	_____
7040 Klingon B-10	7.95	8-9	_____
7042 Klingon C-8 Dreadnought	5.50	6-8	_____
7043 Klingon D-7 Battlecruiser	5.50	6-8	_____
7044 Klingon D-5 Cruiser (1987)	3.95	4-6	_____
7046 Klingon F-5 Frigate (two)	3.95	4-6	_____
7051 Klingon Tug Carrier	5.50	6-8	_____
7053 Klingon Pseudo-Fighters (six) (1987)	3.95	4-6	_____
7060 Romulan Condor	5.50	6-8	_____
7064 Romulan Warbird (two)	3.95	4-6	_____
7071 Romulan Sparrowhawk	3.95	4-6	_____

ROLE PLAYING GAMES

	Issue	Current	Cost/Date
7073 Gorn Tyrannosaurus Dreadnought	5.50	6-8	______
7081 Gorn Heavy Cruiser (two)	3.95	4-6	______
7082 Gorn Destroyer (two)	3.95	4-6	______
7084 Gorn Destroyer (two)	3.95	4-6	______
7100 Kzinti Space Control Ship (1985)	5.50	6-8	______
7101 Kzinti Carrier	3.95	4-6	______
7103 Kzinti Escort Carrier	3.95	4-6	______
7104 Kzinti Striker Carrier	3.95	4-6	______
7107 Kzinti Frigate (two)	4.50	5-7	______
7110 Kzinti Pseudo-Fighters (six) (1987)	3.95	4-6	______
7120 Lyran Lion Dreadnought (1985)	5.50	6-8	______
7122 Lyran Cruiser	3.95	4-6	______
7123 Lyran Jaguar War Cruiser	3.95	4-6	______
7124 Lyran Destroyer (two)	3.95	4-6	______
7126 Lyran Pseudo-Fighters (six) (1987)	3.95	4-6	______
7140 Hydran Paladin Dreadnought (1985)	5.50	6-8	______
7141 Hydran Ranger	3.95	4-6	______
7142 Hydran Horseman Light Cruiser	3.95	4-6	______
7143 Hydran Lancer (two)	3.95	4-6	______
7144 Hydran Hunter/Scout (two) (1985)	3.95	4-6	______
7147 Hydran Pseudo-Fighter (six) (1987)	3.95	4-6	______
7160 Tholian Dreadnought	3.95	4-6	______
7161 Tholian Cruiser (two) (1985)	4.95	5-7	______
7164 Tholian Patrol Cruiser (two)	3.95	4-6	______
7172 Neo-Tholian Dreadnought (1987)	3.95	4-6	______
7174 Neo-Tholian Cruiser (two) (1987)	4.95	5-7	______
7181 Orion Cruiser	3.95	4-6	______
7182 Orion Salvage Cruiser	3.95	4-6	______
7183 Orion Raider (two)	3.95	4-6	______
7211 Commercial Battle Station	3.95	4-6	______
7221 Andromedan Intruder (1985)	3.95	4-6	______
7222 Andromedan Satellite Ships (three)	5.50	6-8	______
7223 Andromedan Conquistador/ Python (1987)	4.95	5-7	______
7250 ISC Dreadnought	5.50	6-8	______
7252 ISC Star Cruiser	3.95	4-6	______
7256 ISC Destroyer & Frigate	4.95	5-7	______
7000.1 Stand Covers (set of 12)	1	1-2	______
7000.2 Plastic Stands (set of 6)	3.50	3-4	______
7000.3 Metal Stands (set of 6)	5	5-6	______

Starships – Starline 2200 Boxed Set
#7300 1982
Five miniature ships in boxed set:
7011 Federation Heavy Cruiser
7043 Klingon D-7 Battlecruiser
7046 Klingon F-5 Frigate
7064 Romulan Warbird
7084 Gorn Destroyer

	Issue	Current	Cost/Date
Complete Set	12.95	12-16	______

Star Trek the Adventure Game, 1985.

	Issue	Current	Cost/Date
• **Star Trek – The Adventure Game Series,** West End Games			
Star Trek - The Adventure Game #11004 (1985) Combination role playing and board game, designed by Greg Costikyan for adult solitaire to 2 players. Pits Federation (Kirk) against Klingon (Koloth). Cardboard fold-out board, two 6-sided dice, cardstock playing pieces, 60-page gaming book detailing 120 adventures. Boxed set. [4]	16	16-18	______
Star Trek - The Enterprise Encounter #20030 1985 Gaming set for 2-4 players. The Squire of Gothos has created 3 false Enterprises and marooned the crew across the galaxy. 22"x17" map, 28 playing pieces, 4 page rules, 4 page original story, 68 color cards, 1 die and 4 crew racks. Boxed. [5]	17	17-20	______
Star Trek III - Exploring New Worlds #20020 1985 Three solitaire games: "Kobayashi Maru" the cadet test; "The Sherwood Syndrome" - save a primitive planet; and "Free Enterprise" - help the Glisten Cluster out-trade the Klingons. Three booklets, two 22"x17" maps, 400 counters, die and plastic tray. Boxed set. [6]	17	17-20	______

4. The box cover for this game set features the cover artwork of Boris Vallejo. The same art was used on Pocket Book's paperback novel *Black Fire.*
5. This game set, as well as game 20020, appeared as a special order promo in Pockets Books paperback novel *Dwellers in the Crucible.*
6. This game was nominated for the H.G. Wells Award for Best Science Fiction Game 1985.

ROLE PLAYING GAMES

	Issue	Current Cost/Date	
• Star Trek - The Correspondence Game Play-by-mail role playing game. Initial fee provides player with the Captain's Guide (24-page 8½"x11" booklet) explaining your Heavy Cruiser, potential Starfleet missions and rules for further submissions. Also includes a Crew Roster, (8½"x44" printout of 400 member crew organized by ship sections, each crewmembers code number and ratings of profession, strength, quickness, endurance and intuition) and first-turn computer printout of the Captain's Log, Starfleet orders and the current adventure. Participation is up to individual.			
Player Kit	6	6-7	______
Additional Turns	4	4-5	______
Additional Starships	4	4-5	______

Klingons Boxed Set, First Edition Release.

Star Trek Role Playing Game, 1983. 1st Edition.

Set #2003, FASA Corp., 1983.

• Star Trek The Role Playing Game, Fasa Corporation
Game sets, sourcebooks, miniatures, updates. Booklets are all in 8½"x11" softbound. [7]

Basic Game Sets (2000's Series)

	Issue	Current Cost/Date	
2001 **Star Trek The Role Playing Game Basic Set,** 1983 All rules, plans, grids and counters to play characters in the Star Trek universe: Rulebook - 128 pages, t.v. series history, photos and playing theme and rules; Deck plan Book - pull-apart to-scale plans for U.S.S. Enterprise and Klingon D-7 Battle Cruiser ships; Adventure Book - "Ghosts of Conscience", "Again, Troublesome Tribbles" and "In the Presence of My Enemies", 56 pages; 224 color counters, two 20-sidced dice, hex grid playing field. Boxed, cover by O'Connell, busts of Kirk and Spock over red planet with front-view t.v. Enterprise overhead. No ISBN number given. [8]	25	30-40	______
Star Trek The Role Playing Game - Basic Rulebook #2001A, only, 1983	10	10-11	______

7. Fasa Corporation issues product ID #'s categorically as games are produced (2001, 2002 . . . 2201, 2202 . . .). The prefixes identify which type of gaming piece is released. Listings here are ordered numerically. Most supplements are fully interchangeable or are convertible.
8. Fasa's press publication entitled *Stardate* ceased printings in early 1986, but is scheduled to re-appear in 1987 under printing by a different publisher name (See Amateur Press listings).

	Issue	Current Cost/Date	
Star Trek The Role Playing Game, Deluxe Edition, 1985 Updated and expanded version, including: Cadet's Orientation Scourcebook Game Operations Manual Star Fleet Officer's Manual Adventure book - three scenerios Deck Plans - Constitution Class and Klingon D-7 Star Trek III Starship Combat Game - intro to starship combat, basic tactics rules to advanced and expert, ship data book (20 ships) and chart book; 78 color counters, dice. Boxed, cover art Kirk and Spock busts over yellow, poxed moon with Enterprise and Klingon Battlecuiser in distance. ISBN 9-831787-01-7	25	25-28	_____
2002 **The Klingons** 1983 Major character supplement, overview of the race, culture, society, political and military objectives: Rule Booklets - character generation, plus "The Natural Order" adventure. Boxed, cover art movie race breed of Klingon Captain sitting in command chair. 0-931787-02-5	15	18-20	_____
The Klingons (Second Edition) 1986 Updated info on this race of alien: Rule Booklet Player's Book - what is believed about the Klingons Gamemaster's Book - what the race knows to be the truth about themselves Cellophane wrapped, same cover art as original release 0-931787-02-5	12	12-14	_____

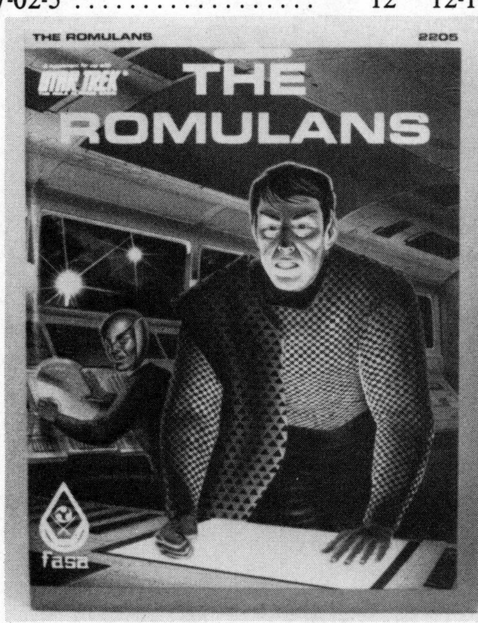

Romulan Character Supplement, 1984.

	Issue	Current Cost/Date	
2003 **Star Trek II Starship Combat Simulator** 1983 Four different games and major rules: Master Control Panel; Command Control Panel; Mapsheet with tactical displays; 78 counters, 112 playing pieces, one 20-sided die; Boxed, cover art black and white, two Klingon Cruisers face off Enterprise and three other Federation ships ..	11	14-18	_____
Star Trek Tactical Combat Simulator, Revised and Expanded, 1987 Four games in one involving Romulans, Klingons, Gorns and Orions, boardgame: Command and Control Rulebook - 80 pages; Control Sheets - 80 pages of records and counters; Printed Forms - 16 pages; Starfield 22-"x33" grid; One 20-sided die; Boxed, cover art Federation Cruiser saucer close-up receiving direct hit from a Klingon Battle Cruiser, two other ships in background 1-55560-009-3	20	20-22	_____
2004 **Star Trek The Role Playing Game Basic Game Set - Second Edition,** 1984 Briefer version, does not include grid sheet, playing pieces or dice: Star Fleet Officer's Manual - 40 pages, glossary and how-to-play, rules for ground-based adventures Cadet's Orientation Sourcebook - 40 pages, photos, races, governments and equipment Game Operations Manual - 48 pages, how to design adventures, character generation Boxed, cover art t.v. McCoy, Kirk and Spock with phasers and red nebula with starboard Enterprise 0-931787-0401	12	12-14	_____
2005 **The Romulans,** 1984 Major character supplement, info about the Romulan Star Empire, Imperial Navy, equipment, creating characters, maps: Romulan Starfleet Intelligence Manual - 32 pages, what is believed about them Romulan Way Game Operations Manual - 48 pages, the truth about this race. Paper slipcover case, cover art shows Romulan officers on the bridge 0-931787-05-x	10	12-16	_____

ROLE PLAYING GAMES

	Issue	Current	Cost/Date
2006 **Star Trek III Starship Combat Game,** 1984 Fast-paced combat strategies for war-gaming: Introduction to Starship Combat - adventure about Lork Kruge and Genesis Basic Starship Tactics - 8 page rulebook on how to use ships Advanced Rules - 24 pages, systems for Command and Control Panels, hints about the Kobayashi Maru scenerio Ship Data Book - details on 8 Fed, 8 Klingon, 4 Romulan, 2 Gorn, 2 Orion vessels Charts and Display Panels - bridge action for the characters; 78 pieces, 22"x33" starfield map, one 20-sided die; Boxed, cover photos SF III Enterprise under fire from Klingon Bird of Prey 0-931787-06-8	8	10-12	_____
Star Trek III Starship Combat Role Playing Game (Second Edition), 1986 Updated combat and role playing edition containing four games in one: Rulebook - 64 pages, ships data and scenerios for Basic, Advanced and Expert Starship Tactics and the Command and Control versions of this game Boxed, cover photos ST III Enterprise under fire of the Klingons Bird of Prey (same as the first edition) 0-931787-06-8	15	15-16	_____
2007 **Triangle,** 1985 Basic game featuring extensive mapping and alien characterizations for races inhabiting "The Golden Triangle," an area of space between three major powers of the galaxy: Rulebook - 96 pages of info, 120 planet descriptions, histories and governments, corporations, trade routes, black markets Color Wall Map - 17"x22" Cellophane wrapped, cover art by David Martin, 7-ship collage and including Klingon Cruiser and phaser power 0-931787-07-6	10	10-12	_____

2008 **The Orions,** 1986
Major character rules, the family and clans, organization of this race whose planet lies between the Federation and Klingon Empire:
Book of Common Knowledge - the Orions as the outworlders know them

Triange, 1985.

	Issue	Current	Cost/Date
Book of Deep Knowledge - the details and facts of Orion society, life and politics as only the Orions understand it Cellophane wrapped, cover art portrays blue-skinned male and green-skinned Orion slave girl 0-931787-08-4	12	12-14	_____
2009 **Star Fleet Ground Forces Manual,** 1987 Major rules supplement to provide background to generate ground-based military personnel and ship-board marines. Systems for all the major races - organization and listing of weapons pieces, plus history of the U.F.P. ground forces. Cellophane wrapped, cover art two platoon, armored soldiers and ground tank. 0-931787-09-2	12	12-14	_____
2010 **Operation Armageddon** 1987 Extensive staff college wargame set detailing the exercise that all officers must take to graduate, four games in one: The Klingons Cross the Line - invasion of Federation Space The Enemies Entangled - war between the Klingons and Romulans Operation Armageddon - four powers at war all at once Rulebooks, 2000 playing pieces, dice, maps of the entire Star Trek universe (78"x66" - total of 35 square feet of playing area) Boxed, cover art small Federation and Klingon ship insert over tactical starchart. 0-931787-10-6	45	45-47	_____

ROLE PLAYING GAMES

	Issue	Current Cost/Date	
2011 **The Federation,** 1986 Sourcebook for the structure, operation and organization of the U.F.P. Backgrounds on founding members and their cultures. Detailed look at Vulcans, Terrans, Andorians, Tellarites, Edoans, Caitians, more. Timeline leading to U.F.P. formation, World Logs. Book cover art is Council Meeting Chamber with Sarek the Vulcan and female Andorian plus 2 other aliens. 0-931787-030-0	12	12-14	_____
2014 **Star Fleet Intelligence Manual,** 1987 Major rules supplement and sourcebook for spies and secret operatives. Background on Intelligence Command, its history, organization and standard methods of operation. Booklet cover art shows two Federation Intelligence Officer's aiming phaser weapons with starship overhead. 0-931878-39-4	12	12-14	_____
2015 **Struggle For The Throne, The Star Trek Game of Klingon Diplomacy and Intrigue,** 1987 Basic game set involving the death of the Klingon Emperor and the power struggle between Thought Admirals. This game depends on player interaction (bribery and deals, treachery wins). Rulebook, playing cards, color map, dice. Boxed, cover art depicts a Klingon at a playing board. 0-931787-45-9 [9]	20	20-24	_____
2016 **Star Fleet Marines,** 1987 Board game set for tactical ground combat in the Star Trek universe. Simulates battles between Marines of S.F.C. and the Klingons at the level of the company/platoon. Rulebooks, full color map sheets, new tanks and personnel cariers, etc. Boxed. 1-55560-010-7	20	20-24	_____

Supplements to the Gaming Sets

Deck Plans (2100's Series)

	Issue	Current Cost/Date	
2101 **U.S.S. Enterprise,** 1983 Set of nine 2-sided interior design sheets, 22"x33" for use with the 15mm role playing gaming figures, includes 12-page Ship Recognition Handbook for Constitution Class Cruiser. Boxed, cover art starboard t.v. Enterprise and three planets. 0-931787-86-6	15	17-19	_____
2102 **Klingon D-7 Battlecruiser,** 1983 Six 2-sided 22"x33" deck plans with interior designs for 15mm figures and 12-page descriptive booklet. Boxed. 0-931787-87-4	12.50	14-16	_____
2103 **U.S.S. Reliant,** 1983 Interior details and plans of this new ship from Star Trek II, includes explanative booklet for 15mm figures. Boxed.	10	10-13	_____
2104 **Space Laboratory, Regula One,** 1983 Details of the interior and exterior of the space station introduced in ST II. Includes booklet. Boxed.	12.50	14-18	_____

Adventures and Sourcebooks (2200's Series)

	Issue	Current Cost/Date	
2201 **The Vanished,** 1983 Adventure scenerio where you must discover the reason behind a deep space research station's evacuation. Includes deck plans and complete crew roster for FDR 39. Black cover, paper pocket, Vulcan and human female Star Fleet Officers with t.v. Enterprise overhead	6	10-14	_____
White cover, fold-out pocket, Sulu and another crewman, art by Dietrick 0-931787-11-4	7	9-10	_____
2202 **Witness for the Defense,** 1983 Return to the planet of the Horta, Janus IV (episode "Devil in the Dark") where young miner is accused of murder and genocide. Can Kirk, Spock and McCoy clear him and find the real killer in time? Paper pocket with matt drawing of the mines as seen on the show. 0-931787-12-2	7	9-10	_____

9. This is a Basic Game set which has the same name as Micro-Adventure 5004 which was released in 1985 in conjunction with Lord Kruge from the ST III movie. Here the format is expanded.

Enterprise Deck Plans, 1983.

"The Vanished", Editions #1 and #2.

Klingon Deck Plans, 1983.

FASA Adventure #2202 with unusual cover art.

ROLE PLAYING GAMES

	Issue	Current Cost/Date	
2203 **Trader Captains and Merchant Princes,** 1983 Sourcebook, 52-pages describing space rougues, pirates and merchants, the economics of commodity trading, financial loans and marketable securities. Paper pocket with cover art of Captain in flight jacket negotiating with a dubious merchant. 0-931787-13-0	7	9-10	_____
Updated release, 1987 Two book edition with rules and charts as before, plus: Book 1 - comments on the ups and downs of a merchant's life in the U.F.P. Book 2 - how to create characters, how to buy and sell, rent, lease or steal a starship, find cargo for hire, the black market dealings. Cellophane wrapped, cover art shows padded security guard and sneaking looking "Harry Mudd" type. 9-931787-13-0	18	18-19	_____

Ship Construction Manual, 1983.

	Issue	Current Cost/Date	
2204 **Ship Construction Manual - Star Trek II The Wrath of Kahn,** 1983 Sourcebook for costs, schedules and combat status designs to build your own armed starship fleet, 56-page booklet, cover art in 3-tone cover showing movie Enterprise inside orbiting repair web as introduced in STTMP.	6	10-12	_____

Art Covers by David R. Deitrick.

	Issue	Current Cost/Date	
Updated release, 1987 Revamped info for use with the **Starship Combat Role Playing Game 2006-2nd Edition.** Material from above in one 96-page sourcebook which adds essays on the design philosophy of major races plus cost, availability and reliability of their starship designs. Cellophane wrapped, book cover art full color Federation Scout inside interior dry dock of space station as introduced in ST III. [10]	12	12-14	_____

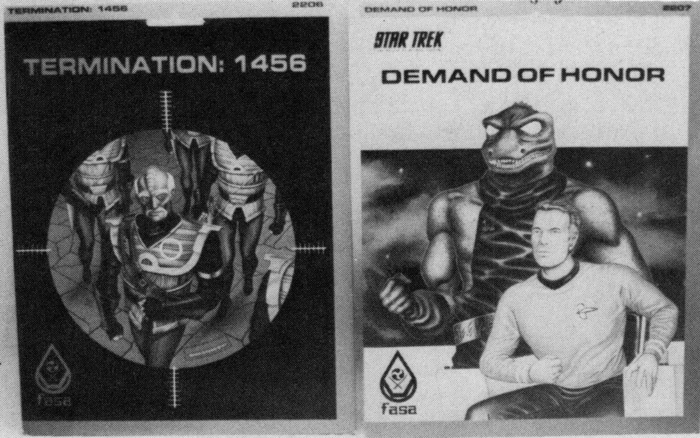

Artwork Covers by Mitch O'Connell.

2205 **Denial of Destiny,** 1983
Adventure to avoid the Prime Detective when doomed planet Aleriad will collide with cosmic debris and its religious fanatic natives refuse to abandon their world. What's peculiar about the one-legged beggar of Kembali? Cover art by Dietrick, t.v. Enterprise, three Federation ships, planet Aleriad and one of its natives. 0-931787-15-7

	Issue	Current Cost/Date	
Fold-out paper pocket	6	9-10	_____
Re-release, cellophane wrapped, 1986	7	7-8	_____

10. This updated 2204 version delete the original box's "Star Trek II Wrath of Kahn" movie affiliation.

ROLE PLAYING GAMES

Artwork by Giberson.

	Issue	Current Cost/Date	
2206 **Termination: 1456,** 1984 Adventure of Thought Admiral Krador Zantai Rrilac who may be plotting the overthrow of the Klingon Emperor. Aboard the warp shuttle KS Vascin you and your crew go to Muldor IV to penetrate his stronghole, notes, maps and character cast in booklet format. 0-931787-16-5			
Paper pocket, art by ROK	6	9-10	_____
Re-release, cellophane wrapped, 1986	7	7-8	_____
2207 **Demand of Honor,** 1984 Adventure aboard the Destroyer U.S.S. Hastings as you carry a Gorn Ambassador (the one who fought Kirk in "Arena") to meet with renegade Gorn smugglers and raiders, maps, vessels, cast, 48-pages. Booklet cover art by ROK shows green Gorn and t.v. Captain Kirk.			
Paper folder-style pocket	6	9-10	_____
Re-release, cellophane wrapped, 1986	7	7-8	_____
2208 **The Orion Ruse,** 1984 The Captain of TransSolar's Eridani Star is just opening trade talks with the Orion settled world of Daros IV when a Federation merchant ship vanishes in its proximal space. S.F.C. now decides to use your ship on a spy mission. 0-931787-18-1			
Paper pocket, art by Giberson	7	7-10	_____
Re-release, cellophane wrapped ...	7	7-8	_____

	Issue	Current Cost/Date	
2209 **Margin of Profit,** 1984 The merchant ship TwoBrothers is having trouble with dilithium hijackings. Could Akalzed, the Orion "trader" be involved? 0-931787-19-X Paper pocket, art by Giberson, has ST II The Wrath of Kahn affiliation	7	7-10	_____
Re-release, cellophane wrapped, 1986	7	7-8	_____
2210 **The Outcasts,** 1985 The Vulcan Agent Salak finds an unwitting accomplice to help him deal with a dangerous Romulan renegade. 0-931787-20-3 Paper pocket, cover art of the Vulcan Salak and Federation Officer by Dietrick	7	7-9	_____
Re-release, cellophane wrapped, 1986	7	7-8	_____
2211 **A Matter of Priorities,** 1985 Tale of the Klingon patrol ship IKV Malevolent and the S.F.C. secret base on Vator III. Cellophane wrapped, art by Dietrick. 0-931787-21-1	7	7-8	_____

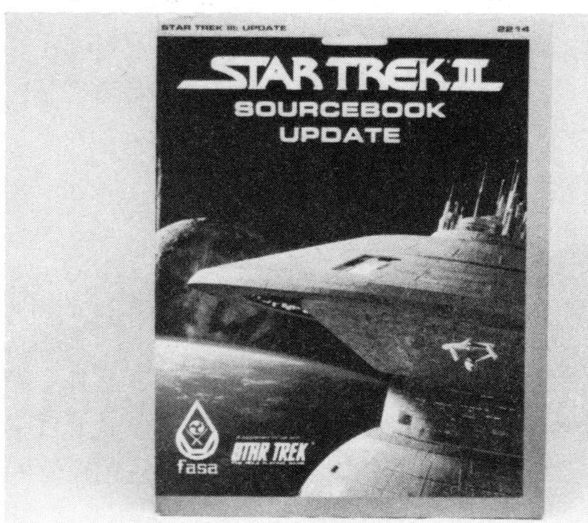

#2214, 1985.

2212 **A Doomsday Like Any Other,** 1985 U.S.S. Exeter receives a distress call from the planet Extair . . . a planet killer like the original one introduced in the episode "Doomsday Machine". Cellophane wrapped, art by Dietrick. 0-931787-22-X	7	7-8	_____
2213 **The Mines of Selka,** 1985 While investigating an Orion smuggling ring, you become involved with ships disappearing in the Selka System. Cellophane wrapped, cover art by Dietrick of an Andorian male and Federation crewwoman. 0-931787-23-8	8	8-9	_____

ROLE PLAYING GAMES

Issue Current Cost/Date

2214 **Star Trek III Sourcebook Update,** 1985
Sourcebook for the changes in alien government since the t.v. series, UFP and Star Fleet updates, starship recognition charts, biography updates on Star Trek crew, 48 p. 0-931878-24-6
Paper pocket, cover photo of the ST III spaceport over Earth with Enterprise outside, blue border .... 6 8-9 ______
Re-release, same photo, no blue border 1987, cellophane wrapped . 7 7-8 ______

2215 **The Triange Campaign (For Gamemasters Only),** 1985
Adventures to serve as the gamemaster's companion to Triangle Game Set 2007. Plots: "Merchant to Death" a Romulan arms dealership called Luxury Apparel; the Klingon Krador in "A Dose of Revenge"; BioResearch a mega-corporation in "The Corporate Grasp"; plus "A Family Affair"; time lines, library computer data, Newsfax bulletins and Star Fleet Intelligence, 60-page booklet, cellophane wrapped, cover art by David Martin shows female Romulan arms dealer with weapon drawn. 0-931787-25-4 .... 8 8-9 ______

2216 **Graduation Exercise,** 1985
Young 16-year-old Klingon cadet faces his first Romulan encounter and a grim Master of Cadets, cellophane wrapped, art by Dietrick shows Klingon Cadet.
0-931787-03-3 .... 8 8-9 ______

2217 **Where Has All The Glory Gone?** 1985
Adventure of the Chandley Class U.S.S. Niwen at the Romulan Neutral Zone as a distress call comes through - other ship has only 24 hours left on life support - will they make it in time? Cellophane wrapped, art by Dietrick of two men in helmeted environsuits.
0-931787-76-9 .... 7 7-8 ______

2218 **Return to Axanar / The Four Years War,** Doublepack. 1986
Two-book package: sourcebook compiled by Academician Sir Kenneth A.F. Brighton of Starfleet Museum, Memory Alpha detailing major battles, political and social economics of the site of the Klingon/Fed. war; plus Axanar adventure of thee U.S.S. Cooper as it transfers scientists to the planet, cellophane wrapped, cover art by Dietrick 0-931787-78-5 .... 12 12-14 ______

2219 **Decision at Midnight,** 1986
Adventure of Tam O'Shanter and the alien (Caitian) Commander Brr'ynn in space, cellophane wrapped, art by Dietrick shows bearded Fed. Officer with a Fed. starship overhead. 0-931787-29-7 .... 8 8-9 ______

2220 **An Imbalance of Power,** 1986
You are a Klingon scout who discovers a duralium planet. Find a way to exploit the natives, includes 22" x 17" color map, 228 counters, boardgame format, cellophane wrapped, art by Dietrick portrays movie race, armored Klingon grappling with a native alien. 0-931787-46-7 12 12-14 ______

2221 **Old Soldiers Never Die /The Romulan War Doublepack,** 1986
Two-book package: sourcebook The Romulan War detailing the Fed's conflict with the Romulan Star Empire over history, plus adventure of the U.S.S. Sparon and a distress call from Memory Alpha - the mothballed U.S.S. Juggernaut has been stolen and may be refitted for enemy duty, cellophane wrapped, cover art of Sulu bust with star cruisers overhead. 0-931787-47-5... 12 12-14 ______

2222 **A Conflict of Interest/Klingon Intelligence Briefing,** Doublepack, 1986
Two-book package: sourcebook on the SFC's latest information on the Klingon Empire plus adventure involving diplomats from Federation and the Klingons trying to convince Sheridan's World to join up with their respective alliances, cellophane wrapped, art by Dietrick.
0-931787-48-3 .... 12 12-14 ______

Klingon Ship Recognition Manuals, 1st and 2nd Editions.

ROLE PLAYING GAMES

Item	Issue	Current	Cost/Date
2223 **The Dixie Gambit,** 1986 Three ships involved in Operation Dixie are lost-and-presumed-destroyed behind the Imperial Line. Now one of those ships has mysteriously turned up within the Triangle, cellophane wrapped, cover art by Dietrick, 2 bearded men at station with Klingon Cruiser targeted for fire on the sensor visuals. 1-55560-001-8	8	8-9	______
2224 **Star Trek IV Sourcebook Update,** 1987 Updated information since the 4th movie: politics of Genesis, state of the Federation, Star Fleet military justice, Operation Armageddon war is simultations, 16 full-color panels showing new movie aliens, World logs descriptions, cellophane wrapped, cover art foil design insignia. 1-55560-002-6	12	12-14	______
2225 **Perish By the Sword/Galaxy Exploration Command,** 1987 Two-book sourcebook and adventure package. 1-55560-007-7	12	12-13	______
2226 **The Strider Incident/Defense Outpost Plans,** 1987 Two-book, sourcebook and adventure with deck plans included. 1-55560-003-4	12	12-13	______
2229 **Operation Buchman/Adventure,** 1987 Two-book, sourcebook and adventure. 1-55560-005-0	12	12-13	______

Data Books (2300's Series)

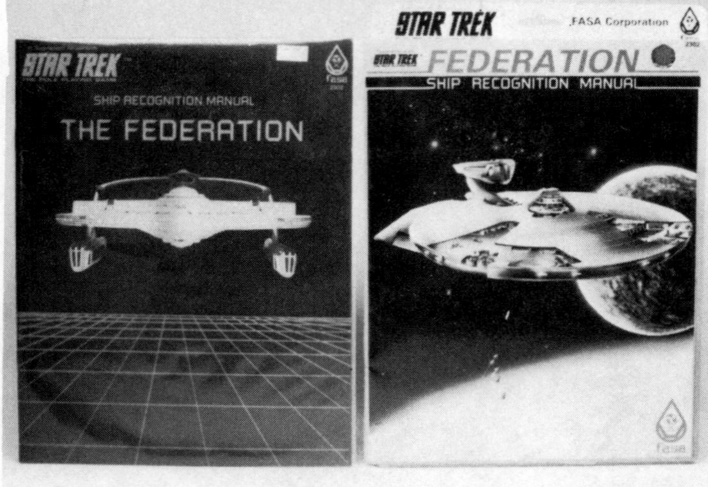

Federation Ship Recognition Manual, 1st and 2nd Editions.

Item	Issue	Current	Cost/Date
2301 **Klingon Ship Recognition Manual,** 1983 40 different ships of the fleet with their many variants, 3-view drawings, history and performance stats, 32-page booklet, 0-931787-41-6 Cover in 3-tone, three frontview Klingon D-7 Battle cruisers over star grid.	6	9-10	______
Re-released material, update info, cellophane wrapped, cover art by Dana Knutson, cut-away schematic of Klingon D-20 Class Cruiser (Death Rite), 1986	8	8-9	______
2302 **Federation Ship Recognition Manual,** 1983 40 different ships with variants in above booklet format. 0-931787-42-4 Cover in 3-tone, frontview U.S.S. Reliant Class scoutship over star grid	6	9-10	______
Re-released material, updated info on Enterprise, Reliant, Constitution and Excelsior class starships, cellophane wrapped, cover art by Knutson, cut-away schematic of Remora Class VII Escort and Scorpio Class II Corvette, 1986	8	8-9	______
2303 **Romulan Ship Recognition Manual,** 1984 Different ships of the fleet and their variants in above format booklet. 0-931787-43-2 Original release	6	8-9	______
Re-release, updated history over the last 40 years, cellophane wrapped, art by Knutson, cut-away schematic of a Romulan Whitewind Cruiser, 1986	8	8-9	______
2304 **Gorn and Minor Races,** 1987 Gorn fleet manual, plus ships from Orion Colonies, independent manufacturers in the Triangle and all the fring races, cellophane wrapped. 0-931787-44-0	8	8-9	______

Miniature Starships (2500's Series)

Starships - 1/3900 Scale [11]
Die-cast metal miniatures for use with Star Trek II and Star Trek III Starship Combat games:

Item	Issue	Current	Cost/Date
2501 (New) U.S.S. Enterprise (1983)	3.50	4-6	______
2502 U.S.S. Reliant (1983)	3.50	4-6	______
2503 Klingon D-7 Battlecruiser (1983)	3.50	4-6	______

11. These starships were Winners of the 1985 and 1986 H.G. Wells Award for Best Vehicle Miniatures.

ROLE PLAYING GAMES

	Issue	Current	Cost/Date
2504 Romulan Bird of Prey (1983)	3.50	4-6	______
2505 (Old) U.S.S. Enterprise (1983)	3.50	4-6	______
2506 Space Laboratory Regula One (1983)	3.50	4-6	______
2507 Larson Class Federation Destroyer (1983)	3.50	4-6	______
2508 Klingon D-10 Class Heavy Cruiser (1983)	3.50	4-6	______
2509 Klingon D-18 Destroyer (1984)	4	4-5	______
2510 Klingon K-23 Escort (1984)	4	4-5	______
2511 Gorn MA-12 Cruiser (two) (1984)	4	4-5	______
2512 Orion Blockade Runner (three) (1984)	4	4-5	______
2513 Klingon L-9 Frigate (1984)	4	4-5	______
2514 U.S.S. Loknar Frigate (1984)	4	4-5	______
2515 Romulan Winged Defender Cruiser (1984)	4	4-5	______
2516 U.S.S. Chandley Frigate (1984)	4	4-5	______
2517 U.S.S. Excelsior Battleship ST III (1984)	4	4-7	______
2518 Klingon Bird of Prey (ST III) (1984)	4	4-6	______
2519 U.S.S. Grissom Research Vessel ST III (1984)	4	4-6	______
2520 Deep Space Freighter (ST III) (1984)	4	4-5	______
2525 21 Romulan Graceful Flyer (1985)	4	4-5	______
2522 Orion Wanderer (1985)	4	4-5	______
2523 Kobayashi Maru Freighter (1986)	4.50	5-6	______
2524 Romulan Gallant Wing Cruiser (1986)	4.50	5-6	______
2525 Gorn BH-2 Battleship (1986)	9	9-10	______
2526 U.S.S. Baker Destroyer (1986)	4.50	5-6	______
2527 Romulan Nova Battleship (1986)	12	12-13	______
2528 Romulan Bright One Destroyer (1986)	4.50	5-6	______
2529 Klingon L-24 Battleship (1986)	12	12-13	______
2530 Klingon D-2 Missle Destroyer (1986)	4.50	5-6	______
2531 Romulan Whitewind Cruiser (1986)	4.50	5-6	______
2532 U.S.S. Northampton Frigate (1987)	4.50	5-6	______
2533 U.S.S. Remora Escort (1987)	4.50	5-6	______
2534 U.S.S. Andor Cruiser (1987)	4.50	5-6	______
2599 Starship Support Stands (in blue, red, purple, green or smoke)	2	2-3	______

Miniature Figures (2600's Series)

25MM Figures (1983) [12]
Die-cast metal figures from ST II, Wrath of Kahn to use in gaming, including painting guides individually packaged in cellophane pockets:

	Issue	Current	Cost/Date
2601 James T. Kirk	1	3-5	______
2602 First Officer Spock	1	3-5	______
2603 Dr. Leonard "Bones" McCoy	1	3-5	______
2604 Lt. Saavik	1	3-5	______
2605 Chief Engineer Montgomery Scott	1	3-5	______
2606 Communications Officer Uhura	1	3-5	______
2607 Mister Sulu	1	3-5	______
2608 Mister Chekov	1	3-5	______
2609 Kahn Noonian Singh	1	3-5	______
2610 Dr. David Marcus	1	3-5	______
2611 Joachim (Kahn's First Officer)	1	3-5	______
2612 Dr. Carol Marcus	1	3-5	______
2613 Captain Terrell (U.S.S. Reliant)	1	3-5	______
2614 Kahn Noonian Singh (Ceti Alpha V)	1	3-5	______
2615 Klingon Officer	1	3-5	______
2616 Klingon 1	1	3-5	______
2617 Klingon 2	1	3-5	______

Miniatures Collections Sets (3000's Series)

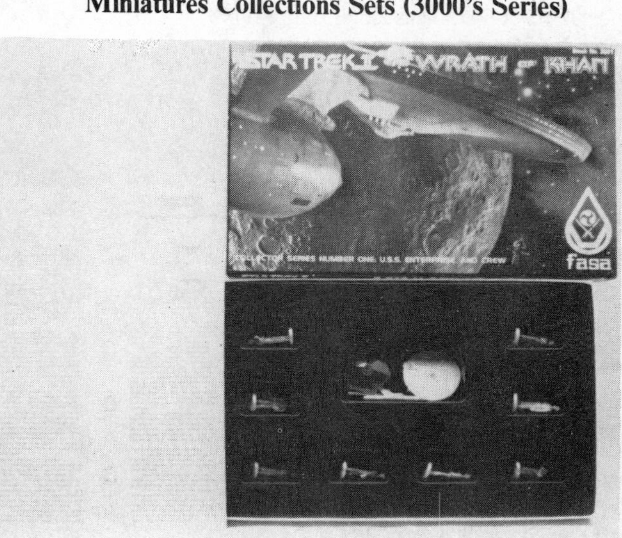

3000 Series Collection Set #1.

Boxed sets of eight die-cast metal figures and one 1/3900 Scale starship. Miniatures are packed in plastic and foam cartons that include a guide to painting. Box cover photos are close-ups of the starships as seen in ST II. Boxes have Star Trek II The Wrath of Kahn affiliation logos. [13]

Collection Set No. 1 3001 (1983)
New Enterprise starship and crew.
New U.S.S. Enterprise (NCC-1701)
Admiral Kirk
First Officer Spock
Dr. Leonard McCoy
Chief Engineer Scott
Commander Chekov

12. Fasa has ceased production of the miniature 25MM crew figures, making these collectibles very hard to find.
13. Figures contained in the Collector Sets have different poses than those sold individually. Production on the Collector Set packages has been discontinued.

	Issue	Current Cost/Date	
Mister Sulu Communications Officer Uhura Lt. Saavik Boxed Set	10	25-35	_____
Collection Set No. 2 3002 (1983) Kahn and his followers take U.S.S. Reliant U.S.S. Reliant Kahn Noonian Singh (Ceti Alpha V gear) Joachim (Ceti Alpha V gear) Kahn Noonian Singh (Normal gear) Joachim (Normal gear) Female Followers (two) Male Followers (two) Boxed Set	10	20-30	_____
Collection Set No. 3 3003 (1984) Regula One Space Laboratory and its staff: Regula One Station Dr. Carol Marcus Dr. David Marcus Jedda (a scientist) Other Project Genesis Scientists (2) Genesis Control Device Computer Console Boxed Set	10	20-30	_____
Collection Set No. 4 3004 (1984) Klingon Battlecruiser and its crew: New Klingon D-7 Battlecruiser Klingon Ship Commander Klingon First Officer Other Klingon Crew (six) Boxed Set	10	20-30	_____

Playing Aids (2800's series)

	Issue	Current Cost/Date	
2801 **Starship Combat Hex Grid, Star Trek II The Wrath of Kahn,** 1983 Five 22"x33" starfield maps for use with the Starship Combat Game 2006	3	3-4	_____
2802 **Gamemaster's Kit,** 1984 A 3-panel screen displaying all the important tables and charts and 16-page booklet for players with character sheets for Star Fleet personnel, Klingons, merchants, etc. ..	6	7-8	_____
2803 **Tricorder/Sensors Interactive Display,** 1985 Hand-held, punch-out for conducting scans and scientific readings. includes instructions, cellophane wrapped.	10	10-12	_____

Micro-Adventure Game Sets (5000's Series)

Differ in basic format from the other Fasa gaming sets in that they are miniature sets in 5"x7" boxes that are fully self-contained rulesbooks and adventures. These stand-alone games are distinct from the extensive role playing line listed above.

	Issue	Current Cost/Date	
5001 **Star Trek III The Search For Spock Game,** 1985 End of the 3rd movie scenerio where you must rescue young Spock from the crumbling Genesis planet, 112 pieces, 76 Event Cards, a modular map to create over 10,000 planets as playing fields, 3 dice and rulebook, game for 1 to 4 players. Boxed, cover photo shows distant Kirk battling Kruge at ledge with close-up photo inset of Spock. 931787-51-3	7	9-12	_____
5002 **Starship Duel Game No. 1,** 1985 Combat mini-game that uses unique Navigation Wheel to plot courses. Adventure of Enterprise versus the Klingon Bird of Prey scoutship from ST III, 2 navigation wheels, conversion wheel for upgrading scout to Klingon I-42 Heavy Frigate, ship stat cards, 75 counters, 2 dice, rulebook, 1 to 2 players. Boxed, cover schematic drawing of Enterprise and Klingon cruiser on star grid. 0-931787-52-1	7	9-12	_____
5004 **Star Trek III - Struggle for the Throne,** 1985 Players are Klingon Thought Admirals vying to bribe, out-deal and influence their way to the Imperial throne, 76 action cards, 112 pieces, modular map, 2 dice, rules, for 2 to6players. Boxed, cover photos close-up of Kruge on Klingon bridge from movie. 9-931787-54-8	7	9-12	_____
5005 **Starship Duel Game No. 2** 1985 Pits ST II U.S.S. Reliant against Klingon L-9 Frigate. Interchangeable wth ships of Starship Duel Game No. 1 and includes conversion wheels, 2 navigation wheels, ship stat cards, 75 counters, 2 dice and rules, for 1 or 2 players. Boxed, cover is schematic drawing of Reliant and Klingon ship on star grid. 0-931787-55-6	7	9-12	_____

HOBBY KITS

(Arts & Crafts)

Every age group enjoys its own level of sophistication in the marketing of Star Trek hobbies and crafts. Manufacturers of activity crafts for children and young adults generally gear their products towards a specific age level of difficulty, dexterity and aesthetic appeal.

Children's Star Trek crafts, for instance, have included paintings, molded castings and poster coloring art kits which feature character profiles or action scenes from T.V. Trek, the animated series and motion pictures. Pre-teens and young adults were likewise presented with string art, needlepoints, paint-by-numbers and plastic model kits of the many spacecraft evolving from the Star Trek universe.

One of the most memorable additions to this category was the development of the **U.S.S. Enterprise** and **Klingon Cruiser Flying Model Rockets** manufactured by Estes Industries in October 1974.

Estes, the largest model rocket manufacturer in the world, devoted great care towards the accuracy of their product. The V-2 rocket used to propel the kit was researched with the help of rocket experts, and the spaceship designs were crafted from pictures donated by the Smithsonian Institution. The result was the production of quality plastiform molds designed to be crafted around the rocket shell.

The only drawback, for both kits, was their packaging which did nothing to illustrate the potential which could be obtained by proper assembly and painting touch-ups. When carefully constructed, the models rival those of A.M.T. and Ertl. Another limitation was the relatively high level of dexterity required for their assembly.

Unfortunately, the lifespan of these Star Trek rockets was short-lived. Within a couple years, Estes abandoned the manufacture of exotic flying rockets other than standard airplane and shuttle types. Retailers report that the kits were not popular and that the spaceships simply didn't fly well. The Enterprise and Klingon rocket, along with various Star Wars novelties succumbed to a retail death, making them desirable collectibles.

Other Star Trek hobby kits are good collectibles, too. The colorful packaging which accompanies them is classic. Most are extremely rare even in poor condition.

Models

Manufacturers have always recognized the popularity of snap-together model car and airplane kits for kids. It was predictable that somebody would create a model kit of the U.S.S. Enterprise for mass production and sale.

In 1966 A.M.T. Corporation of Troy, Michigan produced about 90,000 Enterprise kits by fall of that year, plus a Klingon Cruiser. The sale of the "original" starship was excellent despite numerous shortcomings.

The most noticeable error on A.M.T.'s first Enterprise was the inclusion of circular deck lines on the top of the saucer which don't exist on the television model. This model was also lacking in stability of construction. Due to countless complaints, the model was re-released the same year with slight alterations in superstructure and with new mold revisions that allowed for easier assembly.

Still the perfection of this second Enterprise model was marred by the inclusion of a totally inaccurate decal sheet that not only assigned a questionable call number and name to other starships in the Star Trek universe, but was printed in a style contradictory to that of the T.V. Enterprise.

In 1979, A.M.T. merged with Lesney (Matchbox) to produce the intricately molded **Star Trek The Motion Picture** Enterprise, the Klingon Battle Cruiser and the Vulcan Shuttle Sarek. By 1982, Ertl (a Division of Kiddie, Inc.) purchased Lesney's rights and acquired the logo A.M.T. Ertl. Ertl released the **Star Trek Wrath of Kahn** Enterprise, the older T.V. Enterprise and a second shuttle of the 1966 three-piece **Spaceship Set.**

The **Mr. Spock** model has also had a varied history. This was originally produced by Aurora Plastics, Ltd. of the United Kingdom. In 1966 Aurora traded their toolings of Mr. Spock phasering a three-headed serpent to A.M.T. for the American designs of the Enterprise. In 1973, Mr. Spock was reissued in the U.S. in his series uniform, again, aiming a haser at the dreaded multi-headed snake. Then in 1979, Spock appeared without the snake, standing on a plastic platform and wearing the apparel of STTMP. Instead of a phaser, he held a communicator.

Collectors may be able to identify model sets without their original boxes simply by the characteristics of the assembled parts. A.M.T., Lesney and Ertl had their own design peculiarities.

- A.M.T. Packaged kits contained assembly guides, water transfer decals and display stands. The models were white, gray or blue plastic glue-together or snapped. Models with operating lights required 2 AA batteries.
- Lesney/A.M.T. kits contained assembly guides, no-water, rub-down transfers and display stands. The plastic model pieces were white or gray glue-together and represented revised STTMP version spacecraft of assorted types. Operating models used 2 C cell batteries.
- Ertl/A.M.T. plastic kits included assembly guides, no-water, rub-down transfers and display stands. Some models cite "superceeding" codes referring to original design models of A.M.T. and Lesney vintage.

HOBBY KITS

(Arts & Crafts, Models)

	Issue	Current	Cost/Date
•**Action Fleet - Star Trek The Motion Picture** Mars, Inc. 1980 Cardstock mobile to assemble, five cut-out spaceships from the movie: Enterprise Klingon Cruiser, Vulcan Shuttle, Work Bee Pod and Travel Pod, also includes a fold-out Fleet Specification Guide and ship schematics with weaponry specs. [1]	1.50	15-20	_____

•**Figurines**

Mix and Mold Sets, Catalog Shoppe, 1975
Individual kits to make a statue of characters to stand 6¼" tall, include a mold, casting ingredients and instructions for using the materials, boxed 6½"x9", three different sets:

	Issue	Current	Cost/Date
Kirk	—	9-12	_____
Spock	—	9-12	_____
McCoy	—	9-12	_____

The illfated packaging for the Enterprise Rocket, 1975.

Painting Figurines - Star Trek The Motion Picture Sets
Crafts by Whiting/Milton Bradley, 1979
Kits containing a 4½" tall molded figurine plus five acrylic paints, brush and instructions, 8"x11½" plastic form cardstock mount with cartoon transporter scene artwork, two different sets:

	Issue	Current	Cost/Date
1906-1 Admiral Kirk - holding phaser	2.95	8-12	_____
1906-2 Mr. Spock - in Vulcan robes	2.95	8-12	_____

Search For Spock Kite, Lando Merchandising, 1984.

• **Flying Model Rockets,** Estes Industries, 1975
Cardboard and plastic flying rocket to assemble, engine powered ship that uses a parachute recovery, designed for advanced model rocketry skill levels, two designs; packaged in plastic envelope with cardstock header:

	Issue	Current	Cost/Date
1274 Klingon Battle Cruiser, 15½" long, wing span 10" weight 2½ oz., uses engines B4-2, B6-4 or C6-5	8	15-18	_____
1275 U.S.S. Enterprise, 43" overall length, 17½" saucer disc, weight 4 ozs., uses engines B6-2 or C6-3	8	15-20	_____

1. This mobile required assembly and appeared as a nationally advertised Sunday Comics supplement in conjunction with STTMP movie. It was a special offer item. (See Special Promotions Chapter.)

Issue | Current | Cost/Date

• **Kite - U.S.S. Enterprise, Star Trek The Search For Spock Kit**
Lando Merchandising, Inc., 1984
Diamond shaped plastic kit with assembly required, has purple background with starfield and cartoon rendering of STTMP Enterprise in white. Measures 2'x2" diagonally and has 8" plastic purple fringe along the bottom sides, plastic stays included, plastic bag wrap. [2] . . 3.95 10-12 _____

• **Model Kits**

Command Bridge S950-601, A.M.T. Corporation, 1975
360 degree plastic platform, gray model with eleven bridge stations, viewscreens, chairs and railings. Includes 2½" figures of Kirk, Spock and Sulu. Special Star Trek jacket offer coupon inside. 8½"x10" boxed, with cartoon style lid. . . . . 2.95 18-30 _____

Lid for the Original U.S.S. Enterprise Space Ship #5921-200, 1966.

Enterprise Models
Plastic model Kits by Aurora, A.M.T., Midori, Lesney, Ertl, Milton Bradley.

Star Trek Enterprise, 350-5
Midori Plastik Kit, Japan, 1969
Plastic model features t.v. ship with the addition of a propeller! Box sports Spock and Kirk with laser rifle promo photo from first season, along with Japanese NTV affiliation. Boxed 12½"x17¼" . . . . 3 25-30 _____

Issue | Current | Cost/Date

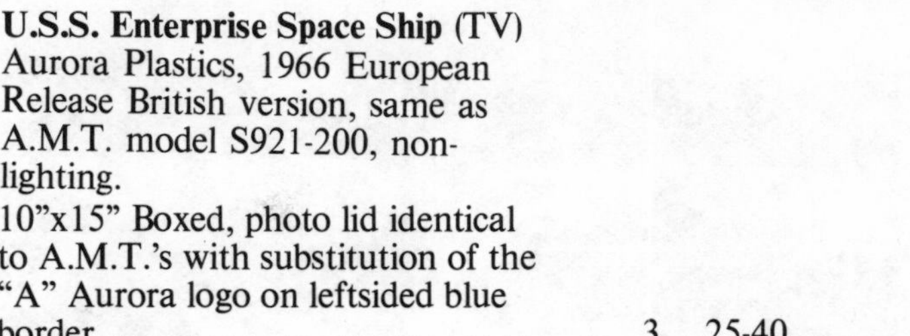

U.S.S. Enterprise Space Ship (TV)
Aurora Plastics, 1966 European Release British version, same as A.M.T. model S921-200, non-lighting.
10"x15" Boxed, photo lid identical to A.M.T.'s with substitution of the "A" Aurora logo on leftsided blue border . . . . 3 25-40 _____

U.S.S. Enterprise Space Ship (TV) S921-200
A.M.T. Corporation, 1966
White plastic, clear domes with upper and lower lighting, nacelle caps white, dish antenna. Length 18".
10"x15" Boxed with cartoon-style lid [3] . . . . 2 75-150 _____

AMT's Enterprise Model #6675-10D0.

U.S.S. Enterprise Space Ship (TV) S951-250
A.M.T. Corporation, 1966
Revised version of AMT model S921-200 with structural and color changes. White plastic model with green tint domes and red nacelle caps, dish antenna. Length 18 inches. No lighting. [4]
8½"x10" Boxed, no color border, photo lid. . . . . 2.50 25-35 _____
10"x15" Boxed, blue border wtih photo lid . . . . 2.50 60-75 _____

U.S.S. Enterprise Space Ship (TV)
6676-10DO Ertl/A.M.T., 1983
Re-release of A.M.T. model S951-250. Includes special decals to construct an entire fleet of starships. Packaged as the original smaller box. 8½"x10" Boxed with photo lid [5] . . . . 4.95 6-9 _____

2. This kite kit was used as a special offer by Lever Brothers during the premiere of **Star Trek III.** (See Special Promotions Chapter.)
3. Where A.M.T. acquired their design specifications for the model is unknown. Rumors that ship plans represented in Ballantine's **The Making of Star Trek** were employed are false. These blueprints hadn't even been drawn at the time.
4. Many early Enterprise models were marketed in either 8½x10" or 10"x15" size boxes. This packaging anomaly corresponds to the fact that the larger boxed kit contained upper and lower deck lighting in some cases, while the smaller kits contained tinted domes or nacelle caps without the optional lighting.
5. In March 1987, Tonka Corporation agreed to buy Ertl Toys of Dyersville, Iowa.

Two rare kits by AMT 1974 & 1975.

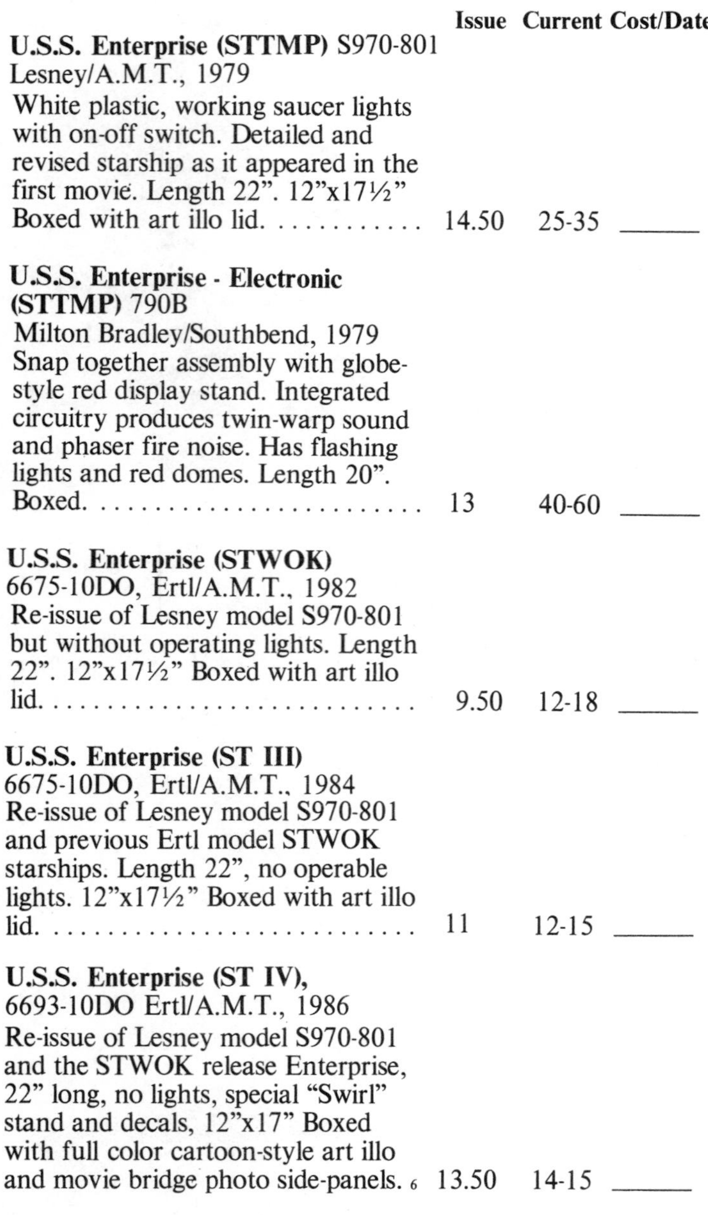

	Issue	Current	Cost/Date
U.S.S. Enterprise (STTMP) S970-801 Lesney/A.M.T., 1979 White plastic, working saucer lights with on-off switch. Detailed and revised starship as it appeared in the first movie. Length 22". 12"x17½" Boxed with art illo lid.	14.50	25-35	_____
U.S.S. Enterprise - Electronic (STTMP) 790B Milton Bradley/Southbend, 1979 Snap together assembly with globe-style red display stand. Integrated circuitry produces twin-warp sound and phaser fire noise. Has flashing lights and red domes. Length 20". Boxed.	13	40-60	_____
U.S.S. Enterprise (STWOK) 6675-10DO, Ertl/A.M.T., 1982 Re-issue of Lesney model S970-801 but without operating lights. Length 22". 12"x17½" Boxed with art illo lid.	9.50	12-18	_____
U.S.S. Enterprise (ST III) 6675-10DO, Ertl/A.M.T., 1984 Re-issue of Lesney model S970-801 and previous Ertl model STWOK starships. Length 22", no operable lights. 12"x17½" Boxed with art illo lid.	11	12-15	_____
U.S.S. Enterprise (ST IV), 6693-10DO Ertl/A.M.T., 1986 Re-issue of Lesney model S970-801 and the STWOK release Enterprise, 22" long, no lights, special "Swirl" stand and decals, 12"x17" Boxed with full color cartoon-style art illo and movie bridge photo side-panels. 6	13.50	14-15	_____

STTMP Klingon Cruiser, 1980.

	Issue	Current	Cost/Date
Exploration Kit S958-601, A.M.T. Corporation, 1974 Original boxed set of miniature to-scale replicas, hand phaser in pistol mount, communicator and tricorder. 8½"x10" Boxed with cartoon-style lid.	2.95	35-75	_____
10"x15" Boxed with cartoon-style lid.	2.95	60-100	_____

Star Trek III, Klingon Cruiser, 1984

	Issue	Current	Cost/Date
Galileo Shuttlecraft S959-602, A.M.T. Corporation, 1974 White plastic, including interior helm console and seats. Length 7¾", Special Star Trek jacket offer coupon inside. 8½"x10" Boxed with cartoon lid.	2.95	50-75	_____
10"x15" Boxed with cartoon lid. . . .	2.95	60-100	_____

6. The **Star Trek IV** Enterprise is tagged as the newly rebuilt starship NCC - 1701A.

HOBBY KITS

Issue | Current | Cost/Date

Klingon Battle Cruisers
Plastic model kits by A.M.T., Matchbox, Ertl

Klingon Battle Cruiser (TV) S952-250, A.M.T. Corporation, 1966
Television series vessel, blue plastic, optional sky hook mount. Available in lighted and unlighted models. Lengths 18".
10"x15" Boxed (forward control and crew's quarters lighted), Magenta border on left reads "Klingon" in yellow, photo lid shows Cruiser over Saturn planet. . . . . 2.50 65-100 ______
8½"x10" Boxed, no color border, no lights . . . . 2.50 30-50 ______

Klingon Battle Cruiser (TV) S952-802
A.M.T. Corporation, 1968
Unlighted version of the series Cruiser. Same model as S952-250 re-packaged. Special Star Trek jacket offer coupon inside.
10"x15" Boxed, Magenta border on left reads "Star Trek" in yellow, photo lid shows central Cruiser with miniature Enterprise in upper right hand corner. 2.50 50-75 ______

Klingon Battle Cruiser (TV)
Ertl/A.M.T., 1983
Re-release of A.M.T. model S952-250. Packaged the same as the smaller kit. 8½"x10" Boxed with photo-style lid. . . . . 4.95 10-12 ______

Klingon Cruiser (STTMP) S971-801
Lesney/A.M.T., 1980
Katanga Class Klingon vessel from the very first movie. Gray plastic, very detailed model, length 15". Special Star Trek poster offer coupon inside. 10"x12½" Boxed with photo-style lid. . . . . 6.95 20-35 ______

Klingon Cruiser/Vaisseau/ Raumkreuzer (STTMP) PK-5111
Matchbox/A.M.T., 1979
European Release Large box movie version model with 32 plastic parts. Measures 38 cm. Model title translates into 3 languages. Instructions read in Italiono, Espanol, Svenska, English, Francais and Deutsch.
10"x12½" boxed with STTMP photo lid and white upper border. . . 6.95 10-18 ______

Issue | Current | Cost/Date

Klingon Cruiser (ST III) 6682-10EO
Ertl/A.M.T., 1984
Super-detailed re-issue of Lesney model S971-801. Length 15", includes display stand, glue together with no painting needed. Boxed 10"x12¼" with photo style lid. . . . . 7.95 9-12 ______

K-7 Space Station (TV) S955-601
A.M.T. Corporation, 1976
White plastic triple-hulled structure with 16" diameter. Includes miniature 2" starship Enterprise.
8½" x 10" Boxed with photo-style lid . . . . 2.95 40-60 ______

Romulan Bird of Prey (TV) S957-601, A.M.T. Corporation, 1975
Gray plastic model, length 7½". Large Bird of Prey decal included.
8½"x10" Boxed with cartoon-style lid. . . . . 2.95 45-75 ______

Space Ship Sets
Plastic models by A.M.T. and Ertl

Space Ship Set (TV) S953-601
A.M.T. Corporation, 1976
Snap together models of three of Star Trek's television spacecraft. Includes Enterprise, Klingon and Romulan ships in miniature.
8½"x10" Boxed with cartoon-style lid. . . . . 2.95 20-40 ______

Space Ship Set (TV) 6677-10EO, Ertl/A.M.T., 1983
Re-release of the original AMT model kit S953-601. Contains Enterprise (3¼"x7⅛"), Klingon Cruiser (3⅞" x 5¾") and Romulan Bird of Prey (5½"x3"). Includes desk stand for displaying all three.
6"x9½" Boxed with photo lid. . . . . . 4.95 6-9 ______

Spock Kits
Plastic kits by Aurora, A.M.T., Lesney

Mr. Spock (TV) 922
Aurora Plastics, 1972
British plastic model kit not distributed in the United States. Platform model of Spock phasering a three-headed serpent. Boxed with cartoon-style lid. . . . . 3 20-35 ______

Mr. Spock (TV) S956-601
A.M.T. Corporation, 1973
Spock from the t.v. series pointing a phaser at a three-headed serpent. Detailed alien landscape platform base. Snap together pieces.
8½"x10" Boxed with cartoon-style lid. . . . . 3.50 20-25 ______
10"x15" Boxed with cartoon-style lid. . . . . 3.50 25-35 ______

HOBBY KITS

	Issue	Current	Cost/Date
Mr. Spock (STTMP) S973-801, Lesney/A.M.T., 1979 STTMP uniform Spock on platform with communicator in hand. 6" tall. Special Star Trek poster offer inside. 8½"x10" Boxed with Art-illo lid....	4.50	10-15	_____
Vulcan Shuttles Plastic models by Lesney, Matchbox, Ertl			
Vulcan Shuttle - Surak (STTMP) S972-801, Lesney/A.M.T., 1979 Gray plastic model of the new interstellar shuttle. Includes detachable passenger module. Length 10". Special Star Trek poster offer inside. 10"x12" Boxed with art illo lid.	4.50	15-30	_____
Vulcan Shuttle/Navette/Raumschiff (STTMP) PK-5112 Matchbox/A.M.T. 1979 European release large box movie vessel "Surak." Model title in 3 languages. Instructions read in Italiano, Espanol, Svenska, English, Francais and Deutsch.	6.50	10-18	_____
Vulcan Shuttle - Surak (ST III) 6679-10EO Ertl/A.M.T., 1984 Re-issue of Lesney model S972-801. Gray plastic model, length 10". No painting required. 10"x12" art illo lid.	7.95	9-12	_____
• **Needlepoint Kits,** Artista Designs, 1980 Individual sewing kits with 14"x18" needlepoint #10 canvas, instructions, needle and black and white yarn, character busts of:			
Captain Kirk	—	20-30	_____
Mr. Spock	—	20-30	_____

Revamped Mr. Spock Kit, 1979

One of two painted Paint By Number Canvases by Hasbro, 1972.

	Issue	Current	Cost/Date
• **Paint-By-Numbers,** Hasbro Industries, 1972			
Small Canvas - 8" x 11" Oil canvas and paints in ten colors, brush and instructions to complete a painting with four quarter panels:			
Enterprise with Saturn planet; Kirk in the command chair; Yeoman and Spock with phaser; and a green-skinned, antennaed alien under phaser blast, boxed 11" square with photo of Enterprise, Kirk and Spock	2	15-25	_____
Large Canvas - 11"x17" Canvas with nine oil colors, brush and instructions, planet action scene with ¾ busts of Kirk and Spock as Enterprise soars overhad, included large red plastic frame with 2" border, boxed 12"x19" with cut-away photo of Kirk, Spock and Enterprise	3.95	20-30	_____

Bridge Kit and Enterprise Kit #S951-250.

Pen-A-Poster #2413.

	Issue	Current	Cost/Date
• **Pen and Poster Sets**			
How Do You Doodle Set 2081 Open Door Enterprises, 1976 Poster coloring set including two of each scene 12"x18" b/w line drawings, five fine-tip markers: "Journeys of the Enterprise" - action "Tour of the Enterprise " - crew, ship Packaged in plastic pocket	3.95	10-15	_____
Pen-A-Poster Kit ST2555 Open Door Enterprises, 1976 Contains four Star Trek pen-a-poster kits which were also sold separately, contains 10 non-toxic felt pens, posters 12"x18", boxed and shrink-wrapped, includes: Enemies of the Federation Journeys of the Enterprise Star Trek Lives Tour of the Enterprise, complete set	4.35	15-25	_____
Pen-A-Poster Kits Open Door Enterprises, 1976 Four individual poster and pen sets, 14½"x22", b/w line drawings to color with six markers and coloring guide included in plastic pocket kits:			
2411 "Star Trek Lives" - crew	3.95	6-9	_____
2412 "Enemies of the Federation - battles	3.95	6-9	_____
2413 "Tour of the Enterprise" - crew, ship	3.95	6-9	_____
2414 "Journeys of the Enterprise" - voyages	3.95	6-9	_____
3-D Poster Bulletin Board - Star Trek The Motion Picture Crafts by Whiting/Milton Bradley, 1979 Preprinted 11"x17" die-cut cardboard canvas with action scene from the movie, includes four non-toxic marker pens	—	10-12	_____
• **String Art Kit** TC-5016 Open Door Enterprises, 1976 Black 18"x24" backboard with copper pins and colored string, silver thread to construct the portraits of Kirk and Spock, boxed with artwork design on cover	10	15-15	_____

HOUSEWARES

With the tremendous popularity of Star Trek on T.V., it was inevitable that, sooner or later, Trek would make the merchandising jump from off the screen and into our very living rooms. And jump it has but not just into our living rooms. Star Trek housewares have innundated our kitchens and our very bathrooms as well!

The first object to invade our homes was the **Star Trek Lunchbox** manufactured by Aladdin Industries in 1968 and it commands a high price as a collectible compared to its original $2 investment.

The merchandising of Star Trek housewares has coincided greatly with the airing of the animated Star Trek series and with STTMP. A plethora of memorabilia has appeared from 1974-1979 directly in the wake of heavy promotional campaigns meant to gain the attention of juveniles.

The most impressive development for Star Trek housewares of the '80's has been the production of **Star Trek Collector Plates, Mugs** and **Steins** by Ernst Enterprises of Escondido, California. The series of eight character plates began in 1984 by subscription and has expanded into another set focusing on scenes from eight of the most favorite Star Trek episodes in the history of the show.

BATH AND LINENS

Item	Issue	Current	Cost/Date
•**Bandages - "Star Trek The Motion Picture"** Adam Joseph Industries, 1979 Assorted sizes of plastic adhesive bandaids, flesh-tone color with STTMP Letter Logo in silver and busts of Kirk, Spock and McCoy with Enterprise in silver and navy. Strips contained in cardstock box with outline figures of Kirk and Spock.	2	4-6	______
•**Beach Towels,** Canon, 1975 Standard large towels in three different designs:			
Spock Portrait	5	15-20	______
Kirk and Spock Portraits	5	15-20	______
Enterprise - t.v. starship and Moon with the lettering "Where No Man Has Gone Before"	5	20-25	______
•**Bed Linens** Pacific Mills, 1975			
Pillowcases Standard size cases designed to match the sheet set. One pair per package, plastic wrapped	2	8-12	______
Sheets Twin size sheets featuring the t.v. Enterprise and crew: Kirk and Spock, in action scene adventures. Polyester and cotton with blue background. Packaged folded and plastic wrapped. Available fitted and flat.	8	15-20	______
•**Cleansing Towelettes - "Star Trek The Motion Picture"** Adam Joseph Industries, 1979 Twenty antiseptic, fragrant and disposable hand or facial towelettes. Ten are sealed in tear-open packet featuring blue photo of movie Enterprise; attached alternately to packets with photo busts of Kirk or Spock. Box is pink and silver, 2"x2¼"x4" bearing picture of STTMP Enterprise.	3	4-6	______
•**Sleeping Bag - "Star Trek"** Alp Industries, 1976 Children's slumber bag, synthetic fiber-filled, reversible pull-tabs and separating zippers. Colorful scenes from the t.v. series feature cartoon front-view Enterprise, portraits of Kirk, Spock and McCoy and the same trio in action pose, 3'x5' packaged in a clear vinyl tote bag with drawstring.	10	35-45	______

Glow in the Dark Cups distributed by Stop 'N' Go Stores, 1986.

BAR ACCESSORIES

Item	Issue	Current	Cost/Date
•**Bottle - "Saurian Brandy Bottle"** Dickel Whisky Co., 1964-1969, 1980 This genuine whiskey decanter was used as a prop in several t.v. episodes and earned itself a "Star Trek" name. Design is powderhorn with leather stopper and handle-band assembly, bottle w/o contents: [1]			
Fifth Bottle		20-35	______
Miniature		10-15	______
•**Bottle Topper - "Mr. Spock"** Star Base Central, distrib. 1986 Hand painted ceramic Spock's head of STTMP vintage. Promotional item.	—	15-20	______

1. Dickel began manufacturing these decanters again in 1980. Newer bottles have vinyl straps in lieu of leather ones.

Promotional Theater Cup STTMP, 1979.

"Mr. Spock" Decanter, Grenadier Spirits, 1979.

•Cups - "Star Trek IV - The Voyage Home"
Coca-Cola, Inc., distributed by Stop 'n Go Stores, 1986.
Set of four large 28 oz. capacity plastic cups with cartoon illos from the ST IV movie. Glow-in-the-Dark. Manufactured by Giacona Container. [2]

	Issue	Current	Cost/Date
Crew- two illo boxes with portraits, over blue and yellow starfield (McCoy, Spock, Kirk), (Sulu, Chekov, Uhura, Scotty)	1.50	2-4	_____
Kirk with portside Enterprise	1.50	2-4	_____
Spock - posed in robe, plus close-up	1.50	2-4	_____
Klingon Bird of Prey ship	1.50	2-4	_____

Star Trek The Motion Picture Cup
Coca-Cola Company, 1979

	Issue	Current	Cost/Date
Large 32 oz. cup sold at STTMP premiere movie theaters with a large coke, white plastic with busts of Decker, Spock, Kirk, McCoy & Ilia against a starscape background, picture of Enterprise over cup blurb, 5½" high, approx. 4" in diameter.	1	2-4	_____

• Decanter - "Mr. Spock"
Grenadier Spirits Co., 1979

	Issue	Current	Cost/Date
STTMP vintage porcelain ceramic bust of Spock, liquor decanter filled with 25.4 ozs. of 48-Proof Cielo Liquer. Box has window-cut cellophane panel, panel features data on Star Trek, Leonard Nimoy and Mr. Spock.	20	20-30	_____

• Glasses - "Star Trek"
Dr. Pepper, 1976
Four pedestal-style drinking glasses, 6¼" tall, each featuring a color decal portrait and a recap from the Animated Series. Boxed promotional set.
T.V. Enterprise
Captain James T. Kirk
Mr. Spock
Dr. Leonard McCoy

	Issue	Current	Cost/Date
Complete set of four glasses. [3]	8	35-50	_____

Glasses - "Star Trek The Motion Picture"
Coca-Cola Company, 1979
Three drinking glasses in a set, each glass 5½" tall and features the STTMP Letter Logo over cartoon scene from the movie.
Bust of Kirk, McCoy and Spock
Enterprise over planet
Bust of Decker and Ilia

	Issue	Current	Cost/Date
Complete set of three glasses. [4]	6	45-60	_____

Glasses - "Star Trek The Search For Spock"
Taco Bell (Division of Pepsico, Inc.)
Four pedestal-style drinking glasses with double-ring base. Each glass is 5-5/8" tall holds 16 ozx. capacity and features a scene and legend from the plot sequence of the third movie. Anchor Hocking manufacturer.

	Issue	Current	Cost/Date
Lord Kruge	1.59	3-5	_____
Enterprise Destroyed	1.59	3-5	_____
Fal-Tor-Pan	1.59	3-5	_____
Complete set of four glasses. [5]	—	15-20	_____

2. The ST IV movie cups were not nationally advertised. They were produced as a promotion for Coca-Cola Classic softdrink and were distributed by Stop 'n Go Stores located in the Southeast. Original prices included a large fill-up of Coke.
3. The written legends for this particular set of glassware were composed by Bjo Trimble.
4. Coca-Cola never found a retail franchise outlet to distribute this glassware set which contributes to its rarity.
5. During the original promotional campaign the $1.59 cost of each glass included a fill-up of Pepsi softdrink in the price. One new glass per week was released in conjunction with the ST III movie premiere month.

Two sides of Star Trek Mugs by Deka Plastics, 1975.

	Issue	Current	Cost/Date
• **Mugs - "Star Trek Collector Set"** Ernst Enterprises, 1986 Eight porcelain mugs featuring the original artwork of Susie Morton as it also appeared on her Star Trek Collector Plate Series. Portraits of those plates appear on one side reproduced over a stargrid; reverse show's character's name in "zoom-in" design, 3-5/8" tall, 10 oz. capacity: Mugs portrait Spock, Kirk, McCoy, Scotty, Sulu, Chekov, Uhura, Beam Down Sold in two packages only			
Set of 4 (Spock, McCoy, Sulu, Scotty)	19.95	20-22	_____
Set of 8 (complete set)	37.90	38-40	_____
Mug - "Star Trek 20th Anniversary Mug" Star Trek Official Fan Club, Mug, 1986 White porcelain coffee mug with 2-tone official Anniversary Letter Logo (circle bearing "20 Years 1966-1986) on one side and Official Club Logo on the reverse.	10	10-12	_____
Mugs - "Star Trek The Wrath of Kahn" Image Products, 1982 Set of four insulated coffee mugs with plastic laminate over photos from the second movie, showed STWOK Letter Logos:			
U.S.S. Enterprise, front view	3	5-8	_____
Spock, in Vulcan robe meditating	3	5-8	_____
Kahn, aboard the U.S.S. Reliant	3	5-8	_____
Kirk, in Admiral's uniform, seated	3	5-8	_____
Complete set of four mugs	12	20-35	_____
• **Mug and Bow Set - "Star Trek"** Deka Plastics, 1975 Two-piece child's place-setting incuding 20 oz. white plastic bowl and 10 oz. mug with square handle. Color decal shows bust of cartoon "Mr. Spock," "Captain Kirk" (labeled) and t.v. Enterprise in starboard profile. Sold as combination set.	3	15-20	_____
Mug and Bowl Set - "Star Trek The Motion Picture" Deka Plastics, 1979 Two-piece set includes 20 oz. white plastic bowl and 10 oz. mug with square handle. Imprinted design features elaborate rainbow background, front-view STTMP Enterprise and photo busts of Decker and Ilia, and Spock, Kirk and McCoy	7	8-15	_____
• **Steins - "Kirk and Spock Collector Set"** Ernst Enterprises, 1986 Glass, mug-style beverage steins that hold 22 oz. capacity. White glass background with cepia-tone drawings:			
Kirk - bust, plus a standing pose	19.95	20-22	_____
Spock - 2 busts, one "ear" profile	19.95	20-22	_____
Steins - "Star Trek The Wrath of Kahn" Image Products, 1982 Set of three ceramic beer-stein mugs. Character busts are set in high-relief on the front, in color. Back reads the movie Letter Logo and the character's name in raised block letters:			
Mr. Spock	29.95	15-35	_____
Adm. Kirk	29.95	15-35	_____
Kahn	29.95	15-35	_____
Complete set of three steins	75.95	45-85	

KITCHENWARE

	Issue	Current	Cost/Date
• **Freezicles - "Star Trek"** Catalog Shoppe, 1975 Six reusable plastic ice treat molds. Two each of Kirk, Spock and McCoy. Boxed set includes mixing and measuring cup, Heinz fruit concentrate mix and 20 individual sticks. Box cartoon illos children enjoying molded treats.	3	10-15	_____
• **Flashlight - "Star Trek The Motion Picture Light Beam"** General Mills, 1979 Blue plastic, palm-size flashlight, 3¾" long with yellow "Star Trek" lettering on both sides. Uses 2-AA batteries.[6]	1	3-4	_____

6. This plastic promotional item was advertised as a special coupon offer from General Mills on the box-backs of Cheerios Cereal. It was never available through retail.

BAR ACCESSORIES

Issue | Current | Cost/Date

• Lunchboxes

"Star Trek"
Aladdin Industries, 1968
Dome-style metal lunch paid with twin clasp metal fasteners. Sidepanels have detailed cartoon scene of starboard profile t.v. Enterprise beneath a ringed planet. Metal soup-style thermos cartoons kneeling Spock and Kirk, as they employ the rarely seen t.v. phaser rifle. . . . 2 45-60 ______

"Star Trek", Aladdin Industries, 1978
Square black plastic lunch pail in solid color vinyl. Front panel illos portside t.v. Enterprise, ringed planet, sun-burst, standing Spock and a bust of Kirk. Soup-style thermos is also plastic and has lettering and starboard profile starship. . . . . 5 20-30 ______

"Star Trek The Motion Picture",
King-Seely Thermos Co., 1979
Square metal lunch pail. Sidepanels show artist's rendering of Kirk and Spock busts, Letter Logo and front-view STTMP Enterprise. Thermos is plastic with a blue and white paper decal of the starship. . . . . 6 15-20 ______

• Magnetic Holders

Star Fleet Headquarters Decal
New Eye, Distrib. 1986
Giant 12" diameter SFC emblem with magnetic backing, for refrigerators, etc. . . . . 12 12-13 ______

Tribble
Lincoln Enterprises, 1975
Furry tribble with magnetic backing. Used as a membership gift.[7] . . — 1-2 ______

Serving Tray - "Star Trek The Motion Picture", 1979
Metal snack/t.v. tray with collapsible tube legs, features photo of Mr. Spock wearing t.v. uniform, although letter reads movie Logo format. . . . . 6 8-10 ______

PARTY WARE

Tuttle Press, 1976
Birthday Cake Topper
Ten edible candy rosebuds and a cardstock centerpiece for cake.

Issue | Current | Cost/Date

design features color cartoon of t.v. Enterprise and running figures with captions: "Dr. McCoy", "Captain Kirk" and "Mr. Spock". Lettering reads "Happy Birthday." Plastic wrapped set backed with cardboard. 2 3-4 ______

Cups
Eight disposable 7 oz. paper party cups featuring the busts only of McCoy, Kirk and Spock, plus t.v. Enterprise. Stacked in plastic wrap. 1.50 3-4 ______

Napkins
Disposable paper napkins to match the other items in the party seet, action scene is the same, but shows only ¾ of the starship:
6½"x6½" Cocktail size (set of 20). 1 3-4 ______
13"x13¼" Dinner size (set of 16). . 1.50 3-4 ______

Plates
White paper plates with color cartoon of t.v. Enterprise over running trio of McCoy, Kirk and Spock. Plastic wrapped:
6" diameter Cake plates (set of 8) . . 1.50 3-4 ______
8" diameter Dinner plates (set of 8) 2 3-4 ______

Tablecloth
Disposable paper tablecloth with a repeating cartoon pattern to match the party set placesettings above, except that busts of the individual Kirk, Spock and McCoy characters are added to the running action-scenes, 54"x88".[8] . . . . 5 7-10 ______

LIVING ROOM DECOR

• Chairs

Inflatable Chair - "Mr. Spock"
K-Mart, 1979
STTMP vintage toy featuring a cartoon imprint of Spock on children's toy chair. Floor bag with arms. 5 10-12

Director's Chair - "The Official Star Trek IV - The Voyage Home', Star Trek Official Fan Club, 1987
White metal-framed director's chair with ST IV Letter Logo and "Star Date: 1986, How On Earth Can They Save the Future?". Blue cloth seat and back. Requires assembly. . 49 50-52 ______

7. This promotional trinket was used as a give-away to the first 1,000 fan members to join Lincoln Enterprises' Star Trek Animated Fan Club (STAFC) which featured updates on the cartoon series during the 1970's. Tribble magnets were free with the $5.50 annual membership fee.
8. The "Star Trek" lettering that appears throughout this paper party set follows the Gold Key Comics letter logo used during the same period.

LIVING ROOM DECOR

Issue | Current | Cost/Date

• Clocks

Alarm Clock - "Star Trek", 1984
Standard alarm clock with large face featuring photo of Kirk, McCoy and Spock, time set and alarm set, second hand.[9] . . . . — 10-15 ______

Star Trek Alarm Clock, 1984

Travel Clock - Insignia Design, Sweda, 1983
Lincoln Enterprises, distrib.
Fold-out travel clock that compacts to fit inside a wallet. Gold-tone finish, digital display and alarm. Includes a leatherette carrying case and jeweler's battery. "Star Trek" version was sold with a plain Command Star Insignia in gold color, mounted in upper left hand corner.. 24.95 25-26 ______

Wall Clock - "Star Trek", ASA, Inc., 1974
Kitchen style clock with 8" diameter face. Plastic case has deep outer rim. Starfield faceplate has lettering over a very stylized t.v. Enterprise firing twin phaser banks. Electric cord is attached. . . . . — 25-35 ______

Wall Clock - "Official 20th Anniversary"
Star Trek Official Fan Club, 1987
Round, kitchen clock with white base and face and red lettering "1966-1986 Star Trek 20-years" official Letter Logo. Movement is analog-quartz. . . . . 28 28-30 ______

• Collector Plates, Ernst Enterprises

Separate collection series of porcelain glass wall plates featuring the original artwork of artist Susie Morton. Series features limited edition, numbered, certified plates that come with registration certificates. Boxed in plain white cardboard shipping packages.

"Star Trek-Collector Plate Series 1984
Eight plate series released in portrature form for the individual stars of the t.v. series. 8½" diameter plates have blue-starred borders reading "The Voyages of the Starship Enterprise . . . To Boldly Go Where No Man Has Gone Before." 90-day firing period.

Issue | Current | Cost/Date

No. 1, July 1984
"Mr. Spock" with t.v. Enterprise. . . 29.50 30-32 ______
No. 2, August 1984
"Dr. McCoy" with backdrop laboratory . . . . 29.50 30-32 ______

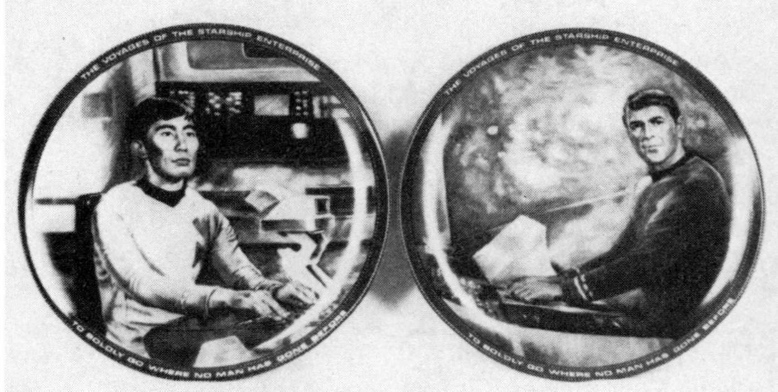

No. 3, October 1984
"Mr. Sulu" at the helm (shows 1st season remote viewer extention device) . . . . 29.50 30-32 ______
No. 4, December 1984
"Scotty" at the transporter console. 29.50 30-32 ______

No. 5, February 1985
"Uhura" at the communications station . . . . 29.50 30-32 ______
No. 6, April 1985
"Chekov" at the helm, Romulan Bird of Prey vessel on the viewscreen . . . . 29.50 30-32 ______

9. The same faceplate appears on a Star Trek theme wristwatch and pocket watch. (See Jewelry listings.)

	Issue	Current	Cost/Date
No. 7, July 1985 "Captain Kirk" over collage of planet, K-7 Space Station and Enterprise	29.50	30-32	_____
No. 8, August 1985 "Beam Us Down, Scotty" transporter room scene with all seven previous characters	29.50	30-32	_____

"Enterprise" Collector Plate

"Star Trek - Commemorative Plate Series", 1986
Beginning of a new series of plates to commemorate the favorite episodes of Star Trek on television, beginning in the year of the 20th Anniversary. 8½" diameter plates feature 24K gold borders with eight miniature etchings of the Enterprise. 90 day firing period.

	Issue	Current	Cost/Date
No. 1, December 1986 "The Trouble With Tribbles" showing Kirk in the famous pile-up of furry creatures	29.50	30-32	_____

"Star Trek- Enterprise Collector Plate"
10¼" diameter plate with gold border, art shows t.v. Enterprise over planet with comet trail containing head portraits of the above seven characters, two releases:

	Issue	Current	Cost/Date
Original Issue - October 1985, as described	39.50	40-42	_____
Signature Edition - 20th Anniversary release, same as above but with additional signatures from the stars in 24K etching on the reverse, along with "Space, the final frontier . . ." legend. Limited 7-day firing period, December 1986.	45	45-47	_____

	Issue	Current	Cost/Date
•**Curtains,** Pacific Mills, 1975 Standard window width curtains in 83" length. Dark blue fabric features cartoon t.v. Enterprise on starfield with Saturn-like planet and busts of Kirk and Spock. Plastic wrapped with cut-away cardstock illo.	—	12-18	_____

Light switch plates, 1985

• **Lighting**

	Issue	Current	Cost/Date
Light Fixture - Enterprise, Prestigeline, Inc. Globe-style swag lamp which replicates a stylized starship. Three-tier metal tubing assembly forms the ship's body and ends in three glass domes. The saucer rises up above these structures on a metal strut. Length 14". Tube suspension rod connects the swag chain and camouflages the electrical cord and plug	79.95	90-115	_____

Light Switch Plate - "Star Flite #   "
American Tack and Hardware Co., 1985
Two different Enterprise-like ships featured on plastic, single-switch wall plate covers. Measure 4½"x5":

	Issue	Current	Cost/Date
Style 1 - Red and yellow Enterprise over a blue planet, backing is 3-D, puffy vinyl.	2.40	3-4	_____
Style 2 - Green Enterprise-like ship with a third added nacelle in the middle, over orange planet, neon-glo paint.	2.40	3-4	_____

"Space Ship Mobile" Note the three Nacelles

	Issue	Current	Cost/Date
• **Mirrors,** Lightline Industries, 1977 Glass mirrors with choice of two character decals in black and silver:			
Kirk	7	12-16	_____
Spock	7	12-16	_____

• **Mobiles**

	Issue	Current	Cost/Date
"Space Ship Mobile #M-312" B.J.C. International, Inc., 1979, Canada Decorator mobile featuring six silver plastic Enterprise-like ships with an added third nacelle attached to the upper portion of rear end of the saucer. Ships measure 3" long. Boxed 3½"x18" silver and blue package. Mobile designer A.Y. Sung	4	5-8	_____
"Space Ship Mobile #N/MO 116-6", Japan Decorator mobile featuring six silver plastic Enterprises identical to ones listed above. Box is 3½"x16" and is black with a white starfield overlay.	4	5-8	_____

• **Plants**

	Issue	Current	Cost/Date
Vulcan Aralia, April Publications, 1984 Living house plant with deep green, wavy leaves and star-like flowers. Plant is reported to be sacred to the Vulcan Masters who use its orange fruits to make wine. Packet containing 20 seeds.	3	3-4	_____
Vulcan Pon Farr Plant April Publications, 1984 Living house plant which reportedly symbolizes the Vulcan mating season, growing instructions included, 15 seeds per packet.	3	3-4	_____

	Issue	Current	Cost/Date
Vulcan Firefly Clip-ons Lincoln Enterprises, 1984 Colorful winged-creatures to adorn your indoor or outdoor garden, or ckip on to any household decor. Reputed to be butterflies of Mt. Seleya on Vulcan. Different colors and patterns insure no two are alike. Choice of sizes:			
Extra Small, 4½"	4.95	5-6	_____
Small, 8"	7.95	8-9	_____
Medium, 11"	9.95	10-11	_____
Large, 15"	14.95	15-16	_____
Extra Large, 23"	19.95	20-21	_____
• **Rugs - Star Trek,** 1976 Synthetic fur throw rugs featuring t.v. cartoon imprints in four styles:			
Bridge action	—	10-15	_____
Action scene collage	—	10-15	_____
Enterprise with Crew- ship firing photon torpedos on a Klingon Cruiser with portrait insets of Spock, Kirk, McCoy, Uhura, Scotty and Sulu mounted inside starbursts.	—	15-25	_____
Enterprise Starship	—	15-20	_____
• **Statues- Lucite Enterprise,** Starlog Magazine, 1985 Limited edition of 5,000 Enterprise models sculptured in crystal clear lucite, hand-polished, includes lucite pedestal display base, measures 7½"x12", weighs 1½ lbs. [10]	29.95	30-35	_____
• **Trashcan - Enterprise and Shuttle Design,** Cheinco, 1977 Metal wastepaper basket featuring t.v. starship and the shuttlecraft Galileo, now reads "NCC-1701, U.S.S. Enterprise" below the illo. Reverse side shows smaller version starship and provides stats and information on the ship	6	12-16	_____

10. The advertisement for this desk-top decorative model pictured the starship with its two nacelles mounted backwards.

ID's

Star Trek fans have always displayed their affection for Star Trek and its characters openly. Of all science fiction genres, Star Trek has been an especially viable medium for the production of token advertisements which proclaim its popularity through assorted cloth, paper or steel constructed expressions of devotion. ID articles, whatever their type, identify a fan and visually associate him or her with Star Trek legions.

There are literally thousands of ID collectibles for an avid collector to acquire. It would be impossible to list them all. Approximately 95% are fan produced, the remaining 5% being professionally issued to small business retailers or catalog traders. The basic types available are:

Badges – Usually card stock calling cards of assorted colors and sizes. They may be slipped into clear plastic pin holders or sold separately in sets. Size 2½" x 3" or 2¾" x 3½".

Buttons – Buttons come in assorted sizes from 1½" diameter to giant-sized 3" diameters. The most common size is 2¼". They are usually laminated with a thin pliable plastic over the design face. The entire affair is crimp-pressed around a circular metal disk with a self-contained latch clip. Button clips for attaching to apparel may either be horizontal, safety-pin types or a cheaper stick-pin variety which rotates along the inner lip of the button's reverse.

Cards – Another name for ID badges.

Membership I.D.'s – These are usually small cardstock cards which indicate a fan's affiliation with a particular Star Trek club or official character fan club. They may or may not display photo insets of the representative actor or actress.

Money – Occasionally some very interesting funny money memorabilia has appeared which toots Star Trek affiliations. A very desirable collectible of this type is the set of personality dollar bills made of uncirculated U.S. tender which were offered through an ad in *Starlog Magazine.*

Patches – Thread design motifs on a heavy cloth backing. Sizes and shapes can vary from circular, oval, rectangular or square. Some patches may be cloth cut-outs. Primarily used as clothing novelties which are sewn on to shirts, jackets or pants.

Transfers – There are two types of transfers, either decal or iron-on. Decal transfers simply reproduce a reverse image onto cloth via heat sensitive dyes. Iron-on transfers actually attach the original design onto the cloth surfaces with heat-bonded glues. Transfers may also be photographic images reproduced from film footage or artwork images.

Stickers – These are produced as bumper stickers (usually 2¼"x11") or as smaller sizes designed for application on any flat surface. Both appear as unlettered design stickers or as clever slogan collectibles. Sticker collection sets are also available.

Wall hangings - This category is comprised of larger ID's used as decorative displays. Certificates, flags, plaques and signs all appear in this area of memorabilia specialties. Aside from the the many fan issue certificates being produced, fan club certificates represent interesting collectibles.

Assorted Fan Club I.D. Cards from L.N.N.A.F.

Buttons

Star Trek has been no stranger to the common circular advertising craze found throughout science fiction fandom. Buttons have been, and always will be, one of the most popular promotional medias for a display of Star Trek's popularity. For this reason, buttons deserve special mention.

Some of the first buttons to appear tooting Star Trek themes were those produced by the Leonard Nimoy National Association of Fans which was founded in October 1967. Their club newsletters offered original logo buttons. The first photo style buttons appeared in the early 1970's. Langley Associates became the first retail dealership for this type of Star Trek button and produced an extensive line of buttons featuring full color cast or guest star close-ups from T.V. Trek, as well as selective spacecraft and alien planetscapes.

Such vintage buttons are good collectibles. With the advent of the motion pictures, the diversity of Star Trek buttons of all kinds has accelerated. Besides **slogan** buttons from fan clubs and fan traders, there are also **artwork** buttons which may be one-of-a-kind drawing miniatures. Some of these are nothing more than mimeographed sketches that are converted to color when button-makers dress them up with colored markers right on the spot.

Photo buttons appear as different types as well. Many fan produced buttons featuring action scenes or character profiles are **photo snips.** They are nothing more than picture cut-outs from old science fiction magazines or promotional advertisements. Still other photo buttons are produced from special light defraction paper which gives the button image a sparkling, multi-colored appearance. These are **gimmick** buttons and are nice additions to a button collector's steel and latch-clip memorabilia.

Star Trek III Photo Buttons and T.V. Series Style, Button Up, 1984

Assorted Fan Issue Slogan Buttons

Taco Bell Buttons, 1984

Assorted Photo Button types. Photo snips, gimmick & hand colored. Spock in lower left is from Langley Assoc.

Badges and Cards

	Issue	Current	Cost/Date
•**Badges and Cards** **Business Cards - Star Trek** April Publications, 1984 Collector's series, colorful raised letter printing on Lusterkote card stock, 2½"x3". Four different sets:			
Set No. 1 includes ten cards: Captain Kirk Mr. Spock Dr. McCoy Scotty Lieutenant Uhura Cyrano Jones! Harry Mudd Bela Oxmyx Kang Gery Seven	1.25	1-2	_____
Set No. 2, includes ten cards: Lieutenant Sulu Ensign Chekov Nurse Chapel Yeoman Janice Rand Landru T'Pring Edith Keeler Sarek of Vulcan Korob and Sylvia Koloth	1.25	1-2	_____
Set No. 3, includes ten cards: Captain Pike Lt. Kevin Riley T'Pau Apollo Trelane Nomad Vaal Hengist Miramanee Garth of Izar	1.25	1-2	_____
Set No. 4, includes ten cards: Admiral Kirk Spock of Vulcan Dr. McCoy, Retired Commander Decker Lieutenant Ilia Dr. Chapel Chief Janice Rand Sonak Admiral Nogura Commander Branch	1.25	1-2	_____

BADGES AND CARDS

	Issue	Current	Cost/Date
• Computer Identification Cards - Star Trek, April Publications			
Set of 8 wallet-sized cards designed to resemble computer-issue cards, black on white card stock, 2½"x3".			
Command Center			
Data #912			
Main Mission #010			
Medical #714			
Security #586			
Technical #254			
Visitor #351			
Sold as set of 8 cards	6.50	7-8	_____
Laminated card with spring clip (you send in your personal I.D. photo) See listing.			
• Identification Badges, April Publications			
Assorted card stock badges in plastic mount holder with secure-lock pin back for wearing on clothing, approximately 2½"x3".			
Enterprise Boarding Pass	1	1-2	_____
Radiation Detector/Engineering Dept.	1	1-2	_____
Regula I Boarding Pass	1	1-2	_____
Regula I Computer Access Pass	1	1-2	_____
Starfleet Cadet I.D.	1	1-2	_____
Starfleet Command Security Pass	1	1-2	_____
Starfleet Division First Aid Certificate	1	1-2	_____
Starfleet Divisional I.D.	1	1-2	_____
Starfleet Headquarters Access Pass	1	1-2	_____
United Federation of Planets	1	1-2	_____
U.S.S. Reliant Planet Exploration	1	1-2	_____
Vulcan Science Academy	1	1-2	_____
• Identification Badges T-K Graphics, 1984			
Assorted ID cards on colored cardstock, displayed in plastic holders with pinback clip, 2¾"x3½".			
Enterprise Shuttle Pilot	1.25	1-2	_____
Imperial Klingon Navy	1.25	1-2	_____
Klingon Diplomatic Corps	1.25	1-2	_____
Star Fleet Academy (UFP Emblem)	1.25	1-2	_____
Star Fleet Command Security Pass	1.25	1-2	_____
Star Fleet Drydock Security Pass	1.25	1-2	_____
Star Fleet Headquarters Access Pass	1.25	1-2	_____
Star Fleet Intelligence Division	1.25	1-2	_____
Star Fleet Recruiting Office (UFP Pennant)	1.25	1-2	_____
Star Fleet Transporter Technician	1.25	1-2	_____
Tribble Inspector	1.25	1-2	_____
UFP Diplomatic Service (UPF Emblem)	1.25	1-2	_____
U.S.S. Enterprise Boarding Pass	1.25	1-2	_____
U.S.S. Enterprise Computer Section	1.25	1-2	_____
U.S.S Enterprise Medical Sections	1.25	1-2	_____
Vulcan Science Academy Visitor's Pass	1.25	1-2	_____

	Issue	Current	Cost/Date
• Identification Cards - Star Trek April Publications, 1983			
Raised lettering on wallet-sized cards of assorted colors with space for adding your name or your photo. 12 different sets available:			
Set No. 1, includes five cards: Starship Captain, Phaser License, Vulcan Academy Membership, Klingon Identification, Galactic Passport	1	1-2	_____
Set No. 2, includes five cards: Starfleet Admiral, Vulcan Master, Air Team Pass, Vulcan Kolinahr Card, Deltan Identification	1	1-2	_____
Set No. 3, includes five cards: Enterprise Boarding Pass, Tribble License, Vulcan Identification, Starfleet Security Card, Library Card - Memory Alpha	1	1-2	_____
Set No. 4, includes five cards: Enterprise Crew Identification, Starfleet Command Identification, Envoy-Babel Conference, Science Officer Identification, Vulcan Blood Donor Card	1	1-2	_____
Set No. 5, includes five cards: Starfleet Officer's Club, Vulcan Space Central, Federation Immunization Card, Starfleet Draft Card, Phaser Marksmanship Card	1	1-2	_____
Set No. 6, includes five cards: Starfleet Academy I. D., Federation Ambassador, Communications Officer I. D., Import License - Saurian Brandy, Membership - Tribble Society	1	1-2	_____
Set No. 7,includes five cards: Medical Officer Identification, Federation Social Security Card, Sub-Space Radio Operator License, Space Trader License, Cabaret Card - Rigel IV	1	1-2	_____
Set No. 8,includes five cards: Vulcan Officer's Club, Starship Engineering License, Klingon War Academy, Shuttlecraft Operator License, Horta Mining License	1	1-2	_____
Set No. 9,includes five cards: Vulcan Ambassador, Starfleet Commodore, Class A-7 Computer Expert, Federation Diplomatic Courier Tribble Breeders Association	1	1-2	_____

BADGES AND CARDS

	Issue	Current	Cost/Date
Set No. 10, includes five cards: Starship First Officer Vulcan Passport Starfleet Academy Honor Society Orion Slave Trader Sehlat Kennel Club	1	1-2	_____
Set No. 11, includes five cards: Starfleet Medical I.D. Card Vulcan Academy Honor Society Starship Passenger's Association Klingon War Crimes Tribunal Mugato Hunting License	1	1-2	_____
Set No. 12, includes five cards: Vulcan Space Trader Enterprise 3-D Chess Club Phaser Sharpshooters Team Restricted Area Pass Federation Diplomatic Corps	1	1-2	_____

• **"Starfleet Divisional ID" Cards - Star Trek**
April Publications
2½"x3" card stock badges which include space for photo, name, rank and status, read "Starfleet Divisional I.D.". Each card has the appropriate printed insignia for its job description, UFP Janus Head Emblem in bottom corner.
Command
Engineering
Medical
Science
Ship Personnel
Star Base

	Issue	Current	Cost/Date
Sold as a set of 6 cards	5.50	5-6	_____

Laminated card with spring clip (you send in your personal I.D. photo)
See listing.

• **Star Fleet Laminated ID Badges**
New Eye, 1986
You send in a personal photo and they will laminate it for you on authentic-looking military ID cards. Read: name, rank and reserve status. Available in many of those identification previously listed:

	Issue	Current	Cost/Date
All six "Starfleet Divisional ID" cards Each, including spring clip	5	5-6	_____
All eight "Computer Identification" cards Each, including spring clip	5	5-6	_____
Plus: Vulcan Science Academy Visitor Pass	5	5-6	_____
Star Fleet Headquarters Access Pass	5	5-6	_____

• **Wallet Identification Cards**
Assorted I.D. cards printed on colored stock, 2"x3":

	Issue	Current	Cost/Date
Imperial Klingon Navy Intelligence	.25	.50-1	_____
Intergalactic union of Transporter Operators and Technicians Member	.25	.50-1	_____
North American Tribble Breeder's Assoc.	.25	.50-1	_____
Phaser Permit	.25	.50-1	_____
Starbase 13X Card	.25	.50-1	_____
Star Fleet Command Intelligence Division	.25	.50-1	_____
Star Fleet Library	.25	.50-1	_____
Star Fleet Medical Association	.25	.50-1	_____
Star Fleet Officer's Association	.25	.50-1	_____
Star Fleet Security	.25	.50-1	_____
Star Fleet Tri-Dimensional Chess Club	.25	.50-1	_____
UFP Diplomatic Service	.25	.50-1	_____
UFP Intelligence	.25	.50-1	_____
UFP Voter Registration	.25	.50-1	_____
Vulcan Diplomatic Service	.25	.50-1	_____
Vulcan Science Academy Student I.D.	.25	.50-1	_____

Photo Buttons

	Issue	Current	Cost/Date
• **Crew Photo Promotional Button** Paramount Pictures, 1974 3¼" x 2¼" rectangle in metal, black and white photo of bridge crew from the t.v. series: Chekov, McCoy, Scotty, Spock and Kirk (seated).	1	3-4	_____
• **Enterprise Schematic** Blue and white button with blue outline of t.v. Enterprise, above blue starfield, bottom reads "Star Trek" in white letters, rotating clip pinback, 1¼" diameter	.50	1-2	_____
• **Spock Photo Button** 1973 Metal with clasp back pin, small black and white photo or Mr. Spock on silver background, 1½" diameter	.25	1-2	_____
• **Spock and Kirk Photo Button Promo** Paramount Pictures Corp, 1966 Color, blue background with black and white photo cut-outs of Spock and Kirk from t.v. series, block letters in white above the profiles reads "Star Trek", 2¼" diameter	.25	2-4	_____

PHOTO BUTTONS

	Issue	Current	Cost/Date
Star Trek Character Photo Buttons			
Lincoln Enterprises, 1976			
Colorful photo buttons featuring portraits from the t.v. series, words "Star Trek" lettered on top with names of the characters beside pictures, 2¼" diameters:			
2470A Kirk	1	1-3	_____
2470B Spock	1	1-3	_____
2470C Dr. McCoy	1	1-3	_____
2470D Scotty	1	1-3	_____
2470E Uhura	1	1-3	_____
2470F Sulu	1	1-3	_____
2470G Chekov	1	1-3	_____
2470H Chapel	1	1-3	_____
2470I Enterprise	1	1-3	_____
• **Star Trek Episode Photo Buttons**			
Assorted Themes and sizes available:			
• **Button-Up Company,** 1984			
Assorted color photo buttons with scenes from t.v. episodes, "Star Trek" appears in white letters along rims or near edges, 1½" diameter:			
Enterprise with second Federation ship	1	1-2	_____
Kirk with communicator	1	1-2	_____
Kirk and Spock in civilian clothes	1	1-2	_____
Sulu, close-up	1	1-2	_____
• **Langley Associates,** 1976			
60 assorted 2¼" diameter full color photos in laminate. Only one button shows lettering, all were officially authorized by PPC.			
1 "Star Trek" title credit with Enterprise	.50	2-4	_____
2 Enterprise firing twin phasers	.50	2-4	_____
3 Enterprise counterclockwise over blue planet	.50	2-4	_____
4 Enterprise clockwise over green planet	.50	2-4	_____
5 Enterprise counterclockwise between magenta planet and its moon	.50	2-4	_____
6 Enterprise apporaching Amoeba (IS)	.50	2-4	_____
7 Romulan Bird of Prey (BT)	.50	2-4	_____
8 Klingon Cruiser	.50	2-4	_____
9 Spock, close-up, in dress uniform	.50	2-4	_____
10 Spock, close-up regular uniform	.50	2-4	_____
11 Spock, laughing (Blooper)	.50	2-4	_____
12 Alternate universe bearded Spock (MM)	.50	2-4	_____
13 Kirk, close-up, in dress uniform	.50	2-4	_____
14 Kirk, close-up	.50	2-4	_____
15 Kirk, buried in tribbles	.50	2-4	_____
16 McCoy, close-up	.50	2-4	_____
17 Scotty, close-up	.50	2-4	_____
18 Chekov at Science Station	.50	2-4	_____
19 Sulu at Helm with remote viewer extension	.50	2-4	_____
20 Uhura at station	.50	2-4	_____
21 Spock, close-up	.50	2-4	_____
22 Natira, close-up (FW)	.50	2-4	_____
23 Spock, close-up	.50	2-4	_____
24 Sarek, close-up (JB)	.50	2-4	_____
25 Sulu, close-up	.50	2-4	_____
26 Romulan Cdr. male, close-up (BT)	.50	2-4	_____
27 Romulan Cdr., female, close-up (EI)	.50	2-4	_____
28 Shuttle docking	.50	2-4	_____
29 Marta, close-up (WGD)	.50	2-4	_____
30 Spock, at station	.50	2-4	_____
31 Chekov and Security Guards	.50	2-4	_____
32 Vina, close-up (Me)	.50	2-4	_____
33 Kirk, on transporter pad	.50	2-4	_____
34 Zarabeth, close-up (AY)	.50	2-4	_____
35 Odona, close-up (MG)	.50	2-4	_____
36 Spock, close-up	.50	2-4	_____
37 Balock's dummy (CMn)	.50	2-4	_____
38 Sulu, close-up	.50	2-4	_____
39 Janice Rand, close-up (CX)	.50	2-4	_____
40 Balok's dummy, close-up (CMn)	.50	2-4	_____
41 Keeper, close-up (Me)	.50	2-4	_____
42 Deela, close-up (WE)	.50	2-4	_____
43 Sylvia, close-up (Cp)	.50	2-4	_____
44 Spock, close-up	.50	2-4	_____
45 Chekov, close-up	.50	2-4	_____
46 McCoy, close-up in Med Tunic	.50	2-4	_____
47 Kor, close-up (EM)	.50	2-4	_____
48 Nurse Chapel, close-up	.50	2-4	_____
48 Losira, close-up (TWS)	.50	2-4	_____
50 Chekov, close-up	.50	2-4	_____
51 McCoy, close-up	.50	2-4	_____
52 Kang, close-up (Dv)	.50	2-4	_____
53 Ruk and Kirk, close-up (LG)	.50	2-4	_____
54 Kahn, close-up (SS)	.50	2-4	_____
55 Alternate universe Marlana Moreau (MM)	.50	2-4	_____
56 Zephram Cochrane, close-up (Mt)	.50	2-4	_____
57 Spock, close-up of his smile (TSP)	.50	2-4	_____
58 Uhura at her station (MM)	.50	2-4	_____
59 Shras, close-up (JB)	.50	2-4	_____
60 Kirk with communicator, close-up	.50	2-4	_____
• **Star Trek The Motion Picture Photo Buttons**			
Aviva, 1979			
Set of seven 2¼" diameter full color enameled buttons. Each has "Star Trek" lettering in new design movie logo on top of the photo:			
1 Admiral Kirk, close-up	1	1-2	_____
2 Kirk, right profile	1	1-2	_____
3 Spock, McCoy and Kirk (seated)	1	1-2	_____
4 Spock, waist-shot, in Vulcan robes	1	1-2	_____
5 Spock, in regulation uniform	1	1-2	_____
6 Eleven members STTMP bridge crew	.50	2-4	_____
7 Admiral Kirk, walking	1	1-2	_____

PHOTO BUTTONS

	Issue	Current	Cost/Date
• Starpost			
2¼" diameter full color photo buttons, laminated:			
Kirk	.69	1-2	______
Spock	.69	1-2	______
Kirk and Spock	.69	1-2	______
Ilia	.69	1-2	______
Chapel	.69	1-2	______
Rand	.69	1-2	______
• Star Trek: The Wrath of Kahn Photo Button Set			
Image Products, Inc., 1982			
Starlog, distributors			
Set of five 3" full color enameled photo buttons, each has letter logo over photo:			
1 Admiral Kirk, close-up	1.20	2-3	______
2 Spock garbed in Vulcan robes, lettering reads "Spock Lives!"	1.20	2-3	______
3 Kahn, close-up	1.20	2-3	______
4 Full nine member STWOK bridge crew	1.20	2-3	______
5 Front view Enterprise	1.20	2-3	______
Price for complete set of five buttons	6	8-10	______
• Star Trek: The Search For Spock Photo Buttons			
Button-Up Company, 1984			
Assorted color buttons featuring the crw, aliens and Klingons of the movie cast, each has a logo reading "Star Trek III" appearing somewhere on its circumference in white letters or black, 1½" diameter:			
Chekov, facing right, close-up	1	1-2	______
Kirk, looking left, close-up	1	1-2	______
Kirk, in uniform	1	1-2	______
Kruge, close-up with red tint	1	1-2	______
Kruge, in command chair	1	1-2	______
Marcus, close-up, black lettering	1	1-2	______
McCoy, close-up with blue tint	1	1-2	______
Saavik, close-up	1	1-2	______
Spock, close-up in white robe	1	1-2	______
Spock, looking left in white robe	1	1-2	______
Sulu, close-up looking upward	1	1-2	______
Uhura, pointing phaser, black lettering	1	1-2	______
• Starpost, distributors			
Two different sets, in different sizes:			
2¼" diameter button:			
David and Saavik	.79	1-2	______
Enterprise	.79	1-2	______
Kirk	.79	1-2	______
Kirk and McCoy	.79	1-2	______
Kirk and landing party on Genesis planet	.79	1-2	______
Kirk and Kruge	.79	1-2	______
Kruge	.79	1-2	______
McCoy	.79	1-2	______
Saavik	.79	1-2	______
Sarek	.79	1-2	______
Spock	.79	1-2	______
Sulu	.79	1-2	______
Uhura	.79	1-2	______
3" diameter full color photo buttons, laminated:			
Chekov	.99	1-3	______
David Marcus	.99	1-3	______
Group on planet Vulcan	.99	1-3	______
Kirk	.99	1-3	______
Kir, Chekov and Scotty	.99	1-3	______
Kirk and landing party on Genesis planet	.99	1-3	______
Kirk and Kruge	.99	1-3	______
Klingon Bird of Prey	.99	1-3	______
Kruge	.99	1-3	______
McCoy	.99	1-3	______
Saavik	.99	1-3	______
Sarek	.99	1-3	______
Sulu	.99	1-3	______
Uhura	.99	1-3	______
U.S.S. Excelsior	.99	1-3	______
U.S.S. Grissom	.99	1-3	______

Slogan Buttons

	Issue	Current	Cost/Date
• April Publications, 1984			
2¼" diameter buttons (unless noted), plastic laminated with metal safety pinbacks, each	1	1-2	______
He Touched Me (Shows profile of Spock giving Vulcan Salute)			______
I have Been Where No Man Has Gone Before			______
I Studied With The Vulcan Masters			______
My Tribble Loves Me			______
Spock It To Me [1]			______
Vulcan Power			______
• Button Up, 1986			
1½" diameter slogan pin, plastic laminated with safety pin latch, black lettering on square, yellow background with blue, lined edging, comes clipped to yellow cardstock back designed for counter rack display,			
Beam Me Up, Scotty!	1	.75-1	______
• Fan Issue			
Assorted slogan buttons produced by fan retailers and distributors, all are 2¼" diameter unless noted, plastic laminated of varying qualities, safety pin latch,			
Each,	1	.75-1	______
And The Adventure Continues			______
Battle Alert			______
Beam Me Up Scotty			______

1. "Sock It To Me!" was the slogan cry of the comedy entertainment series Rowan and Martin's Laugh-In which aired in the early 1970s. This Star Trek derivative has its roots here.

SLOGAN BUTTONS

	Issue	Current Cost/Date
Beam Me Up Scotty, There's No Intelligent Life On This Planet		______
Beware of Romulans Bearing Gifts		______
Can I Cook, Or Can't I?		______
Closet Trekkie		______
Did I Get It Right?		______
Don't Call Me Tiny		______
Exhilarating, Isn't It?		______
Fascinating		______
Feed Him!		______
Federation Funny Farm		______
Fruity As A Nut Cake		______
Give The Word		______
Good Morning, Captain		______
Graduate of Harry Mudd's School of Business Ethics		______
Hailing Frequencies Open		______
He's Dead Jim		______
He's So Human		______
Hell of A Time To Ask		______
Hey, Do You Want To Play With My Phaser?		______
His Was The Most Human		______
How Can You Be Deaf With Ears Like That?		______
How Many Fingers?		______
I AM A Trekker		______
I Don't Believe in the No-Win Scenario		______
I Failed the Kobayashi-Maru Test		______
I Lied		______
I Love Chekov		______
Jim Kirk		______
McCoy		______
Scotty		______
Spock		______
Sulu		______
Uhura		______
I'm A Deforest Kelley Fan		______
I'm A George Takei Fan		______
I'm A James Doohan Fan		______
I'm A Leonard Nimoy Fan		______
I'm A Nichelle Nichols Fan		______
I'm A Walter Koenig Fan		______
I'm A William Shatner Fan		______
I'm Dead Jim		______
I Never Forget A Face		______
I Only Use It For Medicinal Purposes		______
I Passed The Kobayashi-Maru Test		______
I Wanted Prisoners!		______
Illogical But Fascinating		______
It Is Time For Total Truth		______
It's Not Logical		______
I've Missed You		______
Jim Kirk Was Never A Boy Scout		______
Just A Wee Bit Of Shore Leave		______
Klingons Don't Take Prisoners		______
Let Them Eat Static!		______

	Issue	Current Cost/Date
May The Wind Be At Your Back		______
McCoy, Leonard H. Son of David		______
Nothing Happening Here		______
Old Trekkers Never Die, They Just Warp Out		______
Price You Name, Money I Got		______
Project Genesis		______
Rebuild The Enterprise		______
Remember The Enterprise		______
Revenge Of The Tribbles		______
Sit In The Closet		______
Spock, Get Me The Hell Out Of Here		______
Spock Lives		______
Star Trek Forever (black lettering on blue with UFP logo)		______
Star Trek Lives. Paramount Is Dead		______
Target Engines Only		______
That Green Blooded Son of A Bitch		______
The Word Is No. Therefore I Am Going Anyway.		______
The More They Overthing the Plumbing, The Easier It Is To Stop The Drain		______
The Needs Of The One Outweigh The Needs Of The Many		______
The Spirit Of The Enterprise Lives On		______
This Button Boldly Goes Where No Button Has Gone Before		______
This Is The Hind End Of Space		______
This Isn't Reality. This Is Fantasy.		______
Up Your Shaft		______
U.S.S. Botany Bay		______
Waiting For Star Trek III		______
Waiting For Star Trek IV		______
Who's Been Holding Up The Damn Elevator?		______
You Have Been And Always Will Be My Friend.		______

• **LNNAF** (Leonard Nimoy National Associaton of Fans)
Special slogan buttons available through club membership during the years 1969-1971, 1½" diameter with stick pin backs.

	Issue	Current	Cost/Date
I Grok Mr. Spock, 1969, black lettering on bright green [2]	.25	2-4	______
Star Trek Lives! 1971, black letters on orange, the official button of the 1972 Star Trek Con,	.35	2-3	______
Turn On To Nimoy, 1969, green lettering on white, slogan runs in circles [3]	.15	3-4	______
What's A Leonard Nimoy? 1969, black lettering on white. [4]	.25	3-4	______

2. The term "Grok" originated in the early 1970's with the very popular science fiction novel *Stranger In A Strange Land* written by Robert Heinlein. The slogan button "I Grok Mr. Spock" was released during this time period as a dark olive green button with black lettering. More recent duplications have not followed this particular color format, and say simply "I Grok Spock".
3. This early button carrying the familiar 1960's vernacular was released by The Leonard Nimoy National Association of Fans.
4. Promotional button for The Leonard Nimoy National Association of Fans during the early 1970's.

SLOGAN BUTTONS

	Issue	Current	Cost/Date
Lincoln Enterprises, 1984			
Slogan buttons of assorted sizes	.25	.50-1	
It Is Illogical / Star Trek black lettering on blue, 2¼" diameter			_____
Long Live and Prosper black lettering on green, 3" diameter			_____
Paramount Is A Klingon Conspiracy, black lettering on red, 2½" diameter			_____
Star Trek Lives, black lettering on yellow, 1½" diamter			_____
Keep On Trekkin, black lettering on yellow, 2¼" diameter			_____
• **Star Trek Convention Buttons**			
Special buttons made primarily for Trek conventions by promoters, assorted sizes and clip types.			
Riverside Iowa - Future Birth Place of Captain James T. Kirk Trek Fest 1986, 2" diameter	1.50	1-2	_____
Riverside, Iowa - Where The Trek Begins, Trek Fest 1986, Style No. 1 without stars, 2" diameter	1.50	1-2	_____
Style 2 with stars, 2" diameter	1.50	1-2	_____
Star Trek, Specialties Inc., Gaithersburg, Maryland			
White letters beneath t.v. Enterprise, blue background, 1½" diameter	1	1-2	_____
• **Stick Pin Buttons,** circa 1970s			
Assorted stick pin buttons with colorful paper backgrounds, 1½" in diameter,			
Star Trek Is! black lettering on blue	.50	1-2	_____
Vulcan Power blue lettering on white	.50	1-2	_____
• **Taco Bell Buttons,** 1984			
Issued in conjunction with the promotion of Star Trek III glassware by Taco Bell, yellow lettering on blue background, giant 3" diameter size.			
Beam Home With The Crew Of The Enterprise	1	2-4	_____
Beam Home With Kruge	1	2-4	_____
Beam Home With Spock	1	2-4	_____
Beam Home With T'Lar	1	2-4	_____
• **T-K Graphics,** 1985			
A variety of slogan buttons with safety pin style latches, 2¼" diameters, each	1	1-2	_____
Beam Me Up Scotty, This Place Has No Intelligent Life.			_____
Carbon-Based Unit			_____
I Don't Like To Lose			_____
I Exaggerated			_____
I Have Been And Always Will Be			

	Issue	Current	Cost/Date
Your Friend			_____
Kiss Me I'm A Trekker			_____
Live Long And Prosper			_____
Nobody's Perfect			_____
Remember Spock			_____
Revenge Is A Dish Best Served Cold			_____
Space . . . The Final Frontier			_____
Spock Lives, black lettering on gold, has block letters			_____
Star Trek, black lettering on green, shows Enterprise schematic			_____
Star Trek Fans Make Better Lovers			_____
Star Trek Lives, shows Command Insignia			_____
Survivor Kobayashi Maru Test, black lettering on orange			_____
The Human Adventure Is Just Beginning			_____
The Needs Of The Many Outweight The Needs of the Few Or The One			_____
There Are Always Responsibilities			_____
U.S.S. Enterprise Veteran, black lettering on gold			_____
Vulcans' Never Bluff			_____

DECALS

	Issue	Current	Cost/Date
• **Crew Portraits,** Lincoln Enterprises, 1980 Two-tone water mount decals, sheets are 9"x4". Double set. Eight oval portraits include Kirk, Spock, McCoy, Scotty, Uhura, Sulu, Chekov and Chapel. No. 1807 Sheets 6 and 7	3	3-5	_____
• **Gadgetry** Star Trek/Lincoln Enterprises 1968; 1980 Two-tone water mount decals, sheets are 9"x4". Communicator, phaser and 3-D chess game. Silver and black. Includes miniature figures of aliens, etc. No. 1803 sheet 3	.75	3-5	_____
• **Insignia Designs** Star Trek/Lincoln Enterprises 1968; 1980 Silver and black water mount decals, sheets are 9"x4". The three styles of uniform insignias from the series plus miniature aliens, etc. No. 1801 Sheet 1	.75	2-3	_____
• **Monster Portraits** Lincoln Enterprises, 1980 Two-tone water mount decals, sheets are 9"x4". Eight oval portraits of aliens as seen in the series. No. 1806 Sheet 5	1.95	2-4	_____

Decal Sheet, Star Trek Enterprises, 1968.

	Issue	Current	Cost/Date
• **NCC-1701 Letter Logos** Lincoln Enterprises, 1980 Two-tone water mount decals, sheets are 9"x4". The Enterprise call letters in assorted sizes. No. 1805 Sheet 4	1.25	1-2	_____
• **Spacecraft** Star Trek/Lincoln Enterprises 1968; 1980 Silver and black water mount decals, sheets are 9"x4". Enterprise, Klingon Warship and Galileo '7, includes miniature standing figures. No. 1802 Sheet 2	.75	2-3	_____

Star Trek Money

Money

	Issue	Current	Cost/Date
• **Star Trek Money** Fan issue, United Trekkies of Planet Earth, 5½"x12½" giant money, features six different Star Trek character illos. Black design on blue paper stock, 1969 series:			
100 Credits with profile of Kirk	—	1-3	_____
50 Credits with profile of Spock	—	1-3	_____
20 Credits with profile of McCoy	—	1-3	_____
10 Credits with profile of Uhura	—	1-3	_____
5 Credits with profile of Scotty	—	1-3	_____
1 Credit with profile of Chekov	—	1-3	_____
• **Star Trek Money** Fan issue, United Trekkies of Planet Earth Re-issue of the above paper currency in 7¾"x17" format. Black design on gold paper stock, 1975 series features the same Credit/portrait illo denominations.	—	1-2	_____
• **Star Trek Personality Dollar Bills** Starlog Magazine, 1979 Legal mint, uncirculated U.S. currency as permitted by the Government, dollar bills with photo picture of Trek characters in place of Washington, sent in clear acetate presentation covers, four types:			
Captain Kirk	3.98	4-6	_____
Mr. Spock	3.98	4-6	_____
Sulu	3.98	4-6	_____
Lt. Uhura	3.98	4-6	_____
Complete set of 4 bills	13.98	15-20	_____
• **Vulcan Nick-el** Albert Schuster, distributor, 1972 Commemorative solid wood coin from the first Star Trek Convention in NYC in January, 1972. Silver dollar size, featuring ink-stamped bust of Spock and the logo "Vulcan Nick-el". Reverse reads in bold type "In Spock We Trust" with smaller print "Leonard Nimoy Wouldn't Lie."	.50	2-3	_____

Sample Star Trek Patch

Patches and Transfers

Item	Issue	Current Cost/Date	
• **Captain's Sleeve Braid** Star Trek Official Space Emblem, 1975 6" long and 1½" wide, gold and black embroidered t.v. rank braid for designing your own uniform. Packaged on cardstock featuring cartoon Enterprise. Plastic wrapped.	1.50	2-3	_____
• **Enterprise, U.S.S., Insignia** Lincoln Enterprises, 1983 2"x3" embroidered oval, t.v. starship in starboard profile, gold and red on black	1.50	2-3	_____
• **Enterprise, U.S.S** 3"x4" oval with starboard profile STTMP version Enterprise in space, black background	2	2-3	_____
• **Enterprise/"Star Trek" Iron-On** Famous Monsters Magazine, 1980 Television starship in a starboard profile beneath small planet with galaxy backdrop. Circular photo transfer has pennant-style block lettering overhead reading "Star Trek"	1	3-4	_____
• **"Enterprise, U.S.S." Decal Transfer,** Lincoln Enterprise 2¼" x10" heat sensitive decal for transferring to clothing, dark blue block lettering on white	—		_____
• **"Enterprise, U.S.S."** Star Trek Welcommittee, 1976 3½"x4½" fan shaped design of rear view starship over varigated planet, 6 colors embroidered on dark blue .	1.50	3-4	_____
• **"Enterprise, U.S.S." Official Crew's Cap Insignia Patch,** 1980 Circular Patch as it appears on the sports cap by The Thinking Cap Co. Black lettering within a gold border surrounds black starfield with a plain command star insignia, embroidered in gold.	5	5-6	_____

Item	Issue	Current Cost/Date	
• **"Enterprise, U.S.S. - NCC 1701"** Star Trek Welcommittee, 1976 3"x4" oval, port profile starship in white, white and yellow embroidered on choice of white or black backgrounds, lettering and border in red	1	3-4	_____
• **"Enterprise, U.S.S. - NCC 1701"** /Mascot Patch Circular patch with lettering above and below a furry mascot	1.50	2-3	_____
• **Episode Photo Transfers** Lincoln Enterprises, 1979 Ten famous photo scenes from the t.v. series reproduced in full color. Rectangular iron-ons are made to adhere to fabrics that contain at least 50% cotton material.			
1010 Spock holding Vulcan harp . .	1.25	3-4	_____
1011 Kirk and Spock, close-up	1.25	3-4	_____
1012 Spock wearing cranial control device, plus Kirk (SB)	1.25	3-4	_____
1013 Enterprise firing twin phasers	1.25	3-4	_____
1014 Kirk, close-up	1.25	3-4	_____
1015 McCoy, Spock and Kirk dressed as Nazis (PF)	1.25	3-4	_____
1016 Spock and Kirk, bare to waist (PF)	1.25	3-4	_____
1017 Spock and Kirk, at Science Station	1.25	3-4	_____
1018 Spock giving Vulcan salute . .	1.25	3-4	_____
1019 Kirk, action shot	1.25	3-4	_____
• **"Federation" With Enterprise** Star Trek Welcommittee, 1977 3"x3" shield design, starboard profile TV Enterprise in space, silver and black embroidered on orange. .	1	2-4	_____
• **"Galileo NCC-1701'7"** Star Trek Welcommittee, 1977 2" circle, shuttlecraft in starboard profile, 3 colors embroidered on royal blue.	.75	2-4	_____
• **Great Bird of the Galaxy** New Eye, distributors 3"x4" rectangle with rounded corners, graceful avian creature with wings outstretched, stylized Greek letters and laurels. Designed credited to Gene Roddenberry. Copper stitching on black.	2	3-5	_____
• **IDIC / "Peace In Our Galaxy"** Lincoln Enterprises, 1983 3" circle, design credited to Gene Roddenberry. Blue background with gold lettering and central silver and gold embroidered IDIC.	1.95	3-4	_____

PATCHES AND TRANSFERS

Issue Current Cost/Date

• **"Keep On Trekkin' "**
Star Trek Welcommittee, 1977
3½"x3" rectangle, port profile silhouette of Enterprise in center, gold and white embroidered on red. 1 2-4 ______

• **Kirk Figure**
Star Trek Official Space Emblem, 1975
4½" standing figure, hands on hips. Embroidered cut-out. Packaged on cardstock featuring cartoon Enterprise. Plastic wrapped. . . . . 1.50 3-5 ______

• **"Klingon"**
Star Trek Welcommittee, 1977
3"x3" shield design, Klingon Cruiser in overhead angle, silver and black embroidered on orange. Lettering. . 1 2-4 ______

• **Klingon Battle Cruiser Insignia**
Lincon Enterprises, 1980
2"x3½" oval, Cruiser in port profile, gold embroidered on black. . . . 1.50 2-4 ______

• **Klingon Cruiser**
Intergalactic, distributors.
3"x4" oval, port profile STTMP Cruiser in space. Black background 2 2-4 ______

• **"NCC 1701" Letter Logo**
Star Trek Official Space Emblem, 1975
4½" x1" rectangular logo in block letters. Packaged on cardstock with cartoon Enterprise. Plastic wrapped. . . . . 1.50 3-5 ______

• **Phaser Patch**
Star Trek Official Space Emblem, 1975
2"x3" cut-out, left profile of a pistol phaser from the TV series. Black and silver. Packaged on cardstock with cartoon Enterprise. Plastic wrapped. . . . . 1.50 3-5 ______

• **"Romulan"**
Star Trek Welcommittee, 1976
3"x3" sheild design, Romulan Bird of Prey in overhead angle, silver and black embroidered on orange. Lettering. . . . . 1 2-4 ______

Insignia Patches

• **"Space Station K-7"**
Star Trek Welcommittee, 1976
3"x4" oval, K-7 station, starfield and miniature Enterprise, 4 colors embroidered on black. . . . . 1 2-4 ______

Issue Current Cost/Date

• **Spock Figure With Phaser**
Star Trek Official Space Emblem, 1975
4½" standing figure holding phaser, embroidered cut-out. Packaged on cardstock with cartoon Enterprise. Plastic wrapped. . . . . 1.50 3-5 ______

• **Spock Figure With Tricorder**
Star Trek Official Space Emblem, 1975
4½" standing figure wearing tricorder, embroidered cut-out. Packaged on cardstock with cartoon Enterprise. Plastic wrapped. . . . . . 1.50 3-5 ______

• **Starbase Personnel Insignia**
Intergalactic, distributors, 1980
Uniform patch in same style as the earlier TV insignias but never seen. Gold leatherette with black silk embroidery. Pi symbol. . . . . 2 2-3 ______

Special offer flyer for Iron On Transfers 1974-1976

• **Starship Command Insignia**
Lincoln Enterprises, 1968; 1980
Uniform insignia from the series. Gold leatherette with black silk embroidery. Star symbol. . . . . .50 1-3 ______

• **Starship Engineering & Other Services Insignia**
Lincoln Enterprises, 1968; 1980
Uniform insignia from the series. Gold leatherette with black silk embroidery. Stylized spiral symbol. . . . .50 1-3 ______

• **Starship Medical Insignia**
Intergalactic, distributors, 1980
Uniform patch in same style as the earlier TV insignias but never seen. Gold leatherette with black silk embroidery. Block cross symbol. . . . . 2 2-3 ______

• **Starship Sciences Insignia**
Lincoln Enterprises, 1968; 1980
Uniform insignia from the series. Gold leatherette with black silk embroidery. Stylized eye symbol. . . . . .50 1-3 ______

PATCHES AND TRANSFERS

	Issue	Current	Cost/Date
• Starship General Personnel Insignia Intergalactic, distributors, 1980 Uniform patch in same style as the earlier TV insignias but never seen. Gold leatherette with black silk embroidery. Gamma symbol.	2	2-3	______
• Star Trek Iron-On Transfers AMT Corporation, 1974-1976 Four transfer designs, each approximately 6"x9", suitable for application to clothing:			
1. T.V. Enterprise over orange globe, blue lettering on white reads "Keep On Trekkin"	1	3-5	______
2. T.V. Klingon Cruiser in black, starry space with yellow and red block lettering "Klingon Power"	1	3-5	______
3. Miniature t.v. Enterprise over massive yellow, black and orange block lettering "Star Trek Lives", blue background.	1	3-5	______
4. A Collage of Transfers: Righthand Vulcan salute over yellow and black "Vulcan Power"; assorted sizes of "U.S.S. Enterprise" lettering; four ship's insignias and a brown fur ball which reads "How's Your Tribble".[1]	1	3-5	______
• Star Trek The Motion Picture Iron-Ons General Mills, Inc., 1979 Set of five 5"x9" shirt tranfers designed by Roach, Inc. of California.			
1. Spock photo with yellow and black STTMP lettering	.20	4-6	______
2. Capt. Kirk photo with blue and black letters "Capt. Kirk-STTMP"	.20	4-6	______
3. Enterprise and starburst with yellow and white STTMP lettering	.20	4-6	______

STTMP Patch, Aviva, 1979

Aviva Patch

	Issue	Current	Cost/Date
4. Starship Executive Officers - Kirk and Spock photo within gold ring, with magenta and black STTMP lettering	.20	4-6	______
5. A blank transfer to create your own design.[2]	.20	—	______
• Star Trek The Motion Picture Iron-On Transfer Book Wallaby Books, 1979 Softbound book containing assorted STTMP photo decals and transfers for clothing.	5.95	10-16	______
• Star Trek The Motion Picture New Design Uniform Insignias, Lincoln Enterprises Designed for the movie by Bob Fletcher. All are Command Star Insignias encircled by assorted colors which denote different stations. 2¼" diameter patches.			
Cadet Insignia (red)	1.50	1-2	______
Command Insignia (white)	1.50	1-2	______
Medical Insignia (green)	1.50	1-2	______
Navigations & Engineering/ Operations (yellow)	1.50	1-2	______
Science & Communications (orange)	1.50	1-2	______
Security (silver)	1.50	1-2	______
• Star Trek The Motion Picture New Medical Emblem Lincoln Enterprises, 1980 Formal emblem worn by ranking medical officers. 2¼" staff and bar in green.	1.95	2-3	______

1. These transfers were a special coupon offer inside of A.M.T. plastic model kits produced from 1974 to 1976. Items were offered individually at $1.00, or as a set for $3.00.
2. Items were a special promotion coupon on package-backs of Cheerios Cereal. The complete set was available for $1.00 plus two Proof-of-Purchase bottoms. Not offered individually.

UFP Cut-Out Patch

	Issue	Current	Cost/Date
• **Star Trek The Motion Picture Photo Patches** Bordered, transfer-style photo prints on fabric made to be sewn to clothing. Aviva, 1979 Bordered, transfer-style photo prints on fabric made to be sewn to clothing.			
Kirk in Uniform	2	3-4	_____
Kirk in Admiral's Tunic	2	3-4	_____
Kirk and Spock	2	3-4	_____
Kirk, Spock and McCoy	2	3-4	_____
Spock in Uniform	2	3-4	_____
Spock in Vulcan Robes	2	3-4	_____
• **"Star Trek III - The Search For Spock" Emblem** Lincoln Enterprises, 1984 3"x5" all embroidered cut-out. Letter border surrounds Enterprise over Genesis planet. Portside profile. Black, grey, yellow, red and orange. Made to iron-on or sew.	5.95	6-8	_____
• **Star Trek 20th Anniversary 1966-1984 Patch** Lincoln Enterprises, 1984 Commemorative for the 20th anniversary of "The Cage," first t.v. pilot film. Shows STTMP Enterprise in starboard profile with sweeping trail, hexagonal base reads "Star Trek 1964-1984", color embroidery	5.95	7-9	_____
• **Triangle Award Set Patches** Mike McMaster, designer, 1985 Set of 19 different colors and geometrical shapes appliqued to triangular patches. Same as worn by Capt. Kirk on his dress uniform during the t.v. series. Set of 19 patches	10	10-12	_____

	Issue	Current	Cost/Date
• **Uhura Figure** Star Trek Official Space Emblem, 1975 4" standing figure wearing tricorder. Embroidered cut-out. Packaged on cardstock with cartoon Enterprise. Plastic wrapped.	1.50	3-5	_____
• **"U.F.P." Banner** Intergalactic, distributors Double-V banner configuration with the initials surrounded by stars. Choice of red or black backgrounds.	2	2-4	_____
• **"U.F.P." Alpha Centauri Flag Patch** Star Trek Official Space Emblem, 1975 3"x4" galaxy seal of the Federation as seen on the reference book *Technical Manual.* Silver and blue on black background. Packaged on cardstock with cartoon Enterprise. Plastic wrapped.	3	6-8	_____
• **"United Federation of Planets Starfleet HQ" Patch** Intergalactic distributors, 1980 Same patch used on the sports cap by the Thinking Cap Co., lettering is on blue border surrounded by white with blue and silver embroidered galaxy seal.	5	5-6	_____
• **Vulcan Salute/ "Live Long & Prosper"** Intergalactic, distributors Circular patch with imprinted hand and lettering below.	5	5-6	_____
• **Vulcan Salute/ "Live Long & Prosper"** Fan issue Square 3"x3" patch, yellow with black design	3	3-4	_____
• **Vulcan Salute/ "Spock Lives!"** Intergalactic, distributors Circular patch with imprinted Vulcan hand addressing salute. Lettering is over the thumb.	5	5-6	_____
• **"Zap!"** Star Trek Welcommittee, 1976 3½"x3" rectangle, block lettering and port profile Enterprise firing twin phasers, 4 colors embroidered on dark green.	1	2-3	_____

STICKERS

Issue | Current | Cost/Date

- **Ad-Mee-Ral Kirk**
  T-K Graphics
  Black lettering on white, rectangle with rounded corners, 1"x2¾", Set of 20 . . . . 1 | 1-2 | ______

- **Beam Me Up Scotty. There's No Intelligent Life On This Planet.**
  Fantasy Trader . . . . 1 | 1-2 | ______

- **Beam Me Up Scotty. This Place Has No Intelligent Life.**
  T-K Graphics
  1¼" diameter stickers on color stock of bright red, orange or green.
  Singles . . . . .05 | .05-.10 | ______
  Sets (5 each color, 15 stickers) . . . . 1 | 1-2 | ______
  4½"x5½", black lettering on brilliant white stock, includes cartoon of Spock holding communicator by Steve Stiles . . . . .50 | .50-1 | ______
  1"x2¼", black lettering on white rectangle, rounded corners, set of 20. . . . . 1 | 1-2 | ______

- **Beam Me Up Scotty. This Planet Has No Intelligent Life.**
  T-K Graphics
  Black lettering on white, 2¼"x11" . .75 | 1-2 | ______

Sample Sticker

- **Beam Me Up Scotty. This Planet Sucks.**
  Fantasy Traders . . . . 1 | 1-2 | ______

- **Boss. Thee Starship, Thee Starship**
  T-K Graphics
  Black lettering on white, rectangle with rounded corners, 1"x2¾", Set of 20 . . . . 1 | 1-2 | ______

- **Bring Back Our Enterprise**
  William Shatner Fan Club
  Blue letters on white vinyl, 3¼"x11" . . . . 2 | 2-3 | ______

- **Bring Back The Enterprise**
  Lincoln Enterprises
  Black lettering on florescent day-glo yellow stock, 4"x15" . . . . 1.25 | 1-2 | ______

- **Caution – Endangered Species**
  Lincoln Enterprises
  Black lettering on florescent day-glo yellow stock. Pictures the planet Earth, 4"x15" . . . . 1.25 | 1-2 | ______

- **Caution, I Brake For Tribbles**
  April Publications
  Self-sticking, removeable, Saturn blue or gay-glo yellow stock, 3½"x14½" . . . . 1.50 | 1-2 | ______

- **Ceti Alpha V. It's No Fantasy Island.**
  T-K Graphics
  Black lettering on white, 1"x2¾", Set of 20 . . . . 1 | 1-2 | ______

- **Coming Next Episode, Mr. Bill is Captured by Klingons**
  T-K Graphics
  Giant sticker, black lettering on white, 2"x4". Set of 6 . . . . .75 | 1-2 | ______

- **Dispatched: Stardate**
  T-K Graphics
  1"x2¾" sticker, peel-off backing, black lettering on white. Singles . . . .05 | .05-.10 | ______
  Sets (20 per pack) . . . . 1 | 1-2 | ______

- **Don't Honk I only Have Impulse Power**
  Star Base Central
  3"x10" . . . . 1 | 1-2 | ______

- **Don't Tailgate, This Is A Klingon War Cruiser**
  Lincoln Enterprises
  Black lettering on florescent day-glo red stock, 4"x15" . . . . 1.25 | 1-2 | ______

- **Dr. McCoy Doesn't Make Housecalls**
  Aviva
  Shows profile of McCoy on lefthand side, blue and white letters on orange stock, 2½"x11" . . . . 1 | 1-2 | ______

- **Earthers Beware . . . Klingon Battle Cruiser**
  Star Base Central
  Shows picture of Klingon ship on upper right hand side, 3"x10" . . . . . 1 | 1-2 | ______

- **Federation Vehicle: Official Use Only**
  Amateur Press . . . . 1 | 1-2 | ______

- **Follow Me "Where No Man Has Gone Before"**
  Amateur Press
  White lettering on dark background, 3"x10" . . . . 1 | 1-2 | ______

- **Genesis Project / Top Secret**
  T-K Graphics
  Black lettering on white rectangle with rounded corners, 1"x2¾", Set of 20 . . . . 1 | 1-2 | ______

- **Graduate of Starfleet Academy**
  Amateur Press
  Shows three different Starfleet insignia on lefthand side, 2"x9". . . . . 1 | 1-2 | ______

STICKERS

Issue | Current Cost/Date

- **Government Vehicle: Vulcan Embassy**
  Lincoln Enterprises
  Black lettering on florescent day-glo yellow stock, pictures the IDIC, 4"x15" .... 1.25 1-2 _____
- **Happy Holidays**
  T-K Graphics
  Special giant Christmas sticker, red or green ink on white, shows Spock in elf costume giving Vulcan salute, says "To, From", 2"x4", drawing by K. Bartholomew. Set of 6 (one color) .... 1 1-2 _____
- **He's Dead Jim.**
  T-K Graphics
  Black lettering on white rectangle with rounded corners, 1"x2¾", Set of 20 .... 1 1-2 _____
- **Honk If You Like Star Trek**
  April Publications
  Self-sticking, removeable, Saturn blue or day-glo yellow stock, 3¼"x14½" .... 1.50 1-2 _____
- **Honk If You're A Trekker**
  T-K Graphics
  Black lettering on red, green, orange or chartreuse florescent stock, 3¼"x5½" .... .50 .50-1 _____
- **Human Adventure Is Just Beginning, The**
  Lincoln Enterprises
  Black lettering on florescent day-glo stock, 4"x15" .... 1.25 1-2 _____
  T-K Graphics
  1"x2¾" sticker, set of 20 .... 1 1-2 _____
- **I Adore Admiral Kirk**
  T-K Graphics
  1"x2¾" sticker, peel-off backing, black lettering on white, singles ... .05 .05-.10 _____
  Sets (20 per pack) .... 1 1-2 _____
- **I Am A Carbon Unit**
  Lincoln Enterprises
  Black lettering on florescent day-glo, 4"x15" .... 1.25 1-2 _____
- **I Am A Trekkie**
  Amateur Press
  Profile of Spock on lefthand side, 2¾"x 11" .... 1 1-2 _____
- **I Brake For Tribbles**
  T-K Graphics
  Black and red lettering on blue paper stock, 2¼"x11" .... 1 1-2 _____
- **I Don't Believe In The No-Win Scenerio**
  T-K Graphics
  Black lettering on white rectangle with rounded corners, 1"x2¾", set of 20 .... 1 1-2 _____
- **I Grok Spock/Star Trek**
  Lincoln Enterprises
  Black lettering on florescent day-glo red stock, 4"x15". .... 1.25 1-2 _____
- **I Have A One Trek Mind**
  Star Base Central
  Picture of Enterprise in upper left-hand corner, 2"x9" .... 1 1-2 _____
- **I Have Been And Always Will Be Your Friend**
  T-K Graphics
  Black lettering on white rectangle with rounded corners, 1"x2¾", set of 20 .... 1 1-2 _____
- **I Know Engineers. They Love To Change Things.**
  T-K Graphics
  Black lettering on white, rounded corner rectangle, 1"x2¾", set of 20 1 1-2 _____
- **I Operate On Impulse Power.**
  T-K Graphics
  Black lettering on white stock, 2¼"x11" .... .75 1-2 _____
- **I Reserve The Right To Arm Klingons**
  Lincoln Enterprises
  Black lettering on florescent day-glo yellow stock, 4"x15" .... 1.25 1-2 _____
- **I Study Horta Culture**
  Fasson
  Shows picture of Spock examining pile of tribbles on lefthand side, 4"x14" .... 1 1-2 _____
- **I'd Rather Be Watching Star Trek**
  T-K Graphics
  Black lettering on white rectangle with rounded corners, 1"x2¾", set of 20 .... 1 1-2 _____
- **I'm Waiting For Star Trek III**
  T-K Graphics
  Black lettering on white rounded corner rectangle, 1"x2¾".
  Set of 20[1] .... 1 2-3 _____
- **I've Faced The Kobayashi Maru Test**
  T-K Graphics
  1"x2¾" sticker, black lettering on white. Singles .... .05 .05-.10 _____
  Sets (20 stickers per pack) .... 1 1-2 _____
- **I've Visited Vulcan – Home of Spock**
  April Publications
  Lettering on Saturn blue or day-glo yellow stock, 3¼"x14½" .... 1.50 1-2 _____
- **Illogical**
  T-K Graphics
  1"x2¾" sticker, peel-off backing, black lettering on white .... .05 .05-.10 _____
  Sets (20 stickers per pack) .... 1 1-2 _____

1. From a collectibles standpoint, **pre-sequel** items such as this are subject to very limited production, distribution and market time since the period leading up to a movie's release is generally of a very short duration. Pre-sequel advertisements and promotions are interesting collector's items.

STICKERS

	Issue	Current	Cost/Date
Infinite Diversity In Infinite Combinations			
T-K Graphics			
1"x2¾", set of 20 stickers	1	1-2	______
Insignia			
Star Trek/Lincon Enterprises, 1968; 1980			
Black and gold color on pressure-sensitive, gummed, satin-finish paper, reproductions of the main Star Fleet Command insignia from the t.v. series:			
Single Command Insignia	.15	.25-.50	______
Set of three	.50	.75-2	______
It Had The Virtue of Having Never Been Tried			
T-K Graphics			
1"x2¾", set of 20 stickers	1	1-2	______
It Is The Only Logical Thing To Do			
Star Base Central			
Pressure sensitive, adhesive back sticker, shows hand giving Vulcan salute encircled by logo	.10	.10-.25	______
It's 1983 And Star Trek Lives On			
T-K Graphics			
1"x2¾", set of 20 stickers	1	2-3	______
Jaws Is A Klingon Minnow.			
Lincoln Enterprises			
Black lettering on lforescent day-glo, red stock, 4"x15"	1.25	1-2	______
Pressure Sensitives, Inc.			
Black lettering on green day-glo shows black "Shark's Nose" logo from the **Jaws** movie, 2¾"x11"	1	1-2	______
Jim Kirk Was Many Things, But He Was Never A Boy Scout. T-K Graphics			
1"x2¾", black lettering on white			
Singles	.05	.05-.10	______
Sets (20 stickers per pack)	1	1-2	______
Join The Enterprise . . . See The Future			
T-K Graphics			
1"x2¾", set of 20 stickers	1	1-2	______
3¼"x5½", black lettering on red, green, orange or chartreuse florescent stock	.05	.05-.10	______
Keep On Trekkin'			
2"x4" sticker, black lettering on white, single	.20	.20-.50	______
Set of 6 stickers	.75	.75-1	______
2"x9", logo in balloon, lettering with caricature of Spock on lefthand side	1	1-2	______
3"x12", black lettering on green stock, caricature of Spock on lefthand side	.75	.75-1	______

	Issue	Current	Cost/Date
Kirk And Spock Forever			
T-K Graphics			
1"x2¾", black lettering on white, singles	.05	.05-.10	______
Sets (20 stickers per pack)	1	1-2	______
Klingon Battle Cruiser			
T-K Graphics			
Shows schematic of Klingon vessel, giant 2"x4" sticker, black lettering on white, set of 6	.75	.75-1	______
1"x2¾", black lettering on rectangle, set of 20 stickers	1	1-2	______
Klingon Postal Service			
T-K Graphics			
1"x2¾", set of 20 stickers	1	1-2	______
Klingon Property: Violaters Will Be Dismembered			
Fantasy Traders	1	1-2	______
Klingon Staff Car			
T-K Graphics			
Black lettering on white stock, 2¼"x11"	.75	1-2	______
Live Long And Prosper			
T-K Graphics			
1"x2¾" set of twenty stickers	1	1-2	______
2¾"x11", black lettering on white, shows Vulcan Hand Salute	.75	1-2	______
Amateur Printing			
3"x9", shows Vulcan Hand Salute on lefthand side	1	1-2	______
April Publications			
3¼"x14½", saturn blue or day-glo yellow stock	1.50	1-2	______
Fantasy Traders			
Pictures Vulcan Hand Salute on right, encircled by "It is the only logical thing to do"	1	1-2	______
Lincoln Enterprises			
4"x15", black lettering on florescent day-glo yellow stock	1.25	1-2	______
May Your Tribbles Always Purr			
T-K Graphics			
1"x2¾", set of 20 stickers	1	1-2	______
Mr. Spock For President			
Star Trek/Lincoln Enterprises			
4"x13", black lettering on day-glo (1968)	.35	2-3	______
4"x15", black lettering on orange florescent stock (1980)	1.25	1-2	______
Mr. Spock Phone Home			
Lincoln Enterprises			
Black lettering on florescent day-glo stock, 4"x15"	1.25	1-2	______
My Favorite Doctor Is The Real McCoy			
T-K Graphics			
1"x2¾", set of 20 stickers	1	1-2	______

STICKERS

	Issue	Current	Cost/Date
My Hailing Frequencies Are Open			
T-K Graphics			
1"x2¾", set of 20 stickers	1	1-2	_____
(The) Needs of the Many Outweigh The Needs Of The Few			
T-K Graphics			
1"x2¾", black lettering on white, singles	.05	.05-.10	_____
Sets (20 stickers per pack)	1	1-2	_____
No Carbon Based Units Beyond This Point			
T-K Graphics			
Giant 2"x4" sticker, black lettering on white, set of 6	.75	1-2	_____
No Smoking By Order of Star Fleet Command			
T-K Graphics			
Giant sticker, 2"x4", set of 6	.75	1-2	_____
Notice: You Are Entering A Tribble Sanctuary			
T-K Graphics			
Giant sticker, 2"x4", set of 6	.75	1-2	_____
Now More Than Ever, We Need Spock			
T-K Graphics			
1¾" diameter sticker on color stock or bright red, orange or green, singles	.05	.05-.10	_____
Sets (5 of each color, 15 stickers) ..	1	1-2	_____
Now More Than Ever, We Need Spock			
T-K Graphics			
1"x2¾", set of 20	.75	1-2	_____
Old Trekkers Never Die, They Just Warp Out			
T-K Graphics			
1"x2¾", set of 20 stickers	1	1-2	_____
Phasers On Stun			
Amateur Press			
Shows picture of Enterprise firing phasers above log, 4"x14"	1	1-2	_____
Pointed Ears Are A Sign of Intelligence			
T-K Graphics			
1"x2¾", black lettering on white, singles	.05	.05-.10	_____
Sets (20 stickers per pack)	1	1-2	_____
Powered By Tribbles			
Star Base Central, distributors			
Shows Volkswagen Beetle on left-hand side dropping tribbles, 5"x14"	1	1-2	_____
Product of Klingon Science			
T-K Graphics			
Black lettering on white, 2"x4"			
Set of 6 stickers	.75	1-2	_____
Property of Star Fleet Library			
T-K Graphics			
1"x2¾", set of 20 stickers	1	1-2	_____

	Issue	Current	Cost/Date
Property of U.S.S. Enterprise			
T-K Graphics			
1"x2¾", set of 20 stickers	1	1-2	_____
Quarantine/Star Fleet Medical Section			
T-K Graphics			
Giant 2"x4" sticker, black lettering on white, singles	.20	.20-.50	_____
Sets (6 stickers per pack)	.75	1-2	_____
Restricted Area/Star Fleet Headquarters Personnel Only			
T-K Graphics			
Giant sticker, 2"x4", set of 6	.75	1-2	_____
Revents Is A Dish Best Served Cold			
T-K Graphics			
Singles	.05	.05-.10	_____
Sets (20 stickers per pack)	1	1-2	_____
Riverside, Iowa - TREK - "			
Chamber of Commerce, 1986			
4"x12", Future Birthplace of Capt. James T. Kirk	1.50	1-2	_____
4"x12", Where It All Begins [2]	1.50	1-2	_____
(The) Saga Continues			
T-K Graphics			
Red and black lettering on yellow stock, shows Enterprise silhouette, 2½"x11"	1	1-2	_____
Save Star Trek - Write NBC			
Star Trek Enterprises, 1968			
Florescent green letters on black stock. The bumper sticker of the Save Star Trek Campaign, 4"x13" [3]	.35	8-10	_____
Saurian Brandy Bottle Label			
Joy-Miller Enterprises			
Silver-tone Federation Seal of Approval for Galactic Distribution. Label is made to apply to the Dickel Whiky bottles (powderhorn style) which was used as a prop in several of the t.v. episodes.	.50	3-4	_____
Scotty Warps My Engines			
T-K Graphics			
1"x2¾", set of 20	1	1-2	_____
Smile If You Like Star Trek			
Lincoln Enterprises			
Black lettering on florescent day-glo orange stock, shows Smiley with Vulcan ears, 4"x15"	1.25	1-2	_____

2. The proceeds generated from the sale of Riverside's "birthplace" slogan (including T-shirts as well) are designated to go towards the construction of a permanent local monument to the future Captain James T. Kirk.

3. Official bumper sticker for the fan Mail-Drive Campaign to save the Star Trek t.v. series from its projected 2nd season cancellation. (See Promotions-Flyers for more details on this historic fan campaign.)

STICKERS

	Issue	Current	Cost/Date
Space . . . The Final Frontier			
Amateur Printing			
2"x11", shows Enterprise in upper righthand corner on two-tone color stock, upper portion dark, lower portion light	1	1-2	_____
T-K Graphics			
1"x2¾" sticker, set of 20	1	1-2	_____
3¼"x5½", black lettering on assorted colors of red, green, orange and chartreuse, florescent stock . . .	.50	.50-2	_____
Spock For President			
T-K Graphics			
Shows row of nineteen stars beneath log, 2¾"x11"	1	1-2	_____
Spock Is Dead - Long Live Star Trek			
Lincoln Enterprises			
Black lettering on florescent day-glo stock, 4"x15".	1.25	1-2	_____
Spock It To Me!			
Star Trek Enterprises, 1968			
Black lettering on day-glo, 4"x13" [4]	.35	4-6	_____
Spock Lives On			
T-K Graphics			
1"x2¾" stickers, set of 20	1	1-2	_____
2¾"x11", black lettering on white	.75	1-2	_____
Star Fleet Academy			
New Eye, distributors			
1½"x18" peel and stick decal, blue letters on white	4	4-5	_____
2½"x18", college-sticker transparency for car window, block lettering .	3	3-4	_____
T-K Graphics			
1¾" diameter sticker on color stock of bright red, orange or green, singles	.05	.05-.10	_____
Sets (5 each color, 15 stickers)	1	1-2	_____
1"x 2¾", set of 20 stickers	1	1-2	_____
Star Fleet Academy Parking Permit			
Hollywood On Location, 12985			
Bumper Sticker	1	1-2	_____
Star Fleet Command			
T-K Graphics			
Giant sticker, 2"x4", shows Janus Head Emblem, set of 6	.75	1-2	_____
Star Fleet Communique			
T-K Graphics			
1"x2¾", black lettering on white, singles	.05	.05-.10	_____
Sets (20 stickers per pack)	1	1-2	_____
Star Fleet Computer Division			
T-K Graphics			
1"x2¾", set of 20	1	1-2	_____

	Issue	Current	Cost/Date
Star Fleet Freight			
T-K Graphics			
Designed as a shipping label.			
Giant sticker, 2"x4", black lettering on white, set of 6	.75	1-2	_____
1"x2¾", black lettering on white, set of 20 stickers	1	1-2	_____
Star Fleet Headquarters: Classified			
T-K Graphics			
1"x2¾", set of 20 stickers	1	1-2	_____
Star Fleet Headquarters Official Mail			
T-K Graphics			
1"x2¾", set of 20	1	1-2	_____
Star Fleet Headquarters Official Vehicle			
T-K Graphics			
Black lettering on white, 2¾"x11" .	1	1-2	_____
Star Fleet Headquarters Staff Vehicle			
T-K Graphics			
Red and black lettering on green stock, shows UFP Janus Head design, 2¾"x11"	1	1-2	_____
Star Fleet HQ Tactical Operations Center			
T-K Graphics			
1"x2¾", black lettering on white, shows UFP Pennant, singles	.05	.05-.10	_____
Sets (20 stickers per pack)	1	1-2	_____
Star Fleet Postal Service			
T-K Graphics			
1"x2¾", black lettering on white, singles	.05	.05-.10	_____
Sets (20 stickers per pack)	1	1-2	_____
Star Fleet Priority Communique/Rush To:			
T-K Graphics			
Giant 2"x4" sticker, black lettering on white	.20	.20-.50	_____
Starfleet Recruiting Office			
Star Base Central			
Black lettering, 3"x10"	1	1-2	_____
Star Fleet Spacegram			
T-K Graphics			
1"x2¾", set of 20 stickers	1	1-2	_____
Star Fleet Technical Document			
T-K Graphics			
1"x2¾", set of 20	1	1-2	_____
Star Trek Fans Make Better Lovers			
Amateur Press			
Shows tiny heart inside the letter "o" of last word, 2½"x11"	1	1-2	_____

4. This off-shoot slogan stems from the "Sock It To Me" logo of the 1960's comedy series "Rowan and Martin's Laugh-In."

STICKERS

	Issue	Current	Cost/Date
Star Trek Forever			
T-K Graphics			
1"x2¾", black lettering on white, shows Janus Head Emblem, singles	.05	.05-.10	
Sets (20 stickers per pack)	1	1-2	
2"x4", black lettering on white, shows U.S.S. Enterprise silhouette in black, singles	.20	.20-.30	
Sets (6 stickers per pack)	.75	1-2	

Star Trek Convention Bumper Sticker, 1972

	Issue	Current	Cost/Date
Star Trek Lives			
T-K Graphics			
2¼"x11", black and red lettering on green stock, Enterprise silhouette	1	1-2	
Star Base Central, distributors			
3"x9", shows Enterprise in upper lefthand corner firing phasers at Klingon ship in the lower righthand corner	1	1-2	
3"x12", black lettering on green	.75	1-2	
April Publications			
3¾"x14½", black letters on saturn blue or day-glo yellow stock	1.50	1-2	
Star Trek Convention, NYC 1972			
Florescent orange lettering on black stock [5]	.50	2-3	
Lincoln Enterprises			
4"x15", black lettering on florescent day-glo green stock	1.25	1-2	
Star Trek The Motion Picture			
Amateur Press			
Shows picture of Enterprise and Spock giving Vulcan hand salute in lefthand corner, 3"x14"	1	1-2	
Star Trek III - The Search For Spock			
Lincoln Enterprises, 1984			
Title logo and an Enterprise silhouette as seen to promote the movie. Same design that appears on the ST III Letterhead stationery.	2.50	3-4	
There Are Always Possibilities			
T-K Graphics			
1"x2¾", set of 20	1	1-2	
This Car Boldly Goes Where No Car Has Gone Before			
Fantasy Traders	1	1-2	
This Vehicle Equipped With Warp Drive			
April Publications			
Saturn blue or day-glo yellow stock, 3¾"x14½"	1.50	1-2	
This Vehicle Is Powered By Matter/Anti-Matter			
Star Base Central			
Logo centered in dark color swatch with ragged border, 4"x14"	1	1-2	
Trekkers Do It Under The Stars			
William Shatner Fan Club			
Blue lettering on white vinyl, 3½"x11"	2	2-3	
Trekkers Do It With Enterprise			
T-K Graphics			
Singles	.05	1-2	
Sets (20 stickers per pack)	1	1-2	
Tribble Breeding Is A Hairy Experience			
T-K Graphics			
2"x4", set of 6 giant stickers	.75	1-2	
4½"x5½", black lettering on brilliant white stock, includes cartoon drawing by Steve Stiles	.05	.50-1	
UFP Diplomatic Service			
T-K Graphics			
Giant sticker, 2"x4", black lettering on white, set of 6	.75	1-2	
1¾" diameters, stickers in red, orange or green stock, set of 15 (5 each color)	1	1-2	
U.F.P. Janus Head			
T-K Graphics			
1"2¾", black lettering on white, emblem in silhouette only	.05	.05-.10	
1"x2¾", black emblem on white, rectangle with rounded corners, set of 20 stickers	1	1-2	
1¾" diameter, black lettering on bright red, orange or green color stock, singles	.05	.05-.10	
Set (5 each color, 15 stickers)	1	1-2	
Calendar Sticker, black lettering on white set (6 stickers per pack)	.75	1-2	
3¼"x5½", black lettering on red, green, orange or chartreuse, florescent	.50	.50-1	
U.S.S. Enterprise			
Star Base Central, distributors			
1½"x13", lettering only	1	1-2	
T-K Graphics			
1"x2¾" shows ship schematic, set of 20 stickers	1	1-2	
1¾" diameter sticker, black lettering on bright red, orange or green color stock, silhouette only, singles	.05	.05-.10	
Sets (5 each color, 15 stickers)	1	1-2	
3¼"x5½", black lettering on red, orange, green or chartreuse stock, shows ship schematic	.50	.50-1	
U.S.S. Enterprise Official Papers			
T-K Graphics			
1"x2¾", set of 20	1	1-2	

5. The orange and black printing of this prolific Star Trek slogan issued from the original 1972 NYC Star Trek Con held at the Statler-Hilton Hotel in January. In all of its many subsequent printings, it has never reproduced this particular color combination since.

STICKERS

	Issue	Current Cost/Date	
U.S.S. Enterprise Shuttlecraft T-K Graphics Red and black lettering on yellow stock, shows Enterprise silhouette, 2¾"x11"	1	1-2	_____
Vote Yes On Star Trek Lincoln Enterprises Black lettering on florescent day-glo red stock, 4"x15"	1.25	1-2	_____
Vulcan Embassy Official Vehicle T-K Graphics Black lettering on white, 2¾"x11"	.75	1-2	_____
Vulcan Embassy Staff Vehicle T-K Graphics Black lettering on white stock, 2¾"x11"	.75	1-2	_____
Vulcan Power April Publications Black lettering on Saturn blue or day-glo yellow stock, 3¾"x14½"	1.50	1-2	_____
Vulcan Science Academy New Eye, distributors 1½"x18" decal to peel and stick, white letters on red	4	4-5	_____
2½"x18", college-sticker transparency for car window, block lettering	3	3-4	_____
Warp 5: A Speed We Can Live With Fantasy Traders	1	1-2	_____
Watch It. Photon Torpedos Armed Star Base Central Shows picture of Enterprise in dark oval on righthand side, 3"x13"	1	1-2	_____
We Want Star Trek III Lincoln Enterprises Black lettering on florescent day-glo stock, 4"x15"	1.25	2-3	_____

• **Sticker Collection Sets**

Assortment Series - Star Trek
T-K Graphics
Six assortment sets of peel-away stickers, 60 to a set, various sizes with diverse lettering slogans, black on white:

	Issue	Current Cost/Date	
Assortment #1 4/ Star Trek (with emblem) 4/ Enterprise 4/ Kirk and Spock Forever 4/ Keep On Trekkin' 4/ Star Fleet Headquarters Official 4/ Mail 4/ Vulcan Diplomat 4/ Star Trek Lives 4/ Klingon Postal Service 4/ Bring Back Star Trek 4/ Property of the Enterprise 4/ UFP Pennant (Picture) 4/ Property of Klingon Navy 4/ Tribble Spayed 4/ Spock 4/ Kirk Set of stickers	2	2-4	_____
Assortment #2 6/ Space: The Final Frontier 6/ Visit Vulcan 6/ UFP Diplomatic Dispatch 6/ Star Fleet Headquarters Classified 6/ Enterprise (schematic) 6/ May Your Tribbles Purr 4/ Vulcan Power 4/ Vulcan's Never Bluff 4/ Star Fleet Communique 4/ Spock Lusts In Heart 8/ The Human Adventure Is Just Beginning Set of stickers	2	2-4	_____
Assortment #3 6/ Spock Is Laughing 6/ Where No Man Has Gone Before 6/ Ilia Shampoos 6/ Dispatched: Stardate 6/ Tribble Power 6/ Live Long And Prosper 6/ Star Fleet Technical Document 6/ Star Trek Fans Make Better Lovers 6/ Star Fleet Freight 6/ Vulcans Do It Set of stickers	2	2-4	_____
Assortment #4 6/ Adopt A Tribble 6/ I'm A Trekker 6/ Paramount Is A Klingon Conspiracy 6/ Pointed Ears Are A Sign of Intelligence 6/ Hailing Frequencies Open 6/ Janus Head Emblem 6/ Klingon Postal Service 6/ Trekkers Do It With Enterprise 6/ I Am A Carbon Based Unit 6/ Old Trekkers Never Die Set of stickers	2	2-4	_____
Assortment #5 6/ He's Dead Jim 6/ Spacegram 6/ Special Orders 6/ Engineers 6/ I'd Rather Be Watching Star Trek 6/ Star Fleet Computer Division 6/ Survive and Succeed 6/ Star Trek Forever 6/ Tribble Breeding Is A Hairy Experience 6/ Property of Star Fleet Library Sticker set	2	2-4	_____

STICKERS

Issue | Current | Cost/Date

Assortment #6
6/ Spock Lives
6/ Tranquilizer
6/ Ad-Mee-Ral Kirk
6/ Boss - Thee Starship
6/ I Don't Like To Lose
6/ The Needs of the Many Outweigh the Needs of the Few or the One
6/ Jim Kirk Was Never A Boy Scout
6/ Revenge Is a Dish Best Served Cold
6/ I've Passed the Kobayashi Maru Test
6/ There Are Always Possibilities
Sticker set . . . . 2 2-4 ______

"Headline" Labels Set
Lincoln Enterprises, 1980
Assorted pressure sensitized stickers of various shapes, sizes and colors, brilliant day-glo or gold mylar, red and yellow. Slogans matched with Trek episode titles, witty phrases, etc. Examples are:
"That Which Survives" - Star Trek
Neilsen Ratings - "Doomsday Machine"
Paramount Comissary - "Bread and Circuses"
The Bermuda Triangle Is a Klingon Plot
Total of 60 individual stickers
1610, One set, 3 pages . . . . 1.95 2-3 ______
1611, Two sets, 9 pages . . . . 4.95 5-6 ______

Stained Glass Decal Stickers - STTMP
Aviva
Set of six 5" color decals that can be reapplied to surfaces, includes:
"Mr. Spock", profile with encircled insignia
STTMP Enterprise, port profile
Spock with Vulcan Salute
Spock in robes
Vulcan Salute
Kirk with encircled command star insignia
Set of 6 . . . . 2 2-5 ______

Sticker Packet Series - Star Trek Motion Picture
Aviva, 1979
Three sets of cartoon design stickers to peel and stick, mounted against cardstock and plastic wrapped:
Packet 1
Kirk bust with encircled Command Star
Encircle Command Star Insignia
Kirk bust, cut-out
Encircled Enterprise

Issue | Current | Cost/Date

Spock bust with encircled Command Star
Block lettering "Star Trek"
Sticker set . . . . 1.50 2-3 ______

Packet #2
Kirk bust with "Star Trek" lettering
Encircled Command Star Insignia
Encircled Vulcan Salute
Encircled Enterprise
Side profile of Spock, cut-out
Block lettering "Star Trek"
Sticker set . . . . 1.50 2-3 ______

Packet #3
Encircled Spock bust with lettering "Star Trek"
Encircled Command Star Insignia
Vulcan Salute and Spock bust, cut-out
Encircled Enterprise
Encircled ¾ figure Spock in Vulcan robes
Block lettering "Star Trek"
Sticker set . . . . 1.50 2-3 ______

STTMP Sticker, 1979

STTMP Sticker, 1979

PRINTED WALLHANGINGS
(Certificates, Plaques, Flats & Signs)

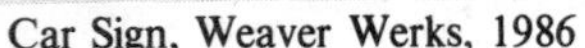
Car Sign, Weaver Werks, 1986

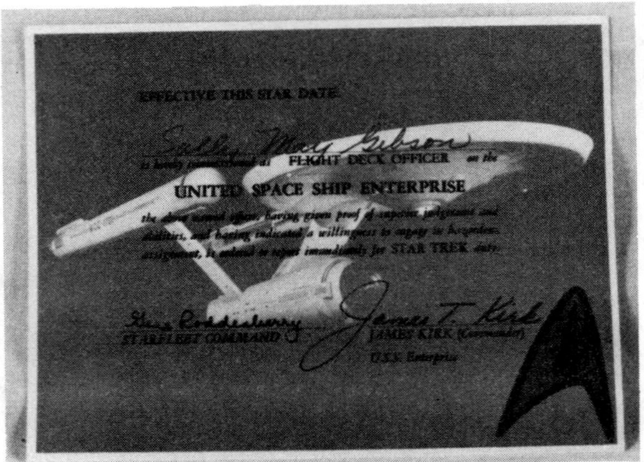

Flight Deck Certificate (regular) 1968

	Issue	Current	Cost/Date
Beam Me Up, Scotty - Car Sign #908			
Weaver Werks, 1986			
Sign designed for vehicular rear windows and patterned after the faddish "Baby On Board" yellow and black caution signs, plasticized 5"x5" sign with clear rubber suction cup included.	1.95	2-3	_____
Beam Me Up Scotty. This Place Has No Intelligent Life.			
T-K Graphics, 1984			
Black lettering on heavy red cardboard stock, drawing by Steve Stiles, 8½"x8½" sign.	1	1-2	_____
Gold litho, 8½"x11"	1	1-2	_____
Gold litho, 8½"x11"	1	1-2	_____
Gold Litho, 8½"x11"	1	1-2	_____
Gold litho on parchment paper, 8½"x11"	1	1-2	_____
April Publications			
Gold litho, 8½"x11"	1	1-2	_____
Gold litho, 8½"x11"	1	1-2	_____
Celebrity Wall Plaques			
Celebrity Prints, Inc., 1985			
Hand and footprints of the Sci-Fi stars. Ivory tinted prints are framed in gold anodized frames and include autograph signatures. Includes certificate of Authenticity and photo of the star, plus actor's bio.			
James "The Beamer" Doohan			
Walter Koenig			
"Galactically Yours," George Takei			
Nichelle Nichols			
Available in two size formats:			
10"x14" handprint and autograph	29.95	30-31	_____
20"x20"' hand and foot print, autographed	49.95	50-51	_____
Delta Oath of Celibacy Certificate			
April Publications			
Lithographed in gold, 8½"x11"	1	1-2	_____
Enterprise Crew Member Certificate			
April Publications			
Gold litho, 8½"x11"	1	1-2	_____
Federation Birth Certificate			
April Publications			
Gold litho, 8½"x11"	1	1-2	_____
Flight Deck Certificate			
Star Trek/Lincoln Enterprises 1968; 1980			
Honorary member of the U.S.S. Enterprise crew, "signed" by James T. Kirk and Gene Roddenberry, two styles			
Regular - Enterprise superimposed on blue paper.[1]	.50	1-3	_____
Deluxe - Enterprise superimposed on parchment-like paper, includes insignia sticker and two-color ribbon	1	2-3	_____
Klingon Captain Certificate			
April Publications			
Gold litho, 8½"x11"	1	1-2	_____
Klingon War Academy Diploma			
April Publications			
Gold litho, 8½"x11"	1	1-2	_____
No Smoking. /By Order of Star Fleet Command			
T-K Graphics, 1984			
Black lettering on red cardboard stock, 5½"x8½" Sign	.75	.75-1	_____

1. During the 1968 Save Star Trek Campaign organized and manned by volunteer fans, special issues of the Regular Flight Deck Certificate which included the addition of a gold insignia sticker were mailed to fans who wrote letters to NBC.

WALLHANGINGS

	Issue	Current	Cost/Date
Only Vulcan Spoken Here April Publications, 1984 Gold litho on card stock. Sign.....	1	1-2	_____
Phaser Marksmanship Certificate April Publications Gold litho, 8½"x11"	1	1-2	_____
Spock's Death Certificate April Publications Gold litho, 8½"x11"	1	1-2	_____
Star Fleet Academy Dipoloma T-K Graphics Black lettering on white card stock, decorated with foil seals, space for name, 8"x10" format			
Unframed	.75	.75-1	_____
Framed with heavy artist's board ..	2.75	2-3	_____
Starfleet Academy Diploma April Publications Gold litho, 8½"x11"	1	1-2	_____
Starfleet Admiral Certificate April Publications Gold litho, 8½"x11"	1	1-2	_____
Star Fleet Headquarters / Restricted Area T-K Graphics, 1984 Black lettering on red cardboard, 5½"x8½" sign	.75	.75-1	_____
Starfleet Oath Certificate April Publications Gold litho on parchment paper, 8½"x11"	1	1-2	_____
Starfleet Officer's Club Certificate April Publications Gold litho, 8½"x11"	1	1-2	_____
Starfleet Operations Officer Certificate April Publications Gold litho, 8½"x11"	1	1-2	_____
Starship Captain's Certificate April Publications Gold Litho, 8½"x11"	1	1-2	_____
"Star Trek Lives!" Pennant Fan issue, 1972 Souvenir from the first Star Trek Convention in NYC, in January 1972. Black felt with white lettering, border and tassels...............	1	8-10	_____
Star Trek Sepia Pictures Ludlow Sales, 1986 Large sepia tint stills mounted on a black mat board, has hole punches for easy hanging, 11"x14":			
Spock & Kirk with Enterprise model	3.99	4-5	_____
Bridge Crew, Kirk, Spock, McCoy, Scotty, Uhura, Chekov, Sulu & Chapel	3.99	4-5	_____

Sepia Picture, Ludlow Sales

	Issue	Current	Cost/Date
Star Trek The Motion Picture Starship Signs General Mills, Inc., 1979 Special promotion items free on the package backs of Cheerios Cereal boxes. All feature portrait photos with captions, ID's and silver borders, 3¼"x6¾", signs cut-out:			
"U.S.S. Enterprise"	—	.50-1	_____
"Danger ... Keep Out"	—	.50-1	_____
Mr. Spock's Quarters"	—	.50-1	_____
"Medical Office - Dr. Leonard 'Bones' McCoy"	—	.50-1	_____
"Engine Room - Do Not Enter" ...	—	.50-1	_____
"Intermix Chamber - Authorized Personnel Only"	—	.50-1	_____
"Captain's Quarters"	—	.50-1	_____
Complete set of 7 cut-out signs	—	4-8	_____
Complete set of package backs [2] ...	—	10-15	_____

STTMP Starship signs on Cheerios Box

2. As in the case of all promotional Package-back premiums, the collectible for this complete set of cards is higher if the cards remain intact on their original package boxes.

WALLHANGINGS

Issue | Current | Cost/Date

"Star Trek The Wrath of Kahn" / "Spock Lives!" Pennant
Image Products, Inc., 1982
Standard size triangular flag. White and red pseudo-felt with yellow and red lettering and a detailed illo decal of Spock in Vulcan robes stamped in black. . . . . 3.50 4-6 ______

"Star Trek The Wrath of Kahn" / "U.S.S. Enterprise" Pennant
Image Products, Inc., 1982
Standard size triangular flag. Black pseudo-felt with white lettering and stamp of front-view starship. . . . . . . 3.50 4-6 ______

Tribble Pedigree Certificate
April Publications
Gold litho, 8½"x11" . . . . 1 1-2 ______

U.F.P. Certificate, 1968

United Federation of Planets Certificate
Star Trek Enterprises, 1968
Grants the bearer full citizenship in the U.F.P. and free passage on any starship. Black lettering in italics printed on parchment-like paper, 8"x11". Free with the annual $3.00 membership to Star Trek Interstellar fan club. . . . . — 2-4 ______

United Federation of Planets Flag
April Publications
12"x20" double-triangle flag in red and silver satin cloth, representing the U.F.P. flag as seen on the t.v. episode "And the Children Shall Lead" . . . . 3 6-10 ______

Vulcan Birth Certificate
April Publications
Gold litho, 8½"x11" . . . . 1 1-2 ______

Vulcan Land Lease Certificate
April Publications
Gold litho, 8½"x11" . . . . 1 1-2 ______

Issue | Current | Cost/Date

Vulcan Marriage License
April Publications
Gold litho, 8½"x11" . . . . 1 1-2 ______

Vulcan Master Diploma
April Publications
Gold litho, 8½"x11" . . . . 1 1-2 ______

Vulcan Officer's Club Certificate
April Publications
Gold litho, 8½"x11" . . . . 1 1-2 ______

Vulcan Science Academy Diploma
April Publications
Gold litho, 8½"x11" . . . . 1 1-2 ______

Vulcan Science Academy
T-K Graphics
Design on white card stock, foil seal decorations, standard diploma design 8"x10":
Unframed . . . . .75 .75-1 ______
Framed with heavy artist's board . . 2.75 2-3 ______

JEWELRY

For many Star Trek fans, especially the more conservative Trekkers who might shy away from neon bumper stickers or flashy transfer shirts, wearing a piece of finely crafted jewelry set in a Star Trek theme is a means of demonstrating their admiration and loyalty.

Many types of metals and their component alloys are used in the art of jewelry making. All varieties and combinations can be found in descriptions of Star Trek merchandise.

	Component Type	Description
Gold	precious metal	Occurs in prescribed units of fineness (purity). One karat equals 1/24th part real gold. 12 Kt. - 50% real gold metal. 14 Kt. - 58% real gold metal. 22 Kt. - 92% real gold metal. 24 Kt. - 100% real gold metal
Gold Filligree (or Silver)	metal	A fine wire of metal is applied over a base metal surface.
Gold Filled (or Silver)	metal	A process where a metal actually surrounds a center composed of a baser metal.
Gold Plated (or Brass, Nickel & Silver)	metal	A fine layer of metal is placed on top of a baser metal, electrically.
Nickel	metal	A metallic element allied to iron & cobalt. It is used chiefly in alloys & in electroplating.
Rhodium	metal	From the platinum family & used to prevent corrosion through electroplating.
Sterling Silver	metal	A metal with a unit of fineness of 0.925 pure silver.
Zinc	metal	An element resembling magnesium which is used in making alloys.
Brass	alloy	An alloy composed of copper & zinc of variable proportions.
Bronze	alloy	A copper-based alloy containing variable amounts of tin.

Generally speaking, five buying points should be considered when collectors deliberate over the purchase of any Star Trek jewelry. This includes belt buckles, bracelets, charms, earrings, keychains, necklaces, pendants, medallions, pins, rings and watches.

These fundamental criteria for jewelry selection are: function, style, exclusivity, artistry and the overall quality of a jewelry piece. Rarity and vintage play a lesser role in evaluating collectible jewelry than they do for Star Trek merchandise of other types.

1. Is an item functional (serves a potentially useful purpose)? Belt buckles, keychains and watches are utilitarian articles. Bracelets, charms, earrings, necklaces, pendants, medallions, pins and rings are more for ornamentation.
2. Does the jewelry have style? Is it aesthetically appealing or does it make a statement? If pieces appear cartoonish, excessively gaudy or are "cheap" looking, they represent nothing but costume jewelry.
3. Is a piece particularly fine or an original work indicating its exclusivity? Custom designs often sell with an accompanying owner's certificate or even a serial registration number indicating that it is a limited edition minting or a commemorative item.
4. Did the manufacture of the jewelry require a large degree of artistry and a mastery of craftsmanship? Well handcrafted jewelry tends to provide fine detail work along with fewer imperfections. Original artistry is also a good selling point.
5. What quality of metals were used to create the jewelry collectible? Certain metals are more expensive to use and the completed price should reflect this.

Serious jewelry collectors should purchase their collectibles by hands-on inspection. Mail-order catalogs often inaccurately describe jewelry merchandise. Vague descriptions such as "heavy" metal, "ornate" detail and the classic, equally nebulous size definition of "large" or "small" riddle most catalogs.

In other cases, words such as "gold," "brass" and "bronze" can refer to an item's color rather than its metal base. Usually words such as brass and bronze indicate a brownish cast or hue. True gold metals are expensive. Inexpensive "gold" pieces probably refer to gold-tone imitations.

Collectors must also be leary of trader slang. Identical jewelry listings can be disguised as something else because they are carefully described by different names. Traders will spice up jewelry columns by substituting clever titles. The "Vulcan Hand of Peace," the "Vulcan Greeting" and the "Vulcan Salute" are obvious examples of misleading nomenclature.

A similar case exists for the retailing of a pendant depicting the fortress planetscape from the episode "The Menagerie." This pendant has names which range from simply "The Rigel 7 Pendant" to the eclectic pseudonym "The Unisex Celestial Pendant."

For the most part, the Starship Enterprise, the Vulcan IDIC, the Starfleet Command Insignia, the U.F.P. Janus Head Emblem and the composite profiles of Kirk and Spock appear over and over again in Star Trek's expansive jewelry lines.

BELT BUCKLES

	Issue	Current	Cost/Date
• Enterprise Design Buckles Assorted metal and enameled buckles featuring the starship Enterprise in profile or relief format:			
Solitary Starship - Without Legend Lee Belts, 1976 Oval brass-tone child size buckle featuring t.v. Enterprise. Includes black or brown leather belt. No legend.	2.99	5-7	______
Starship - without Legend, mounted Triangle Indiana Metal Co. 4149 T.V. Enterprise mounted on a triangular base. Blue enamel background with brasstone or antique silver-tone ship. No legend.	5	6-8	______
Starship - "Space the Final Frontier" Below Saturn Planet, Indiana Metal Co., 1982 2½" diameter brasstone buckle featuring t.v. Enterprise below a ringed planet and its moon. Green enameled background has Froz-n'-color trademark. Reverse has the legend "Space, the final frontier"	10	12-16	______
Starship - "Star Trek Lives" over Globe Rectangular metal buckle. Relief lettering reads "Star Trek Lives" and the "U.S.S. Enterprise" with starboard profile t.v. starship in center over stylized globe	4	6-9	______
Starship - "These Are The Voyages . . ." Bronze-tone oval buckle with t.v. Enterprise and legend on reverse.	4.95	6-9	______
• Insignia Design Buckles Buckles designed after the Star Trek II movie encircled Command Star Insignias on uniforms: also called "Star Fleet Uniform Belt Buckle." Extra-large and authentic size movie buckle with 2¾" diameter, cut-out star. Choice of gold-tone or bronze-tone enamel base	10	12-15	______
Lincoln Enterprises, 1982 also called "Official STWOK Belt Buckle." Standard size buckles for adult and child in flattened base metal with shiny gold surface.			
Adult (2" diameter)	7.60	8-10	______
Child (slightly smaller)	6	7-9	______
Lincoln Enterprises, 1984 also called "Official Uniform Belt Buckle". Molded metal cast from the authentic design used for STWOK and STSFS. 3" diameter in tubular circle base with star mounted on the top.	14.95	16-18	______
• Kirk Profile Tiffany Studios 2½" diameter oval buckle featuring bust of Captain Kirk. Brass-tone buckle.	4.95	9-12	______
• Kirk and Spock Profile Buckles Lee Belts, 1976 Oval buckle in brass-tone. Includes black or brown leather children's belt.	2.95	5-7	______
Lincoln Enterprises, 1980 Antique bronze-tone in right-angle corners. Two right-side face profiles with starboard profile of Enterprise overhead. Letters "Star Trek", 2"x3" rectangle	3.95	5-7	______
• Spock Profile Lee Belts, 1976 Oval buckle in brass-tone. Includes black or brown leather children's belt.	2.95	5-7	______
• Starfleet Belt Buckle Set Heroes World, distrib., 1980 Advertised in Star Trek Marvel Comic No. 2, child's set including STTMP vintage plastic uniform buckle with "Star Trek" lettering, stretch belt. Middle of buckle is "thermal sensor" strip to change color; ID card and encircled command star badge to wear.	6.99	10-12	______
•"Star Trek" Logo and Commemorative Buckles			
"Star Trek" Letter Logo Buckle Lee Belts, 1979 Metal buckle featuring the words "Star Trek" in the new STTMP lettering style. Includes a child's size stretch belt in assorted colors	2	4-6	______
"Star Trek 1980 U.S.S. Enterprise" Commemorative Lincoln Enterprises, the Olde New England Mint, engravers, 1980 Registered, numbered, with mint certificate of authenticity. Features STTMP Enterprise in port profile over a starfield. Rectangular. Logo banner reads "Star Trek - U.S.S. Enterprise." Minted in Bronze	20	25-30	______
Minted in solid sterling silver with highlights in 24 Kt. gold	180	200-215	______
"Star Trek" 1983 200th Anniversary of Man's Flight Commemorative Starlog Magazine, distributors, 1983 Deluxe edition commemorative buckle. 24 Kt. gold-plated STTMP starship wtih "Star Trek" logo lettering. Approximately 3"x4". Includes certificate of ownership and an			

BELT BUCKLES

	Issue	Current	Cost/Date
engraved issue number on the reverse. Packaged in a plastic box. .	19.95	25-30	_____

"Star Trek" 1983 200th Anniversary of Man's Flight Commemorative
Sunday Comics Promotions, Inc., 1983
2⅜"x3½" buckle in brass-tone to commemorate the 200th Anniversary of Man's First Flight. Logo "Star Trek" and STTMP Enterprise on unornamented metal. Special offer price. . . . . 6.88 8-10 _____

Magazine Ad, 1983.

"Star Trek III - The Search For Spock / The Saga Continues" Commemorative
Lincoln Enterprises, 1984
Official movie commemorative buckle. Numbered, registered, with certificate of authenticity. Features STTMP starship in starboard profile between flying banners and triple planet starfield. 2½"x3½" rectangle has deeply etched design. Reverse has the synopsis "The Saga Continues," an 82 word summary of the movie. Package includes an original art drawing. Pewter alloy base, 2445 19.95 22-25 _____

BRACELETS AND CHARMS

• **Enterprise Charms**
Star Trek/Lincoln Enterprises
1970, Introduced in Star Trek Enterprises Catalog No. 2, 1¾" t.v. starship in starboard profile, relief on metal background with hole for a clasp or neckchain on top, 22K gold-plate . . . . 5 8-10 _____

	Issue	Current	Cost/Date
1980, Lincoln's 3-D model of the STTMP movie starship, 1¾" long, gold-plated with chain loop as part of the saucer dome.	4.95	6-8	_____
Gold-plated wrist bracelet, optional	5.50	5-6	_____

• **IDIC Charm**
Lincoln Enterprises, 1980
Charm size rendention in gold and sizer tone metals with synthetic gemstone . . . . 5.50 6-7 _____

• **Insignia Charm**
Lincoln Enterprises, 1980
Charm size rendition of the t.v. series plain Command Star in choice of two metals finishes, ½" in length:
22K gold-plate with 18" gold-plate chain . . . . 4.95 5-7 _____
Sterling silver with 18" sterling chain . . . . 8 8-10 _____

• **Vulcan Salute Charm**
Lincoln Enterprises, 1980
also called "Vulcan Hand of Peace" 3-D righthanded palm and wrist in shiny gold-tone, includes 18" chain. 2414 . . . . 3.95 4-6 _____

• **Wrist Band - Star Trek The Motion Picture**
DuBarry Fifth Avenue, Inc., 1979
Child's, small size identification bracelet with link chain. Available in silver or gold-tones with a capacity to hold 8 letters for a personalized souvenir . . . . 1.25 5-8 _____

EARRINGS

• **Enterprise Design**
Aviva
Starship outlined in black on a clear lucite block, pierced earring style. . . 1 2-4 _____
3-D replica models in gold or silver plate, pierced or clip-on earring styles . . . . 6 6-8 _____

• **IDIC Design**
Circle and triangle with gemstone apex. The Vulcan symbol of Infinite Diversity in Infinite Combinations, as worn by Mr. Spock on the t.v. episode "Is There In Truth No Beauty?"
Lincoln Enterprises, 1980
Lightweight gold and silver-tone replicas, ¾" diameter, pierced or clip-on . . . . 6.50 7-9 _____

EARRINGS

Issue | Current | Cost/Date

• **Insignia Design**
The plain command star as worn on the series.
Lincoln Enterprises, 1980
also called "Star Fleet Dress Ear-rings" t.v. insignia replicas in 22K gold plate or in sterling silver.
Several earring styles:

	Issue	Current	Cost/Date
Pierced, dangle-style, gold plate	8.95	9-10	______
Pierced, dangle style, sterling	15	15-17	______
Pierced, post style, gold plate	8.95	9-10	______
Pierced, post style, sterling	15	15-17	______
Clip-on, dangle style, gold plate	8.95	9-10	______
Clip-on, dangle style, sterling	15	15-17	______

KEYCHAINS

• **Enterprise Designs**
Solitary Starship
New Eye, distributors
Starship over black void of space . . . 2 | 3-5 | ______
Tel Rad Services, 1975
Gold-tone chain and medallion. Features special auto-lock, t.v. Enterprise relief in silver-tone. . . . . 3.50 | 5-6 | ______

Starship with Klingon Cruiser, 1974
Reversible medallion features one relief silhouette on each side. Bronze cast, t.v. starships . . . . 4 | 8-12 | ______

Starship - "Star Trek" with U.F.P. Emblem (Reversible)
Image Products, 1982
Large 1½" oval medallion in solid brass, one side lettered "Star Trek" below STWOK Enterprise, reverse has high relief UFP circle emblem on polished surface . . . . 10 | 10-12 | ______

• **"I Love Star Trek" Letter Logo**
April Publications
Chain and ring holders in choice of two medallions:
White plastic with red heart . . . . . . 1 | 2-3 | ______
Simulated leather texture . . . . 1 | 2-3 | ______

IDIC
Lincoln Enterprises, 1980
Medium size 1" replica in gold and silvertone on a chain . . . . 6.50 | 7-8 | ______

Leonard Nimoy Keychain
Claire Mason, 1973
Fan Issue keyholder. Features photos of Leonard Nimoy, Mr. Spock and Paris from Mission: Impossible embedded in plastic and attached to a keyring . . . . 1 | 4-6 | ______

"Live Long and Prosper" Letter Logo
Blue vinyl pocket key holder with white lettering and the Vulcan Salute. . . . . 2 | 2-4 | ______

S.T.T.M.P. Key Chains, Aviva, 1980

Issue | Current | Cost/Date

Phaser
1974
t.v. phaser pistol charm on a key-ring . . . . 1 | 5-8 | ______

"Starfleet Headquarters"
1986
U.F.P. Emblem plus the S.F.C. HQ 7 pront Insignia cluster in 22K gold-plate, circular medallion with keychain attached. . . . . 6.95 | 7-8 | ______

Star Trek The Motion Picture Keychains
Aviva, 1980
Reversible color decals/transparencies embedded in clear lucite squares approximately 1"x1". Short silver-tone chain and clasp ring:

	Issue	Current	Cost/Date
A101 STTMP Enterprise over star-field	1	3-5	______
A102 Spock, Kirk and Enterprise over planets	1	3-5	______
A103 Righthanded Vulcan Salute	1	3-5	______
A104 "Star Trek" lettering with standing figure of Spock	1	3-5	______
A105 "Mr. Spock" lettering with insignia and Spock's head profile	1	3-5	______
A106 "Live Long and Prosper" lettering with Spock in Vulcan robes	1	3-5	______

Tribble Key Guard
Lincoln Enterprises, 1975
Fuzzy miniature tribble to guard your keys from Klingon nastys!
0404 . . . . 1.50 | 3-4 | ______

Trivia Keychain
Proudline, 1984
2"x3¼" orange and white plastic pocket trivia game. Contains 120 t.v. questions and answers on 24 pull-out plastic cards. Star Trek questions (2) and one question about William Shatner. Metal keyring is attached by a white vinyl loop. . . . . 1.50 | 1-3 | ______

United Federation of Planets
Metal medallion with 1" diameter and thick ¼" braided chain and key ring clasp. Emblem with laurels. . . . 3.50 | 4-5 | ______
Circular metal medallion with enamel finish in full color galaxy emblem with laurels. . . . . 4.95 | 5-6 | ______

PENDANTS

Necklaces, coin-mounts and medallions either fixed to chains or removable settings:

	Issue	Current	Cost/Date

- **Enterprise Design Pendants**

Solitary Starship

Federation Trading Post
t.v. starship, relief done in pewter, includes a chain .... 8 | 9-12

STTMP starship in portside profile, relief done in 14K gold-plate, packaged in a gold colored box .... 6.95 | 8-10

Lincoln Enterprises, 1980
3-D miniature starship from STTMP, gold-plated, 1¾"x1", hangs horizontally from loop on saucer. Also available in a charm. Includes the chain .... 5.50 | 6-8

Starlog distributors, 1980
3-D miniature starship from STTMP, pewter cast with nickel-plating. Includes 18" silver-ton chain. Hangs vertically from loop on hangar bay. Very stylized rendition. .... 4.95 | 6-9

Starship - Orbiting Planet

American Miss, 1974
Metal cut-out of t.v. starship in orbit around a ringed planet with 4 moons. Goldtone, includes chain, mounted on jeweler's style heavy cardstock - flossed. Child's costume jewelry. .... 2 | 4-6

Good Time Jewelry, 1971
Oval dog-tag, thin metal with engraving of Enterprise over planet. Plastic wrapped on cardstock with cartoon portraits of Kirk, Spock and McCoy and Enterprise in battle with Klingons. "An Adventure in Space," child's costume jewelry ... 2 | 4-5

Starship - Phasering

Lincoln Enterprises, 1980
also called the "Enterprise Circle" 1¼" diameter cut-out in 24K gold filigree. Shows STTMP starship in starboard profile using twin phasers on a planet. Includes an 18" chain . 5.95 | 6-8

Original Vulcan Idic, Star Trek Enterprises, 1970.

Starship with Insignia

Hit Line, U.S.A., 1974
2½" diameter white plastic circle with t.v. starship on one side and insignia on the reverse .... 2 | 4-6

- **Holographic Pendants**

Don Post Studios, 1982
Holographic lens encircled by metal ring. Available in double or single image, in three projections. Includes a silvertone heavy link chain.

	Issue	Current
STTMP Enterprise, single lens	19.95	22-25
STTMP Enterprise, double lens	25.95	26-30
Space Shuttle Enterprise, single	19.95	18-20
Space Shuttle Enterprise, double	25.95	20-22
Klingon Warship, single	19.95	22-25
Klingon Warship, double	25.95	26-30

- **IDIC Designs**

Infinite Diversity in Infinite Combinations
Star Trek Enterprises, 1970
Available in only one size, Catalog #2. Large 2" diameter in 22K gold-plate and Florentine Silver (rhodium plate) with gemstone setting. Includes 24" gold-tone chain .... 7.50 | 12-16

Lincoln Enterprises, 1980
Re-released pendants in assorted sizes. Gold-plate and nickel-plate, include gold-tone chain

	Issue	Current
Large 2" diameter with 24" chain	7.50	8-10
Medium 1" with 18" chain	6.50	7-8
Small ¾" with 18" chain	5.50	6-7

- **Insignia Designs**

Sciences Insignia

Federation Trading Post
T.V. insignia as worn by Spock, pewter .... 3 | 5-7

Starship Command

T.V. insignia as worn by Captain Kirk
Federation Trading Post
pewter rendition .... 3 | 5-7

also called "Star Fleet Dress Pendant," t.v. insignia in 14 K gold plate, with chain .... 6 | 6-8

Star Trek The Wrath of Kahn Encircled Command Insignias

Don Post Studios, 1982
also called "Star Fleet Uniform Pendant," design cut-out, brass-plated metal, does not include a chain. Original packaging is a plastic form with foam backing mounted on 4"x6" cardstock featuring the "starburst" logo on front and a photo of the bridge crew on back. Two sizes:

	Issue	Current
Large 2" diameter	8.95	10-12
Small 1½" diameter	6.95	7-9

PENDANTS

Issue / Current / Cost/Date

"Kahn's Pendant"
Broken circle command star, brass-plated metal, 2½" diameter, does not include a chain. Original packaging the same as the jewelry piece above. . . . . 9 15-20 ______

Lincoln Enterprises, 1982
also called "Official Uniform Insignia Medallion," design cut-out of flattened metal with shiny gold surface, includes gold-tone chain. Two sizes: Large 1½" diameter . . . . 5.95 7-9 ______
Small 1" diameter . . . . 4.50 5-7 ______
Also available in a pin.

• **Mount Seleya Temple Peace Symbol**
Lincoln Enterprises, 1984
3-D sculpture of temple on Vulcan, from STSFS. 1" high, polished gold-plate, includes 24" gold-plated chain . . . . 6.95 7-9 ______

• **Rigel 7 Pendant**
Lincoln Enterprises, 1980
also called the "Unisex Celestial Pendant," 1¼" in diamter cut-out in 24K gold filigree, details castle and moon planetscape from "The Menagerie," circular banner reads "Where No Man Has Gone Before," includes 18" chain. . . . . 5.95 6-8 ______

• **Sparkle Necklaces**
Designs on sparkle refraction surface, silver emblems against black backgrounds on 1½" circular medallions, include gold or silver-toned 24" twisted neck chains, with holders:
Enterprise against starfield . . . . 3.50 5-6 ______
Encircled Command Star Insignia . 3.50 4-5 ______
U.F.P. Emblem . . . . 3.50 4-5 ______

• **Spock Profiles**
Spock's Head, Necklace
American Miss, 1974
Metal outline of left-sided profile, cartoonish, includes gold-tone chain. Child's costume jewelry mounted on jeweler's heavy cardstock - flossed . 2 5-7 ______

Spock Over Insignia, Space Jewelry
Good Time Jewelry, 1971
Imposed right profile of Mr. Spock's head. Plastic wrapped on cardstock with cartoon portraits of Kirk, Spock, Scotty and McCoy and Enterprise in battle with Klingon: "An Adventure in Space". Child's costume jewelry. . . . . 2 5-7 ______

Issue / Current / Cost/Date

• **"Starfleet Headquarters"**
1986
Circular medallion with attached chain mount. Front shows U.F.P. Emblem, rear has laurels with 7 prong "insignia" style crest, in 22K gold-plate with chain . . . . 10.95 12-14 ______

• **"Star Trek" Logos and Commemoratives**
Star Trek Comic Logo, Necklace
American Miss, 1974
Solid metal horizontal lettering reads "Star Trek" with bisecting starship Enterprise as seen on the Gold Key comics. Includes gold-tone chain. Mounted on jeweler's style heavy cardstock- flossed. Child's costume jewelry . . . . 2 5-7 ______

Star Trek 1974 Medallion Coin Series
Three commemorative coins issued in the series, differing in metal content and mint cut styles. Front shows bust of t.v. Spock and Kirk, reverse features starboard profile t.v. Enterprise with "Star Trek" lettering, plus the "Where No Man Has Gone Before . . . First Nationally Televised Episode" dedication.
Type 1 Series
Coin minted in .999 Silver, with edge numbers, clean cut, detachable mount . . . . 75 175-300 ______
Type 2 Series
Coin appearance same as above without rim serial numbers, struck in bronze with detachable coin mount setting . . . . 30 35-50 ______
Type 3 Series
High quality fully struck bronze coin without numbers and with chain-mount holder and rim struck as solid part of the coin and non-detachable . . . . 20 30-40 ______

Star Trek 1974 Commemorative Coin
1975 New York Star Trek Convention 12-gauge, bronze coin medal. Front profile t.v. starshp with "U.S.S. Enterprise," rear reads "Star Trek 1975" over a starfield. Not sold with a coin chain mount, $1\frac{9}{16}$" diameter . . . . 5 15-20 ______

Star Trek 1976 - 10th Anniversary Commemorative Coin
Lincoln Enterprises, 1976
Silver dollar size coin medallion in holder. Front reads: "10th Anniversary Commemoration - Star Trek 1966-1976" with busts of Kirk, Spock, McCoy and Scotty. Reverse profiles starboard Enterprise over planet with the legend "Space the

PENDANTS

	Issue	Current	Cost/Date
Final Frontier ... Where No Man Has Gone Before." Includes 24" chain. Bronze cast.	5.50	8-10	_____
Star Trek 1986 - 20th Anniversary Commemorative Coin Lincoln Enterprises, 1986 Solid zinc coin 1½" diameter with antique finish and coated with clear enamel to prevent tarnishing. Front has bas-relief STTMP vintage busts of Kirk and Spock. Read has a starboard movie Enterprise over planets and reads "1966-1986 20th Anniversary Commemorative", 2461	14.95	15-17	_____
Star Trek III The Search For Spock Coin Mount Medallion Lincoln Enterprises, 1984 1½" diameter medallion in gold-plated holder with 24" heavy gauge chain. Cast from solid zinc with antique finish and clear enamel coating. Front portraits Kirk and Spock and reads "ST III: SFS". Reverse profiles starboard Enterprise below the Genesis planet encircled by "Kirk - of all the souls I have encounted, his was the most human."	12.95	14-16	_____
"Trek" Fan Medallions • **"Trekker" or "Trekkie" Medallion** The Ultimate Design Group, 1978 Reversible slogan pewter medallion made for use with a chain. Mail order. Also available as a jacket pin.	4.50	5-7	_____
"Try-Trekkin' " Lincoln Enterprises 1979 Gold-plated block lettering attached to a wire choker	3	4-5	_____
1980 Two words top and bottom of an oval, synthetic "mood" stone that changes between six colors, includes chain	4.95	5-6	_____
• **Unisex Klingon Warning Whistle** Lincoln Enterprises, 1979 Clever name for this standard police whistle with gold-plated surface. Includes 18" gold-plated chain.	2	2-3	_____
• **United Federation of Planets** Federation Trading Post t.v. banner emblem and laurels, pewter	3	4-6	_____
Circular laminate medallion, executed in full color enamel, galaxy emblem with laurels.	4.95	5-6	_____

	Issue	Current	Cost/Date
• **Vulcan Salute** Federation Trading Post also called "Vulcan Hand Greeting". Hand salute rendered in pewter cast	3	4-5	_____
• **"Where No Man Has Gone Before" Necklace** Lincoln Enterprises Four lines of block lettering in gold-plate, includes 24" chain	6.95	7-8	_____

PINS

	Issue	Current	Cost/Date
• **Enterprise Design Pins** Aviva, 1979 Ship pins in different finishes: Movie starship in brass with enameled photo finish, circular background	3	3-5	____
Movie starship in cut-out profile, brass with enameled photo finish	4	4-5	____
T.V. starship cast in bronze	8	8-10	____
Hollywood Commemorative Pin Co., 1986 Part of the ltd. edition Star Trek Collection in cloisonne: No. 3 - "Star Trek/Starship Enterprise" with yellow lettering above and below starboard profile t.v. ship in white, red square background, 1"x1¾"	8	8-9	_____
No. 15 - Same Enterprise as above, but cut-out with no background	6	6-7	_____
• **IDIC** Lincoln Enterprises, 1980 Rendition in ¾" gold and nickel plate, was also available in earrings, pendant and ring formats	4	4-6	_____
• **"I Am A Trekkie" Stickpin** Lincoln Enterprises, 1976 Gold-tone stickpin with a button top with the above slogan.	—	3-5	_____

PINS

- **Insignia Designs**

The original, simple rank insignia as worn on the t.v. uniforms and the later, more elaborate circled designs produced for the four motion pictures in assorted metals and sizes:

Don Post Studios, 1982
Movie version Encircled Command Star also called the "Uniform Insignia" ST II insignia in brass-plate. Original packaging in plastic bubble with foam backing on 4"x6" cardstock with the "Starburst" Movie Design Logo on front and photo of bridge crew on reverse. The pin sizes are slightly smaller than the 2" and 2½" diameter Encircled Star pendants from Don Post:

	Issue	Current	Cost/Date
Large	5.95	8-10	______
Small	4.50	6-8	______

Aviva, 1979

	Issue	Current	Cost/Date
T.V. Command Star superimposed on a circular background, brass with enameled photo finish	3	4-6	______
T.V. Command Star cast in bronze	6	7-8	______
Movie encircled star, cut-out in brass with enameled photo finish	4	5-6	______

Hollywood Commemorative Pins Co., 1986
Starway, distributors
Part of their limited edition cloisonne pins in the "Star Trek Collection":
Encircled Insignias:

	Issue	Current	Cost/Date
10 - Command Star, white and gold on maroon circle, ½" diameter	6.00	6-7	______
12 - As above, 1½" diameter	8	8-9	______
21 - Command Star, white and gold on white circle, ½" diameter	6	6-7	______
22 - Engineering, white and gold star on yellow circle, ½" diameter	6	6-7	______
23 - Operations, white and gold star on orange circle, ½" diameter	6	6-7	______
24 - Security, white and gold star on red circle, ½" diameter	6	6-7	______
25 - Medical, white and gold star on green circle, ½" diameter	6	6-7	______
26 - Science, white and gold star on blue circle, ½" diameter	6	6-7	______
30 - Plain t.v. Command Star in white and gold	6	6-7	______
32 - Plain t.v. Command Star in red and gold	6	6-7	______
35 - Plain t.v. Engineering Swirl in yellow and gold	6	6-7	______
42 - Plain t.v. Sciences "eye" in red and gold	6	6-7	______

Lincoln Enterprises
Plain t.v. Command Star, 1980
½" long in two metals

	Issue	Current	Cost/Date
22K gold-plate	4.95	6-7	______
Sterling silver	8	9-10	______

Encircled Command Star
also called the "Official Uniform Insignia," ST II encircled star in flattened metal with a shiny gold surface, two sizes:

	Issue	Current	Cost/Date
Large, 1½" diameter	5.95	6-7	______
Small, 1" diameter	4.50	5-6	______

Encircled Star
also called "Star Trek Federation Dress Pin," ST Ii insignia in 14K gold-plate with official military twin-pin fastener on back, 2" diameter .. 9 — 10-12 ______

- **Insignia Bar Pins**

ST II introduced Encircled Command Star over an oblong bar mount.

Don Post Studios, 1982
also called "Federation Uniform Jacket Insignia," brass-plated 1½" insignia over a 3" bar. Packaged in plastic bubbled on foam back mounted on 4"x6" cardstock with "Starburst" on front and photos of bridge crew on reverse .. 10 — 15-18 ______

Lincoln Enterprises, 1982
also called "Jacket Insignia," star over bar in authentic movie size, plus and additional smaller version, 14K brushed gold-plate:

	Issue	Current	Cost/Date
2408 Large 2"x3"	7.95	9-10	______
2409 Small 2"x1"	5.95	7-9	______

- **Kirk Pin**

Aviva, 1979
STTMP Admiral Kirk on circular pin in brass with enameled photo finish, letters "Star Trek" .. 3 — 4-5 ______

- **Klingon Empire Pins**

Hollywood Commemorative Pin Co., 1986
Part of Star Trek limited edition cloisonne collection:

	Issue	Current	Cost/Date
150 Klingon Symbol, yellow sphere trisected by red, blue and gray 3-prong geometry, ¾"x1"	6	6-7	______
151 Klingon Symbol, larger size	8	8-9	______
155 Klingon Admiral Rank, 2-star, bisected circle, gold and red, ¾" diameter	6	6-7	______
156 Klingon Captain Rank, central star, gold and red, ¾" diameter	6	6-7	______

- **McCoy Pin**

Aviva, 1979
STTMP Dr. McCoy in brass with enameled photo finish, circular pin with "Star Trek" letters .. 3 — 5-6 ______

PINS

	Issue	Current	Cost/Date
• Romulan Empire Crest Pin			
Hollywood Commemorative Pin Co., 1986			
Part of the ltd. edition Star Trek Collection cloisonne set:			
175 - blue circular pin with gray, dark blue and red "thunderbird-style" design, 1" diameter	8	8-9	______
• Spock Figures			
Assorted busts and standing profiles:			
Aviva, 1979			
Spock - circular brass pin with enameled photo finish and "Star Trek" letters	3	4-5	______
Spock - bust with "Live Long and Prosper" on brass with photo enamel finish	3	4-5	______
Spock - figure wearing Vulcan robes in brass with photo enamel finish	3	4-5	______
Spock - t.v. figure in bronze cast	6	7-8	______
Hollywood Commemorative Pin Co., 1986			
Part of the cloisonne Star Trek set:			
301 - Series 1, full figure t.v. Spock figure in blue, black and gold, ⅝" x 2¼"	6	6-7	______
• Star Fleet Command Branch Pins			
Hollywood Commemorative Pin Co., 1986			
1"x1½" pins showing octagon of various colors with U.F.P. starfield inside, command star in gray and specific branch of the service lettered across bottom. Each branch illos its own individual logo symbol on two sides, overall pin color is blue: limited editon Cloisonne.			
61 - Military	6	6-7	______
62 - Security, red	6	6-7	______
63 - Marines, navy	6	6-7	______
64 - Medical, white	6	6-7	______
65 - Headquarters	6	6-7	______
66 - Intelligence	6	6-7	______
68 - Colonial Operations, pale blue	6	6-7	______
69 - Personnel, red	6	6-7	______
70 - Communications, gray	6	6-7	______
71 - Merchant Marine, olive green	6	6-7	______
72 - Engineering, yellow	6	6-7	______
• Star Fleet Command Rank Pins			
Assorted "spearhead/point" clusters with the number and arrangement of the geometries designating different grades:			
Hollywood Commemorative Pin Co., 1986. Part of the ltd. edition Star Trek cloisonne collection:			
101 - Flag Admiral, six points on a hexagon, gold, white and black, 1¼"x1¼"	8	8-9	______
102 - Admiral, four point, gold and black over a square, ⅞"x⅞"	6	6-7	______
103 - Commodore Bar, rounded ends, one solid inside bar with spearhead ends, ¾"x3½"	8	8-9	______
104 - Captain Bar, pointed with triple inside bars, ¾"x3½"	8	8-9	______
Lincoln Enterprises, 1985			
STTMP rank insignia pins cast in fiberglass and mounted on display cards:			
2413 - Lieutenant, double "Bullets" alone	2.50	2-3	______
2414 - Captain Bar, pointed ends with two spearheads and triple inside bars	3.50	4-5	______
2415 - Rear Admiral, 4-point spearheads over a square	3.50	4-5	______
2416 - Commander, double bars without spearhead points	3	4-5	______
2417 - Petty Officer 1st Class, a barred octogan	2	2-4	______
New Eye, distrib., 1987			
Movie vintage rank pins and bar pins:			
Chrome-high polish finish pins as described in above two listings:			
Lieutenant, double bullets	6	6-7	______
Captain Bar, trible inside bars, points	10	10-11	______
Commander, double bar, without points	10	10-11	______
Admiral, four points on a square	10	10-11	______
Variety II Style Rank Pins, 1987			
Lt. Commander, double bullets inside bar	10	10-11	______
Lt. Commander, solid horizontal bar inside bar	10	10-11	______
Fleet Admiral, four points inside double circle	12	12-13	______
Commodore, triple bar with four spear head points inside bar	12	12-13	______
• Star Fleet Command Sleeve Pins			
Smaller version, slightly curved rank pins designed especially to fit onto jacket sleeves:			
Lincoln Enterprises, 1986			
Fiberglass cast sleeve "Pips," or service recommendation pins:			
2418 - Set of 7 assorted shapes with circles representing 5 year service, oblong bar solids are SFC special commendations	9.95	10-11	______
New Eye, distrib., 1987			
Captain Bar, triple inside bars, points	10	10-11	______
Commander Bar, double inside bars, no points	10	10-11	______
• Star Fleet Uniform Shoulder Strap Pin			
Intergalactic, distrib., 1985			
ST III regalia as worn on the back of the uniforms to hold straps down. Octogonal metal cut-out with two military clutch-back pins, ⅞" diameter	2.50	2-3	______

PINS

	Issue	Current	Cost/Date
• "Star Trek" Series Commemoratives			
Assorted pins with show's title as a series dedication.			
Hollywood Commemorative Pin Co., 1986. Part of the ltd. edition cloisonne Star Trek Collection:			
5 - "Star Trek" above and below red, gold and white encircled insignia on blue rectangle, ⅝"x⅞"	6	6-7	______
6 - "Star Trek" as above, on white rectangle, ⅝"x⅞"	6	6-7	______
203 - "Star Trek 20 Year 1966-1986" pin in circular Anniversary Logo, red, white and blue, 1" diameter	6	6-7	______
205 - "Star Trek 20th Anniversary, To Boldly Go ... Stardate: 1/6609 to 1/8609", 1"x2" rectangle in blue with yellow lettering; white cut-out Enterprise, red moon and blue Earth	8	8-9	______
206 - "Star Trek 20th Anniversary 1966-1986" WOW pin, 1"x1½" in blue with yellow lettering, white Enterprise and red, orange and blue nova	8	8-9	______
210 - "Star Trek Twenty Years 1966-1986" Official Insignia Anniversary Logo as seen on posters, gold and red lettering over gold edged insignia with dark gray background, 1½"x2¼"	10	10-12	______
• "Trekker" or "Trekkie" Pin			
The Ultimate Design Group, 1978 Pewter cast jacket pin with reversible ID's, mail order (also available as a medallion)	3.50	5-7	______
• United Federation of Planets Design			
Assorted crests in different sizes and metals:			
Hollywood Commemorative Pin Co., 1986 ltd. edition cloisonne collection			
250 - gray laurels shield with starfield in blue and white lettering "UFP", ⅞"x1⅛"	8	8-9	______
U.F.P. Emblem Galaxy emblem with laurels, 1" diameter metal	3.50	4-6	______
U.F.P. Emblem Full color blue and silver starfield on black enamel	4	4-6	______
• Vulcan Salute Pins			
Assorted pins with hand salute theme:			
Aviva, 1979 Brass pins with enameled photo finish and three styles of Vulcan hand mounted on a circle	3	4-5	______
Vulcan hand salute cast in bronze	6	6-7	______
Hollywood Commemorative Pin Co., 1987			
Part of the Star Trek ltd. edition cloisonne pin series:			
50 - Circular disc with gold hand, letters "Live Long and Prosper"	6	6-7	______
51 - Blue disc with flesh-tone hand and "LL & P" lettering, spelled out, 1"	8	8-9	______
52 - Red 1" disc, same as 51	8	8-9	______
53 - Maroon 1" disc, same as 51	8	8-9	______

RINGS

	Issue	Current	Cost/Date
• Enterprise Ring			
Starlog, distributors, 1980 3-D miniature model of the STTMP starship cast in pewter and nickel-plate. Very stylized. Smaller than the same design in pendant form. Adjustable.	6.45	7-9	______
• IDIC Ring			
Federation Trading Post Rendition cast in pewter. Adjustable	4	4-6	______
Lincoln Enterprises, 1980 Small ½" rendition in gold and nickel plate. Adjustable. Also available in earrings, pin, charm and keychain	5.50	6-7	______
• Insignia			
Lincoln Enterprises, 1980 ½" rendition in two metal choices. Adjustable t.v. Command Star:			
22K gold-plate	4.95	5-6	______
Sterling silver	8	8-10	______
Also available in charm, earrings, pin.			
• Vulcan Crystal Rings			
Lincoln Enterprises, 1980 Quartz-color, synthetic "mood" rings with stone that changes from six hues, adjustable with various gold-tone designs:			
Stone with "Star Trek" lettering	4.95	5-6	______
Stone horizontally mounted with scrollwork	4.95	4-5	______
Stone horizontally mounted with laurels	4.95	4-5	______
Stone horizontally mounted, plain setting	4.95	4-5	______
Stone vertically mounted, plain setting	4.95	4-5	______

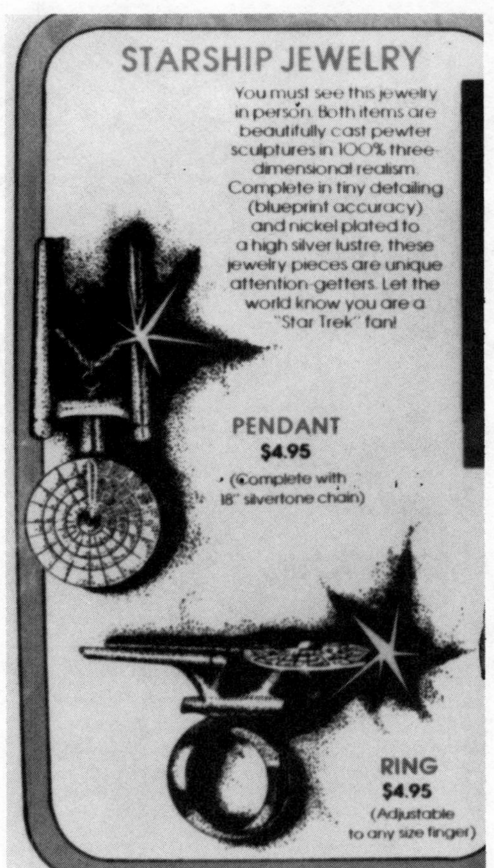

Magazine Ad for Pendant and Ring.

WATCHES

Enterprise Design Watches

ASA Co., 1974
Enterprise design faceplate wristwatch with a striped nylon sports band, analog .... 9.95 15-28 ______

Bradley Time Division/Elgin Ind., 1980-82. Collection of children's and adult's wristwatches with STTMP vintage Enterprise faceplates and assorted bands and casings:
5746-DFE4 Analog Watch
Black dial features central, blue starship and "Star Trek" lettering, white hand sweeps to black numerals on a round chrome ring. Square black plastic case with black vinyl band and silver-tone bezel ring. Packaged in plastic pocket ... 29.95 30-35 ______

5747-ZFE4 Digital L.C.D. Watch
Blue dial features dark blue starship and yellow words "Star Trek" above L.C.D. display, below is yellow Kirk and blue Spock in miniature portraits, large square, chrome case with black vinyl band. Displays time, month, day, nite-lite and seconds. Packaged in plastic pocket 19.95 25-30 ______

Issue Current Cost/Date

5749-YFE4 Digital L.C.D. Watch
Same as the above L.C.D. watch, but with medium size, ladies or children's chrome case and thinner wristband. Packaged in plastic pocket case .... 19.95 25-30 ______

Leader Toys, 1977
3170-3669 Analog Watch
Working children's toy watch with pendulum and visible "inner workings", red vinyl wristband, boxed. 4.95 10-16 ______

"Star Trektennial Watch - 1976"
Tenth Anniversary commemorative wristwatch designed by Uri Geller. Faceplate features starboard Enterprise streaking across a starry black background and trailing streamer of red. Inscription reads "Tenth Anniversary Star Trek 1966-1976", two styles:
Gold-tone frame with black band .. 21 35-40 ______
Clear lucite case .... 20 35-40 ______

STTMP Wristwatch, 1980
Exclusive jewelry design by Doug Little. Features a large faceplate with starship over starburst design, analog works, gold-tone case with black viny band, men or women's sizes .... 29.95 25-35 ______

- **Portrait Designs**

Kirk, Spock and McCoy Triumvirate, 1984
Analog watches with faceplate showing illo drawing of Kirk, McCoy and Spock busts in yellow. Dial is blue with white numbers. Dustproof, stainless steel back. Three styles:
Men's wristwatch, simulated black leather wristband .... 15 20-25 ______
Women's wristwatch, black vinyl band .... 15 20-25 ______
Pocket Watch, standard size, 2" diameter .... 15 20-25 ______

Spock Portrait Watches

Bradley Time Div., Elgin Ind., 1980
5743-DFE4 - Blue dial charicature of STTMP Spock and white numerals. Second hand sweeps a yellow tiny Enterprise and white shuttlecraft around the face. Medium chrome oval casing, black vinyl band, cylinder box. .... 24.95 30-40 ______

	Issue	Current	Cost/Date
Lewco Corp., 1987 "Star Trek Mr. Spock Watch" - 7371 An Hour Classics, quartz L.C.D. wristwatch with grey vinyl band and attached right profile Spock's bust in plastic with starboard t.v. Enterprise and yellow comet trail. Watch itself is a standard black case L.C.D. displaying five function - hour, minute, month, 60-sec. timer, date plus automatic time flash setting	14.95	15-16	_____
• **Radio Watch** Collins Industrial Corp., Ltd., 1982 Digital watch with a built-in micro A.M. radio. Includes earphone attachment and features alarm, month, date, hourly chime and faceplate tuner. Letters "Star Trek" title logo	16	15-20	_____
• **Video Game Watch - ST II** Collins Industrial Corp., Ltd., 1983 L.C.D. display, black plastic square case, white display gaming screen with red control buttons. Features time, day and week, plus a two-level Trek battlegame with sound effects, multi-function alarm (1 to 24 hours), quartz accuracy time. Packaged in window-cut on cardstock that illos the various functions.	49.94	15-20	_____

Star Trek II Watch, 1983.

LITERATURE

Star Trek literature of all types (amateur press, adult and children's books, comics, magazines and prozines) is the most popular category of collectible for Star Trek fans.

Written materials about Star Trek are produced by two editorial groups; either large, commercial publishing houses or small, amateur presses. Books, comics and magazines are professionally produced. Prozines and high-quality nonfiction fan issue books are amateur publications which generally lose money or barely manage to break even on independent titles, unlike their commercial counterparts.

For Star Trek collectors, there is an extensive degree of subject material into which topics have branched. Books may be fiction (an imaginary story told with dialogue) or nonfiction (true narrative and reference). Comics are short stories told through pen and ink drawings. Periodical topics (magazines and prozines) are generally nonfiction subjects though short stories do appear intermittantly in prozine formats.

A brief breakdown of the various literary formats available on Star Trek material is itemized below.

Hardback - Any hardcover book bound together with linen thread, polyvinyl acetate adhesives or animal glue. Covers are composed of either leather (goatskin), Vellum (calfskin), sound binding cloths or heavy-duty paper stock.

Tradepaper - Any oversized or odd-sized softcover book different in form from the common mass market paperback. Usually bound together by glue and paper covers that are slightly laminated or waxed.

Paperback - A mass market book bound by glue and usually measuring only 4¼"x7⅛" or 4½"x6½". Covers are waxed or laminated over a cardstock binding.

Softcover - Any oversized or odd-sized book bound by clips, metal bars, staples, plastic spiral spines, etc. Usually mimeographed, photo copied and of lower quality reproduction. Covers may be waxed or laminated. More often covers are plain paper stock of various types (parchment, bond or construction).

Three important factors determine the worth of literature collectibles. These factors are age, rarity and condition. Of these three characteristics necessary when considering to purchase Star Trek memorabilia in print, condition of an item is the most important.

The condition of a book, comic or magazine when bought, will have the most effect on the potential resale of that same article at some time the in future. Age and rarity factors will always help to appreciate collectible values. Inferior condition factors will always depreciate memorabilia worth.

For those who collect Star Trek literature, there is a definite system for evaluating the face worth of written collectibles. There is a handy check-list for spotting quality materials from second-rate ones. Originally, the 10-point scale below derived from *The Comic Book Price Guide* by Robert Overstreet was established by comic book collectors, but its general guidelines may apply for a myriad of publishing collectibles that Star Trek fans will at some time be puzzling over. Books, magazines and prozines are subject to the same kinds of wear and tear as comics. The condition classifications that follow will aid in matching literature appearance to selling cost.

Pristine Mint - Designates a non-circulated file copy. Pages are extra white and crisp. The cover is flawless.
Mint - In new or newsstand condition. Any defects are attributable to the cutting, folding or stapling process.
Near Mint - Almost perfect copy with a tight spine. Copy is tight and clean. There is possibly some discoloration.
Very Fine - Slight wear signs and some creases. Otherwise a very clean copy.
Fine - Stress lines appear around the binding (staples, spiral spines or glued backs). There is some minor flaking and discoloration.
Very Good - Obviously a read copy. Cover gloss is gone. Any staples present are loosening but there are no tears or browning pages.
Good - An average used copy. Spines may be rolled. Has creases or minor tears.
Fair - Heavily read copy. It is possibly soiled or has multiple wrinkles and tears appearing.
Poor - A damaged copy. Soiled and technically unsuitable for collector purposes.
Coverless - Almost worthless. The cover alone may be worth more than the separated text.

Amateur Press

Aside from the commercially released books on Star Trek by large professional publishing houses, there exists the commendable realm of fan publication and small press. Fan issue materials have offered Star Trek fans some of the best research and writing in the entire history of Trek literature.

Sometimes these independently produced fan publications also appear as commercial editions. Bjo Trimble's *Star Trek Concordance* and Eileen Palestine's *Starfleet Medical Reference Manual* were once fan published ventures which eventually broke into the professional publishing market. Amateur press releases shouldn't be confused with fanzines (fan fiction novels or short stories).

Filk song books - These are unique nonfiction subject books which have arisen solely from fan publishing. The term "filk" is acutally a parody of the word "folk" and refers to a specially written pop tune sung or played to music. Originally, the name filk song occured among Sci-Fi and Trek enthusiasts when a convention flyer was passed around with a misspelled advertisement proclaiming the local "filksingers" were going to perform. Filksongs are original Star Trek song lyrics of a humorous nature.

General reference - Nonfiction books include episode guides, Trek biographies, behind-the-scenes exposes, price guides and writing guides.

Poetry - Poetry and artwork has always been a popular topic with fans.

Reference manuals - Some of these amateur publications rival commercial releases in artwork, technical authenticity and imagination. Reference manuals may be blueprint guides, uniform catalogs or detailed examinations of the inner workings of Starfleet Command and all of its assorted regalia, armament and starship equipment.

Trivia, games and parodies - Amateur press releases come in a variety of guises designed just to be fun or activity oriented.

Adult Books

There is no doubt that the Star Trek universe is the most successful serial science fiction adventure in book form as well as having been one of the most popular television shows in network history.

Of the three general categories of binding format available (paperback, tradepaper or hardback), the best publishing media for Star Trek books has been the paperback. The reasons for this are simple. Paperbacks are attractive to the eye, easy to manipulate and are relatively inexpensive.

In the past 20 years, eleven of thirteen major paperback publishers have published something related to Star Trek themes, either directly or indirectly. A brief listing of publishers who have contributed to Star Trek literature and the most notable work that they produced is discussed briefly below. This impressive catalog of literary history is a tribute to Star Trek's popular appeal and a boon to avid collectors of Star Trek memorabilia.

Ace/Grosset & Dunlap

These companies were owned by Carter Communications, a subsidiary of Filmways.

Star Trek Catalog - Originally released as a tradepaper by Grosset & Dunlap and then as an Ace paperback in 1979. For the most part, this publishing house dabbled with nonfiction Trek during the release of **Star Trek The Motion Picture.**

Shatner: Where No Man Has Gone Before - This paperback received limited exposure and disappeared quickly from retail book racks. It is a rare collectible.

Avon

Avon is owned and operated by Hearst Corporation.

You and I - The only Star Trek related work this company produced. It is not an original issue either but a reprint of the Celestial Arts tradepaper by the same name. It is a notable collectible because it is the only one of Nimoy's poetry books that has a title cover printed in an exaggerated script form.

Ballantine/Random House

Until recently, both these publishing firms belonged to RCA. They now belong to Newhouse Newspapers Publishing Group. Previous to this corporate change, Random House acquired Ballantine paperbacks from Ian and Betty Ballantine during an expansion program.

The Making of Star Trek - This is the first adult nonfiction paperback ever to have been produced and the first promotional tie-in with the television series.

Star Trek Logs - Buoyed by the success of *The Making of Star Trek* and their movie tie-in Star Wars, the Ballantines began publication of the *Logs* in conjunction with the airing of animated Star Trek in 1974. In the late 70's, the Ballantines sold out to Lester and Judy Lynn Del Rey. This managerial shift is reflected in the *Logs*. Editions *Log One* through *Log Eight* originally appear with cartoon covers. After the ownership change, all *Logs* were reprinted with a Del Ray logo including new editions *Log Nine* and *Log Ten.*

The World of Star Trek - Another nonfiction tie-in which comes in both Ballentine and Del Rey printings.

The Trouble With Tribbles - Appears in both Ballantine and Del Rey editions.

Trek or Treat - Ballantine's most memorable tradepaper and one-of-a-kind. This was Ballantine's competitive move to profit with the popular appeal of Star Trek photographs given new life with balloon captions as was proven by Bantam's *Fotonovels* in the same year.

Star Trek Concordance - This is a collector's classic. Ballantine was the first to use gimmick editions on a Star Trek book. Covers can be stamped, pressed or cut-out along their surfaces to make them more attractive. The cover design is composed of a rotating cover wheel which instantaneously pinpoints every episode from the T.V. series with its respective indexed call letters, stardate and page number. It is also the first adult tradepaper devoted to Star Trek.

Star Trek Star Fleet Technical Manual - This is the only tradepaper to have reached the New York Times Bestseller's List. It is also the only book ever released with a hardcover slipcase protector.

Bantam Books

Since 1968 Bertelsmann Publishing Group of West Germany has owned Bantam.

Star Trek Fotonovels - The idea for these books came from Mandala, a California-based company, which offered the concept of using color photos from Star Trek episodes with balloon dialogue to Bantam. This unusual method of story telling has its origins with European novels of the same type. These are much sought after editions and a complete set of twelve is a collector's dream.

Spock Must Die - This 1970 book written by James Blish represents the first adult fiction paperback in print. Blish's premier novel was followed by thirteen other original fiction tales about Star Trek until the year 1980.

Star Trek Maps - Bantam's most memorable nonfiction product is undoubtedly the now sought after *Star Trek Maps.* It is difficult to know whether to classify this product as a poster or a book. Whatever its classification, the cardstock packet which contains them is unique in the packaging world of Star Trek memorabilia.

Berkley/Ace

Berkley has been owned by MCA and just recently took Ace Books under its wing. Since 1975, Berkley has come under the direct supervision of its sister company G.P. Putnam.

Mirror Friend, Mirror Foe - This is a reprint of the original sci-fi novel authored by George Takei and Robert Aspirin which came out in 1979 from Playboy Press. Nothing has changed in this reprint edition except the cover art even though the novel is the first Star Trek related book to have made a cross-conglomerate jump from one defunct major publishing house to another thriving one. It is also the only work of original fiction by a member of the Trek cast to have come into print.

Bluejay Books/St. Martin's

Bluejay Books is a new imprint of St. Martin's Press. It came into conception in 1983 as a specialty house for science fiction and fantasy.

The World of Star Trek - This is a tradepaper reprint of the original Ballantine paperback with the same title. The book has been updated to include information up to **Star Trek The Search For Spock.** This book is unusual because it has not only changed publishing houses, but has enlarged its size format as well. It took eleven years for the transition.

Celestial Arts

Celestial Arts originated out of Millbrae, California and printed only one Star Trek book in 1975.

I Am Not Spock - Of the many tradepaper editions concerning the world of Star Trek in print, *I Am Not Spock* is both rare and original. To add to its desirability, it is not only the first nonfiction adult tradepaper ever released, but the first tradepaper ever produced concentrating on Star Trek themes in publishing history.

Dell/Doubleday

Doubleday is the owner of Dell Books. Prior to the 1960's, all paperbacks with a Dell logo were edited and produced by Western Publishing Company.

Making of the Trek Conventions - This hard to find book by Joan Winston in hardback chronicled the planning, coordinating and tribulations associated with the production of Star Trek conventions of the early 1970's.

Will I Think of You? - This was Dell's one and only literary contribution to Star Trek in written form. This was a reprint of an earlier Celestial Arts tradepaper edition and the book tied in well with Nimoy's association with animated Trek of the middle seventies.

E. P. Dutton

E. P. Dutton is an independent publisher. It is one of the few hardback houses to ever print Star Trek materials. Others include Anima, Doubleday, Gregg Press, Random House and Simon & Schuster.

Star Trek Readers - *Star Trek Reader 1* was the first adult hardback ever printed in the genre. This book and the three succeeding volumes was meant to be an anthology of James Blish's original 12 Bantam paperbacks condensed in number and designed for library use. The *Readers* are good collectibles because they are representative of a book going from paperback to hardback. Generally, this printing procedure is reversed.

Playboy Press

Playboy Press operated out of Chicago, Illinois and was owned by the same corporate publishing house as *Playboy Magazine.* This publishing line is no longer in print.

Mirror Friend, Mirror Foe - The original edition of this book was done by Playboy Press and, strangely enough, fared the best in sales with young readers rather than adult sci-fi fans. Originally Playboy intended to issue two more paperback sequels to this novel, the second to be entitled *Stellar Flower, Savage Flower.* Despite claims of their appearance in 1982, neither sequel materialized. There was also talk of releasing all three novels in a hardback trilogy called *Star Stalker.* Most collectors are unaware of the fact that there was a conscious effort to attract sales through clever manipulation of recognizable Star Trek themes. This included the main character's sword battles and the book's title which alluded to the Trek episodes "The Naked Time" and "Mirror, Mirror" respectively.

Startoons - One of two paperbacks released by Playboy and written by Joan Winston. The other was a reprint of the Doubleday hardback *The Making of the Trek Conventions. Startoons* is a short, humorous book with a high collectibility status.

Pocket/Wallaby/Wanderer/Simon & Schuster

Until 1986 Pocket Books and Wallaby functioned solely as houses under the direct ownership of Simon & Schuster. In 1976, however, Simon & Schuster was acquired by Gulf Western conveniently making this large publishing house and Paramount Pictures Corporation sister companies.

Entrophy Effect - The first book in Pocket Books continuing line of new and original Star Trek fiction novels for adult audiences. It was followed by seven more works on a sporatic timetable up until March 1983. It was the first of the *Timescape* imprints, the last being *The Wounded Sky.*

Yesterday's Son - This was the first novel designed as a sequel to the Star Trek episode "All Our Yesterdays" and the first Trek fiction to reach the top of the New York Times Bestseller's List. It is also the first Trek paperback by Pocket to sport a new gimmick cover with the front title foil-stamped in gold.

Enterprise - *Enterprise* represents another step by Pocket Books to increase their literary repertoire of gimmick covers for public consumption. The use of a cut-away sidestep cover of this book in the upper righthand corner which reveals an artwork picture of the Enterprise from the underlying page is unique. No previous paperback editon about Star Trek has this feature. Also, the full page art behind a narrative cover is so far one-of-a-kind.

Chekov's Enterprise - This was an unusual movie tie-in book associated with **Star Trek The Motion Picture.** Walter Koenig's diary of behind-the-scenes during the filming of a major motion picutre is a nice collectible as well as the only nonfiction paperback Pocket Books has attempted to publish.

Star Trek The Motion Picture Photo Story - This is a very desirable item for Star Trek collectors. Based on the success of Bantam's Fotonovels, Pocket offered this novelization with color pictures and balloon captions with the same intent.

Star Trek II, The Wrath of Kahn Photo Story - This was the second book by Richard Anobile using photos and enclosed captions to tell a movie story. However, instead of color photos Pocket defrayed printing costs by using black and white print inserts. This was the last book of its type since 1982.

Star Trek Speaks - Susan Sackett's nonfiction book is the first of two releases by Wallaby Books that features cover art in narrative form. A narrative cover lacks any photos or artwork and relys only on the author's name and book title to promote sales of the book. The second such tradepaper in the history of Star Trek literature is *The Star Trek Com-*

pendium. Because of this, both books are a collector's oddity. (Only the first edition of The Star Trek Compendium bears this honor. The new 20th Anniversary edition has a full color photo insert on the cover.)
Space Flight Chronology - This is also a collector's gem. It is the only Star Trek book to feature a side-step cover (the front is trimmed short on the right side to reveal a color band from the page beneath) and it includes a huge one-of-a-kind tipped-in gatefold which allows the reader to draw pages out as an extended chart.

Artwork by Eddie Jones.

Artwork by Paul Alexander

Signet

This publishing house is also known as NAL (New American Library). It is a subsidiary of the Times/Mirror Corporation.
Best of Trek - To date, eleven volumes edited by Walter Irwin and G.B. Love have appeared under the Signet imprint. The publishing of *Best of Trek #1* heralded the debut of the first Star Trek anthology of original literature in a paperback edition. All of the volume's covers also display some of the most surrealistic spaceships ever associated with the Trek universe as represented on T.V.
Star Trek Quiz Book - This is the only other Star Trek book published under Signet. Its value is enhanced by the abrupt title change which occurred upon a second printing. The name *Trekkie Quiz Book* helped to attract young readers. A first edition copy is worth holding onto because of its rarity. About 218,975 *Trekkie Quiz Books* on the other hand went into circulation after the title switch.

Warner

Warner Communications owns Warner Books.
Meaning in Star Trek - A narrative cover makes this book a good collectible. It is the first paperback written about Star Trek with this unusual format. *The Making of the Trek Conventions* by Playboy Press comes close to being a narrative title but is excluded because it has a stock photo background beneath the narrative print.

Zebra

Zebra is an imprint of Norfolk Publishing Corporation.
Star Trek Trivia Mania - Released as a specialty book with a succession of other trivia editions, this paperback has been delegated to the bargain tables after a brief shelf life of about one year. Collectors should keep an eye out for it.

Children's Books

Star Trek books for children and young readers comprise about one third of all original and commercially released Star Trek titles in print. In general, children's Trek books are usually activity books. Coloring books, game books, trivia packages, punch-outs and pop-ups dominate this market. An immediate result of this trend, as far as collectors are concerned, is to have made all of the hardcover fiction titles published for kids in the past two decades valuable collectibles.

One of the most desirable collectibles of this type is the book *Mission To Horatius* published by Whitman Publishers in 1968. Written by acclaimed science fiction writer Mack Reynolds and illustrated by Sparky Moore, this large print hardback novel was geared towards the 8-12 year old audience.

With the printing of this book, Star Trek characters for the very first time walked beyond the realms of their television environments into new, imaginary adventures. Today the book has great collectible value because it was the first authorized work of original fiction sanctioned by Desilu Studios and because of the death of its author in 1983. Star Trek as a genre for ficton experimentation owes its long legacy of success directly to this first historical edition born of the children's marketplace.

It was not until nine years later that more fiction for children appeared. In 1977 Random House presented two juvenile books *Prisoner of Vega* and *The Truth Machine.* Both were produced as original fiction for kids in glossy bindings. Of these two books, the highly realistic drawings of Jane Clark's *The Truth Machine* are superior to those of Robert Swanson and to all other Star Trek children's hardbacks to follow.

The first juvenile Star Trek book actually produced by Random House was the tradepaper nonficton title the *Star Trek Action Toy Book* printed a year before. James Razzi's realistic activity book with paper punch-outs of Star Trek equipment, weaponry and starships was the first of its kind.

Two years after Random House abandoned Star Trek material for the children's market, Simon & Schuster began their publishing campaign to fill in the obvious void in juvenile literature for young Trekkers.

In 1979, the most impressive of seven books issued by Simon & Schuster in the Star Trek genre for kids was the *Star Trek Make A Game Book.* Designed by Bruce and Greg Nash, this unique Star Trek game book includes playing pieces, a fold-out paper board and a spinner for use after construction.

Since 1979, all the children's books issued have been movie tie-in promotionals. Media blitzing has cascaded down even into the Star Trek children's market. Some interesting collectibles have surfaced from the glut of tradepaper novels, character biographies and movie adaptations which have engulfed the young readers' bookshelves.

The first children's gift book set issued in a slipcover case appeared with three tradepaper books by William Rotsler. This set included *Star Trek II Short Stories, Star Trek II Distress Call* and *Star Trek II Biographies.* An interesting anomaly to this history-making publication is the fact that the photo of the Enterprise on the cover of Rotsler's *Star Trek II Short Stories* is printed upside-down.

William Rotsler also broke new ground in 1982 when *Star Trek II Distress Call* appeared. This was actually the first time a plot-it-yourself type of gaming book adventure would involve Star Trek themes. Two years later a decision to adopt this concept into a book for older teens produced the Archway paperback *Star Trek – Voyage To Adventure.* Such newly popular adventure/reading game books have made Which-Way books themselves very popular. Approximately 1,900,000 of these serial paperbacks are in print, including nearly 200,000 in bookclub sales.

Just recently, a second Star Trek plot-it-yourself adventure by Archway entitled *Star Trek Phaser Fight* has been released for those interested in literary gaming within the Star Trek universe.

The first paperback ever produced for children also appeared under an Archway logo. *The Monsters of Star Trek* by Daniel Cohen was produced in 1980, twelve years after the first adult paperback *The Making of Star Trek* reached avid fans one generation older. Since that time, Cohen's paperback has gone into reprint and even had a more recent artwork cover facelift.

Glossary

Abridged – this indicates that an interior text has been altered in some way through deletions or typesetting processes. An abridged manuscript is shorter than an unabridged text.

Blurb – the small paragraphs and phrases on the cover of a book stirs a readers curiosity. Blurbs are commissioned by freelance writers. They may be nothing more than a direct reprint of some inner portion of the book itself, abridged quotes or highly-cliched plot summaries worded for dramatic effect.

Cover Art – Refers to the artwork which appears on a book cover and which originated from a drawing or oil painted canvas by an artist. Once photographed by offset lithography (a process used since 1950), and cropped, it is used to be a visual condensation of the content of the book. It is a good idea to collect new cover art editions of reprinted novels. Many older fiction releases are getting a front cover change. Pocket Books in particular produces high-quality artwork covers by Boris Vallejo and Mealo Cintron.

Cover Designs – these are the specific styles of book cover formats used to promote sales of a particular type of book (nonfiction or fiction). There are four styles used most commonly in the publishing business.

1. Symbolic Design - this is the most common. It consists of a single-scene artwork front with a cover blurb on the rear of the book. Ex. *Mudd's Angels.*
2. Typographic - found primarily on nonfiction titles. It is composed of editorial print along with a photo insert representative of the overall content of the book. Typographic styles are used to pinpoint audiences of well-defined fans interested in Star Trek materials. Ex. *The Making of Star Trek.*
3. Narrative - Covers of this type contain no photos or cover art. There is only bold editorial print used to entice Star Trek readers into purchasing it. This is rare in Trek literature. Ex. *Star Trek Speaks.*
4. Vignette - the rarest of all styles found among Star Trek books released so far. This occurs when a cover artwork extends from the front of the book to the back, creating one large and continuous scene. It has only been used once by Random House for an illustrated children's hardback. Ex. *Prisoner of Vega.*

First Edition – the first printing in any format (hardcover, tradepaper, paperback or softcover) of a book.

Gimmick Cover – this is a relatively new sales promotion campaign which has been created by advanced graphics and printing processes. Gimmick covers refers to paperbacks which sport decorative enhancers such as foil-stamping, letter embossing, sidestep, gatefolds and cover cut-aways. Pocket Star Trek novels employ this type of cover enhancement on all of their later titles but only on the first edition. Reprints often lack embossing or foil-stamping.

Imprint – A distinguishing publication mark on the cover and spine of a book that in effect serves as a mascot-type identification for a publisher. Pocket's wallaby, (no, it's not a kangaroo) has undergone many transmutations over the years, including one penned by Walt Disney. She has even been given the name Gertrude in honor of the mother-in-law of her designer Frank J. Lieberman. Just recently Pocket Books has gone back to a previous Gertrude design and their Star Trek novels now sport reprint editions with two different wallaby logos.

Reprint – any subsequent printing of an original first edition, no matter how delayed, which contains the same text and essentially the same cover art.

Second Editions – a reprint of an original first edition. The content of the interior manuscript has not been altered, but the outside cover has. Usually they display altered cover art, cover photos and have a different ISBN.

STAR TREK IN COMICS

Star Trek as a comic format first appeared in 1967 under the auspice of Gold Key Comics, a division of Western Publishing Company. This long-running comic series spanned a total of 12 years and 61 issues, concluding in 1979.

Despite the lengthy lifetime of the Gold Key issues, they were relatively unpopular. Generally, the series as a whole was plagued by numerous formating inconsistancies when compared to the established television series of the Star Trek universe. Problems began with the very first issues which were drawn by Alberto Gioletti.

Gioletti resided in Italy and never saw a Star Trek episode. His interpretation of Trek characters and associated Trek technologies came solely from a limited quantity of episode photographs. The result was an accumulative series of negative factors that destroyed the credibility of the comic's potential. One of the bigger blunders of these early issues was the proposed ability of the Enterprise to land on planet surfaces.

It is no secret that all Gold Key artists involved in these Star Trek comics labored under rigid format specifications, including an edict which proposed a limit of only 25 words per cartoon panel. Also, no character from the television series could be utilized who was not a central character of the cast.

Prime examples of storyline alterations dictated by such strict publishing mandates involved comic writer Len Wein. Originally, the central antagonist conceived as the villian for issue #10, *Sceptre of the Sun,* was Kahn Noonian Singh. Under the imposed guidelines, this character transformed into the evil Chang. A similar transmutation occurred in Wein's issue #12, *Flight of the Buccaneer.* Initial intentions of the comic were to focus on the continued escapades of lovable space rogue Harcourt Fenton Mudd. Since Mudd was not considered a series regular, the idea was abandoned.

While Wein recognized the need for continuity and authenticity between television Trek and comic Trek (he used Stephen Whitfield's book *The Making of Star Trek* as his literary bible), the best drawings of the series were probably drawn by Alden McWilliams. McWilliams' contributions to Gold Key comic panels began with issue #40. His artwork also graced many of the covers.

In 1980, following the release of **Star Trek The Motion Picture,** Marvel Comics Group began a series of Star Trek comics. These were issued monthly and began with a three issue STTMP adaptation. Unfortunately, poor sales and stringent publishing limitations which dictated that only Trek material from the first two motion pictures was usable rather than characters, aliens, etc., from the T.V. series helped to liquidate the comic in less than 2 years.

Presently, Star Trek in comic format is being produced by D.C. Comics. This series began with the continuing adventures of the Enterprise Crew after **Star Trek II, The Wrath of Kahn.** D.C. has diverged from both its predecessors in producing comic issues that may or may not be serial, taking several volumes in order to complete an adventure. D.C. artists have also been able to incorporate T.V. Trek into their storylines along with movie adaptations.

Special Edition Comics

Experimentation with the Star Trek motif in the comic medium is not only limited to comic adventure books. Comic Trek has spilled over into softbound, paperback and hardback formats as well.

In 1970 a British publishing house, World International Publishing Ltd., began yearly hardback editions featuring reprints of the American born Gold Key Comics. In an effort to attract more juvenile interest in the annuals, the books also included added entertainment and activity features such as starfacts, cosmic crosswords and math puzzles.

The first American use of Star Trek comics for a similar purpose initiated by Whitman Publishing Company in 1975. Two softbound Dynabrite comics featured abridged re-hashings of Gold Key issues #33, #41, #34 and #36.

Golden Press followed suit in 1976 by producing the first of four *Star Trek Logs.* Following the example of English publishers six years before, the *Logs* were cleverly designed Gold Key reprints with additional essays referring to the Star Trek universe which included bonus character psychofiles, Federation letters and ship histories.

The first attempt to cross over into the adult market from the young adult category occurred as late as 1979 when Marvel's Super Special Magazine Number 15 containing a comic adaptation of *Star Trek The Motion Picture* was re-issued by Pocket Books as a Stan Lee Presents spectacular.

The last crossover book geared for adult audiences from true comic issue publications is a colorful book by Marvel Illustrated Books. Another Stan Lee Presents paperback appearing in 1982, this included three Marvel Comic stories in one. Star Trek comics #7, #11 and #12 are penned all over again by Luke McDonnell and Tom Palmer, and the result is an attractive collectible.

A more recent development in Star Trek comic literature has been the appearance of comic satires featuring Trek characters or recognizable facsimiles. *Elftrek* is a full scale comic spoof about the entire Trek universe which greatly resembles the well established adult satires prolificated in better known professional periodicals such as *Mad* and *Cracked.*

Comic Syndications

Any discussion about Star Trek comic specials would be incomplete without some mention of Trek as it has appeared in syndicated newspaper comic strips. Clever cartoonists have discovered that Star Trek comic strip adaptations appeal to audiences of all ages, and that they are good "eye-catchers" because virtually everyone is familiar with the stereotypical lines and dialogue which have gone into making the Trek phenomenon as a whole.

Perhaps the most well known strip featuring Star Trek is the exclusive comic syndication initiated by Mandala Productions in 1978 following the direct success of their Fotonovel paperback series published by Bantam Books.

Originally, the comic was to have been issued in a format similar to that of the Fotonovels by incorporating color photos from the actual series. Unfortunately at that time, photo reproduction in the newspaper media was technically unfeasible. It was decided that more conventional drawings should be used.

Star Trek as an original comic strip was released along with the first Trek motion picture in December 1979. Drawn by California artist Thomas Warkentin, the strip went on to be printed in 600 newspapers across the country through distribution by the L.A. Mirror Time Syndicate.

A variety of other comic strip artists have used Trek in their own established universes. They include:

Peanuts – In 1972, Charles Schultz's character Snoopy revelled in the exploits of flying the starship Enterprise from atop his doghouse.

B.C. – A fearless ant from Johnny Hart's comic re-enacted a "Beam me up Scotty" routine upon finding himself hopelessly surrounded by hungry anteaters.

John Darling – Armstrong & Battiuk satirized Leonard Nimoy's dislike of being identified continually as the legendary Mr. Spock.

Bloom County – In the *Washington Post,* Berke Breathed's penguin character took a voyage to the premier showing of the first Star Trek movie.

Funky Winkerbean – In 1979, Tom Battiuk's central cartoon character was an animated school computer which was obsessed with its devotion to Star Trek. In a series of thematic strips running from 1979 to the beginning of 1981, this dauntless computer not only waits in line to buy tickets for STTMP but it goes on to host a self-sponsored Star Trek convention in Toledo, Ohio.

Few fans know that one comic spin-off of Star Trek went on to become a full length tradepaper book. Michael C. Goodwin's pen and ink overlays featuring exterior shots of the Enterprise in deep space began as a serial in a local Salt Lake City newspaper called the *Desert News*. The strips ran from January to September 1977. In 1980, Goodwin's collected comic anthology was compiled into a 125 page tradepaper entitled *My Stars* published by Vulcan Books.

MAGAZINES

For the past two decades Star Trek has flourished with the help of the attention that it has received from commercial periodicals. Star Trek has actually been the topic of interest for the magazine public since 1967 when teen journals and gossip tabloids featured Trek between their covers. Since the birth of the T.V. series, magazine editors have realized that Star Trek in print increased their publication's circulation.

When Star Trek aired on T.V. magazine articles first appeared as black and white photo spreads of the "on-the-set" activities of the cast, biographical essays and attempts to stir up controversy through carefully written title lines. Occassionally, Star Trek articles appeared as full color spreads with gaudy art backgrounds and pop-art montages.

Ironically, after the cancellation of Star Trek, episode guides and subjective technological examinations of the Trek universe began to appear in magazines with a new image. Star Trek was beginning to take on an aura of serious journalism. Until the late 1970's Star Trek was bonded to commercial magazines with definite sci-fi, horror, fantasy and macabre themes.

The appearance of *Starlog* magazine in 1977 was a changing point for Star Trek. The general idea for the periodical was to raise science fiction subjects out of the domain of the "pulp ghetto." *Starlog #1* hit the stands after 3 months of collecting interviews, rare photos and a 3-season episode guide concentrating solely on Star Trek, its cast and trivia from the show.

Originally planned as a quarterly magazine, *Starlog* has become the #1 science fiction magazine in the country. It is now a monthly periodical which has devoted hundreds of pages to information, interviews and photo essays on the Star Trek universe in over 100 issues.

The production of **Star Trek The Motion Picture** helped immensely in revitalizing Trek journalism. Magazine publishers were no longer confined to rehashings of old news from T.V. Trek and were able to elaborate on the special effects, props, costumes and cast interviews associated with the new movie. The same philosophy has been generated with each new successful Star Trek film.

Collectors should keep their eyes open for four different types of magazine articles.

Parody specials - The earliest type of Star Trek periodical spread. This is a comic satire of Star Trek, its characters and technology as spoofed through pen and ink cartoons. *Mad Magazine* produced the first circulated parody story entitled "Star Blecch" in November 1966. Since that time, ten Trek parodies have appeared in *Cracked, Crazy* and *MAD*. A nice collectible parody occurred in *Starlog* Magazine in September 1978. One year after the airing of a **Saturday Night Live** satire about the network cancellation of Star Trek, *Starlog* reprinted the complete original shooting script from the show with commissioned parody drawings by *MAD* artist Jack Rickard. The original **Saturday Night** satire written by Michael O'Donohue is heralded as the best script to have been produced on the show and starred John Belushi (Kirk), Chevy Chase (Spock) and Dan Ackroyd (McCoy).

Spotlight periodicals - Any magazine of commercial status which gives column space to Star Trek topics from 1970 to the present.

Tabloids - Occasionally Star Trek coverage appeared in newspaper type formats such as *Monster Times*. Newspaper articles from syndicated papers have also chronicled information and movie reviews on Star Trek throughout the past two decades.

Vintage periodicals - Magazines which appeared during the years 1966-1969 and gave media coverage to Star Trek as a T.V. phenomenon. These are wonderful collectibles and rare publishing novelties.

PROZINES

Prozines are professional quality periodicals originating from fan factions. These are often very slick publications dealing solely with Star Trek interests and may be issued, monthly, quarterly or bi-annually. The word prozine originates from the words **pro**fessional but of fan**zine** backgrounds.

Prozines are a direct offshoot of early convention programs of the 1970's when convention going was a popular mass activity. Some early convention "booklets" such as those produced at Star Trek Houston (produced in association with the Star Trek '75 Convention) and the International Star Trek Convention '75 are large, colorful souvenir magazines of prozine quality.

Many souvenir program editors expanded their talents into the production of fan periodicals. G.B. Love, who would become the famous editor of the prozine *Trek Magazine,* produced souvenir booklets *Star Trek '74 & '75*. James Van Hise, well known Star Trek author and editor of the original prozine *Enterprise Incidents #1-8,* produced *Star Trek Houston*.

Beginning in 1975, a cluster of Star Trek prozines surfaced. Collectors of prozines of this period will soon notice that many of these early magazines facilitated their page counts with the exact same articles, drawings, photos, etc. It is not unusual to see the same article or interview printed in different prozines, exemplifying the fact that article contributions circulated in a limited publishing/editing circle and in a round-robin manner.

Essentially the same handful of prominent fan authors have attempted to keep the Star Trek prozine market alive in the last decade. Currently, all have appeared to flounder. *Trek Magazine* gained permanent recognition for its quality articles and by having the only prozine to have made it into professional circles via Signet's popular paperback anthologies # 1-11.

Enterprise Incidents underwent a variety of quality and production changes before discontinuing its monthly prozine releases altogether. The same demise occurred with New Media's *Enterprise Magazine*. However, some very nice special editions appeared during the prozine's running. They published extensive interview booklets, movie exposes and even technical manuals.

Collectors shouldn't cut up their prozines, especially very early and hard-to-find copies of the original *Trek* magazines #1-3. These appeared as tabloids. Prozines are worth an escalating value intact and unblemished. The re-sale of clipped pages is usually difficult.

AMATEUR PRESS

	Issue	Current	Cost/Date
A to Zine, The How-To of Fan Publishing Boojums Press, Paula Smith, 1984 Details various printing styles, layouts and pricing calculations useful in beginning your own fanzine, folded pamphlet, 14 p.	1.25	2-3	______
Bartenders Guide 1983 Recipes for Star Trek drinks, drawings, folded and stapled mimeo, black lettering on white, 10 p.	3	3-5	______
Bar Guide, All-New 1986, Updated material, more brain shattering concoctions	4.95	5-6	______
Enterprise Flight Manual Lincoln Enterprises, 1983 Console blueprints for STTMP Enterprise, mimeod, clipped sheets, softbound, 40 p.	4.95	5-6	______
1985 ST II version, functions for all new consoles, details and graphics as used on the film sets. Bridge to engineering sections, interiors, 8½"x11", 40 p.	5.95	6-7	______
Enterprise Sing-Sings Gayle Puhl, 1984 Contains 22 filk songs, plus the music score notes, 27 p.	5	6-8	______
Federation Cookbook 1984 Training manual for cadets containing recipes and drawings, softbound	3	3-4	______
Federation Reference Series Star Fleet Printing Office Eventual series of 6 softbound books designed to expand the Star Fleet Tech Manual by Mandel. Originally intended to be released bi-monthly.			
1984 **Number 1** General Division Index, Star Fleet Reference reports, starship designs, insignia markings ID chart, costume and phaser drawings, glue-bound removeable pages, 30	4.50	6-7	______
Number 2 Drawings and illustrations for more ships plus charts and ID's.	4.50	6-7	______

Starship Designs & Federation Reference Series.

	Issue	Current	Cost/Date
1986 **Number 3** Administrative orders, SFC reorganization, ships dry docks, office complexes, space suits, more vessels	4.95	5-6	______
Federation Trivia Books Trek Publications 1977 Assorted trivia questions on the characters and facts from t.v. Star Trek			
Number 1	1.50	2-3	______
Number 2	1.50	2-3	______
Gorn Guidebook 1984 Historical, psychological and cultural surveys about these aliens, spiralbound	4.95	5-6	______
Highly Illogical Leonard Nimoy Association of Fans 1977 Booklet of puzzles, trivia, quiz pages, etc. dealing with Star Trek and Leonard Nimoy	3	4-6	______
How To Sell A Script Lincoln Enterprises 1984 Formulas for writing and selling t.v. scripts as guided by Gene Roddenberry and D.C. Fontana, mimeod sheets, clipped, 37 p.	3.50	4-5	______
Klingon Joke Book April Publications 1985 Collections of alien jokes directed as the Klingons, softbound, stapled	2	2-3	______

AMATEUR PRESS

Issue | Current | Cost/Date

Officers of the Bridge
Ralph and Valerie Carnes
1976 Biographies of Trek characters, photos and information, illustrations by Kelly Freas, softbound, 56 p. .... 6.95 7-10 ______

Rec Room Rhymes
Omnibus
1982 Contains 61 filk songs (22 are Trek), plus Roberta Rogow's tuneful notes and recitations, softbound, 68 p. .... 5 5-6 ______

Sing-A-Song-of-Trekkin'
Caterpillar Music
1976 20 Trek filk songs by Roberta Rogow, includes musical scores, drawings, 44 p. .... 5.95 6-7 ______

Spock Trivia Book
1985 Questions and answers about Mr. Spock, 8"x10", spiral bound publication .... 5 5-6 ______

Star Fleet Academy Training Manual
John Wetsch
1983 Information for new officers of U.S.S. Columbia; UFP organization, SFC orders, ranks, leadership, technology and a glossary of terms, stapled, 8 p. .... 2.95 3-4 ______

Star Fleet Assembly Manual
1983 Series of publications detailing assembly procedures for converting model kits by AMT/Ertl into sophisticated Star Trek replicas - photos, drawings, digital electronics guides, 8"x10", spiralbounds

Number 1 .... 9.95 10-12 ______
Number 2 .... 9.95 10-12 ______
Number 3 .... 10.95 11-12 ______
Number 4 .... 10.95 11-12 ______

Star Fleet Classified Files
Geoffrey Mandel
1983 Special information on the Klingon and Romulan Empires, uniforms, sequel to **U.S.S. Enterprise Officer's Manual,** spiral bd... 6.95 8-9 ______

Star Fleet Code Book
April Publications
1978 Descriptions for using and deciphering Star Fleet codes, glossy stock softbound, stapled, 16 p. .... 2 3-4 ______

Star Fleet Cookbook
April Publications
1984 Gathering of alien recipes from around the Star Trek universe, softbd., staples .... 2 2-4 ______

Star Fleet Command Files
Star Fleet Historical Archives
1980 Admiral Heihachiro Nogura's intelligence reports of Klingon Empire and Romulans with revision procedure for Constitution Class heavy cruisers, companion guide to **U.S.S. Enterprise Officer's Manual,** spiral bound, 23 p. .... 5.95 7-8 ______

Issue | Current | Cost/Date

Star Fleet Handbook
Geoffrey Mandel, 1976-1977
Sereis of ten technical publications for the SFC universe, softbound
Numbers 1-10, each .... 1.95 2-4 ______

Star Fleet Hand Weapon Familiarization Handbook
1983 Compilation of weapons blueprints from the Federation, Klingons, Romulans and Gorns ... 5.95 6-8 ______

Star Fleet Marriage Manual
1984 Compilation of regulations, customs, etc. for alien weddings, spiral bound, 25 p. .... 5.95 6-7 ______

Star Fleet Medical Reference Manual
Eileen Palestine
1974 Fan edition with white cover, original publishing of the Ballantine mass tradepaper; physiology, diseases and drugs in the Trek universe .... 7.50 25-35 ______

Star Fleet Officer Requirements
1985 **Volume #1**
Compilation of new command equipment, console designs, destruct sequences, etc. for Trek fans, since the movies. For use beyond **U.S.S. Enterprise Officer's Manual.** Spiralbound 38 p. .... 8.95 9-10 ______
1986 **Volume #2**
More details on uniform variations, security deployment, sentry duty, restricted areas, classified info and new ship constructions .... 11.95 12-13 ______

Star Fleet Ship Recognition Manual
Starfleet Publications
1984 Technical drawings of all starships of Trek universe; Warship recognition (SFC vessels), the Constitution Class, alien warships; Klingon, Romulan, Gorn; DY-100 Class and general vessels, spiral, 42 p. .... 8.95 9-12 ______

Star Fleet Technical Manual
1985 Reprint of the famous tradepaper edition by Ballantine; technical drawings, uniforms and info, spiralbound, red paper cover ... 19.95 20-22 ______

AMATEUR PRESS

Issue Current Cost/Date

Star Fleet Uniform Recognition Manual
Noron Group, Shane Johnson
1985 Tech manual tracing the evolution of SFC uniforms from the 5-year mission through Genesis (ST III), drawings of suits and rules for anti-exposure, 8"x10", 77 p. ...... 11.95 12-14 ______

Star Trek - An Epic in Photos, Poetry and Art
Starbase One
1975 Production featuring samplers of artistic creativity in Trek. Cover is satire illo of Spock pointing finger and smiling as Hanock from "Return to Tomorrow," softbd., ... 1.50 3-6 ______

Star Trek Buyer's Guide
April Publications
1983 Where to acquire Trek memorabilia, with addresses, spiral bound, 34 p. .... 3 3-6 ______

Star Trek Concordance of People, Places & Things
Bjo Trimble, compiled by Dorothy Jones
Mathom House Publications
1969 Encylopedic reference guide featuring the work of 20 amateur artists; a definitive text for exploring t.v. Trek during its first two seasons, blue cover, brass-clip ..... 5.25 50-70 ______

1970 **The Third Season Supplement**
Supplemental publication covering t.v. 3rd season episodes. (1969 and 1970 issues were combined in Ballantine's tradepaper Star Trek Concordance published in 1976) ... 3 25-35 ______

1985 **Reprint** of the combined two issues by Trimble, blue cover, spiral bound
First Two Seasons .... 10 10-12 ______
Third Season Supplement .... 10 10-12 ______

Star Trek Episode Guide
Starbase Central
1976 Complete, brief listing of the 3 seasons of t.v. Trek, stapled, mimeod black lettering on blue paper stock, 8 p. .... 1 2-3 ______

Star Trek Fandom Triumphs
Geoffrey Mandel, Doug Drexler, Ron Barlow
1979 September
Detailed account of the making of STTMP, tech drawings, photos and info, softbd, 32p. .... 5 6-8 ______

Star Trek Format
Star Trek/Lincoln Enterprises
1969 Mimeod sheets containing original t.v. episode descriptions for Star Trek as prepared by Gene Roddenberry to sell series to NBC.
Brass-clipped, 16 pages .... 1 5-8 ______
1983 **Reprint** coverless, 16 pages [1] . 1 1-2 ______

Star Trek Fandom Triumphs.

Star Trek Official Biographies Issue Current Cost/Date
Star Trek/Lincoln Enterprises
1968 Double-sheet info and stats from the real life histories of the Star Trek cast, mimeod, 8½"x11" format
2001 **Gene Roddenberry** .... .20 1-2 ______
2002 **William Shatner** .... .20 1-2 ______
2003 **Leonard Nimoy** .... .20 1-2 ______
2004 **DeForest Kelley** .... .20 1-2 ______
2005 **James Doohan** .... .20 1-2 ______
2006 **Nichelle Nichols** .... .20 1-2 ______
2007 **George Takei** .... .20 1-2 ______
2008 **Walter Koenig** .... .20 1-2 ______
2009 **Majel Barrett** .... .20 1-2 ______

1979 Typewritten bio sheets to include two of the most popular characters from Trek animated cartoon episodes
2012 **M'Hress** (Herself) .... .30 1-2 ______
2013 **Arex** (Himself) .... .30 1-2 ______

1980 More updated bio sheets, sold in a set: Histories of the STTMP stars, their hobbies, everyday lives, etc. Roddenberry, Shatner, Nimoy, Kelley, Doohan, Nichols, Takei, Koenig, Barrett, G. L. Whitney, Robert Wise, Persis Kimbata, S. Collins. **13 Set Profile** .... 4.95 5-6 ______

Star Trek Primer, a Child's Garden of Space
Boojums Press, Paula Smith
1975 March
Five Complete primers of original Star Trek verse, illustrated by Phil Foglio, stapled, 15 p. .... .50 2-3 ______

1. Star Trek Enterprises was the original name of Lincoln Enterprises when it started up as the only official mail-order distributor for Star Trek merchandise during the actual 1966-1969 airing of the t.v. series. Many of Lincoln's original souvenir items went into subsequent reprintings which makes determining authenticity of original items of crucial importance to Star Trek collectors.

Star Trek Song Book, First Edition.

	Issue	Current	Cost/Date
Star Trek Songbook			
Ruth Berman			
1971 Summer			
Mimeod compilation of info about the songs and musical scores used on the Trek episodes, includes photos, artwork, b/w photo front cover, stapled, 39 p.	.50	3-5	______
1973 Fall reprinting, 27 p.	.75	2-3	______
1976 Summer reprinting, 27 p.	.75	1-2	______
Star Trek Travel Brochures			
April Publications			
1984 Set of five fold-out brochures depicting tourist attractions in Trek universe, 6p.			
Guardian of Forever	.60	1-2	______
Red Hour Festival of Landru	.60	1-2	______
Discover Vulcan	.60	1-2	______
Tour Amusement Park Planet	.60	1-2	______
Janus IV - The Horta Welcomes You	.60	1-2	______
Complete set of 5	3	5-10	______
Star Trek Trivia Game Book			
April Publications			
1984 Assortment of trivia with answers about Trek, photos, spiral bd., 36 p.	3	3-5	______
Star Trek Writer's Guide			
Star Trek/Lincoln Enterprises			
1968 Gene Roddenberry's guide on hot to write for the Star Trek t.v. series, includes info on characters, the Enterprise, 32 p. Original Edition has orange construction paper cover, stapled	1.25	6-7	______
1983 Reprint Edition	3.50	4-5	______
Star Trek II Writer's Guide			
Lincoln Enterprises			
1983 Mimeod sheets by Roddenberry with updated info on the Trek universe since the series, how to write for Trek movies, softbound, clipped	3.50	4-5	______

	Issue	Current	Cost/Date
Starry Night			
Michael and Lynne Anne Goodwin			
1985 8½"x11" softbound format cartoon book, featuring "Tripping the Light Fantastic" sequel to the My Stars paperback by Mike Goodwin	5	5-6	______
Trek Memorabilia Price Guide			
Emilo Lazzio			
1983 Guide to the t.v. episodes and price book for Trek collectibles, photos	15	15-16	______
1986 Updated and expanded edition	18	18-19	______
Trekker Cookbook			
Yeoman Press, Johanna Cantor			
1977 Trek recipes and drawings, softbound, 80 p.	4.95	6-8	______

Trekkie Toons

	Issue	Current	Cost/Date
Trekkie Toons			
Good Old Grandma's Comics, Terry Lanham			
1976 Trek parody in cartoons, includes "To Save A Dying Race", b/w illustrations, softbound, 25p.	1	3-5	______
Trexindex			
April Publications			
1984 Complete index to Star Trek fanzines, their stories and articles, quality reprint of the original fanzine edition	4	5-7	______
U.S.S. Discovery Officer's Manual			
1985 Officer's manual for the Discovery NCC-3100 Class ships. Personnel files, plans, bridge and engineering, propulsion, gear; Klingon update	6.95	7-9	______
U.S.S. Enterprise Officer's Manual			
Geoffrey Mandel			
1980 Guidelines for SFC Officer's tech drawings, charts, illos by Doug Drexler, spiralbound, 110 p.	10.95	14-16	______
1986 Revised Edition			
Assorted writers and artists update this expanded version. Spiralbound, grey cover with red lettering	12.95	13-14	______

Officer's Manual

	Issue	Current	Cost/Date
Vulcan Book April Publications 1984 Pages are written in Vulcan with language translation code, softbound, b/w print and drawings on white glossy stock, 10 p.	2	2-4	______
Vulcan Language Guide April Publications 1977 Details on the five main Vulcan dialects and when to use them, softbound, blue print on white glossy stock, 16 p.	2	2-4	______
Vulcan Reflections: Essays on Spock and His World T-K Graphics 1977 Vulcan cultural studies according to four articles originally published in the early Trek fanzine **Spockanalia**	4	7-10	______
Weapon and Field Equipment Technical Reference Manual Noron Group 1984 Quality publication with technical drawings of famous t.v. and movie hand props, with Trek Phaser I, II, phaser rifle, Phaser IV and V and communicator, 78p	11.95	15-20	______
1986 Pro-Edition remake titled **Weapons Manual,** 80 pages of film and t.v. hardware and weapons, glossy cover	11.95	12-14	______

ADULT BOOKS

	Issue	Current	Cost/Date
Abode of Life Lee Corey, Pocket Books Paperback, original fiction, 207 p. 0-671-83297-2, first Timescape edition, May 1982	2.50	2-4	______
0-671-47719-6, without Timescape imprint	2.95	3-4	______
0-671-62746-5, with new "Gertrude" logo	3.50	3-4	______
Battlestations! Diane Carey, Pocket Books Paperback, original fiction, sequel to **Dreadnought!,** 274 p. 0-671-63267-1, first edition, November 1986	3.50	3-4	______
Best of Trek Walter Irwin & G.B. Love, Signet Paperback, nonfiction and stories taken from *Trek Magazine,* 239 p. [1] 0-451-11682-8, first edition, 1974	1.75	2-5	______
0-451-11682-8	2.50	2-4	______
Best of Trek No. 2 Walter Irwin & G. B. Love, Signet Paperback, nonfiction & stories, 196 p. First edition, 1977	1.95	2-5	______
0-451-09836-6	2.50	2-4	______
0-451-12368-9	2.75	2-4	______
0-451-12368-9	2.95	3-4	______
0-451-13466-4	2.95	3-4	______
0-451-12368-9	3.50	3-4	______
Best of Trek No. 3 Walter Irwin & G.B. Love, Signet Paperback, nonfiction and stories, 196 p. 0-451-09582-0, first edition, 1979	1.95	2-4	______
0-451-11807-3	2.50	2-3	______
0-451-13092-8	2.95	3-4	______
Best of Trek No. 4 Walter Irwin & G.B. Love, Signet Paperback, nonfiction and stories, 214 p. 0-451-11221-0, first edition 1981	2.25	2-4	______
0-451-12356-5	2.75	2-3	______
0-451-13465-6	2.95	3-4	______
0-451-13465-6	3.50	3-4	______
Best of Trek No. 5 Walter Irwin & G. B. Love, Signet, Paperback, nonfiction and stories, 201 p. 0-451-11751-4, first edition, 1982	2.50	2-5	______
0-451-11751-4	2.75	2-4	______
0-451-12947-4	2.95	3-4	______
0-451-12947-4	3.50	3-4	______
Best of Trek No. 6 Walter Irwin & G.B. Love, Signet Paperback, nonfiction and stories, 191 p. 0-451-12493-6, first edition, 1983	2.25	2-4	______
0-451-12493-6	2.75	2-3	______

1. **Best of Trek** #1-5 and 7 has cover art by Eddie Jones. Numbers 6, 8, 9, 10 and 11 have cover art by Paul Alexander.

ADULT BOOKS

	Issue	Current	Cost/Date
Best of Trek No. 7			
Walter Irwin & G.B. Love, Signet Paperback, nonfiction and stories, 201 p.			
0-451-12977-6, first edition, 1984	2.75	2-3	______
0-451-14204-7	2.95	2-3	______
0-451-14204-7	3.25	3-4	______
Best of Trek No. 8			
Walter Irwin & G.B. Love, Signet Paperback, nonfiction and stories, 221 p.			
0-451-13488-5, first edition, February 1985	2.95	3-4	______
0-451-13488-5	3.50	3-4	______
Best of Trek No. 9			
Walter Irwin & G.B. Love, Signet Paperback, nonfiction and stories, 207 p.			
0-451-13816-3, first edition, September 1985	2.95	3-4	______
Best of Trek No. 10			
Walter Irwin & G.B. Love, Signet Paperback, nonfiction and stories, 204 p.			
0-451-14311-6, first edition, June 1986	2.95	3-4	______
Best of Trek No. 11			
Walter Irwin & G.B. Love, Signet Paperback, nonfiction and stories, 204 p.			
0-451-14576-3, first edition, November 1986	2.95	3-4	______
Black Fire			
Sonni Cooper, Pocket Books, Paperback, original fiction, 220 p.			
0-671-83632-3, first edition, Centered Timescape imprint, January 1983	2.95	3-5	______
0-671-83632-3, Timescape imprint in corner	2.95	3-4	______
0-671-83632-3, without Timescape imprint, numbered cover	2.95	3-4	______
0-451-61758-3, new "Gertrude" logo	3.50	3-4	______
Chain of Attack			
Gene DeWeese, Pocket Books, Paperback, original fiction, 251 p.			
0-671-63269-8, first edition, February 1987	3.50	3-4	______
Chekov's Enterprise			
Walter Koenig, Pocket Books Paperback, autobiography on the making of STTMP, 222 p.			
0-671-832-7, first edition, 1980	2.25	3-6	______
Come And Be With Me			
Leonard Nimoy, Blue Mountain Arts, Tradepaper, poetry, 60 p.			
0-833-96033-8, first edition, September 1978	4.95	5-10	______
0-883-96033-8, May 1979	4.95	5-8	______

Covenant of the Crown, hardback.

	Issue	Current	Cost/Date
Corona			
Greg Bear, Pocket Books Paperback, original fiction, 192 p.			
0-671-47390-5, first edition, April 1984	2.95	3-4	______
0-671-62749-X, new "Gertrude" logo	3.50	3-4	______
Covenant of the Crown			
Howard Weinstein original fiction, 191 p.			
0-671-83307-3, paperback, Pocket Books, first Timescape edition, December 1981	2.50	2-5	______
0-671-83307-3, without Timescape imprint, numbered cover	2.95	3-4	______
04082, hardcover Pocket Books through the Literary Guild or Science Fiction Book Club, 1981			
Publisher's edition	9.99		
Member's price	4.98	5-6	______
Crisis on Centaurus			
Brad Ferguson original fiction, 254 p.			
0-671-61115-1, paperback, Pocket Books, first edition, March 1986	3.50	3-4	______
2436, hardcover Pocket Books through the Science Fiction Book Club, 1986 Member's price	4.98	5-6	______
Death's Angel			
Kathleen Sky, Bantam Books, Paperback, original fiction, 213 p.			
0-533-14703-X, first edition, April, 1981	2.25	2-5	______
0-533-14703-X, June 1981	2.25	2-4	______
0-533-24637-2, April, 1984	2.95	2-3	______
0-533-24637-2, 4th printing	2.95	2-3	______
0-533-24983-5, second edition art with Spectra logo, July 1985	2.95	3-4	______
Deep Domain			
Howard Weinstein, Pocket Books Paperback, original fiction, 275 p.			
0-671-63329-5, first edition, April 1987	3.50	3-4	______

Two cover styles for *Death's Angel*

	Issue	Current	Cost/Date
Demons			
J. M. Dillard, Pocket Books Paperback, original fiction, 271 p.			
0-671-62524-1, first edition July 1986	3.50	3-4	______
Devil World			
Gordon Eklund, Bantam Books Paperback, original fiction, 153 p.			
0-553-13297-0, first edition, November 1979	1.75	2-5	______
0-553-24677-1, January 1985	2.95	2-3	______
Dreams of Raven			
Carter, Pocket Books, Original fiction, 0-671-64500-5, May 1987	3.50	3-4	______
Carmen Carter, Pocket Books, Original fiction, 0-671-64500-5, May 1987	3.50	3-4	______ ______
Dwellers In The Crucible			
Margaret Wander Bonanno, Pocket Books, paperback, original fiction, 308 p.			
0-671-60373-6, first edition, September 1985	3.50	3-4	______
Enterprise			
Vonda N. McIntyre original fiction, 371 p.			
0-671-62581-0, first edition, September 1986	3.95	3-4	______
0927, hardcover Pocket Books through the Science Fiction Book Club, 1986 member's price	5.98	5-6	______
Entrophy Effect			
Vonda N. McIntyre original fiction, 224 p.			
0-671-83692-7, paperback, Pocket Books Timescape edition with white cover, June 1981	2.50	2-4	______
0-671-49300-0, blue cover without Timescape imprint, April 1984	2.95	2-3	______
9-671-62229-3, yellow title	3.50	3-4	______
0-8398-2831-4, hardcover Gregg Press	10.95	10-11	______
Fate of the Phoenix			
Sondra Marshak & M. Culbreath Bantam Books, paperback, fiction sequel to **Price of the Phoenix,** 262p			
0-553-12779-9, first edition, May 1979	1.95	2-6	______
October 1979	1.95	2-5	______

	Issue	Current	Cost/Date
October 1981	1.95	2-4	______
0-553-24638-0, April 1984	2.95	3-4	______
0-553-24638-0, second edition, artwork cover, May 1985	2.95	3-4	______
Final Reflection			
John M. Ford, Pocket Books Paperback, original fiction, 253 p.			
0-671-47388-3, first edition, May 1984	2.95	3-4	______
0-671-62230-7, new "Gertrude" logo	3.50	3-4	______
Galactic Whirlpool			
David Gerrold, Bantam Books Paperback, original fiction, 223 p.			
0-553-124242-9, first edition October 1980	2.25	2-6	______
Second printing, March 1981	2.25	2-5	______
Third printing, October 1981	2.25	2-4	______
0-553-24170-2, second edition cover art, July 1984	2.95	3-4	______

Trade paper, *I Am Not Spock.*

	Issue	Current	Cost/Date
I Am Not Spock			
Leonard Nimoy Autobiography & photos			
0-890-87717-5, tradepaper, Celestial Arts. 135 p., November 1975 [2]	4.95	10-25	______
0-345-25719-7, paperback, Ballantine Books (Del Rey), reprint of Celestial Arts tradepaper, 150 p., May 1977	1.75	5-10	______
Ishmael			
Barbara Hambly, Pocket Books Paperback, original fiction, 255 p.			
0-671-55427-1, first edition, May 1985	3.50	3-4	______
0-671-55427-1, 2nd printing	3.50	3-4	______
Killing Time			
Della Van Hise, Pocket Books Paperback, original fiction, 311 p.			
0-671-52488-7, first edition, recalled by Paramount for objectional clauses, July 1985	3.50	5-8	______
0-671-52488-7, without embossed title	3.50	3-4	______
0-671-52488-7, new "Gertrude" logo	3.50	3-4	______

2. This book is the first Star Trek tradepaper ever produced, the first adult tradepaper in print and the first adult tradepaper on a nonfiction subject.

ADULT BOOKS

	Issue	Current	Cost/Date
Klingon Dictionary			
Mark Okrand, Pocket Books Paperback, language guide to Klingon vocabulary, 172 p.			
0-671-54349-0, Dec. 1985	3.95	3-4	_____
Klingon Gambit			
Robert E. Vardeman, original fiction, 158 p.			
0-671-47720-X, paperback, Pocket Books, centered Timescape imprint, October 1981	2.95	2-5	_____
0-671-47720-X, Timescape imprint in right corner	2.95	2-4	_____
0-671-47720-X, without Timescape, numbered cover	2.95	3-4	_____
0-671-62231-5, new "Gertrude" cover	3.50	3-4	_____
0-8398-2834-9, hardcover, Gregg Press	10.95	11-12	_____
Letters To Star Trek			
Susan Sackett, Ballantine Paperback, interesting letters to the Star Trek cast, 215 p.			
0-345-25522-4, 1977	1.95	5-10	_____
Making of Star Trek			
Stephen Whitfield & Gene Roddenberry, Ballantine Paperback, behind-the-scenes look at making t.v. Trek, 414 p. [3]			
Twenty-two printings up until September 1986, sample printings include:			
73004, first edition, September 1968	.95	5-15	_____
0-345-01621-0, 6th printing, July 1970	.95	5-8	_____
0-345-01705-0	1.50	3-6	_____
0-345-24691-8, silver cover, 14th printing, January 1975	1.95	3-5	_____
0-345-34019-1, 22nd printing, September 1986	4.95	4-5	_____

Making of Star Trek The Motion Picture.

	Issue	Current	Cost/Date
Making of Star Trek The Motion Picture			
Susan Sackett & Gene Roddenberry, Wallaby, Tradepaper, STTMP behind-the-scenes, 221 p.			
0-671-79109-5, 1982	7.95	8-12	_____

Making of Star Trek II.

	Issue	Current	Cost/Date
Making of Star Trek II, The Wrath of Kahn			
Allan Asherman, Pocket Books Tradepaper, filming STWOK, 223 p. 0-671-46182-6, 1982	7.95	7-10	_____

Hardback edition, 1977.

	Issue	Current	Cost/Date
Making of the Trek Conventions			
Joan Winston			
Autobiographical info on Trek convention going, photos			
0-385-13112-7, hardcover, Doubleday, jacket by Peter Rauch, 252 p., 1977 [4]	7.95	8-15	_____
0-872-16573-6, paperback, Playboy Press, reprint of Doubleday hardcover, 254 p., November 1979	2.25	5-8	_____

3. **The Making of Star Trek** is the first paperback written concerning Trek subject material. It is also the first adult nonfiction paperback printed.
4. This book is the first adult hardback for Star Trek material concerning nonfiction themes.

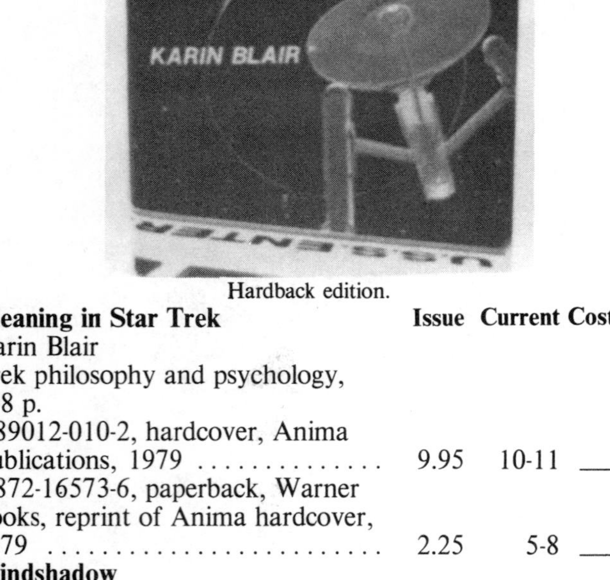

Hardback edition.

Meaning in Star Trek	**Issue**	**Current**	**Cost/Date**
Karin Blair Trek philosophy and psychology, 208 p. 0-89012-010-2, hardcover, Anima Publications, 1979	9.95	10-11	______
0-872-16573-6, paperback, Warner Books, reprint of Anima hardcover, 1979	2.25	5-8	______
Mindshadow J. M. Dillard, Pocket Books Paperback, original fiction, 252 p. 0-671-60756-1, January 1986	3.50	3-4	______
Mirror Friend, Mirror Foe George Takei Paperback, original fiction, co-authored with Robert Asprin, 223p. 0-87216-581-7, Playboy Press, 1979	1.95	2-3	______
0-441-53380-9, Ace, December 1985	2.75	2-3	______
Mudd's Angels J. A. Lawrence, Bantam Books Paperback, original fiction, 177 p. 0-553-11802-1, first edition, May 1975	1.75	2-5	______
0-553-24666-6, Feb. 1985	2.95	3-4	______
Mutiny on the Enterprise Robert E. Vardeman, Pocket Books Paperback, original fiction, 189 p. 0-671-46541-4, Timescape imprint, October 1983	2.95	2-4	______
0-671-46541-4, without numbered cover	2.95	3-4	______
My Enemy, My Ally Diane Duane Original fiction, 309 p. 0-671-50285-9, first edition with numbered cover, July 1984	2.95	2-4	______
0-671-55446-8, second printing	3.50	3-4	______
025908, hardcover, Pocket Books, The Literary Guild & Science Fiction Book Club, Member's price . . .	4.98	5-7	______

My Stars!

My Stars!	**Issue**	**Current**	**Cost/Date**
Michael C. Goodwin, Vulcan Books Tradepaper, Trek Humor portrayed through ink cartoons, 125 p. [5] 0-914350-1, 1980	5.95	6-7	______
Official Star Trek Cooking Manual Mary Ann Picard, Bantam Books Paperback, Trek recipes, 203 p., 0-553-11819-6, July 1978	1.95	2-8	______

Star Trek Quiz Book, Trade paper.

Official Star Trek Quiz Book	**Issue**	**Current**	**Cost/Date**
Mitchell Maglio, Wallaby Tradepaper, trivia questions on Trek history & photo quizzes, 256 p. 0-671-55652-5, May 1985	6.95	7-8	______
Official Star Trek Trivia Book Rafe Needleman, Quizzes on Trek trivia, 205 p. 0-671-83090-X, paperback Pocket Books, January 1980	2.25	5-8	______
3658, hardcover, Pocket Books, Book Club Edition, 1980	3.95	8-12	______

5. The cartoons contained in **My Stars!** previously appeared in Salt Lake City newspaper called the *Desert News.* The comics ran from January to September 1977 before being compiled in this anthology.

Star Trek Trivia Book Book Club edition.

Bjo Trimble's Book

	Issue	Current	Cost/Date
On The Good Ship Enterprise: My 15 Years With Star Trek			
Bjo Trimble, Donning (Starblaze Edition), Tradepaper, autobiography, 285 p.			
0-89865-253-7, 1983	5.95	6-7	_____
Pawns and Symbols			
Majliss Larson, Pocket Books Paperback, original fiction, 277 p.			
0-671-55425-5, Nov. 1985	3.50	3-4	_____
Perry's Planet			
Jack C. Haldeman, Bantam Books Paperback, original fiction, 132 p.			
0-553-13580-5, first edition, February 1980	1.75	2-6	_____
Second printing, March 1980	1.75	2-5	_____
0-553-24193-1, second edition artwork cover, September 1984	2.95	3-4	_____

	Issue	Current	Cost/Date
Planet of Judgement			
Joe Haldeman, Bantam Books Paperback, original fiction, 151 p.			
0-553-11145-0, first edition, August 1977	1.75	3-8	_____
Second printing	1.75	3-6	_____
Third printing	1.75	2-5	_____
0-553-24168-0, second edition, artwork cover, April 1984	2.95	3-4	_____
Price of the Phoenix			
Sondra Marshak & Myrna Culbreath, Bantam Books Paperback, original fiction, prequel to **Fate of the Phoenix,** 182 p.			
0-553-100978-2, first edition, July 1977	1.75	2-8	_____
0-553-10978-2, December 1977	1.75	2-6	_____
0-553-10978-2, April 1978	1.95	2-5	_____
0-553-24635-6, April 1984	2.95	3-4	_____
0-553-24635-6, second edition artwork cover, March 1985	2.95	3-4	_____
Prometheus Design			
Pocket Books, Paperback, original fiction, 190 p.			
0-671-83398-7, with Timescape imprint, March 1982	2.50	2-5	_____
0-671-49299-3, without Timescape imprint, numbered cover	2.95	2-4	_____
0-671-62745-7, new "Gertrude" logo	3.50	3-4	_____
Shadow Lord			
Laurence Yep, Pocket Books Paperback, original fiction, 280 p.			
0-671-47392-1, February 1985	2.95	3-4	_____

This book is very rare.

	Issue	Current	Cost/Date
Shatner: Where No Man Has Gone Before			
William Shatner, Sondra Marshak & Myrna Culbreath, Ace Books (Tempo-Star) Paperback, Shatner biography, with 50 pages of b/w photos, 327 p.			
0-441-88975-1, silver cover with photo inset of Shatner, 1979	2.25	10-20	_____

ADULT BOOKS

Spock Messiah!
Theodore Cogswell & Charles A. Spano, Jr., Bantam Books Paperback, original fiction, 182 p.

	Issue	Current	Cost/Date
0-553-10159-5, first edition, September 1976	1.75	2-10	
0-553-10159-5, October 1976	1.75	2-8	
0-553-10159-5, June 1977	1.75	2-6	
0-553-10159-5, Feb. 1978	1.75	2-6	
0-553-24674-7, second edition artwork cover, October 1984	2.95	3-4	

Spock Must Die!
James Blish, Bantam Books Paperback, original fiction, 188 p.[6]
Eighteen printings through April 1985, assorted issues include:

	Issue	Current	Cost/Date
0-553-05515-0, first edition, February 1970	.60	2-10	
0-553-02245	1.25	2-8	
0-553-10749	1.50	2-6	
0-553-19797	1.50	2-6	
0-553-12589-3, second edition cover artwork, twin Spock, October 1978	1.75	2-8	
0-553-12591	1.75	2-8	
0-553-24634-8, April 1984	2.95	3-4	
0-553-24634-8, April 1985	2.95	3-4	

Starfleet Command Academy Graduates Exam Manual 200: Questions and Answers
Jim Moore, Carlton Tradepaper, Starfleet study questions

	Issue	Current	Cost/Date
0-8062-2281-6, 1985	5	5-6	

Starfleet Medical Reference Manual
Eileen Palestine, Ballantine Books Tradepaper, technical application of Trek universe, 160p.

	Issue	Current	Cost/Date
0-345-27473-3, first edition, October 1977	6.95	7-15	
Second printing, Nov. 1977	6.95	7-12	

Starless World
Gordon Eklund, Bantam Books Paperback, original fiction 152 p.

	Issue	Current	Cost/Date
0-553-12731-8, first edition, November 1978	1.95	2-8	
Second printing, Nov. 1978	1.95	2-6	
Third printing, August 1979	1.95	2-6	
0-553-24675-5, second edition artwork cover, Nov. 1984	2.95	3-4	

Startoons
Joan Winston, Playboy Press Paperback, pen & ink cartoons with sci-fi themes including Star Trek, some in comic strip format, 50 p.

	Issue	Current	Cost/Date
0-872-1659-5, December 1979	1.95	5-15	

Star Trek 1
James Blish, Bantam Books Paperback, novelization of Star Trek episodes "Charlie's Law," "Dagger of the Mind," "The Unreal McCoy," "Balance of Terror," "The Naked Time," "Miri" and "Conscience of the King," 136 p.
Thirty printings until December 1979, assorted issues include:

	Issue	Current	Cost/Date
F3459, first edition, January 1967	.50	2-10	
0-553-07869, 17th printing, 1972	.75	2-6	
0-553-08589, 19th printing, 1972	.95	2-6	
0-553-02114, May 1975	1.25	2-5	
0-553-10835, February 1977	1.50	2-5	
0-553-12589, October 1978	1.75	2-4	
0-553-12591, May 1979	1.75	2-4	
0-553-13869-3, July 1979	1.95	2-4	
9857, paperback, Bantam Books, special Book Club edition, 31st printing, December 1979	.95	2-5	

Star Trek 2
James Blish, Bantam Books Paperback, contains "Arena," "A Taste of Armageddon," "Tomorrow is Yesterday," "Errand of Mercy," "Court Martial," "Operation: Annihilate," "City on the Edge of Forever" and "Space Seed," 122 p.
Twenty-four printings until December 1979, assorted issues include:

	Issue	Current	Cost/Date
F3439, first edition, February, 1968	.50	2-8	
0-553-05559, photo cover	.60	2-7	
0-553-08066, photo cover	.95	2-6	
0-553-02171, photo cover	1.25	2-5	
0-553-10811, photo cover	1.50	2-5	
0-553-13877-4, second edition artwork cover	1.95	2-4	
0-553-13877-4, December 1979	2.50	2-4	

Star Trek 3
James Blish, Bantam Books Paperback, contains "The Trouble with Tribbles," "The Last Gunfight," "The Doomsday Machine," "Assignment: Earth," "Mirror, Mirror," "Friday's Child," & Amok Time," 118 p.
Twenty-one printings until July 1979, assorted issues include:

	Issue	Current	Cost/Date
F4371, first edition, black cover, April 1969	.50	2-8	
0-553-08683, black photo cover	.95	2-6	
0-553-02253, white photo cover	1.25	2-5	
0-553-10818, photo cover	1.50	2-5	
0-553-12312-2, photo cover with rainbow coloring	1.75	2-6	
9068, paperback, Bantam Books, 4th printing, Book Club edition, black photo cover	.95	2-6	
Bantam Books, 16th printing, Special Book Club edition, black photo cover	1.50	2-5	

Star Trek 4
James Blish, Bantam Books Paperback, contains "All Our Yesterdays," "The Devil in the Dark," "The Enterprise Incident," "Journey to Babel," "The Menagerie," & "A Piece of the Action," 134 p.
Fourteen printings until July 1979, assorted issues include:

	Issue	Current	Cost/Date
0-553-07009-0, first edition June 1971	.75	2-7	
0-553-08579, photo cover	.95	2-6	
0-553-2172, photo cover	1.25	2-5	

6. The first adult fiction book in paperback form.

ADULT BOOKS

	Issue	Current	Cost/Date
0-553-10812, photo cover	1.50	2-5	______
0-553-12311-4, second edition artwork cover, July 1979	1.75	2-4	______

Star Trek 5

James Blish, Bantam Books Paperback, contains "Let That be Your Last Battlefield," "Requiem for Methuselah," "The Tholian Web," "The Turnabout Intruder," "The Way to Eden," & "Whom Gods Destroy," 136 p.

Fifteen printings until June 1980, assorted issues include:

	Issue	Current	Cost/Date
0-07300-0, first edition, February 1972	.75	2-7	______
0-553-08180, artwork cover,	.95	2-6	______
0-553-08150, artwork cover,	1.25	2-5	______
0-553-10840, artwork cover,	1.50	2-5	______
0-553-12325	1.75	2-4	______
0-553-14383-2, horizontal title	1.95	2-4	______

Star Trek 6

Paperback, contains "The Apple," "By Any Other Name," "The Cloud Minders," "The Lights of Zetar," "The Mark of Gideon" & "The Savage Curtains," 149 p.

Fourteen printings until 1979, assorted issues include:

	Issue	Current	Cost/Date
0-553-07364-0, first editon, April 1972	.75	2-7	______
0-553-08184-0, artwork cover	.95	2-6	______
0-553-08154, vertical title	1.25	2-5	______
0-553-10815, vertical title	1.50	2-5	______
0-553-11697, vertical title	1.50	2-5	______
0-553-12911, horizontal title	1.75	2-4	______
0-553-13874, horizontal title	1.95	2-4	______
0-553-13874-X, horizontal title	2.50	2-3	______

Star Trek 7

James Blish, Bantam Books, Paperback, contains "The Changling," "The Deadly Years," "Elaan of Troyius," "The Paradise Syndrome" & "Who Mourns For Adonis?", 155 p.

Twelve printings until April 1979, assorted issues include:

	Issue	Current	Cost/Date
0-553-07480-0, first edition, July 1972	.75	2-6	______
0-553-08610, artwork cover with vertical title	.95	2-5	______
0-553-08150, vertical title	1.25	2-5	______
0-553-02240, vertical title with white spine	1.25	2-5	______
0-553-10815, vertical title	1.50	2-4	______
0-553-12907-4, second edition artwork cover with horizontal title	1.75	2-3	______
0-553-13873, horizontal title	1.95	2-3	______

Star Trek 8

James Blish, Bantam Books Paperback, contains "Catspaw," "The Enemy Within," For the World is Hollow and I Have Touched The Sky," "Spock's Brain," "Where No Man Has Gone Before," & "Wolf in the Fold," 170 p.

Eleven printings until December 1978, assorted issues include:

	Issue	Current	Cost/Date
0-553-07550-0, first edition, November 1972	.75	2-5	______
0-553-08170, vertical title	.95	2-4	______
0-553-02250, vertical title	1.25	2-4	______
0-553-10816, vertical title	1.50	2-3	______
0-553-12731-4, horizontal title	1.75	2-3	______

Star Trek 9

James Blish, Bantam Books Paperback, contains "The Immunity Syndrome," "Obsession," "Return of the Archons," "Return to Tomorrow," "That Which Survives," & "The Ultimate Computer," 183 p

Assorted printings include:

	Issue	Current	Cost/Date
0-553-07808-0, first edition, August 1973	.75	2-5	______
0-553-08628	.95	2-4	______
0-553-02238	1.25	2-4	______
0-553-11285	1.50	2-3	______
0-553-11211	1.75	2-3	______

Star Trek 10

James Blish, Bantam Books, Paperback, contains "The Alternative Factor," "The Empath," "The Galileo Seven," "Is There In Truth No Beauty?," "The Omega Glory" & "A Private Little War," 164 p.

Twelve printings until December 1979, assorted issues include:

	Issue	Current	Cost/Date
0-553-08401, first edition, February 1974	.75	2-5	______
0-553-08611, vertical title	.95	2-4	______
0-553-02241, vertical title	1.25	2-4	______
0-553-10796, vertical title	1.50	2-3	______
0-553-11992	1.75	2-3	______
0-553-13866	1.95	2-3	______
0-553-23235, horizontal title	2.50	2-3	______

Star Trek 11

James Blish, Bantam Books Paperback, contains "Bread and Circuses," "Plato's Stepchildren," "The Squire of Gothos," "What Are Little Girls Made Of?" & "The Wink of an Eye," 188 p.

Seven printings until October 1979, issues include:

	Issue	Current	Cost/Date
0-553-08717, first edition, April 1975	1.25	2-6	______
0-553-11417	2.50	2-5	______
0-553-13502-3, horizontal title	1.75	2-4	______
0-553-25169-4 (entitled **Day of the Dove**) second edition artwork cover, Spectra logo, October 1985	2.95	3-4	______

Star Trek 12

James Blish & J. A. Lawrence, Bantam Books Paperback, contains "And The Children Shall Lead," "The Corbomite Maneuver," "The Gamesters of Triskelion," "Patterns of Force" & "Shore Leave," 177 p.

	Issue	Current	Cost/Date
0-553-11382-8, first edition, November 1977	1.75	2-8	______
0-553-11382-8, October 1979	1.75	2-6	______
0-553-25252-6, second edition artwork cover with Spectra logo, November 1985	2.95	3-4	______

Two sizes, tradepaper & paperback.

Old and new.

The valuable *Star Trek Concordance.*

	Issue	Current	Cost/Date
Star Trek Catalog			
Gerry Turnbull			
Trek merchandise listings and sources, 0-448-14053-5, tradepaper, Today Press (Division of Grosset & Dunlap, 240 p., 1979	6.95	8-12	_____
0-441-78477-1, paperback, Ace, reprint of Today Press edition, 140 p., 1979	2.50	3-6	_____

	Issue	Current	Cost/Date
Star Trek Compendium			
Allan Asherman			
Tradepaper, detailed episode guide, 0-671-79145-1, Wallaby Books, first edition, 1981	9.95	10-12	_____
Seven printings bearing same ISBN.	9.95	10-11	_____
0-671-62726-0 Pocket Books, 2nd editon, Sept. 1986	9.95	10-11	_____
Star Trek Concordance			
Bjo Trimble, Ballantine Books			
Tradepaper, dictionary of the Star Trek universe, episode wheel on cover, 256 p.			
0-345-25137-7, October 1976	6.95	25-50	_____
Book Club Edition, yellow imprint on upper right cover, 1976	3.95	20-30	_____
Star Trek Foto Novel No. 1			
City on the Edge of Forever			
Mandala Productions, Bantam Books Paperback, story told through episode clips & balloon dialogue, 150 p.			
0-553-11345-3, first edition, 1977	1.95	6-12	_____
0-553-12564	2.25	5-10	_____
0-553-12564	2.50	4-8	_____
Star Trek Foto Novel No. 2			
Where No Man Has Gone Before			
Mandala Productions, Bantam Books Paperback, 150p.			
0-553-11346-1, first edition, 1977	1.95	6-12	_____
0-553-12726	2.25	5-10	_____
0-553-12726	2.50	4-8	_____
Star Trek Foto Novel No. 3			
The Trouble With Tribbles			
Mandala Productions, Bantam Books Paperback, 150 p.			
0-553-11347-X, first edition, 1977	1.95	6-12	_____
0-553-12689	2.25	5-10	_____
0-553-12689	2.50	4-8	_____
Star Trek Foto Novel No. 4			
A Taste of Armageddon			
Mandala Productions, Bantam Books Paperback, 150 p.			
0-553-11348-8, first edition, 1978	1.95	6-12	_____
0-553-12744	2.25	5-10	_____
0-553-12744	2.50	4-8	_____
Star Trek Foto Novel No. 5			
Metamorphosis			
Mandala Productions, Bantam Books Paperback, 150 p.			
0-553-11349-6, first edition, 1979	1.95	6-12	_____
0-553-12173	2.25	5-10	_____
Star Trek Foto Novel No. 6			
All Our Yesterdays			
Mandala Productions, Bantam Books Paperback, 150 p.			
0-553-11350-X, first edition, 1978	1.95	6-12	_____
0-553-13509	2.25	5-10	_____
0-553-13509	2.50	4-8	_____

	Issue	Current	Cost/Date
Star Trek Foto Novel No. 7			
The Galileo Seven			
Mandala Productions, Bantam Books			
Paperback, 150 p.			
0-553-12041-7, 1978	2.25	8-12	______
Star Trek Foto Novel No. 8			
A Piece of the Action			
Mandala Productions, Bantam Books			
Paperback, 150 p.			
0-553-12022-0, 1978	2.25	8-12	______
Star Trek Foto Novel No. 9			
The Devil in the Dark			
Mandala Productions, Bantam Books			
Paperback, 150 p.			
0-553-12021-2, 1978	2.25	8-12	______
Star Trek Foto Novel No. 10			
Day of the Dove			
Mandala Productions, Bantam Books			
Paperback, 150 p.			
0-553-12017-4, 1978	2.25	8-12	______

Hard-to-find tradepaper.

	Issue	Current	Cost/Date
Star Trek Foto Novel No. 11			
The Deadly Years			
Mandala Productions, Bantam Books			
Paperback, 150 p.			
0-553-12028-X, 1978	2.25	8-12	______
Star Trek Foto Novel No. 12			
Amok Time			
Mandala Productions, Bantam Books			
Paperback, 150 p.			
0-553-12012-3, 1978	2.25	10-15	______
Star Trek IV: The Voyage Home			
Vonda N. McIntyre, Pocket Books			
Paperback, novelization of the movie, 274 p. 0-671-63266-3, December 1986	3.95	4-5	______
Star Trek Intragalactic Puzzles			
James Razzi, Bantam Books			
Tradepaper, puzzles & trivia, 128 p.			
0-553-01083-2, November 1977	5.95	6-10	______
Star Trek Lives!			
Jacqueline Litchenberg, Bantam Books			
Paperback, autobiographical notes & anecdotes, 274 p.			
0-553-02151-6, first edition, July 1975	1.95	5-10	______
0-553-02151-6, 2nd printing	1.95	5-8	______
0-553-02151-6, 3rd printing	1.95	5-8	______
0-553-02151-6, 4th printing	1.95	4-6	______
0-553-02151-6, 5th printing	1.95	4-6	______
0-553-02151-6, 6th printing	1.95	2-5	______
0-553-02151-6, 7th printing	1.95	2-5	______
0-553-02151-6, 8th printing	1.95	2-5	______
Star Trek Log One			
Alan Dean Foster			
Novelization of the cartoon episode series, Paperback, Ballantine, seventeen printings until October 1985, assorted issues include:			
0-345-24014-6, cartoon cover, first edition, 195 p., June 1974	.95	2-6	______
0-345-24014-6, cartoon cover,	1.25	2-5	______
0-345-25042-7, cartoon cover	1.50	2-5	______
0-345-25811-8, second edition artwork cover, yellow with Del Ray logo, May 1977	1.50	2-6	______
0-345-27601	1.75	2-5	______
0-345-33349-7, brown with Del Ray logo, October 1985	2.95	3-4	______
Tradepaper, Aeonian Press 1974	7.95	8-9	______
0-88411-081-8, hardback, Amereon Library, 184 p., 1975	13.95	14-15	______
Star Trek Log Two			
Alan Dean Foster			
Cartoon episode novelization			
Paperback, Ballantine, 177 p.			
Twelve printings until January 1985, assorted issues include:			
0-345-24184-3, first edition, cartoon cover, Sept. 1974	.95	2-6	______
0-345-24388-9, cartoon cover	1.25	2-5	______
0-345-24435-4, cartoon cover	1.25	2-5	______
0-345-25043, cartoon cover	1.50	2-5	______
0-345-28265-5, second edition artwork cover, orange with Del Ray logo, December 1979	1.75	2-6	______
0-345-32646-6, blue with Del Ray logo, January 1985	2.95	3-4	______
Tradepaper, Aeonian Press, 1974	7.95	8-9	______
0-88411-082-6, hardback, Amereon Library, 177 p., 1975	13.95	14-15	______
Star Trek Log Three			
Alan Dean Foster			
Cartoon episode novelization,			
Paperback, Ballantine, 215 p.			
Twelve printings until September 1985, assorted issues include:			
0-345-24260-2, first edition, cartoon cover, January 1975	1.25	2-6	______
0-345-25044-3, cartoon cover	1.50	2-5	______
0-345-25813-4, second edition artwork cover, red with Del Ray logo	1.50	2-5	______
0-345-31553-7, August 1984	2.25	2-4	______

	Issue	Current	Cost/Date
0-345-33318-7, orange with Del Ray logo, Sept. 1985	2.95	3-4	______
Tradepaper, Aeonian Press, 1975	7.95	8-9	______
0-88411-083-4, hardback, Amereon Library, 215 p., 1975	13.95	14-15	______
Star Trek Log Four			
Alan Dean Foster			
Cartoon episode novelization			
Paperback, Ballantine, 215 p., Seven printings until October 1985, assorted issues include:			
0-345-24435-4, first edition, cartoon cover, March 1975	1.25	2-6	______
0-345-25045 cartoon cover	1.50	2-5	______
0-345-25814, second edition artwork cover with Del Rey logo	1.50	2-5	______
0-345-27553-5, purple cover with del Rey logo	1.75	2-4	______
0-345-33350-0, blue with Del Rey logo, October 1985	2.95	3-4	______
Tradepaper, Aeonian Press, 1975	7.95	8-9	______
0-88411-084-2, hardback, Amereon Library, 215 p., 1975	13.95	14-15	______
Star Trek Log Five			
Alan Dean Foster			
Cartoon episode novelizations			
Paperback, Ballantine, 195 p., Seven printings until October 1985, assorted issues include:			
0-345-24532-6, first edition, cartoon cover, August 1975	1.25	2-6	______
0-345-25046, cartoon cover	1.50	2-5	______
0-345-25815-0, second edition artwork cover, purple with Del Rey logo, December 1977	1.75	2-4	______
0-345-33351-9, aqua cover with Del Rey logo, Oct. 1985	2.95	3-4	______
Tradepaper, Aeonian Press, 1975	7.95	8-9	______
0-88411-085-0, hardback, Amereon Library, 195 p., 1975	13.95	14-15	______
Star Trek Log Six			
Alan Dean Foster			
Cartoon episode novelizations, 195 p.			
Paperback, Ballantine, 195 p.			
0-345-25655-1, first edition, cartoon cover, March 1976	1.50	2-6	______
0-345-25816-9, second edition artwork cover in blue, Del Rey logo, Dec. 1977	1.75	2-5	______
0-345-33352-7, mauve cover, October 1985	2.95	3-4	______
Tradepaper, Aeonian Press, 1976	7.95	8-9	______
0-88411-086-9, hardback, Amereon Library, 1976	13.95	14-15	______
Star Trek Log Seven			
Alan Dean Foster			
Cartoon episode novelizations,			
Paperback, Ballantine, 182 p.,			
0-345-24965-8, first edition, cartoon cover, June 1976	1.50	2-6	______
0-345-25817, second edition artwork cover with Del Rey logo	1.50	2-5	______
0-345-27683, with Del Rey logo	1.75	2-5	______
Tradepaper, Aeonian Press, 1976	7.95	8-9	______
0-88411-087-7, hardback, Amereon Library, 1976	13.95	14-15	______
Star Trek Log Eight			
Alan Dean Foster			
Cartoon episode novelizations,			
Paperback, Ballantine, 1983 p.			
0-345-25141-5, first edition, cartoon cover, August 1976	1.50	2-6	______
0-345-25818-5, second edition artwork cover, green with Del Rey logo, Dec. 1977	1.50	2-5	______
0-345-27602, Del Rey logo	1.75	2-5	______
Tradepaper, Aeonian Press, 1976	7.95	8-9	______
0-88411-088-5, hardback, Amereon Library, 1976	13.95	14-15	______
Star Trek Log Nine			
Alan Dean Foster			
Cartoon episode novelizations			
Paperback, Ballantine, 183 p.			
0-345-25557-7, first edition, green artwork cover without Del Rey logo, February 1977	1.50	2-6	______
0-345-27165, with Del Rey logo	1.50	2-5	______
Tradepaper, Aeonian Press, 1977	7.95	8-9	______
0-88411-089-3, hardback, Amereon Library, 1977	13.95	14-15	______
Star Trek Log Ten			
Alan Dean Foster			
Cartoon episode novelizations			
Paperback, Ballantine, 215 p.,			
0-345-27212-9, first edition artwork cover with Del Rey logo, January 1978	1.95	2-6	______
Tradepaper, Aeonian Press, 1977	7.95	8-9	______
8-88411-090-7, hardback, Amereon Library, 1977	13.95	14-15	______
Star Trek Maps			
New Eye Photography, Bantam Books			
Tradepaper, contains official 32 page technical manual and 4 full color wall maps depicting planets of the Federation & Klingon & Romulan neutral zones, includes "Introduction to Navigation" booklet, packaged in slipcover packet, 0-553-01202-9, 1980	8.95	25-45	______
Star Trek Puzzle Manual			
James Razzi, Bantam Books			
Paperback, games & puzzles, 126 p. Eight printings through November 1978, including:			
0-553-11691-6, first edition, November 1976	1.25	2-8	______
0-553-10549, abridged version, August 1977	1.25	2-6	______
Second printing, Oct. 1977	1.25	2-5	______
Third printing, Oct. 1977	1.25	2-5	______
Fourth printing, Oct. 1977	1.25	2-5	______
0-553-16066-1, fifth printing, newly abridged with Scholastic imprint, Jan. 1978	1.50	2-4	______
Sixth printing, March 1978	1.50	2-4	______
Seventh printing, March 1978	1.50	2-4	______
Eighth printing, November 1978	1.50	2-4	______

STTMP Game

Star Trek Game, Ideal

STTMP Pajamas

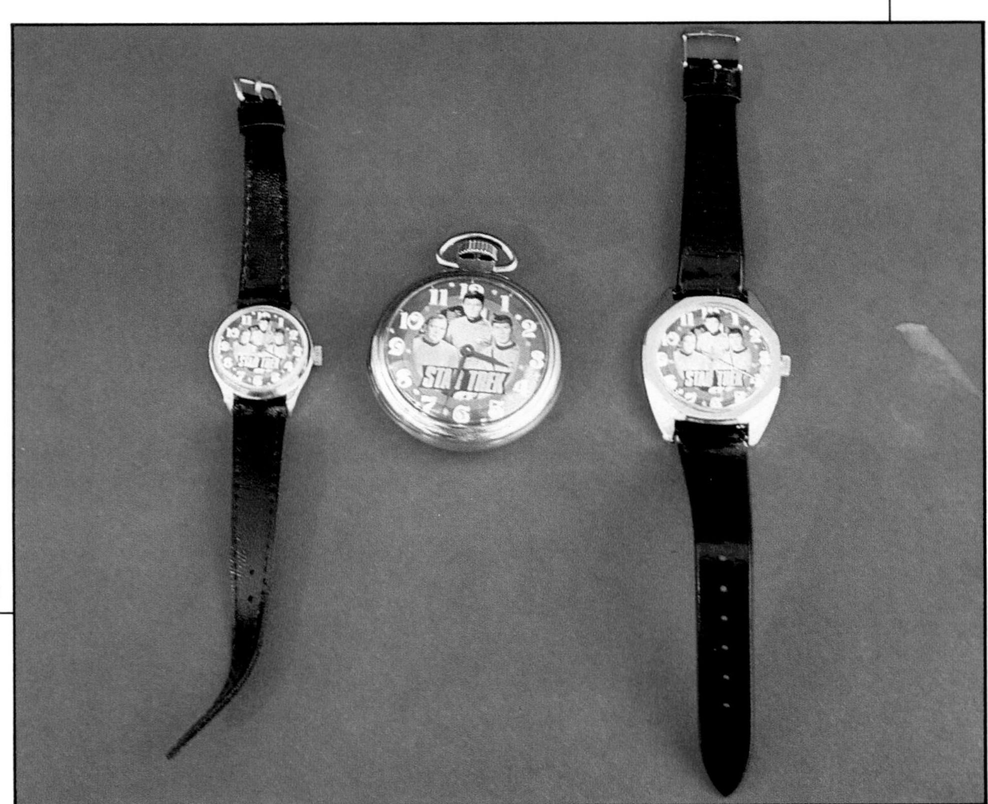

Stopwatch & Matching Men's & Women's Watches

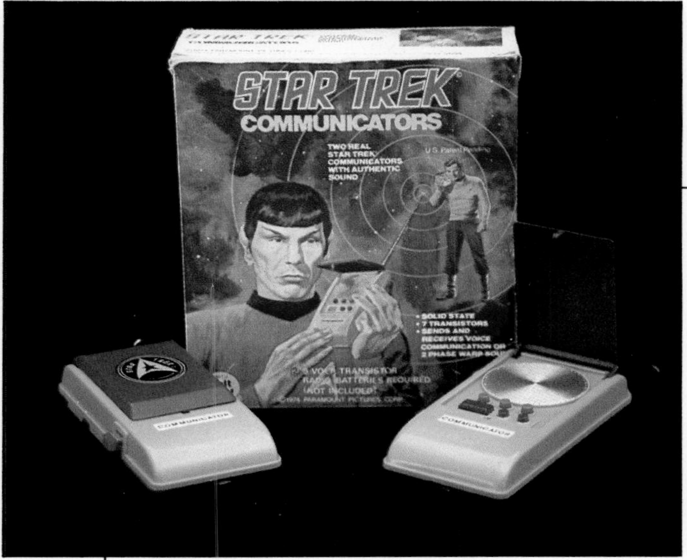

Star Trek Communicators, Mego

Star Trek Phaser Gun

Exploration Kit

Assorted Belt Buckles

Star Trek Medallion

Star Trek Cel

U.S.S. Enterprise Kit, Aurora

Dinky 10″ Die-Cast Toys

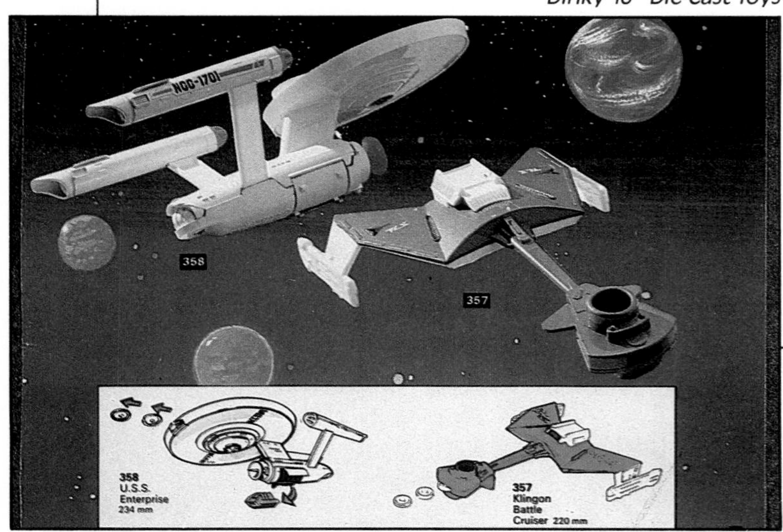

STTMP Lunchbox & Thermos

STTMP Mug & Bowl Set

Collector Plate & Steins, photo courtesy of Ernst Limited Ed.

Freezicles

STTMP Klingon Battle Cruiser

Starline miniatures

K-7 Space Station Kit

Tribble Eater

Spock Bank

Mix & Molds

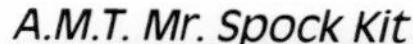

A.M.T. Mr. Spock Kit

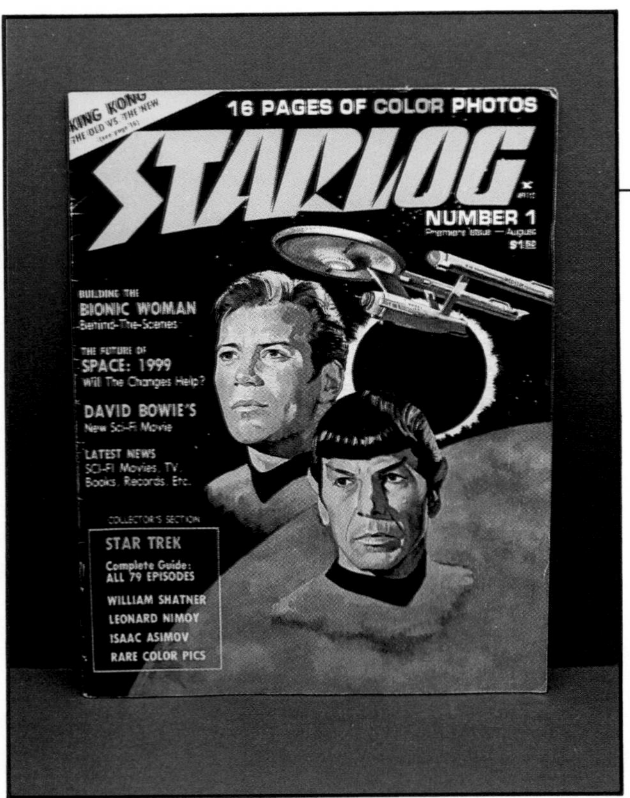

Starlog #1

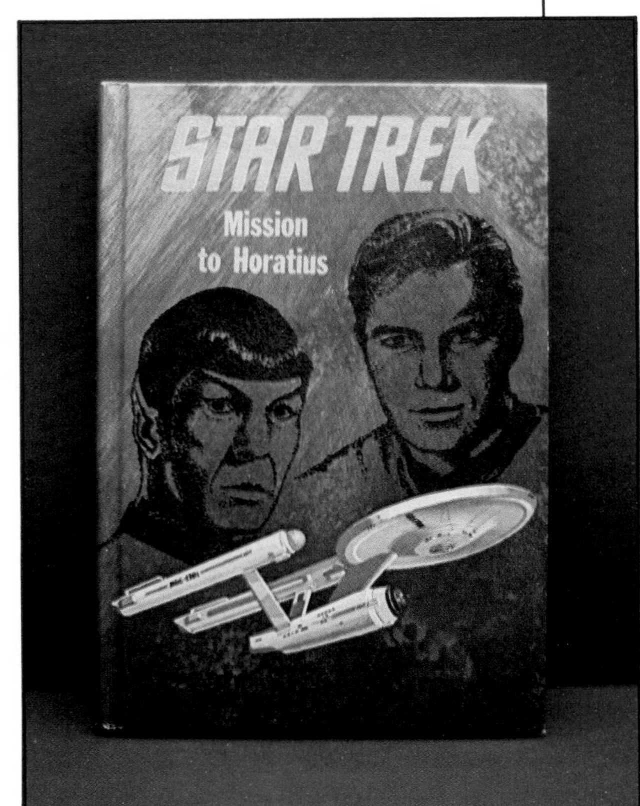

Mission to Horatius

Star Trek Maps

ADULT BOOKS

	Issue	Current	Cost/Date
0-553-12131-6, Special Book Club edition, 1977	1.50	2-5	_____

Star Trek Quiz Book
Bart Andrews, Brad Dunning, Signet Paperback, Trek trivia, later edition released as **The Trekkie Quiz Book,** 150 p.

	Issue	Current	Cost/Date
0-451-074907-1, first edition, June 1977	1.50	2-8	_____
Second printing **Trekkie Quiz Book,** 1977	1.50	2-6	_____
Third printing, **Trekkie Quiz Book,** 1977	1.50	2-5	_____
0-451-08413-6, 4th printing, **Trekkie Quiz Book,** 1977	1.50	2-4	_____

Star Trek Reader Volume 1
James Blish
Hardback, reprint of Bantam paperbacks, **Star Trek** 1-4, 422 p. [7]

	Issue	Current	Cost/Date
Dutton, 1970	5.95	6-12	_____
031369, Book Club Edition, 1970	3.95	4-10	_____
031369, Book Club Edition reprints	5.50	5-6	_____

Star Trek Reader Volume 2
James Blish
Hardback, reprint of Bantam paperbacks **Star Trek** 5-7, 457 p.

	Issue	Current	Cost/Date
Dutton, 1972	5.95	6-12	_____
023515, Book Club Edition, 1972	3.95	4-10	_____
023515, Book Club Edition reprints	5.50	5-6	_____

Star Trek Spaceflight Chronology

Star Trek Reader Volume 3
James Blish
Hardback, reprint of Bantam paperbacks, **Star Trek** 8-10, 447 p. [8]

	Issue	Current	Cost/Date
Dutton, 1973	5.95	6-12	_____
020313, Book Club Edition, 1973	3.95	4-10	_____
020313, Book Club Edition reprints	5.50	5-6	_____

Star Trek Star Fleet Technical Manual

Star Trek Reader Volume 4
James Blish
Hardback, reprint of Bantam paperbacks **Star Trek** 11-12, 472 p. [9]

	Issue	Current	Cost/Date
Dutton, 1974	5.95	6-12	_____
033191, Book Club Edition, 1974	3.95	4-10	_____
033191, Book Club Edition, reprints	5.50	5-6	_____

Star Trek Space Flight Chronology
Stan Goldstein & Fred Goldstein, Illustrated by Rick Sternbach, Wallaby. Tradepaper, space craft chronology with charts & graphs, 192 p.

	Issue	Current	Cost/Date
0-671-79089-7, January 1980	8.95	9-15	_____

Star Trek Speaks
Susan Sackett & Fred & Stan Goldstein, Wallaby, Tradepaper, philosophies of Trek, 160 p.

	Issue	Current	Cost/Date
0-671-79091-9, 1979	2.95	3-5	_____

Star Trek Star Fleet Technical Manual
Franz Joseph, Ballantine
Tradepaper, technical designs & diagrams of uniforms, flags, codes, etc., 180 p. [10]

	Issue	Current	Cost/Date
0-345-24730-2, with hardcover protector and special one-page letter to cadets, 1975	6.95	20-30	_____
0-345-34074-4, special 20th Anniversary edition, September 1986	10.95	11-12	_____

Star Trek The Motion Picture
Gene Roddenberry
Novelization of the movie, Paperback, Pocket Books, 252 p.

	Issue	Current	Cost/Date
0-671-83088-0, first edition, December 1979	2.50	2-5	_____
Second printing through the seventh	2.50	2-4	_____

7. **Star Trek Reader Volume 1** was the first adult hardback and the first adult hardback containing fiction material.
8. Covers on **Readers 1-3** were drawn by Lou Feck.
9. The cover on this **Reader** was drawn by S. Fantoni.
10. This tradepaper had the largest, single first printing in the history of science fiction publishing. After its 3rd week on the bookshelves it went to No. 1 on the New York Times Bestseller's list and remained there for 3 months.

ADULT BOOKS

	Issue	Current	Cost/Date
0-671-54685-6, 8th printing, with silver band on cover	2.95	3-4	
0-686-6088-7, hardback, Simon & Schuster, 151 p., 1980	9.95	10-15	
3830, hardback, Pocket Books Book Club Edition, 1979	5.95	6-10	

Star Trek The Motion Picture Photo Story
Richard J. Anobile, Pocket Books Paperback, movie story told with color photos & dialogue, 160 p.

	Issue	Current	Cost/Date
0-671-83089-9, April 1980	2.95	3-6	

Star Trek: The New Voyages
Sondra Marshak & Myrna Culbreath, Bantam, Paperback, original fiction short stories, 237 p.

	Issue	Current	Cost/Date
0-553-02719-X, first edition, March 1976	1.75	2-8	
0-553-02719-X, second printing, March 1976	1.75	2-6	
0-553-02719-X, April 1976	1.75	2-6	
0-553-02719-X, June 1976	1.75	2-6	
0-553-02719-X, Nov. 1976	1.75	2-6	
0-553-02719-X, April 1977	1.75	2-5	
0-553-02719-X, Dec. 1977	1.75	2-5	
0-553-12753-5, Feb. 1979	1.95	2-4	
0-553-12753-5, Sept. 1979	1.95	2-4	
0-553-14323, June 1980	2.25	2-4	
0-553-24636-4, April 1984	2.95	3-4	
0-553-24636-4, second edition photo cover with Spectra logo, August 1985	2.95	3-4	

Star Trek: The New Voyages 2
Sondra Marshak & Myrna Culbreath Bantam Paperback, original fiction short stories, 252 p.,

	Issue	Current	Cost/Date
0-553-11392-5, first edition, January 1978	1.95	2-8	
0-553-11392-5, second printing, March 1978	1.95	2-6	
0-553-11292-5, July 1978	1.95	2-6	
0-553-11292-5, Sept., 1978	1.95	2-6	
0-553-14959-5, January 1981	2.25	2-5	
0-553-22948-6, June 1982	2.50	2-4	
0-553-22948-6, March 1983	2.50	2-4	
0-553-23756-X, second edition, art-work cover with Spectra logo, April 1984	2.95	3-4	

Star Trek III, The Search For Spock
Vonda N. Mcintyre
Novelization of the movie, 297 p.

	Issue	Current	Cost/Date
0-671-49500-3, paperback, Pocket Books, June 1984	2.95	3-4	
0-8398-2839-X, hardback, Gregg Press (G.K. Hall), 1984	12.95	13-14	
3722, hardback Pocket Books, Book Club Edition, 1984	6.95	7-8	

Star Trek Trivia Mania
Xavier Einstein, Zebra Books Paper-back, 1,000 questions on Trek trivia, 238 p.

	Issue	Current	Cost/Date
0-8217-1732-4, Sept. 1985	2.50	3-4	

Odd sized Poetry Books by Nimoy.

Star Trek II, The Wrath of Kahn
Vonda N. McIntyre
Novelization of the movie, 233 p.
Paperback, Pocket Books,

	Issue	Current	Cost/Date
0-671-45610-5, first edition, July 1982	2.50	2-5	
Second printing	2.50	2-4	
Third printing	2.50	2-4	
Fourth printing	2.50	2-4	
Fifth printing	2.50	2-4	
0-671-47232-1, title in yellow	2.75	3-4	
0-671-55248-1, with silver band on cover	2.95	3-4	
0-671-63494-1, with white band on cover & new "Gertrude" logo	3.50	3-4	
0-8398-2832-2, hardback Gregg Press (G.K. Hall), 1982	10.95	11-12	
03119, hardback, Pocket Books, Book Club Edition, 1982	6.95	7-10	

Star Trek II, The Wrath of Kahn Photo Store
Richard Anobile, Pocket Books Paperback, movie story told with b/w photos & dialogue, 160 p.

	Issue	Current	Cost/Date
0-671-45912-0, 1982	2.95	3-5	

Trek or Treat.

Strangers From The Sky

	Issue	Current	Cost/Date
Margaret Wander Bonnano, Pocket Books, Original fiction, July 1987	3.50	3-4	

Tears of the Singers
Melinda Snodgrass, Pocket Books Paperback, original fiction, 252 p.,

	Issue	Current	Cost/Date
0-671-50284-0, Sept. 1984	3.50	3-4	

ADULT BOOKS

Issue | Current Cost/Date

Thank You For Your Love
Leonard Nimoy, Blue Mountain Arts Tradepaper, 4"x5½", poetry, 30 p
0-88396-114-8, 1980 .... 2.50 3-5 ______

These Words Are For You
Leonard Nimoy, Blue Mountain Press Tradepaper, poetry, 64 p.
0-88396-148-2, first edition, November 1981 .... 4.95 5-8 ______

Trekkie Quiz Book
Bart Andrews & Brad Dunning, Signet Paperback, See **Star Trek Quiz Book**

Trek or Treat
Terry Flanagan & Eleanor Ehrhardt, Ballantine Books Tradepaper, humorous dialogue in balloon captions coupled with b/w episode photos, 96 p.
0-345-25679-4, 1977 .... 2.95 3-6 ______

Trek to Madworld
Stephen Goldin, Bantam Books Paperback, original fiction, 177 p.
0-553-12618-0, first edition, January 1979 .... 1.95 2-8 ______
0-553-14550, August 1980 .... 2.25 2-6 ______
0-553-24676-3, with second edition artwork cover, Dec. 1984 .... 2.95 3-4 ______

Trellisane Confrontations
David Dvorkin, Pocket Books Paperback, original fiction, 190 p.
0-671-46543-0, with Timescape imprint, February 1984 .... 2.95 3-5 ______
0-671-56543-0, without Timescape imprint, numbered cover .... 2.95 3-4 ______

Triangle
Sondra Marshak & Myrna Culbreath, Pocket Books Paperback, original fiction, 188 p.
0-671-83399-5, first edition, Timescape imprint, March 1983 ... 2.95 3-5 ______
0-671-49298-5, without Timescape imprint, numbered cover .... 2.95 3-4 ______
0-671-60548-8, with new "Gertrude" logo .... 3.50 3-4 ______

Trouble With Tribbles
David Gerrold, Ballantine Paperback, behind-the-scenes while making t.v. Trek, 272 p.
0-345-23402-2, first edition, black cover, May 1973 .... 1.50 2-8 ______
0-345-23402-2, Jan. 1974 .... 1.50 2-6 ______
0-345-23402-2, Sept. 1974 .... 1.50 2-6 ______
Fourth printing .... 1.50 2-6 ______
0-345-24942-9, second edition red cover, Sept. 1975 .... 1.95 2-5 ______
0-345-24942-9, sixth printing ..... 1.95 2-5 ______
0-345-24942-9, Dec. 1977 .... 1.95 2-5 ______
0-345-27671-X, red cover with Del Rey logo, Jan. 1978 .... 2.25 2-4 ______

Issue | Current Cost/Date

Uhura's Song
Janet Hagan, Pocket Books Paperback, original fiction, 373 p.
0-671-54730-5, first edition, January 1985 .... 3.50 3-4 ______
0-671-54730-5, with new "Gertrude" logo .... 3.50 3-4 ______

Vulcan
Kathleen Sky, Bantam Paperback, original fiction, 175 p.
0-553-12137-5, first edition, September 1978 .... 1.95 2-10 ______
Second printing, August 1979 ..... 1.95 2-8 ______
0-553-24633-X, April 1984 .... 2.95 2-5 ______
0-553-24633-X, fourth printing .... 2.95 3-4 ______
0-553-24633-X, with Spectra logo, June 1985 .... 2.95 3-4 ______

Vulcan Academy Murders
Jean Lorrah, Original fiction, 278 p., Paperback, Pocket Books,
0-671-50054-6, first edition, November 1984 .... 3.50 3-4 ______
0-671-50054-6, 2nd printing ...... 3.50 3-4 ______
0-671-50054-6, 3rd printing .... 3.50 3-4 ______
0-671-50054-6, with new "Gertrude" logo, ... 3.50 3-4 ______
064121, hardback, Pocket Books, Literary Guild Book Club, 1984 ... 9.50 10-12 ______
01529, hardback, Pocket Books, Science Fiction Book Club, 1984 .. 4.98 5-8 ______

Cartoon Trek by Goodwin.

Warmed By Love
Leonard Nimoy, Blue Mountain Press Hardback, compilation of poetry from previously published works, 157 p.
0-883906-200-4, September 1983 .. 14.95 15-16 ______

We Are All Children Searching For Love
Leonard Nimoy, Blue Mountain Press Tradepaper, poetry, 63 p.
0-88396-024-9, first edition, 1977 .. 4.95 5-10 ______
0-88396-024-9, Dec. 1977 .... 4.95 5-8 ______
0-88396-024-9, January 1979 ..... 4.95 5-8 ______

Second Edition, Cover.

Web of the Romulans
M. S. Murdock
Original fiction, 220 p.
Paperback, Pocket Books

	Issue	Current	Cost/Date
0-671-46479-5, with Timescape imprint, June 1983	2.95	3-5	______
0-671-46479-5, without Timescape logo, 2nd printing	2.95	3-4	______
0-671-60549-6, numbered cover	3.50	3-4	______
0-8398-2833-0, hardback Gregg Press (G.K. Hall)	10.95	11-12	______

Who Was That Monolith I Saw You With?
Michael Goodwin, Heritage Books
Tradepaper (stapled spine), science fiction satire rendered in cartoon strip format & features Trek, prequel to **My Stars!** 110 p.

	Issue	Current	Cost/Date
0-930068-01-7, first edition, April 1976	2.50	2-8	______
Second edition, revised, August 1976	2.50	2-6	______
Second printing, August 1977	2.50	2-5	______

Will I Think of You?
Leonard Nimoy
Poetry & photos

	Issue	Current	Cost/Date
0-912310-70-7, tradepaper, Celestial Arts, 94 p. August 1974	4.95	5-10	______
0-440-05756-125, paperback, Dell Publishers, 50 p., October 1975	1.25	2-6	______

World of Star Trek
David Gerrold
Behind-the-scenes of Star Trek
Paperback, Ballantine, 276 p.

	Issue	Current	Cost/Date
0-345-23403-0, first edition, May 1973	1.50	2-8	______
2nd printing	1.50	2-6	______
3rd printing	1.50	2-6	______
4th printing	1.50	2-6	______
5th printing	1.50	2-5	______
6th printing	1.50	2-5	______
7th printing	1.50	2-5	______
0-345-24938-0, January 1975	1.95	2-4	______
9th printing	1.95	2-4	______
0-345-28571-9, second edition artwork cover, silver with Del Rey logo, Dec. 1979	2.50	3-4	______
Tradepaper, Bluejay Press, 209 p. 0-312-94463-2, first edition, May 1984,	8.95	9-11	______
0-312-94463-2, 2nd printing,	8.95	9-10	______
0-312-94463-2, 3rd printing,	8.95	9-10	______
0-312-94463-2, 4th printing,	8.95	9-10	______

World Without End
Joe Haldeman, Bantam Books
Paperback, original fiction, 150 p., [11]

	Issue	Current	Cost/Date
0-553-12583-4, first edition, February 1979	1.95	2-6	______
0-553-24174-5, second edition, artwork cover, February 1985	2.95	3-4	______

Wounded Sky
Diane Duane
Original fiction, 255 p., [12]
Paperback, Pocket Books

	Issue	Current	Cost/Date
0-671-47389-1, first edition, Timescape imprint, Dec. 1983	2.95	3-5	______
0-671-47389-1, without Timescape imprint	2.95	3-4	______
0-671-60061-3, 3rd printing	3.50	3-4	______
025841, hardback Pocket Books, Literary Guild Book Club, 1983	9.50	10-12	______
025841, hardback Pocket Books, Science Fiction Book Club, 1983	4.98	5-8	______

Yesterday's Son
A. C. Crispin
Original fiction, 191 p. [13]
Paperback, Pocket Books

	Issue	Current	Cost/Date
0-671-47315-8, first edition, Timescape imprint, Aug. 1983,	2.95	3-5	______
0-671-47315-8, without Timescape imprint, numbered cover	2.95	3-4	______
0-671-60550-X, numbered cover	3.50	3-4	______
0-8398-2830-6, hardback, Gregg Press (G.K. Hall)	10.95	11-12	______
022558, hardback, Pocket Books, Literary Guild Book Club, 1983	9.50	10-12	______
022558, hardback, Pocket Books, Science Fiction Book Club, 1983	4.98	5-8	______

You and I
Leonard Nimoy
poetry & photos, 110 p.
0-912310-27-8, hardback, Celestial Arts, 1973

	Issue	Current	Cost/Date
0-912310-26-X, first edition, January 1973	5.95	6-10	______
0-912310-26-X, 2nd printing	5.95	6-8	______
0-912310-26-X, 3rd printing	5.95	6-8	______
0-912310-26-X, 4th printing	5.95	6-8	______
0-912310-26-X, Dec. 1975	5.95	6-8	______
Paperback, Avon Books, 0-380-17616-0, Dec. 1973	1.50	2-6	______

11. This book in the first edition had cover art drawn by Eddie Jones (**Best of Trek 1-5** and **7**).
12. **Wounded Sky** is the last paperback by Pocket to display an original Timescape logo.
13. This book was the first to have a foil-stamped title.

SUBJECT MATERIAL BOOKS

	Issue	Current	Cost/Date
Age of Wonders: Exploring the World of Science Fiction David Hartwell Nonfiction examination of sci-fi literature and media phenomeno, p. 33-35, 89, 133 & 199 review Star Trek and the Trekkie movement, the design of the Enterprise and naming the U.S. shuttle			
0-8027-0808-0, hardback, Walker & Company, 205 p., 1984	15.95	16-17	_____
0-97-026963-7, paperback, McGraw Hill, 224 p., 1985	3.95	4-5	_____
American Monomyth Robert Jewett & John Shelton Lawrence, Anchor Press (Doubleday) Hardback, study of the American myth syndrome, pop culture & the media arts, Chapter 1 "Star Trek and the Bubblegum Fallacy," Chapter 2 "Trekkie Religion and the Werther Effect," pp. 1-39 with 2 b/w photos, 263 p.,			
0-385-12203-9, 1977	8.95	9-12	_____
American Vein Christopher Wicking & Tise VahimagI, E.P. Dutton Biographies of well known t.v. directors contains brief descriptions of Star Trek with bios on Gene Roddenberry, Gene L. Coon, Joseph Pevney, James Daniels, James Goldstone & Ralph Senensky, 261 p.,			
0-525-47603-2, tradepaper, 1979	6.95	7-8	_____
0-525-05420-0, hardback, 1979	9.95	10-12	_____
Celebrity Cookbook Johna Blinn, Playmore Inc., (Moby Books) Tradepaper, illustrated recipes from stars, contains William Shatner's "Steak Picado," pp. 200-201, interview on Star Trek's futuristic diets,			
2301, 1981	7.95	8-9	_____
Complete Directory to Prime Time Network Television Shows 1946-Present Tim Brooks & Earle Marsh, Ballantine Alphabetical directory to t.v. programs, pp. 708-709 summarize Star Trek, its history and following, 1,006 p. 0-345-29587-0, hardback,			
1979	19.95	20-21	_____
0-345-29588-9, tradepaper, revised edition, 1981	12.95	13-14	_____

	Issue	Current	Cost/Date
Cosmic Dancers, Exploring the Science of Science Fiction Amit Goswami, McGraw Hill Tradepaper, investigation of Sci Fi technology as possible fact, Star Trek philosophies include time travel, matter transporters, matter-anti-matter drive & drive logic, pp. 8, 113, 114, 157, 213 & 247			
0-97-023867-7, 1986	7.95	8-9	_____
Encyclopedia of Science Fiction Movies Phil Hardy, Woodbury Press A yearly chronology of science fiction films, reviews & photos, goes through 1985, info on STTMP, ST II & ST III, 408 p.			
Hardback, 1984	12.98	12-13	_____
Famous Spaceships of Fact and Fantasy Kalmbach Publishing Company (editors), Tradepaper No. 12038, how to model famous spaceships, Enterprise on cover, pp. 64-73 detail various models & modifications for the starship, 88 p.			
0-89024-539-8, 1984	8.50	8-9	_____
Fandom Directory Harry A. Hopkins Annual index of over 13,000 computer listings of interest to Trek fans, categories listed by state, fan addresses & general sci-fi interests, special classified section Tradepaper, Fandom Computer Services, approx. 400 p.			
Directory No. 1 1979-1980	3.95	3-6	_____
No. 2 1980-1981	3.95	3-6	_____
No. 3 1981-1982	3.95	3-6	_____
No. 4 1982-1983	5.95	5-7	_____
No. 5 1983-1984	5.95	5-7	_____
No. 6 1984-1985	9.95	9-10	_____
No. 7 0-89379-869-9, 300 p., 1985	19.95	20-21	_____
No. 8 0-89370-532-2, 400 p., 1986	19.95	20-21	_____
Fandom is for the Young: Or One Convention Too Many Karen Flanery & Nana Gramick Vantage Hardback, nonfiction information on attending sci-fi conventions			
0-553-04416-2, 1981	8.95	9-10	_____
Fantastic Television Gary Gerani & Paul Schulman Harmon Books Tradepaper, pictorial history of SF & fantasy on the screen, "Star Trek" chapter pp. 100-114 with 9 pages of commentary and 5 page episode guide, 27 b/w photos, book cover has blue tint photo of Spock, 192 p.			
0-517-52646-8, hardback, 1977	12.95	13-15	_____
0-517-52645-X, tradepaper, 1977	8.95	9-10	_____

SUBJECT MATERIAL BOOKS

	Issue	Current	Cost/Date
Films of the Seventies Robert Bookbinder, Citadel Press Tradepaper, features STTMP, pp 283-288, photos & info, 328 p. 0-8065-0927-9, 1982	9.95	10-11	______
From Jules Verne To Star Trek Jeff Rovin, Drake Publishers Tradepaper, guide to 100 best productions in movie and t.v. sci-fi, includes a synopsis of Trek pp. 139-143, 3 b/w photos of Trek's exotic women & full color portrait of Spock, 147 p. 0-8473-1458-8, 1977	6.95	7-10	______
Model Building Handbook Brick Price, Chilton Craft & Hobby Books, Tradepaper, explores handcraftedmodels & props, includes photos of STTMP helmet of fiberglass & auto putty, phaser's wooden master for vacuum forming & professional machinery used to create prop-quality starships, 176 p. 0-8019-6862-3, 1981	12.95	13-14	______
0-8019-6863-1, 1981	9.95	10-11	______
Omni's Screen Flights, Screen Fantasies Edited by Danny Peary, Dolphin Books (Doubleday). Tradepaper, review of famous SF movies, info on STTMP, ST II & ST III, 310 p. 0-385-19202-9, 1984	17.95	18-19	______
Pictorial History of Science Fiction Films Jeff Rovin, Citadel Press Tradepaper, brief history & photos of t.v. Trek, pp. 205-208, 0-8065-0537-0, 1975	9.95	10-11	______
Science Fiction Edited by Phil Hardy, William Morrow & Co., hardback, pictorial review of SF films, features STTMP page 354, STWOK page 377, contains b/w photos and 2 page color centerfold from STTMP, jacket front is color photo from STWOK, 400 p. 0-688-00842-9, 1984	25	25-26	______
Science Fiction Collector's Catalog Jeff Rovin, A.S. Barnes & Co., Inc. Tradepaper, collector information on SF memorabilia, features Trek comics, magazines & chapter 14, pp. 146-157 devoted to Trek collectibles, 181 p. 0-498-02562-4, 1984	12.95	13-15	______
Science Fiction Fantasy Editor of *Video Times* Magazine Signet Paperback, reviews video releases pp. 92-103 covers Trek disks, tapes & CEDS, 128 p. 0-451-13930-5, 1985	1.95	1-3	______
Science Fictionary Ed Naha, Wideview Books (Putnam) Comprehensive dictionary for t.v. films and writers, bios include Roddenberry, Gerrold, Fontana & former fanzine writer Juanita Coulsen, recaps Trek series, movies & animated cartoons, 200 p. 0-872-23-6196, hardback, 1980	16.96	17-18	______
0-872-23-6293, tradepaper, 1980	10.95	11-12	______
Screening Space: The American Science Fiction Film Vivian Solcak, Ungar Pub. Co. Tradepaper, reviews & analysis ofSTTMP, STWOK & STSFS, revised edition of prev. published title, **Limits of Infinity,** c. 19080, 345 p. 0-8044-6886-9, 1987	14.95	15-16	______
S-F 2: A Pictorial History of Science Fiction Films 1975-Present Richard Meyers, Citadel Press Hardback, a dictionary of films "Where No Man Has Gone Before" review Trek pp. 153-161, 12 b/w photos with one 2 page photo spread, 256 p. 0-8065-0875-2, 1984	12.95	13-14	______
Second Whole Kids Catalog Peter Cardozo, Designed by Ted Menten, Bantam Books. Book of games, activities & crafts, pp. 236-239 devoted to Trek books, posters, etc., 250 p. 0-872-23-6196, hardback, 1980	16.95	17-18	______
0-872-23-6293, tradepaper, 1980	10.95	11-12	______

Something to look for.

SUBJECT MATERIAL BOOKS

Issue | Current Cost/Date

Six Science Fiction Plays
Roger Elwood, Editor, Washington Square Press
Cover title proclaims "Included for the first time anywhere is Harlan Ellison's original script for **City On The Edge of Forever,** the Star Trek smash hit." Features the uncut script pp. 3-138 with intro by Ellison, 388 p.
0-671-48766-3, hardback, library edition, 1976 .... 6.95 7-12 ______
0-671-48766-3, paperback, 1976 ... 1.95 2-8 ______

Space and Science Fiction Plays For Young People
Sylvia E. Kamerman, Editor
Plays, Inc.
Hardback, collection of one-act, royalty-free plays for the classroom, pp. 40-72 feature an abridged screenplay for Gerrold's "The Trouble With Tribbles" designed for Junior & Senior High age students, 220 p.
0-8238-0252-3, 1981 .... 12.95 13-14 ______

Space Trek: The Endless Migration
Jerome Clayton Glenn & George S. Robinson
Historical background explored thru technology & used to project what the future of human migration into space will be, pp. 62-63, pp. 79-84 recount the efforts of fan league Enterprise Frontiers to name the space shuttle after Trek's starship, 223 p.
Hardback, Stackpole Books, 0-8117-1581-7, 1978 .... 9.95 10-11 ______
Paperback, Warner Books, 0-446-91122-4 .... 2.50 2-6 ______

Special Effects in the Movies
John Culhane, Hilltown Press (Ballantine)
Tradepaper, info & photos from STTMP pp. 164-165, 184 p.
0-345-28606-5, 1981 .... 11.95 12-13 ______

Starlog Science Fiction Trivia
Editors **Starlog** Magazine, Signet
Paperback, pp. 40-44 include trivia questions on Trek, 2 b/w photos & cartoon drawing, cover has photo inset of Spock, 208 p.
0-451-14397-3, September 1986 ... 2.95 3-4 ______

Star Wars; Star Trek and the 21st Century Christians
Winkie Pratney, Bible Voice Inc.
Paperback, reviews Christian philosophies as portrayed in Star Wars & Trek, b/w photos, 91 p.
693400, 1978 .... 1.75 2-6 ______

Issue | Current Cost/Date

State of the Art
Pauline Kael, Dutton Tradepaper, reviews of STWOK & STSFS, pp. 196-198, 0-525-48186-9, 1985 ..... 12.95 13-14 ______

Super T.V. Trivia
Bart Andrews, Signet Paperback, compilation of three books in one, **Super Trivia No. 1,** (1975), **Super Trivia No. 2** (1976) and **Super Trivia No. 3** (1977), questions on Trek & assorted photo quizzes, cover drawing has bust of Spock, 154 p. 0-451-13507-5, 1985 ...... 3.95 3-4 ______

T.V. Addict's Nostalgia Trivia and Quiz Book
Bart Andrews, Greenwich House
Hardback, b/w photos & trivia questions about t.v. shows, contains "Trekkie Fever" pp. 134-137,
0-517-44836-X, 1984 .... 6.98 6-8 ______

T.V. In The 60's
Tim Brooks, Ballantine
Paperback, pp. 222-225 discuss T.V. Trek, 271 p.
0-345-31866-8, 19085 .... 3.50 3-4 ______

T.V. Nostalgia Quiz and Puzzle Book
Bruce Nash, Contemporary Books
Paperback, pp. 151-153 features Star Trek "Tube Teasers," 299 p.
0-8092-5425-5, 1984 .... 6.95 7-8 ______

T.V. Theme Song Sing-Along Song Book
John Javna, St. Martin's Press
Tradepaper, lyrics, music & trivia on famous T.V. shows, pp. 102-103 spotlight Star Trek, 64 p.
0-312-78215-2, 1984 .... 5.95 6-7 ______

T.V. Trivia, Thirty Years of Television
Editors of Consumer Guide, Beekman House
Hardback, original book edition of the magazine version by Entertainment Today, pp. 52-53 contain questions & color photos on Trek, 64 p.
0-517-46367-9, 1984 .... 4.98 5-6 ______

Watching T.V.: 4 Decades of American Television
Harry Castleman & Walter Podrazik, McGraw Hill
T.V. synopsis of Trek pp. 195-197, 314 p.
0-07-010268-6, hardback, 1982 ... 22.95 23-24 ______
0-07-010267-4, tradepaper, 1982 .. 14.95 15-16 ______

Yesterday's Tomorrow
Joseph C. Corn & Brian Horrigan
Summit Books
Tradepaper, nonfiction review of the culture and technology of the future as projected by fact, fiction and the Big Screen, p. 31 briefly summarizes T.V. Trek, 158 p.
0-671-54133-1, 1984 .... 17.95 18-19 ______

ADULT BOOK SETS

Book Club Assortment — Issue / Current / Cost/Date

Hardback, Set of five Star Trek novels which include No. 048082 **Covenant of the Crown,** No. 025908 **My Enemy, My Ally,** No. 064121, **Vulcan Academy Murders,** 025841, **Wounded Sky** and 022558 **Yesterday's Son,** Pocket Books,

Literary Guild Set .... 42.50 43-45 _____

Science Fiction Book Club Set .... 22.50 23-24 _____

More Star Trek Adventure Set
Paperback, Pocket Books
Set of four novels including **Shadowland, Vulcan Academy Murders, Web of the Rumulans & Ishmael,** slipcover case features **Killing Time & Vulcan Academy** artwork .... 14 14-15 _____

Star Trek Adventure Set
Paperback, Pocket Books
Set of four novels including **My Enemy, My Ally, Wounded Sky, Tears of the Singers & Uhura's Song,** slipcase artwork cover features first two books,
0-671-91017-5, Nov. 1985 .... 14 14-15 _____

Star Trek Alpha Assortment
Paperback, Pocket Books
Set of four novels including **Black Fire, Covenant of the Crown, Triangle & Prometheus Design,** slipcase features artwork from **Yesterday's Son**
0-671-98548-5, 1983 .... 11.80 12-14 _____

Star Trek Assortment
Paperback, Pocket Books
Set of four novels including **Abode of Life, Wounded Sky, Mutiny on the Enterprise & Trellisane Confrontation,** slipcase features artwork from the first two.
0-671-90086-2, 1984 .... 11.80 11-13 _____

Star Trek Beta Assortment
Paperback, Pocket Books
Set of four novels including **Web of the Romulans, Entrophy Effect, Klingon Gambit & Yesterday's Son,** slipcase artwork features **Prometheus Design**
0-671-098550-7, 1983 .... 11.80 12-14 _____

Star Trek Fotonovel Assortment
Paperback, Bantam Books
Set of four books including the first four fotonovels **City on the Edge of Forever, Where No Man Has Gone Before, Trouble With Tribbles & A Taste of Armageddon,** slipcase features photos from the last two titles
No. ISBN, 1979 .... 7.80 20-40 _____

Scene from Interior **Giants In The Universe.**

Star Trek Logs Assortment — Issue / Current / Cost/Date

Paperback, Ballantine
Contains **Star Trek Logs 1-4,** cartoon covers
9-345-25341-8, 1975 .... 5 10-20 _____

Star Trek Readers Assortment
Hardback, Dutton
Contains four Book Club editions including 031369 **Star Trek Reader No. 1,** 023515 **Reader No. 2** 0230313 **Reader No. 34** & 033191 **Reader No. 4** by Blish
Science Fiction Book Club set .... 19.50 20-21 _____

Star Trek Series Assortment
Paperback, Bantam
Contains Star Trek novelizations 1-5 by Blish, slipcase cover, 1977 . 5 10-25 _____

Star Trek Series Fiction Assortment
Paperback, Bantam
Deluxe library slipcase includes four novels, **Vulcan & Planet of Judgement** available, 1979 .... 7.50 8-20 _____

Star Trek 20th Anniversary Set Volume I
Pocket Books, 1986
Set of four Star Trek novels, "Covenant of the Crown," "Dwellers In The Crucible," "The Final Reflection" & "The Killing Time," slipcover case
0-671-91253-4 .... 13.45 13-14 _____

Star Trek 20th Anniversary Set Volume II
Pocket Books, 1986
Set of four Star Trek novels, "Crisis On Centaurus," "Mindshadow," "Pawns and Symbols" & "The Trellisane Confrontation," slipcover case 0-671-91254-2 .... 13.45 13-14 _____

Two versions of *Planet Ecnal's Dilemma*

CHILDREN'S BOOKS

Issue | Current | Cost/Date

Blast of Activities
Merrigold Press
Softcover, coloring book, cover features full color shot of T.V. Spock holding phaser, 8"x11", 32 p.
1310, 1979 .... .59 1-3 ______

Draw 50 Famous Stars
Lee J. Ames, Doubleday & Co.
Panel outline sketches for drawing the portraits of T.V. & movie stars selected from Rona Barrett's *Hollywood Magazine,* nine panel frames detail a right profile of Mr. Spock, 30 p.
0-385-15688-X, tradepaper, 1983 .. 8.95 9-10 ______
0-385-15689-B, prebound with jacket, 1983 .... 8.95 9-10 ______

Far-Out Fun
Merrigold Press
Softcover, color & activity book with artwork cover of Enterprise over sunburst, STTMP theme, 8"x11", 32 p.
1309, 1979 .... .50 1-3 ______

Rescue At Raylo

Issue | Current | Cost/Date

Futuristic Fun
Whitman Publishing
Softcover, color & activity book with cartoon-style artwork cover, T.V. Enterprise over insets of Spock & Kirk, 8"x11", 60 p.,
1257-1, 1979 .... .40 1-3 ______

Giants in the Universe
Kay Wood, Random House
Hardcover, pop-up book with three dimensional cut-outs, 8 p.,[1]
0-394-83558-1, 1977 .... 4.95 5-15 ______

Jeopardy At Jutterdon
Whitman Publishing
Softcover, story & activity book with stickers, 8½"x12", 16 p.
2169-2, 1979 .... .79 2-5 ______

(A) Launch Into Fun
Merrigold Press
Softcover, color & activity book, red cover with color photo inset of Kirk, Spock & McCoy in STTMP uniforms, 8"x11", 32 p.
1311, 1979 .... .59 1-3 ______

Make-A-Game Book
Bruce & Greg Nash, Wanderer Books
Tradepaper, punch-out board game from STTMP, contains official single sheet letter from Star Fleet Command assigning mission, 20"x32" gaming sheet & playing pieces included, 9 p.
0-671-95552-7, Nov. 1979 .... 6.95 7-10 ______

Make-Your-Own-Costume Book
Lyn Edelman Schnurnberger
Designs & costume patterns from STTMP, includes color illustrations, 188 p.
0-671-25180-5, hardcover, Simon & Schuster, 1979 .... 12 10-15 ______
0-671-79109-X, tradepaper, Wallaby Books, 1979 .... 6.95 7-10 ______

Mission To Horatius
Mack Reynolds, illustrated by Sparky Moore, Whitman Pub.
Hardback, novel for children, "Authorized edition" and the first Star Trek novel ever produced, 210 p.[2] 1968 .... .79 15-25 ______

Monsters of Star Trek
Daniel Cohen, Pocket Books
Paperback, includes descriptions of famous Trek aliens, b/w photos, 117 p.[3]
0-671-56057-3, first edition, January 1980 .... 1.75 2-6 ______
0-671-52360-0, Archway logo, January 1980 .... 1.95 2-4 ______
0-671-63232-9, second edition, artwork cover with mugato .... 2.50 2-3 ______

1. **Giants In The Universe** has so far had a net sale of 11,597.
2. This book is the first Star Trek hardback ever produced. It is also the first children's hardback in a fiction category.
3. **The Monsters of Star Trek** is the first children's paperback ever produced. It is also the first nonfiction paperback written for juvenile audiences.

CHILDREN'S BOOKS

Issue | Current | Cost/Date

Planet Ecnal's Dilemma
Whitman Publishing
Softcover, coloring book, cartoon cover features front view of t.v. Enterprise & Yeoman with a tricorder, photo inserts of Spock & Kirk, 8"x11", 58 p.
1081, 1978 .... .49 1-3 ______
1035-1, 1978 .... .49 1-3 ______

Planet Ecnal's Dilemma
Merrigold Press
Softcover, abridged reprint of the above coloring book, purple cover with photo inset of Spock, Uhura, McCoy, Scotty & Kirk on T.V. bridge, 8"x11", 32 p.
1306, 1979 .... .50 1-3 ______

Prisoner of Vega
Christopher Cerf & Sharon Lerner
Illustrated by Robert Swanson, Random House, original fiction, 45 p.
0-394-83576-X, hardback, 1977 ... 2.95 5-10 ______
0-394-93576-4, hardback, Gibraltar Library binding, 1977[4] .... 3.99 4-5 ______

Rescue at Raylo
Whitman Publishing
Softcover, coloring & activity book, cartoon artwork of T.V. Enterprise (rear view) & Mr. Spock, photo inset of Kirk on bridge, 8"x11", 58 p.
1261, 1978 .... .49 1-3 ______

Rescue at Raylo
Merrigold Press
Softcover, abridged reprint of the above color & activity book, green cover has photo inset of Spock on STTMP bridge, 8"x11", 32 p. 1307, 1979 .... .59 1-3 ______

Star Trek Action Toy Book
James Razzi, Random House
Tradepaper, paper punch-outs of phaser, tricorder, Klingon Cruiser, the Enterprise, translator, communicator, Vulcan ears & standing figure of Kirk. 6 p.[5]
0-394-83277-9, 1976 .... 2.95 5-10 ______

Star Trek Activity Book
Peter Lerangis, illustratred by Carlos Garzon, Wanderer Softcover, puzzles, mazes, etc., full color artwork cover with Kirk, McCoy & Spock from t.v. series, 8½"x11", 32 p. 0-671-63246-9, 1986 .... 1.49 1-2 ______

Star Trek Adventure Coloring Book
Ellen Steiber, illustrated by Paul Abrams, Wanderer
Softcover, story & coloring book, color artwork cover features Sulu, Kirk, Spock and Enterprise, 32 p.
0-671-63244-2, 1986 .... 1.49 1-2 ______

Star Trek Alien Coloring Book
Peter Trewin, illustrated by Paul Abrams, Wanderer
Softcover, story & coloring book, color artwork cover shows STTMP Klingon, Spock & T'Lar, 8"x11", 32 p. 0-671-63245-0, 1986 .... 1.49 1-2 ______

Star Trek Coloring Book
Lincoln Enterprises
Softcover, includes 24 scenes from Trek animated cartoons, monsters, action scenes, phasers, communicators, etc., one illustration per page, detachable, 24 p.
0101 .... 3 3-4 ______

Star Trek Coloring Book No. 1
Saalfield Publishing Company
Softbound, cover with cartoon style drawing of Kirk & Spock, 8"x11", 64 p. C1856, 1975 .... .49 2-5 ______

Star Trek Coloring Book No. 2
Saalfield Publishing
Softbound, cover with bust of Spock rendered in oil paint medium, includes dot-to-dot, mazes, etc., 8"x11", 64 p.
C1862, 1975 .... .49 2-5 ______

Star Trek IV The Voyage Home
Peter Lerangis, Wanderer
Tradepaper, movie novelization with color photos, 92 p.,
0-671-63243-4, 1986 .... 5.95 6-7 ______

Star Trek Giant Coloring Book No. 1
Wanderer Books
Tradepaper, contains characters from STTMP, 1979 .... — 2-4 ______

Star Trek Giant Coloring Book No. 2
Wanderer Books
Tradepaper, features STTMP scenes & characters, 1979 .... — 2-4 ______

Star Trek Guide
J. Ed Clauss, Aeonian
Softcover, episode guide for the Star Trek T.V. series & info, 36 p.
0-88411-079-6, 1976 .... 2.95 3-5 ______
0-88411-079-6, 1978 .... 3.95 4-5 ______
0-88411-079-6, ... 5.95 5-6 ______

Star Trek Illustrated
James A. Lely, Creative Education
Guide to the Star Trek t.v. series, 32 p.[6]
Softcover edition, 1979, ... 3.95 4-6 ______
0-87191-718-1, hardcover, 1979 ... 7.95 8-9 ______

Star Trek: Phaser Fight
Which Way Books No. 24
Barbara & Scott Siegel, Archway
Paperback, adventure game in book form, you are a cadet Ensign assigned to the Enterprise & your actions determine your fate, 118 p.,
0-671-63248-5, 1986 .... 2.50 2-3 ______

4. This book has had a total of 16,890 sales in a regular edition. Gibraltar book sales number 6,097.
5. This is the first children's tradepaper devoted to Star Trek themes. Its nonfiction category in this format is also a first. Net sales measured a large 179,406.
6. **Star Trek Illustrated** was the first children's hardback in a nonfiction category.

First and Second Edition Covers

Star Trek by Creative Education

	Issue	Current	Cost/Date
Star Trek Puzzle Book Peter Lerangis, illustrated by Carlos Garzon, Wanderer Softbound, mazes, rebus & tracing activities etc., color artwork cover shows t.v. Kirk, Spock & Uhura on planetscape, 8"x11", 32 p. 0-671-63247-7, 1986	1.49	1-2	______
Star Trek The Motion Picture Peel-Off Graphics Book Lee Cole, Wanderer Tradepaper, sticker book containing removeable stickers featuring graphic designs, door signs & logos from the movie, 10 p.	6.95	7-12	______
Star Trek The Motion Picture Pop-Up Book Wanderer Hardback, fiction novelization of the movie told with 3-D cut out figures	4.95	5-10	______
Star Trek The Motion Picture U.S.S. Enterprise Punch-Out Book Tor Lokvig, illustrated by Chuck Murphey, Wanderer Books Tradepaper, paper cut-outs to assemble, makes STTMP Enterprise, 32 p. 0-671-95560-8, 1979	5.95	6-10	______
Star Trek The Motion Picture U.S.S. Enterprise Bridge Punch-Out Book Tor Lokvig, illustrated by Chuck Murphey, Wanderer Books Tradepaper, paper cut-outs to assemble, makes STTMP bridge, 32 p. 0-671-95544-6, 1979	5.95	6-10	______
Star Trek III, The Search For Spock Movie Trivia William Rotsler, Wanderer Softbound, flip pad containing puzzles, word games & trivia quizzes on the movie, includes yellow marker pen which makes invisible answers visible 0-671-50135-6, June 1984	2.95	3-4	______
Star Trek III, The Search for Spock More Movie Trivia William Rotsler, Wanderer Softbound, flip-pad with more puzzles, word games & trivia quizzes, yellow marking pen included, 0-671-50137-2, June 1984	2.95	3-4	______
Star Trek III, The Search for Spock - The Vulcan Treasure William Rotsler, Wanderer Tradepaper, Plot-it-yourself adventure book, 117 p. 0-671-50138-0, 1984	3.95	4-5	______
Star Trek III, The Search for Spock Short Stories William Rotsler, Wanderer Tradepaper, contains five original fiction stories "The Azphari Enigma," "The Jungles of Memory," "A Vulcan, A Klingon and an Angel," "World's End" & "As Old As Forever," 126 p. 0-671-50139-9, 1984	3.95	4-5	______
Star Trek III, The Search For Spock Story Book Lawrence Weinberg, Simon & Schuster Hardback, novelization of the movie with full color photos, 32 p. 0-671-47662-9, blue cover edition, 1984	6.95	7-8	______

CHILDREN'S BOOKS

	Issue	Current	Cost/Date
4887, Doubleday Book Club & Literary Guild Book Club, black cover with white spine & 5 photo insets on cover, 1984	5.95	6-9	______
Star Trek II Biographies William Rotsler, Wanderer Tradepaper, biographies of the Trek characters updated to the Wrath of Kahn timeframe, 159 p.			
0-671-46391-8, 1982	3.95	4-6	______
Star Trek II Distress Call William Rotsler, Wanderer Tradepaper, choose your own adventure in the Star Trek universe, 126 p.			
0-671-46389-6, 1982	2.95	3-5	______

Star Trek III Storybook

	Issue	Current	Cost/Date
Star Trek II Short Stories William Rotsler, Wanderer Tradepaper, fiction stories with Trek characters from the Wrath of Kahn movie, 159 p. [7]			
0-671-46390-X, 1982	2.95	3-5	______
Star Trek: Voyage To Adventure Which Way Book No. 15 Michael J. Dodge, Archway Books Paperback, plot-your-own adventure sequences aboard the Enterprise, illus. by Gordon Tomei, 118 p. [8]			
0-671-50989-6, white cover, first edition 1984	1.95	2-4	______
0-671-62492-X, yellow cover	2.50	2-3	______
Strange & Amazing Facts About Star Trek Daniel Cohen, Archway Paperback, history, trivia & photos on 20 years of Trek, 113 p.			
0-671-63014-8, 1986	2.50	2-3	______
Trillions of Trillig Christopher Cerf & Sharon Lerner illustrated by Kay Wood, Random House, Hardback, fiction pop-up book with story told in 3-D cut-outs. [9]			
0-394-83558-1, 1977	2.50	5-15	______
Truth Machine Christopher Cerf & Sharon Lerner illustrated by Jane Clark, Random House, Original fiction [10]			
0-394-93576-6, hardback, 1977	3.99	4-10	______
0-394-83575-1, tradepaper, 1977	2.95	3-8	______
0-394-83575-1, Gibralter Library Binding	3.99	4-10	______

CHILDREN'S BOOK SETS

	Issue	Current	Cost/Date
Star Trek II Gift Set William Rotsler, Wanderer Tradepaper, includes **Star Trek II Short Stories, Star Trek II Distress Call & Star Trek II Biographies,** slipcover case			
0-671-93230-6, 1982	9.95	10-12	______

7. **Star Trek II Short Stories** is the first children's tradepaper in a fiction category. It made publishing history, however, because of the photo of the inverted Enterprise on its front cover.
8. **A Voyage To Adventure** is the first children's fiction title in a paperback format.
9. This book had a net sales of 12,537.
10. Net sales for **The Truth Machine** have been 18,345 for the regular edition and 6,788 for the Gibraltar binding.

COMIC BOOKS

Gold Key Comics

A div. of Western Publishing Company. Complete comic set consists of 61 issues, 1967-1979:[1]

	Issue	Current	Cost/Date
Number 1, 1967 "Planet of No Return," Part I & Part II, cover photo of Kirk, Sulu, Enterprise & Spock holding beaker	.10	15-40	_____

First Gold Key comic. #1 & #2.

	Issue	Current	Cost/Date
Number 2, 1968, 10210-806 "The Devil's Isle of Space," Part I, "The Secret of Execution Asteroid," Part II, photo cover	.12	10-20	
Number 3, 1968, 10210-112 "Invasion of the City Builders," Part I, "The Bridge to Catastrophe" Part II, photo cover	.15	8-15	_____
Number 4, June 1969, 10210-906 "The Peril of Planet Quick Change," Part I "The Creatures of Light," Part II "The Sinister Guest," photo cover, reprinted in issue #35	.15	8-15	_____
Number 5, September 1969, 10210-909 "The Ghost Planet," Part I & II, photo cover, reeprinted as issue No. 37	.15	8-15	_____
Number 6, December 1969, 10210-912 "When Planets Collide," photo cover	.15	8-12	_____
Number 7, March, 1970, 10210-003 "The Voodoo Planet," Chapter I & Chapter II, photo cover, reprinted as issue #45	.15	5-10	_____
Number 8, September 1970, 10210-004 "The Youth Trap," Part I & Part II, photo cover	.15	5-10	_____
Number 9, February 1971, 10210-102 "The Legacy of Lazeus," Part I & Part II, photo cover	.15	5-10	_____
Number 10, May 1971, 10210-105 "Sceptre of the Sun," Part I & Part II, first artwork cover with photo insets of Kirk & Spock	.15	5-10	_____
Number 11, August 1971, 10210-108 "The Brain Shockers," Part I & Part II, artwork cover	.15	4-8	_____
Number 12, November 1971, 10210-111 "The Flight of the Buccaneer," Part I & Part II, artwork cover	.15	4-8	_____
Number 13, February 1972, 10210-202 "Dark Traveler," Part I & Part II, artwork cover	.15	4-8	_____
Number 14, May 1972, 90210-205 "The Enterprise Mutiny," Part I & Part II, artwork cover	.15	4-8	_____
Number 15, August 1972, 90210-208 "Museum at the End of Time," Part I & Part II, artwork cover	.15	4-8	_____
Number 16, November 1972, 90210-211 "Day of the Inquisitors," Part I & Part II, artwork cover	.15	4-8	_____
Number 17, December 1972, 90210-302 "The Cosmic Cavemen," Part I & Part II, artwork cover	.15	4-8	_____
Number 18, January 1973, 90210-305 "The Hijacked Planet," Part I & Part II, artwork cover	.15	4-8	_____
Number 19, July 1973, 90210-307 "The Haunted Asteroid," Part I & Part II, artwork cover	.20	4-8	_____
Number 20, September 1973, 90210-309 "A World Gone Mad," Part I & Part II, artwork cover	.20	4-8	_____
Number 21, November 1973, 90210-311 "The Mummies of Heitus VII," Part I & Part II, artwork cover	.20	3-6	_____
Number 22, January 1974, 90210-401 "Seige in Superspace," Part I & Part II, artwork cover	.20	3-6	_____
Number 23, March 1974, 90210-403 "Child's Play," Part I & Part II, artwork cover	.20	3-6	_____
Number 24, May 1974, 90210-405 "The Trial of Captain Kirk," Part I & Part II, artwork cover	.20	3-6	_____
Number 25, July 1974, 90210-407 "Dwarf Planet," Part I & Part II, artwork cover	.25	2-5	_____
Number 26, September 1974, 90210-409 "The Perfect Dream," Part I & Part II, artwork cover	.25	2-5	_____
Number 27, November 1974, 90210-411 "Ice Journey," Part I & Part II, artwork cover	.25	2-5	_____
Number 28, January 1975, 90210-501 "The Mimicking Menace," Part I & Part II, artwork cover	.25	2-5	_____
Number 29, March 1975, 90210-503 "The Planet of No Return," Part I & Part II, reprint of issue #1 with artwork cover	.25	2-5	_____
Number 30, May 1975, 90210-505 "Death of a Star," Part I & Part II, artwork cover	.25	2-5	_____

1. There was an occasional interchange between Gold Key and Whitman. Cover coloration may differ between the same issue number in these particular comics. In rarer cases, cover printings were actually reversed. There is no appreciable value difference between logo editions.

COMIC BOOKS

	Issue	Current	Cost/Date
Number 31, July 1975, 90210-507 "The Final Truth," Part I & Part II, artwork cover	.25	2-4	______
Number 32, August 1975, 90210-508 "The Animal People," Part I & Part II, artwork cover	.25	2-4	______
Number 33, September 1975, 90210-509 "The Choice," Part I & Part II, reprinted in 1978 as Whitman Dynabrite Comic with issue #41, artwork cover	.25	2-4	______
Number 34, October 1975, 90210-510 "The Psychocrystals," reprinted in 1978 as Whitman Dynabrite Comic with issue #36, artwork cover	.25	2-4	______
Number 35, November 1975, 90210-511 "The Peril of Planet Quick Change," Part I & Part II, reprint of issue #4, artwork cover	.25	2-4	______
Number 36, March 1979, 90210-603 "A Bomb in Time," reprinted in 1978 as Whitman Dynabrite Comic with issue #34, artwork cover	.25	2-4	______
Number 37, May, 1976, 90210-605 "The Ghost Planet," Part I & Part II, reprint issue #5 with artwork cover	.25	2-4	______
Number 38, July 1976,, 90210-607 "One of Our Captains is Missing," artwork cover	.25	2-4	______
Number 39, August 1976, 90210-608 "Prophet of Peace," artwork cover	.25	2-4	______

Gold Key & Whitman imprints.

	Issue	Current	Cost/Date
Number 40, September 1976, 90210-609 "Furlough to Fury," artwork cover	.30	2-4	______
Number 41, November 1976, 90210-611 "The Evictors," reprinted in 1978 as Whitman Dynabrite Comic with issue #33 artwork cover	.30	1-3	______
Number 42, January 1977, 90210-701 "World Against Time," artwork cover	.30	1-3	______
Number 43, February 1977, 90210-702 "The World Beneath the Waves," artwork cover	.30	1-3	______
Number 44, May 1977, 90210-705 "Prince Traitor," artwork cover	.30	1-3	______
Number 45, July 1977, 90210-707 "The Voodoo Planet," Chapter I & Chapter II, reprint of issue #7 with photo cover	.30	1-3	______
Number 46, August 1977, 90210-708 "Mr. Oracle," artwork cover	.30	1-3	______
Number 47, September 1977, 90210-709 "This Tree Bears Bitter Fruit," George Kashdan, A. McWilliams & Doug Drexler, artwork cover	.30	1-3	______
Number 48, October 1977, 90210-710 "Murder on the Enterprise," Arnold Drake, A. McWilliams & Doug Drexler, artwork cover	.30	1-3	______
Number 49, November 1977,90210-711 "A Warp in Space," George Kashdan & A. McWilliams, artwork cover	.30	1-3	______
Number 50, January 1978, 90210-801 "Planet of No Life," Arnold Drake & A. McWilliams, artwork cover	.30	1-3	______
Number 51, March 1978, 90210-803 "Destination Annihilation," George Kashdan & A. McWilliams, artwork cover	.35	1-3	______
Number 52, May 1978, 90210-805 "And A Child Shall Lead Them," George Kashdan & A. McWilliams, artwork cover	.35	1-3	______
Number 53, July 1978, 90210-807 "What Fools These Mortals Be," George Kashdan & A. McWilliams, artwork cover	.35	1-3	______
Number 54, August 1978, 90210-808 "Sport of Knaves," George Kashdan & A. McWilliams, artwork cover	.35	1-3	______
Number 55, September 1978, 90210-809 "A World Against Itself," Arnold Drake & A. McWilliams, artwork cover	.35	1-3	______
Number 56, October 1978, 90210-810 "No Time Like The Past," George Kashdan & A. McWilliams, artwork cover	.35	1-3	______
Number 57, November 1978, 90210-811 "Spore of the Devil," Arnold Drake & A. McWilliams, artwork cover	.35	1-3	______
Number 58, December 1978, 90210-812 "The Brain Damaged Planet," George Dashdan & A. McWilliams, artwork cover	.35	1-3	______

COMIC BOOKS

	Issue	Current	Cost/Date
Number 59, January 1979, 90210-901 "To Err is Vulcan," Arnold Drake & A. McWilliams, artwork cover	.35	1-3	______
Number 60, February 1979, 90210-902 "The Empire Man," John Warner & A. McWilliams, first of two cartoon art style covers	.35	1-3	______
Number 61, March 1979, 90210-903 "Operation Con Game," George Kashdan & A. McWilliams, second of two cartoon art style covers	.35	1-3	______

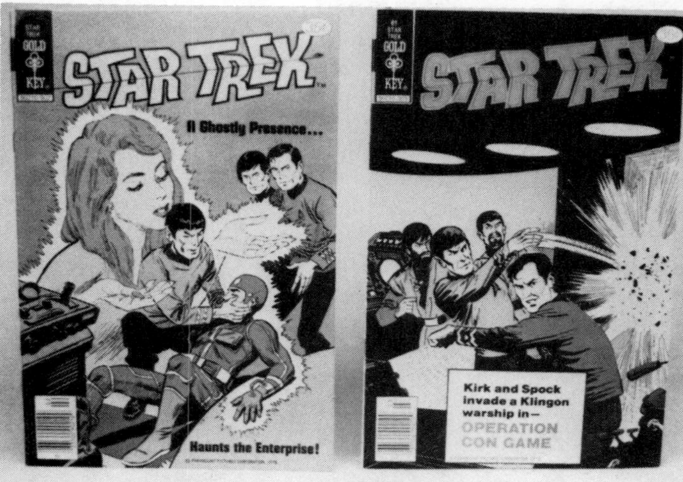

Gold Key comics #60 & 61. Note cover art.

Marvel Comics

Marvel Comics Group

Complete comic set consists of 18 issues, 1980-1982 [2]

	Issue	Current	Cost/Date
Number 1, April 1980 Stan Lee Presents "Star Trek The Motion Picture," Part I, Mary Wolfman, Dave Cockrum, Klaus Johnson & Marie Severin, movie adaptation	.40	1-2	______

Marvel Comics, #1 & 2.

	Issue	Current	Cost/Date
Number 2, May 1980 "V'ger," Mary Wolfman, Dave Cockrum, Klaus Janson, John Constanza & Marie Severin, STTMP adaptation Part II	.40	1-2	______

Spiderman logo vs. its counterpart

	Issue	Current	Cost/Date
Number 3, June 1980 "Evolutions," Mary Wolfman, Dave Cockrum Klaus Johnson, John Constanza & Marie Severin, STTMP adaptation Part III	.40	1-2	______
Number 4, July 1980 "The Haunting of Thallus," Mary Wolfman, Dave Cockrum, Klaus Johnson, Carl Gaff & Jim Novak	.40	1-2	______
Number 5, August 1980 "The Haunting of the Enterprise," Mike Barr, Dave Cockrum, Klaus Janson, John Costanza & Carl Gafford	.40	1-2	______
Number 6, September 1980 "The Enterprise Murder Case," Mike Barr, Dave Cockrum, Klaus Janson, Rick Parker & Carl Gafford	.50	1-2	______
Number 7, October 1980 "Tomorrow or Yesterday," Tom DeFalco, Mike Nasser, Klaus Janson & Ray Burzon	.50	1-2	______
Number 8, November 1980 "The Expansionist Syndrome," Martin Pasko, Dave Cockrum, Ricardo Villamonte, Ray Burzon & Carl Gafford	.50	1-2	______
Number 9, December 1980 "Experiment in Vengence," Martin Pasko, Dave Cockrum, Frank Springer, John Constanza & Carl Gafford	.50	1-2	______
Number 10, January 1981 "Domain of the Dragon God," Michael Fleiner, Leo Duranona, Klaus Janson, Rick Parker & Carl Gafford	.50	1-2	______

2. Marvel Comic covers may have issue number enclosed either in diamond boxes with a Spiderman logo or numbers enclosed within square boxes with vertical bar codes. Spiderman covered issues were sold directly from the publisher to a comic book dealership. Bar coded comics were those purchased by retail outlets from licensed, independent distributors. There is no distinction in collector prices between the two types.

	Issue	Current	Cost/Date
Number 11, February 1981 "Like a Woman Scorned," Martin Pasko, Joe Brozowski, Tom Parker, Carl Gafford & Joe Rosen	.50	1-2	______
Number 12, March 1981 "Eclipse of Reason," Alan Bremmert, Martin Pasko, Luke McDonnell, Tom Palmer, Joe Rosen & Carl Gafford	.50	1-2	______
Number 13, April 1981 "All the Infinite Ways," Martin Pasko, Joe Brozowski, Tom Palmer, Joe Rosen & Carl Gafford	.50	1-2	______
Number 14, June 1981 "We Are Dying, Egypt, Dying," Martin Pasko, Luke McDonnell, Gene Gray, John Morelli & Carl Gafford	.50	1-2	______
Number 15, August 1981 "The Quality of Mercy," Martin Pasko, Gil Kane, John Morelli & Carl Gafford	.50	1-2	______
Number 16, October 1981 "There's No Space Like Gnomes," Martin Pasko, Luke McDonnell, Day, Sal Trapani, Janice Chang & Carl Gafford	.50	1-2	______
Number 17, December 1981 "The Long Night's Dawn," Mike Barr, Ed Hannigan, Palmer, Simons, Parker, Blomfield & Gafford	.50	1-2	______
Number 18, February 1981 "A Thousand Deaths," D.M. DeMatteis, Joe Brozowski, Sal Trapani & Shelly Leperman	.60	1-2	______

D.C. Comics
D.C. Comics, Inc.
1983 to present

D.C. Comic #1.

	Issue	Current	Cost/Date
Number 1, February 1984 "The Wormhole Connection," Mike Barr, Tom Sutton, Ricardo Villagran, John Constanza & Michele Wolfman, Chap. I continues adventures after the events of ST II	.75	1-2	______
Number 2, March 1984 Chap II "...The Only Good Klingon ...," Mike Barr, Tom Sutton, Ricardo Villagran, John Constanza & Michele Wolfman	.75	1-2	______
Number 3, April 1984 Chap. III "Errand of War," Mike Barr, Tom Sutton, Ricardo Villagran, John Constanza & Michele Wolfman	.75	1-2	______
Number 4, May 1984 "Deadly Allies," Mike Barr, Tom Sutton, Ricardo Villagran, John Constanza & Michele Wolfman	.75	1-2	______
Number 5, June 1984 "Mortal Gods," Mike Barr, Tom Sutton, Sal Amendola, John Constanza & Michele Wolfman	.75	1-2	______
Number 6, July 1984 "Who is Enigma?" Mike Barr, Tom Sutton, Ricardo Villagran, John Constanza & Michele Wolfman	.75	1-2	______
Number 7, August 1984 "Pon Far," Mike Barr, Ed Barreto, Ricardo Villagran, John Constanza & Michele Wolfman	.75	1-2	______
Number 8, November 1984 "Blood Fever," Mike Barr, Tom Sutton, Ricardo Villagran, John Costanza & Michele Wolfman	.75	1-2	______
Number 9, December 1984 "...Promises To Keep," Mike Barr, Tom Sutton, Ricardo Villagran, John Constanza & Michele Wolfman, "New Frontiers," Chapter 1	.75	1-2	______
Number 10, January 1985 "Double Image," Mike Barr, Tom Sutton, John Constanza & Michele Wolfman, Chapter 2	.75	1-2	______
Number 11, February 1985 "Deadly Reflection," Mike Barr, Tom Sutton, Ricardo Villagran, John Constanza & Michele Wolfman, Chapter 3	.75	1-2	______
Number 12, March 1985 "The Tantalus Trap," Mike Barr, Tom Sutton, Ricardo Villagran, John Constanza & Michele Wolfman, Chapter 4	.75	1-2	______
Number 13, April 1985 "Masquerade," Mike Barr, Tom Sutton, Ricardo Villagran, Carrie Spiegel & Michele Wolfman, Chapter 5	.75	1-2	______
Number 14, May 1985 "Behind Enemy Lines!" Mike Barr, Tom Sutton, Ricardo Villagran, John Constanza & Michele Wolfman, Chap. 6	.75	1-2	______
Number 15, June 1985 "The Beginning of the End..." Mike Barr, Tom Sutton, Ricardo Villagran, John Constanza & Michele Wolfman, Chapter 7	.75	1-2	______

	Issue	Current	Cost/Date
Number 16, July 1985 "Homecoming. . ." Mike Barr, Tom Sutton, Ricardo Villagran, John Constanza & Michele Wolfman, Chapter 8 . . .	.75	1-2	______
Number 17, August 1985 "The D'Artagnan Three", L. B. Kellogg, Tom Sutton, Ricardo Villagran, John Constanza & Michele Wolfman	.75	1-2	______
Number 18, September 1985 "Rest & Recreation!", Ricardo Villagran, Agustin Mas & Michele Wolfman .	.75	1-2	______
Number 19, October 1985 "Chekov's Choice", Walter Koenig, Dan Speigle, C. Speigle, Michele Wolfman & Marv Wolfman, special adventure set between the events of STTMP and ST II	.75	1-3	______
Number 20, November 1985 "Giri," Wenonah Woods, Tom Sutton, Ricardo Villagran, Augustin Mas & Michele Wolfman	.75	1-2	______
Number 21, December 1985 "Dreamworld," Bob Rozakis, Tom Sutton, Ricardo Villagran, Agustin Mas & Michele Wolfman	.75	1-2	______
Number 22, January 1986 "Wolf on the Prowl," Tony Isabella, Tom Sutton, Ricardo Villagran, A. Mas-Layi & M. Wolfman, Part I	.75	1-2	______
Number 23, February 1986 "Wolf At the Door," Tony Isabella, Tom Sutton, Ricardo Villagran, A. Maslayi & M. Wolfman, Part II . . .	.75	1-2	______
Number 24, March 1986 "Double Blind," Diane Duane, Tom Sutton, Ricardo Villagran, Agustin Mas & Michele Wolfman, Part I	.75	1-2	______
Number 25, April 1986 "Double Blind" Part II, Diane Duane, Tom Sutton, Ricardo Villagran, Agustin Mas & Michele Wolfman	.75	1-2	______
Number 26, May 1986 "The Trouble with Transporters," Bob Rozakis, Tom Sutton, Ricardo Villagran, Agustin Mas & Michele Wolfman	.75	.75-1	______
Number 27, June 1986 "Around the Clock," Robert Greenberger, Tom Sutton, Ricardo Villagran, Agustin Mas & Michele Wolfman	.75	.75-1	______
Number 28, July 1986 "The Last Word," Diane Duane, Gray Morrow, Agustin Mas & Michele Wolfman	.75	.75-1	______
Number 29, August 1986 "Last Stand," Tony Isabella, Tom Sutton, Ricardo Villagran, Agustin Mas & Michele Wolfman	.75	.75-1	______

	Issue	Current	Cost/Date
Number 30, September 1986 "Uhura's Story," Paul Kupperbers, Ricardo Villagran, Carmine Infantino, Agustin Mas & Michele Wolfman	.75	.75-1	______
Number 31, October 1986 "Maggie's World," Tony Isabella, Len Wein, Tom Sutton & Ricardo Villagran . .	.75	.75-1	______
Number 32, November 1986 "Judgement Day," Len Wein, Tom Sutton, Ricardo Villagran, Agustin Mas & Michele Wolfman	.75	.75-1	______
Number 33, December 1986 "Vicious Circle," Len Wein, Tom Sutton & Ricardo Villagran, special anniversary issue celebrating 20 years of Star Trek, 37 p.	1.25	1-2	______
Number 34, January 1987 "The Doomsday Bug," Len Wein, Tom Sutton, Ricardo Villagran, Agustin Mas & Michele Wolfman, Chapter 1 "Death Ship"	.75	.75-1	______
Number 35, February 1987 "The Doomsday Bug," Len Wein, Gray Morrow, Agustin Mas & Michele Wolfman, Chapter 2 "Stand-off!" . .	.75	.75-1	______
Number 36, March 1987 "The Doomsday Bug," Len Wein, Gray Morrow, Agustin Mas & Michele Wolfman, Chapter 3 "The Apocalypse Scenario"	.75	.75-1	______
Number 37, April 1987 "Choices," Len Wein, Curt Swan, Pablo Marcos, Agustin Mas & Shelley Eiber . .	.75	.75-1	______
Number 38, May 1987 "The Argon Affair," Michael Fleisher, Adam Kubert, Ricardo Villigran, Agustin Mas & Michele Wolfman	.75	.75-1	______
Number 39, June 1987 "When You Wish Upon A Star," Len Wein, Tom Sutton, Ricardo Villagran, Agustin Mas & Michele Wolfman .	.75	.75-1	______
Star Trek III The Search For Spock, 1984 Mike Barr, Tom Sutton, Ricardo Villagran, John Costanza & Michele Wolfman, special movie adaptation, 64 p.	1.50	1-3	______
Star Trek IV The Voyage Home 1987, D.C. movie Special #2 Mike Barr, Tom Sutton, Ricardo Villagran, Agustin Mas & Michele Wolfman, movie adaptation, 64 p. . .	2	2-3	______

Star Trek Annuals by D.C.

Special D.C. Editions.

	Issue	Current Cost/Date	
Enterprise Log Volume 1 Golden Press, Western Publishing Co. Tradepaper edition containing a compilation of Gold Key Comic reprints, original issues No. 1-8, also includes Kirk's psychofile, portrait of a starship, a page from Scotty's diary & Trek artist profile, 233 p. 0-307-11185-7, 1976 [3]	1.95	3-6	______
Enterprise Log Volume 2 Golden Press Tradepaper compilation of Gold Key Comics No. 9-17, 224 p. 0-307-11188-1, 1977	1.95	3-6	______

Comic parody.

Special Comic Editions

	Issue	Current Cost/Date	
Dan Curtis Give-A-Ways Western Publishing Co., 1974 Comic premiums issued in 3"x6" format with abridged 24 page Gold Key Comic reprints. Nine issues were released in a series, two of which were Star Trek.			
No. 2, reprint of Gold Key No. 14 "The Enterprise Mutiny".	free	2-5	______
No. 6, reprint of Gold Key No. 13, "Dark Traveler"	free	2-5	______
Complete set of nine comics	free	15-30	______
Elftrek, Part 1 Dimension Graphics, July 1986 Satiric graphics based on Star Trek characters, Marcus Lusk, Mark Poe, Greg Legat & Jayne Sisson, 32 p. . .	1.75	1-2	______
Elftrek, Part 2 Dimension Graphics, August 1986 Comic satire, continuation of story from Part 1, 32 p.	1.75	1-2	______
Enterprise Log Volume 3 Golden Press Contains reprints of Gold Key Comics No. 18-26, tradepaper, Spock's psycho-file, 224 p. 0-307-11188-1, 1977	1.95	3-6	______
Enterprise Log Volume 4 Golden Press Tradepaper, includes Gold Key reprints of comics No. 27, 28, 30, 31, 32, 36, 34 & 38 despite cover claim of containing 37-35, also includes history of the Enterprise 0-307-11189-X, 1977	1.95	3-6	______
Star Trek Stan Lee, Marvel Comics Group Paperback, three stories told in comic format, reprints original Marvel Comics No. 12 "Eclipse of Reason," No. 11 "Like A Woman Scorned" & No. 7 "Tomorrow or Yesterday," 159 p. 0-939766-00-0, 1982 [4]	2.50	3-6	______

3. The **Star Trek Logs** are valuable collectibles. A Boston warehouse fire destroyed half the supply intended for U.S. distribution.
4. This comic adaptation in paperback form is the last of its type since 1982.

Star Trek Logs #1 & 2.

Logs #3 & 4.

	Issue	Current	Cost/Date
Star Trek Annual #1, 1985 "All Those Years Ago," Mike Barr, David Ross, Bob Smith, Carl Gafford & Marv Wolfman, special flashback adventure to before STTMP, 50 p.	1.25	1-3	______
Star Trek Annual #2, 1986 "The Final Voyage," Mike Barr, Dan Jurgens, Bob Smith, Agustin Mas & Michele Wolfman, special edition chronicles last mission of the Enterprise before STTMP, 46 p.	1.25	1-2	______

Dynabrite reprints.

Star Trek Annuals	Issue	Current	Cost/Date
World International Publishing Ltd. Hardback, British re-issues of Gold Key Comic stories, full color artwork, includes assorted games, crosswords & activities, two comic stories per volume, 96 p.			
0-7235-008-8, 1970	—	25-30	______
0-7235-083-5, 1971	—	20-25	______
0-7235-010-9, 1972	—	15-20	______
0-7235-016-6, 1973	—	15-20	______
0-7235-021-3, 1974	—	12-15	______
0-7235-032-5, 1975	—	12-15	______
0-7235-036-1, 1976	—	10-15	______
0-7235-041-9, 1977	—	10-15	______
0-7235-650-6, 1978	—	10-15	______
0-7235-655-1, 1979	—	10-15	______
1980	—	8-12	______
1981	—	8-12	______
1982	—	8-12	______
1983	—	8-12	______
1984	—	8-10	______
1985	—	8-10	______
0-7235-6765-4, 1986	7.95	8-9	______
Star Trek Dynabrite Comic 11357 Whitman Publishing Softbound reprint of Gold Key Comic No. 41 "The Evictors" & No. 33 "The Choice," heavy gauge paper, 48 p., 1978	.69	3-5	______
Star Trek Dynabrite Comic No. 11358 Whitman Publishing Softbound reprint of Gold Key Comic No. 36 "A Bomb in Time," & No. 34 "The Psychocrystals," heavy gauge paper, 48 p., 1978	.69	3-5	______
Star Trek The Motion Picture Marvel Super Special Magazine Number 15, Marvel Comics Group Softbound, official comic adaptation of STTMP, also includes photos, features, art & a new Concordance glossary, 130 p. No. 02077, December 1979 [5]	1.50	2-4	______

5. The $1.50 price tag on this comic special was a printing error. The adaptation was originally meant to sell for $2.00.

SPECIAL EDITION COMICS

	Issue	Current Cost/Date
Star Trek The Motion Picture Stan Lee Presents Pocket Books Paperback, comic novelization of STTMP in conjunction with Marvel Comics, 250 p. 0-671-83563-7, 1980	1980	3-6 _____

S.T.T.M.P. Comic Special.

Star Trek Annual.

Comic Story Books.

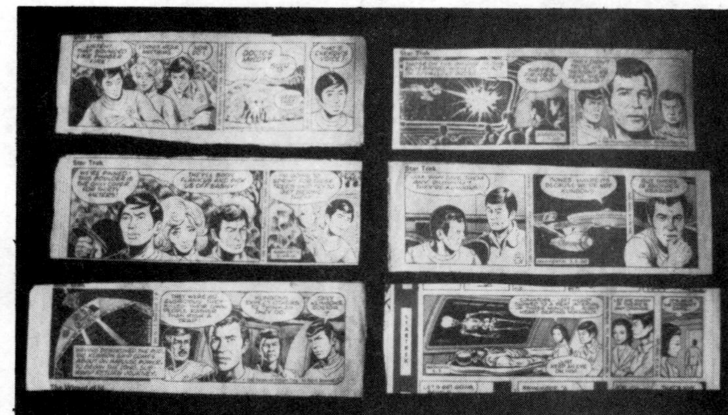

Star Trek Syndicated Comic Strips.

	Issue	Current Cost/Date
Who's Who In Star Trek #1 March 1987 Allan Asherman, Steve Bove, Carl Gafford & Michele Wolfman, character bios of the Star Trek universe (A-M) 48 p..	1.50	1-2 _____
Who's Who In Star Trek #2 April 1987 Allan Asherman, Steve Bove, Carl Gafford, Michele Wolfman & Howard Chaykin, character bios continued (M-V), 48 p.	1.50	1-2 _____

ADULT MAGAZINES

Vintage Magazine article, 1967

Star Trek covers.

	Issue	Current	Cost/Date
Air & Space Museum Smithsonian Institute 1986 October 11 Star Trek museum display.	3.95	4-5	_____
American Cinematographer ASC Holding Corporation 1980 February, Vol. 61, Number 2 Detailed examination of the making of Star Trek The Motion Picture . .	2.50	6-10	_____
1982 October, Vol. 63, Number 10 Special effects for Star Trek II, Warp speed, beyond Genesis effect	2.50	5-6	_____
1984 September, Vol. 65, Number 8 Visual effects for Star Trek III	2.50	3-4	_____
1986 December The Voyage Home, a work of thousands, Full color ST IV cover, special effects, planetscapes, under-water shots, etc., p. 50-74	2.95	3-4	_____
Castle of Frankenstein Gothic Castles Publishers 1967 Color cover photos Spock. Feature story studies Trek crew, actors and 1st season effects. Allan Asherman. [1]	.50	10-15	_____

	Issue	Current	Cost/Date
1969 Number 11 Special Star Trek issue, t.v. show . .	.50	8-12	_____
1969 Number 15 Star Trek is back, The ST debate, full color cover Kirk and Spock. . . .	.50	8-10	_____
Christian Century 1982 August 18-25, Vol. 99, No. 26 ST III movie review	.75	1-2	_____
Cinefantastique F.S. Clark Publishers Vol. 8, Number 2/Number 3 STTMP interview with Roddenberry on filming the movie	2.50	3-6	_____
Vol. 9, Number 1 Star Trek The Motion Picture report.	2.95	3-6	_____
Vol. 9, Number 2 Full color productions article on the release of Star Trek Motion Picture.	2.95	3-6	_____
Vol. 9, Number 3/Number 4 Review of STTMP and comparison photos with the t.v. series	5.95	6-9	_____
Vol. 12, Number 5/Number 6 Special double issue on making ST II and Blade Runner. Exhaustive coverage of filming and special effects by ILM. Star Trek II Cover Edition	7.95	8-12	_____
Blade Runner Cover Edition	7.95	6-10	_____
1984 July Leonard Nimoy in Star Trek III. . .	4.50	5-6	_____
1987 Vol. 17, Number 1 Preview of ST IV, the best yet	4.95	5-6	_____
Cinefax Valley Printers, Calif. 1980 March, Number 1 Designing V'ger for STTMP by Douglas Trunbull	3.50	6-10	_____
August, 1980, Number 2 Star Trek special effects.	3.50	6-10	_____
August, Number 18 Final voyage of the starship Enterprise 25 pages on special effects, rear cover color photo from ST III .	4.75	6-8	_____
Co-Ed Magazine 1969 January Mr. Spock conquers new frontiers, article on Leonard Nimoy, photos .	.50	3-5	_____
Commodore Power Play 1986 April/May Vol. 5, Number 2, Issue 20. Review of Simon & Schuster software "The Koybayashi Alternative."	—		_____
Coronet Magazine 1969 May Up to his ears - Leonard Nimoy. . .	.50	2-3	_____
Cracked Major Magazines			

1. Fans will recognize this very early magazine's author, Allan Asherman as being the author of the recent tradepaper **The Star Trek Compedium.**

Cracked magazines.

	Issue	Current	Cost/Date
Cracked			
1975 September, Number 127 Features ST parody from t.v. series called "Star Tracks." Full cover Trek artwork.	.50	4-6	______
1984 October, Number 207 Spock cover, features Michael Jackson parody using ST motif.	1.00	2-4	______
1985 January, Number 209 ST III parody containing "Star Drek III"	1.25	2-3	______
1986 February Cracked Collector's Edition - Best Movie Satires of the 80's, Number 65 "Star Drek The Moving Picture" feature is re-released	1.25	2-5	______
March 1986 Giant Cracked Sci-Fi Special No. 43 Cartoon satires two Trek specials: "Scotty Sulu McNimoy- Trekker King" dedicated to world's foremost fan; plus "Star Yeech" salute to 20th anniversary	1.95	2-4	______
1987 April Cracked Digest 3: TV Satires T.V. Guide clone comic digest, includes "Star Yecch" t.v. show spoof	2	2-3	______
July 1987 Cracked No. 228 Globe Communications Corp., Parody of **Star Trek IV** entitled, "Star Drek IV," full color cover spoofs Spock, Kirk & McCoy	1.35	1-2	______
Crawdaddy Magazine			
1976 December Ed Naha, producer of the album *Inside Star Trek,* is interviewed in teen music magazine	.75	2-3	______
Crazy			
Marvel Comics Group 1982 December, Number 92 Movie parody "Star Blech II," full color cover artwork Spock, McCoy and Kirk	1.25	3-5	______
Cue			
New York Weekly Entertainment Magazine 1975 December 26 Can Space 1999 match Star Trek? by Mike Jahn, full color cover caricature Kirk and Spock facing off two 1999 stars	.60	3-5	______
1979 December 7 Spock has the right stuff. Review Nimoy in STTMP. Full color Spock cover	.75	3-6	______
Famous Monsters			
Warren Publications Number 145 Star Trek The Motion Picture	1.75	2-4	______
1980 Number 161, April STTMP movie special	1.75	2-4	______
1984 Number 185, July Star Trek II Wrath of Kahn	2	2-4	______
Number 187 Star Trek II review, color cover front	2.25	3-4	______

Two spotlight periodicals

	Issue	Current	Cost/Date
Fantastic Films			
Blake Publishing Company 1973 August, Vol. 1, Number 3 Interview with Susan Sacket.	2	4-6	______
1978 December, Vol. 1, Number 5 Spock Speaks article and the Vulcan language decoded. Cover photo inset of Spock.	2	4-6	______
1979 September, Vol. 2, Number 10 Interview with Robert Wise of STTMP	2	4-6	______
1980 January, Vol. 2, Number 14 Special collector's issues, costumes and designs of STTMP	2.95	3-6	______
February 1980, Vol. 2, Number 15 Part II of ST costume designs	2.95	3-6	______
1982 August, Number 30 Behind the scenes of ST II, special effects and movie review	2.95	3-5	______

ADULT MAGAZINES

	Issue	Current	Cost/Date
November 1982, Number 22 Special Edition - Best of Fantastic Films, including ST II.	3.50	5-10	______
1983 September, Number 31 Interview with William Shatner.	2.95	3-5	______
1984 June, Number 39 Star Trek III photo review.	2.95	3-4	______
July, 1984, Number 40 Interview ith Leonard Nimoy of ST III.	2.95	3-4	______
September, 1984, Number 41 Interview James Doohan of ST III	2.95	3-4	______
November 1984, Vol. 7, Number 6 ST III special effects	2.95	3-4	______
Fantasy Image			
Number 1 In search of Star Trek, reviews all three films	2.50	3-4	______
Number 2 Color cover of Spock mannequin, Gene Roddenberry interview	2.50	4-5	______
FAVE Teen Magazine			
1968 March Star Trek production, photos on the t.v. set, 4 b/w photos	.35	3-5	______
1969 January Nimoy interview, 2 b/w	.35	2-3	______
April The Trek cast, Koenig, Doohan and Takei on horseback, 4 b/w, color pin-up; plus Koenig interview, 1 b/w, 1 color photo	.35	4-5	______
May 1969 Spock as a teenage outcast, 3 b/w; plus Koenig interview, 7 b/w photos	.35	4-6	______
June 1969 Koenig interview, plus FAVE forum panel including Koenig, 8 b/w	.35	3-5	______
July through September 1969 Cast bios, 5 b/w, 1 color pin-up poster of Spock and Chekov	.35	3-5	______
Fifteen Magazine			
1968 Nimoy interview, 6 b/w, 1 orange cepia	.40	2-4	______
1968 April through June Koenig interview, 4 b/w	.35	3-5	______
Koenig, 4 b/w plus color pin-up of Spock and Scotty from show	.35	3-5	______
1968 July Nimoy interview, 4 b/w plus Koenig 3-page photo spread	.35	3-5	______
October through December 1968 Cast biographies, 5 b/w photos	.35	3-5	______
Koenig, 4 b/w	.35	3-5	______
Koenig interview with color pin-up, 4 b/w	.35	3-5	______

	Issue	Current	Cost/Date
1970 January through March Nimoy interview, 1 b/w	.35	3-4	______
April through June 1970 Nimoy photo spread on his new Pet Pad pet shop venture in L.A., 10 b/w	.65	3-4	______
Ford Times			
Ford Motor Company 1982 December, Vol. 74, No. 12 The Best Known Face in Outer Space, article on Shatner. Free publication for client patronage	Free	2-3	______
Future			
March, 1979, Number 9 Spock on cover, on the movie set of STTMP	2.25	4-6	______
November 1979, Number 14 Enterprise on cover, Designing STTMP	1.95	3-6	______
December 1979, Number 15 New faces of STTMP	1.95	3-5	______
1980 February, Number 16 Enterprise on cover, Star Trek Takes Off.	2.25	4-6	______
March 1980, Number 17 Second anniversary issue, review STTMP	2.50	3-5	______
Future Fantasy			
1978 Number 1 William Shatner interview.	1.75	3-5	______
1978, Number 2 Battle between Star Wars and Star Trek	1.75	3-5	______
1979 Number 3 The resurrection of Star Trek	1.75	3-5	______
Hollywood Screen			
1968 April through June Nimoy interview, 2 b/w photos	.40	3-5	______
Home Viewer			
1985 February, Vol. 3, No. 3 Sci-fi Fever, previews new ST III tape and first 10 episode videos. Full color cover photo of STTMP Spock	1.50	4-6	______
Humanist			
1984 Sept./Oct., Vol. 44, No. 5 ST III movie review	2.50	3-4	______
IN Magazine			
1967 October Nimoy interview, 3 b/w photos	.40	3-4	______
1968 April Nimoy interview, 2 b/w, 1 color	.40	3-4	______
MAD Magazine			
E.C. Publications, Inc. 1966 November Star Trek t.v. series parody "Star Blecch." First Trek magazine satire	.25	8-10	______
1980 July, Number 216 STTMP parody "Star Blecch The Motion Picture."	.75	4-6	______

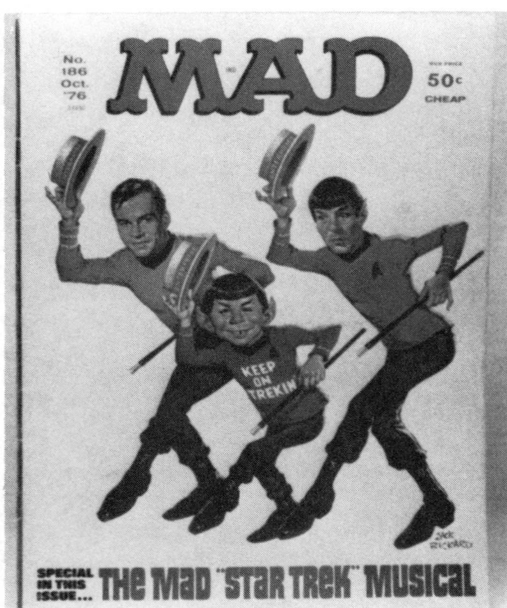

Full color art cover.

	Issue	Current	Cost/Date
1983 January, Number 236 "Star Blecch II The Wrath of Korn" plus Star Trek II out-take by Don Martin	1	3-5	______
1984 December, Number 251 "Star Blecch III" parody, plus Don Martin looks at ST III	1.25	3-4	______
Maclean's			
1982 June 14, Vol. 95, No. 24 ST II movie review, illustrated	1	2-3	______
1984 June 11, Vol. 97, No. 24 ST III movie review	1.25	2-3	______
Mediascene Preview			
Supergraphics 1978 Dec./Jan., Vol. 1, No. 31 Filming the final frontier, STTMP		3-6	______
1980 February Review of STTMP		3-6	______
Modern Screen			
Sterlings Magazines, Inc. 1970 Jan. through March Nimoy interview, 7 b/w photos	.65	3-5	______
Monsters of the Movies			
Magazine Management, Inc. 1975 Summer, Number 9 Full color cover of Spock pointing phaser at caterpillar-like monster, Leonard Nimoy interview	1.25	4-6	______
Monster Magazine			
1976 February Spock special, "His Story," Part I	1.75	3-5	______
April 1966 Spock cont'd. "An Analysis," Part II	1.75	3-5 3-5	______ ______
Monster Times			
Monster Times Publishing Company Number 2, Vol. 1, Feb. 1972 Special Star Trek Edition. Star Trek saga with Shatner, Nimoy interview, comics update, Gray Morrow art centerfold pull-out.	.50	6-10	______

	Issue	Current	Cost/Date
Number 20, Vol. 2, March 1973 12-page ST pull-out includes "Keep on Trekkin' " poster, filmography, yellow pages, book review and Spock model Kit.	.50	4-8	______

Art cover.

Monster Times.

	Issue	Current	Cost/Date
Number 25 The trouble with Star Trek.	.50	3-5	______
Number 26 Star Trek exclusive. The Return of ST	.50	4-6	______
Number 34 ST convention report, interview Shatner-Captain Kirk Speaks.	.50	3-4	______
Number 36 An exclusive interview with Nimoy	.50	3-4	______
Number 42 Star Trek returns	.50	2-4	______
Number 43 Star Trek's Captain Kirk	.50	2-4	______

ADULT MAGAZINES

	Issue	Current	Cost/Date
Number 45 Star Trek interview - Big Bill Shatner	.75	2-4	______
Number 46 Star Trek - The Final Frontier	1	4-6	______
Monster Times People of Star Trek Collector's Issue Number 2 Inside stories on the cast and characters of Star Trek, illustrations, photos	1	4-6	______
Monster Times TV Sci-Fi Special Salute Special 40-page magazine devoted to Star Trek, includes 6 color sci-fi ST posters, stories and info on 1972 ST fan convention	1.50	—	______
Motion Picture			
1968 April through June Nimoy photostory, 12 b/w, 1 color	.35	3-5	______
July through September 1968 Nimoy interview, 1 b/w	.35	3-5	______
Movie Life			
1967 Nimoy interview, 8 b/w	.35	3-5	______
November Shatner interview, 5 b/w	.35	3-5	______
1968 January Nimoy photostory, 25 b/w; Shatner photostory, 35 b/w	.35	4-6	______
April through June 1968 Shatner interview, 11 b/w	.35	3-5	______
September 1968 Nimoy interview, 8 b/w	.35	3-5	______
1970 April Nimoy interview, 1 b/w	.65	2-4	______
September 1970 Nimoy interview, 2 b/w	.65	2-4	______
Movie Mirror			
1968 April through June Shatner interview, 4 b/w	.35	3-5	______
Movie T.V. Photo Stars			
1967 October through December Nimoy interview, 11 b/w	.35	3-5	______
1968 January Shatner interview, 1 b/w	.35	3-5	______
February through March 1968 DeForest Kelley, interview, 8 b/w	.35	3-5	______
Nimoy interview, 3 b/w Nichelle Nichols interview, 3 b/W 1968 April through June Shatner interview, 2 b/w	.35	3-5	______
August 1968 Shatner, 3 b/w; Walter Koenig, 2 b/w	.35	4-6	______
1969 January through March Nimoy interview, 2 b/w	.45	3-4	______
1970 July Nimoy interview, 3 b/w	.65	2-4	______
October 1970 Nimoy photostory, 50 b/w	.65	3-5	______

	Issue	Current	Cost/Date
December 1970 Nimoy interview, 4 b/w	.65	2-4	______
1971 January through March Nimoy interview, 4 b/w, p. 42-43	.75	2-4	______
Nimoy interview, 4 b/w, p. 28-29	.75	2-4	______
April through June 1971 Nimoy interview, 4 b/w, p. 10-11	.75	2-4	______
Nimoy interview, 4 b/w, p. 34-35	.75	2-4	______
Nation			
Nation Company, Inc. 1982 August 21-28, Vol. 235, No. 5 ST II movie review, photos	1	1-2	______
National Enquirer			
1986 January 13, Vol. 61, No. 24 Nimoy interview, Kelley interview	.65	1-2	______

Spock From Star Trek IV reviews.

	Issue	Current	Cost/Date
Newsweek			
Newsweek Inc. 1984 June 11, No. 24 ST III movie review, illustrated	1.75	2-3	______
1986 December 22 The Enduring Power of Star Trek feature article, p. 66-71, color photos and full color cover of Spock	2	3-4	______
New York			
1982 June 21, Vol. 15, No. 25 ST II review, illustrated	1.25	2-3	______
1984 June 11, Vol. 17, No. 24 ST III movie review	1.50	2-3	______
New Yorker			
New Yorker Magazine, Inc. 1982, June 28, Vol. 58, No. 19 ST II review, 3 pages	1.25	1-2	______
1984 July 9, No. 21 ST III review	1.50	1-2	______

ADULT MAGAZINES

	Issue	Current Cost/Date	
Omni			
Omni Publications, International			
1974 June			
Film review of STTMP, b/w photo	2	2-3	______
Parade Magazine			
1979 December 10			
Full color cover, review of STTMP	1.25	2-5	______
Photo Screen			
1967 December			
Nimoy interview, 5 b/w	.35	3-5	______
1968 April through June			
Nimoy interview, 10 b/w	.35	3-5	______
October through December 1968			
Walter Koenig, 6 b/w photos of his new son, Joshua Andrew	.35	3-5	______
1969 July through September			
Nimoy interview, 2 b/w	.45	3-4	______
Pizzazz Magazine			
1978 April			
Star Trek versus Star Wars	1.25	2-3	______
Playboy			
1980 January			
Gene Roddenberry and STTMP review	2	2-5	______
Popular Science			
Times Mirror Magazines, Inc.			
1967 December			
"TV's Star Trek: How They Mix Science Fact with Fiction," gadgetry and effects photos. One of the first special effects articles about Trek .	.50	6-10	______
Progressive			
Progressive, Inc.			
1980 March, Vol. 44, No. 3			
STTMP movie review, 2 pages	1.75	1-2	______
Quasimoto's Monster Magazine			
Number 6			
William Shatner interview	1.50	2-4	______
Number 7			
Leonard Nimoy of Star Trek	1.50	2-4	______
Number 8			
Star Trek biographies	1.50	2-5	______
Questar			
William Wilson Publishing			
1979 November, Number 5			
Preview of STTMP, Spock and Kirk photo insets on cover	2	2-5	______
1980 February, Number 6			
STTMP Review, Spock and Kirk photo insets on cover	2	2-5	______
READ Scholastic			
1968 "Star Alien" article about Nimoy as Mr. Spock	.25	2-4	______
1970 "Who Zapped the Enterprise?" article on the t.v. show's cancellation	.25	2-4	______

	Issue	Current Cost/Date	
Rolling Stone			
1982 July 22			
ST II review, photo		1-2	______
September 2, 1982			
Nicholas Meyer on ST II		1-2	______
Rona Barrett's Hollywood			
Winter Annual, Vol. 1, No. 9, Laufer Publishing Co., 1979			
Sneak preview of STTMP & William Shatner up close	2	2-4	______
Scene Magazine			
1968 October 25			
School scholastic publication, explored the then current teenage t.v. rankings, photo from "The Menagerie" episode 1	.25	2-3	______
Scholastic Voice			
Scholastic Magazines			
1973 January 29, Vol. 54, No. 1			
T.V. play for classroom - "The Menagerie - Part I" from Star Trek	.25	2-3	______
February 5, 1973, Vol. 54, No. 2			
Part II - "The Menagerie" play. Full color cover artwork busts of Kirk, Spock and Enterprise, Trek essay contest	.25	3-4	______
April 30, 1978, Vol. 54, No. 12			
Science fiction and Star Trek, plus winners of essay contest.	.25	2-3	______
 **Science Fantasy Film Classics**			
Byte Publications			
1978 July, 3rd Edition			
Special ST issue featuring the computers, technology and characters of Trek, old and new. Special blueprints of the future includes 22"x32" centerfold. Photo inset of Enterprise on cover	2	4-6	______
Screenland			
1968 January through March			
Nimoy interview, 5 b/w	.35	3-5	______
Shatner interview, 2 b/w	.35	3-5	______
April through June 1968			
Nimoy Interview, 11 b/w	.35	3-5	______
Shatner interview, 1 b/w	.35	3-5	______

ADULT MAGAZINES

	Issue	Current	Cost/Date
Screen Stars			
1970 July through September			
Nimoy interviews: 1 b/w p. 34-35	.65	2-4	_____
1 b/w p. 32-33	.65	2-4	_____
2 b/w p. 26-26	.65	2-4	_____
1970 October through December Nimoy interview, 2b/w	.65	2-4	_____
Space Gamer			
1981 August, No. 42 Color cover with Enterprise. Review of Star Fleet Battles Game. Also, Trek computer talk	2.50	3-4	_____
1983 July/August Review of Star Trek the Correspondence Game	3.50	4-5	_____
1983 September/October Star Trek The Role Playing Game review	3.50	4-5	_____
Space Odysseys			
Countrywide Communications, Inc.			
1977 April Super heroes of outer space - Star Trek, artwork Kirk, Spock and Enterprise	1	2-4	_____
Space Stars			
Number 3 Star Trek Motion Picture article	1.75	2-4	_____
Space Trek			
Stories, Layouts & Press, Inc.			
1978 Special Edition STTMP movie preview	1.75	2-4	_____
1978 Winter Issue Nichelle Nichols interview	1.75	2-4	_____
1979 Spring issue STTMP article	1.75	2-4	_____
Space Wars			
Stories, Layouts & Press, Inc.			
1977 October The stars of Star Trek	1.75	2-4	_____
1977 December-Collector's Edition Star Trek Mania	1.75	2-4	_____
1979 May Kirk battles Mr. Spock	1.75	2-4	_____
1979 November Star Trek Update	1.75	2-4	_____
1980 March STTMP preview	1.75	2-4	_____
1980 May The secret message of Star Trek	1.75	2-4	_____
SPEC-16 Magazine			
1967 February Introducing Nimoy as Star Trek's Mr. Spock! 2 b/w	.35	4-6	_____
1967 July Nimoy's recording session for Mr. Spock's Music from Outer Space album, 4b/w	.35	4-6	_____
1968 January through March Koenig, Meet Mr. Chekov, 4 b/w	.35	4-6	_____
Koenig interview, 1 b/w; plus full color pin-up poster of him	.35	4-6	_____
April through June 1968 Faces of the Trekkers, 10 b/w, 12 cepia	.35	5-6	_____
Trek'ers answer 50 spaced-out questions, 6 b/w	.35	5-6	_____
Trek'ers and special focus on Koenig, 7 b/w, 1 color pin-up of Koenig	.35	5-6	_____
Koenig interview, 5 b/w	.35	2-4	_____
September 1968 Star Trek Special: the Trek'ers' hates and loves; SPEC-tickles focus on Trek; 2 pages with 8 b/w photos of the Enterprise crew with balloon sayings over episode film cuts. Includes Koenig interview	.35	8-12	_____
November 1968 Trek'ers on the town and at home, 5 b/w		3-5	_____
December 1968 Koenig and Sajid Kahn on the Star Trek t.v. set, 11 b/w	.35	5-6	_____
Star			
1986 December 8 ST IV movie review, illustrated	.65	1-2	_____
Star Blaster			
Windsor Communications, Inc.			
1983 March Spock lives once more, review ST III	1.95	2-4	_____
Starblazer			
Liberty Communications			
1985 Summer Special Collector's Issue, Spock is dead, exploring life and death in Trek	2.50	2-3	_____
August 1985 Issue Unseen Star Trek, Part II, filming STTMP	2.50	2-3	_____
Star Encounters			
Number 3 Beyond Star Trek, the t.v. series	1.75	2-4	_____
Starforce			
1978 July, Number 1 Star Trek article	1.75	2-4	_____
Star Invaders			
Liberty Communications			
1985 Spring, Vol. 1, Number 2 The courtmartial of Admiral Kirk, Star Trek in Russia	2.25	2-4	_____

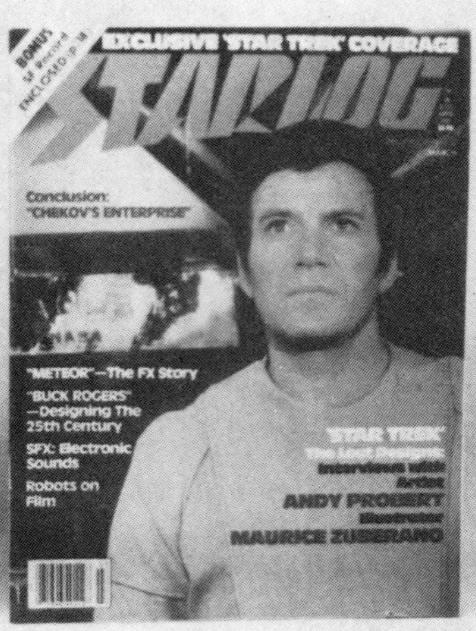

Full color photo covers.

Starlog
O'Quinn Publications

	Issue	Current Cost/Date	
1977 August, Number 1 Special premier issue, full color cover featuring Lanley Associates poster of Kirk and Spock busts and Enterprise, rare pictures and complete t.v. episode guide	1.50	5-15	______
September, Number 2 STTMP movie news with Gene Roddenberry	1.50	5-10	______
October, Number 3 Color cartoon cover of Trek series characters, NASA unveils Enterprise shuttle, Centennial Con, ST conventions, ST animated series and Nichelle Nichols interview	1.50	5-8	______
November, Number 4 Original story "Arena" by Harlan Ellison with accompanying photo story from episode	1.50	2-6	______
December, Number 5 STTMP report	1.50	2-6	______
1978 January, Number 6 STTMP movie report	1.50	2-6	______
February, Number 7 STTMP report	1.50	2-6	______
April, Number 9 Interview with William Shatner	1.75	5-8	______
July, Number 12 Gene Roddenberry and STTMP Enterprise designs	1.75	2-5	______
September, Number 14 Trek Report and Star Trek series spoof from **Saturday Night Live,** as written by Michael O'Donohue [2]	1.75	2-5	______
November, Number 16 Nimoy on the set of "Invasion of the Body Snatchers."	1.75	2-5	______
December, Number 17 Gene Roddenberry interview	1.95	2-4	______
1979 January, Number 18 Star Trek Report, monster make-up from STTMP	1.95	2-5	______
February, Number 19 Nimoy and "Invasion of Body Snatchers"	1.95	2-5	______
May, Number 22 Star Trek Report with aliens of STTMP	1.95	2-5	______
June, Number 23 Star Trek and Nichelle Nichols in blacks in science fiction	1.95	2-5	______
July, Number 24 Special 3rd anniversary edition, Star Trek Report, STTMP review and interview with Nimoy and Shatner	2.95	3-7	______
August, Number 25 Full color cover of Enterprise, Star Trek Report, lighting the Enterprise and Mike Monor from STTMP	1.95	2-5	______
October, Number 27 Special effects behind STTMP	1.95	2-5	______
1980 January, Number 30 Full color cover of Kirk, Spock and Enterprise, interview Robert Wise of STTMP, Gene Roddenberry's "The Questar Tapes," Harold Michaelson of STTMP and **Chekov's Enterprise,** Part 1	1.95	2-5	______
February, Number 31 David Gerrold on Captain Kirk and **Chekov's Enterprise** Part II	1.95	2-5	______
March, Number 32 Full color cover of Kirk, Star Trek Report, Maurice Zuberana (Storyboard Artist for STTMP), Andy Probert lost designs of Enterprise, **Chekov's Enterprise** Part III	2.95	3-7	______
April, Number 33 Harlan Ellison reviews STTMP, Star Trek premier article, Trek costumes and aliens, Gerrold with "Spockalyse Now" and the new Marvel Comic books	2.25	2-5	______
July, Number 36 Interview with Nichelle Nichols	2.95	3-7	______
August, Number 37 Interview Persis Kimbatta of STTMP	2.25	2-5	______
September, Number 38 Interview DeForest Kelley	2.25	2-5	______
October, Number 39 Interview Fred Freiberger (Producer of Star Trek t.v. series)	2.25	2-5	______
November, Number 40 Interview with Gene Roddenberry on STTMP and Star Trek books by Bjo Trimble	2.25	2-5	______

2. A video release of "The Last Voyage of the Starship Enterprise" is now available in **The Best of John Belushi Vol. I,** an anthology of this comedian's best-loved skits from "Saturday Night Live."

ADULT MAGAZINES

	Issue	Current Cost/Date	
1981 January, Number 42 Full color cover of Mark Lenard as Klingon from STTMP. Lenard interview, Star Trek Cons by David Gerrold and Trimble on the convention Equicon	3	3-7	_____
May, Number 46 Star Trek Log, Trek in science fiction comics	2.50	2-5	_____
June, Number 47 STTMP hand props, interview Takei, Part I	2.50	2-5	_____
August, Number 49 Interview George Takei, Part II	2.50	2-5	_____
October, Number 51 Music scores of Gerry Goldsmith (STTMP), interview with Roddenberry and Shatner	2.50	2-5	_____
November, Number 52 William Shatner interview, Part II	2.50	2-5	_____
1982 January Number 54 Star Trek bloopers, Part I, Star Trek filksongs	2.50	2-5	_____
February, Number 55 Star Trek bloopers, Part II	2.50	2-7	_____
March, Number 56 Star Trek bloopers, Part III	2.50	2-5	_____
May, Number 58 Should Spock die? by David Gerrold	2.50	2-6	_____
June, Number 59 Free Star Trek pull-out poster, Trimble on Star Trek Wrath of Kahn and Kirstie Alley interview	2.50	2-7	_____
July, Number 60 Color cover with the Enterprise, remaking Star Trek Wrath of Kahn Part I, the real Trimbles	3.95	4-7	_____
August, Number 61 Remaking STWOK Part II, Walker Loenig on making ST II, full color cover with Enterprise, Kirk, Spock and Kahn	2.50	2-5	_____
September, Number 62 James Doohan interview, Ricardo Montalban (Kahn), Koenig on Roddenberry, Bjo Trimble on Trek fan mail and Gerrold on ST II	2.50	2-5	_____
October, Number 63 Nimoy on ST II, James Horner on ST II music, ST II review by Gerrold and Trek letters to Trimble	2.50	2-6	_____
November, Number 64 The Genesis Effect, Ultimate Fantasy report (Star Trek con) and the ST II experience by Gerrold	2.50	2-7	_____
1983 February, Number 67 Interview with Jack Sowards "The Man Who Killed Spock", painting for ST II and Gerrold on Star Trek computer games	2.50	2-5	_____
March,Number 68 Interview with Harve Bennett on ST II, Bjo Trimble on Star Trek fans	2.50	2-5	_____
June, Number 71 Star Trek II props	2.95	3-5	_____
July, Number 72 Shatner interview, talk with Sam Nicholson of Zenon Light Company on STTMP	2.95	3-7	_____
November, Number 76 Trek actors at Space Trek II Con in St. Louis, MO.	2.95	3-7	_____
December, Number 77 Interview with Robin Curtis of ST III	2.95	3-5	_____
1984 January, Number 78 Interview with Nicholas Meyer of ST II	2.95	3-5	_____
March, Number 80 On the set of Star Trek The Search for Spock	2.95	3-5	_____
April, Number 81 David Gerrold on ST III	2.95	3-5	_____
May, Number 82 Full color cover of Christopher Lloyd (Kruge) of ST III, Lloyd interview	2.95	3-5	_____
June, Number 83 Interview Robin Curtis on ST III, Star Trek novelizations and interview with A. C. Crispin (author "Yesterday's Son")resurrection of Star Trek	1.75	3-5	_____
July, Number 84 Interview Nimoy on directing ST III	2.95	4-7	_____
August, Number 85 Interview Dame Judith Anderson (T'Lar) of St III	2.95	3-5	_____
September, Number 86 Interview Mark Lenard (Sarek) of ST III	2.95	3-5	_____
October, Number 87 Kirk photo inset on cover, readers' review ST III, "Bones" McCoy remembers	2.95	3-6	_____
November, Number 88 DeForest Kelley interview, Part II	2.95	3-5	_____
1985 February, Number 91 Chekov's choice-Koenig reviews the making of ST III	2.95	3-4	_____
March, Number 92 Pull-out poster No. 23, scene from ST III	2.95	3-4	_____
May, Number 94 James Doohan interview - Keeps on Trekkin'	2.95	3-4	_____

ADULT MAGAZINES

	Issue	Current	Cost/Date
1985 June, Number 95 Merritt Butrick interview (ST II), "The Search for David"	2.95	3-4	______
November, Number 100 Roddenberry interview, Nichelle Nichols and Nimoy profile	2.95	3-4	______
December, Number 101 George Takei interview	2.95	3-4	______
1986 January, Number 102 Kirsty Alley interview	2.95	3-4	______
February, Number 103 Harve Bennett interview, preparing Star Trek IV-The Voyage Home	2.95	3-4	______
March, Number 104 Stephen Collins (STTMP) interview	2.95	3-4	______
April, Number 105 Grace Lee Whitney (Yeoman Rand) interview	2.95	3-4	______
May, Number 106 Leonard Nimoy interview	2.95	3-4	______
June, Number 107 Alexander Courage (Trek music) interview	2.95	3-4	______
July, Number 108 Roddenberry interview, The Voyage Home	2.95	3-4	______
August, Number 109 George Takei interview on ST IV	2.95	3-4	______
September, Number 110 Leonard Nimoy on beginning the Voyage Home	2.95	3-4	______
October, Number 111 Trek for t.v. again, and making the Voyage Home	2.95	3-4	______
November, Number 112 Special Star Trek 20th Anniversay Spectacular - full color cover Kirk, Spock and McCoy; interviews Shatner, Nimoy, Kelley; episode recap, salute to Trekdom; photos	2.95	4-6	______
December, Number 113 James Doohan on ST IV	2.95	3-4	______
1987 January, Number 114 ST IV, Nimoy launches Voyage Home, full color cover of Spock	2.95	3-4	______
February, Number 115 Kelley a part of history, Ted Cassidy (Ruk) featured as special guest interview	2.95	3-4	______
Starlog, Best of Volume 1 Includes interview with Leonard Nimoy	3.95	4-6	______
Starlog, Best of Volume 2 Includes Gene Roddenberry interview and STTMP reveiw	3.95	4-6	______
Starlog, Best of Volume 3 Full color cover of Spock from ST II, includes Leonard Nimoy interview	3.95	5-8	______
Starlog, Best of Volume 4 Includes William Shatner inteview and review of ST II	3.95	4-6	______
Starlog, Best of Volume 5 Includes a bloopers reveiw and information on ST III	3.95	4-5	______
Starlog, Best of Volume 6 Why Star Trek failed the fans story	3.95	4-6	______
Starlog, Best of Volume 7 Leonard Nimoy and Kirstie Alley interviews, preparing for ST IV	3.95	4-6	______
Starlog, Science Fiction Trivia, 7/85 Contains two pages of trivia questions on Star Trek with b/w photos, cover has color photo inserts	2.95	3-4	______
Starlog, Science Fiction Trivia, 9/85 Softbound 5" x 8" re-release with 4 pages of Trek trivia	2.95	3-4	______
Starlog Scrapbook, Volume 1 Best photos selection, includes Star Trek photos and pin-ups from STTMP	2.95	3-4	______
Starlog Scrapbook, Volume 2 Best photos collection, contains photos and pin-ups from ST II	2.95	3-4	______
Starlog Scrapbook, Volume 4 Rare and unusual color or b/w photos from Starlog files, includes full color shots of Uhura, Saavik, Kirk, plus more	2.95	3-4	______
Starlog Scrapbook, Volume 5 Captain's Logs, Trek pin-ups and t.v. episode guide	3.95	4-5	______
Starlog Scrapbook, Volume 6 1987, Star Trek, the 20 year voyage, b/w and color photos from 20 years of Trek	2.95	3-4	______
Starlog Poster Magazine, No. 2 Contains pull-out from ST II, 16"x22"	2.95	3-4	______
Starlog Poster Magazine, Volume 3 Pull-out poster from ST III, 16"x22"	2.95	3-4	______
Starlog Poster Magazine, Volume 4 Contains pull-out from the Star Trek t.v. series, 16"x22"	2.95	3-4	______
Starlog Poster Magazine, Volume 6 Full color poster of Nichelle Nichols, bio information, 16"x22"	2.95	3-4	______
Starlog Poster Magazine, Volume 7 Information on Leonard Nimoy, William Shatner & DeForest Kelley plus 3 pull-out posters, 16"x22"	2.95	3-4	______
Starlog - Star Trek The Wrath of Kahn, Official Movie Magazine Complete, exclusive behind-the-scenes articles, photos and interviews, 66 p.	3.50	4-6	______

Poster Magazines.

Special Edition Movie Magazines.

	Issue	Current	Cost/Date
Starlog - Star Trek The Search For Spock Official Movie Magazine Includes behind-the-scenes articles, photos and interviews, 66 p.	3.50	4-6	_____
Starlog - Star Trek The Search For Spock, Official Poster Magazine Contains ten 16"x22" pull-out posters from ST III	3	4-5	_____
Starlog - Star Trek The Voyage Home, Official Movie Magazine Movie behind-the-scenes interviews and photos	3.50	4-5	_____
Starlog - Star Trek The Voyage Home, Official Movie Special, 12/86 Deluxe Edition: cast bios, histories, photos and eight posters	5.95	6-7	_____
Starlog - Star Trek The Voyage Home, Official Poster Magazine Movie behind-the-scenes articles, and ten 16"x22" pull-out posters	3.95	4-5	_____
Star Warp Stories, Layouts, & Press, Inc. 1976 June The girls of Star Trek by Allan Asherman	1.50	2-3	_____
Super Star Heros Ideal Publishing **1979** January, Number 2 Spock and Kirk STTMP color cover inset, Star Trek hits the big screen	1.75	2-3	_____
May, Number 7 Collector's Issue - Spock on cover, Spock puts his ears back on for STTMP	1.75	3-4	_____
October, Number 10 Persis Kimbatta interview about STTMP	1.75	2-3	_____
December, Number 11 Collector's Issue - Cover has color photo inset of Kirk and Spock beneath the Enterprise, rebuilding the STTMP ship, plus Star Trek pull-out poster	1.75	4-6	_____
Superteen Magazine 1968 May The Spock characterization, 10 b/w	.40	4-6	_____
Teen Life 1968 May Mr. Spock characterization, 10 b/w	.40	4-6	_____
Teen Screen 1968 April through June Koenig interview, 7 b/w	.35	2-4	_____
Teen Stars Yearbook 1969 January, Issue No. 15 The World of the Space Trekkers, 3 b/w	.50	4-6	_____
Time 1979 January 15 STTMP movie review, illustrated	1.25	1-2	_____
1982 June 7, Vol. 119, No. 23 ST II movie review, illustrated	1.50	1-2	_____
1984 June 11, Vol. 123, No. 24 ST III movie review, illustrated	1.75	2-3	_____
1986 December 8 **ST IV movie review, illustrated**			

Syndicated & Local T.V. Guides

	Issue	Current	Cost/Date
T.V. Guide **1966** October 15-21 Interview with William Shatner, "No One Upsets the Star"	.15	6-10	_____

ADULT MAGAZINES

	Issue	Current Cost/Date	
1967 March 4-10 A look at Leonard Nimoy and Spock, "Product of Two Worlds"	.15	5-8	______
March 25-31 Cleveland Armory review t.v. Star Trek [3]	.15	5-8	______
April 29-May 5 Article by Isaac Asimov reflecting on his daughter's comment: "Mr. Spock is Dreamy!"	.15	5-8	______
July 15-21 Nichelle Nichols interview, "Let Me Off At The Next Planet"	.15	4-6	______
October 14-20 Photo feature titled "4x4 = 2,000 Androids," the twins and sets used in filming "I, Mudd" episode	.15	5-8	______
November 18-24 Color front features profile of Kirk and Spock, "Star Trek Wins the Ricky Swartz Award," Trek's growing fandom	.15	5-10	______
1968 June 22-28 William Shatner, "Intergalactic Golden Boy"	.15	4-6	______
August 24-30 DeForest Kelley interview, "Where is the Welcome Mat?"	.15	4-6	______
October 5-11 "Do Stars Dress Well on T.V.?" interviews with fashion experts Cardinali, Blackwell, Edith Head, Bill Theiss (ST t.v. designer)	.15	2-3	______
1969 October 18-24 Leonard Nimoy interview	.15	4-6	______
1970 April 25-May 1 Leonard Nimoy on his role as Paris on "Mission: Impossible", the "Great Impersonator Refuses to Strip Off the Last Disguise"	.15	2-3	______
June 6-12 "...And Then Came the Dawn," Star Trek bought the first t.v. script Judy Burns ever wrote, the screenplay for "Tholian Web" episode	.15	4-5	______
1972 March 25-31 Article covering the first official, exclusively Star Trek fan convention Star Trek Con held in New York City in January 1972	.20	5-8	______
1976 October 14-20 Star Trek in review	.25	4-6	______

T.V. Movie Screen

	Issue	Current Cost/Date	
1967 July through September Shatner interview, 1 b/w, plus a b/w pin-up with color border	.35	3-5	______
November A psychologist reveals the primitive sex appeal of Mr. Spock, two 4-tone photos; plus Kelley article, two 2-tone photos	.35	8-10	______
1968 January Nimoy interview, 8 b/w photos	.35	3-5	______
February Shatner interview, 1 b/w; plus James Doohan article, 6 b/w and 1 cepia photo	.35	4-6	______
May DeForest Kelley, 2 b/w photos	.35	3-5	______
June William Shatner interview, 1 b/w	.35	3-5	______
August Shatner article, 1 b/w; plus Kelley picture article, 7 b/w photos	.35	4-6	______
1968 September Nimoy photostory, 11 b/w pictures	.35	3-5	______
December Nimoy interview, 1 color cepia photo	.35	3-5	______
1970 February Nimoy interview, 1 b/w photo	.65	2-4	______
1971 October through December Nimoy interview, 4 b/w photos	.75	2-4	______

T.V. Movies Today

	Issue	Current Cost/Date	
1970 July through September Nimoy interview, 4 b/w photos	.65	2-4	______
1971 August Nimoy interview, 5 b/w photos	.75	2-4	______

T.V. Picture Life

	Issue	Current Cost/Date	
1968 January through March Shatner, 5 b/w, p. 38-39	.35	-35	______
Nimoy, 2 b/w, p. 48-49	.35	3-5	______
2 b/w, p. 26-27	.35	3-5	______
Kelley, 5 b/w, p. 36-38	.35	3-5	______
1968 April through June "How the Fans Saved Star Trek," article on the campaign against NBC, 3 b/w p. 22-23	.35	6-8	______
Shatner, 8 b/w, p. 26-28	.35	3-5	______
2 b/w, p. 24-25	.35	3-5	______
Nimoy, 2 b/w, p. 24-25	.35	3-5	______
Kelley, 9 b/w, p. 29-31	.35	3-5	______
1968 July through September Nimoy, 5 b/w, p. 22-23	.35	3-5	______
Walter Koenig, 9 b/w photos of Joshua Andrew the new Koenig baby, p. 24-26	.35	4-5	______
1968 September Shatner interview, 6 b/w photos	.35	3-5	______
1968 October Deforest Kelley story, 2 b/w photos	.35	3-5	______
1969 January through March Nimoy article, 7 b/w photos	.45	3-5	______

3. This was television Trek's first official review as a series, by a t.v. critic.

ADULT MAGAZINES

	Issue	Current Cost	Date
1970 July through September Nimoy interview, 1 b/w, 1 color photo	.65	2-4	______

T.V. Radio Show

	Issue	Current Cost	Date
1967 October through December Feature article about Peggye Vickers the first president of the LNNAF (Leonard Nimoy National Association of Fans) club; photos on the t.v. Trek set, 12 b/w and 1 color, p. 40-43	.35	8-10	______
Shatner and Nimoy's stardom popularity, 4 color photos, p. 22-23	.35	4-6	______
Nimoy interview, 7 b/w photos	.35	3-5	______
1968 January through March Shatner interview, 5 b/w, p. 33-35	.35	3-5	______
Nimoy interview, 1 cepia, 1 color, p. 26-27	.35	3-5	______
1968 April through June Shatner, 1 color, 1 cepia photo, p. 21-22	.35	3-5	______
1 color, 1 cepia photo, p. 20-21	.35	3-5	______
Nimoy, 2 b/w, 1 color, p. 26-27	.35	3-5	______
1968 July through September Shatner interview, 2 b/w, p. 40-41	.35	3-5	______
1968 October Nimoy interview, 3 color, 10 b/w; plus full cover photo featuring the Nimoy family	.35	8-12	______
1969 January through March Shatner interview, 6 b/w, p. 39-41	.45	3-5	______
Nimoy interview, 5 b/w, p. 33-35	.45	3-5	______
1969 April through June Nimoy interview, 6 b/w, 1 color, p. 56-59	.45	3-5	______
Nichelle Nichols, 1 b/w, p. 18	.45	3-5	______
1970 October through December Nimoy interview, 3 b/w, p. 34-35	.65	2-4	______
1971 August Nimoy story, 1 b/w	.75	2-4	______

T.V. Screen Album

	Issue	Current Cost	Date
1968 July through September Star Trek production, on the set, 3 b/w, 1 color photo; plus color pin-up of Nimoy and pet dachsund	.40	5-8	______

T.V. Star Annual

	Issue	Current Cost	Date
1967 Issue No. 23 Nimoy interview, plus b/w pin-up of him signed "Spock"	.50	4-6	______
1968 Issue No. 24 Cast stories, 11 b/w photos; Nimoy photostory, 12 b/w; Plus inside front cover color glossy of Spock on the bridge	.50	6-8	______
1969 Issue No. 25 How Can We Forget Star Trek? article, 4 b/w; Shatner photostory, 18 b/w; plus Nimoy interview, 4 b/w photos	.75	6-8	______

T.V. Star Parade

	Issue	Current Cost	Date
1967 July How Mr. Spock's make-up is applied on the Trek t.v. set, 18 b/w	.35	8-10	______
August Nimoy story, 2 b/w; Shatner, 5 b/w; Plus color art style rendering of Spock, Kirk and Enterprise on the front cover	.35	12-15	______
September Trek cast bios, 3-tone photo spread; Shatner interview, 4 b/w; and Nimoy, 4 b/w	.35	8-10	______
October Nimoy and Mike Barrier (Lt. DeSalle) as real life friends, 7 b/w	.35	4-6	______
December Lunch with the stars on the Star Trek t.v. set, 16 b/w photos	.35	6-8	______
1968 January Nimoy, full b/w photo spread, 2 pages	.35	3-5	______
February Trek cast zodiac forecasts, 7 b/w; Kelley interview, 6 b/w; Nichols story, 6 b/w; Plus color cover featuring cut-outs of Kelley and Nichols with insets of Nimoy and Shatner	.35	8-12	______
April Shatner story, 4 b/w, 4 cepia; Plus color cover portrait of the Shatner family	.35	8-12	______
June Shatner story, 1 b/w; Nimoy, 10 b/w; plus James Doohan interview, 1 b/w	.35	6-8	______
July Nimoy, 2 b/w, 3 red-cepia; Nichols, 3 b/w, 4 red-cepia photos	.35	6-8	______
August How the special effects of Star Trek really work, 9 b/w photos	.35	8-10	______
September Shatner inteview, 1 b/w; Nimoy photostory, 13 b/w pictures	.35	6-8	______
November Shatner, 3 b/w; Nimoy, 1 cepia; and Doohan, 2 b/w photos	.35	6-8	______
1969 January Nichols, 4 b/w; Kelley, 3 b/w photos	.35	4-6	______
1970 January through March Nimoy interview, 9 b/w photos	.65	3-5	______

T.V. Stars Trivia

	Issue	Current Cost	Date
Harris Publications 1985 Pages 42-43 contain 15 trivia questions on Star Trek, b/w photos, photo insets of Kirk and Spock on cover	1.95	2-3	______

ADULT MAGAZINES

	Issue	Current	Cost/Date
T.V. Trivia, Thirty Years of Television Entertainment Today Magazine 1985 January Slick special featuring trivia questions and info on Star Trek, 2 color inserts, 1 b/w crew portrait and full color pin-up 9"x11", 64 pages	2.95	3-5	______
Twilight Zone 1984 August Full color cover of Cathie Sheriff as Klingon from ST II, Nimoy directs ST II	2.50	2-4	______
US Magazine 1980 January 8 Color cover of Persis Kimbatta (Ilia) with Enterprise, interview Kimbatta from STTMP	.75	2-5	______
U.S.A. Today 1982 September, Vol. 111, No. 2448 ST II Review, illustrated	3.50	4-5	______
Video Review Viare Publishing 1985 March Critic's Choice: the ten most tapeable episodes of Star Trek, a review of the Trek phenomenon and a complete 79-episode guide to Trek video cassettes	1.95	3-4	______
1986 October Twenty years of Trek and news on the new television series; Cut-out Kirk and Spock on cover	1.95	2-3	______
Video Times Publications International, Ltd. 1985 February, Vol. 1, Number 2 Star Trek beams into casettes, ST III review and the Trek following; color cover photo	2.95	4-6	______
Woman's Day CBS Magazines, Inc. 1970 October "Mr. & Mrs. Leonard Nimoy: Fun with Pottery," article on their home handicrafts, 14 b/w, 3 color	.75	2-3	______

JUVENILE MAGAZINES

Full Color Cover Star Trek III

	Issue	Current	Cost/Date
Enter Magazine Children's Television Workshop 1984 September, Volume 1, No. 10 Computer moviemakers- digital dazzlers from Lucasfilms special effects, cover full color Enterprise, spacestation and Excelsior from ST III	1.75	2-4	______
G.I. Joe Lorimar Telepictures Publications, Inc. 1987 Winter, Volume 1, Issue 1 "I Left My Vulcan in San Francisco," article on ST IV with movie and t.v. photos	1.95	2-3	______
Go Bots Lorimar Telepictures Publications, Inc. 1987 Winter, Volume 2, Number 1 ST IV Beams Down, movie review and photos	1.95	2-3	______
Muppet Magazine Lorimar Telepicutres Publications, Inc. 1984 Summer Mr. Spock and ST III article incorporating Muppets, "Crazed Pigs Mob Spock"	1.50	2-3	______
Stars Turman Publishing Co. 1986 No. 101, Volume 1, Number 8 Educational stories and essays for various reading levels, pages perforated and removeable, includes questions about Shatner 1 b/w Trek photo, Level 3.5 Grades	2.95	3-4	______
Wierd Worlds Scholastic Magazine 1979 Number 3 Special Star Trek challenge, 15 multiple choice questions, answers and photos	1	2-3	______

FOREIGN MAGAZINES

Foreign Magazines.

	Issue	Current	Cost/Date
Space Voyager Argus Specialist Publications, Ltd. England			
1984 October/November, Number 11 Full color photo front featuring the Enterprise, full color review ST III and pull-out poster	1.50	4-5	_____
1985 December/January, No. 12 "Have Tribble Will Travel" interview with David Gerrold and Roddenberry's thoughts on man's future	1.50	4-5	_____
Starburst Marvel Comics, Ltd. London, England			
1978 No. 1, Vol. 1, No. 1, January Star Wars versus Star Trek with rare photos, "The Writers of Star Trek"- and episode guide, Spock insert on cover	.50	3-5	_____
No. 3, Volume 1, Number 3 STTMP movie review		3-5	_____
No. 4, Volume 1, Number 4 Star Trek Update		3-5	_____
1979 No. 10, Vol. 1, No. 10, June Str Trek interviews, Part I, Persis Kimbatta article		3-6	_____
No. 11, Vol. 1, No. 11, July Star Trek interviews, Part II		3-6	_____
No. 17, Vol. 2, No. 5 Preview for STTMP movie		3-5	_____
No. 19, Vol. 2, No. 7 Review of STTMP		3-5	_____
1982 No. 49, Vol. 5, No. 1, Sept. Interview with producer of ST II		3-6	_____
Robert Sallen interview, ST II review and Spock color cover		4-8	_____
1984 No. 73, Volume 7 No. 1, Aug. Review of ST III		3-6	_____
No. 79, Vol. 7, No. 7 Special t.v. issue, Dr. Sally Gary on Star Trek, full color cover of Kirk and Spock	2.50	4-8	_____
Starlog -Japanese Editions O'Quinn Publications			
1979 No. 2 Special U.S. import issue available through Starlog magazine back-order dept. Highlights S.F. television and focuses on Star Trek. Includes Enterprise poster fold-out and blueprints	10	10-15	_____
No. 3 Special import, focuses on S.F. special effects including those used on Trek	10	10-15	_____

PROZINES

	Issue	Current	Cost/Date
All About Star Trek Fan Clubs [1] Ego Enterprises			
1976 December, Number 1 Star Trek stars portfolio, fantastic fan clubs news, Mark Lenard profile and The Federation Trading Post Gallery	1	6-10	_____
1977 April, Number 2 Book review "Spock Messiah," Trek action toys, Nimoy narrates "In Search of . . ." and Trek facts	1	4-6	_____
June, Number 3 Filmbiography of William Shatner, the aliens of Star Trek, Spock relaxes, and the women of Star Trek	1	4-6	_____
August, Number 4 Leonard Nimoy fan clubs, pul-out poster, photos and artwork	1	4-6	_____
October, Number 5 Animated Star Trek review, Koenig interview, Leonard Nimoy party	1	4-6	_____
December, Number 6 Star Trekkers speak out on Star Wars, Shatner live, Nimoy profile	1	4-6	_____
Blueprinting the Science Fiction Universe Book I New Media Publishing			
1985 softbound collection of Shane Johnson's ships, weapons and equipment from Star Trek, Star Wars, Battlestar Gallactica and more	12	12-16	_____
Cinemagic Cinemagic Publishing Company, Inc.			
1976 Spring Special Star Trek production "Paragon's Paragon" and "A Romulan Encounter."	1.50	4-8	_____
Comics Feature New Media Publishing			
1984 March Star Trek returns to comics, D.C. comic interview with Marv Wolfman and Mike Barr	2.95	3-5	_____

1. This was the first serially produced Star Trek prozine available on national newsstands.

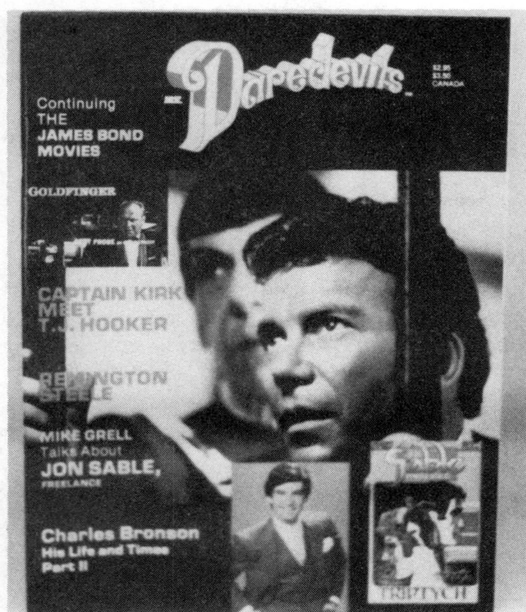

Cover from Daredevils

	Issue	Current	Cost/Date
Daredevils New Media Publishing **1984** January, Number 3 Color cover with Kirk and Spock, interview Shatner - Captain Kirk meets T.J. Hooker	2.95	4-6	______
February, Number 4 Beginning of Star Trek episode guide, reviews of two pilots "The Cage" and "Where No Man Has Gone Before"	2.95	4-6	______
March, Number 5 Episode guide includes "Corbomite Maneuver," "Mudd's Women," "Enemy Within," "Man Trap" and "Naked Time"	2.95	3-5	______
April, Number 6 Episodes: "Charlie X," "Balance Terror" "What Are Little Girls," "Dagger of the Mind," "Miri," "Conscience of King," "Galileo 7"	2.95	3-5	______
May, Number 7 Episodes: "Court-Martial," "Menagerie," "Shore Leave," "Squire Gothos," "Arena," and "Alternative Factor"	2.95	3-5	______
June, Number 8 Guides: "Tomorrow Is Yesterday," "Return Archons," "Taste Armageddon," "Space Seed," and "This Side Paradise	2.95	3-5	______
July, Number 9 Guide: "Devil in Dark," "Errand Mercy," "City Edge of Forever," and "Operation: Annihilate"	2.95	3-5	______
August, Number 10 Guide: "Cats-paw," "Metamorphosis," "Fridays Child," "Who Mourns Adonais" and "Amok Time"	2.95	3-5	______

	Issue	Current	Cost/Date
September, Number 11 Guide: "Doomsday Machine," "Wolf in Fold," "Changeling," "Apple" and "Mirror, Mirror"	3.50	4-5	______
October, Number 12 Episodes: "Deadly Years," "I, Mudd," "Trouble Tribbles," "Bread and Circuses" and "Journey Babel"	3.75	4-5	______
November, Number 13 Guide: Private Little War," "Gamesters Triskelion," "Obsession," "Immunity Syndrome" and "Piece of the Action"	3.75	4-5	______
1985 January, Number 14 Guide: "By Any Other Name," "Return to Tomorrow," "Patterns Force," "Ultimate Computer," "Omega Glory" and "Assignment: Earth"	3.75	4-5	______
Divisions, Rank and Insignia Robert Fletcher, Lincoln Enterprises 1986 Drawings and descriptions explaining movie line of uniforms and hardware. Includes STTMP through ST III production notes. No. 2425	2.95	3-5	______
Doctor and The Enterprise New Media Press, Jean Aurey story, 1985. Complete story and drawings from this story as it was serialized in issues No. 1-3 of **Enterprise** prozine. Dr. Who and Star Trek cross-over	9.95	10-12	______

Enterprise 1 and 2.

	Issue	Current	Cost/Date
Enterprise Magazine New Media Press **1984** May, Number 1 Full color cover, building a starship, Star Trek comics, review of Pocket Book Star Trek novels	3.50	15-25	______
July, Number 2 Building a starship Part II, Trek in comics Part II, ST III Movie review	3.50	12-15	______
August, Number 3 ST III novelization review, ships of Star Trek, adventures in fandom, bloopers, Starfleet in miniatures	3.50	4-6	______

PROZINES

	Issue	Current	Cost/Date
October, Number 4 Trek by mail, the transporter-how it effects life, make an ST II cadet uniform, technical drawings	3.75	4-6	______
November, Number 5 Costume designs ST III, Gerry Finnerman (Trek Director of Photography), propulsion of the future, Enterprise dossier and Captain's bookshelf	3.75	4-6	______
December, Number 6 Endurance of Trek, ST II make-up, Romulan society and culture, artificial gravity and technical drawings	3.75	4-6	______
1985 January, Number 7 The Vulcan's progress, Trek leisure wear, Takei interview, Trek design patents, Romulan society, tech drawings. [2]	3.75	4-6	______
September, Number 11 A. C. Crispin interview, 3rd season review, Robert Wise (STTMP) interview and Spock profile	3.75	4-6	______
November, Number 13 Takei interview, Will Decker interview, Which Side of Paradise-review of continuing episodes, James Cook - **James Kirk** comparison	3.75	4-6	______

Last Issues.

New magazine format - name changes to:
Science Fantasy T.V.

	Issue	Current	Cost/Date
1986 Volume 1, Number 2, January Compiled by **Enterprise Incidents** and **Fantasy Empire** productions. Includes the complete first season Trek episode guide as was serialized in **Daredevils** prozines, Issues No. 1-9 .	8.95	10-12	______
Volume 1, Number 3, February D. C. Fontana interview [3]	3.75	4-6	______

Van Hise's Publication and reprint by New Media Publications.

Enterprise Incidents
James Van Hise Publishers [4]

	Issue	Current	Cost/Date
1976 Number 1 Cover art of Spock with Lirpa by Steve Fabian, interviews Roddenberry, Takei and John (Kor) Collicos; pictorial review "Amok Time"			
Original First Edition	3.50	15-25	______
Xerox reproduction	3.50	3-6	______
Number 2 Cover art "Mirror, Mirror" recap of cover episode with 30 stills, Kelley interview and Star Trek models			
Original First Edition	3.50	12-16	______
Xerox reproduction	3	3-6	______
Number 3 Covert art from "Menagerie" with story recap with 50 stills, Jeffrey Hunter interview and Star Trek Bloopers			
Original First Edition	3.50	12-16	______
Xerox reproduction	3	3-6	______
Number 4 Recap "Doomsday Machine," the shuttlecraft mock-up, Ralph Fowler art, interview and profile William Shatner			
Original First Edition	3.50	10-15	______
Number 5 The banned episodes of Star Trek, Trek vs. Star Wars, recap "This Side Paradise" and Trek bloopers			
Original First Edition	3.50	10-15	______
Xerox reproduction	3	3-6	______
Number 6 Cover drawing "Balance of Terror" by Ralph Fowler, recap episode, profile Nimoy and some fan fiction . . .	3.50	8-10	______

2. After Issue No. 7, this magazine's coverage diverged away from being solely dedicated to Star Trek and included other SF media, such as Dr. Who. Trek was not featured in Issues No. 8, 9, 10 or 12.
3. With the magazine re-name New Media Press combined **Enterprise, Fantasy Empire and elements from Daredevils** publications. Issue No. 3 of **Science Fantasy T.V.** ended the revamped series.
4. **Enterprise Incidents** began as a local prozine produced in Florida. Xerox reproductions listed here were sold through the publisher.

PROZINES

	Issue	Current	Cost/Date
Number 7 Cover art of Romulan invasion of Earth by Fowler, with story, Roddenberry interview, D.C. Fontana and George Takei	3.50	8-10	______
Number 8 Special Star Trek the Motion Picture issue; Greg Jein interview, bloopers	3.50	6-10	______
• (New format - New Media Publishing title appears) [5]			
1982 Number 9, Summer Special First of new format – book review of **Death Angel** and **Entropy Effect,** reprint Geoffrey Mandel's **Star Trek Fandom Triumphs** amateur press release, bloopers	2.50	5-10	______
Number 10 Review Bantam Star Trek books, Roddenberry's speech at Berkeley, Nimoy as Van Gogh in "Vincent"	2.50	5-8	______
Number 11 Buck Price movie miniatures, review Gerrold's **Galactic Whirlpool** novel and more bloopers	2.95	4-8	______
Number 12 Franz Joseph and Doohan interviews, day with Leonard Nimoy	2.95	4-8	______
1984 Number 13, January First all-color interior and exterior issue; review ST II, Shatner's pre-Trek days and visual effects of STTMP	2.95	5-10	______
Number 14, February Making the Galileo 7 episode, Mike Minor (ST II) and Nicholas Meyer	2.95	4-8	______
Number 15, March Vulcans and Romulans compared and the history of Romulan Society	2.95	4-6	______
Number 16, April Behind the scenes ST II, tech drawings of Enterprise, Romulan society and Star Trek The Role Playing Game	2.95	4-6	______
Number 17, May Computer graphics of Genesis Effect, STTMP visuals, Angelique (Shahna) Pettyjohn interview	2.95	4-6	______
Number 18, June Mark Lenard of ST III, movie review and the new Trek models	2.95	4-6	______
Number 19, July Takei interview, color preview ST III	2.95	4-6	______
Number 20, August ST III review and make-up on the movie	2.95	4-6	______

	Issue	Current	Cost/Date
Number 21, September Interview with Mark Lenard of ST III	2.95	4-6	______
Number 22, October William Shatner interview	2.95	4-6	______
Number 23, November Interview Christopher Manley (ST III young Spock), Kelley interview	2.95	4-6	______
Number 24, December Harve Bennett looks at ST II and II, gives hints about upcoming ST IV	2.95	4-6	______
1985 Number 25, January Nimoy directing ST III	2.95	4-6	______
Number 26, February Harve Bennett and Nimoy discuss how to make a movie	2.95	4-6	______
• New magazine format - name changes to: **Science Fiction Movieland)** [6]			
Number 27, March Leonard Nimoy interview	2.95	3-5	______
Number 28, April Ralph Winston (ST III) interview	2.95	3-5	______
Number 29, May Nichelle Nichols interview	2.95	3-5	______
Number 30, June Nichelle Nichols story - Life Beyond Trek	2.95	3-5	______
Number 31, July William Shatner interview	2.95	3-5	______
Number 36, December Roger C. Carmel interview	2.95	3-5	______

ENTERPRISE INCIDENTS – SPECIAL EDITIONS

	Issue	Current	Cost/Date
Alien Cookbook N.M.P. 1984 A compendium of space recipes, chapter one features Vulcan recipes including Plomeek Soup, Vulcan Main Dish, Vulcan Spices, Dragon's Breath, Dessert Hi-R-Tar and Romulan Ale	3.50	4-5	______
Enterprise Incidents Special Collector's Editions, NMP			
1983 Number 1, November Reprint of Van Hise's Enterprise Incidents No. 1 and 2	3.50	5-8	______
1984 Number 2, January Reprint of Van Hise's Enterprise Incidents No. 3 and 4	3.50	4-6	______
Number 3, April Reprint of Van Hise's Enterprise Incidents No. 5	3.50	4-6	______
Number 4 Reprint of Van Hise's Enterprise Incidents No. 6	6	6-8	______

5. In 1982 the original artwork cover format changed to color photo covers and expanded interviews with Star Trek stars. These issues were mass-produced by New Media Press and were available on national newsstands.
6. With this name change, the old format of **Enterprise Incidents** expanded to include all elements of S.F. fandom. Note that Star Trek was not featured in Issues No. 32-35. Issue No. 36 ended the last of the **Science Fiction Movieland** series.

PROZINES

	Issue	Current	Cost/Date
Number 5 Reprint of Van Hise's Enterprise Incidents No. 7	3.95	4-6	______
• (New title - changes to **Enterprise Collector's,** deletes Enterprise Incident's affiliation) [7] **1985** Number 6, January Reprint of Van Hise's **Enterprise Incidents No. 8.** Plus, Star Trek The Motion Sickness parody of first movie, Greg Jein and D.C. Fontana interviews, Trek Bloopers. Expanded format	4.50	6-8	______
Enterprise Incidents Special Summer Issue 1983 Gene Roddenberry interview, story on Kahn Noonian Singh and the mechanical affinities of Star Trek	2.95	5-8	______

Special Editions.

	Issue	Current	Cost/Date
Enterprise Incidents Spotlight Series **1984** On Interviews Interviews with the personalities of Star Trek: Roddenberry, Takei, Kelley and Doohan	3.50	4-6	______
On Leonard Nimoy Interviews, profiles and photos	3.50	4-6	______
On the Technical Side Interview with Franz Joseph and Brick Price about Trek miniatures	4.50	5-7	______
• **1985** (Retitled, delete **Incidents**) [8] Enterprise Spotlight No. 2, January Star Trek trivia memory book, primarily a reprint of Trek articles published in 1966-1969 magazine articles; features Shatner and Nimoy	3.95	5-8	______
Enterprise Spotlight No. 3, February Reprints of early Trek articles and clippings. Roddenberry tapes, New Voyages book review, spirit of Trek, fan fiction, Tomorrow's World, transporter	3.95	5-8	______

More Special Editions.

	Issue	Current	Cost/Date
Enterprise Incidents, The Technical Book of Science Fiction Films, Star Trek and Star Wars 1984 October, New Media Press Softbound production of patented costumes, models and logo designs from the Trek t.v. series and movies, 55 p.	7.95	8-10	______
Fantasy Enterprises New Media Press 1985 Winter, Number 1 Roddenberry interview and analyzing the Enterprise	3.75	4-5	______
Future Threads 1986 Photos, patterns, interviews with the designers of Star Trek t.v. and films to create your own fantasies: Trek, Star Wars, Dr. Who, "V" 8"x10"	9.95	10-12	______
Illustrated Editor Lori Brown and Sherilyn Bruun 1984 February, Volume 1, No. 1 Premiere issue, a salute to Star Trek, poems, stories and artwork, special centerfold poster included. Limited Edition of 543 copies	5	8-10	______
Media Spotlight Irjax Enterprises 1975 Number 1, Summer Special salute to Star Trek, first of four issues devoted to Trek. Includes Trek t.v. articles, photos, profiles	1.25	6-9	______
1976 Number 2, Fall Star Trek Lives Again! Spock photo story, Trek as part of sci-fi, and porno in Trek. Full color cover of Enterprise	1.25	5-8	______
1977 Number 3, March Roddenberry tapes and the spirit of Star Trek, photos, profiles	1.25	4-6	______
Number 4, May Color cover with Spock, Star Trek fandom and Nichols interview	1.25	4-6	______

7. Name change deletes "Incidents" from the original series title. This is because **Enterprise Magazine** was still producing under its original title, while **Enterprise Incident's Magazine** had just changed its name to **Science Fiction Movieland Magazine.**
8. The **Enterprise Incidents Magazine** affiliation was deleted because of that publication's name change to **Science Fiction Movieland. Enterprise Magazine** was still publishing under its original title.

Media Spotlights.

Monsterland

	Issue	Current	Cost/Date
Movieland Publishing, Inc. 1987 Number 6 Spring Issue, February, (Van Hise and Al Schuster production) Exclusive interview with Nimoy on directing ST IV, Doohan interview, Spock insert on cover.	2.50	3-4	______

Gaming Prozine.

Nexus - The Gaming Connection

Task Force Games

Gaming publication designed to augment the Task Force **Star Fleet Battles** space gaming sets and miniatures. 40 to 50-page magazines provide special game updates, explanations, product information and fictional stories in "Star Fleet Universe" sections,

	Issue	Current	Cost/Date
1982 No. 1, Vol. 1 Vol. 1	2.50	3-4	______
No. 2, Vol. 1, June/July (bi-monthly)	2.50	3-4	______
No. 3, Vol. 1	2.50	3-4	______
1983 No. 4, Vol. 1, Jan/Feb	2.50	3-4	______
No. 5, Vol. 1, Mar/Apr	2.50	3-4	______
No. 6, Vol. 1 Special Star Fleet Issue, fiction, products, cover art by G.A. Kalin of Gorn and 3 Fed ships	2.50	4-5	______
No. 7, Vol. 2	2.50	3-4	______
1984 No. 8, Vol. 2 (Begins qtrly. release and expanded format)	3	3-4	______
No. 9, Vol. 2 Features Star Fleet ficton and a gaming scenerio, cover art by G.A. Kalin of Klingon Battlecruiser and t.v. Enterprise	3	4-6	______
No. 10, Vol. 2	3	3-4	______
1985 No. 11, Vol. 2	3	3-4	______
No. 12, Vol. 2	3	3-4	______
No. 13, Vol. 2	3	3-4	______
No. 14, Vol. 2	3	3-4	______
1986 No. 15, Vol. 2	3	3-4	______
No. 16, Vol. 2	3	3-4	______

Star Trek Prozines

RBCC

	Issue	Current	Cost/Date
James Van Hise, publisher 1975 Number 118 Special Trek issue: an evening with Nimoy, "The Cage"/"Menagerie" comparison, review "Where No Man Has Gone Before" and Trek beyond the pilots. Enterprise cover art by Mike McKenney, back cover by Steve Fabian	1.25	5-8	______

Stardate [9]

Fasa Corporation, publisher

1984 through 1986; role playing game supplement.

	Issue	Current	Cost/Date
1984 Number 1 Special Star Trek III issue; photos from the movie, treatise on Starfleet regulations, the space dock and column "Ask Star Fleet Command"	2	4-7	______
Number 2, December Special on the Vulcans, their planet and people, writing SF, the trials and tribbles of William Campbell and the Trek menagerie of creatures	2	4-6	______

9. **Stardate** magazine as it was published by Fasa Corp. ceased distribution in early 1986. In early 1987 the publication resumed again under Reluctant Publishing, Ltd. titled **Stardate - The Science Fiction Gaming Resource.** Newly formated and expanded, this Volume 3 series will feature ads, mail questions, game updates. To be published monthly at a cover price of $3.50 on newsstands.

PROZINES

	Issue	Current	Cost/Date
1985 Number 3/4 Double Issue More on Star Trek The Role Playing Game, robots in Trek, gaming the Captain, Vulcans and mixed blood. Larger expanded format	4	5-6	______
Number 5/6 Double Issue Expanded, larger issue format	4	5-6	______
Number 7/8 Double issue Expanded, large issue format	4	4-6	______
Number 9 Single issue, smaller format	2	2-4	______
Number 10 Single issue format	2	2-4	______
1986 Number 11 Single issue format	2	2-4	______

Starship Design
Starstation Aurora

	Issue	Current	Cost/Date
1984 Softbound, glossy magazine format to replicate a 23rd Century periodical. Tech drawings and articles on Star Fleet, military advertisements, etc. Limited edition, individually numbered, 39 pages	7.95	10-15	______

Original Edition.

Star Trek: An Analysis of a Phenomenon [10]
S.C. Enterprises
Softbound, glossy page production discussing Trek in relation to scientific fact and theory, photos and drawings,

	Issue	Current	Cost/Date
First Edition, 1968	.75	20-25	______
Reprinted Edition, white border, 1978	2.95	5-8	______

Star Trek File, Files Spotlight On
Psi Fi Movie Press, Inc. (New Media Press) [11]

	Issue	Current	Cost/Date
Where No Man Has Gone Before, 1985 Beginning of series of Star Trek in-depth stories, character profiles, actor biographies and seasonal episode guides, edited by John Peel, 8½"x11" softbound with color episode photo on cover, 94 p.	9.95	10-14	______

Star Trek Files.

Issues No. 1 and No. 2.

No. 3 and No. 4.

	Issue	Current	Cost/Date
ST -1, The Early Voyages, 1985 Photos, Takei interview, Sulu character profile, episode guide, 56 pages	4.95	6-10	______
Deluxe Limited Edition Hardcover, 1986	19.95	20-22	______
ST-2, Time Passages, 1985 Photos, shuttlecraft info, Ted Sturgeon interview, Yeoman Rand character profile, pin-up, episode guide, 56 pages	4.95	6-8	______

10. This was the very first Star Trek publication produced in prozine format. It was not available on local newsstands.
11. New Media Press is currently reprinting older issues.

PROZINES

	Issue	Current	Cost/Date
ST-3, A Taste of Paradise, 1985 Photos, Doohan interview, Scotty character profile, photo fiction, episode guide, 56 p.	4.95	6-8	______
ST-4, On The Edge of Forever, 1985, Photos, 1st season episode guide, John Callicos interview, the Klingons, Harlan Ellison biography, pin-ups, 56 p	4.95	5-7	______
ST-5, Mission: Year Two, 1985 Photos, Jerome Bixby interview, Sarek character profile, Mark Lenard story, episode guide, 56 p.	4.95	6-7	______
ST-6, Journey to Eternity, 1986 Photos, interview Norman Spinrad and Mark Lenard, in-depth look at Trek, episode guide, 56 p.	4.95	5-7	______
Second printing, 1986	4.95	5-6	______
ST-7, The Deadly Years, 1986 Episode guide, photos, character profile and interviews, 56 p.	4.95	5-7	______
Second printing	4.95	5-6	______
ST-8, Return to Tomorrow, 1986 Episode guide, planet Vulcan, interviews with David Gerrold, Robert Bloch and Dorothy Fontana, 56 p.	4.95	6-7	______
Second printing, 1986	5.95	6-7	______
ST-9, Assignment: Earth, 1986 Photos, Kelley interview, McCoy character profile, Nimoy interview, episode guide	4.95	6-7	______
Second printing, 1986	5.95	6-7	______
ST-10, Enterprise Incidents, 1986 Nimoy interview, Spock character profile, Kelley interview, photos, episode guide	4.95	6-7	______
Second printing, 1986	5.95	6-7	______
ST-11, Tholian Web, 1986 Uhura character profile, Nichelle Nichols biography and interview, photos, episode guide	4.95	6-7	______
Second printing, 1986	5.95	6-7	______
ST-12, Whom Gods Destroy, 1986 Episode Guide, Mike Minor interview, photos	4.95	6-7	______
Second printing, 1986	5.95	6-7	______
ST-13, That Which Survives, 1985 Episode Guide, directing films, Star Trek and return to t.v., photos	4.95	6-7	______
Second printing, 1986	5.95	6-7	______
ST-14, All Our Yesterdays, 1985 Third season episodes, James T. Kirk character profile, the Trek actor's index	5.95	6-7	______

	Issue	Current	Cost/Date
Star Trek: Houston Phantom Empire 1975 Reprints a lot of **R.B.C.C.** prozine material, "The Cage"/"Menagerie" comparison, and evening with Roddenberry, interviews Koenig and Doohan	2	3-5	______
Star Trek ('74 and '75) Galaxy News Service 1974 Koenig on Trek, Shatner interview, Spock review, evening with Nimoy, photo story of "Menagerie," Trek the way it was and bloopers	1.50	3-5	______
1975 Cover art by Morris Scott Dollens, interview with Doohan, Koenig profile, Nimoy interview and starship chronicles	1.50	3-4	______
Star Trek - 20th Anniversary Tribute New Media Press, Hal Schuster, Editor 1986 September Trek in episodes, animation and movies I to IV, the bloopers, photos and more	7.95	8-10	______

Trek Prozines.

	Issue	Current	Cost/Date
Trek G. B. Love, Editor[12] 1975 Number 1 Tabloid size issue, episode index, history of the Klingons, fan club listings, Morris Scott Dollens front/back covers	1.25	15-30	______
Number 2 Tabloid, special "City Edge Forever" issue: photos, monsters of Trek Original First Edition	1.25	15-20	______
Reprint Edition Magazine Format	2.50	4-5	______
Number 3 Front cover by Steve Fabian, bloopers, Romulans and Chicago-Con, tabloid	1.25	10-15	______
• New Format – 8½"x11" Magazine			
Number 4 Full color cover of Spock from "Amok Time," changing Nimoy into Spock	2.50	8-10	______

12. Anthologies of this prozine publication appear in Signet's paperback series entitled **The Best of Trek.**

PROZINES

	Issue	Current Cost	Date
Number 5 Trek miniatures, the Enterprise, behind the scenes of Trek, the fandom and the Trek Roundtable			
Original First Edition	2.50	8-10	
Reprint as Double Issue (with No. 6)	6	7-9	
Number 6 Trek miniatures, Trek comic books, Star Trek's grade-A girls and Trek Roundtable			
Original First Edition	2.50	6-10	
Reprint Double Issue (with No. 5)	6	7-9	
1977 Number 7, February Interview Grace Lee Whitney, Star Trek comics, Part III, the Spock scrapbook			
Original First Edition	2.50	5-10	
Reprint Double Issue (with No. 8)	6	7-9	
Number 8 Trek animated series review, the psychology of Spock, evening with Roddenberry			
Original First Edition	2.50	5-10	
Reprint Double Issue (with No. 7)	6	6-9	
Number 9 Evening with Takei, McCoy profiles, the Trek Roundtable	2.50	6-10	
Number 10 Special Kirk issue: news on STTMP, the psychology of Kirk, career profiles	2.50	6-10	
Number 11 "City Edge of Forever" story and photos, original Harlon Ellison script and the making of Bantam **Fotonovels**	2.50	6-10	
Number 12 Special Federation issue: Klingon-Romulan alliance, psychology of Spock-rebuttal article	2.50	5-10	
Number 13 Covers by Monica Miller, the 88 character universe, photos	2.50	5-8	
Original First Edition	2.50	5-8	
Reprint Double Issue (with No. 14)	6	6-9	
1979 Number 14, Fall Issue Women in the Federation, speculation on Spock's past, subspace radio and space warps			
Original First Edition	3	5-8	
Reprint Double Issue (with No. 13)	6	6-9	
Number 15 Special STTMP issue: Koenig interview, review and cast lists, the Klingons			
Original First Edition	3	8-15	
Limited Edition Reprint	10	10-12	
Number 16 Vulcan as a patriarchy, Trek mysteries solved, Trek geneology, Star Trek alternative universes and Roundtable	3	5-8	
1981 Number 17, Winter Issue Command decision crisis, Spock's career, the Promethian Star Trek, Sulu's profile	3.25	5-8	

TREK MAGAZINE
Special Releases

Trek Special Series
G. B. Love, Editor

	Issue	Current Cost	Date
1977 Number 1, February Reprint articles from issue No. 1, includes the Klingons, Star Trek then and now, Trek trivia, Star Trek index, evening with Nimoy. New articles - Klingon update, Shatner			
Original First Edition	3	6-10	
Reprint Second Edition	5	6-7	
1978 Number 2, November Reprints from issue No. 4, includes Spock Scrapbook, NYC Star Trek Con review, Spock's personal memoris and new - Trek Around the World, Federation fashions	3	6-8	

Trek Movie Special Series
G. B. Love, Editor

	Issue	Current Cost	Date
1984 Number 1 Special ST II issue: Why Spock died, movie review, the "No-Win" scenerio, photos, art, full color covers, 60 p.	5	6-8	
Number 2 More ST II, Spock resurrected, "Raiders of the Lost Trek," Kirk and Spock's death, photos, art, 64 p.	5	5-8	
Number 3 An all-letters issue, jeers and sheers from the best of Trek magazine, 64 p.	5	5-6	

Warp Factor 2
D.C. Graphics

	Issue	Current Cost	Date
1976 August A day at Equicon, Pleides Survey Vessel technical drawings, Star Trek animation and 4 short stores	3	4-6	

MUSIC

Every Star Trek fan is familiar with the single, melodic musical theme which accompanies the beginning of Star Trek episodes. The symbolic representation of Star Trek's theme is the second most associated token to the show aside from the appearance of the starship Enterprise.

The Star Trek theme song has since found its way onto LP albums, 45 RPM singles and audio cassettes. It has been reproduced as a compliment to space hit theme collections, as background music or as lead-off music to the record releases of major Star Trek actors. Written by Alexander Courage, the Star Trek theme is everything that fans feel and love about the show played in two minutes.

Star Trek as explored in music has branched out in the last two decades to include a variety of formats designed for listening pleasure.

RECORDS AND TAPES

Three Audio & Book Sets, Buena Vista

Unusual 8 track for Star Trek The Motion Picture

Star Trek records have appeared as both adult and juvenile recordings in 45 singles or 33⅓ LPs. Audio cassettes are available for both age groups as well in either standard stereo cassettes or 8-track cartridges.

Amateur Bands – Independently manufactured records which usually make their debut as 45's and are presented at science fiction conventions. **Solar Sailor** by the Dehorn Crew is an unusual fan album produced as an LP.

Cast Recordings – Several members of the original Star Trek cast have tested the waters with their own personal recordings. In 1968 Leonard Nimoy produced the first independent recording **Leonard Nimoy Presents Mr. Spock's Music From Outer Space.** This was the beginning of a long series of Nimoy albums made by Dot Records (a division of Paramount Pictures Corporation) which concluded in 1972. Soon after this first record's success, Decca Records (a division of Universal Studios) released William Shatner's **The Transformed Man.** Since then, both Nichelle Nichols and Grace Lee Whitney have produced 45 singles or audio cassettes as well.

Episode Scores – These are products of the 80's and feature the music of Star Trek as it was aired on television. Star Trek music was both created specifically for certain scenes and borrowed as excerpts from popular and classical compositions. For example, "Charlie is My Darling" from **Charlie X** is an original song while "I'll Take You Home Again Kathleen" from **The Naked Time** and portions of "Goodnight Sweetheart" in background music for **The City On The Edge of Forever** were traditional scores. Recently two music companies (Varese Sarabane Records Inc. and Fifth Continent Music Corp.) have begun a series of Star Trek episode LPs and tapes.

Juvenile Recordings – Records for kids began around the appearance of Star Trek the animated series and were re-released in different covers for **Star Trek The Motion Picture.** With the advent of successive movie films, high quality book and record or book and tape sets have been made by Buena Vista Records.

Movie Soundtracks – Now entire albums or tapes of stereophonic enjoyment has become available since the release of the first Star Trek film in 1979. Jerry Goldsmith, who wrote the score for **Star Trek The Motion Picture,** was nominated for an Academy Award and is still thought to be the best movie album produced. James Horner wrote the score for **Star Trek II** and **Star Trek III.** Leonard Rosenman composed the music for **Star Trek IV.**

Narratives – Narratives occur as behind-the-scenes examinations, biographies, inquiries into Star Trek philosophies, live speeches or as fiction classics told by prominent Trek actors. **Inside Star Trek** and **The Star Trek Tapes** are examples of fine narrative reviews. The most prolific manufacturer of adult narrative recitations is Caedmon Records. They have produced a quality series of science fiction excerpts recited from classic novels using both Leonard Nimoy and William Shatner. Narrative recordings may also be comedy releases. The **Star Trek Bloopers** verbally re-iterate the infamous reels of scrapped Star Trek out-takes found in a Hollywood garbage pail.

Taped Interviews – These are available on cassettes by small commercial sources. Basically they are recordings of vintage television interviews given by actors and actresses of the Star Trek cast.

Theme Song Anthologies – Numerous space theme LPs and tapes have featured Star Trek on their disks.

Sheet Music

Sheet music for Star Trek has generally followed in the wake of the motion picture releases since the late 1970's. A memorable collectible in this category is the Filk Song book **Sing-A-Song of Trekkin'** by Caterpillar Music Corp. This book contains the scores to 20 Star Trek Filk songs and humorous drawings of superior quality.

In conclusion, no discussion of Star Trek music would be complete without mentioning the fact that Gene Roddenberry wrote the lyrics to the Star Trek Theme composed by Alexander Courage. For those who don't know them, here they are:

Beyond
The rim of star-light
My love,
Is wand'ring in star-flight
I know
He'll find in star-clustered reaches
Love
Strange love a star woman teaches.

I know
His journey ends never
His Star Trek
will go on forever,
But tell him
While he wanders his starry sea
Remember, remember me.

Star Trek The Motion Picture Sheet Music

Star Trek II Theme Score

Star Trek III Sheet Music

Spiral Bound Sheet Music

Item	Issue	Current	Cost/Date
Ballad of Bilbo Baggins/Cotton Candy Dot Records, 1968, No. 45-17028 45 RPM, pre-release for Leonard Nimoy's Dot album **Two Sides of Leonard Nimoy**	.79	3-5	______
Beyond Antares R-Way Productions, 1979 45 RPM, Nichelle Nichols sings "Beyond Antares" and "Uhura's Theme," color sleeve front pictures Nichols over starfield, lyrics are on the reverse	4	5-7	______
Captain of the Starship No. NU 9400 K-Tel Presents, Imperial Music House, 1978, Double Album set. Narratives and music. [1]	6	20-30	______
Star Trek Book n' Record Set, PR-26 Peter Pan pressing, 1979. Jacket cover photos Kirk, Spock and McCoy on STTMP Enterprise bridge.	1.98	7-10	______
Star Trek Book n' Record Set BR-522 Peter Pan, 1979 Children's 12" 33⅓ RPM album with 12" square comic book, 16 pages. Other titles include Passage to Moauv. Bookcover jacket photos McCoy, Kirk, Decker and Spock from STTMP bridge; rear photos Enterprise	3.98	15-20	______

"The Crier in Emptiness" - LP and book set.

Book and Record Sets - "Crier in Emptiness" Photo cover.

"The Crier in Emptiness" - 45 RPM & book set.

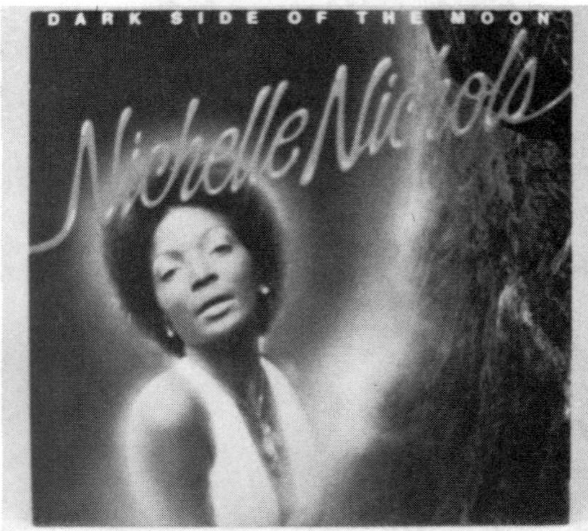

Dark Side of the Moon - 45 RPM

Item	Issue	Current	Cost/Date
Crier in Emptiness TV Power Records, 1975, Peter Pan Star Trek Book n' Record Set No. PR-26 Children's 7" 45 RPM with 20-page heavy paper comic book. 7"x10" cardstock jacket cover has cartoon Kirk, Spock and Uhura on bridge.	1.49	10-12	______
Dark Side of the Moon Americana Records, 1974 45 RPM, Nichelle Nichols sings on this double record set: "Dark Side of the Moon," "It's Been On My Mind," "Starry Eyed" and "Let's Trip" Includes fold-out mini poster, 7" extended play. [2]	2	8-10	______

1. This album was advertised as a K-Tel television offer in certain locales. K-Tel reports that only 900 pressings were made before the record went out of production.
2. It's reported that only 5,000 copies of this Nichelle Nichols record were released before Americana Records went out of business.

ALBUMS & COVERS

Issue | Current | Cost/Date

Dinosaur Planet
Peter Pan Records, 1979
Star Trek Book n' Record Set PR-45
Children's 7" 45 RPM with 20-page comic book. 7"x10" jacket cover photos comic montage of STTMP Kirk and Spock with a fantasy dinosaur . . . . 1.98 7-10 ______

Star Trek Five All-New Action Adventures, 1110
Children's 12" 33⅓ RPM album. Other titles include Passage to Moauv, Time Stealer, In Vino Veritas, To Starve A Fleaver. Slipcover jacket photos Kirk, Spock beneath cartoon STTMP Enterprise; rear shows STTMP movie photo collage . . . . 3.89 6-8 ______

Foundation: The Psychohistorians TC 1508
Caedmon Records, 1976
Album, abridged version (Chap. 1-8) of Issac Asimov's novel, read by William Shatner, TT: 59.24, slipcover front has blue cartoon moonscape with sun and rocket at touchdown. . . . . 8 9-12 ______

Future Games - A Magic Kahuna Dream 1133
Mercury Records, (Div. Phonogramm Inc.) 1977
Album, splice and cut future-shock performed by the group "Spirit". Radio broadcasts, TV excerpts, folk songs and original music by Randy California in league with the Dr. Demento Radio Show. Brief trailers: "Star Trek Dreaming," "Gorn Attack," "The Romulan Experience" and "Journey of Nomad." Slipcover has b/w photo of Randy California.[3] 4.99 6-8 ______

Greatest Science Fiction Hits
Crescendo Records
Vol. 1, GNPS 2128
Neil Norman and His Cosmic Orchestra album of sci-fi themes produced and arranged by Les Baxter and Neil Norman. Tracks from "Alien," "Outer Limits," "Godzilla," "Star Trek (t.v.) Theme" and 14 more . . . . 9.98 10-12 ______

Vol. 2. GNPS 2133
Sixteen more themes including the STTMP movie theme . . . . 9.98 10-12 ______

Green Hills of Earth and Gentlemen, Be Seated TC-1526
Caedmon Records, 1976
Album, Robert Heinlein's stories read by Leonard Nimoy, slipcover jacket . . . . 8 9-12 ______

(The) Human Factor
Star Trek Original Stories for Children 1516
Peter Pan Records, 1979
Children's 7" 45 RPM record in 7"x8" slipcover, front has red border with close-up photo of Kirk and Spock from STTMP. . . . . .99 4-6 ______

I'd Love Making Love To You/ Please Don't Try To Change My Mind
Dot Records, 1969
45 RPM, pre-release for Leonard Nimoy's album entitled **The Way I Feel** . . . . .79 3-5 ______

Illustrated Man TC-1479
Caedmon Records, 1976
Album, story recitals from Ray Bradbury's "The Illustrated Man," "The Veldt" and "Marionettes, Inc." as read by Leonard Nimoy. TT 46:00. Slipcover jacket portrays green jungle planetscape, green alien and brown lions. . . . . 8 9-12 ______

In Vino Veritas
T.V. Power Records, 1975, Peter Pan
Star Trek Little LP F2296
Children's 7" 33⅓ RPM, slipcover jacket cartoons Kirk, Spock, McCoy and the t.v. Enterprise . . . . .79 5-7 ______

Star Trek Original Stories for Children 1513
Peter Pan pressing, 1979. Re-release in 7" 45 RPM. 7"x8" slipcover front has a green border and photos Kirk, Spock and Uhura on STTMP bridge. . . . . .99 4-5 ______

Inside Star Trek PC-34279
Columbia Records (Div. of C.B.S.), 1976
Album, narratives produced by Ed Naha and Russ Payne. Gene Roddenberry narrates tales and anecdotes about Star Trek, TT 56:04. Slipcover jacket blueprints the Enterprise . . . . 8 12-15 ______

Leonard Nimoy Presents Mr. Spock's Music From Outer Space DLP 25794
Dot Records, 1968
Album, Charles L. Green's clever collection of music and narratives in theme for Vulcan Mr. Spock. Includes "Theme from Star Trek," "Beyond Antares," "Twinkle, Twinkle Little Earth" and "Where No Man Has Gone Before." TT 22:43. Slipcover jacket features famous Paramount promo poster of Spock holding model Enterprise.[4] . . 3.50 20-30 ______

3. "Dr. Demento" was a popular late-night music and radio show that was aired in California during the 1970's.
4. "Beyond Antares" was used in the Star Trek episode **"The Conscience of the King."**

Inside Star Trek

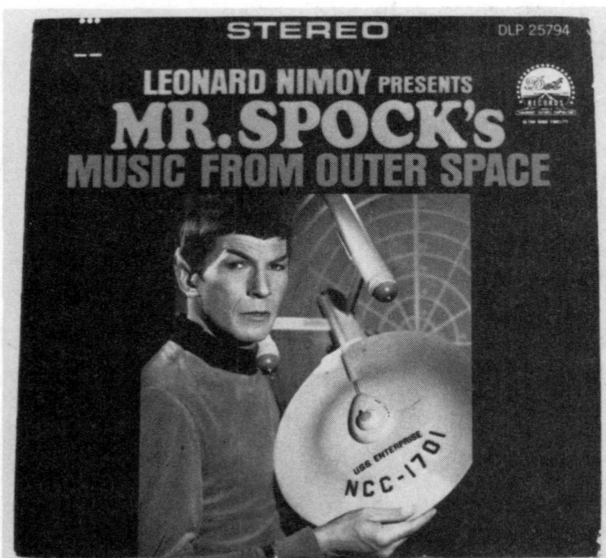

The First Star Trek Record

Issue Current Cost/Date

Man Who Trained Meteors
Star Trek Four Exciting All-New Action Adventures 8236
Peter Pan Records, 1979
Children's 12" 33⅓ RPM album, other titles include Robot Masters, Dinosaur Planet and Human Factor. Slipcover jacket has orange border with close-up photo of Kirk, Spock and McCoy on STTMP bridge; rear photos Andorians, Rigelians and Enterprise from movie 2.98 6-8 _____

Martian Chronicles TC-1466
Caedmon Records, 1976
Album, Ray Bradbury's (abridged) novel as read by Leonard Nimoy . . 8 9-12 _____

Issue Current Cost/Date

Mimsy Were The Borogoves TC-1509
Caedmon Records, 1976
Album, narrative of the story by Henry Kutner (a.k.a. Lewis Padgett) as read by William Shatner. TT 62:35. Slipcover jacket has gold cartoon lanterns and a young child in pajamas gazing at the stars. . . . . . . 8 9-12 _____

Mirror For Futility
Star Trek Book n' Record Set BR-513
Children's 12" 33⅓ RPM album with 12" square 16-page comic book. Other title is Time Stealer. Bookcover jacket cartoons t.v. bridge scene with Kirk, Spock and McCoy . . . . 3.98 7-10 _____

Music From Return of the Jedi and Other Hits 79065-1
SQN Cassettes and Records, 1983
Album, Digitally recorded musical scores by The Odyssey Orchestra. Includes Star Wars movies, Raiders of the Lost Ark, 2001, Close Encounters, Superman and Star Trek theme. Slipcover jacket front cartoons orange planet, twin moons, spacecraft and station by Sam Gallentree. . . . . 7.99 8-9 _____

Mysterious Golem
JRT Records, 1976
Album, story narrated by Leonard Nimoy. A supernatural being is created by the secrets of the Kabbalah. The story that inspired "Frankenstein" to be written. Slipcover jacket with color illustration. 7 8-9 _____

The New World of Leonard Nimoy

New World of Leonard Nimoy DLP 25966
Dot Records, 1970
Album,, Leonard Nimoy sings songs by Steve Clark and Ben Benay. Popular folksongs such as "The Sun Will Rise" by Nimoy included. TT 23:41, slipcover jacket comprised of 5 photo collage of Nimoy . . . . 3.99 15-18 _____

ALBUMS AND RECORDS

Issue | Current | Cost/Date

Outer Space, Inner Mind PAS 2
Famous Turnset, 1976
Double album, Leonard Nimoy renders material taken from Star Trek and Mission Impossible. Bookcover front shows Enterprise on blue backdrop. . . . . 7.50 10-15 ______

Book and Record Sets

Passage to Moauv
T.V. Power Records, 1975, Peter Pan Star Trek Book n' Record Set PR-25
Children's 7" 45 RPM with 20-page heavy paper comic. 7"x10" card-stock jacket cover cartoons Kirk, Spock, Uhura on bridge . . . . 1.49 10-12 ______

Star Trek Book n' Record Set PR-25
Peter Pan pressing, 1979. Re-release, jacket cover photos front-view STTMP Enterprise and busts of Kirk and Spock, pink backdrop . 1.98 7-10 ______

Star Trek Three Adventure Stories 8158, T.V. Power Records, 1975
Children's 12" 33⅓ RPM album. Other titles include Crier in Emptiness and In Vino Veritas. Slip-cover jacket cartoons Kirk, Spock, McCoy and t.v. Enterprise . . . . 2.49 7-9 ______

(The) Robot Masters
Star Trek Book n' Record Set PR-46
Peter Pan Records, 1979
Children's 7" 45 RPM record with 20-page comic book. 7"x10" jacket cover is a photo and cartoon montage of STTMP Kirk with fantasy robot . . . . 1.98 7-10 ______

Solar Sailors
Bandersnatch Press, 1977!
Album, by the Dehorn Crew, originally produced Star Trek thematic songs and narratives, slip-cover jacket front photo of the crew in Federation uniform. . . . . 9.95 10-12 ______

Space Odyssey

Issue | Current | Cost/Date

Space Odyssey SPC-3199
Pickwick International Release, 1972
Album, nine re-releases from the Dot albums by Leonard Nimoy. TT 20:18. Slipcover jacket has pop poster art by "Daniel." Rear has zodiac wheel and intro of Nimoy as Paris on Mission: Impossible . . . . . . 3.99 8-10 ______

Spaced-Out Disco Fever WLP-315
Wonderland Records, 1977
Children's 33⅓ RPM album. The Wonderball Disco Orchestra plays disco version space themes for children's parties. Includes disco Star Trek theme, Star Wars, Close Encounters (this is the cover cartoon art, too) . . . . 3 5-6 ______

Space Themes - Star Wars WLP-313
Wonderland Records, 1977
Album, 33⅓ RPM themes from Star Trek (t.v.), Bionic Woman, Six Million Dollar Man, Superman, 2001, etc. . . . . 3 4-6 ______

Spectacular Space Hits SQN 7808
Sine Qua Non Productions, 1980
Album, movie scores performed by the Odyssey Orchestra. Themes from Star Wars, Close Encounters, 2001, Superman and Star Trek. Slip-cover jacket front cartoons Earth, moon, scout ship and orbital platform by Sam Gallentree. Rear cover introduces the legend of Star Trek as a t.v. series . . . . 6.49 7-8 ______

Star Drek
Fan produced, Malibu California, 1978
45 RPM. Hilarious spoof of Star Trek. . . . . 2 4-5 ______

ALBUMS AND RECORDS

	Issue	Current	Cost/Date
Starship Federation Records East, 1986 Rock n' Roll battle scenerio aboard the starship Enterprise. Features music, sound-effects and voice-over dialogue. [5]	4	4-5	_____

Special Episode Soundtrack

	Issue	Current	Cost/Date
Star Trek 6001 Synthetic Plastics, Inc., 1981 Album, The Now Sound Orchestra presents musical scores by "Bugs" Bowers. Contains themes from Star Wars, Close Encounters, 2001 and Trek. Includes theme from STTMP, "Ilia's Theme" and the theme from the Star Trek series. Slipcover jacket has front starscape by Hatzikalfas and Barrall.	3.99	4-6	_____

Episode Scores by Varese Sarabande

	Issue	Current	Cost/Date
Star Trek Varese Sarabane Records, Inc. 1985 **Volume I,** 1985 Digital album series of newly recorded music from Trek t.v. Performed by The Royal Philharmonic Orchestra, conducted by Fred Steiner. Episodes: "Charlie X," "Corbomite Maneuver," "Mudd's Woman" and "Doomsday Machine." Front slipcover photos t.v. Enterprise firing phasers. Rear shows 1 color photo from each episode with story recaps by Bjo Trimble. 704.270 Album	9	9-19	_____
VCDE 47235 Compact Disc	18	18-19	_____
Volume II, 1986 Episodes: "Mirror, Mirror," "By Any Other Name," "Trouble With Tribbles" and "The Empath". Slipcover photo shows Enterprise; rear has color photos and recaps from episodes. 704.300 Album	9	9-10	_____
Star Trek Label X, Fifth Continent Music Corp. **Volume 1,** 1985 Digital album series produced by Clyde Allen and John Lasher. Royal Philharmonic Orchestra conducted by Tony Bremner. Composed by George Duning and Gerald Fried. Original scores: "Is There In Truth No Beauty" and "Paradise Syndrome." Deluxe package with insert. Front shows blue art Enterprise, back has 16 color episode photos. LXDR 703 Album	9.95	10-11	_____
LXCD 703 Compact Disc	12	12-13	_____
Volume 2, 1985 Scores from "Conscience of the King," "Spectre of the Gun," "Enemy Within" and "I, Mudd." Composers Joseph Mullendore, Jerry Fielding, Sol Kaplan, Samuel Matlovsky. Deluxe package with insert. Front has magenta art ship, back has 16 photos. LXDR 704	9.95	10-11	_____
LXCD 704 Compact Disc	12	12-13	_____
Volume 3, 1986 Scores from "Return to Tomorrow" and "Metamorphosis" by George Duning. LXDR 705 Album	9.95	10-11	_____
Volume 4, 1986 Scores from "Cat's-Paw" and "Shore Leave" composed by Gerald Fired. LXDR 706 album	9.95	10-11	_____

5. This record's producers advertised in **Starlog Magazine** in late 1986 and promoted their release by a unique "Dial-A-Sample" phone call. Callers could hear prerecorded samples of the record's music and dialogue.

ALBUMS AND RECORDS

	Issue	Current	Cost/Date
Star Trek Bloopers Blue Pear Records Album, set of out-takes from third season Star Trek shows. Edited from 6 original on-set tapes found in a trashcan! Slipcover jacket has pen and ink satirical sketch of Mr. Spock	8.95	10-12	_____

Star Trek Tapes

	Issue	Current	Cost/Date
Star Trek Tapes Jack M. Sell Enterprises, 1978 Album, compilation of official press recordings featuring the cast of Star Trek. TT 29:05. Slipcover jacket is blue with Spock giving Vulcan salute. [6]	7.95	10-12	_____

Interesting 45 RPM by Federation Earth Band

	Issue	Current	Cost/Date
Star Trek Theme/Vulcanization Federation Earth Band, 1976 45 RPM stereo production featuring a pop rendition of the t.v. show theme, plus an original composition. [7]	2	4-5	_____

STTMP Soundtrack.

	Issue	Current	Cost/Date
Star Trek The Motion Picture JS 36334 Columbia Records, 1979 Album, Music from the original soundtrack composed and conducted by Jerry Goldsmith. TT 37:47. Includes full-color insert of Enterprise and full-color record sleeve. Slipcover jacket has "rainbow" promo poster	9.99	10-12	_____
Star Trek The Motion Picture Read-Along Adventure 461 Buena Vista Records, 1979 7" 33⅓ RPM record with photo book featuring scenes from the movie. Bookcover jacket has a photo collage of Spock, Kirk and Enterprise.	2.49	4-6	_____

Star Trek II Soundtrack

6. This record was produced in a limited quantity. Only 1,000 albums were ever cut.
7. The Federation Earth Band made their debut appearance at the Space The Final Frontier Convention No. 2 in Oakland, California.

ALBUMS AND RECORDS

Issue Current Cost/Date

Star Trek The Wrath of Kahn Original Soundtrack
SD-19363
Atlantic Records, 1982
Album, Digital recordings from the movie composed and conducted by James Orner. TT 40:33. Slipcover jacket front has new Enterprise on black. Rear photo collages the 14 scenes seen on the promo posters ... 9.98 10-12 _____

Star Trek II 45 RPM Buena Vista Records.

Star Trek II - The Wrath of Kahn Read-Along Adventure
462
Buena Vista Records, 1982
7" 33⅓ RPM record with 24-page photo book of scenes from the movie. Bookcover jacket photos Enterprise and the U.S.S. Reliant in space battle .... 2.49 4-6 _____

Star Trek III The Search For Spock SKBK 12360
Capital Records, 1984
Double album set, Music from the original soundtrack composed and conducted by James Horner and Band 87. TT 41:34. Centerfold slipcover jacket. Includes Star Trek T.V. series theme by Courage and a special 12" single recording of the Main Theme TT 3:40. Jacket front has "neon-glo" promo poster ...... 9.98 10-12 _____

Star Trek III - The Search For Spock Read-Along Adventure
463
Buena Vista Records, 1984
7" 33⅓ RPM record with 24-page photo book of scenes from the movie, sound effects and music. Bookcover jacket photo .... 2.49 4-6 _____

Star Trek IV - The Voyage Home 6195
MCA Records, 1986
Music scores for the original soundtrack composed and conducted by Leonard Rosenman. Song titles include "Ballad of the Whale" and "Market Street," new originals by The Yellow Jackets. Album in slipcover jacket featuring "zoom-in" official movie poster of artwork San Francisco Bay, Earth 1986 .... 10.49 10-11 _____

Star Trek IV Soundtrack

Issue Current Cost/Date

Starve A Fleaver
T.V. Power Records, Peter Pan
Star Trek Little LP 2307 1975
Children's 7" 33⅓ RPM slipcover jacket cartoons Kirk, Spock, McCoy and an alien on t.v. bridge .... .79 5-7 _____

Star Trek Original Stories For Children
1515, 1979
Peter Pan pressing, in 7"x8" slipcover with blue border and photos of Spock, Kirk and McCoy on STTMP bridge. 7" 45 RPM ...... .99 4-5 _____

Theme From Star Trek and Planet of the Apes
WLP-301
Wonderland Records, 1975
12" 33⅓ RPM collection of television themes including Batman and Superman as well. Produced by Ralph Stein and performed by "The Jeff Wayne Space Shuttle" orchestra. Slipcover jacket has yellow and red "Star Trek" title and an orange cartoon of a Gorilla Soldier. 3.29 7-9 _____

Take A Star Trip! Yeoman Janice Rand
Star Enterprises, Inc., 1976
45 RPM, Songs written and performed by Grace Lee Whitney. Premiered at Equicon in California. Includes "Disco Trekkin' " and "Star Child." [8] .... 1.50 8-10 _____

Time Stealer
T.V. Power Records, Peter Pan
Star Trek Little LP 2305, 1975
Children's 7" 33⅓ RPM, slipcover jacket cartoons Kirk, Spock, McCy and a Viking on t.v. Enterprise bridge .... .79 5-7 _____

8. This private label record premiered at the 1976 West Coast Space Con fan convention.

Unusual Theme Song Anthology

Touch of Leonard Nimoy

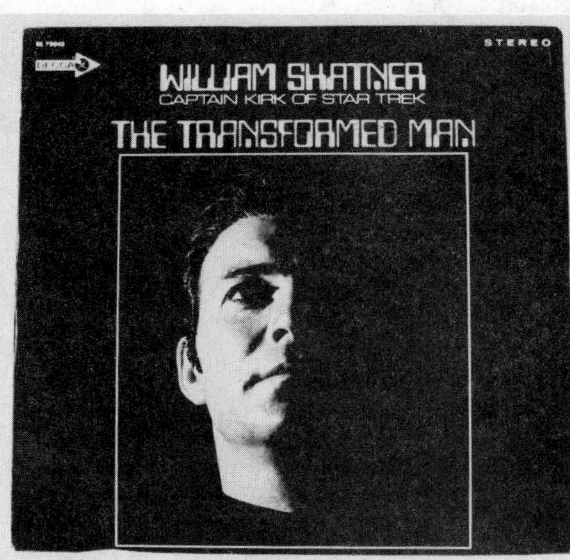

The Transformed Man

Time Stealer

	Issue	Current	Cost/Date
Star Trek Original Stories For Children 1514, 1979 Peter Pan pressing, 7" 45 RPM in 7"x8" slipcover, front has orange border with group photo of the eight cast members on STTMP bridge	.99	4-5	______
Star Trek Four all-New Action Adventure Stories 8168 T.V. Power Records, 1975 Children's 12" 33⅓ RPM album, slipcover jacket cartoons McCoy, Kirk, Spock and a crewman on the t.v. bridge. Rear is cartoon collage of crew with Enterprise overhead	2.49	7-9	______
T.V. (Television's) Greatest Hits, Vol. 1 TVT1100 Tee Vee Toons, 1986 Two record 33⅓ RPM set containing 65 t.v. themes, including Star Trek and featuring announcer Don Pardo	15.96	15-16	______
T.V. Themes WLP-306 Wonderland Records, 1977 Album, 33⅓ RPM including Star Trek, Baretta, Happy Days, Welcome Back Kotter, Laverne and Shirley and more	3	6-8	______
T.V. Theme Sing-Along Album RNLP 703 Rhino Records, 1985 CBS Special Products, 15 popular themes including Dobie Gillis, Mission: Impossible and Star Trek	9.50	9-10	______
Touch of Leonard Nimoy DLP 25910 Dot Records, 1969 Album, Leonard Nimoy sings musical scores and poetry by Charles Grean and George Tipton. Three original songs by Nimoy, including "Maiden Wine" as performed by Spock on "Plato's Stepchildren" episode. TT 25:46. Slipcover jacket front photos Nimoy among the trees.[9]	3.99	15-20	______
Transformed Man, William Shatner DL 75043 Decca Records, 1970 Album, Shakesperean narratives, chorales and instrumentals. A Don Ralke & Son production featuring couplet banding of duets to express multiple perspectives of the same theme. TT 34:07. Slipcover jacket front photos portrait of William Shatner	4.79	20-25	______

9. The original song "Maiden Wine" which was performed by Spock in **Plato's Stepchildren** was personally composed by Leonard Nimoy.

Two Sides of Leonard Nimoy

The Way I Feel

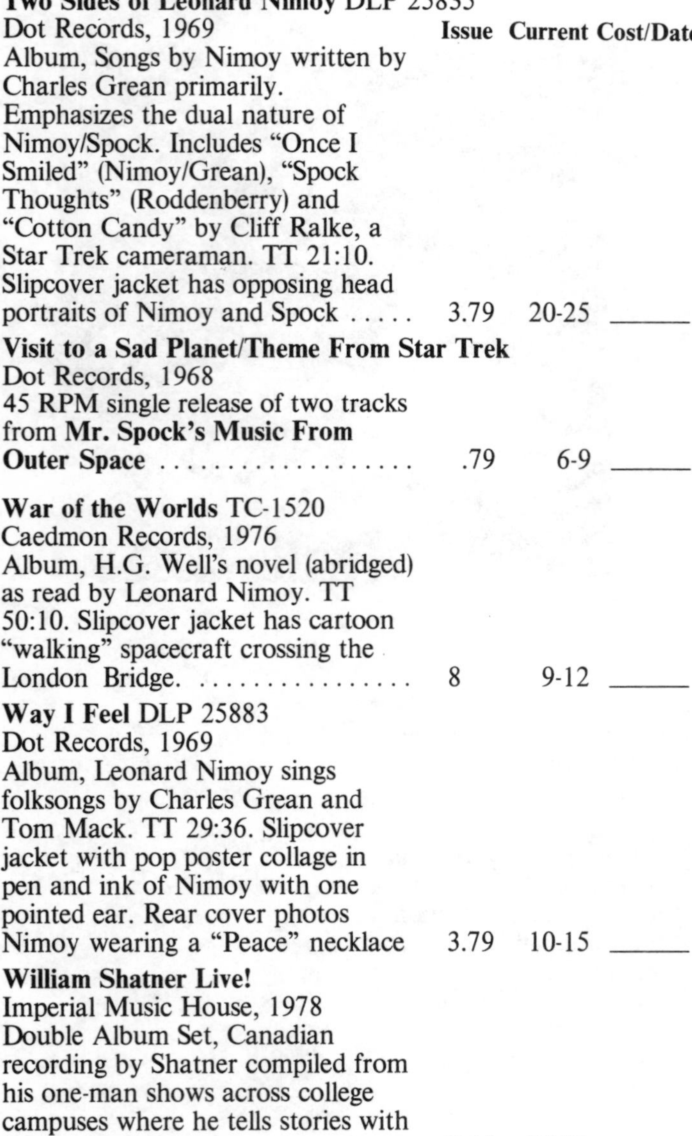

	Issue	Current	Cost/Date
Two Sides of Leonard Nimoy DLP 25835 Dot Records, 1969 Album, Songs by Nimoy written by Charles Grean primarily. Emphasizes the dual nature of Nimoy/Spock. Includes "Once I Smiled" (Nimoy/Grean), "Spock Thoughts" (Roddenberry) and "Cotton Candy" by Cliff Ralke, a Star Trek cameraman. TT 21:10. Slipcover jacket has opposing head portraits of Nimoy and Spock	3.79	20-25	______
Visit to a Sad Planet/Theme From Star Trek Dot Records, 1968 45 RPM single release of two tracks from **Mr. Spock's Music From Outer Space**	.79	6-9	______
War of the Worlds TC-1520 Caedmon Records, 1976 Album, H.G. Well's novel (abridged) as read by Leonard Nimoy. TT 50:10. Slipcover jacket has cartoon "walking" spacecraft crossing the London Bridge.	8	9-12	______
Way I Feel DLP 25883 Dot Records, 1969 Album, Leonard Nimoy sings folksongs by Charles Grean and Tom Mack. TT 29:36. Slipcover jacket with pop poster collage in pen and ink of Nimoy with one pointed ear. Rear cover photos Nimoy wearing a "Peace" necklace	3.79	10-15	______
William Shatner Live! Imperial Music House, 1978 Double Album Set, Canadian recording by Shatner compiled from his one-man shows across college campuses where he tells stories with music	7.95	25-30	______

AUDIO TAPES

	Issue	Current Cost/Date	
Academy Awards Startone Recordings, New York, 1980 Excerpts of Bill Shatner and Persis Kimbatta with STTMP's nominations in three awards categories, 11 minutes	3	3-4	_____
Animated Star Trek Startone Recordings One cassette contains a 24 minute episode. A-1 Yesteryear A-2 One of Our Planets is Missing A-3 The Lorelei Signal A-4 The Survivor A-5 Mudd's Passion A-6 The Ambergist Element A-7 Slaver Weapon A-8 Beyond the Farthest Star A-9 BEM A-10 Albatross			
24 minute, single episode	3.50	3-5	_____
24 minutes, double episode	4.75	5-6	_____
Bill Talks Startone Recordings **Number 1,** 1977 to 1983 Collection of talk show interviews with William Shatner, includes: 2 interviews from Mike Douglas, 1977 1 Tonight Show, 1979 1 Kidsworld, 1980 1 Merv Griffin, 1980 1 Toni Tenille, 1980 1 Over Easy, 1980 2 John Davidson, 1981 1 Hour Magazine, 2 Tonight Show, 1982 1 Good Morning America, 1982 1 Merv Griffin, 1982 1 Madame's Place, 1982 1 Merv Griffin, 1983 Also contains ads for Commodore, Kerosun, Visiting Hours, ST II, 183 minutes	10	10-12	_____
Number 2, 1982 to 1983 More recent interviews with William Shatner including: 1 Good Morning America 2 Tonight Show 1 Merv Griffin 1 Madame's Place 1 Merv Griffin, 1983 Also ads for his movie "Visiting Hours," Commodore, Kerosun and ST III, 81 min.	6.50	7-8	_____

	Issue	Current Cost/Date	
Episode Tapes Startone Recordings From the television series, all available in 45 minute formats or 50 minute formats, one cassette with one or two episodes.			
45 minute single episode	4	4-6	_____
50 minute single episode	4.75	5-7	_____
45 minute double episode	7.25	8-9	_____

ST-1 The Man Trap
ST-2 Charlie X
ST-3 Where No Man Has Gone Before
ST-4 The Naked Time
ST-5 The Enemy Within
ST-6 Mudd's Women
ST-7 What Are Little Girls Made Of?
ST-8 Miri
ST-9 Dagger of the Mind
ST-10 The Corbomite Maneuver
ST-11 The Menagerie, Part I
ST-12 The Menagerie, Part II
ST-13 The Conscience of the King
ST-14 Balance of Terror
ST-15 Shore Leave
ST-16 The Galileo 7
ST-17 The Squire of Gothos
ST-18 Arena
ST-19 Tomorrow is Yesterday
ST-20 Court-Martial
ST-21 The Return of the Archons
ST-22 Space Seed
ST-23 A Taste of Armegeddon
ST-24 This Side of Paradise
ST-25 The Devil in the Dark
ST-26 Errand of Mercy
ST-27 The Alternative Factor
ST-28 The City on the Edge of Forever
ST-29 Operation-Annihilate
ST-30 Amok Time
ST-31 Who Mourns for Adonais?
ST-32 The Changeling
ST-33 Mirror, Mirror
ST-34 The Apple
ST-35 The Doomsday Machine
ST-36 Catspaw
ST-37 I, Mudd
ST-38 Metamorphosis
ST-39 Journey to Babel
ST-40 Friday's Child
ST-41 The Deadly Years
ST-42 Obsession
ST-43 Wolf in the Wolf
ST-44 The Trouble with Tribbles
ST-45 The Gamesters of Triskelion
ST-46 A Piece of the Action
ST-47 The Immunity Syndrome
ST-48 A Private Little War
ST-49 Return to Tomorrow
ST-50 Patterns of Force
ST-51 By Any Other Name
ST-52 The Omega Glory
ST-53 The Ultimate Computer
ST-54 Bread and Circuses

AUDIO TAPES

ST-55 Assignment: Earth
ST-56 Spock's Brain
ST-57 The Enterprise Incident
ST-58 The Paradise Syndrome
ST-59 And the Children Shall Lead
ST-60 Is There in Truth No Beauty?
ST-61 Spectre of the Gun
ST-62 Day of the Dove
ST-63 For the World is Hollow and I Have Touched The Sky
ST-64 The Tholian Web
ST-65 Plato's Stepchildren
ST-66 Wink of an Eye
ST-67 The Empath
ST-68 Elaan of Troyius
ST-69 Whom Gods Destroy
ST-70 Let That Be Your Last Battlefield
ST-71 The Mark of Gideon
ST-72 That Which Survives
ST-73 The Lights of Zetar
ST-74 Requim for Methuselah
ST-75 The Way to Eden
ST-76 The Cloud Minders
ST-77 The Savage Curtain
ST-78 All Our Yesterdays
ST-79 Turnabout Intruder

	Issue	Current	Cost/Date
Greatest Sci-Fi Hits Crescendo Records, 1985			
Vol. I, GNPS 2138 Neil Norman & His Cosmic Orchestra play 16 themes, including theme from t.v. Star Trek	9.50	9-10	_____
Vol. II, GNPS 2133 16 movie themes, including theme from STTMP	9.50	9-10	_____
Halley's Comet: Once In A Lifetime S1788 Geodesium, 1986 Original music and sound effects, notes by Dr. William Gutsch, Chairman of American Museum - Hayden Planetarium. History and diagrams on viewing the comet, narrated by Leonard Nimoy	7.95		_____
Inside Star Trek Startone Recordings, 1976 Same as the LP by Columbia Records, Gene Roddenberry discusses various aspects of Trek and science fiction, 60 minutes	4.75	5-7	_____
John Davidson Startone Recordings, 1982 Entire original cast of STWOK with Bibi Besch are assembled in a tribute to the motion picture, 42 minutes	4	4-6	_____
Leonard Nimoy Presents Mr. Spock's Music From Outer Space Star Base Central, 1985 Tape cassette of this 1968 classic album of music and narratives, stereo	8	8-9	_____

	Issue	Current	Cost/Date
Leonard Talks Startone Recordings			
Number 1, 1976 to 1982 Recordings Collection of talk show interviews with Leonard Nimoy, including: Mike Douglas 1976 and 1980 Hot Hero Sandwich, 1980 Merv Griffin, 1980 John Davison, 1981 Toni Tenille, 1981 Entertainment Tonight, 1982 Today, 1982 Good Morning America, 1982 Also contains ads for ST II and Magnavox promotion, 1982. 92 minutes	7.25	7-8	_____
Number 2, 1982 Recordings Collection of more recent Leonard Nimoy interviews and television ads, short tape, 16 minutes	3.50	4-5	_____
Martian Chronicles CP-1466 Leonard Nimoy, Caedmon Records, 1979 Single cassette narration of Ray Bradbury's classic, Dolby System. Also includes "There Will Come Soft Rains" (7:55) and "Usher II" (26:35). "Martian Chronicles" (14:15), boxed	8.98	9-12	_____
Merv Griffin Startone Recordings, 1982 A salute to STWOK, includes guests Shatner, Nimoy, Kelley and Bibi Besch, 45 minutes	4	4-5	_____
Midday Live Startone Recordings, 1979 William Shatner reveals his thoughts on Star Trek, Kirk, and more, in-depth discussion of STTMP, 35 minutes	4	4-5	_____
Music From Return of The Jedi and Other Space Hits 79065, Odyssey Orchestra, 1983 Sine Qua Non productions, one stereo cassette which includes Star Trek T.V. theme	4.75	5-6	_____
Saturday Night Live Startone Recordings, 1975 Recording of Trek spoof with John Belushi as Kirk, Chevy Chase as Spock and Dan Ackroyd as McCoy and Scotty, 12 minutes	3	3-4	_____
Sci-Fi Spectacular Stage & Screen Productions, 1983 Movie music from ET, Close Encounters, Star Trek and many more, performed by the Cinema Sound Stage Orchestra, clear case	2.98	3-4	_____

AUDIO TAPES

Issue | Current | Cost/Date

Science Fiction Soundbook SBC 104
Caedmon Records, 1977
Packaged set of 4 cassette tapes plus a program booklet. 7"x10" library case includes Foundation - Shatner, Green Hills - Nimoy, Martian Chronicles - Nimoy and Mimsy Were the Borograves - Shatner .... 15 15-25 ______

Space Movies SSCX716
Stage & Screen Productions, 1986
Dolby stereo cassette of movie themes: ET, Tron, Star Wars, Planet of the Apes and STTMP......... 2.99 3-4 ______

Star Trek 704-270
Varese Sarabande Records, Inc. 1985
Digital cassette recording of four t.v. episode scores: "Charlie X," "Corbomite Maneuver," "Mudd's Women," and "Doomsday Machine," Fred Steiner & the Royal Philharmonic Orchestra .... 7.95 8-9 ______

Star Trek
Fifth Continent Music Corp., 1985

Volume 1 LXDC-703
Original t.v. scores from t.v. series: "Is There In Truth No Beauty" and "Paradise Syndrome." (See records listings for production details) ..... 7.95 8-9 ______

Volume 2, LXDC-704
Original scores from episode: "Conscience of the King," "Spectre of the Gun," "Enemy Within" and "I, Mudd." (See records listing for production details) .... 7.95 8-9 ______

Star Trek Tapes
Startone Recordings, 1978
Same as the LP by Sell Enterprises, excerpts from convention appearances by Shatner, Nimoy and cast, 30 minute .... 3.50 4-5 ______

Star Trek: The Motion Picture
Startone Recordings, 1979
One cassette featuring the movie, 132 minutes .... 8 8-9 ______

Star Trek The Motion Picture JSA-36334
Columbia Records, 1979
One Columbia TC 8 stereo cartridge with music from the motion picture soundtrack, 4"x5" in cut-out slipcase. 8 track format .... 7.98 9-12 ______

Star Trek The Motion Picture Read-Along Adventure 161DC
Buena Vista Records, 1983
Story and photos from the movie with 24-page booklet and story tape cassette featuring character dialogue, sound effects and music. Identical recordings on both sides of the cassette. 7¼"x11½" plastic pouch and cardboard mount. Booklet is 7"x7". .... 3.96 5-7 ______

Issue | Current | Cost/Date

Star Trek II: The Wrath of Kahn
Startone Recordings, 1982
One cassette featuring the story from the movie, 113 minutes ..... 7.50 8-9 ______

Star Trek II - The Wrath of Kahn Read-Along Adventure 162 DC
Buena Vista Records, 1983
Story and photos from the second movie with 24-page booklet and story tape cassette featuring character dialogue, sound effects and music. Identical recording on both sides of the cassette. 7¼"x11½" plastic pouch and cardboard mount. Booklet is 7"x7" .... 3.96 5-7 ______

Star Trek II Interviews
Startone Recordings, 1982
STWOK is discussed with Ricardo Mantalban on Merv Griffin and the Tonight Show, Kirstie Alley talks on Merv Griffin, 34 minutes .... 4 4-5 ______

Star Trek II Radio Special
Startone Recordings, 1982
The voyage of Star Trek, a detailed history of the t.v. series phenomenon up to STWOK, comments by all major characters, Roddenberry, etc., 51 minutes .... 4.75 5-6 ______

Star Trek III - The Search For Spock Read-Along Adventure 163 DC
Buena Vista Records, 1984
Story and photos from the third movie with 24-page booklet and story tape cassette featuring character dialogue, sound effects and music. Identical recording on both sides of the cassette. 7¼"x11½" plastic pouch and cardboard mount. Booklet is 7"x7" .... 2.97 4-6 ______

Star Trek III: The Search For Spock 4XKK-12360
Capital Records, 1984
Soundtrack for the movie, composed and conducted by James Horner, expanded dynamic range, TT 41:00 .. 8.98 9-10 ______

Themes From E.T. The Extra Terrestrial And More
MCAC-6114
MCA Records, Inc., 1982
Theme songs arranged and conducted by Walter Murphey, includes the Theme from Star Trek (t.v. series), clear plastic case .... 2.99 4-5 ______

Today Show
Startone Recordings, 1982
Preview of ST II with Shatner, Montalban, Nicholas Meyer, Bob Sallin and Ken Ralston of Industrial Light and Magic, 16 minutes ..... 3.50 4-5 ______

Trek Bloopers
Startone Recordings, 1979
Same as the LP by Blue Pear Records. Rare third season out-takes from Star Trek T.V. series, 55 minutes .... 4.75 5-6 ______

AUDIO TAPES

Issue Current Cost/Date

T.V. Themes C64166
Stage & Screen Productions, 1983
Instrumentals and vocal recreations from favorite television themes. Includes Star Trek, M*A*S*H, Mission: Impossible and Hillstreet Blues, plus 18 more. Performed by the Video Theatre Orchestra. Plastic case photos J.R. from the series Dallas .... 2.98 3-4 ______

20/20
Startone Recordings, 1979
In-depth look at Trek fandom with Roddenberry, Shatner, Nimoy, Kelley, Doohan, Nichols, Joan Winston, Bjo Trimble, Lee Cole and more, 15 minutes .... 3 4-5 ______

Uhura Sings
aR-Way Productions, 1986
Single tape cassette featuring old and new songs by Nichelle Nichols, includes new version Star Trek theme, Space Rock, Ode to the Space Shuttle and Beyond Antares . 8.50 8-9 ______

War of the Worlds
Leonard Nimoy, Caedmon Records, 1979
Single cassette narration of H.G. Well's classic, Dolby System, TT 23:38 side one, 26:24 side two, boxed .... 8.98 9-10 ______

You & I
Leonard Nimoy, Petunia Productions, 1978
Leonard Nimoy speaking the words of love from his book by Celestial Arts .... 5 6-9 ______

SHEET MUSIC

Follow Your Star
Caterpillar Music Corp., 1979
Lyrics and music as recorded by Leonard Nimoy .... 1.50 2-4 ______

Sing A Song of Trekkkin'
Caterpillar Music Corp., 1979
Roberta Rogow. Fun-filled folio of twenty Trekker filk songs as composed and arranged by the fen. .... 4.95 5-8 ______

Space Medley
Screen Gems/Columbia Pictures
Full score conductor arrangement by Fox Fanfare Music, Inc. Concert Band Medley by John Tatgenhorst for a 19 piece orchestra. Scores incluce "Theme from Star Trek (Bruin Music)" "Close Encounters" and "Star Wars - Main Title." 9"x12" jacket cover contains individual scores. Black cover with pink lettering. C0070B1X, 1979 .... 40 40-42 ______

Star Trek Theme
Bruin Music Co., 1966
Single-sheet musical score from the t.v. series as composed by Alexander Courage .... 1 6-8 ______

Issue Current Cost/Date

Star Trek The Motion Picture
Star Beyond Time, the Love Theme From Star Trek The Motion Picture
Ensign Music Corp., 1979
Lyrics by Larry Kusik, music by Gerry Goldsmith, three pages of lyrics and the score, 8½"x11" sheets .... 2.50 4-6 ______

Star Trek - The Musical Themes
Charles Hensen II, Music & Books of California, Inc., 1979
Movie score from STTMP (Goldsmith, Ensign Music Co.) and the "Love Theme from STTMP," also includes the t.v. Theme (Courage, Bruin Music Co.) Plastic spiral bound book has heavy cardstock pages with b/w and color promo photos. Front cover shows "Rainbow" promo poster designed by Bob Peak, 8½"x11", F812la ... 4.95 12-16 ______

Star Trek II - The Wrath of Kahn

"Highlights of Star Trek II The Wrath of Kahn"
Famous Music Corp., 1982
Full score conductor's arrangement. Concert band medley transcribed by Jack Bullock, music by James Horner, for 21-piece orchestra. Jacket contains individual instrument scores. Black cover with "Starburst" movie logo, 9¼"x12", 2755HB1X .... 50 50-52 ______

"Paramount Presents The Main Theme From Star Trek II The Wrath of Kahn"
Famous Muisc Corp., 1982
Music scores in assorted packages:
Children - The Robert Schultz "Big Note - Color Me" Series with simple score on three-page fold out, heavy paper. Includes a spirograph galaxy to color. Cover has a clown holding a crayon, balloon and piano keyboard, 9"x12" 0237MP3X ..... 2 2-3 ______
Adult Beginning to Intermediate - nine pages of sheet music as composed by Jamesd Horner. Cover features the movie "Starburst" logo, 9"x12" 0237MSMX .... 2.50 4-6 ______
Popular Music - the Robert Schultz "Popular Music Made Easy" series with score from the movie on four glossy sheets. Cover has multi-colored grand piano against white background, 9"x12" 0237MP2X ... 2.25 2-3 ______

Star Trek III - The Search For Spock

"Star Trek III - The Search For Spock"
Columbia Pictures Publications, 1984
Softbound book collection of nine musical scores from the movie arranged for piano/vocal/chords, by Ed McLean. Includes four pages of color and b/w photos. Front cover shows cropped "Neon-glo" movie promo poster, 52 pages, P0578SMX 9.95 12-16 ______

SHEET MUSIC

	Issue	Current	Cost/Date
"Paramount Presents The Search For Spock, Theme From Star Trek III" Famous Music Corp., 1984 Music arranged by James Horner, seven page score title theme for medium level piano solo. Glossy stock, cover has a cropped "Neon-glo" poster listing credits, 9"x12" 1528SSMX	2.50	3-5	_____
200-Broadway, Motion Picture and Television Songbook Columbia Pictures Publication Tradepaper, plastic spiral bound songbook containing 200 assorted scores. Edited by Carol Cuellas for Central Litho press in Miami. Includes: Theme from Star Trek by A. Courage, pp. 270-273 Main Theme Star Trek II by James Horner, pp. 232-240 Main Theme Star Trek III by James Horner, pp. 657-663 Music compositions are adapted for piano/vocal/chords, 703 pages, 1984	29.95	30-32	_____

	Issue	Current	Cost/Date
You Are Not Alone Music and lyrics by Don Christopher Performed by Leonard Nimoy on the album **Leonard Nimoy Present's Mr. Spock's Music From Outer Space** Petunia Sheet Music Co., 1967 Sheet music arrangement	.50	3-5	_____
Caterpillar Music Co., 1979 New arrangement for this song. ...	1.50	2-4	_____
Visit To A Sad Planet Caterpillar Music Co., 1979 Narration and music by Don Christopher from the album **Leonard Nimoy Presents Mr. Spock's Music From Outer Space**	1.50	2-4	_____

POSTERS AND POSTERBOOKS

For the collector of Star Trek posters, three distinct varieties exist. There are t.v. posters (portraying characters or scenes from three seasons of episodes) movie posters (scenes and characters from the movies) and theater posters (official film promos).

Posters can be purchased in two design medias: photographic portraits and enlarged photo stills or special artwork renditions. Usually Star Trek character shots and action scenes are simply stock film footage photos blown up to poster dimensions. Unusual art posters drawn by hand are fan generated in most cases. However, theater posters often appear as colorful artwork drawings as a result of the need to be able to reproduce them over and over again in magazines and newspapers.

Theater posters are probably the most popular memorabilia among Star Trek fans. They also tend to raise in value in a minimum number of years. For theater poster enthusiasts, there is an established delineation of type which is standard within the movie industry.

One-Sheet – A theater poster with a general size of 27½" x 43" in size.
Half Sheet – Theater poster with the dimensions of 22" x 28" or 22¼" x 30".
Insert poster – Theater poster with the usual size of 14"x36" or 14¼"x38".
Theater window card – This runs 14⅛" x 22⅛" or 14⅜" x 24⅛".

Posterbooks

Few Star Trek posterbooks were produced. The most valuable as a collectible is the set of 17 posterbooks issued by Paradise Press in 1976. These were issued monthly until late 1978.

Perhaps the most interesting posterbook for collectors to keep an eye out for is the Paradise Press 1979 **Star Trek The Motion Picture Poster Book.** Inside the text portion a Klingon Battle Cruiser appears as a photo inset, but it's upside down.

Posters

Star Trek T.V. Series Posters

	Issue	Current	Cost/Date
Action Collage - "Stardate 7431.09" (Art) Jim Steranko, 1974 Color action scenes from the series, heads of Kirk, Spock, McCoy and Enterprise with Klingon ships either side, lettered, 23"x32"	3	5-8	______
Action Collage P69 (Art) Monster Times Magazine, 1974 Color on glossy paper, portraits of Sulu, Enterprise, Dr. Severin, transporter scene, Spock, Uhura, Chekov, Kang, Marta, Scotty, Kirk and McCoy, 17"x22"	2	10-15	______
Action Collage (Art) Monster Times Magazine, 1974 Color on glossy paper, Sulu, t.v. Kahn and McCoy in corners, large bust Spock and Kirk in the middle, 17"x22"	2	8-10	______
Action Collage - "Star Trek" P51 (Art) Monster Times Magazine, 1976 B/w, by Greg Morrow, collage with Kirk forecenter holding phaser, Spock at right shoulder, wavy lettering in upper right corner, 22"x34"	1.50	7-10	______
Action Collage - P1012 (Photo) Langley Associates, 1976 Color, 52 action scenes from the t.v. series, 20"x24"	3	7-9	______
Action Collage - Fantasy Universe (Art) Starlog Poster Gallery, 1977 Full color by famed sci-fi artist Ken Barr, shows wispy montage of Kirk in forefront holding phaser and communicator, also has Spock, McCoy, Sulu, Uhura and Scotty behind him, Enterprise above firing twin phasers, planetscape near bottom, 20"x28"	3	6-8	______

	Issue	Current	Cost/Date
Action Collage (photo) Carsan, 1977 Color, 18 photos insets, shows Enterprise firing phasers center, Spock with phaser in lower right and Kirk with tribble pile in upper left, 23"x34" [1]	4.29	6-8	______
Action Collage - "Enterprise Incidents" (Art) Starbase Central, 1982 Full color, high quality poster print, busts of Kirk, Spock and female Commander from this episode, also various fantasy action scenes, 22"x30"	4	6-8	______
Calendar Posters - 1975 (Photo) Starbase Central B/w 12-month calendar on bottom with photo montage of series' episodes inserted throughout, reads "A Calendar for the Crew of the Starship Enterprise," 23"x35"	2	3-6	______
Calendar Poster - 1976 (Photo) Star Base Central B/w, similar to the above 1975 edition, reads "Live Long and Prosper," 23"x35"	2	3-6	______
Crew (Art) 1976 B/w, group shot with Kirk holding communicator, Uhura, Spock and Sulu around, 19"x28"	1.50	3-4	______
Crew P1014 (Photo) Langley Associates, 1976 Color, transporter pads, shows Kirk, Spock, Uhura, Sulu, Chekov, Chapel, Scotty and McCoy, 20"x24"	3	5-6	______
Starbase Central STP001, smaller, 17½"x23" and in black and white	3	3-4	______

1. An advertisement for this poster appeared in the magazine Super Heroes.

POSTERS

Issue | Current | Cost/Date

Crew-Mini Posters (Photo)
Fantasy House, 1974
Color, six mini-posters sealed in transparent plastic bag with card-stock top; Kirk, Spock, McCoy, Scotty, Uhura, Sulu, 4"x6" .... 1 3-5 ______

Crossword Puzzle Poster. Photo courtesy of Running Press.

Crossword Puzzle Poster - "Incredible Intergalactic Star Trek," (Art)
Running Press, 1976
Color, unusual fill-in shape of the Enterprise, drawing of Kirk and Spock firing phaser right hand corner, mailed folded, flat, 24"x36" ... 2.95 4-6 ______

Enterprise, Bridge of P2181 (Art)
Lincoln Enterprises, 1967; 1983
Full color promo poster based on the episode "Where No Man Has Gone Before," shows Enterprise circling planet with busts of Kirk and Spock in foreground, bridge scene center, 16"x20"[2] .... 2.50 4-5 ______

Enterprise P1008 (Photo)
Langley Associates, 1976
Full color, starship in deep space firing twin phasers, 24"x36" .... 3 4-6 ______

Enterprise (Photo)
Smithsonian Institution, c. 1970's
Color, blue and white background with model Enterprise from the series flying upward, 18"x24" ..... 2 4-6 ______

Enterprise 2160 (Art)
Lincoln Enterprises, 1976
Original color wall poster of this catalog number (2160). Background is flocked to give 3-D effect of soft velvet, starship is the t.v. version, 24"x36" .... 4 10-15 ______

Enterprise (Art)
Carsan, 1977
Starship facing forward and hovering over planet in lower left, 23"x34" .... 3.29 4-6 ______

Issue | Current | Cost/Date

Enterprise (Art)
Dynamic Publishing Company, 1976
Black Light poster, color with black flocking, starship center, reads "Star Trek" above the ship, 21"x31" .... 2.99 5-7 ______

Enterprise (Firing Phasers) (Art)
1976
B/w, starship in upper left corner, Kirk, Spock, Chekov, McCoy, Scotty, Sulu and other crew below, 19"x28" .... 1.50 3-4 ______

Enterprise and Crew (Photo)
Fantasy House, 1975
B/w, shows starship center, circular photo inserts of Kirk in upper left, Spock in lower left and McCoy in lower right, Limited Edition, 17½"x22½" .... 1 4-8 ______

Enterprise and Crew P1009 (Photo)
Langley Associates, 1976
Color, starship against starry sky with photos insets of Kirk, Spock, McCoy, Scotty, Sulu, Chekov and Uhura, 20"x24" .... 3 5-7 ______

Enterprise and Crew P84 (Photo)
Monster Times Magazine, 1976
B/w, starship center, circular photo insets of Kirk, Scotty, Rand and Chekov above, and Spock, Uhura, Sulu and McCoy below, 24"x36" .. 2.50 5-8 ______
Smaller re-release 17½"x30" ...... 3 3-4 ______

Enterprise and Crew "Star Trek Keeps On Trekkin!"
STP004 (Photo)
Starbase Central, 1984
B/w, block lettering over t.v. Enterprise and cut-outs of McCoy, Chapel, Scotty, Chekov, Uhura, Sulu and Spock around Kirk in command chair, 16"x24" .... 3 3-5 ______

Enterprise/Klingon Cruiser P1007 (Art)
Langley Associates, 1976
Color rendering of starship and battle cruiser engaged in phaser battle, blue and white, 20"x24" .... 3 4-6 ______

Enterprise/Klingon Cruisers P1010 (Photo)
Langley Associates, 1976
Color, starship firing twin phasers at cruiser while second enemy hovers below, 20"x24" .... 3 4-6 ______

"Enterprise, U.S.S. Space Cruiser/Battle Cruiser Klingon Empire" Reversible (Photo)
Star Trek Con, 1972
B/w, first reversible Trek poster. One side starship with bridge schematics, second side blueprint-style overlay and comparison chart of starship and Klingon craft, 18½"x22½" .... 1.50 8-12 ______

2. This poster also appeared as the cover art for the original printing of James Blish's **Star Trek 1,** episode novelization released in 1967.

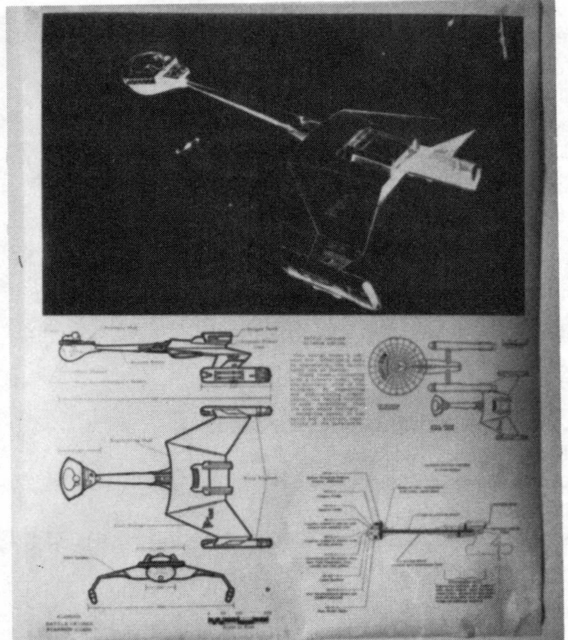

The first reversible Star Trek Poster. Reverse is Enterprise. 1972.

	Issue	Current	Cost/Date
Episode Scene - "Day of the Dove" (Photo) Star Trek Galore, 1977 Color, 19"x23" Klingon Landing Party	2	4-6	______
Kang and Klingons surrounding Kirk, McCoy, Chekov and other crew	2	4-6	______
Episode Scene - "Gamesters of Triskelion" (Photo) Paramount Pictures, 1984 Pictures Shahna (Angelique Pettyjohn) holding weapon and standing by battle sheild	3	4-6	______
Episode Scene - "Journey to Babel" (Photo) Star Trek Galore, 1977 Color, 19"x23" Feast Scene and table spread, with Spock, Amanda, McCoy and Kirk	2	4-6	______
Group Shot of Spock, Amanda and Kirk	2	4-6	______
Episode Scene - "The Menagerie - Rigel IV" (Photo) Langley Associates, 1976 Color, moonrise over planetscape, Pike and Vina before gothic palace, 20"x24"	3	6-8	______
Episode Scene - "Taste of Armageddon" (Photo) Star Trek Galore, 1977 Color, low-story modernistic cityscape with landing party on righthand side, 19"x23"	2	4-6	______
"Kirk" Blacklight Poster (Art) Dynamic Publishing, 1976 Color with black flocking, 4 poses of Kirk with Enterprise on top, lettering on bottom, 20"x24"	2.99	8-12	______
Kirk, Captain (Photo) Darghis Associates, 1976 Black and white format Kirk in command chair (Spock in background with arms crossed), 3390, 17½"x30"	1	4-6	______
Close-up, holding phaser pistol, 17¼"x23"	1	4-6	______
Kirk - As Romulan P2171 (Art) Lincoln Enterprises, 1983 Color art by Doug Little, bust of Kirk as Romulan officer from "Enterprise Incident," 17"x23"	3.95	4-6	______
Kirk - Many Faces P2161 (Photo) Lincoln Enterprises, 1983 Color, 13 poses of Kirk through the 3 t.v. episode seasons, insets in ovals around a central close-up, blue background	4.95	5-7	______
Kirk - With Lirpa (Photo) Star Trek Galore, 1977 Color, waist shot of Kirk holding Vulcan weapon and facing forward, 19"x23"	2	4-6	______
Kirk - "United Federation Command Wants You" (Art) F. Boichot, 1975 Color, waist-shot of Kirk in yellow shirt pointing finger, with lettering	3	5-8	______
Kirk - Lifesize Poster LS1000 (Photo) Langley Associates, 1976 Color, vertical poster of Kirk on transporter pad, velour shirt over black T-shirt (2nd season), phaser on belt, 21"x72"	3.50	5-8	______
Kirk-Mini Poster P86 (Photo) Monster Times, 1976 Color, bust of Kirk in dress uniform, 9"x12"	1	1-3	______
Kirk - Personality Poster (Photo) Stephen Sally/Jeri of Hollywood, 1967 B/w reproduction of Paramount publicity still, Kirk wearing heavy velour rib-neck tunic with braided cuffs. Studio matt background, mailed flat and folded in 6"x9" envelope, 22½"x33" poster, thin paper	2	15-20	______
Kirk and Spock P1017 (Art) Langley Associates, 1976 Color, rendering of Kirk and Spock busts and background Enterprise, orange planet and eclipsed sun, 20"x24"[3]	2.99	7-10	______
Kirk and Spock - Door Poster (Art) Carsan, 1977 Color, busts of Kirk and Spock center, with Enterprise overhead, Klingon ship below, planetscape in lower left, very long, vertical format, 36"x96"	5.95	8-12	______

3. This poster appeared as the cover art for the premiere issue of **Starlog** magazine in August, 1977.

Vintage Poster, Jeri of Hollywood, 1967

Issue Current Cost/Date

Kirk and Spock - "Keep On Trekkin' " Centerfold (Art)
Monster Times Magazine, 1975
7-tone centerfold poster from magazine Vol. 1, No. 20. Features caricature of Spock followed by Captain Kirk, both in the exaggerated "Truckin' " mode, newspaper stock, 16½"x23" ...... .50 4-6 ______

Kirk and Spock - "Space ... The Final Frontier" Centerfold (Art)
Monster Times Magazine, 1972
Color, 6-tone centerfold poster from Vol. 1, No. 2. Features central Kirk in comic art drawing holding phaser rifle and close-up of Spock with tricorder; also 6 other character profiles. The entire t.v. teaser into is printed, newspaper stock, 16½"x23" .... .50 5-8 ______

Kirk and Spock - "Star Trek" P1012 (Photo)
Langley Associates, 1976
Color, surrealistic overlay of Kirk and Spock busts in reverse negative effect. Lettering on top, 22"x24" .. 3 5-8 ______

Kirk and Spock - With Yeoman Rand P67
Monster Times Magazine, 1976
B/w, reprint of Paramount publicity still, Yeoman Rand, Kirk and Spock holding out lighting devices defensively .... 1 5-7 ______

Issue Current Cost/Date

Klingon - Battle Cruiser P1011 (Photo)
Langley Associates, 1976
Color, ship in deep space, 20"x24". 3 5-7 ______

Klingon- Cruiser Blueprint 417 (Art)
Paraside Press, 1978; Geoffrey Mandel
Print shows exterior dimensions of ship, four views plus special cross-section of bridge, mailed flat and folded, 24"x36" .... 2.50 4-6 ______

Klingon - Recruiting Poster (Art)
F. Boichot, 1975
Color, chest-shot of Kang from "Day of the Dove," reads "Klingons, your duty is to serve the Empire" .... 3 6-8 ______

Koenig, Walter - "Peace" Poster (Photo)
Starbase Central, 1984; distributor
B/w, 60's vintage photo of Walter against a galaxy background. Row of 8 profile poses line the bottom, signed "Peace, Walter Koenig" .... 3 5-6 ______

McCoy (Photo)
Darghis Associates, 1976
B/w, close-up, looking left, 17½"x23" .... 3 4-6 ______

McCoy - Personality Poster (Photo)
Stephen Sally/Jeri of Hollywood, 1967
B/w, reproduction of Paramount publicity still, shows 2nd season McCoy, mailed flat and folded in 6"x9" envelope, 22½"x33", thin paper stock .... 2 10-15 ______

Leonard Nimoy Personality Poster - 1970s Style.

POSTERS

Vintage poster of Mr. Spock, Personality Posters, 1967.

	Issue	Current	Cost/Date
Spock - "Leonard Nimoy" 231 (Photo) Personality Posters Mfg., 1967 Color, the now-classic portrait of Spock holding the model Enterprise over gridwork background.[4]	1.75	10-15	______
Spock - Lifesize Poster LS1001 (Photo) Langley Associates, 1976 Color, vertical poster of Spock on transporter pad, 21"x72"	3.50	5-8	______
Spock P50 (Art) Monster Times Magazine, 1976 B/w, drawing by Virgil Finlay, shows head-shot of pilot episode Spock, facing right, 17"x22"	1.50	5-8	______
Signed artist's drawing	3	10-12	______
Spock, First Officer, P83 (Photo) Monster Times Magazine, 1976 B/w, waist-shot of Spock holding tricorder, 17"x22"	1	4-6	______
Spock, Mister P64 (Photo) Monster Times Magazine, 1976 B/w, low quality photo of Spock in early make-up from pilot film, working over console, 17"x22"	1	3-5	______
Spock, Mister 3391 (Photo) Darghis Associates, 1976 B/w, waist-shot of Spock holding phaser, Galileo shuttlecraft in back, from "Metamorphosis," 17½"x23"	1	3-5	______
Paradise Studios, 1983 **Mr. Spock** ST-12 Color reprint, 24"x36"	3.95	4-6	______
"Spock" Blacklight Poster (Art) Dynamic Publishing Company, 1976 Color, with black flocking, 4 poses of Spock with Enterprise circling planet in upper right, lettering on bottom, 21"x31"	2.99	8-12	______
Spock - Many Faces P2162 (Photo) Lincoln Enterprises, 1983 Color, 13 poses of Spock through the three t.v. seasons, photo insets in ovals around a central close-up, orange background	4.95	5-7	______
Spock Personality Poster (Photo) Stephen Sally/Jeri of Hollywood, 1967 B/w, reproduction of Paramount publicity still, Spock with early make-up, short bangs, heavy velour tunic, right hand on computer console, backdrop is galaxy swirl, mailed flat and folded in 6"x9" envelope, 22½"x33"	2	15-20	______
Spock - "I Am Not Spock" (Art) Celestial Arts, 1975 Gold on black, poster size edition of the cover art from the tradepaper by the same title. Shows Spock in close-up giving the Vulcan salute, 24"x36"[5]	2	5-8	______

"Spock In Pain" by Mattewillis Baird, 1973.

4. This poster appeared as the slipcover jacket photo for Leonard Nimoy's first record album, *Leonard Nimoy Presents Mr. Spock's Music From Outer Space,* released by Dot Records in 1968.
5. This poster was offered through special order from the publisher of the **I Am Not Spock** autobiography, Celestial Arts.

POSTERS

	Issue	Current	Cost/Date
"Spock in Pain" (Art) Huckleberry Designs, 1973 B/w, print of the charcoal artwork by Mattewillis Baird contest entry; caption reads "Grand Prize Star Trek Convention Art Show NYC 1972," heavy gauge paper, 23"x29" [6]	1.50	20-30	______
Spock - "Keep On Trekkin' " P82 (Art) Monster Times Magazine, 1975 Color, reprint of the Kirk and Spock poster previously listed. Abbreviated version shows only Spock, towards the left, lettering on right, 17"x22", not a centerfold	2	2-4	______
Spock - "Star Trek" (Photo) Familiar Faces, The W.O.R.K.S., 1974 Heavy Guage chrome mylar film in ultra gloss, black photo stencil of Spock holding communicator, black block lettering is on lefthand side, 19¾"x24"	5	15-20	______
Spock- and Nixon P2178 (Art) Lincoln Enterprises, 1983 Color, humorous rendering by Doug Little, shows Spock performing Vulcan Mind Meld on President Nixon, 17"x22"	3.95	5-7	______
Shuttlecraft, Galileo (Art) Darghis Associates, 1976 Color, drawing by John Carlance, Galileo in deep space, 23¼"x35"	3	4-6	______
Shuttlecraft, Galileo ST-14 (Art) Paradis Studio, 1983 Color, shuttlecraft lifting off of moonscape, craft is against black starfield, craters below, 22"x34"	3.95	5-7	______
Sulu, Lt. (Photo) Darghis Associates, 1976 B/w, close-up of Sulu with arms crossed, looking left, made from Paramount publicity photo, 17½"x23"	1	3-5	______
Takei, George (Photo) Starbase Central, distributors, 1984 B/w, campaign poster for Takei while he was running for City Council, 10th District, shows Takei in shirt and tie	3	4-5	______
Wanted Poster - "Dead or Alive - Harcourt Fenton Mudd, 10,000 Credits" (Photo) Paradis Studios, 1983 B/w on yellow-tan paper, shows old style wanted poster with photo inset of Mudd, includes character description, aliases, etc., 10½"x17"	1	2-3	______

Star Trek The Motion Picture Posters

	Issue	Current	Cost/Date
Commedy Calendar Poster P2166 (Art) Lincoln Enterprises, 1983 Full color, whimsical montage of characters and scenes from STTMP, shows Enterprise circling planet in center with 12 month calendar at bottom, 24"x36"	3.95	5-6	______
Enterprise P2160 (Photo) Lincoln Enterprises, 1983 Full color new Enterprise against black, starry sky, 24"x36" [7]	4.95	5-6	______
Enterprise (Premium Poster) (Photo) Proctor and Gamble, 1979 Full color Enterprise in center with square photo inserts of the various other movie vessels, 17"x22"	—	3-5	______
Kirk P2156 (Photo) Lincoln Enterprises, 1983 Color bust of Kirk wearing white and gray uniform, facing right, 17"x22"	2.50	3-5	______
Kirk P2172 (Art) Lincoln Enterprises, 1983 Full color rendering by Doug Little, chest shot of Admiral Kirk facing right, 17"x22"	3.95	4-6	______
Kirk and Spock P2158 (Photo) Lincoln Enterprises, 1983 Full color bust of Spock on left, Kirk on right, with Enterprise in the background flying through nebula, no writing (also issued as Procter and Gamble Premium, 1979), 17"x22"	2.50	3-5	______
Kirk and Spock P2176 (Art) Lincoln Enterprises, 1983 Full color drawing by Doug Little, busts of Kirk and Spock in grey-blue uniforms, facing left, 17"x22"	3.95	4-6	______
Klingon and Reagan P2179 (Art) Lincoln Enterprises, 1983 Color artwork by Doug Little, humorous scene of Reagan in STTMP uniform and a Klingon, Enterprise and Klingon Cruiser in upper left corner, 17"x22"	3.95	4-6	______
McCoy P2154 (Photo) Lincoln Enterprises, 19083 Color featuring close-up of STTMP Doctor wearing white uniform and holding medical device, white borders, 17"x22"	3.95	4-6	______
Nurse Chapel (Art) Lincoln Enterprises, 1985 STTMP bust of Chapel by Doug Little, with Enterprise on right side	3.95	4-6	______

6. The New York City Star Trek Convention held in January, 1972 was the very first public fan convention dedicated exclusively to Star Trek.
7. This is a re-released No. 2160 featuring the movie version starship Enterprise. The original No. 2160 showed the t.v. ship with an unusual "flocked" background (See T.V. Posters Listing).

POSTERS

Issue | Current | Cost/Date

Spock In Kolinar P2174 (Art)
Lincoln Enterprises, 1983
Duel busts of Spock by Doug Little, one in black robe, other in Vulcan dress, 17"x22" . . . . 3.95 4-6 ______

"Star Trek" (Photo)
Star Base Central, 1984
STTMP color portside Enterprise with lettering overhead, printed on color mylar film . . . . 10 12-16 ______

Star Trek Crew P2155 (Photo)
Lincoln Enterprises, 1983
Color, group shot of the STTMP characters, eleven original crewmembers standing or sitting on the bridge, 17"x22" . . . . 2.50 3-4 ______

"Star Trek The Motion Picture" Action Poster
Coca-Cola Company, 1979
Premium poster featuring 3-panel photos and Coke trademark . . . . . . — 4-6 ______

"Star Trek The Motion Picture" Characters
Sales Corp. of America, 1979
Full color art planetscape with Enterprise and Vulcan Shuttle with horizontal bottom photo inserts of Acturian, Sulu, Scotty, Decker, Ilia, Kirk, Spock, McCoy, Uhura and two other aliens.
Sales Corp. Mail Order (same as above) . . . . 3 4-5 ______
Lesney/AMT model box order (above poster with reversible second side picture in 3-D litho; 3-D glasses included) . . . . 3 6-10 ______

Issue | Current | Cost/Date

Sales Corp. of America, 1979; 22"x48" printed on full color chrome mylar . . . . 5 6-8 ______
Coca-Cola Company, 1979; 11"x23", includes movie character busts Ilia, Spock, Kirk, McCoy, Decker lower right corner . . . . 2.50 4-5 ______
Star Base Central, 1979; 24"x48" Wall Size: derivative of Kimble's work, top reads "Starship U.S.S. Enterprise," bottom "Interior/ Exterior Specifications and Data Systems Data" . . . . 4 5-7 ______

"Star Trek The Motion Picture" Movie Cast Poster (Photo)
Paramount Pictures, 1979
Full color advance promotional poster, shows Enterprise turning towards right with horizontal photo insets of cast along bottom: Kirk, Spock, McCoy, Scotty, Uhura, Chekov and Decker, 18"x25" . . . . . 3 10-20 ______

Star Trek The Motion Picture - The Human Advanture Is Just Beginning" Movie Cast Poster
Lincoln Enterprises, P 2157, 1979; PPC (Photo)
Full color promo poster with busts of McCoy, Kirk, Spock, Ilia and Decker on the bottom; Enterprise on top right, lettering over a starburst center, 17"x22" [9] . . . . 2.50 4-6 ______

"Star Trek The Motion Picture - The 23rd Century Now" Movie Cast Pictures, (Photo)
Paramount Pictures, 1979
Full color poster featuring Enterprise and cast with full credits along the bottom, large size 27"x41" . . . . 8 10-20 ______

Enterprise Cut-Away, S.T.T.M.P.

"Star Trek The Motion Picture" Enterprise Cutaway Poster (Art)
Four-color cutaway of the STTMP Enterprise drawn by David Kimble; dark background with specifications lists along bottom; interior layout of the vessel.
Sales Corp. of America, 1979; 22"x48" printed on glossy paper stock [8] . . . . 3 4-6 ______

"Star Trek The Motion Picture - There Is No Comparison" Movie Publicity Poster (Art)
Paramount Pictures, 1979
Nicknamed the "Rainbow" poster; full color art featuring busts of Kirk, Spock and Ilia beneath rainbow-like color effects, 24"x36" . . . . 4.95 10-15 ______
Foreign Release - Finland, 1980, smaller 16'x23" . . . . — 12-15 ______

8. The glossy stock rendition of this prolific poster was used as a Give-A-Way premium by FotoMat, a distributor of the Paramount Home Video "Classics" Star Trek episode tape in 1980. It was also a special $3.00 mail-in order in boxed Lesney/AMT Star Trek model kits through 1981.
9. This poster was used as a Proctor & Gamble premium gift.

POSTERS

Star Trek The Motion Picture — Issue | Current | Cost/Date

"Star Trek The Motion Picture - Starship U.S.S. Enterprise Poster (Photo)
Sales Corp. of America, 1979
Color frontview Enterprise against blue field, printed on mirror-finish chrome mylar, lettering split between top and bottom, 22"x29"[10] . . . . 6 — 8-10 ______

8½" x 11" Foldout Poster, Starburst Design.

STAR TREK II – THE WRATH OF KAHN POSTERS

Kahn and Gonzo P2177 (Art)
Lincoln Enterprises, 1983
Color drawing by Doug Little, humorous drawing of Kahn grasping Gonzo Muppet, blue-gray background, 17"x22" . . . . 3.95 — 4-6 ______

Spock P2173 (Art)
Lincoln Enterprises, 1983
Color rendering by Doug Little, bust of Spock in red and white uniform, facing right, 17"x22" . . . . 3.95 — 4-6 ______

Spock and Enterprise P2175 (Art)
Lincoln Enterprises, 1983
Color art by Doug Little, shows Spock giving Vulcan Salute on right, Enterprise circling Genesis planet on left, black, starry background, 17"x22" . . . . 3.95 — 4-6 ______

Spock Friend Poster P2195 (Art)
Lincoln Enterprises, 1984
Full color by S. Catherine Jones, Official Commemorative poster features dual busts of Spock, surrounded by border which reads "Of all the souls I have met in my encounters, his was the most human" 3.95 — 4-6 ______

Spock Is Dead? P2170 (Art)
Lincoln Enterprises, 1983
Full color shows busts of Spock facing left with small tear on cheek, 24"x36" . . . . 6.95 — 6-8 ______

Kirk P2167 (Art)
Lincoln Enteroprises, 1983
Full color, bust of starship Admiral in red and white uniform, looking left, 24"x36" . . . . 4.95 — 5-7 ______

Star Trek II Action Poster P2168 (Photo)
Lincoln Enterprises, 1983
Full color, shows group shot of Sulu, McCoy, Uhura, Chekov, Kirk, Scotty, Saavik and Spock in the center with 11 photo insets around the borders, showing action shots, 24"x36" . . . . 4 — 4-6 ______

Star Trek II Stars (Photo)
New Eye Distributors, 1984
Central View shows full rear-view Enterprise over Movie Title Logo. Square inserts, one on each corner photo Kirk, McCoy, Spock and Kahn . . . . 5 — 5-7 ______

"Star Trek II - The Wrath of Kahn, At The Beginning Of The Universe, Lies the Beginning of Vengence," Movie Publicity Poster — Issue | Current | Cost/Date
Paramount Pictures, 1982
Full color publicity release featuring center artwork of starburst with Movie Title Logo, borders comprised of 10 photo insets of action scenes from the movies.
Lobby poster, 40"x60" . . . . — — 20-40 ______
One-sheet, 27"x41" . . . . — — 12-16 ______
Standard print, 24"x36" . . . . 4.95 — 8-10 ______
Fold-out brochure, 11"x17", reverse includes photo of bridge crew and credits . . . . 3 — 4-5 ______

Star Trek II Poster.

"Star Trek II - The Wrath of Kahn" Movie Title Logo Poster
Paramount Pictures, 1982
Full color, single sheet with only the logo and starburst logo effect, 22"x31" . . . . 2.95 — 3-5 ______

10. Used as a special offer Lesney/AMT order in boxed Star Trek model kits through 1981.

POSTERS

	Issue	Current	Cost/Date
Star Trek II Wanted Posters (Photo) Paradis Studios, 1983 Old or new style wanted posters with black and white photo of individual character, includes character description and criminal information, black lettering on tan paper.			
James T. Kirk, Bounty 35,000 Credits	1	1-3	______
Kahn Noonian Singh, 20,000 Credits	1	1-3	______
Kruge, 15,000 Credits	1	1-3	______
Montgomery Scott, 20,000 Credits	1	1-3	______
Valkris, 20,000 Credits	1	1-3	______

STAR TREK III - THE SEARCH FOR SPOCK POSTERS

Star Trek III Theater Poster (Spock's Head).

	Issue	Current	Cost/Date
"Star Trek III - The Search For Spock" Movie Publicity Poster (Art) Paramount Pictures, 1984 Color, featuring blue and red Spock's head center, with Enterprise firing phasers and Klingon vessel, cast pictures in portrait style along the bottom, 22"x29"	3	4-6	______
German release - lobby poster, one-sheet 23"x33"	—	12-15	______
French release - lobby poster, one-sheet 23"x33" "A La Recherche De Spock"	—	12-15	______

	Issue	Current	Cost/Date
"Star Trek III - The Search For Spock" Movie Logo Poster (Art) Paramount Pictures, 1984 Full color, neon-glo Spock's head in center, small Enterprise and Klingon ship on either side, movie credits and Letter Logo on bottom			
Theatre Size, 40"x60"	—	20-30	______
One-Sheet, 27"x41"	—	8-10	______
Standard, 24"x36"	4.95	5-7	______
"Star Trek III - The Search For Spock" Set Larido Merchandising, Inc., 1984 Licensed poster set of four one-of-a-kind photo/art releases, full color with "ST III" Letter Logo, 16"x22"			
Port profile Klingon Bird of Prey	—	2-3	______
Landing party on Genesis (Sulu, Chekov, Scotty, Kirk, McCoy) watch Enterprise flame-out	—	2-3	______
Front-view Enterprise over Star-burst (Art)	—	2-3	______
Close-up of Kirk offering hand to Kruge on ledge	—	2-3	______
Special offer complete set of four	2.95	8-10	______

STAR TREK IV - THE VOYAGE HOME POSTERS

	Issue	Current	Cost/Date
"Star Trek IV - The Voyage Home" Advance Movie Promo Poster Paramount, 1986 The official color artwork "Zoom-in" poster with the ST IV Letter Logo falling in towards planet Earth and additional lettered header: "Beaming Down to Earth December 12, 1986."	10	10-12	______
"Star Trek IV - The Voyage Home" Movie Promo Poster Release Paramount, 1986 Official artwork advertising release with Movie Letter Logo on bottom and full casting credits. Center shows Golden Gate Bridge tower and San Francisco skyline with Klingon Bird of Prey scout vessel superimposed. Oval design overhead features Kirk and Spock heads with Chekov-Sulu and McCoy-Scotty-Uhura on side flanks; lettered header "Star Date 1986. How on Earth can they Save the Future?"	15	15-17	______
"Star Trek IV - The Voyage Home" Pre-production Promo Poster Paramount, 1986 San Francisco Bay art collage with Golden Gate Bridge tower to far left and starship Enterprise overhead; two whales below, trailing streamer portraits Kirk, Spock, McCoy, Scotty, Sulu, Chekov and Uhura going from upper left to lower right-hand corners.	10	10-12	______

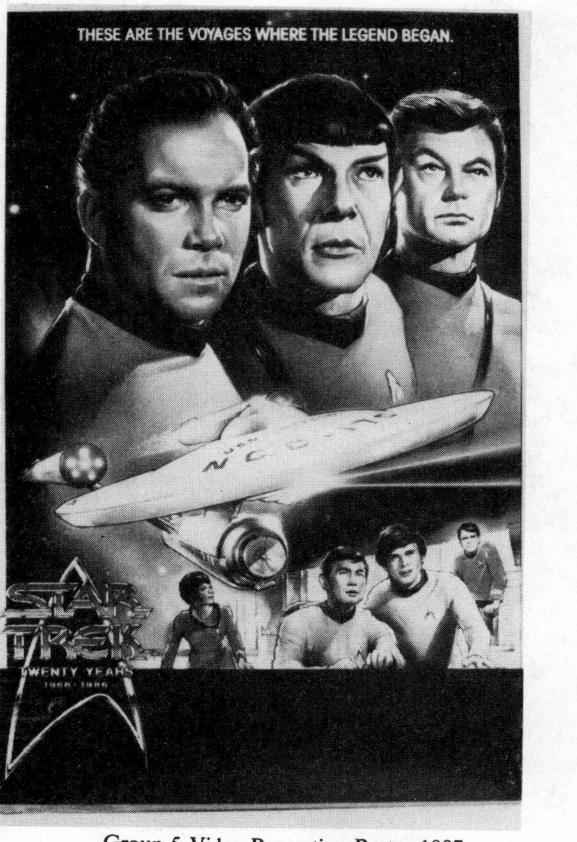

Group 5 Video Promotion Poster 1987

Issue Current Cost/Date

"Star Trek IV - U.S.S. Enterprise NCC-1701A"
David Kimble, 1986 Mind's Eye Press (Art)
Six-color printing of the rebuilt Enterprise from the fourth movie, cutaway profile like the original Kimble STTMP poster:
Standard, 24"x36" 12.50 13-14
Limited Edition, 1,500 signed and numbered prints "1/500 David Kimble" .... 50 50-55 ______
Order through manufacturer only.

Star Trek Anniversary Commemorative Posters

"Star Trek 20th Anniversary" Poster
New Eye, distrib., 1987
Poster showing 2nd season publicity poster with studio-posed Spock and Kirk, seated; with Uhura and McCoy (wearing a tricorder) standing behind them. Backdrop is a "Spirograph" type of art-deco design, dark solid header bears the Official "Star Trek Twenty Years 1966-1986" Insignia Design Logo on upper left. .... 10 10-12 ______

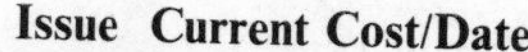
Issue Current Cost/Date

"Star Trek, 1966-20-1986" Commemorative
Personalties, Inc., 1987 (Art)
Design by Wash. D.C. illustrator Barbara Gibson, busts of Chekov, Scotty, Spock, Kirk, McCoy, Uhura, Sulu above lettering. Below is movie starship between planets, silver border, printed on heavy gauge paper, 23"x34" .... 29.95 30-32 ______

Star Trek Merchandise-Promotional Posters [11]

Atlantic Records SD 19363, 1982
Star Trek II The Wrath of Kahn Record
Full color poster showing title logo with starburst over starship that is blurred in a full warp drive. Bottom artwork illos a large ringed planet rising over black lunarscape, 17½"x25½" .... — 10-15 ______

D.C. Comics, 1983
Color, comic-style poster shows Kirk and Enterprise in center, 3-panel display along bottom features Sulu and Chekov, McCoy and Saavik. Large white borders, reads "Star Trek - Coming in November, the New D.C., There's No Stopping Us Now," 17"x22" ... — 12-16 ______

Star Trek The Role Playing Game Promo
Fasa Corporation, 1984
Color, exact same cover as is found on the first edition of Star Trek The Role Playing Game 2001, Kirk and Spock busts over planet with frontview Enterprise overhead, 17"x22" .... — 8-10 ______

Star Trek Home Video Releases
Paramount Pictures Corporation
"The Cage" Video Promo, 1966
Full color artwork blow-up of the boxed video cover, bust of Captain Pike with starship crew, 26"x39", info on bottom .... — 5-7 ______

Episode Videos - "Classics", 1980
Black bordered posters released as commercial displays for advertising Paramount's episode video cassettes. Bold yellow letters read "Star Trek" on top with "Television Classics" printed in red type beneath. Full color photo insets measure 11"x14" and feature two episodes contained per cassette. Bottom lists the episode titles in red, over white bold type "Paramount Is Going Home." Total poster size 12½" x22".
"Amok Time" and "Journey to

11. Product promo posters are made available to distributors and retailers as advertising aids for Star Trek related merchandise. Since they are not meant for public sale, no issue prices are given.

POSTERS

	Issue	Current	Cost/Date
Babel" Features color close-up of Spock as he lunges with the lirpa, crudgel weapon	—	12-16	______
"Let That Be Your Last Battlefield" and "The Trouble With Tribbles" Features close-up of Bele from Cheron	—	12-18	______

Video Promo For Television Classics.

Another Early Video Promo Poster.

	Issue	Current	Cost/Date
Episode Videos - Group 1 Releases, 1985 Color, special promotion for the first 20 television episode videos in the complete video series of tapes offered by Paramount. Contains 11 color photo inserts from various shows with Enterprise along bottom, 23"x32"	—	6-8	______
Episode Videos - Group 4 Releases, 1986 Color, promo poster for the 4th group of tapes, "The Changeling" through "The Deadly Years," with 7 photo inserts from the shows, 17"x22"	—	5-7	______
Episode Videos - Group 5 Releases, 1987 Full color artwork, Busts of Kirk, Spock and McCoy over t.v. frontview Enterprise. Bottom shows Uhura, Sulu, Chekov and Scott in bridge scene. Reads "These Are The Voyages Where the Legend Began," lower left corner bears official Anniversary Insignia Logo "Star Trek Twenty Years 1966-1986" Store promo, 26"x39"		7-9	______
Smaller 12½"x19" retailed version .	3	3-4	______
Star Trek The Motion Picture Movie Video Special Longer Version Promo, 1985 Color "rainbow" logo movie poster with art style Kirk, Spock and Ilia over Enterprise. Heavy, dark border with Paramount Home Video title and logo on bottom, 17"x22"	—	3-4	______

Video Promo For Star Trek III. Note artwork Spock's head design.

	Issue	Current	Cost/Date
Star Trek II The Wrath of Kahn Movie Video, 1985 Color photo poster with black lettering and three close-up insets: Spock and Admiral Kirk (top), Kahn with two female followers (bottom), and Paramount Home Video title and logo, 17"x22"		3-4	______
Star Trek III Movie Video, Advance Publicity Poster, 1984 Color, unusual color artwork showing Kirk facing Spock through glass Engine Room partition as the Vulcan dies, top reads, "Before the Search For Spock Began . . ." bottom reads, "See Star Trek III, The Search For Spock At A Theater Near You." Righthand, lower corner shows photo of STTMP video tape, Star Trek II. tape and the special god edition "Space Seed" episode tape, 17½"x25"		8-12	______
Star Trek III Movie Video Promo, 1984 Color, size-reduced version of the ST III Movie Publicty Poster which includes video purchasing info along bottom, 17"x22"		4-5	______
Star Trek III Movie Video - Vertical Poster, 1984 Color with shades of gray, black, blue and white, shows Spock's head artwork on left, reads "Star Trek III The Search For Spock" in large letters in center, video purchasing information below, 12"x36"		6-7	______

POSTERS

Unusual Book Promo Poster, Pocket Books.

	Issue	Current Cost/Date
Pocket Books Promo Poster, 1983 Color, with black and white photos, top half features scene from ST III, Kirk looking at computer screen with image of Spock and McCoy, top reads, "Case 49500-3," bottom briefly reviews Pocket's Star Trek promotions, 14"x22"		4-6 ______
Sega Games Promo Poster, 1983 Special promotion for the video professional arcade games, full color artwork of Enterprise doing battle with Klingon Cruiser, Regula Lab to the right; top reads "Strategic Operations Simulator," bottom Sega-The Arcade Experts," 22"x33½" [12]		8-12 ______

POSTERBOOKS

Sci-Fi Posterbook.

	Issue	Current Cost/Date
Sci-Fi Blockbusters Poster Book Volume 1, Number 3 Megastars Magazine, Fall 1984 Articles include the real story behind the Search For Spock, double-sided poster features photo montage of Spock from the series and ST III movie scenes, folded 8½"x11½"	1.95	3-4 ______
Sci-Fi T.V. Monthly Sportscene Pub. Ltd., England 1976 Series of posterbooks featuring focused t.v. character articles, profiles, photos and pin-ups. British issue price - .50p.		
Issue No. 1 Star Trek story, Spock's boyhood, Enterprise pin-up, Spock cover	2	5-6 ______
Issue No. 2 More on Spock's life, Enterprise blueprints, Gene Roddenberry interview, Spock cover	2	3-4 ______
Issue No. 3 Star Trek's evid Empires - the Klingons and Romulans, Spock and Kirk cover	2	3-4 ______
Issue No. 4 The Kirk story, Enterprise bridge blueprint	2	3-4 ______
Issue No. 5 The Enterprise Crew profiles, Part I	2	3-4 ______
Issue No. 6 The Enterprise Crew Part II, Star Trek alien poster, tricorder poster, Enterprise and Kirk cover	2	3-4 ______
Issue No. 7 More on the Star Trek crew and ship	2	3-4 ______
S.F. Color Posterbook - T.V. and Motion Picture Science Fiction, No. 2 Starlog Publications, Lamplight Studios, 1978 Star Trek The Motion Picture in review	1.50	2-3 ______

Starlog Poster Magazines
(See Magazine listings - "Starlog Special Magazine Editions section")

Star Trek - The Voyages Poster Book Series
Paradise Press, Inc., 1976-1978
Set of seventeen posterbooks featuring full color phtoos, articles and character profiles and pin-ups from the t.v. series, folded 8½"x11" format.

12. This poster is also the cover art for the **Sega Star Trek Owner's Manual** (Part No. 420-0855) that serves as the operations handbook for the video arcades.

POSTERS

The very collectible Poster Books by Paradise Press.

	Issue	Current Cost/Date	
Voyage One 7609.01, 1976 Special Collector's Issue, Enterprise on cover, Spock's evolution, Enterprise, City in Space, "The Cage" review, poster with Enterprise in the Tholian Web	1	8-12	_____
Voyage Two 7610.01, 1976 Harlan Ellison's "The City On The Edge of Forever," special effects, Kirk, Spock and McCoy relationships, poster of Kirk, Spock and McCoy from "The Specre of the Gun" episode	1	5-10	_____
Voyage Three 7611.01, 1976 Star Trek blooper shots, "Trouble With Tribbles" review, how to play fizzbin game, poster of Spock at bridge console	1	5-10	_____
Voyage Four 7612.01, 1976 Super aliens of Trek - Klingons and Romulans, "Journey to Babel" critique, poster of Kirk and Kang from "The Day of the Dove"	1	5-10	_____
Voyage Five 7701.01, 1977 Spock interview, inside the Vulcan mind, planet Vulcan revisited, poster of Spock with Vulcan lyre	1	5-10	_____
Voyage Six 7702.01, 1977 "Amok Time" review, the art of Star Trek, the equipment of the Trek universe, poster of Kirk, Spock, McCoy and bridge crew from "Shore Leave"	1	5-8	_____
Voyage Seven 7703.01 "For the Love of Jim" issue, "The Enemy Within" critique, analysis of James T. Kirk, poster of Kirk in dress uniform with drink in hand . .	1	5-8	_____
Voyage Eight 7704.01, 1977 McCoy interview, McCoy's medical miracles, medical technology, poster of Yeoman Rand, McCoy and Kirk from "Miri" episode	1	5-8	_____

	Issue	Current Cost/Date	
Voyage Nine 7705.01, 1977 "Assignment: Earth" review, the music of Star Trek, Vulcan Logic and how to use it, poster of Uhura from "Mirror, Mirror"	1	6-8	_____
Voyage Ten 7706.01, 1977 Smithsonian Museum report, pictorial inspection of Star Trek miniatures, "This Side of Paradise" review, poster of Kand and his Klingon landing party from "Day of the Dove"	1	6-8	_____
Voyage Eleven 7707.01, 1977 Leonard Nimoy interview, the miniatures of Star Trek, "The Enterprise Incident" critique, poster of Spock at computer console	1	6-10	_____
Voyage Twelve 7708.01, 1977 Profiles of Chapel, Rand and Uhura, the heroines of Star Trek, critique of "The Paradise Syndrome," poster of Yeoman Rand	1	8-12	_____
Voyage Thirteen 7709.01, 1977 Starship engineering, Montgomery Scott interview, poster of Scotty leaning on command chair	1	8-12	_____
Voyage Fourteen 7710.01, 1977 The Rules for three-dimensional chess, history of the Federation, "Where No Man Has Gone Before" review, poster of Kirk and Spock on bridge	1	8-12	_____
Voyage Fifteen 7801.10, 1978 The non-human aliens, "Conscience of the King" review, Sulu as helmsman, poster of Kirk and Sulu	1	8-10	_____
Voyage Sixteen 7802.21, 1978 Starfleet Imperialism, "Mirror, Mirror" critique, poster of "Mirror" crew on the bridge	1.25	8-10	_____
Voyage Seventeen 7804.4, 1978 The costumes of Star Trek, review of "Space Seed: Kirk and McCoy on cover	1.25	8-10	_____
Star Trek The Motion Picture Poster Book Exclusive Collector's Issue Paradise Press, 1979 Color, features behind-the-scenes news by Chris Rowley, plus Paramount promotion poster fold-out, 8½"x11" folded [13]	1.50	5-7	_____
Star Trek II - The Wrath of Kahn Posterbook British release, 1982 Posterbook with articles that opens up to a horizontal format movie poster. Limited U.S. distribution. . .	4	8-12	_____

13. This promotion poster fold-out is the same as Lincoln Enterprises' Poster P2157. An interesting misprint inside this posterbook shows a photo of the Klingon Battle Cruiser placed upside-down.

PROPS

(Adult Weapons & Equipment)

The fine attention which Star Trek's producers have paid to creating realistic-looking props on television and in the motion pictures has given birth to a very wide range of both amateur and professionally manufactured replicas of Trek apparatus for teens and adults. Kits are still available for many of the smaller, hand-held devices which appeared during the airing of the series.

Communicators, tricorders, phasers (types I and II) as well as other miscellaneous equipment are samples of the sophisticated line of Star Trek hardware which exists today to accommodate the needs of older fans. These items can be purchased preassembled and ready for display or bought as unassembled kits. Many trader catalogs offer a broad selection of models. Usually prop-quality merchandise appears on price lists which exceed the $100 mark in the case of working models with electronic sound effects.

In recent years the props which were made for use in the making of the Star Trek movies resulted from special machinery which plastiformed a mold from a wooden master. Very detailed prop-quality replicas of these collectibles are now available from manufacturing houses equipped to follow this basic procedure. Generally the price of such props varies according to the level of technology used in producing the model's assembly kit.

For fans wishing to create their own Star Trek hardware, books such as **The Model Building Handbook** by Brick Price offer invaluable tips and techniques for designing models out of fiberglass resin and auto body putty. Articles on the subject have also appeared in magazines dealing with methods of customizing plastic model kits from spacecraft. For less adventurous collectors, original prop designs and spacecraft miniatures can be ordered from individuals who specialize in custom-made artifacts.

PROPS

	Issue	Current	Cost/Date
Agonizer Richard Coyle, designer Lincoln Enterprises, distributors 1980, 3" solid cast polyurethane plastic, replica of the device as introduced in the t.v. episode "Mirror, Mirror." P-2494	5.95	8-16	_____
Communicator (Belt) Richard Coyle, designer Lincoln Enterprises, distr., 1980 Also called the "Belly Warmer" STTMP vintage close-range communications device as worn on formal attire during the movie. Solid cast polyurethane with snap post fasteners, approx. 2"x4". P-2495	5.95	7-9	_____
Communicator (Hand-held) Richard Coyle, designer Lincoln Enterprises, distr., 1980 Device used in the series and Star Trek III motion picture, polyurethane plastic with metal grill and trim. H-2492	55	55-65	_____
Communicators (Hand-held) Numerous manufactured flip-top, epoxy resin, metal and polyurethane cast types with varying degrees of detail and operability. Based on the t.v. series models, these come available as optional kits, unpainted or painted, approx. 2½"x4".			
Pre-assembled replicas		50-65	_____
Kits, with electronics for sound effects		45-60	_____
Kits, non-functional		30-40	_____
Communicator (Wrist) Richard Coyle, designer Lincoln Enterprises, distr., 1980 STTMP vintage communicator that straps to the wrist. Hand painted and labeled, solid cast polyurethane with metal wristband. Non-functional. H-2493	30	30-35	_____
Klingon Sonic Disruptor Tim Calloway, designer Starbase Central, distr., 1983 Nonfunctional prop, unbreakable, heavy-duty casting with hand-painted accents. Also known as the Disruptor Pistol.	60	60-75	_____
Phaser, Type I (Hand-phaser) Richard Coyle, designer Lincoln Enterprises, distr., 1980 Hand-held phaser unit, hand-painted and assembled, urethane cast. Battery operated for sound effects. H-2491	25	25-30	_____
Phaser, Type II (Pistol-phaser) Richard Coyle, designer Lincoln Enterprises, distr., 1980 Urethane cast unit. Hand-painted and assembled. Phaser I unit inserts into a plastic handle mount. Trigger produces light and sound effects, setting knob adjusts variable sound, uses 9-volt battery. H-2490	100	100-125	_____
Phaser, Type II (Pistol-phaser) M-5 Productions, 1974 Hand-made pistol phaser replica out of balsa wood and plastic coating, metal accents and detailed painting.	50	75-90	_____
Tricorder James Kirk, designer Life-size prop with functional L.E.D. lights, video screen with light and sound effects, vacu-form plastic with metal accents, tape storage compartment and hinged cover, shoulder strap is included, measures 8" long x5½" wide x 2" deep. Available in two styles.			
Functional (sound effects, lights)	150	150-200	_____
Non-functional	75	75-90	_____

SCHOOL AND OFFICE SUPPLIES

Quite an assortment of Star Trek collectibles have been manufactured for utilitarian purposes in the school and office setting. Items in this category include bookmarks, bookplates, calendars, checkbook covers, erasers, greeting cards, letter openers, memo holders, memo pads, notebooks, notecards, pencils, pens, pen holders, portfolio pouches, postcards, stamps, stationery and writing tablets.

Good collectibles in this area are early calendars and stationery of the '60's and '70's. A set of all four Ballantine **Stardate Calendars** produced from 1976-1979 in their original mailing boxes is classic memorabilia of high professional quality. Hundreds of stationery designs displaying fan artwork have existed throughout the years and there has been no attempt to list them though they are readily available to Star Trek collectors. Some of the most beautiful stationery comes directly from Paramount itself or from the offices of Star Trek staffers.

School and Office Supplies

	Issue	Current	Cost/Date
Address Book			
Reproductions, 1987			
Checkbook size A-Z address book with special telephone number section and a second pocket for inserting papers. Clear vinyl plastic cover has outside b/w photo sheet insert from t.v. series showing Scotty, Chekov, McCoy, Chapel, Uhura, Sulu and Spock gathered around Kirk in command chair, 3"x6½"	4.99	5-6	______
Address Labels			
T-K Graphics, 1984			
Customized labels with assorted Star Trek designs and slogans, have 4-lines to personalize items, sets include 4 packs with 20 stickers to a pack:			
"Beam Me Up Scotty. This Place Has No Intelligent Life."	4	4-6	______
UFP Janus Head Emblem	4	4-6	______
UFP Pennant Design	4	4-6	______
U.S.S. Enterprise Command Insignia	4	4-6	______
U.S.S. Enterprise, ship schematic	4	4-6	______
U.S.S. Enterprise, ship silhouette	4	4-6	______

Bookcovers

T-K Graphics

Vinyl, polyester-lined book covers in several sizes, brown and tan with designs and logos silkscreened on the front:

"Imperial Klingon Fleet"

"Star Fleet Academy" with Janus Head Emblem

"Star Fleet Command" with Janus Head Emblem

"Star Fleet Command-Intelligence Division"

"Star Fleet HQ - Technical Operations Center"

"Star Fleet Pilot's Association" w/Enterprise

"UFP Diplomatic Service" with Janus Head

"U.S.S. Enterprise" with ship schematic

"U.S.S. Enterprise/NCC-1701"

	Issue	Current	Cost/Date
"Vulcan Science Academy"			
Each in 5"x7½" paperback size	2	3-4	______
Each in 6½"x9½" hardback size	3	4-5	______

Bookmarks

	Issue	Current	Cost/Date
Antioch Publishing Co.			
Groan-Ups H-847, 1985			
"Beam Me Up Scotty, There's No Intelligent Life Down Here," red lettering on yellow with blue and white planetscape border, choice of purple or blue tassel.	.99	.50-1	______
T-K Graphics			
2" x 4" bookmarks, black lettering or design on colored card stock:			
"Tribble Breeding is a Hairy Experience"	.25	.50-1	______
"Star Trek Forever" with Janus Head	.25	.50-1	______
"Star Fleet Tactical Operations Center" with UFP Pennant	.25	.50-1	______
"U.S.S. Enterprise" with schematic	.25	.50-1	______

Bookplates

	Issue	Current	Cost/Date
T-K Graphics, 1984			
Self-sticking plates with space for personalization, reads "From the Library of", 2" x 4" format, 15 plates per packet:			
Kahn design, drawing by Bob Suh	1.75	2-3	______
"Star Fleet Academy Library"	1.75	2-3	______

Calendars

	Issue	Current	Cost/Date
1968 "Your Star Trek Pictorial Calendar"			
Star Trek Enterprises, 1968, Six-page claendar featuring scenes from the series in color-cepia hues, two months per page with one overhead photo, 9¾" x 7¾", stapled, includes: B/w chess scene Kirk and Spock "Where No Man Has Gone Before" Green - Spock and Kirk "Assign: Earth" Brown - Kirk, Uhura, McCoy on bridge Purple - Kirk, McCoy aboard sleeper ship "Space Seed" Blue - Spock with Nomad "Changeling," Red - Kirk and Uhura, bridge included as part of a kit	—	35-40	______

1. This first of many subsequent Star Trek photo calendars was sold by insert flyers included inside the envelopes containing b/w Star Trek publicity glossies mailed to 1960's fans who wrote to their favorite stars for autographed pictures. (See the Special Promotions chapter.)

The First Star Trek Calendar

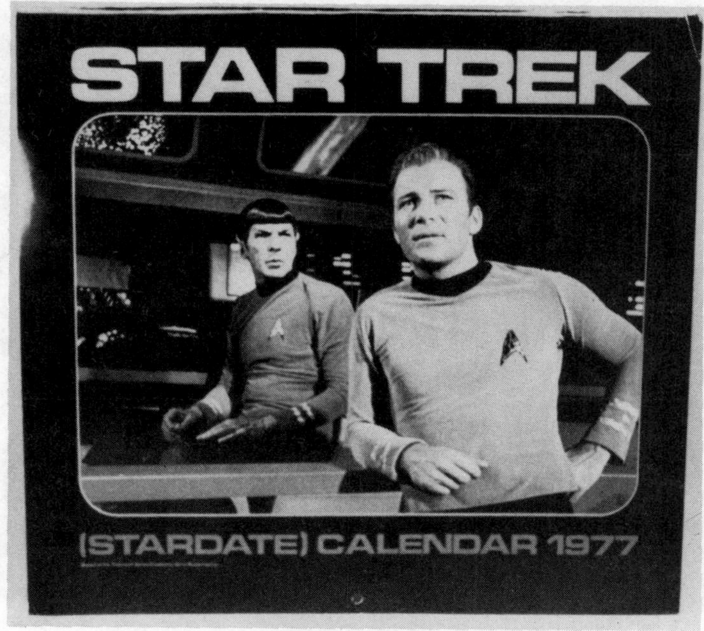

The Second of Ballantine's Boxed Calendars

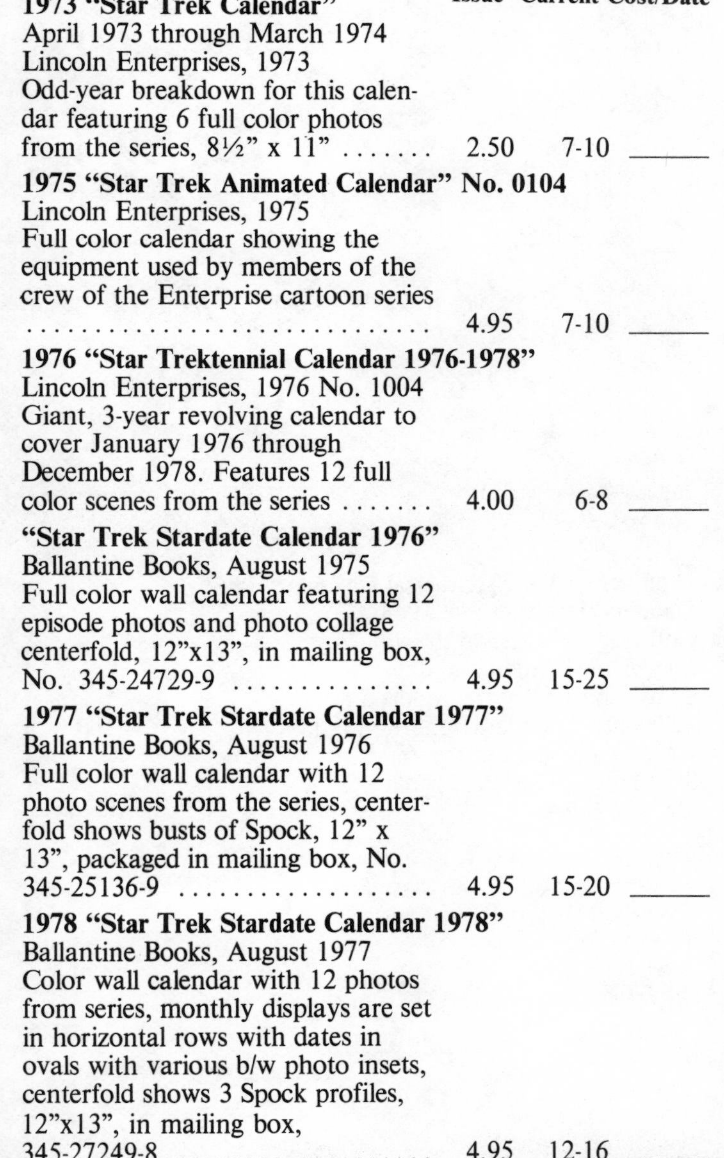

Issue Current Cost/Date

1973 "Star Trek Calendar"
April 1973 through March 1974
Lincoln Enterprises, 1973
Odd-year breakdown for this calendar featuring 6 full color photos from the series, 8½" x 11" .... 2.50 7-10 _____

1975 "Star Trek Animated Calendar" No. 0104
Lincoln Enterprises, 1975
Full color calendar showing the equipment used by members of the crew of the Enterprise cartoon series .... 4.95 7-10 _____

1976 "Star Trektennial Calendar 1976-1978"
Lincoln Enterprises, 1976 No. 1004
Giant, 3-year revolving calendar to cover January 1976 through December 1978. Features 12 full color scenes from the series .... 4.00 6-8 _____

"Star Trek Stardate Calendar 1976"
Ballantine Books, August 1975
Full color wall calendar featuring 12 episode photos and photo collage centerfold, 12"x13", in mailing box, No. 345-24729-9 .... 4.95 15-25 _____

1977 "Star Trek Stardate Calendar 1977"
Ballantine Books, August 1976
Full color wall calendar with 12 photo scenes from the series, centerfold shows busts of Spock, 12" x 13", packaged in mailing box, No. 345-25136-9 .... 4.95 15-20 _____

1978 "Star Trek Stardate Calendar 1978"
Ballantine Books, August 1977
Color wall calendar with 12 photos from series, monthly displays are set in horizontal rows with dates in ovals with various b/w photo insets, centerfold shows 3 Spock profiles, 12"x13", in mailing box, 345-27249-8 .... 4.95 12-16 _____

1979 "Star Trek Stardate Calendar 1979"
Ballantine Books, September 1978

Issue Current Cost/Date

Color wall calendar with 12 scenes from the series, dates in ovals, no b/w photo insets, monthly displays are horizontal, centerfold Enterprise orbiting red planet, 12"x13", in mailing box, No. 345-278121-6 ... — 9-13 _____

1980 "Star Trek The Motion Picture Calendar 1980"
T-K Graphics, 1979
Wall calendar, top has full color photo of the eleven member movie bridge crew, bottom lists the entire year's dates with holidays shown, 11" x 17" format .... 2.00 5-7 _____

"Star Trek The Motion Picture Stardate Calendar 1980"
Wallaby (Pocket Books), 1979
Full color wall calendar, 12 photo scenes from the movie, dates in horizontal rows, centerfold of movie cast, 12" x 13", cellophane wrap No. 671-79098-6 .... 5.95 8-12 _____

"U.S.S. Enterprise Officer's Official Date Book - 1980 Desk Calendar"
Wallaby, 1979
White spiral bound weekly engagement book, STTMP pictures. Right pages feature daily dates one week at time; left illustrated with b/w or color photos, approx. 41 photos b/w, 12 color, 5½" x 8" format .... 6.95 8-12 _____

1981 "Star Trek Stardate Calendar 1981"
Wallaby (Pocket Books), 1980
Full color wall calendar with 12 scenes from STTMP, horizontal monthly dates, centerfold Mr. Spock and Capt. Kirk, 12" x 13", cellophane wrap, No. 671-79142-7 . 5.95 8-12 _____

2. This 1976 calendar re-appeared in 1982 as a re-release revolving calendar for the years 1983 to 1984. It was re-sold by Lincoln Enterprises.

Three Year Calendar, Lincoln Enterprises

	Issue	Current	Cost/Date
"Star Trek Calendar 1982-1984" Lincoln Enterprises, 1982 Re-release of the 3-year revolving calendar from 1976, dates coincide again. Features 12 scenes from the t.v. series, No. 1004	4.95	6-8	_____
"Star Trek Stardate Calendar 1982" Pocket Books, 1981 Color wall calendar with 12 scenes from STTMP, monthly dates in horizontal rows, 12" x 13", cellophane wrap	5.95	7-10	_____

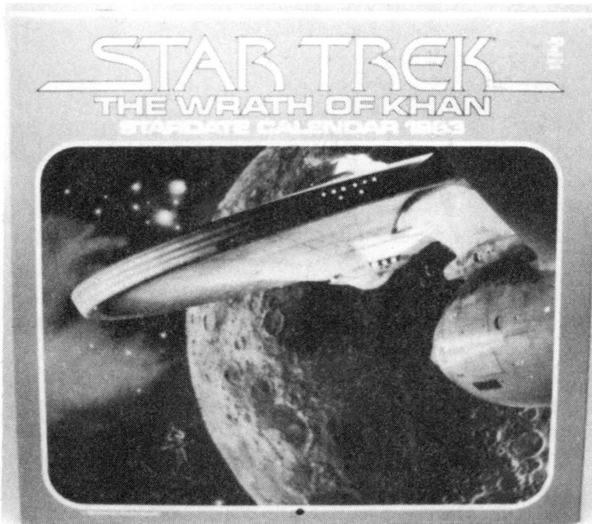

Star Trek II Calendar

	Issue	Current	Cost/Date
1983 "Star Trek The Wrath of Kahn Stardate Calendar 1983" Pocket Books, 1982 Color wall calendar with 12 photo scenes from ST II, dates in horizontal rows, centerfold Enterprise firing on Reliant, 12" x 13", cellophane wrap, No. 671-45611-3	6.95	8-12	_____
1984 "Star Trek" Pocket Calendars 1984 T-K Graphics, 1984 Mini-calendars, printed on colored cardstock, wallet size, 2¾" x 4¼":			
UFP Janus Head Emblem	.25	.50.1	_____
U.S.S. Enterprise (silhouette)	.25	.50-1	_____
"Star Trek Stardate Calendar 1984" Timescape (Pocket Books), 1983 Color wall calendar featuring 12 photo scenes from the t.v. series, dates in vertical rows, crew centerfold, 12" x 13", cellophane wrap No. 671-47939-3	6.95	8-10	_____
1984 "William Shatner Calendar 1984" William Shatner Fan Club, 1983 Full color, 12 "never-before-seen" shots of Bill, glossy litho with special date reminders, 8" x 10", staple binding	15.00	18-20	_____

Datazine Publications

	Issue	Current	Cost/Date
1985 "Star Trek Historical Calendar 1985" Datazine Publications, 1984 Collection of cartoon drawings by artist Don Harden and data compiled by Tim Farley, reproduced as a 12 month calendar. Important data posted daily as events pertain to Star Trek, 2-page centerfold drawing, 24 pages	4.95	7-10	_____

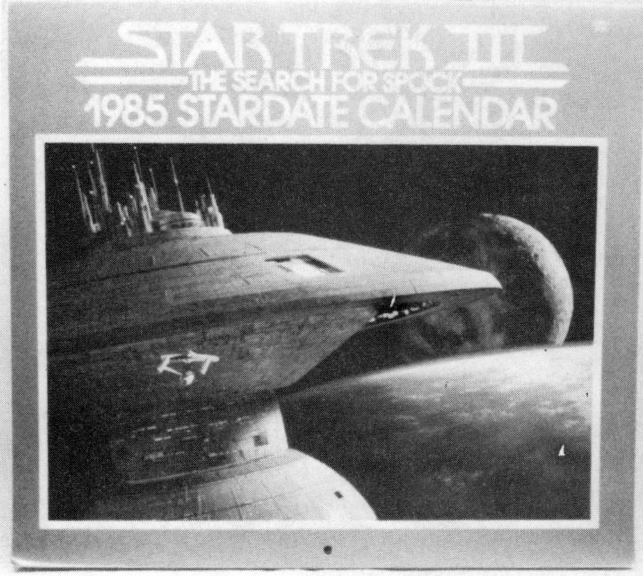

Star Trek III Calendar

	Issue	Current Cost/Date	
"Star Trek The Search For Spock Calendar 1985" Pocket Books, 1984 Color wall calendar with 12 photos from St III, dates in vertical rows, centerfold of Enterprise at space dock, 12" x 13" cellophane wrap No. 671-52789-4	6.95	8-10	_____
"William Shatner Calendar 1985" William Shatner Fan Club, 1984 Color, 12 never-seen photos of Bill in different environments, including him break-dancing, glossy litho with 12 cartoons by fan artist LaVena K. Kidd, 8" x 10", staple binding	15.00	16-18	_____
1986 "Star Trek Historical Calendar 1986" Intergalactic, distrib., 1985 2-color cover cartoons a cigar smoking Kirk and Spock with main character "Federation rebels" from ST III. Subtitled "The 'E' Team", b/w drawings with important dates for Trekkers	4.95	6-9	_____

Star Trek Calendar 1986

	Issue	Current Cost/Date	
"Star Trek Stardate Calendar 1986" Pocket Books, 1985 Color wall calendar with 12 photo profiles from the 3 movies. Centerfold Kirk and Spock from STTMP promo poster, dates in horizontal rows, 12" x 13", cellophane wrap, No. 671-60435-X	7.95	6-8	_____

Star Trek 1987 Calendar

	Issue	Current Cost/Date	
"Star Trek 1987 Calendar - The Stars Pick Their Favorite Episodes" Wallaby (Pocket Books), 1986 20th Anniversary issue, glossy stock wall calendar with photos from the Trek stars own favorite episodes, centerfold chart lists 70 episodes by title, airdate and production number, 11¾" x 10⅝", cellophane wrap No. 0-671-62907-7	7.95	8-9	_____

Checkbook Covers

	Issue	Current Cost/Date	
Lincoln Enterprises, 1983 Plush vinyl cover with built-in pocket calculator and pen holder. Maroon color with tiny gold-colored insignia on the lower lefthand corner of the cover	19.95	19-22	_____
T-K Graphics Vinyl, polyester-lined covers in brown and tan with silkscreened designs, 3¼" x 6½" folder style:			
"Star Fleet Academy"	2.50	3.4	_____
"Star Fleet Command Intelligence Div."	2.50	3-4	_____
"Star Fleet HQ Tactical Operations"	2.50	3-4	_____
"UFP Diplomatic Service" with Janus	2.50	3-4	_____
"U.S.S. Enterprise" with schematic	2.50	3-4	_____
"U.S.S. Enterprise"/NCC-1701"	2.50	3-4	_____
"Vulcan Science Academy"	2.50	3-4	_____

Star Trek Erasers, Deiner Industries

Erasers

Item	Issue	Current	Cost/Date
Enterprise Design Rectangular book eraser in assorted colors with portside profile of t.v. starship imprinted on top	.50	1-2	______
Star Trek The Search For Spock Eraser Tips Deiner Enterprises, 1984 Small pencil toppers in seven different mold styles, four colors include magenta, lime green, yellow and sky blue. Head profiles and ships:			
Kruge	.40	.75-1	______
Kirk	.40	.75-1	______
Spock	.40	.75-1	______
Scotty	.40	.75-1	______
McCoy	.40	.75-1	______
Enterprise	.40	1-2	______
Excelsior	.40	1-2	______

Greeting Cards

Item	Issue	Current	Cost/Date
Leonard Nimoy Poetry Card Celestial Arts, 1981 Special greeting booklet featuring Nimoy's poem "Thank You For Your Love" accompanied by pastel, shadow-form drawings, 30 page booklet, 4" x 5½"	2.50	3-4	______
Star Trek Greeting Cards Starlog Magazine, 1976 Set of 24 different cards with a Star Trek theme, assorted sizes with different sayings (Get Well, Sorry, I Didn't Write, Thinking of You, etc.), some cards featuring pop-out ships and equipment, sold as a set of 24 cards	15.95	20-30	______
Star Trek Photo Greeting Cards California Dreamers, 1985 Designers Sam and William Rittenberg of LL & P Enterprises, set of 25 cards featuring episode shots over a black starfield with witty headers and inside sayings (Birthday, Devotion, Sympathy, Congratulations, etc.), sold individually:			
Spock - seated with templed fingers and wearing slave tunic "Bread and Circuses"	1.25	1-2	______

Star Trek Greeting Cards, California Dreamers

Item	Issue	Current	Cost/Date
Spock - c/u at Science Station	1.25	1-2	______
Spock - c/u giving Vulcan Salute	1.25	1-2	______
Spock - playing Vulcan Harp	1.25	1-2	______
Spock - c/u, bemused expression	1.25	1-2	______
Spock - c/u in 1st season radiation suit, "Naked time"	1.25	1-2	______
Spock - c/u holding Isis cat "Assign: Earth"	1.25	1-2	______
Spock - wearing shielded visors "Is There In Truth No Beauty?"	1.25	1-2	______
Spock - another c/u at Science Station	1.25	1-2	______
Kirk - in Romulan disguise "The Enterprise Incident"	1.25	1-2	______
Kirk - prone, being attacked by Gorn "Arena"	1.25	1-2	______
Kirk - at destroyed outpost "Arena"	1.25	1-2	______
Kirk - in harness, wagering with brains from "Gamesters of Triskelion"	1.25	1-2	______
Kirk - in defensive posture	1.25	1-2	______
Kirk - c/u with Nomad "Changeling"	1.25	1-2	______
Kirk - c/u	1.25	1-2	______
Kirk - arms crossed and swaggering	1.25	1-2	______
Kirk and Spock - command chair	1.25	1-2	______
Kirk, Spock, McCoy - in gangster garb "A Piece of the Action"	1.25	1-2	______
McCoy - tortured face "The Empath"	1.25	1-2	______
McCoy - contemplative	1.25	1-2	______
McCoy, Uhura with Kirk in command chair	1.25	1-2	______
Chekov - c/u, pained	1.25	1-2	______
Sulu - over the shoulder shot at viewscreen with planet	1.25	1-2	______
Enterprise - frontview starship	1.25	1-2	______

Trivia Greeting Cards

"Whaddayaknow" Trivia Cards

Crabwalk, Inc., 1984 — Issue / Current / Cost/Date

Two trivia greeting cards with questions about Star Trek, written by Sal Piro, 10 questions on front, answers inside, 4½" x 6½":

Science Fiction Trivia Quiz No. W213/100 Question No. 1 - Who created Star Trek? plus nine SF questions .... 1.00 1-2 ______

Star Trek Trivia Quiz No. W250/100 Ten questions include:
1. What is the I.D. number on Enterprise?
2. Who played Scotty?
3. What is Kirk's middle name?
4. Where is Spock from?
5. Who played Ilia in STTMP?
6. What is the simple name for polygeminus Rex?
7. Which episode inspired STWOK?
8. In what episode did Joan Collins appear?
9. Who played Saavik in STWOK?
10. What is the length of Enterprise?

Card .... 1.25 2-3 ______

Letter Opener - Enterprise Design

New Eye, distrib.

Metal gold-tone letter opener, 7" notched blade, topped by an oval lucite knob containing a decal of the Enterprise .... 3.00 5-7 ______

Memo Holder

Tel Rad Services, 1975

Standard style, plastic holder for memo sheets, black, pictures the t.v. Enterprise .... 1.50 2-4 ______

Memo Pads

T-K Graphics, 1984

Pads with 25 sheets on cardboard in assorted color stock, black printing, 4½" x 5½":

	Issue	Current	Cost/Date
Kahn Design - drawing by Bob Shu	1.25	1-2	______
"Space: The Final Frontier"	1.25	1-2	______
"Star Fleet Headquarters" - with UFP Janus Head Emblem ...	1.25	1-2	______
"Star Fleet Spacegram"	1.25	1-2	______
"Star Trek Forever" - with Enterprise silhouette	1.25	1-2	______
"Star Trek Lives" - with Enterprise	1.25	1-2	______
"Vulcan Science Academy"	1.25	1-2	______

Lincoln Enterprises, 1968-1983

Gummed pads with letterhead as used by NBC during the t.v. series, in miniature size, blue sky with black Enterprise .... .40 1-2 ______

Notebook - Crew Photo

Reproductions, 1986

Spiral bound, 4" x 6" lined notebook with b/w photo cover of the t.v. bridge crew: Scotty, Chapel, McCoy, Chekov, Uhura, Sulu, and Spock around seated Kirk .... 2.99 3-4 ______

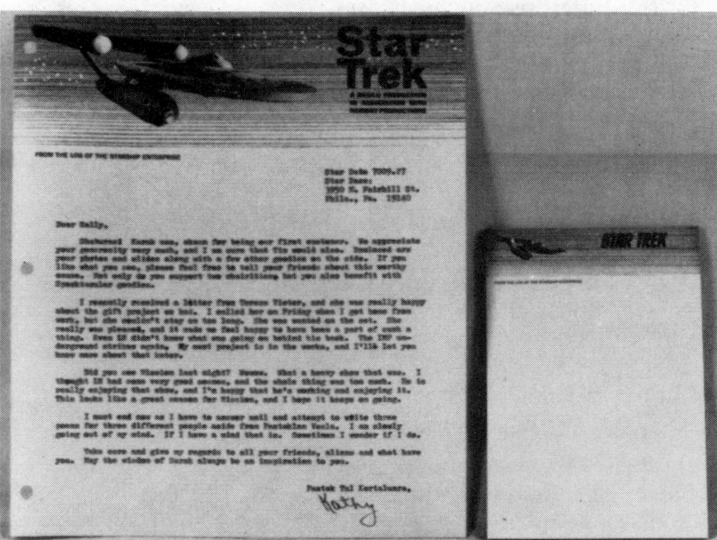

Official Star Trek letterhead and retail version memo pad from Lincoln Enterprises.

Notecards

T-K Graphics, 1984

Assorted color cards with white envelopes for mailing, 4½" x 5½" cardstock:

	Issue	Current	Cost/Date
"Beam Me Up, Scotty, This Place Has No Intelligent Life" - cartoon Spock by Steve Stiles as the Vulcan is surrounded by Reagan and his staff, 6 cards in 3 different colors .	1.25	1-3	______
Spock as Santa's Helpers Design - by Kathryn Bartolomew, 10 cards .	1.25	1-3	______
"Star Fleet Headquarters" - with Janus Head Emblem, 6 cards in 3 colors	1.25	1.2	______
"Tribble Breeding is a Hairy Experience" with drawing by Steve Stiles, 6 cards	1.50	1-3	______

SCHOOL AND OFFICE

Issue | Current | Cost/Date

Pens and Pencils

"Beam Me Up, Scotty, There's No Intelligent Life on This Planet" Pen
Hollywood on Location, dist. 1985
Heft, rainbow-colored pen with ballpoint tip, refillable barrel ..... 3.50 4-5 ______

"Star Trek Lives" Pencils
Lincoln Enterprises
Set of 6 No. 2 lead pencils, blue with gold colored lettering .... 1 1-2 ______

"U.S.S. Enterprise, National Air and Space Museum" Pen [3]
Smithsonian Institute, 1979
6" souvenir pen, clear plastic with a miniature floating Enterprise in assorted color barrels .... 5 8-12 ______

Pen Holders

Enterprise Desk Set
Tel Rad Services, 1975
Smoke-colored lucite pen with decal of t.v. Enterprise, includes desk stand and name plate to personalize 5 7-9 ______

Tribble
Lincoln Enterprises, 1975
A tribble furball cannister No. 0405 .... 6 7-8 ______

Portfolio Pouches

T-K Graphics, 1984
Vinyl, lined carrying pouches for papers, zipper closures, brown and tan with silk screened designs, 10½"x7½":

Item	Issue	Current	Cost/Date
"Imperial Klingon Fleet"	6.25	7-8	______
"Star Fleet Academy" with Janus Head	6.25	7-8	______
"Star Fleet Command Intelligence Division"	6.25	7-8	______
"Star Fleet HQ Tactical Operations Center"	6.25	7-8	______
"Star Fleet Pilot's Association" w/Enterprise	6.25	7-8	______
"UFP Diplomatic Service" with Janus Head	6.25	7-8	______
"U.S.S. Enterprise" with schip schematic	6.25	7-8	______
"Vulcan Science Academy"	6.25	7-8	______

Postcards

Cardstock designs, suitable for mailing

Enterprise Postcard
Trotter Photo, 1977
Color episode photo of the starship firing blue twin phasers, James Keith photo, Exeter Press, 3"x5" format .... .25 1-2 ______

Issue | Current | Cost/Date

Enterprise Crew Postcards P87
Monster Times, 1976
Color cards with portraits from the t.v. series, set of six includes:
Spock - close up
McCoy - close up
Kirk - close up
Crewman at helm
Kirk and Chekov
Sulu and Crewman at helm
Set of 6 postcards .... 1 3-6 ______

"Star Fleet Headquarters Official Mail" Postcards
T-K Graphics, 1984
Standard USPS cards with black lettering, 8 cards in set, assorted colors, 3¼"x5½"............... 1.25 1-2 ______

"Star Fleet Headquarters Tactical Operations Center"
T-K Graphics, 1984
Black lettering on 3¼"x5½" cards, 8 card set, assorted colors .... 1.25 1-2 ______

First Postcards, sold by Star Trek Enterprises, 1967

Star Trek Color Postcards 2100
Star Trek/Lincoln Enterprises, 1967-1983
Color postcards featuring seven early T.V. photos of the Star Trek crew, portraits, 5"x7",

Item	Issue	Current	Cost/Date
Kirk	.15	.25-.30	______
Spock	.15	.25-.30	______
McCoy	.15	.25-.30	______
Scotty	.15	.25-.30	______
Uhura	.15	.25-.30	______
Chekov	.15	.25-.30	______
Sulu	.15	.25-.30	______
Set of 7 cards	1	2-3	______

3. The production model Enterprise starship is still on permanent display at the Smithsonian Institute in Washington, D.C. (See the Special Promotions chapter.)

Fantasy Trade Card Set (postcards), 1982

Bridge Crew Post Card

	Issue	Current	Cost/Date
Star Trek Fantasy Card Set Starfleet Imports, 1982 Set of three extra large postcards, each an extracted head shot taken from the cover of the fan novel "Courts of Honor" written by Syn Fergusen, postcard art by Sat Nam Kaur, 5½"x7½"			
STF002 Kirk (STTMP)	1	2-3	_____
STF003 Spock (STWOK)	1	2-3	_____
STF004 Female Romulan Commander (S.T. series)	1		_____
Star Trek Greeting Postcards California Dreamers, Inc. 1987 Set of 8 standard size postcards with photos from the t.v. series and witty headers, 4"x5¾", sold individually:			
Spock in mind-meld with Horta, no title	.75	.75-1	_____
Kirk and Tellurite Ambassadors in banquet scene (Journey to Babel) - "Call me, we'll have lunch"	.75	.75-1	_____
Enterprise, rearview approaching planet - "To Seek out strange new worlds ... like you"..........	.75	.75-1	_____
Helmsman Sulu - "Control systems out, navigational systems out, directional systems out ... I am so confused!".....................	.75	.75-1	_____
Kirk, waist-shot with communicator - "Lock me in, and beam me out ... baby I'm yours"..........	.75	.75-1	_____
Kirk, in command chair - "Screens up for magnification 10 ... you're so good to look at!"...........	.75	.75-1	_____
Spock waist-shot with mind-control headset from 'Spock's Brain' - "Universes may fall ... but rock and roll will never die!"........	.75	.75-1	_____
Star Trek Sepia Fotocards Ludlow Sales, 1986 Sepia-tone postcards with T.V. scenes from Star Trek 4"x6"			
FC-127-50, Bridge Scene, shot of Scotty, Chekov, Chapel, Uhura, Sulu, McCoy, Kirk & Spock	1	1-2	_____

Sepia Postcard, Ludlow Sales

	Issue	Current	Cost/Date
FC-170-50, Mr. Spock, waist-shot of Spock holding phaser and standing in front of Galileo 7........	1	1-2	_____
Star Trek The Motion Picture Color Postcards 2109 Lincoln Enterprises, 1983 Color postcards with portraits of the crew, 5"x7"			
Kirk	1.30	.50-.75	_____
Spock	1.30	.50-.75	_____
McCoy	1.30	.50-.75	_____
Scotty	1.30	.50-.75	_____
Sulu	1.30	.50-.75	_____
Uhura	1.30	.50-.75	_____
Chekov	1.30	.50-.75	_____
Chapel	1.30	.50-.75	_____
Rand	1.30	.50-.75	_____
Ilia	1.30	.50-.75	_____
Decker	1.30	.50-.75	_____
Enterprise	1.30	.50-.75	_____
Complete set of 12 cards	3.95	6-8	_____

SCHOOL AND OFFICE

Star Trek III Postcards 2101
Lincoln Enterprises, 1984
Set of 10 color postcards featuring portraits of stars from the movie cast, 5"x7"

	Issue	Current	Cost/Date
Kirk	.40	.40-.50	______
Spock	.40	.40-.50	______
McCoy	.40	.40-.50	______
Scotty	.40	.40-.50	______
Sulu	.40	.40-.50	______
Chekov	.40	.40-.50	______
Uhura	.40	.40-.50	______
Saavik	.40	.40-.50	______
T'Lar	.40	.40-.50	______
Complete set of 10 cards	3.95	4-5	______

Postcard Books

Collections of detachable cards, suitable for mailing with photo or design fronts.

Postcard Book, Prime Press

Star Trek Postcard Book
Gary Gerani, Prime Press
Oversize softbound containing 48 full-color postcards, inside cover features an index of Star Trek episodes. Titled postcards:

1. Seeking new horizons
2. Leonard Nimoy as Mr. Spock
3. Men of the Enterprise
4. Dr. Leonard "Bones" McCoy
5. William Shatner as James T. Kirk
6. Science Officer Spock
7. "Amok Time"
8. The Vulcan Mr. Spock
9. The Parallel Spock
10. Spock with lyre
11. Science Officer Spock
12. "Spock's Brain"
13. Captain Kirk on the bridge
14. Captain James T. Kirk
15. Kirk disguised as Romulan
16. Kirk on mining planet
17. "The Trouble with Tribbles"
18. Kirk and Spock
19. Enterprise orbits Delta Vega
20. The U.S.S. Enterprise
21. The Enterprise
22. Enterprise orbiting planet
23. "The Tholian Web"
24. Enterprise firing phasers
25. Balok's alter-ego
26. The Gorn
27. The Vians
28. The Mugato
29. Telerite
30. The Taolsians
31. Science Officer Spock
34. Dr. Leonard "Bones" McCoy
35. Spock in Command
36. McCoy and Spock
37. Planet Delta Vega
38. Janus VI mining complex
39. The Rigel Fortress
40. Starbase II
41. Starbase II
42. Planet Eminar VII
43. Terrifying Illusion
44. Kirk using the communicator
45. "This Side of Paradise"
46. The Guardian of Forever
47. The bridge viewing screen
48. The Shuttlecraft Galileo

	Issue	Current	Cost/Date
Postcard Book of 48 cards 0-87897-048-7, 1977	4	5-12	______

Star Trek III The Search For Spock Postcard Book
Wanderer Books
Tradepaper, contains 22 color card-stock postcards with scenes from the movie, 11 pages. Titled cards:

1. David, Saavik, young Spock in snow
2. The Spacedock
3. David Marcus
4. Members of the Enterprise crew
5. Klingon bridge
6. Bird of Prey lands on Vulcan
7. Captain Spock
8. James Tiberius Kirk
9. Sarek and Kirk mind meld.
10. Klingon Sergeant with knife
11. Spock, close-up
12. First sighting of the Bird of Prey
13. Saavik and David
14. Enterprise approaches the Bird of Prey
15. Katra Ritual begins
16. Enterprise crew on Genesis
17. Kirk during Fal-Tor-Pan
18. Bird of Prey attacks
19. Ambassador Sarek

SCHOOL AND OFFICE

	Issue	Current	Cost/Date
20. Kirk and Kruge fighting			
21. Cast of the movie			
22. Sarek in prayer			
Postcard book of 22 cards 0-671-501-2, 1984	4.95	5-7	______

Stamps

Rubber Stamps

T-K Graphics, 1984
Sturdy, high quality wooden base stamps with handles, 1"x2½" format:

	Issue	Current	Cost/Date
Approved: Star Fleet Command	1	1-2	______
Beam Me Up Scotty. This Place Has No Intelligent Life	1	1-2	______
Dispatched: Stardate ____	1	1-2	______
He's Dead Jim	1	1-2	______
Live Long and Prosper	1	1-2	______
Space: The Final Frontier	1	1-2	______
Star Fleet Computer Division	1	1-2	______
Star Fleet Headquarters/Classified	1	1-2	______
Star Fleet Headquarters/Official Mail	1	1-2	______
Star Fleet Spacegram	1	1-2	______
UFP Janus Head Emblem	1	1-2	______
U.S.S. Enterprise Schematic	1	1-2	______

Character Stamps

United Trekkies of Planet Earth, 1975
144 stamp sheet featuring 6 famous Star Trek characters. Adhesive back, yellow color with busts of Kirk, Spock, McCoy, Scotty, Uhura and Chekov, 12"x12" sheet . . . 1 — 4-5 ______

Enterprise Local Postage Stamps

Northville, Michigan, 1973
LNNAF distributors
Special local issue postage stamps. First day cancels and commemoratives honoring:

	Issue	Current	Cost/Date
William Shatner as Captain Kirk Dated August 19, 1973	.25	4-6	______
Leonard Nimoy as Mr. Spock. Dated September 20, 1973	.25	4-6	______

Gummed Stamps

Lincoln Enterprises, 1976
40 full color stamps per sheet, each with assorted different scenes, characters, aliens, etc. from Star Trek t.v. series, 8½"x11" sheets.

	Issue	Current	Cost/Date
1030 one sheet	1.25	2-4	______
1030A three sheets	3	5-8	______

Photo Stamps

Micro Co., 1972
1"x1½" postage size stamps, head profiles reproduced on gummed paper. Each stamp style has a white and color border to match the color of the photo, sets of 50:

	Issue	Current	Cost/Date
1. "William Shatner" lettering below portrait of Kirk in black and white	.50	2-3	______
2. "Wm. Shatner" lettering below portrait of Kirk in cepia-tone brown and white	.50	2-3	______
3. "Leonard Nimoy" close-up of Spock with lettering below cepia-tone brown and white photo	.50	2-3	______
4. Spock photo, no lettering, black and white	.50	2-3	______
5. "Leonard Nimoy" photo of Nimoy as himself above black and white photo	.50	1-3	______

Star Trek Portrait Miniatures

Lincoln Enterprises, 1976
The entire cast of Star Trek characters including Kirk, Spock, McCoy, Scotty, Uhura, Sulu, Chapel, Chekov and the Enterprise in postage stamp size photos. 100 miniatures per sheet, perforated.
0110 One sheet . . . 1 — 3-5 ______

Star Trek Stamp Album - Official

Celebrity Stamps, 1977
Collection 1, softbound book with info, photos and stamp outlines from the series, 24 pages, 8½"x11". Also includes 6 subject packets containing 10 different collector stamps each and one jumbo panorama stamp which divides into four section

	Issue	Current	Cost/Date
Package 1 - features U.S.S Enterprise	—	3-6	______
Package 2 - features Kirk and Crew	—	3-6	______
Package 3 - features Mr. Spock	—	3-6	______
Package 4 - features Klingons and Romulans	—	3-6	______
Package 5 - features Aliens of the Galaxy	—	3-6	______
Package 6 - features Creatures of the Galaxy	—	3-6	______
Complete Unassembled Albums	7.25	20-30	______
Assembled Albums	—	15-20	______
Album only, unused	—	6-10	______

Stationery

Single sheets, 8½"x11" format in assorted color stock and printing, suitable for mailing [4]

"Captain's Quarters"

Starbase Central, 1984
Dark blue ink on light paper, with Comman Star Insignia in lower right corner, 10 sheets . . . 1.25 — -3 ______

Crew Illustrations

Alicia Austin, Star Trek Enterprises, 1968
6 pen and ink designs with imaginative scenes of aliens and crew, black on white, 30 sheets . . . 1 — 4-6 ______

4. Star Trek has been the theme for hundreds of fan produced stationery and letterhead sets over the years. The following listings detail those items which were marketed through mail-order distributors.

SCHOOL AND OFFICE

	Issue	Current	Cost/Date
"From the Bridge of the U.S.S Enterprise" T-K Graphics, 1984 Black lettering on white, 10 sheets plus printed envelopes reading "U.S.S. Enterprise/NCC-1701"	2.25	2-4	______
"Message From the Klingon Empire" Starbase Central, 1984 Rust print on tan paper, Klingonese letters along the borders, 10 sheets.	2	3-4	______
"Star Fleet Academy" April Publications, 1984 Blue print on quality white bond, 25 sheets	3	3-4	______
"Star Fleet Command" T-K Graphics, 1984 Black on white paper, large Janus Head Emblem on 10 sheets, plus envelopes with smaller Emblem in circle	2.25	3-4	______
"Starfleet Command Communications" Starbase Central, 1984 Dark grey ink on light grey paper, place for stardate, Janus Head Emblem in lower left corner, 10 sheets	2	2-4	______

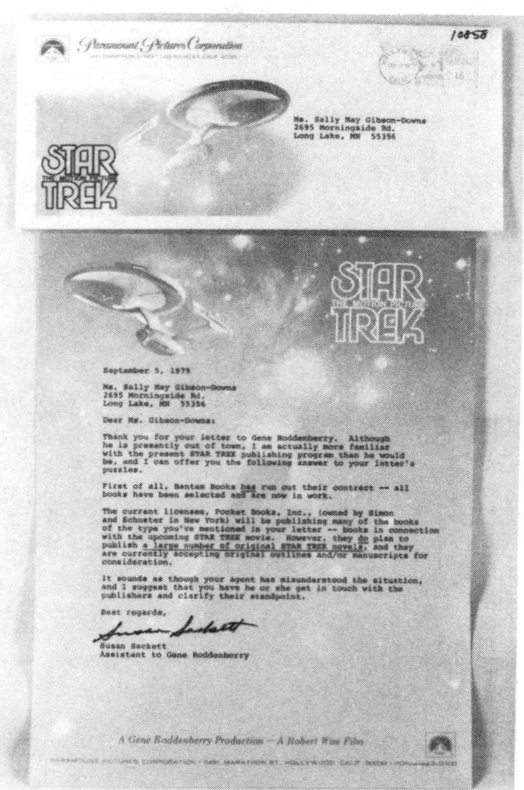

September 5, 1979

Ms. Sally May Gibson-Downs
2695 Morningside Rd.
Long Lake, MN 55356

Dear Ms. Gibson-Downs:

Thank you for your letter to Gene Roddenberry. Although he is presently out of town, I am actually more familiar with the present STAR TREK publishing program than he would be, and I can offer you the following answer to your letter's puzzles.

First of all, Bantam Books has run out their contract -- all books have been selected and are now in work.

The current licensee, Pocket Books, Inc., (owned by Simon and Schuster in New York) will be publishing many of the books of the type you've mentioned in your letter -- books in connection with the upcoming STAR TREK movie. However, they do plan to publish a large number of original STAR TREK novels, and they are currently accepting original outlines and/or manuscripts for consideration.

It sounds as though your agent has misunderstood the situation, and I suggest that you have he or she get in touch with the publishers and clarify their standpoint.

Best regards,

Susan Sackett
Assistant to Gene Roddenberry

A Gene Roddenberry Production — A Robert Wise Film

This STTMP Promotional stationery was never made available through retail. It was used by PPC.

	Issue	Current	Cost/Date
"Star Trek" Official Letterhead Star Trek/Lincoln Enterprises, 1968-1980 As used in the NBC offices during the t.v. program, starship in starry sky, black			
1000 printed envelopes, set of 20 ..	1	2-3	______
1001 printed letterhead, 20 sheets ..	1	2-3	______
"Star Trek III The Search For Spock" Official Letterhead Lincoln Enterprises, 1984 As used by the production staff, ST III Movie Letter Logo in dark print on white paper			
0990 paper	2.95	3-5	______
0991 envelopes, 15	2.50	3-4	______
0992 one set of each	4.95	6-9	______
"UFP Diplomatic Service" T-K Graphics, 1984 Black lettering on white with Janus Head Emblem, 10 sheets	2.25	3-4	______
"U.S.S. Enterprise" Starbase Central, 1984 Red on grey paper with silhouette of starship (top-view) centered in grey, 10 sheets	2	2-4	______
"Vulcan Academy" April Publications, 1984 Blue ink on quality bond, 25 sheets	3	4-5	______
"Vulcan Science Academy" T-K Graphics, 1984 Black on white, including envelopes, 10 sheets	2.25	3-4	______

Spock Writing Tablet, 1970

	Issue	Current	Cost/Date
Writing Tablet - Spock/"Leonard Nimoy" 1970 Ruled writing table for children with coarse grain school paper, thin stock on gummed pad. Cover is glossy print of Spock holding Enterprise poster, signature script in lower left corner signs Nimoy's name, 58 sheets	.30	3-4	______

Scripts

Star Trek Enterprises, in 1968, began what would amount to two decades of the sale of shooting scripts from the 78 episode television series. These original Final Drafts were identical to those used by the production staff and actors or actresses of the show during the first season.

Halfway through the second season, Star Trek Enterprises offered fans the additional opportunity to receive T.V. scripts as the shows were being aired by subscription. Each week a new show script would arrive at their doors for the modest price of $5.50 a piece. The scripts appeared as unmarked, mimeographed copies clipped between the pages of colored construction paper.

Star Trek scripts now exist in so many different formats that listing them all would be impossible. Star Trek Enterprises' scripts first appeared with plain red typewritten cover sheets. There was no exterior ornamentation. Later copies carried stenciled "Star Trek" lettering and sported a variety of construction cover colors. Movie scripts have varied in cover format as well. Different design fronts include: "Star Trek" stenciling with bar and prong clips; embossed "Star Trek" lettering with PPC logos on posterboard; and drafts with plastic, spiral bound spines.

Every script goes through a succession of re-writes and changes that are tagged with an established nomenclature peculiar to the movie industry. Any plot begins as a **Script Outline.** This is a written synopsis of the story which a writer submits to his producer for the initial review. After this, the outline proceeds through a succession of re-writes known as **Drafts.** Slowly, an outline becomes further altered by another series of **Final Revisions** until it is considered an **Incompleted Final.** The last formal layout for the story is a **Shooting Script.** Even at this stage, when the script is hand-carried around a set during filming, changes are constantly being made which transform it into the last draft, which is recognized as being the show.

Basically, there are four types of scripts for collectors to purchase.

Annotated Scripts – These are the most valuable Star Trek scripts. They apear as typed **originals** containing heavy personal commentaries or annotated notes. A price range of $100 is easily reached because of their relative rarity. Such scripts are more valuable than typed originals of scripts that were never produced.

Originals – Original, typewritten scripts sell at premium as well, despite the fact that they are produced in bulk (sometimes numbering in the hundreds for production purposes. Individually, each is still considered one-of-a-kind. Original scripts carry identifying **Copy Numbers** written on their covers as well as special revision dates. Collectors should note that succession of use is not necessarily as important to collectible value as the predominant format of the script. For instance, a First Draft Original is not worth less than a Final Original. Some original scripts may also contain photocopied sections. As long as the script is mostly a typewritten original, some photocopied sections shouldn't affect the sale price.

Script Copies – Script copies are always mimeographed or photocopied. Some bear a P.P.C. trademark. As copies, they accrue the least collectible value over a period of time. However, those produced during the '60's by Star Trek Enterprises are worth more than their contemporary counterparts. The best script copies are those that are the cleanest. T.V. scripts of this caliber should range between $8-13. Longer movie versions should retail in the $12-18 range.

Script Partials – These are combination scripts which contain partial dialogues from several different drafts of a single story. An Original Script Partial can achieve the same value as a typed original in completed form even though the storyline is fragmented.

To date, the record price tag for a script in the Star Trek field belongs to a typed and mimeographed original marked as a "Duplicate Work Copy." It is the script entitled, "Voyage One - The Cage" and contains light, penciled annotations. This work copy for Star Trek's **first pilot episode** written by Gene Roddenberry, commands and impressive retail price of $200.

Clean original scripts containing no annotations should be priced between $30-$40. Identical texts with brief comments sell for around $45-$50, while the average heavily annotated original can reach $60-$75.

Of special interest to fans is the fact that an abundance of well known science fiction writers authored Star Trek episode scripts.

Russell Bates, collaborating with David Wise, produced "How Sharper Than A Serpent's Tooth" (animated).

Jerome Bixby penned "Day of the Dove," "Mirror, Mirror," "Requiem for Methuselah" and "By Any Other Name" with D.C. Fontana.

Robert Bloch wrote "Catspaw," "What Are Little Girls Made Of?" and composed "Wolf In The Fold" which was actually a sequel script for his original fiction entitled "I, Jack the Ripper."

Frederic Brown wrote "Arena" which was adapted by Gene L. Coon into script format.

Mike Dolinsky (a.k.a. Meyer Dolinsky) produced "Plato's Stepchildren."

Max Erlich, with Gene Goon, penned "The Apple."

Harlan Ellison wrote "City on the Edge of Forever."

Dorothy C. (D.C.) Fontana - produced "By Any Other Name," "The Enterprise Incident," "Friday's Child," "Journey To Babel," "Charlie X," "Tomorrow is Yesterday," "The Ultimate Computer" with Lawrence N. Wolfe, "This Side of Paradise" with Nathan Butler and "Yesteryear" (animated).

David Gerrold - penned "I, Mudd" with Stephen Kandel, "The Cloud Minders" with Oliver Crawford," "The Trouble With Tribbles," "More Troubles, More Tribbles" (animated).

George Clayton Johnson - produced "The Man Trap."

Richard Matheson - wrote "The Enemy Within."

Larry Niven - penned "The Slaver Weapon" (animated).

Jerry Sohl - wrote "The Corbormite Maneuver" and "Whom God's Destroy" with Lee Irwin.

Norman Sturgeon - wrote "Amok Time" and "Shore Leave."

Howard Weinstein - penned "The Pirates of Orion" (animated).

SCRIPTS

Original Collector Copies

Sample list of the various formats of original Star Trek scripts in First Draft, Revised, Outline and Shooting Copy editions. Such scripts are available in xerox, partial mimeograph and original typed texts, some with annotations, commments, etc.

Item	Issue	Current	Cost/Date
Assignment: Earth - by Gene Roddenberry The original script for a First Draft Pilot film dated November 14,1966, 47pp. Includes one full page of personal annotation. This was the script for the projected spin-off from the Star Trek episode of the same title. This series pilot film never materialized.	—	60-65	______
Balance of Terror - Paul Schneider First Draft, June 21, 1966, 68pp, Copy 76, annotations.	—	60-65	______
(The) Cage - by Gene Roddenberry The script for the original Star Trek Pilot film which was later encorporated into Parts I & II of the episode "Menagerie." "Duplicate Work Copy," revised Nov. 16, 1964, 67 pp, typed and mimeo'd with pencil annotations Collector Books, CA	—	200-225	______
(The) Changeling - John Meredyth Lucas Final Draft, May 29, 1967, Copy 2, 66 pp	—	40-45	______
Revised Draft, April 7, 1967, with annotations, 72pp.	—	45-50	______
Charlie X - D.C. Fontana July 8, 1966, 72 pp, part xerox, part original type, some real annotations, some xerox annotations, plus a xerox copy of the second draft dated June 27, 1966, 68pp.	—	50-55	______
City on the Edge of Forever - Harlan Ellison Shooting Script, January 27, 1967, 70pp, half-typed, annotated	—	100-110	______
Day of the Dove - Jerome Bixby June 27, 1968, 67pp, Xerox copy with the Star Trek Office stamp and a receiving signature.	—	16-20	______
(The) Empath - Joyce Muskat First Draft, July 17, 1968, copy 2, first three acts only. 42pp.	—	25-30	______
Journey To Thantos Reproductions, 1972 Completed, authentic episode script under consideration when the t.v. series was cancelled. "Starships Enterprise and Exeter are captured by alien computrons who take over the ship's computers for their own devices." Xerox copy	—	20-30	______
(The Menagerie, Part I & II - Gene Roddenberry First Draft, Sept. 21, 1966, 82pp, typed and annotated.	—	75-80	______
Mudd's Women - Stephen Kandel, Gene Roddenberry First Draft, May 23, 1966, "rewrite by John D.F. Black," 75pp, Xerox	—	20-25	______
Power Play - by Jerry Sohl Early script version of "This Side of Paradise." First Draft, Sept. 1, 1966, 74pp, typed plus 23pp typed correspondence on the progress of the script. Includes the aired version of the teaser.	—	75-80	______
Tomorrow the Universe - by Paul Schneider Unfilmed television script. Schneider produced three Trek scripts. This unproduced episode is dated January 20, 1967, 67pp, typed.	—	35-40	______
Turnabout Intruder - Arthur H. Singer and Gene Roddenberry Dec. 27, 1967, 30pp- (with blue "changes") Incomplete (full script goes to page 61).	—	15-18	______
(The) Way of the Spores - by Jerry Sohl First Final Draft (or "polish script") for "This Side of Paradise." Dated October 11, 1966, 64pp, typed with light annotation, plus 4-page typed discussion of the later script dated October 18th.	—	50-55	______

REPRODUCTIONS

Mimeographed or xeroxed copies without original annotations, markings, etc. Copies retailed for distribution and mass marketed.

Item	Issue	Current	Cost/Date
Adventure Series Scripts Star Trek/Lincoln Enterprises 1968; 1980 Mimeographed copies of the actual Final Draft Shooting Scripts as used for each episode of Star Trek. All 78 episodes (including the two-part show "menagerie") are available. Scripts are ordered by individual titles.	5.50	8-15	______
Animated Series Scripts Lincoln Enterprises, 1980 Mimeographed copies of the final shooting drafts, available for each of the 22 cartoon episodes.			
More Tribbles, More Troubles - D. Gerrold	4.50	5-8	______
The Infinite Vulcan - Walter Koenig	4.50	5-8	______
Yesteryear - D.C. Fontana	4.50	5-8	______

SCRIPTS

	Issue	Current	Cost/Date
Beyond The Farthest Star - Sam Peeples	4.50	5-8	______
The Survivor - James Schmerer	4.50	5-8	______
The Lorelie Signal - Margaret Armon	4.50	5-8	______
One of Our Planets is Missing - M. Daniels	4.50	5-8	______
Mudd's Passion - Stephen Kandel	4.50	5-8	______
The Magicks of Megus-Tu - Larry Brody	4.50	5-8	______
Time Trap - Joyce Perry	4.50	5-8	______
The Slaver Weapon - Larry Niven	4.50	5-8	______
The Jihad - Stephen Kandel	4.50	5-8	______
The Ambergris Element - Margaret Armon	4.50	5-8	______
Once Upon A Planet - Lynn Janson and Chuck Menville	4.50	5-8	______
The Terratin Incident - David Harmon	4.50	5-8	______
The Eye of the Beholder - David Harmon	4.50	5-8	______
BEM - David Gerrold	4.50	5-8	______
Albatross - Darlo Finelli	4.50	5-8	______
Pirates of Orion - Howard Weinstein	4.50	5-8	______
Practical Joker - Chuck Menville	4.50	5-8	______
How Sharper Than A Serpent's Tooth - Russell Bates and David Wise	4.50	5-8	______
Counter-Clock Incident - John Culver	4.50	5-8	______
Pilot Episode Script - "The Cage" Lincoln Enterprises, 1984 Mimeographed copy of the Final Shooting Script	12.95	13-16	______
Star Trek The Motion Picture Lincoln Enterprises, 1980 First Draft - story as written by Gene Roddenberry with characters never portrayed in the movie: "Xon" the young Vulcan navigator, and "Alexandria" the woman Kirk loves, mimeographed	12.95	13-16	______
Shooting Script - script used to produce the first movie, 400 scenes in 130 p. mimeographed.	12.95	13-16	______
Star Trek II The Wrath of Kahn Lincoln Enterprises, 1982 Shooting Script - script by Harve Bennett, Jack B. Sowards and Samuel A. Peeples, 250 scenes in 155 p., used to produce movie, beige cover with embossed P.P.C. Logo, mimeographed	12.95	13-16	______

	Issue	Current	Cost/Date
Star Trek II The Wrath of Kahn Lincoln Enterprises, 1982 Dialogue Release Script - total movie footage including dialogue, camera action, edited musical score and the events exactly as they appeared on the screen, mimeographed	12.95	13-16	______
Star Trek III The Search For Spock Lincoln Enterprises, 1984 First Draft	12.95	13-16	______
Final Draft	12.95	13-16	______
Dialogue Release Script	12.95	13-16	______

TOYS

Star Trek toys come in two varieties: action figures and stuffed dolls (animals) or die-cast and plastic playtoys. This is almost exclusively a children's market. In retrospect, dolls and action figures representing the Enterprise crew were a latent merchandising gimmick of the middle 70's, appearing five years after the T.V. show's demise. T.V. Trek also generated more functional playtoys for children such as an amazing array of Star Trek field equipment and weapon gadgetry.

Action Figures, Dolls & Stuffed Toys

NBC's launching of the Star Trek animated series in fall 1973 programming awakened new interest in Star Trek, especially with the children's marketing industry. The cartoon series produced by Filmation Studios ran from September 8, 1973 until August 30, 1975. The animated show also won the 1974-75 Emmy Award in children's animation as a series.

In 1974 Mego produced a line of fourteen, 8 inch, vinyl dolls as well as the accessories **Starship Enterprise Flight Deck** (1974), **Mission to Gamma VI** (1976) and **Telescreen Console** (1977). At the same time, Mego produced several plastic playtoys, too. Everything Mego produced is a rare item if complete and in good condition. Collectors may notice that there is an anomaly associated with Mego's **Enterprise Flight Deck.** The call letters on the picture Enterprise displayed on the back of the carry case are not NCC-1701 but NCC 171.

Especially rare are the hard-to-find 3¾" alien action figures from **Star Trek The Motion Picture** which were produced in 1979. The Arcturian, Betelgeusian, Klingon, Meganite, Rigelian and Zaranite advertised on the reverse of the action figure blister packs sold in the U.S. were mainly issued in Europe alone.

Die-Cast & Plastic Playtoys

Children love action toys. Star Trek has matched the need to the demand with a dizzying assortment of die-cast or plastic toys that roll, fly, flash, inflate or discharge sound. All that most toys needed was an accompanying "Star Trek" decal, stocker or card-stock backing to connect it with the T.V. show or animated series and it became promotionally marketable.

The quality of these collectibles varies from the extremely sophisticated to the cheap. Issue prices echo this quality status fairly well.

It should be pointed out that sometimes the most interesting thing about inexpensive playtoys is the package, box or blister wrapping that they appeared in. These were usually very colorful selling trademarks which featured Star Trek artwork, photo insets and T.V. logos. In some cases, such as the **Tracer Gun** made by Ray Plastics in 1967, the actual item is still being produced in identical type and the only thing that separates a new article from the vintage one is the accompanying Star Trek packaging in a sealed, untampered condition.

DOLLS AND STUFFED TOYS

- **Star Trek Dolls - 8 Inch**
  Mego Corp. 1974
  Vinyl dolls with articulated limbs and moveable heads. Removeable cloth uniforms from the t.v. series and plastic boots. Accessories include plastic utility belt, tricorder, pistol phaser and communicator. Uhura doll has page-boy style fiber hair. Very detailed faces. 90¼"x8½" cardboard plastic-form mount with cartoon illos of the dolls. Back advertises the Mego Playcase and Mego Communicators.

Mego's 8 inch vinyl dolls, 1974

Mego's 8 inch vinyl dolls, 1974

	Issue	Current	Cost/Date
51200/1 Capt. Kirk	2.99	14-20	______
51200/2 Mr. Spock	2.99	14-20	______
51200/3 Dr. McCoy (Bones)	2.99	16-25	______
51200/4 Lt. Uhura	2.99	16-25	______
51200/5 Romulan	2.99	35-60	______
51200/7 Klingon	2.99	25-35	______
51200/8 Gorn	2.99	40-60	______
51200/9 Andorian (Fringed shirt, knee boots and tights)	2.99	30-40	______
51200/10 Talosian (Bald, white uniform)	2.99	25-35	______

DOLLS

	Issue	Current	Cost/Date
51200/11 Cheron (White/black face and jumpsuit)	2.99	30-35	_____
51200/12 Mugato (Unicorn simian, belted tunic)	2.99	30-40	_____
51200/13 The Keeper (Horned, high collar robe)	2.99	30-40	_____
51200/14 Neptunian (Jumpsuit with red boots)	2.99	30-35	_____

8-Inch Dolls Accessories

Mission to Gamma VI
Mego Corp., 1976
Mountain terrain alien landscape action play set including an acto-glove to operate moving jaw "Vaal" idol. Includes a man-eating plant and a secret trap door. 20½"x18½"x16" Boxed. Cover cartoons a child playing with the set . . . . 12 40-60 _____

Starship Enterprise Flight Deck 51210
Mego Corp., 1974
Washable vinyl playcase for carrying the dolls. Replicates the flightdeck (bridge) with Captain's chair navigations console and transporter above which spins by means of a dial to allow characters to disappear. Six interchangeable scenes attach onto the front viewscreen. Boxed. . . . . 8 35-80 _____

Telescreen Console
Mego Corp., 1977
Command center action set which operates with 4 "D" cell batteries. Viewscreen targets "beep" when hit. Plastic console with Captain's chair for dolls. Features phaser aiming controls and battle sounds, scoring device light and projection targets. Boxed 14¼" x 9½", cover cartoons the head of Spock and the actual toy. . . . . 15 60-95 _____

Star Trek Motion Picture - 3¾ Inch Figures
Mego Corp., 1979
STTMP vintage plastic molded dolls with moving arms and legs. Painted. 6"x9" cardstock plastic-form mount cartoons the first six action figures on front. Rear photos the movie characters from the picture. [1]

3¾" Action Figures, Star Trek The Motion Picture

	Issue	Current	Cost/Date
91200/1 Capt. Kirk	2.99	5-8	_____
91200/2 Mr. Spock	2.99	5-8	_____
91200/3 Decker	2.99	5-8	_____
91200/4 Ilia	2.99	6-8	_____
91200/5 Scotty	2.99	5-8	_____
91200/6 Dr. McCoy	2.99	5-8	_____
91200/7 Klingon (with skull ridges)	2.99	8-10	_____
91200/8 Zaranite (split-skull, respirator	2.99	8-12	_____
91200/9 Betelgeusian (Blue-skinned, samari)	2.99	8-12	_____
91201/1 Arcturian (Scaled)	2.99	8-12	_____
91201/2 Meganite (Hooded, folds on face)	2.99	8-12	_____
91201/3 Rigelian (Pink skinned, reptilian	2.99	8-12	_____
91200/1 through 91200/6 as a set	—	20-30	_____

The aliens on this reverse promotion were released in Europe.

1. The 3¾" Star Trek The Motion Picture alien action figures were primarily released in Europe. They were very hard to find in the U.S. It was reported that certain stocks came from Italy.

Star Trek III Action Figures, 1984

3¾ Inch Doll Accessories

	Issue	Current	Cost/Date
U.S.S. Enterprise Bridge 91233 Mego Corp., 1980 Bridge replica playset for the dolls. 24"x12" theatre with working dock port, helm and navigations console, science and communications station and Captain's chair. Plastic shell snaps together (top and bottom) and uses sticker press-tabs. Not functional as a carrying case. Box photos the miniature dolls on the action set. [2]	9	15-25	______

- **Star Trek Motion Picture - 12-Inch Dolls**

Mego Corp., 1980
STTMP vintage cloth uniforms on vinyl dolls with articulated limbs. Includes an assortment of plastic accessories. Window cut cardstock box shows the same illos as those found on the packaging for the 3¾" dolls.

	Issue	Current	Cost/Date
92101/1 Kirk (Gray and white uniform)	10	10-30	______
91210/2 Spock (Science Officer uniform)	10	20-30	______
91210/3 Klingon (with skull ridges)	10	30-40	______
91210/4 Ilia (white shirt-dress with high heel shoes	10	20-35	______
91210/5 Decker (Gray uniform)	10	20-35	______
91210/6 Arcturian (Fleshy head, beige uniform)	10	25-35	______

- **Star Trek III Search For Spock - 3¾ Inch Figures**

Ertl Company, 1984
STSFS vintage plastic molded dolls with posable arms, elbows, legs and knees. Each doll contains individual accessories inside blister pack wrapping. Dolls are painted.

	Issue	Current	Cost/Date
331 Mr. Spock with phaser	2.95	3-5	______
332 Captain Kirk with communicator	2.95	3-5	______
Klingon Leader (Kruge) and Dog	2.95	3-5	______

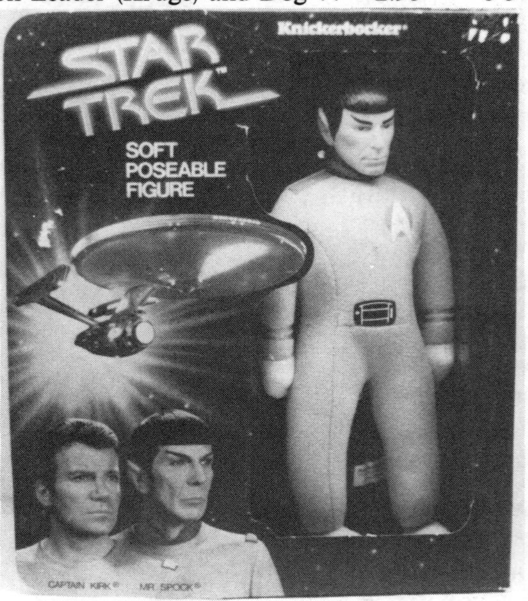

Knickerbocker Spock Doll

Puppets
Manning, 1976
5-Inch painted, wooden puppets. Two-dimensional, flattened operable arms and legs, operate by strings.

	Issue	Current	Cost/Date
Kirk Puppet	3	12-15	______
Spock Puppet	3	15-18	______

Stuffed Dolls

Grammy's Little Trekkers
Berry Patch Dolls, 1986
Hand-sewn, soft body cloth dolls, dressed in t.v. Star Trek uniforms and patterned after the Cabbage Patch Doll series.

	Issue	Current	Cost/Date
Kirk	49.95	50-51	______
Spock	49.95	50-51	______
McCoy	49.95	50-51	______

Berry Patch Clothes, 1986
Designed to fit Cabbage Patch Dolls as well:

	Issue	Current	Cost/Date
Red, yellow blue t.v. uniform with booties for male or female	19.95	20-22	______
Star Trek III movie version uniform with booties	25	25-27	______

Poseable Figures
Knickerbocker, 1979
12-inch stuffed, flannel dolls for young children. Vinyl heads are non-removeable, velcro strips along the body allow for posing of the limbs, STTMP uniforms

	Issue	Current	Cost/Date
Kirk, gray and white uniform	4	15-18	______
Spock, blue-gray uniform	4	12-15	______

2. This playset became very fragile after the paper tabs were applied and the toy was put to use. It has become a rare collectible in good to mint condition.

Tribbles and Their Kin

	Issue	Current	Cost/Date
Dreebles New Eye, distributors, 1986 Electronic tribble that purrs and chirps. Includes a pedigree certificate and a story book.	19.95	20-22	_____
Tribbles, Star Trek David Gerrold Co., 1973 Early producers of assorted furry tribbles in various colors, located in Hollywood, California.			
Small	3	5-6	_____
Large	5	6-8	_____
Tribbles - Assorted Kinds Produced over the years by Aviva, Lincoln Enterprises, Dage Co., and numerous individuals; average price ranges:			
Normal (Long or short hair, approx. 6")	—	4-5	_____
Squeaking	—	5-6	_____
Attack Tribbles (open mouths, fangs)	—	6-7	_____
Babies (approx. 3")	—	2-3	_____
Tribble Preemies New Eye, distributors, 1986 Miniature furry animals, with or without safety pins to be worn (carried) with you	2	2-3	_____
Tribble-Eater 1975 Plush stuffed toy representing the Glommer creature from the animated Star Trek episode "More Tribbles, More Troubles". Beast has four legs with mushroom-like head, small eyes rest on head beneath two antenna-like eye stalks, small plastic "horn" protrudes from the center of the forehead. Orange color, approx. 11" tall		30-40	_____

DIE-CAST AND PLASTIC PLAYTOYS

	Issue	Current	Cost/Date
• **Banks** Play Pal, Inc., 1975 Standing figures of Kirk or Spock in front of bridge command chair, molded plastic, 11½" tall			
Kirk, holding communicator	3	10-15	_____
Spock	3	10-15	_____
• **Binoculars** 9239 Larami Corp., 1968 5½"x5½" white plastic binoculars with orange eyepieces, lens rims and focal adjuster. Words "Star Trek" appear across the two barrels in black decals. Black plastic neck strap, 7½"x10¾" blister packed, photos scene from "Shore Leave" and the "Spock holding Enterprise" poster, boasts NBC affiliation	1	8-12	_____
• **Bop-Bag** 1073 Azrak-Hamway International (AHI) 1975 Mr. Spock cartoon figure imprinted on an inflatable plastic punching bag; floor standing 50" tall. 6"x2"x5" box features "Star Trek" letter logo from the Gold Key series of comics, cartoons Enterprise and photos the actual inflated bag	3	15-18	_____

• Communicator/Walkie-Talkies

	Issue	Current	Cost/Date
Astro Walkie-Talkies 872 Remco Industries, 1967 Oval, hand-held microphone set. 2"x4" mikes have blue hand-grips and a single plastic extention antenna. Paper decals read "Star Trek" and show uniform insignia. Waxboard mount 8¼"x11" cardboard with blue outline drawings of the Enterprise, Kirk and Spock, using toy [1]	1	20-25	_____
• **Communicators** 51214 Mego Corp., 1974 7-transistor walkie-talkies that replicate the hand-held t.v. communicators. Send and receive messages up to ¼ mile. Twin warp sound, telescoping antenna. Two-tone blue plastic with silver and black insignia design. Each requires one 9-volt battery. Includes a belt clip. Box front cartoons Spock holding communicator with Kirk in background.	19	35-65	_____

1. This toy carries a 1967 Desilu Productions affiliation as well as an NBC Letter Logo. The simplicity of the toy-style is a carry-over from the "space-age" children's toy craze so popular in the late 1950's and early 1960's.

PLAYTOYS

	Issue	Current	Cost/Date
• Communicators			
(Command) Communications Console Mego Corp., 1976 Base control station for use as relay station with Mego Communicators set. Sends and receives signals, 5 sound effects, flashing lights, telescoping antenna, uses one 9-volt battery.	12	25-40	______
Wrist Communicators 91238 Mego Corp., 1980 STTMP movie vintage wrist communicators, straps on and is powered with two 9-volt batteries in pack attached to wrist. Flexible antenna sends and receives voices up to 20 feet indoors, 50 feet outdoors. Box 6½"x3½"x4¾".	12	20-35	______
• Dilithium Crystals 1970's Solid, opaque plastic crystal set on a revolving base. 3" squared. Spins clockwise and then reverses itself, choice of three different colors	2	5-8	______
• Flight Game, U.S.S. Enterprise Controlled Space Remco, 1976 Starship flight controls for retrieving space objects, start/stop, hover/glide, accelerate, altitude course, orbit/transport controls. You fly the Enterprise. Boxed.	20	60-120	______
• Frisbee - Flying U.S.S. Enterprise Remco, 1967 Yellow frisbee toy, 8½" diameter with decal of Spock's head and "Star Trek" lettering	.79	8-10	______
• Guns and Phasers			
Flashlight - Ray Gun 9238 Larami Corp., 1968 Traditional gun style in white plastic; 4"x6", orange handgrip, site and barrel tip. Logos "Star Trek" in black decals along the body. Operates by trigger, requires two AA batteries (included). 7½"x10¾" cardboard mount features "Spock holding model Enterprise" photo and color scene from "Shore Leave." Package boasts NBC affiliation, blister packed.	.70	10-15	______
Flashlight - Phaser Ray Gun 6369 Azrak-Hamway International (AHI) 1976 Flashlight pistol with "Star Trek" in black decals along the barrel, 3¾" x 3", requires penlight AA battery. Cardboard mount cartoons alien planetscapes and the Enterprise.	1.50	8-10	______
Phaser Battle, Electronic Target Game 51220 Mego Corp., 1976 Pre-video game with plastic console and 16" diagonal screen for projection Klingon and Romulan ship targets; LED scoring, battle and phaser sounds, battle status report, port and starboard deflectors and adjustable 3-speed control lever. Enemy returns fire. Operates on AC-100 current or six C-cell batteries. Large red box.	24	80-150	______
Phaser Gun, The Official Electronic Remco Industries, 1975 Black plastic rendition of a t.v. phaser pistol with sound and light beam, three beam discs and target projections. Uses one 9-volt or two AA batteries. Cardboard box features small photo busts of Kirk and Spock	3	30-40	______
Phaser Guns, Electronic Dueling Set 7902E Southbend/Milton Bradley, 1979 STTMP stylized with plastic pistols with "Star Trek" imprinted on the barrel. Infrared beam passes through window glass, bounces off mirror and produces explosive "hit" sound on solid impact. Battery operated. Boxed and sold as set of two guns. [2]	30	60-90	______
Phaser, Saucer Gun, The Official 6269 Azrak-Hamway International (AHI), 1976 Black and chrome-colored plastic replica of the t.v. series phaser pistol. Tip shoots a 2¼" colored saucer disc (3 are included); 7"x9" cardboard mount photos busts of Kirk and Spock and cartoons the Enterprise	1.59	7-10	______
Phaser Gun, Super Phaser 2 Target Game Mego Corp., 1976 Type II plastic phaser toy with a sonic buzzer that sounds out when aim strikes Klingon target reflector badge	10	15-18	______
Phaser Gun, Star Trek III Daisey-Lights, 1985 Plastic toy replica with beeping sound effects, battery operated.	3	4-6	______
Photo Blaster Larami Corp., 1979 STTMP vintage pistol gun emits three different color flashes, batteries required	3.50	8-10	______

2. This "dueling set" comprised an early form of laser-tag game, the same type of battle-action set that is so popular today.

PLAYTOYS

Issue Current Cost/Date

Rocket Pistol 870-450
Remco Industries, 1967
5½"x13" blue and black plastic rifle gun in old style 007 format. Features one yellow plastic grenade which bayonet mounts, flip-up target site and retractable handle grip for loading toy caps. Cardboard decal displays the Command Insignia. 7½"x15". Shows photos from the interior of the Enterprise[3] 2.49 35-50 ______

Original Star Trek Tracer Gun Packages, not package for tracer gun still being sold.

Tracer Gun (Rapid Fire) 31[4]
Ray Plastics, 1967
Choice of gold or blue plastic pistols with brown handle grip, 4¼"x6" size, loads up to 20 plastic multi-colored discs (35 included). 8½"x10¾" cardboard mount in two package styles, both boast NBC affiliation:

Cartoon hand holding tracer with head photos of Kirk and Spock .... 1 8-10 ______

Cartoon Enterprise in sky with full bust photos of Spock and Kirk from the original publicity photos ...... 1 8-10 ______

Tracer Scope (Jet Disc) 35
Ray Plastics, 1968
4½"x19" blue plastic rifle with brown handle grip and barrel scope. Loads up to 20 plastic discs (100 included). 8¼"x24" cardboard and blister packed. Cartoons Enterprise in the sky and head photos Kirk and Spock. Boasts NBC affiliations.[5] .. 3 12-18 ______

Package back for the rare Jet Disc Tracer Scope

Issue Current Cost/Date

Tracer Jet Disc Refills 31-JD
Ray Plastics, 1967
5¼"x7¼" cardboard and plastic pack containing 100 refill discs for the above Tracer toys. Pictures the pistol toy in action, labeled "Star Trek". .... .40 2-3 ______

Water Gun - Mini Phaser
1976
Type II t.v. pistol phaser, blue plastic miniatures, blister packed .. 1 3-5 ______

Water Gun - Phaser Pistol
Azrak-Hamway International, 1975
Black and chrome-colored rendition of a phaser pistol, 5¾" in length. Body identical to the AHI Phaser Saucer Gun 6269. 7"x9" cardstock mount, plastic form mount. ...... 1.79 7-10 ______

Star Trek The Motion Picture Water Pistol by Aviva

Water Gun (STTMP)
Aviva, 1979
Movie vintage replica of a phaser in molded gray plastic. Has 20 foot shooting range. .... 4 5-8 ______

3. This boxed toy gun carries a 1967 Desilu Productions affiliation. It is the only package label ever produced with an actual photo of a Star Trek star (Leonard Nimoy as Mr. Spock) posing in action with the real toy.
4. The Tracer Gun remains in production from Ray Plastics. The "Star Trek" affiliation packaging, however, disappeared after the release of the below two cardstocks. The Jet Disc Refills also labelled "Star Trek" affiliation in the late 1960's. Since the toy is still available, this item illustrates the primary importance of retaining original packages to authenticate a toy's value as an original release.
5. This rifle version of the above Tracer Gun enjoyed only a limited distribution, making it a much rarer find. It is not currently in production under a different packaging.

PLAYTOYS

• Guns and Phasers

	Issue	Current	Cost/Date
Water Gun - U.S.S. Enterprise Toy Azrak-Hamway International, 1976 Traditional gun-style water pistol in white plastic with finger-press trigger. Gun barrel forms a stylized rendition of the starship Enterprise's primary hull. Water squirts out of the dish antenna! Saucer dome and nacelles are mounted to the barrel. 7"x9" plastic form mount. Cardstock top cartoons character head portraits and the starship. Bottom cartoons planetscape.	2	15-20	_____
• Helmet Enco Industries, 1976 White plastic motorcyle-style helmet with sun visor, flashing light and telescoping antenna. Snap-on chin strap and stick on names (Kirk, Spock, etc.) included. Box is 10"x7½"x8" and photos kid in uniform wearing the helmet toy. ..	5	25-40	_____

Star Trek Silly Putty

	Issue	Current	Cost/Date
Putty Larami Corp., 1979, No. 8348-5 STTMP vintage play putty. Non-toxic, non-sticking, non-staining putty with special transfer solution vial for adhering images to skin surfaces. Fluid refills available. Putty packaged inside a blue plastic egg. 5"x7" plastic-formed cardstock photos STTMP busts of Kirk, Spock and Enterprise. Ages 3 and over.	1	2-3	_____

Die-Cast Enterprise

Space Ships

	Issue	Current	Cost/Date
Enterprise, U.S.S. 358 Dinky Toys, 1977 234mm (9-inch) white die cast metal replica of the t.v. series starship. Includes a miniature plastic shuttlecraft which locks into forward fuselage hatch. Hand-wind bridge dome fires plastic discs from the saucer. Boxed, 10⅛"x5⅜".	7	30-55	_____
Enterprise, U.S.S 804 Dinky Toys, 1979 STTMP vintage 2"x4" white die cast metal replica of the starship. Plastic decal "NCC-1701". 5"x7" plastic form cardstock mount photos Kirk and Spock and advertises the Dinky Klingon Cruiser toy. Made in England.	2.50	6-8	_____
Enterprise, U.S.S. 248-A1 Corgi, 1982 STWOK vintage starship, 3"x1¾" white die cast replica with plastic struts and pylons. White cardboard plastic form mount photos busts of Kirk and Spock. [6]	2	3-5	_____

Star Trek III Toys by Ertl

6. Note that the Corgi toy starships, both Enterprise and Klingon Battle Cruiser models, are smaller than the Dinky versions, and have plastic structural parts attached to die-cast metal.

PLAYTOYS

Issue Current Cost/Date

Enterprise, Star Trek III 1372
Ertl Company, 1984
Third movie vintage die cast replica, 1¾"x4¼", white paint with black registration letters. Blister packed on 4½"x6½" cardstock with drawings of Spock, Kirk and Kruge busts. . . . . 2.95 3-4 ______

Enterprise, U.S.S. and Klingon Battle Cruiser Boxed Set 309
Dinky Toys, 1977
Boxed set contains large size Dinky replicas 357 and 358 as described above. Window-cut box illos busts of Kirk and Spock and cartoons the two toy ships in battle, includes the landscape artwork and cut-outs in the packaged set. . . . . 15 65-100 ______

Unusual Corgi Double Pack

Enterprise, U.S.S./Klingon Cruiser Two-Pack, Star Trek II 2542
Corgi, 1982
Contains both Corgi Enterprise 148 and Klingon Cruiser 149 die cast metal castings, sealed in plastic form mount on cardstock with busts of Kirk and Spock. . . . . 4 6-9 ______

Excelsior, Star Trek III 1373
Ertl Company, 1984
Die cast metal replica of the Excelsior ship from the third movie; 1½"x4" model with black letters and black plastic display stand. Blister packed, 4½"x6½" cardstock with drawing of Spock, Kirk and Kruge busts. . . . . 2.95 3-4 ______

Klingon, Battle Cruiser 357
Dinky Toys, 1977
220mm (9-inch) t.v. version cruiser in blue and white die cast metal. Hand-wind bridge section fires plastic discs from the forward hull. Boxed, 10⅛" x 5⅜". . . . . 7 30-55 ______

Die-Cast Klingon Cruiser by Dinky

Issue Current Cost/Date

Klingon, Battle Cruiser 803
Dinky Toys, 1979
STTMP vintage replica, 2¾"x4" die cast metal, painted blue, foil decals for insignia of the Klingon Empire. Cardstock plastic form mount on 5"x7", photos Kirk and Spock and advertises the Dinky Enterprise 804. Made in Engalnd. . 2.50 6-8 ______

Star Trek II Klingon Battle Cruiser, Corgi

Klingon, Cruiser-Star Trek II Wrath of Kahn 149-Al
Corgi, 1982
Movie vintage replica, 3"x1¾" blue die cast metal with white plastic power cabin. Plastic form mount to cardstock with photos of Kirk and Spock . . . . 2 3-5 ______

Ertl Bird of Prey

	Issue	Current	Cost/Date
Klingon, Bird of Prey, Star Trek III, 1374 Ertl Company, 1984 2"x3" die cast metal replica of the ship from the third movie; blue paint, reads "Star Trek" across the wings, includes black plastic stand. Blister packed on 4½"x6½" card-stock with drawings of Kirk, Spock, Kruge busts	2.95	3-4	_____
• **Trekulator** Mego Corp., 1974 Functional 9-digit display calculator with six functions (add, subtract, divide, multiply, percent and square root), LED display pictures Enterprise scenes, requires four AA batteries. Boxed, front cartoon Spock at the science statoin and Enterprise; rear illos the calculator toy	10	45-70	_____
• **Tricorder** 51218 Mego Corp., 1976, No. 51218 Functional tape recorder replica with a flip top, plays and records on cassette. Includes a 30-minute tape with sound effects from Star Trek and portions of "The Menagerie" episode. Boxed, cartoons Kirk holding the toy alongside Mr. Spock	12	55-90	_____
• **Utility Belt** 203 Remco Industries, 1977, No. 203 Black plastic belt hold essential Star Fleet field equipment: a disc firing phaser (Tracer Gun) with 8 plastic discs, a molded replica tricorder and communicator. Includes an adjustable belt.	5	12-18	_____
• **Yo-Yo** Aviva, 1979 STTMP metallic-flake blue toy with decal of Kirk and Spock on one side and the starship Enterprise on the other	2	5-7	_____

TRADING CARDS

Star Trek bread cards and gum cards are called non-sports cards by trading card collectors because they deal with subject matter other than professional sport activities such as baseball and football. Star Trek cards of this type display scenes and character shots from the t.v. episodes and **Star Trek The Motion Picture.**

A new trading card style which has appeared since 1982 is the action scene photo card on heavy cardstock paper. Movie theme sets featuring **Star Trek II** and **Star Trek III** have been issued by Fantasy Traders. These are essentially limited edition trading cards that lack the detailed story-line legends on their reverse that is typical of bread cards and gum cards.

Bread Cards & Gum Cards

Star Trek bread and gum cards incorporate three painting formats in their set designs. These are plain panel cards (a photo and caption enclosed within a colored border frame), poster or puzzle reverse pieces and preview cards which contain a promotional illustration of what the completed Star Trek puzzle will look like. They may also comprise a checklist of all the numbered cards contained in the series.

The value of a trading card is determined by several factors. The most important determinant of value is the physical condition of the card. Also of consideration should be the current popularity of the item as a collectible and its relative supply or rarity. Two companies produced Star Trek trading cards during the years 1967 through 1979.

Leaf Brand – This black and white photo set of 72 cards was produced in 1967 and suffered a contractual dispute early in its distribution. They are also the first Star Trek gum cards ever made. Their extremely escalated price tag reflects their novelty status as the most expensive Star Trek collectible ever publicly marketed.

Topps A & BC – Two years after the unsuccessful marketing venture by Leaf Brands in the U.S., this English subsidiary produced a 55 card set from the Star Trek series. Of the 55 cards issued, 12 cards scattered throughout the set contained a sequential storyline for the T.V. episode "What Are Little Girls Made Of?".

Topps T.V. cards – In 1976 Topps released a photo gum card set containing 88 individual scenes or character profiles from television Trek for release in the U.S.

Topps STTMP – Another set of 88 full color cards was issued in 1979 to help promote the release of STTMP. As with the earlier television set, 22 stickers were also included in the series.

Topps & Campbell-Taggert – Reprints of the original Topps STTMP cards were packaged inside loaves of bread from Campbell-Taggert subsidiary bakeries. Four different logo sets identified as Colonial, Kilpatrick's, Manor and Rainbo were printed, each containing the same 33 card sequences.

Limited Edition Sets

The three trading card sets produced by Fantasy Traders in 1982 and 1984 are unusual collector sets which collectors should invest in. The larger size of the 1982 **Wrath of Kahn card** set is especially a trading card oddity. Unlike bread cards or gum cards, these sets are sold only through specific dealers as complete sequential packages. Wrappers issued for the sets are also novel collectibles which may sell individually.

Same STTMP (Bread) Card with different bakery logos.

Bread Cards

Topps Chewing Gum - 33 Card Bread Promos, 1979
Made for distribution for Campbell-Taggert Bakeries: Rainbo, Colonial, Kilpatrick and Manor Breads. Photo cards without stickers. Reverses have character profiles or yellow border crew photo. Cards carry oval with "bakery" name on lower left reverse. One card per loaf of bread offer:

	Issue	Current Cost/Date
1. Star Trek logo		_____
2. Toward the Unknown		_____
3. "Our Starcrafts - Annihilated!"		_____
4. Filming Drydock Sequence		_____
5. James T. Kirk		_____
6. Captain Kirk's Mission		_____
7. Dr. "Bones" McCoy		_____
8. Executive Officer Decker		_____
9. Navigator Ilia		_____
10. Helmsman Sulu		_____
11. Security Chief Chekov		_____
12. Dr. Christine Chapel		_____
13. Janice Rand		_____
14. The Vulcan Mr. Spock		_____
15. Lizard-like Diplomat		_____
16. Andorian - Close-up		_____
17. Return to the Bridge		_____
18. The Senior Officers		_____
19. Scotty's Domain		_____
20. Investigating a Malfunction		_____
21. Starship Under Attack		_____
22. Assault on Chekov		_____

TRADING CARDS

Bread Cards

	Issue	Current	Cost/Date
23. The Surak Craft			______
24. Transporter Malfunction			______
25. Zero Gravity Adventure			______
26. Ilia in Sickbay			______
27. The Landing Party			______
28. Spectacular Starship			______
29. Welcoming Dr. McCoy Aboard			______
30. Klingon Warship - Rear View			______
31. The Unearthly Mr. Spock			______
32. Woman from Planet Delta			______
33. New Starfleet Uniforms			______
Complete Set of Rainbo Cards	—	6-10	______
Complete Set of Colonial Cards	—	6-10	______
Complete Set of Kilpatrick Cards	—	6-10	______
Complete Set of Manor Cards	—	6-10	______

Gum Cards

- **Leaf Brands - 72 Card Gum Set,** 1967 Black and white, very rare card set. Set was withdrawn from the market because of contractual problems with copyrights. Thin card stock, photos captioned in a bottom black panel on front, feature characters and scenes from the episodes. Horizontally lined backs contain the card number inside an insignia plus recap story summary, 2 3/8"x3 7/16".

	Issue	Current	Cost/Date
1. No Time For Escape			______
2. Attempted Mutiny			______
3. A Grup Appears			______
4. Come In, Captain Kirk			______
5. Murasaki Mischief			______
6. Beam Down to Dawn			______
7. Back Himself			______
8. Back Through Time			______
9. Horta Emerging			______
10. Spock's Box			______
11. Spock in Command			______
12. Spock in Command			______
13. Befuddled Bones			______
14. Prepare to Fire Phasers			______
15. Command Decision			______
16. Kirk Battles a Gorn			______
17. Phaser Daser			______
18. Space Race			______
19. Fight Fire with Fire			______
20. Captain's Bluff			______
21. Underground Pursuit			______
22. The Bird			______
23. Teeny Booper			______
24. Time Warp			______
25. You're Kidding			______
26. Beam Out			______
27. Burn Out			______
28. Interference Out			______
29. Not So Funny			______
30. Prisoner of the Mind			______
31. Stalking a Killer			______
32. The Earth Killer			______
33. Fight for Lithium			______
34. Destruction Decision			______
35. "Return My Ship"			______
36. Frozen at the Controls			______
37. Christmas Present			______
38. Amnesia Victim			______
39. Decoy			______
40. Beyond Tomorrow			______
41. Trapped			______
42. Kirk Outside, Spock Inside			______
43. Spock Takes a Job			______
44. Kirk Held Hostage			______
45. Big Joker			______
46. A Scream of Pain			______
47. Captain's Salute			______
48. Call Me Senator			______
49. Into A New World			______
50. Tranquilized			______
51. Time For Shore Leave			______
52. Ice Age			______
53. Ambushed			______
54. Pain of Victory			______
55. Cornered			______
56. Jungle Hunt			______
57. Collision Course			______
58. Corbomite Maneuver			______
59. You Give Me A Headache			______
60. Shore Leave Surprise			______
61. Killer Aboard			______
62. Mindless Man			______
63. Pirates at Bay			______
64. Off Course			______
65. Attack by Nothing			______
66. Funny Little Enemies			______
67. Poison Attack			______
68. Warp Out for Rescue			______
69. Out of Control			______
70. Return to the Living			______
71. Space Prisoner			______
72. Raspberries			______
Individual Cards	—	2-5	______
Complete Set of 72 Cards	—	150-350	______

Wrapper package for the 72 card set of black and white photos from the t.v. series. Wrapper front reads "Official Star Trek Bubble Gum." Words "Star Trek" are inside oval and are bisected by the Enterprise and a rocket trail, similar to the

TRADING CARDS

	Issue	Current	Cost/Date
Gold Key Comics logo. Bottom features black and white head photos of Kirk and Spock. Package included hoto cards and gum stick. Waxed.			
Wrapper alone	—	6-10	_____
Wrapper package intact	—	30-50	_____

Topps Chewing Gum - 88 Card Gum Set, 1976
Gum card and sticker set, color photos from the series, fronts have white borders with captions included. Vertically lined reverses read "Captain's Log" with cartoon Enterprise, bordered narratives and character profiles, 2½"x3½"

	Issue	Current	Cost/Date
1. The U.S.S. Enterprise			_____
2. Captain James T. Kirk			_____
3. Dr. "Bones" McCoy			_____
4. Science Officer Spock			_____
5. Engineer Scott			_____
6. Lieutenant Uhura			_____
7. Ensign Chekov			_____
8. The Phaser - Tomorrow's Weapon			_____
9. The Shuttle Craft			_____
10. Opponents			_____
11. Energize			_____
12. The Alien Mr. Spock			_____
13. Men of the Enterprise			_____
14. Story of Voyage One			_____
15. "Live Long and Prosper"			_____
16. Enterprise Orbiting Earth View From The Bridge			_____
17. Toward the Unknown			_____
18. Enterprise Orbiting Earth			_____
19. The Purple Barrier			_____
20. Outwitting a God			_____
21. Planet Delta Vega			_____
22. Charlie's Law			_____
23. Mysterious Cube			_____
24. Dwarfed By The Enemy			_____
25. Balok's Alter-Ego			_____
26. Last of Its Kind			_____
27. Frozen World			_____
28. Spock Loses Control			_____
29. The Naked Time			_____
30. The Demon Within			_____
31. "My Enemy ... My Self!"			_____
32. Monster Asteroid			_____
33. Korby's Folly			_____
34. The Duplicate Man			_____
35. Balance of Terror			_____
36. Attacked by Spores			_____
37. Spock Unwinds!			_____
38. Duel at Gothos			_____
39. Timeship of Lazarus			_____
40. Dagger of the Mind			_____
41. The Lawgivers			_____
42. The Tunnel Monster			_____
43. Battling the Horta			_____
44. Strange Communication			_____
45. A Startling Discovery			_____
46. McCoy ... Insane!			_____
47. The Guardian of Forever			_____
48. Visit to a Hostile City			_____
49. Mystery at Starbase 6			_____
50. Fate of Captain Pike			_____
51. The Talosians			_____
52. Ordeal on Rigel Seven			_____
53. Capturing the Keeper			_____
54. Blasted by the Enemy			_____
55. Trapped by the Lizard Creature			_____
56. The Gorn Strikes			_____
57. Earthman's Triumph			_____
58. Specimen: Unknown			_____
59. Mirror, Mirror			_____
60. Spock's Wedding			_____
61. Strangled by Mr. Spock			_____
62. Grasp of the Gods			_____
63. The Monster Called Nomad			_____
64. The Companion			_____
65. Journey to Babel			_____
66. Death Ship			_____
67. The Tholian Web			_____
68. The Architects of Pain			_____
69. The Mugato			_____
70. The Deadly Years			_____
71. Ancient Rome Revisited			_____
72. The Melkotian			_____
73. The Vulcan Mind Meld			_____
74. Possessed by Zargon			_____
75. Creation of a Humanoid			_____
76. Captured by Romulans			_____
77. A War of Worlds			_____
78. Space Brains			_____
79. I, Yarneg!			_____
80. Death in a Single Cell			_____
81. The Uninvited			_____
82. The lights of Zetar			_____
83. Invaded by Alien Energy			_____
84. Kirk's Deadliest Foe			_____
85. The Trouble With Tribbles			_____
86. The Nazi Planet			_____
87. The Starship Eater			_____
88. Star Trek Lives!			_____
Complete Set of 88 cards	—	35-45	_____
Individual Cards	—	.40-.50	_____

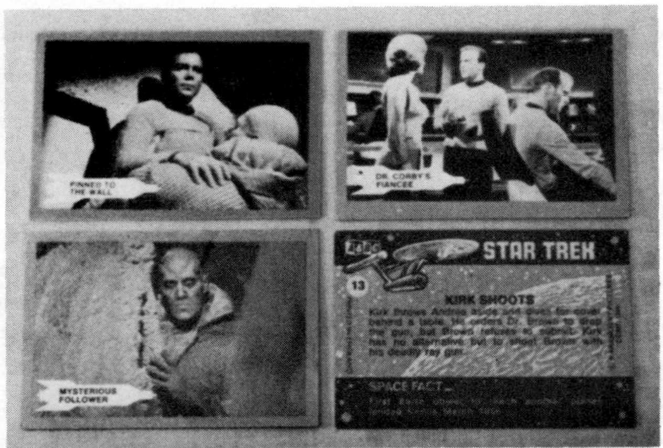

Topp's British release gum cards.

STTMP Gum Cards, Topps, 1979

STTMP Gum Card Stickers

Issue | Current | Cost/Date

Sticker Set of 22
Color photo sticker, numbered and captioned with photo surrounded by borders of green, orange or yellow, peel-off style against a red galazy background, feature aliens, monsters and characters, 2½"x3½"

	Issue	Current	Cost/Date
1. James Kirk			______
2. Mr. Spock - Unearthly			______
3. Spock of Vulcan			______
4. Dr. "Bones" McCoy			______
5. Engineer Scott			______
6. Lieutenant Uhura			______
7. Ensign Chekov			______
8. The Starship Enterprise			______
9. Kirk Beaming Up!			______
10. Star Trek Lives!			______
11. "Highly Illogical!"			______
12. The Keeper			______
13. Commander Balok			______
14. The Mugato			______
15. Lai! The Interrogator			______
16. The Parallel Spock			______
17. Ambassador Gav			______
18. Alien Possession!			______
19. Spock Lives!			______
20. Evil Klingon Kang			______
21. Spock Forever!			______
22. The Romulan Vessel			______
Complete Set of 22 Stickers	—	10-20	______
Individual Stickers	—	.50-1	

Wrapper Package for the 88 card set of color photos from the t.v. series. Wrapper front reads "Star Trek". Included one stick of bubble gum. Illo cartoons close-up portraits of Spock and Kirk drawn in outline below starboard profile Enterprise. "ST" lettering is white inside broad black, diagonal band. Waxed paper.

	Issue	Current	Cost/Date
Wrapper alone	—	2-4	______
Wrapper package intact	—	6-9	______

• **Topps Chewing Gum - 88 Card Gum Set,** 1979
Color photo card set of 88 cards with 22 stickers with scenes and characters from the movie. Scenes are surrounded by a blue, red or yellow frame line and white borders. Numbers and captions appear on frame lines. Card backs contain: 68 puzzle pieces (depicting one Enterprise, one crew photo), 5 story summaries, 12 actor profiles and 2 "Star Quotes," plus one checklist card, 2½"x3½".

	Issue	Current	Cost/Date
1. Star Trek Logo			______
2. Toward the Unknown			______
3. Space Intruder			______
4. Fate of the Klingons			______

TRADING CARDS

	Issue	Current	Cost/Date
5. Warning From Space			
6. "Our Starcrafts/Annihilate!"			
7. Enterprise in Drydock			
8. Rebuilding the Enterprise			
9. Filming Drydock Sequence			
10. James T. Kirk			
11. Captain Kirk's Mission			
12. Dr. "Bones" McCoy			
13. Executive Officer Decker			
14. Navigator Ilia			
15. Uhura			
16. Helmsman Sulu			
17. Engineer Scott			
18. Security Chief Chekov			
19. Dr. Christine Chapel			
20. Janice Rand			
21. The Vulcan Mr. Spock			
22. Spock on Planet Vulcan			
23. The UFP Assembled			
24. Being From Beyond			
25. The Face of Terror			
26. Lizard-Like Diplomat			
27. Not of this Earth			
28. Alien Insectoid			
29. The Unearthly			
30. The Andorians			
31. Advanced Life Form			
32. Betel's Attendant			
33. Andorian - Close-up			
34. The U.S.S. Enterprise			
35. Back in Operation!			
36. Refurbished Starship			
37. Enterprise - Rear View			
38. Return to the Bridge			
39. The Senior Officers			
40. View From the Bridge			
41. Scotty's Domain			
42. Fantastic New Devices			
43. The Engineering Deck			
44. Investigating A Malfunction			
45. Heart of the Starship			
46. Incredible Explosion			
47. Starship Under Attack			
48. Assault on Chekov			
49. Half Human			
50. Spock's Fight For Life			
51. Into The Nameless Void			
52. Terror In The Transporter Room			
53. The Surak Craft			
54. Transporter Malfunction			
55. Zero Gravity Adventure			
56. Symbol of Her People			
57. Exotically Beautiful			
58. Spock's Discovery			

	Issue	Current	Cost/Date
59. The Phaser Battle			
60. Ilia in Sick Bay			
61. Stamina of the Alien			
62. Filming of the Shuttlecraft			
63. Star Explorer			
64. Alien Menace			
65. Star Challengers			
66. "Beam Me Down, Scotty"			
67. The Landing Party			
68. Portrait of a Vulcan			
69. Beyond Infinity			
70. The Encounter			
71. It's Secret Revealed			
72. On Spock's Native World			
73. Spectacular Starship			
74. Welcoming Dr. McCoy Aboard			
75. Kirk's Last Stand			
76. Landscape of Vulcan			
77. Klingon War Ship - rear view			
78. The Final Frontiersmen			
79. Klingon Warship			
80. Vulcan Starship - overhead view			
81. Pride of the Starfleet			
82. Duo for Danger			
83. The Unearthly Mr. Spock			
84. Woman From Planet Delta			
85. New Starfleet Uniforms			
86. Men with a Mission			
87. The Deltan Beauty			
88. Klingon Commander			
Complete set of 88 cards	—	7-12	
Individual cards	—	.10-.15	

Sticker Set of 22

22 color stickers set with scenes and characters from the movie, peel-off cut-out profiles on oval stickers, purple borders with numbers, captions. Reverses puzzle a red border photo of the Enterprise flying above Kirk and Spock, 2½"x3½".

	Issue	Current	Cost/Date
1. Scotty			
2. Janice Rand			
3. Mr. Spock			
4. Chekov			
5. Ilia			
6. Sulu			
7. Kirk			
8. Dr. Chapel			
9. Captain Spock			
10. Dr. McCoy			
11. Uhura			
12. Ilia			
13. Meganite			
14. Bird Alien			
15. Advanced Alien			

	Issue	Current	Cost/Date
16. Decker			______
17. Alien			______
18. Rigellian			______
19. Enterprise			______
20. Klingon Warship			______
21. Surak Vessel			______
22. Enterprise			______
Complete Set of 22 Stickers	—		______
Individual Stickers	—	.20-.35	

Wrapper Package for the 88 card set of color photos from the first movie. Wrapper is purple. "STTMP" letter logo is inside yellow frame box containing PPC credits. White, orange & yellow busts of Kirk and Spock are below. Contained 10 photo cards plus a flattened, rectangular cut of Topps bubble gum.

	Issue	Current	Cost/Date
Wrapper alone	—	.50-1	______
Wrapper package intact	.35	1-2	______

Star Trek II Limited Edition Card Set, Fantasy Traders

Limited Edition Cards

• Star Trek II The Wrath of Kahn Cards

Fantasy Trade Card - 30 Card Set, 1982
Set of 30 cards, numbered individually on heavy stock with white borders, reverse shows b/w "Starburst" movie logo, limited edition of 7,500 sets, 5"x7":

	Issue	Current	Cost/Date
1. Admiral Kirk			______
2. Sulu			______
3. Scotty			______
4. Uhura			______
5. Kirk			______
6. David Marcus			______
7. Kahn			______
8. Saavik			______
9. Saavik, close-up			______
10. Chekov, with phaser			______
11. Kahn			______
12. Captain Terrell			______
13. Kirk and Spock			______
14. Kirk with phaser, Spock, David and Carol Marcus in background			______
15. McCoy			______
16. Injured Kahn			______
17. Chekov			______
18. Carol and David			______
19. Saavik with communicator			______
20. Kirk and David			______
21. Orbiting Space Lab			______
22. Kahn and Chekov			______
23. Reliant in space			______
24. Enterprise group shot on bridge			______
25. Kirk with Spock and Saavik			______
26. Spock and Saavik			______

TRADING CARDS

	Issue	Current	Cost/Date
27. Sulu, Kirk, Uhura and McCoy			
28. Kirk restrained by Scotty and McCoy			
29. Spock on bridge			
30. Saavik			
Individual Cards	—	.50-.75	
Complete set of 30 cards	11.00	15-20	

Wrapper Packages designed to distribute two of the above ST II photo cards, yellow and red illo on black with white borders, 5"x7" plastic pouches, four styles:

	Issue	Current	Cost/Date
Enterprise - over starfield	1		
Kahn - bust	1		
Kirk - bust	1		
Spock - bust	1		

- **Star Trek III The Search For Spock Cards**

Fantasy Trade Card - 60 Card Action Set, 1984
Character and scenes from ST III, color photos, reverses are individually numbered with ST III movie letter logo and brief picture caption, fronts have white borders and no lettering, 2½"x3½" format: [1]

1. William Shatner stars as James Kirk
2. Leonard Nimoy as Captain Spock
3. Deforest Kelley as Dr. McCoy
4. Engineer Scott played by James Doohan
5. Captain Sulu played by George Takei
6. Commander Chekov played by Walter Koenig
7. Nichelle Nichols as Uhura
8. Robin Curtis as Lt. Saavik
9. Ambassador Sarek played by Mark Lenard
10. Priestess T'Lar played by Dame Judith Anderson
11. Commander Morrow played by Robert Hooks
12. Kruge played by Christopher Lloyd
13. Warrigul
14. Enterprise returns for repairs
15. Enterprise berthed next to Excelsior
16. Sarek mind-melds with Kirk
17. Kirk replays flight records
18. Kirk watching film
19. Morrow and Kirk - Genesis is off-limits
20. Conspirators in conference
21. Visiting Bones in prison
22. Liberating Bones from prison
23. Sulu sabatoges prison console
24. Kirk and crew confront Klingons
25. Chekov at the helm
26. Saavik and Marcus view Genesis
27. Saavik and Marcus on planet Genesis
28. Locating Spock's coffin
29. No body in the coffin
30. Saavik and Marcus view burial robe
31. Saavik and Marcus tracking Spock?
32. Spock child lost in snow
33. Rescuing the Spock child
34. Klingon ship fires on the Grissom
35. Spock child resting
36. Klingon landing party
37. Kruge subdues a Genesis mutation
38. Kruge planning against the Enterprise
39. Deadly enemies crippled in space
40. Scotty and Chekov worry over controls
41. Young Spock in Pon farr
42. Saavik and young Spock during Pon farr
43. Spock as young adult
44. Klingon with weapon
45. Marcus and Klingon battle
46. Kirk and crew watch Enterprise explode
47. Enterprise blazes across the horizon
48. Kruge enraged
49. Kirk and Kruge duel
50. Fighting on the brink of destruction
51. Death throes of Genesis
52. Kirk bargains for life of crew
53. Escaping Genesis
54. Kirk and crew land on Vulcan
55. Kirk and crew take Spock to Vulcan
56. Sarek at Mount Seleya
57. McCoy's friendship for Spock is tested
58. T'Lar performs fal-tor-pan
59. Kirk and Spock face to face

1. This Fantasy Trade card set was marketed in the U.S. as a complete packaged collectible which included the 20 card ship set. This made a total of 80 **Star Trek III** cards. In Canada, 4 action cards and 1 ship card were enclosed in an individual wrapper, displayed in small cardstock dumps and sold as if they were ordinary gum cards. These were distributed by the Sports Connection in Toronto, Ontario.

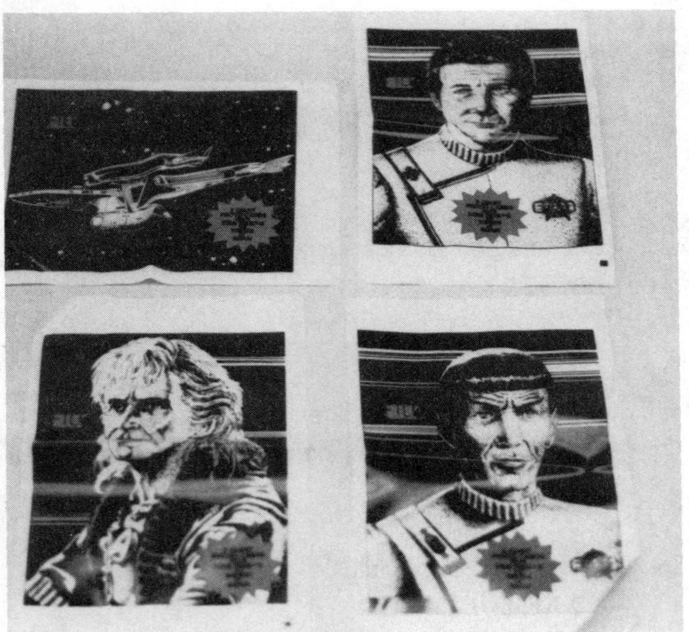
Star Trek II Wrappers

	Issue	Current Cost/Date	
60. Spock's memories restored			______
Complete Set of 60 Action Cards . .	5	7-10	______
Individual Cards	—	.10-.15	

Fantasy Trade Card - 20 Card Ship Set, 1984
Second set of color photo cards from ST III focusing on the starships from the movie. Same format as above, white borders without lettering, reverse individually numbered with movie letter logo and brief caption naming the vessel, 2½"x3½" format:

	Issue	Current Cost/Date	
1. U.S.S. Enterprise			______
2. Enterprise rear view			______
3. Enterprise leaving spacedock . .			______
4. Enterprise front view			______
5. Spacedock top view			______
6. U.S.S. Excelsior			______
7. Excelsior rear view			______
8. Spacedock side view			______
9. Excelsior top view			______
10. Excelsior bottom view			______
11. Merchantman			______
12. Merchantman bottom view			______
13. Merchantman top view			______
14. Merchantman rear view			______
15. Klingon Bird of Prey			______
16. Kruge's ship under Kirk's control			______
17. U.S.S. Grissom			______
18. Grissom rear view			______
19. Grissom top view			______
20. Grissom bottom view			______
Complete Set of 20 Cards	3	4-6	______
Individual Cards	—	.20-.30	

Fantasy Trade Card - 60 and 20 Card Sets
Wrapper for the 60 card set of color photos from the third movie, plus 20 laminated spaceship cards. Wrapper is made of lightweight plastic, heat-pressed at top and bottom. White plastic front shows rectangular black inset of the STSFS "neon-glo" promo design with etchings in white. Below reads black letters in solid or outline "ST III TSFS". No gum.

	Issue	Current Cost/Date	
Wrapper alone	—	.50-1	______
Wrapper intact with 5 photo cards .	.35	1-2	______

Promoting Star Trek – The Best of Both Worlds

Official promotions for Star Trek began before the airing of the premiere television episode, "The Man Trap," on September 8, 1966 and, in one form or another, Star Trek has continued to be promoted for over twenty years. Even during the lean decade of the 1970's when studio and network interest in the canceled series waned to its lowest point, there was always some latent spark of newsworthiness about Star Trek that kept it on the forefront of being a media concern.

This unique and very enviable position in the entertainment field – the "Star Trek Phenomenon" as it has come to be called, owes its evolution to the very unusual double-nature of Star Trek promotions.

There have always been twin forces at work to keep public awareness keenly attuned to the slogan "Star Trek Lives!". The first force is a direct and measurable one stemming from the practical and business side of Trek. It is represented by a running series of assorted media campaigns designed specifically to direct public attention to Star Trek's continuing success and rather remarkable marketing longevity. Here are the familiar publicity photo releases, press kits, contests, premiums and offers that sequentially occur in each stage of Star Trek's production. Here, also, are a limited number of superbly executed Star Trek reproductions and exhibits which, because they exist for the public's enjoyment, fit into this promotional category as well. Many of these scale model displays have been painstakingly sponsored and produced exclusively by Star Trek fans.

The second force of continuous promotion for Star Trek operates from an internally generated energy which is much harder to define and quantify. Basically, it is the real promotional appeal of "belonging" which is projected by the Star Trek fans. This effect of belonging to a united Star Trek network is a self-perpetuating phenomenon in itself. One which has drawn in the highest celebrities of Star Trek.

"Why is Star Trek so **popular?"** the familiar query goes. Further to the point, what mysterious "connection" exists between Star Trek's insiders (the producer and cast who actually work to create the show) and their vast peripheral following. What cement bonds the thousands of Trekkers who have over time lent substantiation to the meaning of the Star Trek philosophy?

Nowhere is the twin-force more noticable than on those special occassions when live performances bring the stars and their fans together. Fan conventions serve a critical part in the continuing popularity of Star Trek. And, for the Star Trek cast of actors and actresses, the Star Trek phenomenon has spun-off a devoted legion of fans who have followed the independent careers of the stars far and beyond their original 3-year stint as actors working on a t.v. drama/adventure show.

Whatever this special glue is that binds together the "official" and unofficial sides of Star Trek's double nature, the breadth and quality of the promotion Star Trek has enjoyed over the last two decades must lie somewhere near the heart of the answer to what makes lasting popularity. In this last chapter, the bits and pieces of Star Trek's promotional history are closely examined. Promotional memorabilia is a collectibles realm all its own. One final frontier for fans and Star Trek collectors.

PART I

Special Promotions

"Is there anything Star Trek has that you would like to have?

The people concerned with your favorite show Star Trek and T.V. Star Parade (Magazine) have received many requests as to where they can purchase copies of the shirts worn on the show by Bill Shatner, Leonard Nimoy, DeForest Kelley, James Doohan and George Takei. They even have requests for Nichelle Nichols' yeoman costume. So we've been asked to have all of you write in to us on the coupon below telling us whether or not you'd be interested in a nylon velour exact copy of the U.S.S. Enterprise crew's shirts. And what price you'd be willing to pay? Do you have favorite colors you'd like to select from? Would you like HIS and HERS shirts? Is there anything else on the show which appeals to you and which you'd like to see on the market? Write and let us know. We'll pass the information on and who knows? Maybe someday real soon you'll be able to buy your favorite item."

(excerpted from T.V. Star Parade Magazine)

The ingenuity demonstrated by the above "market feeler" coupon printed in 1967 ushered in two decades of advertising zeal for promoters involved in selling Star Trek. Everything from glossy publicity shots to redemptive coupons and commercial store displays has been used to promote Star Trek and its assorted affiliated wares. There are six different categories of Star Trek special promotions, each of which exhibits an advertising strategy uniquely its own. Listed alphabetically these six categories are: contests, displays/exhibits, offers and specials, premiums, publicity releases and souvenirs.

CONTESTS

Contests and competitions are effective promotional tools because of their unique ability to stimulate audience participation. During the 1960's, when Star Trek and its cast were favorite topics of movie star and teen star magazines, a wonderful variety of readership contests began to appear on the national newsstands. For the most part, these published promotional contests consisted of parodies on Star Trek's fictional characterizations (particularly Mr. Spock) or were designed to serve the higher purpose of providing readership feedback from Star Trek's fans to the program's producers and sponsors. Contestants were asked only token questions with winners being selected by random drawings. Early contest prizes were inexpensive momentos such as photos, books or records.

In recent years, Star Trek readership contests have grown to be somewhat more elaborate as the following listings will testify. Likewise the prizes being awarded in the 1980's can amount to winnings with considerable value.

Another contest format which lends itself well to Star Trek application is the radio Phone-in event. In this situation, trivia questions are posed over the airwaves and the listening audience's responses are tabulated immediately. Radio contest promotions are enjoying renewed popularity in the wake of Star Trek movies. Collectors can find souvenirs of such events in the advance promotional flyers, trivia fact sheets and newspaper clippings which may report on the progress of ongoing matches.

In the past, some radio contests became media events. One such contest broadcasted in San Diego, California in 1975 awarded its Grand Prize winner with $5,000 in cash and merchandise. The reward was presented in person by Nichelle Nichols.

The premiere week for the release of each new Star Trek motion picture now brings about a great variety of local and regional contest promotions. Television stations have come on the scene by broadcasting consecutive Star Trek episodes and airing special Star Trek taped documentaries. These Trek-A-Thons are usually advertised in newspapers and local television program guides and can include mail-in or coupon drawings as well. Often the prizes for these events assume the form of free passes to a special advance premiere of the new movie – an occassion for collectors to find additional publicity promotions (flyers, programs, posters and even glassware) that are making their marketing debut.

DISPLAYS/EXHIBITS

The term displays is used to describe the commercial side of special promotions as they are used to display wares and promote retail sales. In today's world of fast retail, high turn-around and relatively short-lived consumer appeal, virtually no sales promotion is complete without its attendant entourage of visual displays. Advertising agencies have elaborated on what was once the simple kingdom of leaflets and posters to embark upon such colorful dioramas as book dumps, table tents, ceiling danglers, floor-model "standees", menuboard transparencies and even an inflatable toy Enterprise!

For collectors, such enticing displays become tenuous and fleeting treasurers. Most display items vanish within weeks to be randomly distributed among retail store employees or discarded into refuse bins. Over a very short span of time, display items can evolve into one-of-a-kind gems for observant collectors.

Certainly this wealth of collectible objects is far too vast in its scope to be catalogued in its entirety. But Star Trek collectors are advised that there is collectible potential waiting in this largely unexplored line of momentos and memorabilia.

Some commercial displays afford the opportunity of accruing real value later on. For example, there is the three foot square cardboard standee produced by Dot Records in 1968 to promote its release of Leonard Nimoy's album **The Way I Feel**. This was a full color reproduction of the album jacket cover in striking 3-D format. Dot Records also distributed small 2½"x3" b/w photo glossies of Nimoy made available at local record and department stores. When William Shatner's **The Transformed Man** LP was made available in 1970, Decca Records provided its retail outlets with an attractive kind of lobby card which photographed the album.

Metal give-away buttons promoting Star Trek novels

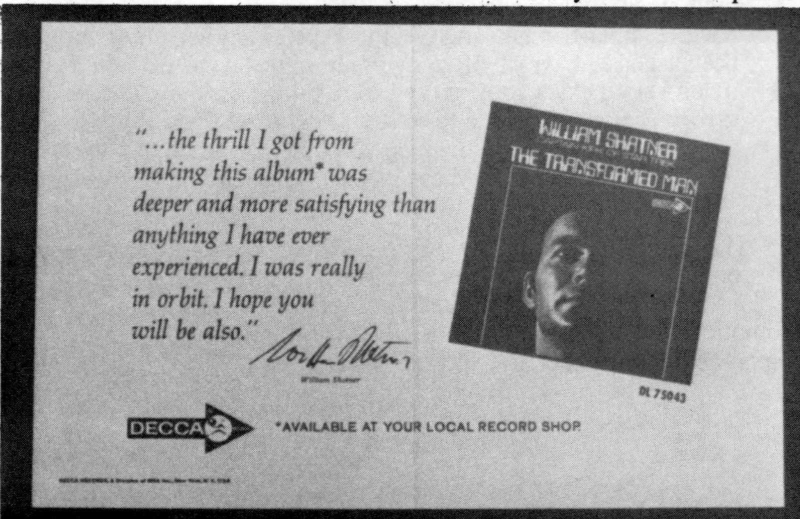

Early ad card for *The Transformed Man* album

In recent years there have been numerous product accessories and posters that advertise specific Star Trek wares. Fantasy Trade Card Company produced two 9¾"-square photo cards to display in conjunction with its ST III 80-card trading card sets. Simon & Schuster's colorful pocketbook display dumps even added an imprinted metal button that consumers could take away with them. The button photos Spock and reads "Star Trek - The Only Logical Books to Read."

Still by far the most extravagant commercial Star Trek display promotion to date was devised by the Tracy Locke Advertising Agency in conjunction with the Taco Bell Star Trek III premium glassware. Franchises in some locations displayed cardboard standees of Mr. Spock holding onto one of the glasses! One particular, life-size 5½ foot floor model was nothing less than spectacular.

To offset the commercial nature of displays and the role they play in product advertising, there are also Star Trek promotional exhibits. Here the exhibit itself is the main attraction.

Official Star Trek exhibits probably had their beginnings during the early 1970's which heralded the heydey for large-scale, fan-sponsored Star Trek conventions. The very first Star Trek Con which was held in January 1972 in New York City, proudly showcased its cherished Star Trek momentos (one of Spock's pointed ears and a superbly hand-crafted replica of Galileo '7) by exhibiting them under glass, for the viewing public. That was, of course, only the beginning.

Over the intervening 15 years, Star Trek's exhibits have been cultivated to the point of professional sophistication. Commercial exhibits devoted to Star Trek can be viewed at two wax museums and in the halls of the reknown Smithsonian Institution. There is also increasing interest among fan clubs and community groups to fund a major Star Trek project of their own. From 20' starship replicas on exhibit in shopping malls and an Enterprise "Star Trike" which is licensed as road-legal, to one dedicated fan's determination to restore the original prop-shell of the Galileo '7, Star Trek has found its way into a parade of privately funded exhibitions.

Of course, like the aforementioned exhibits, even some advertising displays cannot be collected and stored away as memorabilia. This was certainly the case for the original Desilu advertising placard that adorned one section of the exterior studio building. It was equally true for the sensational Heineken Beer roadside billboard that presented Mr. Spock as having only limp and floppy ears until he got a taste of that sudsy brew! Collectors are urged not to be discouraged. In the case of such an irretrievable, yet absolutely priceless collectible, a quick shutter finger will do! For Star Trek's grander displays and professional exhibits, one picture is worth more than a thousand words.

OFFERS AND SPECIALS

Special offer products not only promote the sale of a primary Star Trek ware (as is the case of the Star Trek AMT Model kits), they also offer the collector the chance to purchase a second item which may gain considerable collectible value over time. In the example above, collectors who returned the AMT package coupon during the promotion of 1974-1976, received at discounted cost, a special Star Trek windbreaker jacket.

The redemptive coupon offer has also been a good promotion for the manufacturers of many types of non-Trek related wares when they have added Star Trek merchandise as their special offer gift. Star Trek paraphernalia from trinkets to articles of clothing has been the subject matter for promotional offers for many years.

As collectibles, special offer gifts tend to be both off-beat and rare. In many cases, the offers are only regionally advertised and are not made available everywhere. Furthermore, since many of these gifts occur in the form of punch-outs, iron-ons and other types of plastic toy disposables, few of them have remained intact inside of their original packaging. This is especially the case for children's gadgets and special offers that feature personalized items which will forever bear the namesake of their original owner.

PREMIUMS

A premium is something which is given free, or for only a nominal charge (such as the cost of shipping and handling), with the purchase of a product or service. Because of this close product association, premiums tend to advertise their sponsors with easily identifiable logos or trademarks that are conspicuously placed somewhere on the gifted item. Premium ID's appear as visible imprints and decals applied directly to posters, plastic-wares and glasses.

Premium gifts can also occur as small-scale objects which can be easily inserted inside of a product's final packaging. This is the case for gifts such as bread cards and plastic toys and trinkets. Sometimes the wrapper itself (its photograph or illustration) is the premium.

In the latter case, collectors should be careful to maintain the premium intact upon its original box or package. Cardstock trading cards and signs are especially popular premium promotions with children, as are brightly colored, decorative carrying boxes. Rather lavish box-backs and side-panels have been produced in theme with Star Trek The Motion Picture. When the premium exists as an integral part of a cereal or candy box, the food contents can be removed by opening the top and bottom end-panels and then folding the package so that it will lie flat. In this manner, the premium box can be stored in the same fashion as other perishable paper products.

PUBLICITY RELEASES

Publicity can be generated in a number of different fashions, with the common denominator being the sale or promotion of a specific product or service. Publicity releases can assume a wide range of physical formats – from the studio photographs which are choreographed to promote a series to the catalog mailings which a distributor or a manufacturer might use to stimulate the sale of toys. Selecting an appropriate publicity format is of foremost concern in marketing anything.

Star Trek, as a commercial enterprise, began its storm of publicity releases long before the debut of its 1966 television program. **Publicity kits** containing photographs of the new show's cast along with advance story information and biographical data was circulated to networks and t.v. broadcasting stations. A similar program for the organized dissemination of information occurs today, well in advance of the premiere dates for each Star Trek motion picture. Perhaps the most wide-spread examples of Star Trek publicity releases are the photographic promotions which are launched by Paramount - the theatre promos (lobby cards, poster flyers and full-size marquee posters) that are so liberally distributed across the countryside.

A secondary meaning to the term "publicity" defines it as **information with a news value** which is issued as a means of gaining public attention or support. In 1968, with NBC's initial threat of cancellation for the Star Trek t.v. series, fan organizations began a systematic campaign to rouse public support for the continuation of the show. The SST (Save Star Trek) Campaign, chaired by John and Bjo Trimble, sent out thousands of individual mailings in the form of postcards and flyers that served very well to publicize the goals of this newly united fan movement.

Publicity letters and bulletins continue to be the mainstay of Star Trek's numerous fan clubs. Through the monthly publishing of newsletters, newszines and annual yearbooks, fan clubs work to publicize Star Trek's healthy alliance of fen and broadcast its accomplishments to all corners of the globe. Literally each Star Trek star, and many of its most popular guest stars as well, have an established fan club with a membership dedicated to following and publicizing their independent careers. One volunteer organization, The Star Trek Welcommittee, acts as a fan directory service by providing free information about Star Trek's many clubs, chapters and charters.

Display prop promoting *Mr. Spock's Music From Outer Space* Album

For fans who desire closer contact with the ongoing movie productions and other official "behind-the-scenes" information, Star Trek/Lincoln Enterprises, established in the late 1960's by Gene Roddenberry and his wife, Majel Barrett, has offered fans the opportunity to enroll in a continuing series of Star Trek clubs, each aligned with Star Trek's present phase of production; from the series, to the animated cartoon, through the release of the first motion pictures. There is also the Aurora, Colorado based club called "Star Trek The Official Fan Club" which since the release of ST II has gained rights to exclusive interviews and publicity news about the upcoming **new** Star Trek television series which is slated for an October 1987 debut.

The last two varieties of publicity releases deal directly with the **marketing of Star Trek affiliated merchandise.** They are the newspaper and magazine ads which manufacturers and distributors use to market individual items; and the catalogs they might also issue to publicize their entire line of wares.

Langley Associates Catalog

Original Star Trek Enterprise mail order catalogs

Printed newspaper and magazine ads make very interesting collectibles in themselves. Since they are literally made to be thrown away, printed advertisements and flyers are rare among most Star Trek collections. They also have the intrinsic value of being able to function as "snapshots" into the extinct pop cultures of the past. A prime example of this is the advertising slogan for Leonard Nimoy's first album *Mr. Spock's Music From Outer Space.* The pop-art style of advertising that promoted this 1967 album release went all the way in one particular ad which was published in *GO*, a newsprint record's advertising specialty magazine. The slogan for Nimoy's album reads "Spock It To Me!" in the very colorful vernacular of the teenage sixties!

There are a great number of **manufacturer's catalogs** which contain some reference to Star Trek wares. AMT Models, Dinky Toys and Estes Model Rocketry are just a sample of the manufacturers which have, at one time or another publicized their Star Trek merchandise inside of a catalog. Generally speaking, a catalog is best sought after for its relative **wealth** of pertinent Star Trek listings. Most manufacturers do charge for copies of their catalogs. This means that even if the catalog does contain one very good photo of a particular Star Trek item, its cover price can outweigh the value of the contents you will receive. It is also possible that in order to secure a copy, you will have to compete with other non-Trek collectors in the market which will result in an inflated collectible price. A good example to illustrate this is the Corgi catalog that shows a little boy in a Star Fleet uniform on the cover, playing with a die-cast Enterprise toy. Star Trek fans will have to compete with a throng of avid Corgi toy collectors in order to obtain this issue. Since Corgi toys are, in themselves, considered to be collectibles, this catalog will demand an inflated value because of the hundreds of other non-Trek Corgi toy illustrations that it contains inside.

Sometimes a particular catalog's historical value will increase its worth. The original catalogs issued in 1968 by Star Trek Enterprises are certainly examples of a universally accepted Trek collectible as they represent the very first in a long line of mail-order Star Trek catalogs. There is also the lavishly produced 1976 Langley & Associates Catalog which documents the entire line of Langley Star Trek photos, posters and slides for that year in full color miniature reproductions. Both of these distributor's catalogs are considered rare and valuable. As a rule, however, distributor catalogs can only be expected to accrue minimal value. Usually they are available in mass quantities and for only a nominal charge. Unless such catalogs possess some intrinsic quality which makes them stand out as hallmarks in their field, they will not become valuable collectibles.

Convention flyers like this have nostalgic value

SOUVENIRS

In the broadest sense of the term, most Star Trek memorabilia could be considered to be a souvenir. As a subcategory of Star Trek Special Promotions, however, souvenirs have a much narrower range. Souvenirs, as they are discussed here, are those particular **items which were released in conjunction with one of the other five categories** of Star Trek special promotions. This would include certificates of commendation or awards from organizations or clubs; the postcards and trinkets which might be sold on location at different Star Trek exhibits; and a variety of reprinted materials.

Probably the most familiar kind of souvenirs under this definition are the Movie Program Souvenir Books produced by Parafen Publishing Co., which are designed for distribution primarily at the theatre locations where Star Trek motion pictures are making their debut.

A distinction between **souvenirs** and original **publicity releases** becomes important at this point. Publicity releases comprise collectibles which attain high future value due to their rarity and extremely limited public distribution. They represent **contemporary** issues of items that have as their origin date the exact date of their initial release.

Souvenir items result after-the-fact. They are distributed not as primary promotions, but as secondary momentos which function to call to mind a formerly publicized exhibit or event. In some cases the distinction between publicity releases and souvenirs becomes difficult to judge. However, the distinction is an important one since the bottom-line of all collectibles rests on a priority of originality.

The *Movie Handbooks of Production Information* and the *Shooting Schedules* that Lincoln Enterprises distributes are categorized as being souvenirs. This is also true for the *Season Press Books* and *Season Outlines* published by Archival Marketing Associates. This is so because although the information contained in these booklets may reproduce the articles which were, originally, publicity releases, the booklets themselves are compilations of reprinted material. Also, since they are now being mass produced, these booklets cannot be expected to accrue significantly high retail values.

A secondary source of collectibles to be gleaned from special offers are the **mailings, flyers, newspaper ads and glossy magazine inserts** which generally accompany the opening of a special offer drive. Illustrated artwork or photos on flyers that specifically picture the Star Trek gift being offered can be very desirable. Such printed promotions arrive in the mail for free and are well worth snipping out and preserving intact and in good condition.

If you are sending away for the special offer, photocopy the original or hand-write your own mailing coupon on a separate piece of paper and save the flyer intact. It is also desirable to clip out the newspaper/magazine title and date of issue, as well, if such information is supplied. Otherwise be sure and note in pencil and on the reverse of the promotion the exact date and location in which the advertisement appeared.

SPECIAL PROMOTIONS LISTING

The listings which follow differ in context from all the other listings recorded in this book due to the unusual nature of Star Trek's promotional items.

1. ISSUE PRICES HAVE BEEN INTENTIONALLY OMITTED. Most promotional items have an original price of zero by default, since they were never intended for public consumption, or were distributed at no cost, for free. Where such was not the case, original prices are noted at the close of the item's descriptive text.
2. RETAIL PRICES APPLY TO THE **PRINTED ARTICLES** (FLYERS, COUPONS, INSERTS, ETC.) WHICH ACTUALLY PROMOTED SPECIAL GIFTS. For further information on the value of the gifts to be received appropriate collectibles sections found elsewhere in the book are referenced.
3. NA (NOT APPLICABLE) MAY APPEAR IN THE RETAIL PRICE COLUMN. This occurs for public exhibits and in the odd cases where no retrievable printed material exists to advertise the gift that was a premium or special offer. It also appears for those promotions that occur as an integral and inseparable part of a primary and previously listed collectible (i.e. a coupon printed inside the jacket cover of a book).

The following abbreviations are used in the Special Promotion section:

(C) - Contest
(D) - Display/Exhibit
(P) - Premium
(R) - Publicity Release
(S) - Souvenir
(O) - Offers and Specials

Issue Current Cost/Date

1966

(C) Bill Shatner Contest
T.V. Star Parade Magazine, expired 10/30/67, 1 page promo with coupon: "Star Trek's Bill Shatner asks for your help! Suggest five to ten songs you'd like to hear Bill sing at his first recording session! If you match five, you win." Prize - first pressing of Bill's Gold Star album. Winner announced in Feb. 1968. 5-10 ______

(C) Star Trek's Design-A-Costume Contest
Two pages - rules, coupon and photo spread of some provocative ST women's outfits. T.V. Star Parade Magazine, expired 12/30/67. "Design a costume for any one of the ST stars or even something you'd like to see a guest star wear. Use the wierdest designs you can think of! Note exactly what fabric is being used and the colors." Prize - judged by Bill Theiss (ST Costume Designer), a shirt like Shatner, Nimoy, Kelley, Doohan, Takei or Yeoman's tunic . . . . . 5-10 ______

(R) Advanced Information of 1966-67 Programming Book
Paramount Television Sales
The first Star Trek promo flyer, cover - Kirk and Yeoman Smith from WMN, pg. 4 intros Spock but photo has pointed ears and brows airbrushed out so they won't offend! . . . . 75-100 ______

Rare assorted publicity stills with autographs

Issue Current Cost/Date

(R) Star Trek Intestellar Fan Club
Star Trek Lincoln Enterprises. Official club publishing news flyer. **Inside Star Trek,** edited by Ruth Berman. 12 issues chronicle the progress of the t.v. series as seen from the sets. Original, stapled editions, free with club membership, set of 12 . . . . ______

Reprints, available 1980
1103, set of all 12, cost $6.00 . . . . ______
1103A Six issues only, cost $3.50 . . . . ______

SPECIAL PROMOS - 1966

	Issue	Current Cost/Date
(R) Studio Publicity Photographs Desilu/Paramount Pictures, 1966-1968, b/w and color glossies from the t.v. series, sizes 2½"x3" to 8"x10", unsigned or "autograph" stamped copies. Some were sent free to fans who wrote the actors, later ones were distributed through mail-order Hollywood Souvenir houses:		
Original, unsigned stills	20-25	______
Original, autographed stills (facsimile)	30-35	______
Original, hand-autographed copies	50-75	______
(R) Enterprise - 8"x10" b/w glossy, white frame borders autos "Gene Roddenberry"		______
(R) Kirk - in 1st season, velour shirt with ribbed collar, posed against transporter chamber backdrop		______
(R) Kirk - waist-shot, shouldering phaser rifle		______
Original, unsigned stills	**20-25**	
Original, autographed (facsimile)	**30-35**	
Original, hand-autographed copies	**50-75**	
(R) Kirk - black-collar, velour shirt posed with starglobe, "My Best, William Shatner"		______
(R) Kirk - black-V-collar against white drop, "My Best, William Shatner"		______
(R) Kirk - black-V-collar, behind Enterprise model on a stand		______
(R) Kirk - against starfield, holding Enterprise model		______
(R) Kirk - seated in a captain's chair		______
(R) Spock - waist-shot, holding unusually bulky laser device		______
(R) Spock - in ribbed-collar velour, against control panel with galaxy backdrop, "Leonard Nimoy"		______
(R) Spock - waist-shot, 1st season, holding Enterprise model against grid backdrop, "Best Wishes, Leonard Nimoy"		______
(R) Spock - waist-shot, science station with stylus and board, "Logically, Leonard Nimoy"		______
(R) McCoy - c/u, against white backdrop, "DeForest Kelley"		______
(R) McCoy - seated next to med-scanner		______
(R) McCoy - seated, satin pull-over tunic, wall grid, "Best Wishes, DeForest Kelley"		______
(R) McCoy - in V-collar velour, c/u at bridge "With Emotion, DeForest Kelley"		______
(R) McCoy - standing waist-shot, holding a hypo on bridge set		______
(R) Uhura - c/u at station," Nichelle Nichols"		______

	Issue	Current Cost/Date
(R) Uhura - c/u a above, "Love and Peace" translated from Swahili to English		______
(R) Scotty - c/u, against black "Best Wishes, 'Scotty' James Doohan"		______
(R) Sulu - waist-shot, at helm, "George Takei"		______
(R) Chekov - waist-shot, against Engineering ladder, "Fondly, Walter Koenig"		______
(R) Gene Roddenberry - waist-shot at communications set, script in hand		______
(R) Kirk & Spock - standing, with tricorder and communicator		______
(R) Kirk & Spock - waist-shot, against galaxy		______
(R) Kirk & Spock - seated, 3-D chess game		______
(R) Kirk & Spock - standing, behind Enterprise model		______
(R) Kirk & McCoy - waist-shot, phaser and tricorder		______
(R) Kirk - science station, McCoy seated with stylus and board		______
(R) Kirk & Rand - waist-shot, side-by-side with a starglobe		______
(R) Kirk & Sulu - posed still from NT, Kirk restrains shirtless Sulu by holding fencing foil at his throat		______
(R) Kirk, Spock & Rand - waist-shot, all standing with "ray" gun props		______
(R) Kirk, Spock & Rand -against planet backdrop, Rand seated		______
(R) Kirk, Spock & McCoy - Kirk in Captain's chair, others standing		______
(R) Kirk, Spock & McCoy - waist-shot in front of Galileo '7, with phasers and communicators drawn		______
(R) Kirk, Spock & Uhura - Kirk seated with others standing		______
(R) Bridge Crew - 1st season compliment - Scotty, McCoy, Chekov, Chapel, Kirk, Uhura, Spock and Sulu (Kirk seated)		______
(R) Landing Party - assembled on the pads: Chekov, Uhura, Scotty and Sulu		______
(R) Toy Truck Billboard Promo Tonka Toys, 1968 Paramount promo used for display at t.v. network stations, die-cast trailer truck painted orange and bearing two side-panel billboard decals along trailer sides: one reads "Desilu" and advertises time change for Star Trek, other reads time change for "Mission Impossible"	80-100	______

SPECIAL PROMOS - 1966

The following abbreviations are used in the Special Promotion section:

(C) – Contest
(D) – Display/Exhibit
(P) - Premium
(R) - Publicity Release
(S) - Souvenir
(O) - Offers and Specials

Issue Current Cost/Date

(S) Star Trek Souvenir Kit
Preview, Star Trek Enterprises
Choice of 3 different kit combinations advertised inside publicity photo mailings, Deluxe Kit included all of the items:
3 embroidered Insignia Patches
3 Command Star Insignia Stickers
1 Starship Flight Deck Certificate (plain blue with Enterprise and your own name)
8½"x11" cast sheets and bios of the stars plus Roddenberry
8½"x11" pen and ink blueprints of Enterprise and Galileo by Matt Jeffries
1 official Star Trek letterhead memo pad
"Your Star Trek Pictorial Calendar 1968"
Packaged Kits arrived in manilla, clasp envelope with 1023 North LaBrea, Hollywood, Calif. address. Price $5.00 45-55 ______

1968

(C) Double Giveaway Contest
Movie Stars Magazine, expired 11/30/68
1 page, double coupon, star photos: Guess the number of songs Leonard Nimoy songs on **The Way I Feel** album; or the color of Barbra Streisand's "Funny Girl" blouse.
Prize- copy of LN's album, or a blouse 3-6 ______

Early contest announcement

Issue Current Cost/Date

(C) Mr. Spock's Computer Contest
Fave Magazine, running one month, 1-page with computer card coupon and Spock photo:
"Leonard Nimoy and Mr. Spock now have so many dedicated fans it's getting very hard to keep track of them all! But Leonard has found a way . . . your personal information card will be added to the Star Trek computer's memory tapes - which never forget anything! Then whenever Mr. Spock wants to know about you, he asks the Computer and ZING! There you are!"
Prize - three winners receive new portable record player, personal message from LN and album **Mr. Spock's Music From Outer Space.** 47 others get autographed copy of the new album. Winners announced in full spread article along with their photos. . . . . 5-10 ______

Barnabas vs. Spock Contest Form

(C) Outasite Space Joke Contest
Fave Magazine, expired 3/30/69; 2 pages with Spock, Chekov, photos and sample jokes, plus top 10 space hits including "Spock! In The Name of Love!": "Mr. Chekov got together with his boss, Mr. Spock and let us Outasiters in on the laffs goin' round in Outaspace! Know any space jokes? Send in the coupon. The joke that breaks up the Enterprise crew most win a groovy prize."
Prize $5.00 cash . . . . 5-10 ______

(C) Pick Your Choice - Spock vs Barnabas!
Movie Life Magazine, expired 12/31/68
1 page with star photos and coupon: Popularity test pitting fangs against ears, Spock vs "Dark Shadows" vampire. Choice includes - "Mr. Spock is the only one for me! How could anyone like a vampire?" or "Barnabas is the greatest. How could anyone like a Vulcan?" Prize - autographed star photo . . . . 5-10 ______

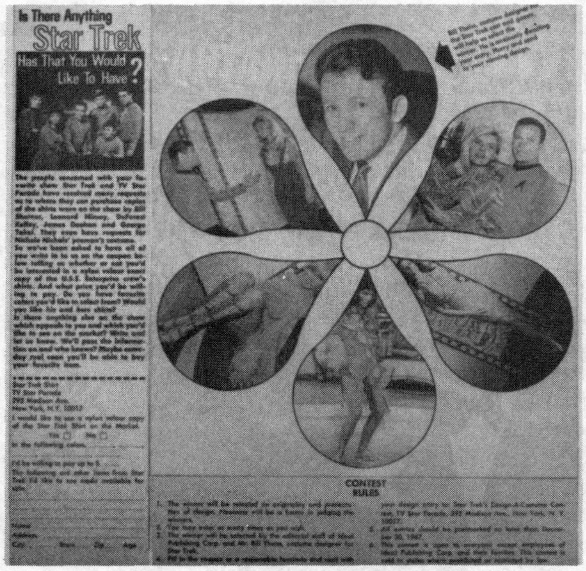

Left: Very important form which asked fans if they'd like to buy Star Trek memorabilia. The result was the establishment of Star Trek Enterprises.
Right: Design A Costume Contest

Issue Current Cost/Date

(C) Pick Your Choice - Rematch Spock vs Barnabas
Movie Life Magazine, expired 3/28/69; Since first match was too close to count (Barnabas won!) - reprint of the original coupon contest with prize the same and promised feature article about the winning star .... 5-8 ______

(C) Star Shadow Contest
Flip Magazine, expired 7/30/68
1 page photo of LN, t.v. host Dick Clark and "mystery guest" shadowed out with only pointed ears showing, prose reads: "Solemn Spock's mood has changed, it appears The Vulcan hasn't laughed so in years! Spock's enjoying the show but he wants to know; If you'll guess who is wearing his ears!
Prize - total of ten, not disclosed
Answer - Paul Revere of Paul Revere and the Raiders .... 5-10 ______

(R) Is There Anything Star Trek Has That You Would Like To Have?
T.V. Star Parade Magazine, no expiration, one column query and coupon, photos the bridge crew:
Originated by Bill Theiss and Gene Roddenberry as survey to potential Star Trek products and merchandise .... 10-15 ______

(R) Star Trek Enterprises Introductory Letter
Star Trek Enterprises
Mimeographed cover letter that accompanies the first printing of Star Trek Enterprises, Majel and Gene Roddenberry's official mail-order distributorship. Letter was stapled to front page of Catalog No. 1 (a 3 page, double-sided typewritten catalog of t.v. merchandise available to fans. In this letter, Gene introduces the company and thanks the fans for their support of Star Trek. Subsequent catalogs would arrive in a more sophisticated accordian-type of fold out. .... 10-12 ______

(R) SST Committee to Save Star Trek
Bjo Trimble
A series of promotional flyers and notices dedicated to alerting Star Trek's fandom of the threat to cancel the t.v. series and a nationwide fen commitment to prevent it: 7¼"x11" Official Newsletter - black SST Letterhead, details goals of campaign .... 5-7 ______
3½"x5½" postcard - how to establish an SST Chapter in your community, who to write to at NBC, Paramount, etc. ... 2-3 ______

(S) SST Honorary Flight Deck Award
Produced by Bjo Trimble, Frederick Pohl/Galaxy & Analog Magazines
Special award sent to fans who responded to the SST mail-in campaign. Certificate the same as the regular Flight Deck Certificate sold by Star Trek Enterprises, but with the addition of gold insignia sticker in the corner. Your name was enrolled on the Starship Enterprise crew rosters. .... 8-10 ______

1970

(P) Sugar Smacks Cereal - Star Trek Back
British release premium; Cereal box back illos artwork Spock holding phaser - blurps relate the "energy" of the Star Trek phaser "pistol" and the "transcicator" (described as having translator functions, although a communicator is shown!) - all this relates to the energy found in every bit of Sugar Smacks cereal! .... 10-12 ______

1971

(P) Dan Curtis Give-Aways
Western Publishing Co. Small edition comic reprints of assorted Gold Key issues. Numbers 2 and 6 were taken from the Star Trek series (See Comics listings) .... ______

(P) Star Trek Stamps
Primrose Confectionary Co., Ltd.; British release set of 12 stamps based on the t.v. series, box premium .... 10-15 ______

SPECIAL PROMOS

	Issue	Current Cost/Date

1972

(O) Photographs by Leonard Nimoy
LNAF/Leonard Nimoy Association of Fans Exclusive 1972 Yearbook Offer - b/w photos each taken, developed, matted and signed by Nimoy himself. Arrived mounted on cardboard, mailed flat in a bond clasp envelope. Many of these prints appeared on a 1973 segment of The Dinah Shore Show: All are 8"x10" photos mounted on 11"x14", unless noted otherwise cost $3.00 each:

"Portrait of Almeria" Set
Six titled works from Almeria, Spain

	Issue	Current Cost/Date
Wagon Wheels	25-35	______
Meson deLeon (5"x10", mounted 7"x14")	25-35	______
Cross In Shadow	25-35	______
St. Anthony	25-35	______
Rainy Street	25-35	______
Portly Passenger (5"x10")	25-35	______

"The Haunted House" Set
Photographed in North Carolina:

	Issue	Current Cost/Date
Broken Window	25-35	______
Haunted House	25-35	______
Barn	25-35	______

"Grafi-Eyes" Set
Photographed in Los Angeles:

	Issue	Current Cost/Date
For Short Therefore	20-30	______
Julie's Eyes	20-30	______
I Am	20-30	______

1973

(C) Essay Contest
Scholastic Voice Magazine, Feb. 5, Vol. 54, Number 2; Star Trek student's essay contest. Winners announced in April 30th, No. 12 publication. Cost 25¢ .... NA ______

(D) Smithsonian - Air & Space Museum
Washington, D.C.
The Enterprise 11-foot wood and plastic filming model was donated in 1974. It has appeared in numerous titled displays at the museum. Also in storage are the Klingon Battlecruiser, the Tholian scoutship from TW, the Enterprise in plastic cube from CP. The Smithsonian plans a special 1991 featuring the drawing of Robert McCall and Trek artifacts to commemorate the series' 25th anniversary. Free museum admission .... NA

(R) A Piece of the Action
Star Trek Welcommittee, Feb. 1973, Newsletter organization of fans that began a Trek-central information and distributions network for current and historical news, facts and updates about Star Trek. Subscription - $3.30 annually. Individual newsletters cost 30¢ each ... 5-7 ______

(R) Directory of Star Trek Organizations
(also called the Yellow Pages of Star Trek) Star Trek Welcommittee
Stapled information director edited by Allyson Whitfield and published by Kay Johnson. Irregular publications - updates on Star Trek wares, fan club and fanzine listings, commercial products, and other miscellaneous information, cost $1.00. .... 2-4 ______

(R) Star Trek Animated Fan Club (STAFC)
Lincoln Enterprises, - Official fan club to promote the Star Trek Animated (cartoon) series from 1974 to 1976. Featured star interviews with the original t.v. cast, behind-the-scenes facts associated with the making of the animated series, story blurbs, etc. The membership package included an ID card, certificate granting full citizenship in the U.F.P. and free passage on any starship, a Trek stickpin, assorted commemorative stamps and a "Star Trek Lives" blue and gold pencil, membership fee $3.50, set of newsletters, flyers. .... 7-9 ______

1974

(O) Photographs by Leonard Nimoy
LNAF/Leonard Nimoy Association of Fans, Exclusive 1974 Yearbook offer - b/w individually titled photos, produced and signed by LN; packaged same as the 1972 sets were, 8"x10", mounted 11"x14" unless noted: cost $4.00;

	Issue	Current Cost/Date
Couple in Doorway (5"x9½", mounted 7"x14")	20-25	______
Seagulls	20-25	______
Siesta of Old Wagons	20-25	______
Workshop	20-25	______

(O) Star Trek Iron-On Transfers
AMT Corporation, ltd. offer 1974-76, Box-insert inside plastic Star Trek model kits, 5¾"x11" flyer illos four transfer sheets (approx. 6"x9"), to apply to clothing, cost $1.00 per sheet or all for $3.00 (See Patches and Transfers listing) 1-2 ______

(O) Star Trek Jacket
AMT Corporation, ltd. offer 1974-76. Coupon included as part of the model kit instructions inside boxes for the Command Bridge, Galileo '7 and Bird of Prey kits. Jackets manufactured by Great Lakes Sportswear Industries, cost $7.95 (See Outerwear listings) .... 1-2 ______

(S) Smithsonian Air & Space Museum
Washington, D.C.
Souvenir "Enterprise" pen and "Enterprise" postcard (see School/Office Supplies listings) .... — ______

Issue Current Cost/Date

1975

(O) I Am Not Spock Poster
Celestial Arts
Poster-size edition of the book by this same title and written by Leonard Nimoy, poster offered through the publisher for $2.00 plus handling, inside book cover (See Posters and Posterbooks listings) .... NA _____

1976

(D) The Star Trike
Loch David Crane, designer/owner
San Diego, CA 1976-Present
Operational 3-wheel trike replica of the t.v. Enterprise constructed from the 1600cc engine mounted on half-frame from 1968 VW Squareback and a Honda CB 360 front end. Starship's saucer and secondary hull are fiberglass over plywood; nacelles (function as twin 2½ gal. gas tanks) are capped in auto headlamps. Features include deck lights, bridge dome lights, and navigational markers. Averages 38 mpg and warps at 100 mph. Indash stereo plays Star Trek tapes. Fully road legal and appears at custom motorcycle shows and parades, charity functions around the West Coast. Estimated present conversion cost $14,000. .... NA

(P) Spock Pops
Monster Times Magazine
Giant, round chocolate flavored sucker featuring a Spock wrapper premium, wrapper shows b/w Spock profile drawing by Virgil Finlay, blister-packed to cardstock, two pops per pack, cost $1.00. .... 4-6 _____

(P) Star Trek Candy Boxes
Pheonix Candy Co.
Cardstock boxes printed with eight different photo poses and scenes from the t.v. sereis, 1"x2½"x5" in size with plastic trinket toys inside, cost 40¢ .... 2-3 _____

(P) Star Trek Glasses
Dr. Pepper
Four drinking glasses featured in a boxed set and promoting the Star Trek animated cartoon series (See Bar Accessories listings) .... NA _____

(S) Space Shuttle Enterprise
Palmdale, California, Sept. 17, 1976
First Day Cover mail souvenir of the "Roll-out of Space Shuttle Enterprise OV-101" with cancelled 13¢ postage stamp on illustrated envelope: shuttle, first 4-man crew and Leonard Nimoy. Blurbs "named after Star Trek spaceship, LN, GT, DK and producer GR attend ceremonies. President Ford and Sen. Goldwater speak," cost 18¢ .... 4-5 _____

Issue Current Cost/Date

1977

(D) Star Trek Stars Wax Display
Hollywood Wax Museum
Hollywood, California
Exhibit featuring wax sculptures of Mr. Spock (seated) and Capt. Kirk (standing with his hand on Spock's shoulder). Backdrop is painted panel with graphic designs, lighted boards and dial inserts to simulate Engineering section. Admission $5.00 .... NA _____

Glossy 9"x11¾" fold-out brochure with close-up color photo of the Spock and Kirk exhibit. .... .50-1 _____

(O) Star Trek Animated Cels Special Offer
Bantam Books, November 1977
Cardstock insert between p. 84-85 in **Star Trek No. 12** paperback by Blish and Lawrence. Ltd. edition hand-painted cels by Filmation Studios, cels No. 1A, 4, 5, 8, 9, 12, 14, 15, 16 and 20. Cost $21.50 plus handling. (See Artwork and Cels listing) .... .50-1 _____

(O) U.S.S. Enterprise Wall Plaque Offer
Science Fiction Book Club
Advertised in Starlog Magazine No. 14. Membership offer including 5½"x7½" color ship on metallic background, serrated edges, white border, ship over planet firing phasers, top reads "Naval Construction Contract 1701"; New Members offered 4 books and plaque for 10¢ .... 10-12 _____

1978

(R) Starlog Records Ballet Query
Starlog Magazine
Coupon ballot with 27 soundtrack titles and 15 t.v. themes. Help Starlog determine which previously unrecorded movie/t.v., scores you would like to see released as records in the future. Check 5 favorite movie, 3 t.v. themes. Checkbox reads "I am eager to see these scores released in record album format and would be willing to pay $6.95 to $7.95 each." .... .50-1 _____

1979

(C) Star Trek Pinball Art Contest
Starlog Magazine, expires 9/14/79
1 page rules, prizes and Bally Pinball Table photo: "Design your own pinball backglass art", original artwork contest for the upright box at the top of the pinball playfield, amateur artist solicitation. Prizes - (1st) Bally Pinball Table; (2nd) 5 sets of nine Trek paperbacks; (3rd) 10 Bradley ST Watches No. 5743-DFE4; (4th) 15 AMT/Lesney STTMP Enterprise models; (5th) 15 Bantam pocketbooks sets of 4-pack gift box;

The following abbreviations are used in the Special Promotion section:
(C) – Contest
(D) – Display/Exhibit
(O) - Offers and Specials
(P) - Premium
(R) - Publicity Release
(S) – Souvenir

Issue Current Cost/Date

(6th) 25 STTMP calendars by Pocket-book; (7th) 30 glossy prints of Starlog Magazine No. 1 cover; (8th) 100 STTMP movie novelization by Roddenberry .... 1-2 _____

(O) Enterprise Mailing List Offer
Pocket Books
1 page ad in Starlog Magazine - if you'd like to be the first to know about Star Trek publishing events of the future and news about STTMP sign on for inclusion on special list. You'll receive advance notice of books, projects and events. Offered in conjunction with Pocket Books media blitz from October 1979 to February 1980. Ad featured complete listing of new Trek title releases and b/w photos. .... 1-2 _____

(O) Starlog Magazine No. 1 Cover Print
Starlog Magazine
8"x10" color glossy reprint of the first cover as published in August 1977. Features Kirk and Spock illo as produced by Langley & Associates in ltd. edition offer direct from publisher, cost $4.95 .... 8-10 _____

(O) Star Trek Dinky Toys Offer
Peter Pan Records
Slipcover jacket insert inside record No. 8168, 4¼"x5½" order form for the special purchase of Dinky's No. 338 (9" Enterprise) or No. 357 (9" Klingon ship) plus membership in Dinky Club of America, cost per item $10.00. (See Diecast and Plastic Playtoys listings) ...... .50-1 _____

(O) Star Trek Jigsaw Puzzle Offer
Starlog Magazine
1 page offer for customized puzzle of your choice from print, slide or negatives you submit, ad shows photo of STTMP Spock, Kirk and McCoy converted to puzzle (See Board Games and Puzzles listings) .... NA _____

(O) Star Trek The Motion Picture Posters Offer
Lesney/AMT Corporation, expires 6/30/81 7"x10" glossy coupon insert inside STTMP Klingon Cruiser and Vulcan Shuttle model kits. Wall sized color posters in three designs, for $3.00 or $6.00 depending on style. (See Posters and Posterbooks listings) .... .50-1 _____

Issue Current Cost/Date

(O) Star Trek The Motion Picture Poster Set
Proctor & Gamble
Store coupon offer for set of posters from the movies, $2.00 with label redemption from Crest Toothpaste, Secret Deodorant or Prell Shampoo (See Posters and Posterbooks for listings) ... .50-1 _____

(O) Star Trek The Motion Picture Stickers Discount Offer
General Mills, Inc., expires 11/30/80
Cardboard coupon on box-back of Trix cereal. Discount on **Peel-Off Graphics Book** designed by Lee Cole, 24 pages of pre-gummed stickers in theme to STTMP. Cost $3.00 plus proof of purchase seals from Trix cereal (See Juvenile Books listings) .... 1-2 _____

(P) Star Trek The Motion Picture Bread Cards 33 Card Set
Topps Chewing Gum, Campbell-Taggart Bakeries
Premium cards include inside of subsidiary bakery bread loaves. Total of 33 trading cards featuring scenes from STTMP. Participating bakeries include Rainbo, Colonial,Kilpatrick and Manor (See Trading Cards listings) .... 6-10 _____

(P) Star Trek The Motion Picture Cereal Premium - Action Shots and Close-Ups
General Mills, Inc.
Set of 18 different color cards included as cardboard box-backs. Action scenes and character photos in 3½"x5" with ⅛" silver borders, individually numbered. Cereals - Count Chocula, Booberry, Frankenberry, Trix, Lucky Charms and Cocoa Puffs. .... 10-15 _____

(P) Star Trek The Motion Picture Cereal Premiums - Starship Signs
General Mills, Inc.
Cardboard door signs appearing as box-back premiums, 3¾"x6¾" cardboard with photo busts and comical admittance slogans, one each on 8-oz. or 20-oz. Cheerios boxes, total of 7 (See Wall-hangings listings) .... 5-7 _____

(P) Star Trek The Motion Picture Cup
Coca-Cola, Inc.
Theatre sales promotional premium offered with the purchase of a drink. (See Bar Accessories listings) .... NA _____

(P) Star Trek The Motion Picture Glasses
Coca-Cola, Inc.
Three drinking glasses with cartoon illos from the movie and descriptions on back. This set of premium glassware never found a franchise and was never advertised. (See Bar Accessories listings) . NA _____

Cereal special offer

Two secret compart rings from inside Happy Meals

Two McDonald's Happy Meal Boxes, 1979

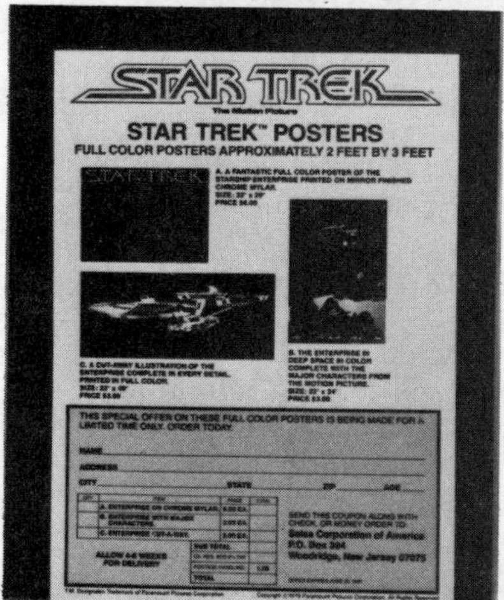

A.M.T. Special offer, insert, STTMP

Issue Current Cost/Date

(P) Star Trek The Motion Picture Happy Meals
McDonalds Corp.
Children's packaged meal boxes including regular hamburger, small drink and small fries inside colorful cartoon and photo carrying container with handles. Four different boxes available with assorted plastic trinkets and game cards inside (compartment rings, trivia); cost included the meal $1.10. . . . . 4-8 ______

(P) Star Trek The Motion Picture Posters
Coca-Cola Company
Two posters released in conjunction with the movie, bear Coca-Cola trademark:
STTMP Action Poster - 18"x24" . . . . . . 4-6 ______
STTMP Enterprise Cut-Away - 11"x23" 4-5 ______
(See Posters and Posterbooks listings)

(R) Star Trek 50 Most Asked Questions
Lincoln Enterprises
Printed booklet answering the most frequently asked questions about t.v. series Star Trek, 1007, $2.00 . . . . 2-3 ______

(R) Star Trek Stage 9 & 10 Stage Blueprints
Lincoln Enterprises
Reproductions of the set and stage blueprints used in the Paramount t.v. filming studio. Two-print set details

Issue Current Cost/Date

Enterprise interior design sets, plus exterior landscapes and settings used in making the series, 24"x36" each, 2191 set $3.00 . . . . 3-5 ______

(R) Star Trek The Motion Picture Official Letterhead
Stationery designed by Michael Minor and used for office correspondence during production, never offered to the public:
Paper - 8½"x11" pastel blue front, white back, port profile STTMP Enterprise in starfield, bottom reads "A Gene Roddenberry Production - A Robert Wise Film," white outline STTMP Letter Logo . . . . 4-5 ______
Envelope - 4½"x9½", white, left side shows **starboard** Enterprise, blue outline STTMP Letter Logo . . . . 3-4 ______

(R) Star Trek The Motion Picture Lobby Cards
Paramount Pictures
Color cardstock photos with scenes from the first movie. Contain brief scene description, PPC Logo and full casting credits, for display in theatres, 11"x14", set
Set of 8 cards . . . . 25-30 ______
Individual cards . . . . 3-4 ______

SPECIAL PROMOS - 1979

	Issue	Current Cost/Date
(R) Star Trek The Motion Picture Matchbooks Paramount Pictures 1½"x1¾" flip-top matchbook, has frontview Enterprise over starburst with "The Human Adventure Is Just Beginning"	.50-.75	______
1½"x1¾" flip-top, features "Rainbow" promo, inside special offers coupons for Spock Ears, Playing Cards, Water Pistol, promo poster, Yo-Yo or a Jacket	.50-.75	______
2"x1¾" World Premiere glossy flip-top dated 12/6/79. Cover is white with gold embossed letters, souvenir from Washington, D.C. theater opening	1-1.50	______
(R) Star Trek The Motion Picture Press Kit Paramount Pictures Corp. Packet of information in folder, not generally available to public, contains 8"x10" b/w glossy prints promoting the movie, actor biographies and production notes.	35-40	______
(R) Star Trek The Motion Picture Publicity Photographs Paramount Pictures Corp. Assorted b/w and color stills from the first movie, action shots and posed star portraits, some with date/time shooting frame identification along the border, 5"x7" and 8"x10"	4-15	______
(R) Star Trektennial Newsletters Lincoln Enterprises Set of 12 newsletters edited by Susan Sackett following the production and progress of shooting STTMP. Single issues numbered 13-24 (follow in sequence to **Star Trek Intestellar** series,		
1103C All 12 issues, cost $6.00	10-12	______
1103D Any 6 Issues, cost $3.50	5-6	______
1103E Any Single issue, cost $ .75	1-2	______
(S) Star Trek The Motion Picture Program Souvenir Book Parafen Publishing Corp. Glossy-page photo book released during the premiere, containing cast credits, movie character profiles, bios, production notes, etc. 9"x12", 16 pages. Cost $2.25	4-6	______

1980

	Issue	Current Cost/Date
(D) Bridge of the Enterprise Movieland Wax Museum Bueno Park, California Wax figures exhibit featuring seven Star Trek characters: standing Spock, Uhura, McCoy and Scotty, seated Kirk, Chekov and Sulu. Figures are at their stations on a detailed platform replica of the t.v. studio set bridge. Exhibit includes illuminiated sensor monitors and lighted consoles, turbo lift doors, chairs and railings in an authentic reproduction. General adult museum admission $5.00.	NA	______
(O) Star Trek (The Motion Picture) Action Fleet Official Offer Mars, Inc. expires 12/31/80 10"x13" color Sunday Comics supplement with newsprint photos and cartoon of a child playing with the assembled ships-mobile. Offer for 5 cardstock, cut-out spacecraft from the movie, plus guide assembly sheet and specs info. Cost $1.50 with redemption of five candy wrappers from Snickers, 3 Musketeers, Milky Way, M & M's, Twix or Summit. (See Living Decor listings)	1-2	______
(O) Star Trek (The Motion Picture) Starfleet Belt Buckle, Official Offer Heroes World, May 1980 Full page color comic book insert in Issue 2 of the Star Trek Marvel Comic series. Mail-order offer featuring kit containing STTMP vintage uniform buckle, a belt, an ID card and an insignia badge. Comic illo plus coupon. Cost $6.69 for the set. (See Belt Buckles listings)	NA	______
(O) Star Trek The Motion Picture Iron-Ons Ltd. Offer General Mills, Inc., expires 12/31/80 Cardboard coupon on box-back of Cheerios cereal. Premium Starship Signs also included on this box-back. Set of five 5"x9" shirt transfers for $1.00 plus 2 Proof of Purchases from Cheerios box bottoms. (See Patches and Transfers listings)	1-2	______
(O) Star Trek (The Motion Picture) Jacket, Official Ltd. Offer D. D. Bean & Sons, expires 12/31/80 Matchbook cover coupon for ordering a Star Trek logo windbreaker inside the STTMP souvenir matchbook with "rainbow" promo cover. (See Outerwear listings)	NA	______
(O) Star Trek The Motion Picture Light Beam Ltd. Offer General Mills, Inc., expires 11/30/80 Cardboard coupon on box-back of Cocoa Puffs cereal. Premium Collectors Shots also included on this box-back. Blue plastic palm-size flashlight for $1.00 plus 2 Proof of Purchases from Cocoa Puffs, Count Chocula, Frankenberry or Booberry cereals. (See your School/Office Supplies listings)	1-2	______

SPECIAL PROMOS - 1980

Issue Current Cost/Date

(O) Star Trek (The Motion Picture) Pajamas Special Ltd. Offer
Mars, Inc., expires 8/31/80
9"x11" glossy flyer insert, newspaper supplement. Photos boy and girl wearing the PJ's and pictures the candy products with redeemable packages. Two transfer photo styles available. Cost $4.50 plus the Proof (Guarantee of Satisfaction) statement from two 8-oz. bags of miniature Milky Ways, Snickers or 3-Musketeers. (See Underwear and Pajamas listings) . . . . 1-2 ______

(O) Star Trek The Motion Picture Personalized Wristband Ltd. Offer
General Mills, Inc., expires 11/30/80
Cardboard coupon on box-back of Lucky Charms cereal. Premium Collector Shots also included on this box-back. Child's size ID bracelet for $1.25 plus 2 Proof of Purchases from Lucky Charms cereal. (See Bracelets and Charms listings). . . . . 1-2 ______

(R) Great Scenes from Paramount Brochure
Paramount Home Video, Vol. 1, No. 3, Nune 1980
Sales promotion for the first series of ten Star Trek episode tapes distributed for rental/purchase by Paramount Home Video. Five VHS/Beta tapes with **two episodes per tape.** 4-page accordion fold-out flyer, front photos Enterprise "... to boldly go where no man has gone before," inside pages show 6 color episode shots and Enterprise over red planet with episodes recaps, ordering, rental info. (FotoMat was a distributor for these early video packages) . . . . 2-3 ______

(R) Star Trek The Motion Picture Newsletters
Lincoln Enterprises
Series edited by Virginia Yaple, all phases of the making of STTMP: field analysis for production, photos, interviews, fan news:
1103F All 6 issues, cost $5.00 . . . . 8-10 ______
1103G Any single issue (numbers 25-30 as a continuation of the **Star Trek Interstellar/Trektennial** series), cost $1.00 . . . 1-3 ______

(S) Movieland Wax Museum
Souvenir items from the gift shop featuring the above "Bridge of the Enterprise" exhibit: (Cover Photo)

Museum Brochure
Glossy 11"x17" color fold-out with promo photos of the major exhibits. 1984 release features the exhibit in color with 60-word blurb beginning - "Fasers on stun ...", free . . . . .50-.75 ______

Issue Current Cost/Date

Postcard, Mike Roberts Color Productions B13428; 4"x6" mailing postcard showing the entire Trek exhibit, cost 35¢ . . . . .40-1 ______

Slide, Pana-Vue by View Master Star Trek bridge exhibit, omitting McCoy and Scotty wax figures. One of a set of five color slides promoting the museum, cost $1.75 . . . . 2-3 ______

Viewmaster, View Master Internat'l Group,
Reel entitled "Six Flags Movieland Wax Museum" No. 5343; three reels, 21 pictures of different museum exhibits, Star Trek Bridge is on Reel B, cost 4.25 . . . . 4-5 ______

1982

(R) Star Trek II The Wrath of Kahn Lobby Cards
Paramount Pictures Corp.
Color cardstock photos featuring scenes, descriptions, PPC Logo and credits for theatre lobby displays, 11"x14"
Set of 8 cards . . . . 30-40 ______
Individual card . . . . 4-5 ______

(R) Star Trek II The Wrath of Kahn Press Kit
Paramount Pictures Corp.
Advance promotional folder containing photos, bios and plot information on the ST II motion picture. Not generally made available to the public. . . . . 30-35 ______

(R) Star Trek II The Wrath of Kahn Publicity Photographs
Paramount Pictures Corp.
Assorted b/w and color stills from the production of the movie and used for media promotion, 5"x7" or 8"x10" . . . . 4-10 ______

(S) Star Trek II The Wrath of Kahn Program Souvenir Book
Parafen Publish Corp.
Glossy-page photo book promotion used as theater souvenir, credits, inside production notes, bios and storyline, 9"x12", 16 pages. Cost $3.00 . . . . 4-6 ______

1983

(C) Science Fiction Celebrity Treasure Hunt No. 6
Starlog Magazine, March 1983, deadline for submissions 3/31/83
Contest to identify the sci-fi celebrity from Starlog back issues and use the A,B,C crossword clues in remaining squares to make a word. (The words have been hidden somewhere in this issue -excluding ads). Number beneath each word line indicates that word's order in making a complete sentence. The three words from Treasure Hunt 6

	Issue	Current Cost/Date
combine with words from the previous five puzzles to make the final solution to the contest. (The three clues associated were: A. Turning death into life (7 words); B. T.V. ghost story (7 words); C. Not a war or a log (4 words). Spread showed partial photo of Gene Roddenberry.	1-2	______

First season press book compilation

(O) U.S.S. Enterprise Commemorative Belt Buckle Ltd. Offer

	Issue	Current Cost/Date
Sunday Comics Promotions, Inc. 2"x6" Sunday Comics advertisement with illo of the buckle and a coupon. STTMP version starship to commemorate the 200th Anniversary of man's first flight. Cost $6.88 plus $1.75 postage with coupon.	.50-.75	______

(S) Adventure Series Publicity Compilations

Archival Marketing Associates, 1983
8½"x11" mass-produced fan souvenirs of the original publicity booklets released by Paramount Television Sales during the series' production:

Season Press Books
Episode synopses, background stories, character and actor bios, spiral-bound compilation, 8½"x11", cost $9.95:

	Issue	Current Cost/Date
First Season Press Book	10-12	______
Second Season Press Book	10-12	______
Third Season Press Book	10-12	______

Third Season Outlines
Outlines as they were originally presented to NBC before use in making of 3rd season shows, 8½"x11", spiral-bound compilation, cost $9.95:

	Issue	Current Cost/Date
Third Season Outline, Volume 1	10-12	______
Third Season Outline, Volume 2	10-12	______

(S) Movie Handbooks of Production Information

Lincoln Enterprises, 1983
Softbound booklets containing bios, date breakdowns, synopses of scenes, stories, on the set info plus facts and figures, everything about the making of the individual motion pictures as it was originally produced by Paramount publicity department for interested newsmedia, mass produced, 8½"x11" compilations, cost $5.95:

	Issue	Current Cost/Date
1110 Star Trek The Motion Picture, 40p.	6-8	______
1111 Star Trek The Wrath of Kahn, 40p.	6-8	______
1112 Star Trek The Search For Spock, 45p	6-8	______

Star Trek Movie Lobby Books

Issue Current Cost/Date

1984

(C) Rebuilding of the Enterprise Contest
Starblazer Magazine, begins Nov. 1984 2 pages with 2 b/w photos of Enterprise and 1 art-style work of Excelsior. Your new orders from Starfleet Command are to designs the New Enterprise II, Constitution Class III, using the latest Trans Warp technology. Submit illustrations (preferably ink on Bristol board), invites NASA and M.I.T. Engineers to submit work. Illustrations become property of the magazine, not returned. Prize - 1st, copy of **Star Trek Compendium;** 2nd, model kit of U.S.S. enterprise from Ertl; 3rd, three winners, copies of the ST III novelization paperback. Winners' photos and designs are to appear in upcoming issue. .... 1-2 ______

(D) Bridge Set Replica - U.S.S Kasimar Starfleet Chapter XIV, Bangor Maine official fan organization composed of Maine, New Hampshire, Vermont, Massachusetts, Rhode Island, Connecticut and Eastern Canada - full-size bridge mock-up with over 400 working lights, 4'x5' main viewscreen, "wrap-around" sound system, 30'x37', approximate cost $4,000. .... NA ______

(O) Paramount Home Video Holiday Offer
Paramount Pictures Corp., expires 2/28/85; Heavy cardstock, folded coupon inside VHS Scotch Brand T-120 Video tape cassettes. Season special that lists 25 home movies for $24.95 each. Offer redeemable through dealerships or the mail, in VHS or Beta format, coupon 3½"x5¼".
Star Trek The Motion Picture (Special Longer Version) cost $24.95
Star Trek II The Wrath of Kahn, $24.95
(See Videos listings) .... .10-.20 ______

(O) Star Trek Strategic Operations Simulator Discount Offer
Proctor & Gamble, expires 9/30/84
Store display coupon, 3"x5" paper on tear-off pad, contains rules for obtaining the new Sega Star Trek video arcade game cartridge for home computers at a special offer price of $9.95 plus Proof of Purchase from any 3 - Crisco (3 lb. can), Crisco Oil (48-oz. bottle), Duncan Hines Cake Mix or Frosting, or Pringles Potato Chips. (See Gaming Programs listings) .... .10-.20 ______

Issue Current Cost/Date

(O) Star Trek III The Search For Spock Poster Offer
Lever Bros., Co.
8½"x4¼" glossy coupon available in tear-off display in stores. Four color posters featuring scenes from the 3rd movie. Coupon illos posters, cost $2.95 plus two wrappers from Shield, Lifebuoy, Caress, Lux or Dove bars of soap. (See Posters and Posterbooks listings) .... .50-1 ______

(O) Star Trek III The Search For Spock Exclusive U.S.S. Enterprise Kite offer
Lever Bros., expires 11/30/84
"Take it to the skies with Shield and Star Trek III," 8¾"x11¼" color glossy newspaper insert that appeared in the Sunday supplements section. Flyer illos black space field illuminated by blue, holographic-style busts of McCoy, Spock and Kirk. Illos boy holding the assembled Enterprise kits, purple and white. Includes 20¢ store coupon and redeemable coupon. Cost $3.95 plus two wrappers from any size Shield Deodorant Soap bar. (See Hobby Kits listings) .... 1-2 ______

(P) Star Trek III The Search For Spock Glasses
Taco Bell, Div. of Pepsico, Inc.
Set of four drinking glasses featuring promo scenes and legends from the third movie. Premium gift for the purchase of a medium size Pepsi at participating Taco Bell franchises, cost 69¢ plus drink. (See Kitchen and Bar listings) .... ______

(R) Star Trek The Official Fan Club
Aurora, Colorado; Pres. Dan Madsen; - 1987 Officially licensed fan club featuring glossy-stock, stapled magazine, bi-monthly, accompanied by special release 8"x11" b/w newsletters. Color photos, exclusive interviews, new Star Trek merchandise info, new t.v. series updates, book reviews, facts, etc. Membership includes printed certificate and card signed by Madsen; membership $15.00 annually.
Individual booklets, 30-pages, $3.00 .... 2-3 ______
Back Issues through Club, $5.00 each .. 4-5 ______

(R) Star Trek III The Search For Spock Poster Card
Paramount Pictures Corp.
Color, unusual glossy stock card given away as a promo at certain movie premieres, front features full reproduction of "neon glo" movie promo poster and reads "Join the Search," reverse shows complete cast and supporting staff list, 8½"x11" .... 3-5 ______

SPECIAL PROMOS - 1984

Issue Current Cost/Date

(R) Star Trek III The Search For Spock Publicity Photographs
Paramount Pictures Corp.
Assorted b/w and color stills from the production footage of the third movie distributed for promotion, 5"x7" and 8"x10" . . . . 3-7 ______

Star Trek III Lobby Card Give-away

(S) Star Trek II The Wrath of Kahn Souvenir Shooting Schedule
Lincoln Enterprises
Softbound, lists what scenes will be in the day's shooting for production days 14-54 during the filming of the second movie. Includes info on props to be used, the character scenes, etc. 8½"x11", 1109, cost $2.00. . . . . 2-4 ______

(S) Star Trek III The Search For Spock Lobby Cards
Paramount Pictures Corp.
Color cardstock photos with scenes, credits and legends from the third movie, PPC Logo, 11"x14"
Set of 8 cards . . . . 15-25 ______
Individual cards . . . . 2-3 ______

(S) Star Trek III The Search For Spock Official Press Release Souvenir
Lincoln Enterprises
Softbound compilation in transparent cover containing dates, facts and figures, plus phases of the production as were originally sent to various newspapers, magazines, t.v. shows and radio stations to promote the movie's premiere, 15 pages, 0770 cost $3.95 . . . . 4-5 ______

(S) Star Trek III The Search For Spock Program Souvenir Book
Parafen Publishing Corp.
Glossy-page theater souvenir containing photos, legends, interviews, behind-the-scenes and bio information for the third movie, 9"x12", 16 pages, cost $3.25 . . . 3-4 ______

1985

Issue Current Cost/Date

(C) Star Trek 20th Anniversary Favorite Episode Poll
D.C. Comics, (Issue No. 22, Jan. 1986) but released on earlier newsstands, contest expires 11/30/85
Postcard entry format for voting for your favorite t.v. episode. Name, address, zip, etc. winner drawn at random for most favorite selection. Prizes: 1st, complete set of 26 novels from Pocket Books (including **Star Trek Quiz Book,** plus original plot and dialogue from Issue 22 comic autographed by Tona Isabella and 1-year subscription to D.C. Star Trek comic series; 2nd (four), set of four Trek novels (**Final Reflection, My Friend, My Enemy, Tears of the Singers),** plus 1-year subscription to the D.C. One entry per person. Notification by 12/30/85. . . . . NA ______

1986

(C) Star Trek IV Trivia Contest
Star Trek The Official Fan Club, sponsor
D.C. Comics, co-promoter
Entry forms in Issue 33 D.C. Special, 12/86 or Publication 51 Star Trek Official Fan Club expires 10/15/86.
1. What is the serial number on saucer of the U.S.S. Enterprise?
2. Who was the first captain of the Enterprise?
3. What does the "T" stand for in James T. Kirk?
Prizes – the grand prize, trip for 2 for 2 days, 1 night in NYC for advance screening of ST IV movie, plus tour of D.C. Comics by the editor; 1st runner up (30), new **Star Trek The Adventure Game** by West End; 2nd runner up (125), new updated **Star Trek Compedium** from Pocket Books, 3rd (125), 1987 Star Trek Calendar from Pocket; 4th (1,000). ST IV poster from Paramount. Grand Winner announced D.C. issue 37 - Dwight McKay. (See Comics listings) . . . . NA ______

(D) The Enterprise Ride
Hauss Manufacturer's, Germany
Pompano Beach, Florida
Carnival, traveling circus amusement ride originally designed by Hauss in Germany in 1968. The ride currently in Pompano Beach is one of 8 such rides in the United States. Owner is Greg Link who has run the ride four years. Features a fast-ferris wheel style ride with cabs set against backdrop mural of space battle Enterprise and Klingon ships, stars and space. Overhead bulb marquee reads "The Enterprise." . . . . . . NA

SPECIAL PROMOS - 1986

Issue Current Cost/Date

(D) Galileo '7 Shuttlecraft Prop
Owner, restorer Stephen Haskins
Originally made for Paramount by AMF Phoenix for $65,000, recently refurbished for $8,500, this prop has had no usable interior but is currently being revamped by volunteer fans at the California Museum of Space & Technology. . . . . NA

(D) U.S.S. Kasimar Bridge
Starfleet Chapter XIV, John Supranovich Starfleet Rear Admiral, 30'x37' portable bridge prop, features 400 working lights, a 4'x5' main screen, wrap-around stereo sound system and carpeting, built as an exact working replica of the Enterprise bridge for $5,000 in materials. . . . . NA

(O) Simon & Schuster Software Discount Offer
8½"x11" glossy page flyer with b/w promo photos of Simon's Star Trek software packages **The Kobayashi Alternative** and **The Promethean Prophesy.** Special offer coupon at bottom is for $5.00 off the normal $39.95 cost of each diskette. (See Gaming Programs listings) .30-.50 ______

(O) Star Trek Collector Pin Club (Special Offer series)
Starway Distributors for Hollywood Commemorative Pin Co.
8½"x11" glossy page flyer. Front shows actual size, color cloisonne pins produced by Hollywood. Reverse is a full page order blank for Starway with optional coupon for membership in an exclusive collector pin club. Ongoing drive is to enroll a minimum of 1,000 founding members. Fee is $10.00 for the right to receive an exclusive membership mailing list that offers one Ltd. Edition Star Trek pin per offering. Members can purchase up to 5 pins. Ltd. editions will then be produced to the number awarded on a one-time-only basis. Membership also includes a printed collector's guide and notebook. (See Pins listings) . . . . . . .30-.50 ______

(P) Star Trek IV The Voyage Home Glow-Cups
Stop 'N Go Stores, distributors
Set of four 28-oz. plastic drinking cups with scenes and characters from the 4th movie. Premium gift with the purchase of a giant 28-oz. Coca-Cola drink. (Cups logo Classic Coke), cost $1.59 each with softdrink. Regional promotion only during the premiere weeks of ST IV;

Set of 4 cups . . . . 5-7 ______

Individual cups . . . . 1-2 ______

Inflatable Enterprise, Video Display Promo

Issue Current Cost/Date

(R) Star Trek IV The Voyage Home "Call the Crew" Promotion
Starlog Telecommunications
Advertisements released in newspapers nationwide on Sunday, 11/23/86 and ran five weeks. Dial 1-900-720-TREK to hear pre-recorded dialogue as written by Walter Koenig for these original scripts. Voices include those of Chekov, Uhura, Dr. McCoy and Mr. Spock. Charge of the call 50¢ plus specific long-distance charges. Ads for this special promotion appeared inside the theatre ads running ST IV newspaper coverage. . . . . .20-.40 ______

(R) U.S.S. Enterprise Inflatable Ship Promo
Sun Unlimited, Inc./Paramount Home Video 20"x24" inflatable starship produced as a mobile-style display item for the 11/86 release of Star Trek episode videos 44-52. "Star Trek" appears on the upper and lower side saucer disk, with "The Video Connection." Gray toy with black letters and red decal stamp-marks. 8-12 ______

(S) "Future Birthplace of Captain James T. Kirk" - Riverside, Iowa Vials of Dirt
Riverside Area Community Club
Municipal promotion with proceeds to go towards the construction of a permanent statue commemorating Kirk and located in Riverside, Iowa. Cost $4.00 for container of dirt from behind the barbershop where Kirk will be born and includes a numbered certificate of authenticity, suitable for framing. . . . . . 4-6 ______

SPECIAL PROMOS

Issue Current Cost/Date

1987

(O) Creation Con Star Trek Booklets Special Offer

Starlog Magazine, Issue 117, 4/87

Offers appeared in conjunction with the Creation Con advertising promo for area conventions and includes the following three printed poetry and photo books by two of the Star Trek stars:

Deforest Kelley - "Big Bird's Dream," his poem about Star Trek accompanied by photos from his personal collection, cost $5.00 plus $1.00 postage . . . . 5-6 ______

Deforest Kelley - "The Dream Lives On," Kelley's Sequel to the previous title with more photos, autographed copy collection, cost $5.00 plus $1.00 postage . . . . . 5-6 ______

Nichelle Nichols - "Poetry and Prose," her own verses and rare photos from her private collection, autographed copy, cost $5.00 plus $1.00 postage . . . . 5-6 ______

Star Trek Play Program

PART II
Conventions and Live Performances

The year is 1971 and the Star Trek television series has been off the network channels for years, but is struggling for syndication rights is assorted larger cities. Commercial interest in Star Trek has dwindled dangerously low. Even Bantam Books, the progenitor of the James Blish Star Trek novelization paperbacks has halted its production of the series with Volume 4 (the finished collection will eventually total 12 volumes of books). Trek merchandising lies dead in the water, with the noteworthy exception of the fan-published presses and the production of annuals by the many Star Trek fan club memberships.

There are rumblings and rumors . . . but many fear these are only the wishful-thinkings of die-hard fans who began their interest in Star Trek as youthful teens and are now ready to move off themselves to go to college or join the work force. With their lives and careers ahead of them, is anyone really interested in reviving Star Trek anymore? Is anyone really **out there?**

The duration of plaintive wondering was answered, and with a vengence, by the Star Trek Fan Convention of January 1972. Once and for all Star Trek was proved beyond a shadow of doubt to be unique in the annals of television history. Not only had the stalwart fans of the deceased series survived the period of marketing malaise, they had increased in numbers, in average age and in the level of the sophistication of their communication channels. In short, they had evolved into a network alliance!

The first Star Trek Convention proved all of this, but it also did something more. It brought together for the first time the creators of the show (Gene Roddenberry, the producer; Majel Barrett, one of its prominent stars, and even Oscar Katz, programming director from NBC) and no less than 4,000 individual Star Trek fans. This totaled up to an attendance record which shattered all prior convention records to-date. Certainly this publicity event was one of the crowning hallmarks of Star Trek lore. The camera crews from the major network affiliates came, the media responded, and the name "Trekkie" or Star Trek-Groupie, was coined by the press practically on the spot.

Conventions continued to be a driving force behind Star Trek's growing fandom throughout the 1970's where attendance records reached the staggering heights of 14,000 Trek conventioneers. To this day, the conventions serve as the ultimate gathering place for Star Trek fans from every walk of life and each regional part of the United States. Conventions in other countries are beginning to catch on as well. The importance that conventions play in joining together the dual-nature of Star Trek's identity – its "official" production side and its peripheral fen, cannot be overstated. The conventions provide the setting for Star Trek's most popular format of public exhibit - conventions unite the fans with the stars.

For collectors who attend the convention gatherings there is an unsurmounted wealth of merchandise and memorabilia. Special souvenirs which originate at the cons, the so-called "Memory Books" and their attendant regiment of progress reports, convention slogan stickers, buttons and bags and product advertising flyers provide a unique source for obtaining collectibles with very limited distributions. No definitive count exists for the total number of convention programs now in existence since virtually any size fan gathering can generate at least a printed-pamphlet souvenir to commemorate its passing. But certain grand-scale conventions held during the 70's produced professional quality photo-books which are recognized as being truly valuable editions.

Conventions as a primary source of distributor displays have been discussed earlier in the book. Suffice it to say that no visit to a fan convention is complete without at least one trip to the Huckster's Room.

There are also other types of Star Trek live performances. Leonard Nimoy fans have been treated to this actor's live stage performances in numerous programs during the intervening years between the original t.v. series and the production of the movies. Nimoy has appeared in Broadway, regional theatre and summer stock productions in such stage roles as Fagin ("Oliver"), Goldman ("The Man in the Glass Booth", McMurphy ("One Flew Over the Cuckoo's Nest") and Tvye ("Fiddler on the Roof"). He also appeared in productions of "Equus," "Visit to a Small Planet," "My Fair Lady" and "Full Circle." Nimoy held the title role in the Royal Shakespeare Company's national tour of "Sherlock Holmes." Nimoy fan collectors, in particular, can delight in collecting the many flyers, program souvenirs and publicity releases pertaining to this actor's very active stage career. One especially popular performance by Nimoy is the stage production "Vincent," a one-man play which this actor also wrote and produced.

William Shatner's followers have had the opportunity to catch his appearances at one of several campuses during his traveling tour that culminated in the release of his LP album titled "William Shatner: Live!"

Gene Roddenberry, the creator and producer for Star Trek, was recently engaged in touring campus locations as well. His tour included a narrative-style dissertation on "Futurism" and its positive global outlook. This presentation, combined with various slides and films from the Star Trek television series fits nicely with the overall view of Star Trek, namely that mankind in the future will learn to co-exist in peace.

The real importance of live participation in Star Trek has not been overlooked by the fans who have been actors and sponsors of the Star Trek performing arts. "HMS Trekastar" was one such play that was written and performed on the fan stage through the artistic talents of Karen Anderson (the wife of science fiction writer Pohl Anderson) and Bjo Trimble. Another example of fan-sponsored theatre, although one in a slightly different vein, was the immensely popular slide show presentation entitled "City on the Edge of Whatever" which was hosted by writer David Gerrold.

Plays thematic to Trek have also been produced by both university and community theatre groups. "One Cube or Two?" was a three-act play produced on the Baltimore campus of the University of Maryland. This play ran three consecutive nights in March of 1973. Performances were promoted by the 1973 International Star Trek Convention (ISTC) in New York City, and the play received media coverage in **Monster Times,** a professionally published, SF oriented magazine. The door price of $2.00 included a souvenir tribble!

Charles Gibson was the producer of two successful Star Trek plays which were performed on stage at the Denham Springs Community Theatre in Louisiana during the mid-1970's. The first was titled "Star Date 3113.7". The second play, "Romulan Encounter" was a 3-act play written by L.E. Wallace, Jr. The plot involved the United Star Ship Esquire NCC-1705 and its voyages into the star system Lagos. The Star Trek consulant for this production was Bjo Trimble and the story featured Romulan characters, as well as a Klingon adventure sequence which occurred as a pre-recorded "Viewscreen" segue on film.

Fans and collectors are wholeheartedly invited to come and participate in all of Star Trek's live performances. There is no better way to demystify the forces of the Star Trek Phenomenon, than to come and experience it for yourself!

The Star Trek Convention and International Star Trek Conventions Program Series, 1972-1976

Issue Current Cost/Date

1972

Star Trek Convention, New York

The very first convnetion dedicated completely to Trek. . . . . 20-30 ______

Memory Book - 6"x9", black photo cover featuring the Enterprise, 29 pages of b/w photos and bios . . . . 25-30 ______

Convention Bag - White plastic with red and blue star and black Spock's head profile. Slogan is "In Spock We Trust." 6-7 ______

International Star Trek Con '73 Program Book

1973

International Star Trek Convention, New York

8½"x11" large format program with black cover and color photo inserts of Sulu and Scotty. 39 pages including the comic "Star Truckin" by Howski Comix and program schedule insert. . . . . 30-35 ______

Bag - Yellow plastic with black Spock's head print and the "ISTC" lettering . . . 5-6 ______

1974

International Star Trek Convention, New York

6"x9" book with cover photo close-up of Spock. 40 pages including stills from the Bloopers. . . . . 10-15 ______

Program Schedule - 8½"x11" pamphlet with stenciled lettering "Welcome to the 1974 ISTC" and a designated area for autographs. Righthand cover border illustrated for planet, Enterprise and Spock's head. Slogan "Star Trek Lives!" 3-4 ______

Bag - plain black plastic. . . . . 4-5 ______

Convention Slogan Notepaper and Pen Set - 5"x6" sheets with outline drawing of planet and Enterprise with the con slogan printed along the bottom. Pen is a black and silver ball point with the printed convention slogan. Set . . . . 6-8 ______

Final Frontier Con '76 and International Star Trek Con '75 Booklets

Star Trek Con '74 and '75 Program Books

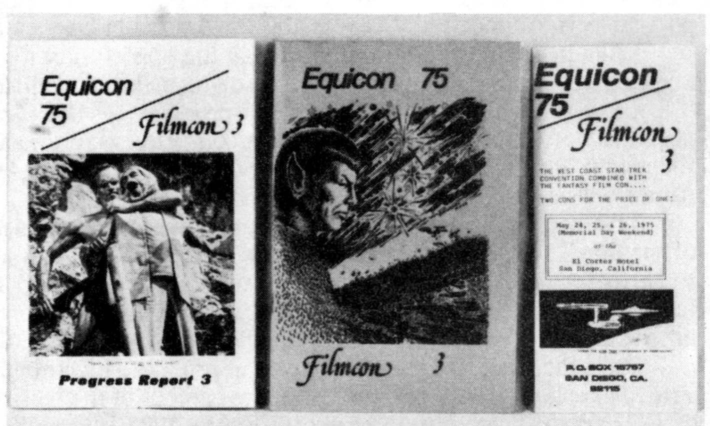

Euicon '75 Conventon Program and updates

Issue Current Cost/Date

1975

Star Trek Convention, New York

6"x9" book with cover photo of Kirk with the Enterprise model in the background. . . . . 8-19 ______

	Issue	Current Cost/Date
Program Schedule – Plain, white 8"x10" cover with blue title stenciling	1-2	_____
Bag - Blue plastic with black print of Spock and Kirk heads.	4-5	_____

International Star Trek Convention, New York
8½"x11" book, 24 pages with cover photo of seated Kirk, McCoy and Spock on the bridge. Shatner, Doohan and Koenig are guests .... 5-8 _____

International Star Trek Convention, Philadelphia
8½"x11", 20 pages, full color cover art by F. Biochet. Front displays the Starfleet Command Recruiting Poster, rear shows the Klingon Recruiting Poster. Contains b/w photos, bios and classified ads. .... 5-8 _____

Star Trek Houston Program & International Star Trek Con 1976

1976

Star Trek Convention, New York
6"x9" booklet with color close-up cover photo of McCoy outside of Cochrane's home from the episode "Metamorphosis." Contains b/w photos. .... 5-8 _____

Pocket Program – large format 8½"x11" schedule, white cover with blue lettering 1-2 _____

Bag - silver plastic with black elongated oval con emblem featuring a very stylized starburst and silhouette of the Enterprise .... 4-5 _____

International Star Trek Convention, New York
Memory book containing photos, bios, etc. .... 4-6 _____

International Star Trek Convention, Washington, D.C.
Memory book containing photos, information .... 4-6 _____

Alphabetical Sampler of Other Star Trek Convention Program Books

August Party, 1976-1981 .... 2-4 _____

Boston Star Trek Convention, 1976
48 pages, full color wraparound cover booklet. Shatner, Kelley, Whitney and Harlan Ellison .... 4-6 _____

Issue Current Cost/Date

Equicon/Filmcon Series, 1973-76
These two conventions merged in 1975. Large West Coast convention series with a production staff including John and Bjo Trimble, Rita Ractliffe and D.C. Fontana. Stenciled cover memory books, progress bulletins and flyers. .... 2-5 _____

KWest Con 1974 .... 2-4 _____

Media West Con, Michigan 1981-84 .... 2-4 _____

Omicon, Miami 1976-86 .... 2-4 _____

Palm Beach Con 1 1975
36 pages, 8½"x11" with cover art by Jack Kirby, other artists include Adams and Bode. James Doohan guests. .... 4-6 _____

Pittsburgh Star Trektacular 1975 .... 2-4 _____

Shoreleave, Maryland 1979-84 .... 2-4 _____

Shuttlecon Columbus 1978 .... 2-4 _____

Space . . . The Final Frontier, 1974-78
Oakland, CA
From the largest Star Trek cons on the West Coast. Programs included STTMP movie news, bios on Trek cast, Trek animation and articles on space exploration. 5½"x8½" formats. .... 4-6 _____

Star Con, Dallas 1979
48 pages, Grace Lee Whitney guest. .. 2-4 _____

Star Trek America, 1977-80 .... 2-4 _____

Star Trek Bi-Centennial-10, New York 1976
32 pages, 8½"x11", Shatner, Kelley, Doohan, Nichols, Takei, Koenig and Grace Lee Whitney .... 3-5 _____

Star Trek Cleveland 1979 .... 2-4 _____

Star Trek Expo, Washington, D.C. 1976 .. 2-4 _____

Star Trek Houston 1975 .... 2-4 _____

Star Trek Orlando 1976 .... 2-4 _____

Star Trek Philadelphia 1977 .... 2-4 _____

Star Trek Space Expo 1978 .... 2-4 _____

Stellar Voyage 1982 .... 2-4 _____

T'Con 1978 .... 2-4 _____

Toronto Star Trek 1976 .... 2-4 _____

Trekcon I, West Palm Beach 1975
32 pages, cover art by C.C. Beck, Takei Kelley Freas and Noel Neill guests .... 3-5 _____

Ultimate Fantasy, Houston 1982
Laser light and orchestrated performance billed as the ST con of all time. Guests included the full cast from STTMP. .... 4-6 _____

Episode Abbreviations Guide

All Our Yesterdays (AY)
Alternative Factor (AF)
Amok Time (AT)
Apple, The (Ap)
Arena (Ar)
Assignment: Earth (AE)
Balance of Terror (BT)
Bread and Circuses (CB)
By Any Other Name (AON)
Cats-paw (Cp)
Changeling, The (Cg)
Charlie X (CX)
Children Shall Lead, And The (CL)
City on the Edge of Forever (CEF)
Cloud Minders, The (Cms)
Conscience of the King, The (CK)
Corbomite Maneuver, The (CMn)
Court-Martial (Cml)
Dagger of the Mind (DMd)
Day of the Dove (Dv)
Deadly Years, The (DY)
Devil in the Dark (DD)
Doomsday Machine, The (DMa)
Elaan of Troyius (ET)
Empath, The (Em)
Enemy Within, The (EW)
Enterprise Incident, The (EI)
Errand of Mercy (EM)
For the World Is Hollow (FW)
Friday's Child (FC)
Galileo Seven (GS)
Gamesters of Triskelion, The (GT)
Immunity Syndrome, the (IS)
I, Mudd (IM)
Is There In Truth, No Beauty? (TB)
Journey to Babel (JB)
Let That Be Your Last Battlefield (LB)
Lights of Zetar, The (LZ)
Man Trap, The (MT)
Mark of Gideon, The (MG)
Menagerie, The (Me)
Metamorphosis (Mt)
Miri (Mi)
Mirror, Mirror (MM)
Mudd's Women (MW)
Naked Time, The (NT)
Obsession (Ob)
Omega Glory, The (OG)
Operation - Annihilate! (OA)
Paradise Syndrome, The (PSy)
Patterns of Force (PF)
Piece of the Action, A (PA)
Plato's Stepchildren (PSt)
Private Little War, A (PWL)
Requiem for Methuselah (RM)
Return of the Archons, The (RA)
Return to Tomorrow (RT)
Savage Curtain (SC)
Shoreleave (SL)
Space Seed (SS)
Spectre of the Gun (SGn)
Spock's Brain (SB)
Squire of Gothos, The (SG)
Taste of Amageddon, A (TA)
That Which Survives (TWS)
This Side of Paradise (TSP)
Tholian Web, The (TW)
Tomorrow is Yesterday (TY)
Trouble With Tribbles, The (TT)
Turnabout Intruder, The (TI)
Ultimate Computer, The (UC)
Way to Eden, The (WEd)
What Are Little Girls Made Of? (LG)
Where No Man Has Gone Before (WNM)
Whom Gods Destroy (WGD)
Who Mourns for Adonais? (WM)
Wink of an Eye (WE)
Wolf in the Fold (WF)

Abbreviated references to specific episodes contained in this guide follow in accordance with those developed by Bjo Trimble, as they appear in her **Star Trek Concordance,** published by Ballantine.

Bibliography

Comic Book Price Guide, No. 15
Richard M. Overstreet
Overstreet Publications, 1985

Non-Sports Card Price Guide
James Beckett and Dennis Eckes
Sports Americana, 1984

Science Fiction & Heroic Fantasy Author Index
Stuart W. Well III
Purple Unicorn Press, 1978

Under Cover, An Illustrated History of American Mass Market Paperbacks
Thomas L. Bonn
Penguin, 1982